GROSSMAN'S GUIDE
to Wines, Beers, & Spirits

SEVENTH REVISED EDITION

GROSSMAN'S GUIDE TO WINES, BEERS, & SPIRITS

SEVENTH REVISED EDITION

HAROLD J. GROSSMAN

Revised by

HARRIET LEMBECK

CHARLES SCRIBNER'S SONS

New York

This book is dedicated to William Lembeck, who generously put aside his own important work to lend his support and many skills to this enormous project.

Library of Congress Cataloging in Publication Data

Grossman, Harold J.
  Grossman's guide to wines, beers, and spirits.

  Previous editions published under title:
Grossman's guide to wines, spirits, and beers.
  Bibliography: p.
  Includes index.
  1. Alcoholic beverages. I. Lembeck, Harriet
II. Title. III. Title: Guide to wines, beers, and
spirits.
TP505.G76   1983   641.2   83-9524
ISBN 0-684-17772-2

1 3 5 7 9 11 13 15 17 19 F/C 20 18 16 14 12 10 8 6 4 2

Printed in the United States of America

Frontispiece: Handsome Sangiovese grapes at Montemasso vineyard
near Florence. (*Courtesy I. L. Ruffino, Pontassieve, Italy*)

CONTENTS

PREFACE

In the many years since *Grossman's Guide to Wines, Beers, & Spirits* was first published in 1940, Harold J. Grossman's book has been accepted as the definitive reference and textbook for everyone interested in this field, professional and amateur alike. The continued growth of the alcoholic beverage industry has sparked a need for knowledge by a wide range of professional people who are concerned with the industry, whether in finance, advertising, legal work, or production. This knowledge is, of course, essential for all marketing levels of the industry. *Grossman's Guide* is to be found in the working library of almost every executive in the industry as well as in hotel schools, buying offices, and retail stores, including those operated by the various control states.

The *Guide* has necessarily been updated and revised periodically over the years. Reference books, unlike some wines, do not improve through aging, and Harold Grossman recognized his responsibility to keep his work as useful as possible by making the necessary changes and additions dictated by new technologies, revisions of laws and regulations, and changing taste trends in the marketplace. This dedication to keeping *Grossman's Guide* as current as possible is the primary reason for this new edition.

To assume the challenging responsibility of editing the sixth edition of *Grossman's Guide,* Scribners chose Harriet Lembeck, whose credentials are highly impressive. One of Mr. Grossman's star pupils eleven years ago, she has since been closely identified with the Beverage Program, which he started. For the past six years she has conducted four courses each year, and from this vantage point she knows the *Guide* page by page and line by line. She is aware of the reactions and needs of the students who use it as a text. In scanning reader letters to *Vintage* Magazine she has found many questions repeated again and again, and the answers to most of them have been incorporated into the revised edition of the *Guide.*

James Beard maintains that those fortunate people who have perfect pitch in music are likely to be equally sensitive to the aroma and flavor nuances of food and wine. This may explain some of the abilities of Harriet Lembeck, who was a major in music at Bryn Mawr College and is distinguished for her perception of tone and pitch as well as for her taste memory.

Harriet Lembeck is chairman of the Wine Committee and a director of the Wine and Food Society of New York, a Commandeur of the Confrérie des Chevaliers du Tastevin, on the faculty of the Sommelier Society of America, Vice-Chairman of the N.Y. Wine Writers' Circle, and a member of many other wine societies. She has devoted countless hours to the meticulous editing of this new edition, which entailed revising obsolete material and recognizing improved technology, tightened quality controls in various countries, the impact of economic factors on our imported wine profile, and the ever-changing taste preferences of the American public (for example, the rapid expansion of the use of white wines as apéritifs). With all this Harriet Lembeck has done an admirable job of preserving the tone and character of Harold Grossman's original work.

We have also enjoyed and benefited from the ability and experience of Harriet's husband, William Lembeck, Professional Engineer. With a wide knowledge of wines and spirits added to his repertoire, he has been most helpful in researching the appendices and contributing specialized information on such subjects as fermentation.

The task of updating and revising the various chapters of the *Guide* was aided immeasurably by the cooperation and suggestions of many industry executives and veterans who were long-time friends of Harold Grossman. I am proud to be a member of the editorial team for this new edition of *Grossman's Guide*. It is as comprehensive, up-to-date, and accurate as many months of effort can make it.

GORDON BASS

A TRIBUTE TO GORDON BASS

While I was writing the seventh revised edition of this book, my good friend, Gordon Bass, died at the age of eighty-two.

Gordon Bass spent his life in service to the wine and spirits industry, helping people wherever he could. He was especially involved with this book, and continually sent notes and documents for the various chapters and appendices.

There were many occasions after his passing when I was able to refer to correspondence from Gordon to clarify something in the text. In fact, I had so much material from him that it was as if he was still here, helping with this revision.

Obviously, I am grateful for the wealth of information that he provided. I am even more grateful for his legacy of a passion for fairness, accuracy, honesty, and loyalty.

HARRIET LEMBECK
April 1983

FOREWORD

There are few books that can be read for pleasure, provide satisfactory browsing, be prized as an encyclopedia, be useful as a pronouncing dictionary and technical manual, and, withal, constitute an ideal textbook. *Grossman's Guide* is one of those rarities and is a direct reflection of the author, his profound knowledge of any and all alcoholic beverages, and his lifelong endeavor to gain more and more information and to pass it on to others, consumers and industry members alike.

Harold Grossman was born in Cuba and grew up in Champaign, Illinois—prophetic even though the spelling of his native town is not exactly vinous. As a young man he returned to Cuba to work in the family-owned Hotel Plaza in Camaguey, and eventually he became its owner-manager. The wine cellar of the hotel was his particular pride and joy, and to build and replenish it young Harold made many buying trips to Europe, thus becoming a firsthand expert. These were the years of Prohibition, and while Harold became a knowledgeable enthusiast, the rest of his countrymen in the United States suffered from legal aridity. During this period he became friendly with Richard L. Blum, who then resided in Havana.

When Repeal came in December 1933, Blum, who was back in New York, persuaded Harold to leave the hotel and become education director of Julius Wile Sons & Co., Inc. His job was to teach what had been forgotten for a generation. Harold shared his knowledge with the entire industry—his employers, distributors and their sales staffs, retailers, hotel and restaurant personnel, and the press. He lectured and wrote and consulted and advised and above all answered questions. He appeared on radio and television programs and for over five years conducted the hotel training course for the International Geneva Association.

With the encouragement, aid, and collaboration of his wife, Florence, this book was written and first published in 1940, when it was eagerly purchased by a public still starved for information.

During World War II Harold went on a mission to Argentina with fluent Spanish as part of his equipment. He remained there for some years in the import-export business—dealing in wines and spirits, of course, among other things. Eventually he returned to New York, became a consultant to the trade, and resumed his writing on alcoholic beverages. In 1959 he instituted a series of tasting lectures using his own book as a text. This fifteen-week series was given twice a year. Upon Harold's death in 1967 volunteers continued the course in session, and it then came under the trusteeship of three of his close industry friends. Until Florence Grossman died it was called the Grossman Memorial Lectures. Today the course still goes on under the same trustees but is now called the Wine & Spirits Program. It is conducted by Harriet Lembeck, Harold's pupil, acolyte, assistant, and friend.

Those of us who knew and admired Harold Grossman, who believe, as he did, that the liquid products of grapes and fruits and grains exist for man's well-being, health, and pleasure, derive much satisfaction from the knowledge that his long years of education and instruction continue in this book and in the lectures based upon it.

JULIUS WILE

As the seventh edition goes to press, these words mourn the passing of Gordon Bass, who died in 1982.

In writing for both of us, I am pleased and happy that Harriet Lembeck has again updated and expanded this Guide.

During the past few years, Harriet's knowledge and stature in the beverage industry has continued to grow. She became a founding member of the Society of Wine Educators and was one of its first Directors.

She continues the Wine & Spirits Program and instituted the advanced wine course, lectures frequently to sales organizations, appears on radio and TV, consults, writes, and travels the wine roads of the world.

These activities and her mounting general and specific knowledge are all reflected in this latest edition.

J.W.
April 1983

ACKNOWLEDGMENTS
TO THE SIXTH EDITION

It is a tribute to the vision of Harold J. Grossman that a thorough revision of his book has taken more than two years and has involved the help of so many people in all facets of the wine and spirits industry. That a book of this breadth, with no models or predecessors, was written in 1940 by a man who taught himself about wines and spirits is most impressive.

With this revision I have tried to update technical material and to bring older attitudes more in line with current thinking. I also have tried to maintain Harold Grossman's passion for accuracy and objectivity. For example, brand names have been deliberately omitted except where they have historical significance.

Knowing that this book was designed to be a handy tool for quick reference as well as for more detailed study, the appendices, especially, have been expanded to include material needed for today's market. I hope that *Grossman's Guide* will be the book reached for first when the need for such material arises.

My interviews with so many people in the wine and spirits industry and related hospitality fields have served to reinforce for me just how widely respected Harold Grossman was and how much cooperation he inspired. Many people have given a great deal of time and effort to all the editions of *Grossman's Guide* since the 1940s. To all those go our continued thanks. Many industry leaders helped me now as they helped Harold Grossman in the past, and often my assistance has come from the next generation of authorities. For this totally and completely revised sixth edition go my sincere thanks to all those who are specifically involved.

Two close industry friends of Harold Grossman, Gordon Bass and Julius Wile, ensured the continuation of Harold Grossman's classes in wines and spirits after his passing. They have kept a weather eye on them as trustees and have now been closely involved with this book. They have given immeasurable time and talent, not only by checking all of the material but by drawing on their own vast experience and contacts to obtain and verify information. No point was too small to be overlooked. They are true educators and have been a source of inspiration and guidance.

Gordon Bass has been in all phases of the alcoholic beverage industry since Repeal in 1933. Having been a retailer, wholesaler, distiller, and importer, he is now wine marketing consultant to Schenley Affiliated Brands. He is chairman of The Tastevin Wine Library and Museum at the Culinary Institute of America, an outstanding wine reference library to which he has generously contributed rare wine books and antique wine bottles. He is a past president and board chairman of the Wine Spirits Wholesalers of America, a past director of the Licensed Beverage Industries, and a past member of the National Association of Alcoholic Beverage Importers (N.A.A.B.I.).

Gordon Bass's membership on the board of the Sommelier Society of America and his guest lectures at the Culinary Institute of America are a special source of pleasure, since there is nothing he likes more than to share his knowledge of wines and spirits and their place in the good life. In 1975 he received the honorary degree of Master of Aesthetics of Gastronomy from the Institute.

Not content to be simply a member of various societies, Gordon Bass has risen to Grand Officier of the Confrérie des Chevaliers du Tastevin and Sénéchal Honoraire for the United States of the Confrérie de la Chaîne des Rôtisseurs. He is a forty-year member of the New York Wine & Food Society, and in 1977 he was awarded the Cross of the Chevalier du Mérite Agricole.

Julius Wile represents the third generation of the wine and spirits business founded in 1877 by his grandfather, Julius Wile. He served his apprenticeship in the important wine and spirits areas of Europe, and after an outstanding forty-year career with Julius Wile Sons & Co., Inc., he recently retired as senior vice-president.

Since 1952 he has been on the faculty of the Cornell University School of Hotel Administration and has lectured for the Sommelier Society of America, as well as for other courses. Perhaps his most important educational role is that of chairman of the Board of Trustees of the Culinary Institute of America.

Julius Wile was also chairman of the Table Wine Committee of N.A.A.B.I. for seventeen years. He contributed annually to the *Encyclopaedia Britannica* on the subject of alcoholic beverages and updated the authoritative Schoonmaker *Encyclopedia of Wine*.

He is a governor and founding member of the Commanderie de Bordeaux and a director of the New York Wine & Food Society. In 1962 he received from the French government the Cross of Chevalier de l'Ordre de l'Économie Nationale, and in 1972 he was awarded the Cross of the Chevalier de l'Ordre National du Mérite.

Special thanks must also go to my husband, William Lembeck. His talents as a Professional Engineer combined with his love of wines and spirits have been of immeasurable help with the technical aspects of this book. His artistic style and abilities as a draftsman are demonstrated by the custom-drawn wine maps throughout the book. With the public's increased interest in the technical aspects of wines and spirits, it has been very helpful to have an engineer-in-residence.

Another friend who has assumed overall involvement with the text is Richard L. Becker, of the import department of Julius Wile Sons & Co., Inc. His painstaking accuracy, collection of data, and careful research have been most valuable.

The complex chapter on the wines of France received the help of Jean-Pierre Gachelin of the French Commercial Consulate of New York and Jean Fourcade of the French Commercial Consulate in Washington, D.C. Mary Lyons, of Food and Wines from France, helped with the Burgundy section; Alain Blanchon and Judy Platt, of Bell & Stanton, helped with the material on Bordeaux and Alsace, as did Michael Buller of *Vintage* Magazine. Irving Smith Kogan and Marie-Claude Stockl of the Champagne News and Information Bureau assisted with the material on Champagne. Robert Tinlot, of the Service de la Repression des Fraudes in Paris, was helpful with some of the finer points of the *Appellation Contrôlée* regulations. Special thanks must go to Charles S. Mueller, executive vice-president of Kobrand Corp., who gave his time generously to review the entire chapter on French wines.

The Wines of Italy had the help of Mary Mulligan of the Italian Trade Commission and industry members John Mariani, Jr., of the House of Banfi and Donald St. John Sozzi of the Jos. Garneau Co. Earlier editions of *Grossman's Guide* mention help given to Harold Grossman by Ercole Sozzi, Donald Sozzi's father. Paul F. Hille, Jr., a friend and wine lover, made good suggestions for this chapter as well. Mario Daniele, of C. Daniele & Sons, graciously made himself available for questions and discussions on the wines of Italy.

For the Wines of Germany, special thanks go to Peter M. F. Sichel for all of the information he provided. His help in organizing the material was invaluable. John Woodford Rapp, Jr., of the offices of H. Sichel Sohne, also contributed his time. Alan Olson, able director of the German Wine Information Bureau, and his assistant, Brenda Mezrahi, were always ready to help with the information gathering. Anne P. Griffiths, a graduate of the German Wine Academy, also checked the material.

The major part of the sherry information was reviewed by Arthur Humbert of Williams & Humbert and his very good friend Julian Jeffs of London. Good source material was provided by the Sherry Institute of Spain, headed first by Luther Conant and then by his successor, Smitty Kogan. Don José Ignacio Domecq, of the famous Domecq family in Jerez, and Antonio Montes, Consejo Regulador of Jerez, both answered many technical questions.

The chapter on the wines of Portugal was strengthened by Victor Espirito Santo, of the Portuguese Government Trade Office. Kenneth L. Onish, of Château and Estate Wines Co., was particularly helpful with the material on Vintage Porto.

The material on the wines of smaller countries was also checked carefully. For Hungary, the task fell to Alexander Campbell McNally and Thomas J. Martin, both authorities from Heublein, Inc. The wines of Israel were reviewed by Yehudah Levinberg, of the Carmel Wine Co.

The names of the people who helped with the Wines of the United States chapter reads like a *Who's Who* of all phases of the American wine business. The wines of California were checked by Dr. Maynard A. Amerine, Harvey

Posert, Brian St. Pierre, and James M. Seff, all of the Wine Institute. Gerald Asher, vice-president of "21" Brands, Inc., provided his usual good sense and perspective with many creative suggestions. Darrell F. Corti, an innovative retailer in Sacramento, contributed an overview of the wines of his state. The information gleaned from Fromm & Sichel's *Data Annual,* sent by Jim Lucas, also contributed to this overview. Dr. Richard G. Peterson, president of the American Society of Enologists and Monterey Vineyard, Inc., provided technical information on the winemaking process. Joseph Concannon of Concannon Vineyards, Inc., was helpful with the regulations on sacramental wines. John W. McConnell made valuable comments on the book as a whole and especially on the grape varieties of California.

The wines of Washington State were reviewed by Joel K. Klein and Vic Allison of Ste. Michelle Vineyards. Information on the wines of Oregon came from Bill Fuller of Tualatin Vineyards and from the staff at Oregon State University.

For the section on the wines of the eastern United States Dr. John R. McGrew of the U.S. Department of Agriculture in Maryland provided well-documented technical information.

From the American Wine Society, Margaret Jackisch, executive secretary, and Philip Jackisch, consulting enologist, also carefully reviewed the material on the wines of the eastern United States, which have changed tremendously since Harold Grossman first wrote about them.

The chapter on beers was reviewed by Desmond G. Sharp-Bolster, of the Guinness-Harp Corp. Material was also obtained from Pat Jones, librarian, and Gary M. Nateman, head of the Legal Department, of the United States Brewers' Association, Bill Siebel of J. E. Siebel & Co., Inc., Jack Varick and James D. Ritchie of Jos. Schlitz Brewing Co.

The chapters on spirits were read by many industry members. Of great assistance on whiskies were John L. Brady, Jr., George W. Pacowski, and Merce Maleski, all of Joseph E. Seagram & Sons, along with Alice Gross, librarian; Weil Herzfeld and Marsha Lane of Schenley Affiliated Brands Corp.; and Jack McGowan, of Irish Distillers, Ltd. Rums were checked by William A. Walker of Bacardi Imports, Inc. Tequila and vodka were reviewed by Christopher W. Carriuolo and Erik J. Pierce of Heublein, Inc. French brandies were checked by the aforementioned Messrs. Jean-Pierre Gachelin and Jean Fourcade of the French Commercial Consulates, and American brandies were reviewed by James R. McManus of the California Brandy Advisory Board. Michel Garnier of the Fleischman Distilling Corp. and W. Ray Hyde of Schieffelin & Co. offered assistance on liqueurs.

For the material on cocktails and mixed drinks, menu and wine list making, beverage control, and bar operation, much help was given by members of the Hilton Corporation: Eugene R. Scanlan, manager of the Waldorf-Astoria

Hotel, Norbert Rademaker, Guenther Richter, Réné R. Varela, Michael R. Cross, and Louis Pappalardo. These sections were also reviewed by the Culinary Institute of America, directed by its president, Henry Ogden Barbour.

The photographs of how to open bottles of wine were made possible by Kevin Zraly and Barbara Kafka, of Windows on the World, and photographer Andrew B. Wile. Information on recorking old bottles of wine was provided by specialist Roger Mason.

Retailing practices were explained by Michael Aron of Sherry-Lehmann, Inc., and Arthur Amster of Manhattan Château Wine & Liquor Corp. In the section on merchandising I was ably assisted by Margaret Stern and Stephanie Shames of Schieffelin & Co., Jim Angelone and Gary Tobin of United Vintners, Alan Schwartz of *Liquor Store* Magazine, and many others.

Laws and regulations were meticulously checked by Eiko Narita of the National Association of Alcoholic Beverage Importers. Alan Graham of the Bureau of Alcohol, Tobacco, and Firearms answered questions relating to regulations. George W. McRory, Jr., of the American Wine Society and a consumer advocate on this subject, was also helpful. Marvin R. Shanken, of Impact, provided reliable statistical information.

Some reference books that have been constant companions throughout this project are *The Encyclopedia of Wines and Spirits* by Alexis Lichine, the *Encyclopedia of Wine* by Frank Schoonmaker, *The World Atlas of Wine* by Hugh Johnson, and the *Great Book of Wine*.

Thanks must also go to the good people of Julius Wile Sons & Co., Inc. They provided the use of their Wine Library and many other facilities to help with this important project. They have not forgotten their long-time associate Harold J. Grossman, who was their original director of education. Special thanks must go to chairman Richard L. Blum, Jr., president Neil Bianchini, vice-president Brian Abbott, and office manager Arlene Duvin.

A book of this encyclopedic nature requires immense coordination on the part of the publisher. To Charles Scribner, Jr., goes special appreciation for undertaking the project when the need for thorough revision became apparent. His loyal staff put in many extra hours to ensure that the accuracy and care put into the manuscript were not lost to the gremlins of production. To Barbara Wood, who makes a specialty of precision, and to Doe Coover, my editor, who became a great friend in the process, go particular, heartfelt thanks.

HARRIET LEMBECK
1977

ACKNOWLEDGMENTS
TO THE SEVENTH EDITION

When the revisions for the Sixth Edition of *Grossman's Guide* in 1977 took more than two years, it was not that surprising, since Harold Grossman's last revision had been done in 1964.

When the revisions for the Seventh Edition, completed in 1983, also took two years, it was a little more surprising. But the wine explosion has been such, and most likely will continue to be such, that it has become naive to expect that the job can be anything else but Herculean.

The United States is undergoing major revisions in its labeling laws and in its acknowledgement of unique appellations. Even the stolid Bottled-in-Bond Act of 1894 has been shaken. European countries are modifying their laws to conform to Common Market specifications. All of this has had to be updated.

The excitement of restaurateurs and retailers about wines has led to new ways of wine service and merchandising. New wineries in the United States have enlarged that listing in the Appendices, as have all of the new wine books

Special thanks go, of course, to the many experts who contributed their talents to the Sixth Edition. Whatever of their work that is still current has been retained in the Seventh Edition.

In addition to all of those, here are some of the good friends who provided information for this edition. The chapter on French wines received help from John Gillespie of the Bordeaux Wine Information Bureau; Jeffrey M. Pogash of the *Comité Interprofessionnel du Vin d'Alsace;* and Mereille Guiliano and Irving Smith Kogan of the Champagne News and Information Bureau. "Smitty" Kogan also provided help in the section on Spanish sherries as well.

The wines of Italy were reviewed by Fenella Pearson, U.S. Editor for *Italian Wines & Spirits* (*Civiltà del bere*), and Barbara Edelman, Director, and Frank di Falco of the Italian Wine Center. New reference books that were particularly helpful were those of Burton Anderson and Victor Hazan. Ms. Pearson, incidentally, also provided up-to-date information on the wines of England.

For the chapter on German wines, help came from, of course, Peter M. F. Sichel, officially of H. Sichel Söhne, Inc., but, more accurately, a citizen of the wine world. The German Wine Information Bureau, led by Alan Olson and Lamarr Elmore provided assistance, as did Kerry Stewart of the *Stabilisierungfonds Fuer Wein* in Mainz, Germany.

New regulations in Madeira were described by David Pamment of the Madeira Wine Association, Ltda; and Alexander Campbell McNally and Erik J. Pierce again reviewed the chapter on Hungarian wines.

The chapter on the wines of the United States was completely rewritten. Special thanks go to the Wine Institute in San Francisco, particularly to Patricia Schneider, Brian St. Pierre, Robert Brown, and Jean E. Valentine, the Fromm and Sichel *Data Annual,* and Phyllis van Kriedt's *California Wineletter.*

Joel Klein developed a great deal of information on Washington state, which he graciously shared; and Philip Jackisch kept a careful check on the wines of the East, where it is entirely possible that things are changing faster than anywhere else.

Angela Seracini of the Wine Spectrum and Charles Fournier of Gold Seal Vineyards also provided much information. John W. McConnell reviewed the grape varieties of the United States, as well as of other countries.

The wines of Canada were reviewed and updated by Michael Vaughan.

Much information on Argentina came from Byron Tosi, Vinos Argentinos; Evelina Alhadeff; the *Instituto Nacional de Vitivinicultura,* and Ing. Alberto J. Alcalde and Ing. Agr. Carlos Tizio Mayer of the National Institute for Agriculture Technology (*INTA*). In addition, gracious help came from Raul de la Mota of Bodega Weinert; Sigifredo A. Alonso of San Telmo; Carlos A. Lopez of Bodegas Lopez; Rodolfo R. Rutini of La Rural; Dr. Carlos M. Basso of Bodega Santa Ana; and Isaac Flichman of Finca Flichman.

The wines of South Africa were checked by David L. Hughes of the Stellenbosch Farmers' Winery, and author of the delightful newsletter "Drink."

From Australia, help came from John Parkinson and David Shear from the Australian Wine & Brandy Corp., and from David Rush and Joseph Strear in New York. Information on the wines of New Zealand was supplied by D. J. Robertson and Michael R. Godfrey, from the New Zealand Commercial Consul, and Neil F. Campbell of Kiwi Wine Imports, Texas.

The wines of Japan and Egypt were researched by Jane Levere of *Travel Weekly,* and winemaking in Hawaii was described by Dmitri Tchelistcheff.

The process of making aromatized wines in California was clearly explained by Joseph Stillman, retired head winemaker at Paul Masson Vineyards.

Some information on beers and ales was supplied by Matthew P. Reich of The Old New York Beer Company.

General information on spirits came from many industry members. They include Harold Barg of Schenley Industries, Inc.; Merce Maleski and Gregory Altschuh, both of Joseph E. Seagram & Sons, and Richard Grindal, Executive Director of the Scotch Whisky Association. Cognacs were checked by Jean-Marie Beulque-Schaub, of the *Bureau National du Cognac,* Colin Campbell of Jas. Hennessy & Co. in France, and William Houlton in New York. American brandies were updated by James R. McManus and John Poimiroo of the California Brandy Advisory Board. Michel Pierre Roux, president of Carillon Importers Ltd., provided assistance with liqueurs, as did Don Gregory from James Burrough, Ltd. of London, for gins. Robert L. McKee, of Heublein/Spirits Group, was extremely helpful on the subject of Tequila.

Many restaurateurs and hoteliers helped with the section on menus and wine lists. Some of them are Paul Kovi and Tom Margittai of The Four Seasons, N.Y.; Willis S. Knight, Assistant Director of Food and Beverage, and Paul C. Lasley of the Century Plaza Hotel, Los Angeles; Michael S. Turback of Turback's of Ithaca, N.Y.; Pat Cetta of Sparks, New York; Richard Lavin of Lavin's, N.Y., Narsai David of Narsai's in California; Michael Klauber of the Colony Beach and Tennis Resort in Longboat Key, Florida; James Hutton of La Colline in Washington, D.C.; and Michael R. Nowlis, School of Hotel Administration, Cornell University, Ithaca, N.Y.

Creative retailers who supplied information include Michael Aron of Sherry-Lehmann, N.Y.; Stanley Greenberg of Town Wine & Spirits, R.I.; Draper & Esquin, San Francisco, and Darrell Corti of Corti Brothers, Sacramento.

Beverage control was reviewed by Eugene R. Scanlan of Eugene R. Scanlan Enterprises and William de Weese of the Waldorf-Astoria Hotel.

Complicated regulations were simplified by Eiko Narita, National Association of Beverage Importers, and George W. McRory, Jr., American Wine Society. Statistical information came from Michael Moaba of M. Shanken Communications, Inc. Research on the Appendices was aided by two thoroughly capable assistants—Julie Morrison of American Classics Wine Co. and Kenneth Alan Zuckerman of Tele-Rep.

Clearly, special thanks must go to my husband, William Lembeck, PE, whose engineering skills were applied to maps, charts, and interpretation of both chemical and statistical information.

Special thanks must also go to Julius Wile, whose enormous contributions to the wine and spirits industry must include being at the ready whenever I called with questions on this volume.

In addition, there are a few members of the industry with whom I did not particularly consult on this volume, but from whom I always learn whenever I speak to them. Their wise words have most certainly influenced the contents of this book, whether or not they were aware of it. They are, in alphabetical order since I admire them all, Gerald Asher, Louis P. Martini, Charles S. Mueller, Robert Mondavi, Abdallah H. Simon, Warren Winiarski, and John Wright.

Certainly my editor and liaison with Charles Scribner's Sons, Louise Ketz, deserves my thanks and gratitude for her painstaking attention to detail, and commitment to the highest standards for this *Guide*.

HARRIET LEMBECK
1983

GROSSMAN'S GUIDE
to Wines, Beers, & Spirits

SEVENTH REVISED EDITION

1
INTRODUCTION

The liquor "industry" is almost as old as man himself, and our knowledge of it is made up of widely scattered information in every language written or spoken. The subject is continually developing and consequently is always intriguing.

The development and improvement of the quality of alcoholic beverages have been the natural results of the advance of science and civilization. The role of science has been limited to ensuring uniformity of quality and sound products year in and year out, for nature still insists on having something to say in the matter, even when it comes to distilled spirits.

The vine, the brewing kettle, and the still have accompanied the spread of Christianity, establishing certain honorable traditions that the trade proudly upholds today. It is also interesting to note the esteem in which the wine trade is held abroad. It was the first "trade" considered sufficiently honorable and dignified for a member of the aristocracy to engage in, and many of the leading European firms are directed by members of noble families.

In England a wine merchant is consulted in matters pertaining to wines, beers, or spirits just as a lawyer is in legal matters. The confidence thus placed in him gives the merchant a keen consciousness of his responsibility. Also, as he knows that his descendants will continue the business he builds, family pride leads him to pass on an impeccable reputation. It is not unusual to find firms that have been doing business under the same name in the same place for hundreds of years—in some cases more than four hundred years. This is the European custom, and we are happy to note that it is beginning to take hold in the United States.

One of the leading Champagne shippers illustrated this point when he told us: "When I ship my wine, my name appears on the label. It is I who guarantee the quality. My reputation is more important to me than any pecuniary profit I may derive from the sale. It took my forebears two hundred years to establish this reputation for shipping wines of quality, and rest assured that I am going to

1

pass on as good a name to my successors as I received." It is men of this type who have placed the wine and spirit trade on the high plane that has become traditional.

Based on these traditions, certain firms have established their brands so well that the public asks for their product by the name of the shipper. This has been particularly true in the case of Cognac and whiskies, but since the American public is "age conscious," many people buy dates rather than brands in whose names we have confidence. This has happened in the case of wines, as well. It is true that certain wines do improve with age—up to a point—but there are other wines that are more pleasant if drunk when young, as in the case with light white wines, whose charm lies in their freshness.

The industry as a whole today is a most important part of our business life, employing, directly or through allied enterprises, millions of men and women. It is one of the three most important sources of tax revenue for the federal and state treasuries.

Just as prohibition is bad, so is excess, and in no case is this more evident than in the use of alcoholic beverages. There is no better word of advice on this point than that which Lord Chesterfield gave to his son in a letter from London, dated March 27, 1747: "Were I to begin the world again with the experience I now have of it, I would lead a life of real, not imaginary, pleasures. I would enjoy the pleasures of the table, and of wine; but stop short of the pains inseparably annexed to an excess of either."

The leaders of the industry unanimously prefer that more people drink and enjoy beverages, rather than that individuals drink more.

It is gratifying to note the moderation exercised by the public in the use of alcoholic beverages. A per capita consumption in the United States of slightly over two gallons of wine per year indicates an average of three-quarters of an ounce per day. Wine has recently surpassed spirits consumption, which averages seven-tenths of an ounce per day, but this amount of wine consumption is still extremely low when compared with other countries. Beer consumption has increased to slightly more than ten times that of wines or spirits, averaging eight and one-half ounces per capita per day. The new low-alcohol and low-calorie wines and beers most likely account for much of these increases, while enabling the public to maintain its standards of moderation.

The *Guide* has been divided into five main sections: wines, beers and ales; spirits; uses, merchandising, and control; and, finally, the appendices, which contain useful, quick-reference data. All of the material has been carefully indexed to make the book easier to use for reference purposes.

Condensed information on the entire industry is given, including the description of a product, its method of production, selling, care, and uses in public and private places. The practices described are those generally used in the United States, unless otherwise specified.

It is our hope that libraries will find the *Guide* a comprehensive source of information on all phases of the subject; that producers, vintners, distillers, and brewers will find it valuable as a general reference and as a means of equipping their sales representatives with information about the other phases of the industry; and that the wholesale distributor will find it invaluable as a training manual for his staff and as a reference book. The various appendices also have been compiled with a view to practical use.

Particular care has been taken to provide information on every phase of the industry for retail establishments, whether off-premise (stores) or on-premise (hotels, restaurants, or clubs).

After reading the book, it may be useful for store owners to review certain chapters when promoting particular products. For example, during the Christmas season there is an opportunity to sell liqueurs in their fancy bottles. It is good business to be aware of these details and to refer to the *Guide* if one is asked, for example, for a liqueur whose style or character may have been forgotten.

It is also advisable for the hotel, restaurant, or club manager to keep his service personnel well informed. They are his sales staff and cannot be expected to increase the sale of beverages if they are not familiar with them. This applies equally to the wholesaler and distributor. The sales staff that is trained and can give information will become salesmen instead of order takers.

While the *Guide* has been designed primarily to be of use to the trade, it is our earnest hope that it will be read by the person who is most important to the entire industry: the consumer. It is to please and serve him that the industry constantly strives. A greater familiarity with the beverages discussed in this book, we believe, not only would aid him in purchasing with assurance, but would, perhaps, point out to him many intriguing qualities he may have overlooked and therefore increase his enjoyment.

To provide the reader with practical information, to increase his knowledge and enjoyment, and, above all, to impart something of the fascination of the subject are the purposes of this *Guide*.

2
DEFINITIONS

It is important to explain the various terms we use, so that there may be no misconceptions or confusion. The definitions and axioms that follow are important because they are the basic elements on which the book is built.

what is alcohol? Alcohol is a volatile, colorless liquid with an ethereal odor, obtained through fermentation of a liquid containing sugar. There are many members of the alcohol family, but ethyl is the best-known alcohol and the one that concerns us most, as it is the principal alcohol to be found in all alcoholic beverages. The chemical formula for ethyl alcohol, or ethanol, is C_2H_5OH. Chemically, alcohols are hydroxides of organic radicals. There is nothing in ethyl alcohol that in itself is poisonous or injurious to a person's health.

what is an alcoholic beverage? Literally, any potable liquid containing from $\frac{1}{2}$ to 80 percent ethyl alcohol by volume is an alcoholic beverage. However, for the purposes of taxation, the federal and state governments have set certain definite standards as to what constitutes an alcoholic beverage. Whereas beers containing as little as 2 percent alcohol by volume are taxable, certain bitters and medicinal compounds, which often contain upward of 40 percent alcohol, are not taxed because they are not considered alcoholic beverages. In 1919 Congress established by law that an alcoholic beverage containing more than $\frac{1}{2}$ percent alcohol by volume was intoxicating, yet in later years liqueurs containing 12 percent alcohol by volume were permitted to be sold as "nonalcoholic" cordials. One may draw the conclusion that by 1930, which was still during Prohibition, the government held that 12 percent alcohol in a permissible liqueur was not as intoxicating as beer, a forbidden beverage, with as little as 1 percent alcohol.

what is wine? Wine is the naturally fermented juice of ripe grapes. Ideally these have been freshly gathered and crushed at or near the place where gathered.

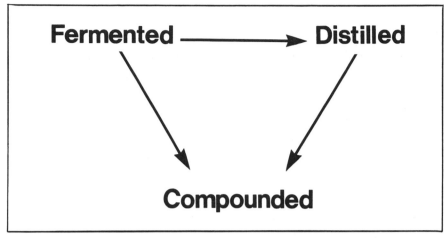

All alcoholic beverages fall into one of three basic categories: (1) fermented beverages, which are made from agricultural products such as grains and fruits and have alcoholic strengths ranging from 3 to 16 percent; (2) distilled or spirit beverages, which result from a pure distillation of fermented beverages; and (3) compounded beverages, which are made by combining either a fermented beverage or a spirit with flavoring substances.

Regulations under the Federal Alcohol Administration Act, however, apply the term more broadly to the fermented juice of other fruits, such as black-berry, elderberry, and peach, and of other agricultural products. Wine is more than just water and alcohol, however; it is a complex liquid in a constant state of change.

Beer is an alcoholic beverage fermented from cereals and malt and fla-vored with hops.

what is beer?

A spirit is a potable alcoholic beverage obtained from the distillation of a liquid containing alcohol. It makes little difference whether the original liquid contains a small or a large amount of alcohol. Once the principles of distilla-tion are applied, nearly all of the alcohol may be separated from the liquid. In addition, certain other flavor compounds may also be separated from the orig-inal liquid, and carried along with the alcohol. These are called "congeners," and they give spirits their distinct characteristics. If spirits are aged in wood, the wood also imparts congeners of its own.

what is a spirit?

There are only two colors in wine: red and white. Any wine containing the slightest tinge of red is a red wine. A rosé wine, therefore, is considered a red wine.

axioms

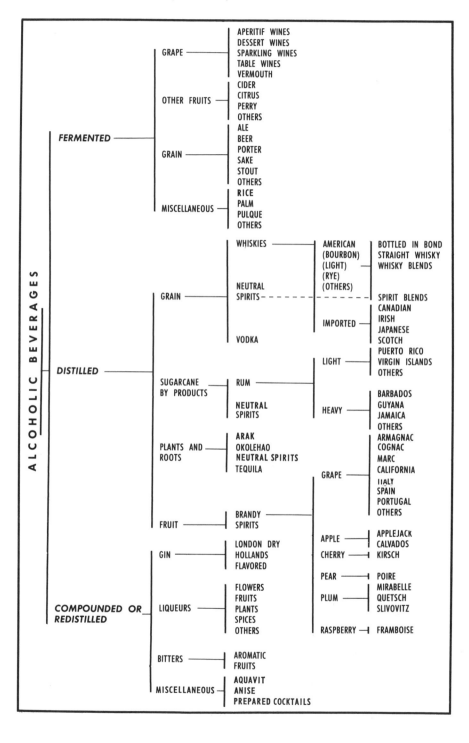

White wines range from the very palest straw color to deep, dark brown.

White wines vary in sweetness, from the extreme dryness of a Manzanilla Sherry, to the rich, sweet lusciousness of a Tokay Eszencia.

The word *dry* is used in the wine trade to describe the opposite of sweet. Literally, it means "lacking in sugar."

Red wines are generally dry. (Exceptions are Porto and port-type wines, Lambrusco, sweetened kosher wines, and a few other specialties from various countries.) Rosé wines can be very dry, but more often are somewhat sweet.

FOUR MAIN CLASSIFICATIONS OF WINES

TABLE (still wines). White and red (including rosé) from all wine-producing countries, most of which have more than one important wine region. Examples: Bordeaux, Burgundy from France; Rhine, Moselle from Germany; Chianti, Veronese from Italy; etc. Alcohol content usually less than 14 percent.

SPARKLING. Champagne, *vin mousseux*, Asti Spumante, Sekt, etc. Alcohol content 14 percent or less.

FORTIFIED.° Sherry, Porto, Madeira, Marsala, Málaga, etc. Alcohol content over 14 percent, but not over 24 percent.

AROMATIZED. Vermouth (Italian and French types), quinined wines, etc. Alcohol content $15\frac{1}{2}$ to 20 percent.

° The U.S. government classified these as dessert wines.

Standard shapes of bottles generally used in the wine trade for packaging products. LEFT TO RIGHT: Champagne and sparkling wines; Burgundy wines; Bordeaux wines; Alsatian and most German wines; *Bocksbeutel* for Franconian wines; sherries and Portos; vermouths. (*Photo by Norman Schaffer, Montclair, New Jersey*)

Some wines containing less than 14 percent alcohol may improve after bottling. Fortified and aromatized wines improve very little or not at all, with the exception of Vintage Portos and Madeiras.

CLASSIFICATIONS OF MALT BEVERAGES

BEERS.   Light-colored brews commonly called lager. Alcoholic strength about 4 percent by weight.

ALES.   Darker and more bitter brews. Alcoholic strength about 4½ percent by weight.

PORTER AND STOUT.   Very full-bodied, rich malt brews. Alcoholic strength about 6 percent by weight.

SAKÉ.   A specially treated and fermented brew made from rice, produced in Japan and Hawaii. Alcoholic strength 14 to 16 percent by volume.

CLASSIFICATIONS OF SPIRITS

BRANDIES.   Cognac, Armagnac, Spanish, Greek, Italian, American, etc.

FRUIT BRANDIES.   Kirsch (cherry), Calvados (apple), Slivovitz (plum), etc.

WHISKIES.   Scotch; Irish; Canadian; American: straights (Bourbon, Corn, Rye, etc.), blends, etc.

RUMS.   Jamaican, Demeraran, Cuban, Puerto Rican, Martinique, Haitian, etc.

GINS.   English, American, Hollands, etc.

VODKAS.   American, Russian, Polish, etc. Unflavored and slightly flavored.

OTHER SPIRITS.   Tequila, Akvavit, bitters, etc.

LIQUEURS.   Generic types, such as menthe, cacao, anise, blackberry, curaçao, etc., are produced in many countries. In addition there are a large number of proprietary specialties that have earned international popularity, such as Bénédictine, Chartreuse, Drambuie, Galliano, Southern Comfort, Kahlúa, etc.

Spirits mature—improve—as long as they are stored in porous containers, usually wood, although sometimes, notably in Holland, they are stored in earthenware crocks, where the action of air mellows the spirit through oxidation.

Spirits do not improve in glass. Once bottled with an airtight closure, they remain unchanged.

METRIC BOTTLE SIZES

The Bureau of Alcohol, Tobacco, and Firearms (B.A.T.F.) of the U.S. Treasury Department has declared metric standards of fill for wines and spirits sold in the United States. For wines, the mandatory compliance date was January 1, 1979. The basic number of bottle sizes is seven, reduced from the sixteen sizes previously allowed for American wines and twenty-seven sizes for imports.

For spirits, the mandatory compliance date was January 1, 1980. The number of bottle sizes permitted for spirits has been reduced from thirty-nine to six.

While the contents must be shown using the metric system, producers may voluntarily add U.S. fluid-ounce contents as well.

The alcoholic beverage industry was a pioneer in adopting the metric system in the United States. The metric measures for wines and spirits are shown below.

PRE-METRIC TERMINOLOGY	METRIC CAPACITY	FLUID-OUNCE CAPACITY	BOTTLES PER CASE	LITERS PER CASE
		WINES (*Still and Sparkling*)		
Miniature	100 ml†	3.4	60	6
Split	187 ml	6.3	48	9
Tenth	375 ml	12.7	24	9
Fifth	750 ml	25.4	12	9
Quart	1.0 liter§	33.8	12	12
Magnum	1.5 liters	50.7	6	9
Jeroboam	3.0 liters	101.4	4	12
———	4.0 liters	135.2	4	16
———	18.0 liters	608.4	1	18

At present, 4.0 liters is the largest that appears in glass. New lightweight packaging, such as the bag-in-the-box, have made sizes of up to eighteen liters practical for on-premise service. The popular 187 milliliter (ml) size is often convenience-packed in multiples of from three to six, in cans or bottles.

		SPIRITS		
Miniature	50 ml†	1.7	120	6
Half-Pint	200 ml	6.8	48	9.6
Pint	500 ml	16.9	24	12
Fifth	750 ml	25.4	12	9
Quart	1.0 liter§	33.8	12	12
Half-Gallon	1.75 liters	59.2	6	10.5

† *ml* means milliliters, or 1/1000 liter.
§ 1 liter equals 1,000 milliliters.

3
FERMENTATION

The story of alcoholic beverages must begin with an understanding of the process whereby alcohol is obtained. Alcohol is produced from sugar or from a product that can be changed into a sugar. Once sugar is present, it can be transformed into alcohol by the natural process of fermentation.

Essentially, fermentation is the result of chemical changes in which a molecule of sugar is split into two molecules of ethyl alcohol and two molecules of carbon dioxide gas. The gas escapes into the air and the alcohol remains. The metamorphosis that takes place is similar to that which changes milk into cheese. Nature provides its own chemical agents to see that the job is accomplished efficiently in each case. The agent in fermentation is a yeast. Yeast, a living plant organism capable of self-reproduction, has many individual strains, a number of which have been identified and given scientific names. The yeast in grape juice, whose job it is to change the juice into wine, is called *Saccharomyces*.

It might be said that transforming grape juice into wine by fermentation could be left entirely to nature without any interference from man, except in the case of sparkling, fortified, or other such wines. And this is true—up to a point. Grass grows quite naturally in the fields in a wild state, but it takes constant care to make an attractive lawn. Wine allowed to ferment upon its husks will draw color from the skins, if they are those of black grapes. But if left too long it will also draw from the pips, stalks, or the small peduncles excess tannin, and more of the unsuitable acids, which would prove objectionable later. It is man's job, therefore, to control fermentation, leaving most of the work to the yeast, or *Saccharomyces*.

The *Saccharomyces* spores, dormant during the winter, settle on the outside of the grape skins as the grapes begin to ripen. When the grapes are gathered and the juice is expressed, the yeast creates enzymes that cause the grape juice to ferment and become wine. The grapes themselves are not affected by the yeast's presence, since its action does not commence until the juice is expressed. In the grape must (unfermented grape juice), with sugar and other necessary nutrients present, the yeast begins to multiply at a prodigious rate. This early

10

yeast growth, while stimulated by the presence of oxygen in the surrounding air, will not produce alcohol if it continues to grow in an atmosphere rich in oxygen. In other words, air is needed to get the yeast to start its rapid multiplication, but further fermentation to produce alcohol must be carried on in the absence of oxygen.

Saccharomyces works violently at first, when there is an abundance of grape sugar to work on, and then more quietly as the sugar is changed into alcohol and carbon dioxide. When all the sugar has been used up or the wine attains an alcoholic strength of approximately 14 percent, the action of the yeast is inhibited and the fermentation process complete. The violent phase is accompanied by the release of much heat, and because *Saccharomyces* works most efficiently between 65 and 80 degrees Fahrenheit, with some white wines fermenting at even lower temperatures, the winemaker tries to control the temperature level at all times during this period.

Saccharomyces performs its job of fermentation by creating catalytic agents called enzymes. The enzymes are nonliving complex chemicals that cut, chop, and change the sugar into ethyl alcohol and carbon dioxide. What was originally must has now become wine. But the importance of the yeast does not end with its function of producing alcohol. It has a definite influence on the character of the wine itself. It is a living plant organism and is influenced by

Grape must fermenting. (*Courtesy Paul Masson Vineyards, Saratoga, California*)

climate, soil, and geographical conditions existing in each wine-producing region. In some areas winemakers use specially propagated strains of yeast to eliminate undesirable characteristics without losing environmental character, instead of, or in addition to, the natural yeasts present on the grapes.

A good case in point is that of some of the white wines of Burgundy and Champagne. In both instances the Chardonnay grape is used, yet two more distinct and different white wines are hard to find. Admittedly, the difference in soils is a contributing factor, but the character of the *Saccharomyces* has much to do with explaining this phenomenon.

Still another example appears in the sherry district at Jerez, Spain, where the yeast that develops a film on the surface of the wine, known as the flower, is entirely different from that in the manzanilla warehouses of Sanlúcar de Barrameda on the seacoast.

To sum up, the process known as fermentation is one that consists mainly of the splitting up of each molecule of grape sugar present in grape juice into two molecules of carbon dioxide and two molecules of ethyl alcohol. But it must be remembered that there are other fermentable substances in grape juice besides grape sugar and that there are enzymatic catalysts that render possible secondary reactions that take place at the same time or later; these are responsible for the presence, in wine, of compounds that did not exist in the grape juice.

Grape juice, indeed, is a very complex aqueous solution. It contains, besides water and grape sugar, acids and numerous other substances, most of them in very small quantities, of both vegetable and mineral origin:

1. Substances, other than water, that are the same in must and in wine, such as grape sugar, *Saccharomyces*, acids, tannins, pigments, essential oils, proteins.

2. Substances, other than ethyl alcohol, present in wine but not in must, such as glycerine, various acids, alcohols other than ethyl, esters, aldehydes. (See Appendix H for a more technical explanation of fermentation.)

We have been discussing fermentation in wine, in which sugar is naturally present in the form of grape sugar in the grape juice. It is also present in other fruits, most particularly in sugarcane, whose juice, when properly treated, gives us the sugar we use in our coffee and, as a by-product, molasses, which when fermented produces the alcohol we distill off and call rum.

Alcoholic beverages are often obtained from basic ingredients that contain no natural sugar but that are rich in starch, such as grains, cereals, and potatoes. This is possible because, under the proper conditions, the starches can be converted into sugar (maltose and dextrin) by the action of diastase (amylase), which is the principal enzyme contained in malt (usually barley malt). Once the sugar is there, the yeast enzymes finish the job of fermentation. This will be explained in more detail in Chapter 17.

4
WINE
IN GENERAL

The winemaker's life is not a happy one, even when nature is most cooperative. Making wine is not merely a matter of gathering grapes, crushing
them, and leaving them to ferment. It is not the simplest and most
profitable of agricultural pursuits, when one considers that every vine must be
carefully watched, pruned back so that all its strength will not go into the stalk
or excess grapes or foliage but into producing grapes of rich quality, and
sprayed against the many diseases always waiting to attack. The producer
must take care that birds, which love the grapes, do not eat up the entire crop;
he must gather the grapes when just ripe, crush and press them, and see that
conditions favorable to a perfect fermentation are present. He must watch
carefully over the casks of new wine to make sure that *Mycodermae aceti*
(vinegar yeasts) that are in the air do not get in and ruin his product; and after
the wine gets in the bottle, he hopes that eventually it will reach an appreciative buyer. Add to this his eternal worry over too much rain or too little
sunshine, and it is a wonder that men have the courage to carry on such an
arduous task.

Man has made wine almost as long as he has husbanded the earth. Paleon-
tologists have found evidence of masses of grape pips, skins, and stems that
apparently had been crushed by prehistoric man. No one knows when wine
was first made. It is possible that a cliff dweller who had gathered wild grapes
to use their sweet juice as a thirst quencher returned from a hunting trip,
picked up the vessel he had left, and discovered, to his amazement and de-
light, that the grape juice had become a different drink, one that made him
happy—the grape juice had fermented and become wine.

The Egyptians credit Osiris, and the Greek Dionysus, with the gift of wine,
while the Hebrews say Noah first introduced it. The numerous references in the
Bible indicate that not only wine but also stronger beverages were made, as

indicated by the following words: *yayin,* the Hebrew word most often used to describe wine; *homer,* fresh, young, unmixed wine; *tiros,* strong wine; *sekhor,* strong drink; and *meseg,* mixed wines.

Phoenician traders introduced the vine into Europe at the Mediterranean coastal trading posts they established, and later the Roman legions carried it into Gaul, Germany, and across the Channel into England. Although England is one of the best markets for wine, the English have never been able to produce wine successfully in commercial quantities.

The greatest single influence upon wine has been the Church. Indeed, the development of the vine has accompanied the spread of Christianity. Wine was needed for sacramental functions, and the priests recognized its food value. Since they made the wine for their own use and not for commercial purposes, they were more interested in quality than in quantity and their every effort was directed toward improving the vines and perfecting the wines they made. As a result, the winemakers outside the Church began to follow their example, and the general standard of winemaking was raised to a higher level.

Evidence of the priests' work still exists in France today. The vineyards of Châteauneuf-du-Pape near Avignon were started by Pope Clement V in the early fourteenth century, and they still produce wines that we enjoy. Dom Pérignon, the Bénédictine monk of the Abbey of Hautvillers, probably did more for Champagne than any other man, and as we lift the sparkling wine we still hear echoed in our ears his rapturous cry as he first sipped Champagne, "Oh, come quickly! I'm drinking stars!"

It was men of the Church, too, who first made elixirs from wine and brandy, combined with herbs and plants, that were originally used for medicinal purposes. The two most notable examples, with their secret formulas still in use today after hundreds of years, are the famed Bénédictine and Chartreuse liqueurs.

Even the vinicultural history of California begins with the efforts of Padre Junipero, a Dominican missionary, who planted vines he had brought from Spain around the missions.

But while the development of viniculture was greatly stimulated by the Church, the making of wine antedates it by thousands of years. Among the Laws of Hammurabi, the lawgiver-king of Babylonia, handed down over four thousand years ago, are regulations governing innkeepers and the manner in which their hostelries could be conducted. The penalties called for the loss of a limb—and in extreme cases death—for permitting riotous drinking on the premises. The penalties seem to have been rather trying for the unfortunate violators, but they indicate, as did our more recent "noble experiment," that man will not be made temperate by force or by stringent prohibitory laws. It is apparent that, from the beginning, the majority of people have enjoyed alcoholic beverages temperately and that there has always been a small minority who abuse the privilege to their own and their fellows' detriment.

Attempts to protect this minority have led to periodic restrictions on the rest for more than four thousand years.

The vine has played an important part in our own land, as well as throughout the world. One of the first concerns of the early European settlers on our eastern seaboard was the cultivation of the vine, both native and imported. These efforts, unfortunately, were doomed to failure for reasons discussed in Chapter 11. However, it is interesting to note that some twenty grape varieties, or more than half of the known species of the world, are indigenous to North America.

The American influence, oddly enough, has been felt in every viticultural region in Europe, not because of our taste for wine or our lack of it, but because of a certain grape pest (*Phylloxera vastatrix*) that reached Europe with a shipment of American vine plants imported for experimental purposes. In every part of viticultural Europe havoc was caused by the insatiable appetite of *Phylloxera* before an effective remedy was found. Chemicals, sprays, and turning over the land were of no avail. After twenty-odd years of suffering and experimentation, it was found that *Phylloxera* did not attack the American plants, which have much hardier roots. Thereupon, the European varieties (*Vitis vinifera*) were grafted onto American roots (*Vitis aestivalis, Vitis riparia,* or *Vitis rupestris*). There are people who say that for this reason our wines must be just as good as European wines because "their grapes grow from American vines." It is important to understand that the grape continues to have the identical character it had before being grafted onto American roots, since these particular rootstocks do not impart any of their own characteristics.

Although man had been making wine and beer since time immemorial, it was not until the early 1860s that anyone actually knew how the miracle occurred. It was the great scientist Louis Pasteur who, by his revolutionary research in the field of vinous and malt fermentation, proved that fermentation was caused by the presence of minute organisms called ferments. He further demonstrated that if grape juice or brewer's wort is exposed to air from which these minute organisms have been removed, no change takes place; but if ordinary air is present, fermentation begins. Based on Pasteur's studies the business of winemaking and brewing began a new era. Exact scientific knowledge replaced guesswork. Certain things no longer "just happened"; the winemakers understood at last how they happened and why, and they knew at last what to do.

Wine, like a human being, is born, passes through adolescence, matures, grows old, and, if not drunk in time, becomes senile and finally dies. Its life span, like that of a person, is unpredictable at the time of birth. It suffers from maladies to which some wines succumb but from which others recover. Some wines are aristocrats, some plebeians, but most wines are just sturdy, honest, good fellows. Yet all are interesting, more so as one gets to know them better, because no two vintages of the same wine, or any two wines, are ever identical.

Each has individuality. There are family resemblances and characteristics that can be recognized quite readily, but the more one studies the subject and notes these intriguing differences, the greater will be the enjoyment from wines.

tasting—what to look for

Three factors govern the appreciation of wine—color, aroma, and taste. Wine offers a threefold sensory appeal. That is why those who love wine first hold the glass to the light, then smell it, and finally taste it. The pleasure of anticipation is half the fun, and in drinking wine each step in the process adds to the enjoyment.

A wine must be clear and brilliant, have a clean, pleasant bouquet, and have a clean, sound, pleasant taste on the palate. There is beauty in its brilliant color, whether it be the pale gold of a white wine, reminding us of sunshine, or the warm ruby depth of a red wine. The color also gives the first indication of the wine's body; the deeper the color, the fuller the wine will be. Naturally, this applies to wines of the same type. Two totally dissimilar wines cannot be compared.

After the appeal to the eye, the sense of smell is pleased by the subtle, pleasant perfume a wine gives off in the form of esters. As a matter of fact, more than three-fourths of our sense of taste is actually our ability to smell. The bouquet, aroma, perfume—call it what you will—of a wine tells much of what the taste will be. In subsequent chapters, in describing the taste of wines, we shall be forced to use what may seem to be strange comparisons. We shall refer to some wines as having a strawberry, violet, or flowery bouquet, trying to give a taste picture in terms of familiar experiences.

Finally, after the aroma of the wine has promised a certain taste, the palate should confirm it and add the aftertaste that is experienced after the wine has been swallowed.

If wine is being tasted critically, with a view to purchasing or judging salability, it should be compared with a similar wine of the same price to establish its quality. Is the taste more pleasing? Is the quality better than the wine with which it is being compared? Tasting is a business and should be carried out very carefully and seriously. But in drinking wine for pleasure, enjoyment should not be encumbered by any critical analysis of its delicate nuances. The important thing, in this instance, is the pleasure the wine gives. Do not be hypercritical.

CULINARY USES OF WINE

It is not necessary to be a professional chef in order to use wine in cooking. A knowing dash of wine in the pot seasons, tenderizes, and imparts rare flavor and bouquet. The alcohol quickly boils off when heat is applied, leaving the wine's flavorful bouquet.

The use of wine in cooking goes back to the first viniculturists—and that is a long, long time. They looked upon wine as food and used it as naturally in cooking as they would any other ingredient.

Why do you use herbs? For flavoring, of course. Jars of dried herbs of every description are found in every kitchen. If you use them with a heavy hand, all you taste is the herb and every dish seems to taste the same. If you look upon wine as the most delicate of all flavorings you will realize its potential in cooking. Knowing how to use it is easier than you think.

The French are recognized as the world's best cooks. They make the most of the ingredients they use to create superb dishes from soups to desserts. Their use of wine in cooking gives the simplest dish an elusive, subtle flavor. They know from long experience that wine will produce the best results if handled delicately. It is not the wine you taste in the finished dish but rather the goodness of the food itself that the wine enhances.

Carême, who was chef to George IV of England and later to the Rothschilds, wrote in his memoirs that his thoughts were first turned to the art of cuisine by the delightful aroma that tantalized him as he stood one day, all but starving, outside a Paris restaurant. That aroma was produced by the wine in which the dishes were being cooked. From that moment on his course was set. Carême became the greatest of all chefs. He was able to produce a thousand different tastes with his seasonings, just as a painter with a few colors can create an infinite variety of nuances and tones. Wine was one of the principal ingredients he used.

In the United States one can find every type of food. Many dishes have been adapted and simplified, but we also have our own heritage. In colonial days sherry, port, and Madeira were the favorite wines of hospitality, and soups, shellfish, and desserts were prepared with these wines. (See Appendix T for a list of recommended modern cookbooks that feature cooking with wine.)

WINE AND HEALTH

"Wine," said Pasteur, "is the most healthful and hygienic of beverages." From the earliest days it has been looked upon as a natural remedy for man's ills. In ancient times it was invaluable to physicians whose medical knowledge was limited, and many doctors today recommend it for various ailments.

For example, wine has a positive role in the prevention of heart attacks, according to a recent study done at the Cardiovascular Research Institute, University of California. Wine's consumption is associated with high levels of high density lipoproteins (HDL), and it is HDL that acts to scour cholesterol plaque from arterial walls and prevent hardening of the arteries. Heart attack risk for moderate wine drinkers (one or two glasses a day) is 30 percent less than for those who either don't drink wine at all or drink heavily.

In wine-drinking nations, wine is considered a food and is taken at mealtimes. The absorption of such minerals as potassium, calcium, phosphorus, magnesium, iron, and zinc is aided by taking wine with meals. This may be of special importance to vegetarians who need to get the most nutrition from their more limited diets. Moderate wine consumption with meals also aids digestion. In France wine is called the milk of the aged.

"Heightened interest in matters of health and moderation have particularly favored wine," according to John de Luca, president of the Wine Institute in San Francisco. "An informed constituency enlightened by winegrower and winemaker, wine writer and wine educator, is the keystone in the arch of wine's growth and progress."

More important, however, than wine's medicinal properties is the fact that throughout the ages man has looked upon it as a food. The Bible refers to it in this sense time and again, for example, in Isaiah: "Until I come and take you away to a land like your own land, a land of corn and wine, a land of bread and vineyards."

calories   The calories in a glass of table wine will vary with the amount of sugar in the grapes at harvest. Calories come from alcohol or sugar. If the wine is fermented dry, all of the sugar will be converted to alcohol. If all of the sugar is not converted and some sugar is left in the wine (residual sugar), the calorie content will still be the same. The amount of sugar at harvest is rarely on the label of a table wine, varying with the year and the grape variety.

Wines that have more sugar at harvest than normal, and are usually consumed with desserts, will be sweet even after fermentation is completed, and, therefore, higher in calories than wines that are normally consumed with the main part of the meal. High sugar at harvest is often written on the label, since this achievement is highly prized by the grower and winemaker.

Besides table wines, there are wines that have been sweetened, or have had additional alcohol added at some point in their production. These will have more calories than dry or sweet table wines.

It can readily be seen that exact calorie counts cannot be given for wines, and the following chart can only be a guide. The only exceptions are wines that fall into a new category called "light wines," where a maximum of 60 calories per 100/ml (about 3½ ounces) is permitted. These lower-calorie wines are created either by removing some alcohol when the wine is made, or by picking the grapes when they are less ripe (or a combination of both). Calorie content appears on the label of light wines, whose minimum alcohol is 7.1 percent.

TYPE OF WINE	APPROX. CALORIES PER OUNCE	TYPE OF WINE	APPROX. CALORIES PER OUNCE
Light wine	17	Vermouth (dry)	35
Dry red or white table wine	25	Sherry (dry)	35
Champagne (brut)	25	Sherry (sweet)	50
German *Auslese* wine	30	Port	50

THE WINE LABEL IN GENERAL

Every label that appears on the bottle of an alcoholic beverage sold in the United States must be approved by the B.A.T.F. of the U.S. Treasury Department. It is mandatory that the public be furnished with clear, correct information as to the product: brand name, type of wine, country of origin, name and address of the bottler of a domestic wine or the importer of a foreign wine, and the net contents. A generic wine (see page 199) must state any qualifying place of origin, for example, New York State Chablis.

If the wine is over 14 percent alcohol, the percentage must be stated. If under, the words *table wine* may be substituted.

Among the items that may be mentioned or included on a label are:

1. Vintage date, the year in which the grapes used to make the wine were gathered, pressed, and the juices fermented into wine
2. Appellation of origin, such as the country, political subdivision, or viticultural area in which the grapes were grown
3. Vineyard in which the grapes were grown
4. Wine made from a specific grape
5. Wine made from special-quality grapes
6. Special quality wine, according to the producer
7. Vineyard owner's name
8. Bottling: estate, château, or shipper
9. Shipper's name and address
10. Official government guarantee of the wine's authenticity and proper labeling
11. Local trade association seal of authenticity of origin

WINE IN THE ECONOMY

In the United States a score of years ago, less than one-third of the wine consumed was still or sparkling wine, while wines containing more than 14 percent alcohol constituted over two-thirds. In recent years, wine has become more and more a part of the U.S. regular diet; by 1980 wines under 14 percent alcohol constituted over 75 percent of U.S. consumption, while wines of higher alcohol fell to just under 25 percent. U.S. per capita annual consumption of all wines is just over 2 gallons, a significant increase over the $9/10$ gallon that was the average in 1960, but still far from the consumption figures of other leading wine-producing countries.

One of the world's greatest wine-producing and wine-consuming nations, for example, is France. Annual per capita consumption is now about twenty-five gallons. Consumption figures of other important wine-producing and wine-consuming countries, such as Italy, Spain, and Portugal, are comparable.

Even though these countries are large consumers of their own wine, they are large exporters as well, and these wines enter U.S. shores under favorable tariff regulations.

Now that American production has outstripped consumption, domestic wines are looking for export markets, but the tariffs are restrictive. Efforts are being made to make the situation more equitable.

In the United States, however, the government has traditionally looked to the alcoholic beverage industry as a source of revenue, with taxes levied from both federal and state authorities.

The present tax rates are:

	FEDERAL	STATE
Light wines under 14 percent	$0.17 per gal.	$0.10 per gal.
Fortified wines up to 21 percent	0.67 per gal.	0.10 per gal.
Natural sparkling wines under 14 percent	3.40 per gal.	0.53⅓ per gal.

The state tax rates shown are those levied in New York. Each state levies its own taxes, and there is some variation; in most of the so-called controlled or monopoly states there is no specific tax as such, since the state sells to its citizens at a profit. See Appendix R for a list of federal taxes and import duties on all alcoholic beverages.

In 1939, when the federal excise taxes were $0.05 and $0.10 per gallon on light wines and fortified wines respectively, the federal and state governments

OPPOSITE PAGE. There are six basic types of wine labels.

TOP LEFT: Estate- or château-bottled wines are those for which the grapes are grown, processed, and bottled on the same property.

TOP RIGHT: Domaine labeling refers to wines for which the grapes are grown, processed, and bottled by the owner but not necessarily on one property.

CENTER LEFT: Regional labeling refers to wines made from grapes grown in one parish or region. If wine or grapes from out of the area are used, local custom or law controls the percentage.

CENTER RIGHT: Varietal labeling indicates the wine by the grape from which it is made. The proportion of wine from that grape may vary from 75 to 100 percent, depending on local law.

BOTTOM LEFT: Generic labeling refers to wines that use the name of a famous wine or wine area that has now come into general use. These names have no legal meaning but identify the general type of the wine. Terms such as Burgundy, Sauterne, or claret indicate the general type of wine and are always preceded by the name of the place of origin.

BOTTOM RIGHT: Monopole or brand labeling is used where the actual name of the wine has no real significance but gains consumer identification and acceptance through advertising or other consumer marketing techniques.

MIS EN BOUTEILLE AU CHATEAU

CHATEAU COS D'ESTOURNEL
GRAND CRU CLASSÉ EN 1855
SAINT-ESTÈPHE
APPELLATION SAINT-ESTÈPHE CONTROLÉE
1979   750 ml
SOCIÉTÉ FERMIÈRE DES DOMAINES PRATS A SAINT-ESTÈPHE (GIRONDE) FRANCE

VIN DE BORDEAUX
PRODUCED AND BOTTLED IN FRANCE
PRATS   ALCOHOL 12% BY VOL.
PRATS FRERES NEGOCIANTS-ÉLEVEURS, SAINT-ESTÈPHE (GIRONDE) FRANCE

Joseph Drouhin
RED BURGUNDY TABLE WINE   CONTENTS 1 PINT 8 FLUID OZS.
                                ALCOHOL BY VOLUME 13°
Beaune
APPELLATION BEAUNE CONTROLÉE
Clos des Mouches
RÉCOLTE DU DOMAINE
MIS EN BOUTEILLE PAR
JOSEPH DROUHIN
A BEAUNE, COTE-D'OR, AUX CELLIERS DES
ROIS DE FRANCE ET DES DUCS DE BOURGOGNE
Dreyfus, Ashby & Co
PRODUCE OF FRANCE

SOAVE
DENOMINAZIONE D'ORIGINE CONTROLLATA
CLASSICO SUPERIORE
PRODUCED AND BOTTLED BY
AZ. SANTA SOFIA S.A.S.
PEDEMONTE (VERONA) ITALIA

ALCOHOL 11.80%   750 ml. (25.4 FL. OZ.)
BY VOLUME   WHITE TABLE WINE
IMPORTED BY KOBRAND CORPORATION NEW-YORK, N.Y.
SOLE UNITED STATES IMPORTERS

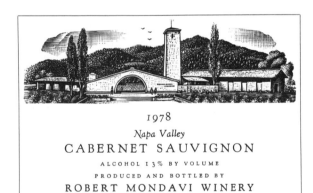

1978
Napa Valley
CABERNET SAUVIGNON
ALCOHOL 13% BY VOLUME
PRODUCED AND BOTTLED BY
ROBERT MONDAVI WINERY
OAKVILLE, CALIFORNIA

PAUL MASSON.
Rare Premium California
CHABLIS

Paul Masson Chablis is a light-bodied white wine with a charming bouquet. Its
distinctive, well-balanced taste is captured by picking the grapes at just the right
time and then fermenting the wine at ideally cool temperatures. Chablis is an ideal
cocktail or dinner wine and should be served well chilled. Alcohol 12% by Volume.
MADE & BOTTLED BY PAUL MASSON VINEYARDS, SARATOGA, CALIF.

MATEUS
PRODUCE
OF
PORTUGAL
ROSÉ
STILL WINE

This composite bottle shows the placement of some of the labels used by the wine trade.

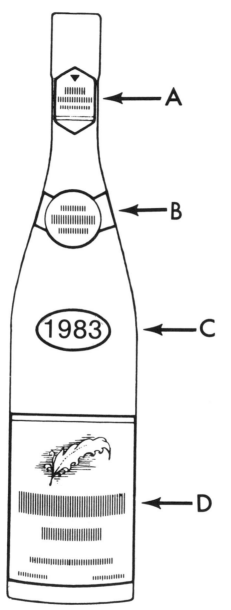

A. Identification seal or label sometimes used by regional groups or associations of shippers as a supplementary guarantee of origin and authenticity

B. Shipper's or importer's label (sometimes included in or placed above or below main label)

C. Vintage label, if applicable and if the vintage date does not appear on the main label

D. Main label, which bears the name and type of the wine, country of origin, contents (if not molded in the glass), and alcoholic strength or equivalent designation.

collected $15 million through wine excise and fortifying taxes. In 1952, when total volume had almost doubled and the federal taxes had been increased by more than three times over those of 1939, tax collections increased to a little over $100 million. In the first five years of the 1970s, federal wine tax collections averaged $180 million a year. The prospect for the 1980s is that, at current rates, because of increased plantings and consumption, federal and state revenues from wine sales will double in less than a decade.

The only increase in federal taxes on wine since 1952 was a jump from $2.72 to $3.40 per gallon for natural sparkling wines, exactly twenty times the 17-cent rate for light wines. This is the most illogical excise tax rate. But all in all, the tax from wine is rarely as much as 4 percent of the total tax revenue from alcoholic beverages. Generally speaking, these taxes are low and quite reasonable when compared with those levied on spirits. However, it is the high license fees, for both production and sale, that are the greatest hindrances to a more rapid expansion of winemaking and that tend to increase the cost of wine to the consuming public.

As long as wine is looked upon as an alcoholic beverage and not as a food, its wide use will be curtailed. When the day arrives that wine can be made and sold freely with a minimum of special tax and license burdens, when it can be distributed through outlets that sell other foods, much as coffee and tea are sold today, then and only then is our country likely to become a wine-drinking nation. Then the federal and state treasuries will derive an increased revenue from wine through the larger income tax payments of the farmers, who will turn to winemaking when they find it profitable.

The picture is not entirely discouraging. Annual wine consumption has reached about 500 million gallons—five times as much as in 1939—according to Wine Institute figures. This means many more acres planted to vineyards and greater employment in vineyards, wineries, and every phase of the industry. It is to be hoped the wine industry will continue to prosper.

In the following chapters we will discuss the wines produced throughout the world, devoting a chapter to each of the major wine producers and consumers of Europe and North America. Most of the wines these countries produce are enjoyed in the United States and are readily available on the larger markets. There are many wines of the world, however, that, regardless of the quantity made, are not among the major imports to the United States. Some, such as those from Chile, used to be more important years ago. Others, such as the Iron Curtain countries of Romania, Bulgaria, and Hungary, are becoming more of a factor because their governments are subsidizing their entry into the U.S. market. The wines of the southern hemisphere are also making themselves known north of the equator. The situation varies with international marketing, value, and production ability to fulfill the demand for quality and consistency.

These smaller wine-producing countries have been separated into four chapters: Other Wines of Europe, Other Wines of the Americas, Wines of the Middle East and Africa, and Wines of Australia, New Zealand, and the Far East. Within each chapter the countries will be discussed in alphabetical order. Appendix Q lists the quantity of wine produced in each country. Appendix R tells which of these nations enjoy most-favored-nation status, which affects import taxes and duties.

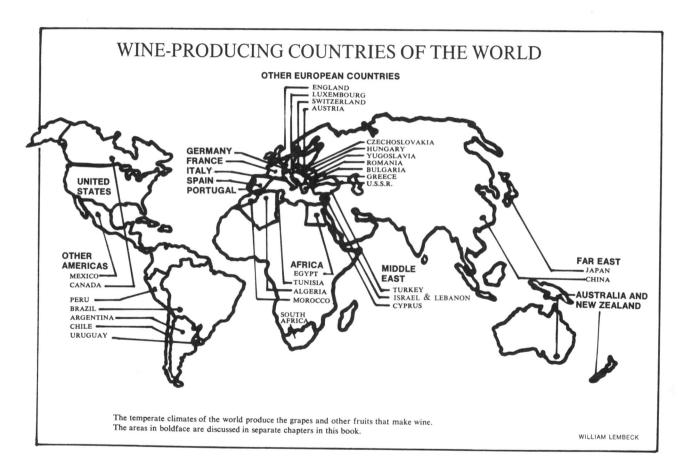

WINE-PRODUCING COUNTRIES OF THE WORLD

OTHER EUROPEAN COUNTRIES

- ENGLAND
- LUXEMBOURG
- SWITZERLAND
- AUSTRIA

GERMANY
FRANCE
ITALY
SPAIN
PORTUGAL

- CZECHOSLOVAKIA
- HUNGARY
- YUGOSLAVIA
- ROMANIA
- BULGARIA
- GREECE
- U.S.S.R.

UNITED STATES

OTHER AMERICAS
- MEXICO
- CANADA

- PERU
- BRAZIL
- ARGENTINA
- CHILE
- URUGUAY

AFRICA
- EGYPT
- TUNISIA
- ALGERIA
- MOROCCO

SOUTH AFRICA

MIDDLE EAST
- TURKEY
- ISRAEL & LEBANON
- CYPRUS

FAR EAST
- JAPAN
- CHINA

AUSTRALIA AND NEW ZEALAND

The temperate climates of the world produce the grapes and other fruits that make wine. The areas in boldface are discussed in separate chapters in this book.

WILLIAM LEMBECK

5
THE WINES OF FRANCE

In any discussion of wines it is natural that France should be uppermost in our minds. Although vying with Italy as one of the largest wine-producing nations in the world, France continues to be a major importer as well as a major exporter of wine.

It is her fine wine that France exports, and it is this policy of exporting only such goods as will enhance the nation's reputation, whether wine or chefs or fashion, that has made the French among the most astute merchandisers in the world and given France a position from which she sets the fashion in the art of good living. Poor wine, badly made clothes, and downright bad cooking may be found in France, but they stay there.

It is not, however, because of the quantity of wine she produces or drinks, but because of the quality and variety of wines she offers to the world, that France comes at the head of our list.

France is politically subdivided into ninety-five departments (states), which are further subdivided into communes or parishes (counties). The three most important departments, in which are produced the most famous wines, are the Gironde (red and white Bordeaux), the Côte d'Or (red and white Burgundy), and the Marne (Champagne). After these leaders come the departments of Yonne (Chablis), Bas-Rhin and Haut-Rhin (Alsace), Saône-et-Loire (Pouilly-Fuissé and Mâcon), Rhône (Beaujolais), and various departments along the Rhône River, which produce Côte Rôtie, Hermitage, and Châteauneuf-du-Pape, as well as those along the Loire River, which produce, going from east to west, Pouilly-Fumé, Vouvray, Saumur, Anjou, and Muscadet. In every department but two the vine is cultivated.

MAKING THE WINE

The harvest in France usually begins at the end of September or early October. The *vendangeurs* ("vintagers")—men, women, and children— are organized in groups under a foreman, who supervises the work to see that only ripe, sound grapes are picked and that the work is done thoroughly and conscientiously. The bunches of grapes are cut off the vine with special pruning shears and are placed in small baskets, which, when full, are emptied into large, wooden, hodlike receptacles known as *hottes*. The *porte-hotte* ("hod carrier") takes his full *hotte* to a wagon or a truck that has two tubs, called *douils*, into which he dumps the grapes. The driver of the truck pushes the grapes down firmly until the *douil* is filled. (A solidly packed *douil* will produce a *barrique* ["cask"] of 225 liters of wine.) When both *douils* are filled, the wagon or truck proceeds to the *pressoir* or *cuvier* ("pressing house"), where the grapes are unloaded and weighed.

Here the grapes are passed through a mechanical destemming, or *égrappage*, and crushing device. The purpose of crushing is simply to break the skins so that the juice will run out freely. The yeast can then begin the fermentation. Some winemakers still destem by hand, grasping bunches of grapes and rubbing them back and forth over wooden slats. The grapes, crushed and loosened from the stems, fall through the slats into the vat below. Otherwise the mechanically crushed grapes, along with their juice, which is now called must, are pumped into the fermenting vat.

At this point the winemaking processes differ for making red, white, and rosé wines. The juice of the usual wine grapes is colorless, and the color in red wine is actually obtained from the inside of the grape skin. The juice of the grape does not dissolve the pigments—it is the alcohol and heat created during fermentation that extracts the color from the skins.

Red wine is made by fermenting the juice with the grape skins and pips still in it, to give the wine color, body, and tannin. Tannins are complex compounds that give stability and longevity to the wine. When fermentation first begins, not much color is dissolved by the small amount of alcohol produced. After about a day, a red wine is only pink in color. If the must is separated from the skins at this point, with the balance of fermentation continuing away from the skins, a rosé wine will result. Because rosé wines begin as red wines do, and have some red color in them, they are considered red wines.

White wine is made by drawing off the free run juice immediately after crushing. This juice is placed in a holding tank for settling. The remaining skins are pressed and this juice is held separately. The winemaker can ferment these two batches separately or together. Fermentation takes place in closed vats to avoid oxidation. White grapes are used almost exclusively, but black-skinned grapes can be used if the must is separated from the skins before any color is extracted. The most notable example of this occurs in Champagne.

Saccharomyces, or wine yeast, whether naturally present on the skins or provided by the winemaker from specially propagated strains, begins to multiply with amazing rapidity in the favorable elements of grape juice and some air, and fermentation begins almost at once. At first it is violent and quite boisterous. In fact, the verb *to ferment* comes from the Latin *fervere*, "to boil," and a vat of fermenting must looks like boiling liquid. The escaping gas causes the surface to boil, bubble, and hiss. During the period of violent fermentation in making red wine, the skins, pips, and all the other residue in the must float to the top, forming a cap three or four feet thick. The cap is broken up with wooden appliances to allow carbon dioxide to escape, to let out excess heat, and to recirculate the skins with the must. Fermentation gradually simmers down and stops when the alcohol content is about 14 percent or when the yeast dies. (Sometimes there is still some sugar left, as with the sweet wines of Sauternes. This is called residual sugar.)

Fermentation of red wines usually takes from seven to ten days, while fermentation of white wines, accomplished at a lower temperature, takes longer. As soon as the fermentation is completed, the new wine is "racked" (drawn off) into clean, sulfured *barriques* of 225-liter capacity, along with press wine obtained by pressing the skins remaining in the fermenters. Press wine is usually aged separately, and is often blended with the new wine in judicious amounts because of its extra richness. The *barriques* are placed in the *chai* ("above-ground warehouse"), or cellar, if the vineyard boasts such a luxury.

During the first few months, because of evaporation, there will be a certain loss of wine, which will leave *ullage* ("air space"), into which the bacteria are prone to penetrate, ready to undo all the work of the yeast, making the wine sick or turning it to vinegar. The preventive is to keep the cask filled up to the top with sound wine. The casks are topped off twice a week during the first two months and every two weeks thereafter until the wine falls "bright" (clear) five or six months later.

During this period of continued activity, the wine throws off certain impurities and superfluous solid matter, which are deposited at the bottom of the cask and are known as the lees, consisting principally of cream of tartar, yeast cells, coloring, and other proteins.

At this point, while the wines are still in the cask, most red wines undergo a malolactic fermentation, in which the harsh malic acid is converted into the softer lactic acid. Since carbon dioxide is also formed, a special water seal is used to permit the gas to escape without allowing any air to enter.

It is not good for the new wine to remain in contact with the lees too long, so the new wine is racked into fresh casks three times during the first year: in the early spring, March or April; in June, when the vine flowers; and in October.

After the third racking a wooden bung is driven home and the cask stored so that the bung is on the side, entirely covered with wine. This ensures complete closures and prevents the entrance of any air. Of course, while the wine is in the cask, it is in contact with the air it breathes through the porous wood, and its development continues.

Changes in vinification methods have made it possible to bottle red wines earlier than had been customary. The lighter-bodied red wines are ready for bottling after two years in wood. The fuller-bodied red Bordeaux and red Burgundies, in big years, may require two and a half years' development in cask, but the traditional three or more years are no longer generally practiced.

The heavier solids precipitate of their own weight to form the lees, but a few lighter particles may remain in suspension, floating in the wine. To ensure only perfectly clear, bright wine, it must be fined. This clarifying process is done as follows: a small amount of albuminous material, which may be isinglass, gelatin, or white of egg, is mixed with a little wine and poured into the cask. This albuminous matter coagulates the solids in the wine, forming a heavy film, which slowly precipitates, acting as a filter and carrying with it all extraneous matter, leaving the wine in a brilliant condition for bottling. The fining process takes one or two weeks and is usually done twice. Just before bottling the wine may be filtered to ensure clarity.

On the day selected for bottling the cask is broached, the entire contents bottled, and the bottles corked. Much as a human being accustomed to an active outdoor occupation dislikes the confinement of an office job, so the wine reflects the change from the cask to the confinement of the bottle. It usually takes several months for it to accustom itself to the change. During this period the wine is not in prime condition since it is suffering from a malady known in the wine trade as bottle-sickness. After the bottle-sickness period the wine resumes its slow development in the bottle, which will continue as it develops toward its prime. The wine will reach a plateau that can last for several years under good storage conditions.

It is difficult to say how long a red Bordeaux, for example, will live. No two vintages are alike. While the less successful vintages reach their peak in five to ten years, better vintages will continue to improve for twenty, thirty, or forty years. If the wine is not drunk, it will gradually become senile and die. Red wines that have suffered man's ingratitude in this manner can easily be recognized. They have lost color, bouquet, body, and flavor; they have become dead and lifeless.

Normally, the older the wine, the greater the amount of deposit there will be in the bottle, and the more delicate it will be. Sediment is a natural phenomenon and can be expected of most wines, particularly red wines. In the course of time the wine throws off some of its bitartrates, and in the case of red wines a certain amount of tannin also; these make up the deposit that settles on the side or bottom of the bottle, depending on how it is stored. The sediment in no way affects the quality of the wine; it is simply one proof of age.

An extremely old red Bordeaux or Burgundy, recently arrived and fit to drink, would be a rarity in the United States today because of the rigors of an ocean voyage. However, there is no reason why a wine sent here when young and laid down in this country should not mature just as well as in France and be just as enjoyable. Experience shows that the ocean trip accelerates the maturing of the wine by at least a year.

WINE REGIONS
OF
FRANCE

BELGIUM

ENGLISH CHANNEL

LUXEMBOURG

Seine R.

Marne R.

Moselle R.

GERMANY

Paris

CHAMPAGNE

ALSACE

Loire R.

Rhine R.

CHABLIS

LOIRE

JURA

*ATLANTIC
OCEAN*

BURGUNDY

SWITZER-
LAND

BORDEAUX

Dordogne R.

BERGERAC

Garonne R.

CAHORS

**CÔTES
DU
RHÔNE**

ITALY

BEARN

MIDI

Rhône R.

CÔTES DE PROVENCE

SPAIN

*MEDITERRANEAN
SEA*

WILLIAM LEMBECK

APPELLATION CONTRÔLÉE

Although the vine has been cultivated commercially in France since the Roman occupation, and with greater care and intelligence than in other countries, it is only since the 1930s that regulatory laws have been passed, guaranteeing the authenticity of origin and place names commonly found on wine labels.

The first delimitative laws were passed after the 1911 "Champagne Wars," in which the *vignerons* who were making their wine exclusively from grapes grown within the province of Champagne rose up in arms against certain merchants who imported grapes at low prices from outside the traditional Champagne region and sold their champagne at cut prices. The riots resulted in laws that fixed the boundaries within which the grapes must be grown to produce wine legally entitled to the name Champagne.

Since then further laws have fixed the geographic limits of all the major wine- and brandy-producing districts. More recently these laws have been refined to fix the physical limits of the world-famous vineyards and have set the maximum quantity of quality wine each may produce of a given vintage. Setting the legal maximum of quantity assures the maintenance of quality. Under this law, called *Appellation d'Origine Contrôlée* (A.O.C.), the production of each vineyard is controlled. The vineyard owner is obliged to report to his local board, which in turn reports to the central or national board of *Appellation Contrôlée* wines, located in Paris. Wines produced under this system of control of origin and quality will bear on their labels the phrase *Appellation Contrôlée*, which has become a French government guarantee of origin and, to a certain degree, of quality as well.

The basic conditions for a wine to be entitled to an *Appellation Contrôlée* are set up by the *Institut National des Appellations d'Origine des Vins et Eaux-de-Vie* (I.N.A.O.), an official body whose members belong either to the French civil service or to the wine industry.

controls of A.O.C. Some of these conditions pertain to district boundaries according to the nature of the soil, grape varieties, maximum quantity of wine per acre allowed to be produced, minimum alcohol content of the wine, and viticultural and vinicultural methods. Growers and shippers must follow these regulations if they wish to label their wines with the name of the vineyard, the commune, or the district. There are exceptions: very old bottles of wine do not carry the *Appellation Contrôlée* statement because most of the laws date only from 1935.

Technicians exercise controls to enforce these regulations. The quality regulations, of course, increase in stringency in relation to the fame of the place of origin of the wine. For example, a wine entitled to be labeled *Appellation Pommard Contrôlée* must come from any vineyard of the Pommard zone and have a minimum of $10\frac{1}{2}$ percent alcohol. But for the wine to have the legal right to be labeled *Appellation Pommard Les Épenots Contrôlée*, it must be made entirely from grapes grown in the Les Épenots vineyard of the Pommard zone. It must also have a minimum alcohol content of 11 percent. In both cases the maximum quantity of wine that may legally be produced each year is 35 hectoliters per hectare (equivalent to 374 gallons per acre).

Some wines bear on their labels the letters *V.D.Q.S.* (*Vins Délimités de Qualité Supérieure*), which indicate that they are a second classification of high-quality wines of specified origin. They are subject to regulations similar to those of *Appellation Contrôlée* wines; that is, these wines have been harvested from strictly defined vineyards and vines, by traditional methods. The label shows that the wine conforms to standards set jointly by the I.N.A.O. and the Ministry of Agriculture. V.D.Q.S. wines, about sixty of them, are grouped into seven general places, where reds, whites, and rosés are produced. Someday the V.D.Q.S. wines may be absorbed into the *Appellation Contrôlée* classification.

The wines from each section are so markedly different and have such individual characteristics that they have been accepted as basic types. Their names are often misused and the wines imitated in almost all wine-producing countries, so in order to study the wines of the country properly, we must take each geographical division separately. Each will be considered in the order of its importance to the wine trade in general.

1. BORDEAUX

If France is the most famous wine-producing country, then the Bordeaux district (Gironde) is the most famous in the production of great red wines. The district produces three distinct varieties of wines, equally distinguished: magisterial clarets; clean, dry, white Graves; and luscious, golden Sauternes.

Fifty years before the birth of Christ, Burdigala (Bordeaux) was the chief *history* town and commercial center of Biturigis Vivisi. Later, in the fourth century, it was made the capital of Aquitanica Secunda. Its fame, then as now, was irrevocably linked with the excellence of its wines, which were praised by Columella, renowned Roman writer of the first century.

Through his marriage to Eleanor of Aquitaine in 1152, Henry of Anjou acquired the Sénéchaussée of Bordeaux (Gascony) and the vast Duchy of Guyenne. Two years later he became King Henry II of England, and for three hundred years Gascony belonged to the English crown. Its wines enjoyed wide popularity in the British Isles, a taste that exists to this day.

The history of the famous wines of Bordeaux began more than two thousand years ago. We do not know who first produced a wine of the claret type, but the poet Ausonius sang of its charms and virtues during the Roman occupation. The famous Château Ausone is supposed to have been his vineyard.

What is claret? The term was originally used by the English when they referred to the red wines of Bordeaux. The English made up a large part of the market for Bordeaux wines, and many English words have gained common usage in the wine world, not only in Bordeaux. The word *claret* has definite geographic origins in Bordeaux, but it is not a legal term in France. Many other countries use the term to describe a red wine they feel is similar to the type made in Bordeaux. This usage, unfortunately, has detracted from the elegant connotation of a château-bottled red wine.

geography   The Bordelais (Bordeaux country) viticultural region is divided into five main (left) and four lesser (right) districts:

Médoc (includes Haut-Medoc)	Premières Côtes de Bordeaux
Graves	Côtes de Bourg
Saint-Émilion	Côtes de Blaye
Pomerol	Entre-deux-Mers
Sauternes	

There is a further subdivision, the commune, or parish. The parish is a geographical, political, and, formerly, religious subdivision, as a parish priest and church were required to administer to the spiritual needs of a community. The Church worked out such a perfect geographical subdivision that the state saw no reason to change it and took it over.

Médoc   The most important district is the Médoc, a triangular peninsula stretching north some fifty miles from Bordeaux to Soulac and varying in width from six to ten miles. It lies between the Gironde River on the east and the Atlantic Ocean on the west and is divided into Médoc and Haut-Médoc. Of the appellation wines produced in the area, Médoc accounts for 25 percent and Haut-Médoc produces 75 percent. With few exceptions (for example, the dry white wines of Pavillon Blanc du Château Margaux, Château Loudenne, and Château La Dame Blanche), only red wines are produced in the fifty-three communes that make up the entire Médoc. The four most important—Pauillac, Saint-Julien, Margaux, and Saint-Estèphe—are all located in the Haut-Médoc, which extends thirty miles from Bordeaux to just north of Saint-Estèphe.

Graves   The Graves takes its name from the gravelly or pebbly quality of the soil. The district stretches for twenty-five miles in the southwest corner of Bordeaux and is for the most part level plain that becomes hillier to the south. Here are produced both red and white wines. The most important communes of the Graves are Pessac, Léognan, and Martillac.

WINE REGIONS OF BORDEAUX

Soulac

Gironde R.

MÉDOC

ATLANTIC OCEAN

SCALE

0   25 km

Borders
of Bordeaux
Appellation

BLAYE

SAINT-
ESTÈPHE

PAUILLAC

SAINT-
JULIEN

BOURG

MARGAUX AND
CANTENAC

HAUT-
MÉDOC

POMEROL

SAINT-ÉMILION

Dordogne R.

Garonne R.

Bordeaux

PREMIÈRES CÔTES
DE BORDEAUX

ENTRE-DEUX-MERS

GRAVES

BARSAC
PREIGNAC
SAUTERNES { BOMMES
SAUTERNES
FARGUES

WILLIAM LEMBECK

*Saint-Émilion
and Pomerol*

Saint-Émilion and neighboring Pomerol are in the eastern part of Bordeaux, north of the Dordogne River in the vicinity of the town of Libourne. Saint-Émilion can be considered as two distinct sections: the Graves section (not the Graves region previously discussed) on a plâteau that extends into Pomerol, and the Côtes to the southeast, around the town of Saint-Émilion. The main grape is the Merlot, which ripens earlier than other Bordelais grapes, and which produces wines that are fruity, scented, and mature earlier than their Médoc counterparts. Pomerol, a single commune northwest of Saint-Émilion, boasts many famous vineyards for its small size.

Sauternes

In the southern portion of the Graves we come to a district smaller than the island of Manhattan but viticulturally favored as are few regions in the world. The rich, luscious, highly perfumed wines of the Sauternes are entirely distinct from all the other wines of Bordeaux and have an excellence all their own. The Sauternais (Sauternes country) lies in the southeast of Graves and on the left bank of the Garonne River. Five communes compose Sauternes country: Sauternes, Barsac, Bommes, Fargues, and Preignac. The wines from any of these communes are known by the regional names of Sauternes. Barsac, however, even though it is a Sauternes, has its own appellation, and many of its châteaus prefer to use it rather than the larger Sauternes appellation.

*Premières Côtes de
Bordeaux, Bourg, Blaye,
and Entredeux-Mers*

In these districts are produced useful wines, both red and white, that are generally shipped as Bordeaux Blanc or Bordeaux Rouge. Some petits châteaus travel under their own names, but many are blended into branded, commercial wines.

soil

One would think that rich soil would be required to produce fine wine. Nothing could be further from the truth. In fact, the soil of the Bordeaux wine region is mainly gravel, limestone, or sand with a clay subsoil. More unfriendly soil for agriculture would be difficult to find, and yet the vine flourishes best in just these types of soil. Where no other crop can be grown successfully, the vine gives the best quality of wine grape. This is equally true in the other famous viticultural regions of the world.

grape varieties

The principal vine used in the production of the great clarets of the Médoc and Graves is the Cabernet Sauvignon. Growing in small, close-set bunches, its violet-scented grapes are small and sweet and give the wine its vinosity. Other vines, such as Merlot, Petit Verdot, and Carmenère, are planted to give special qualities to the wines. In Saint-Émilion and Pomerol, however, the principal grape is the early-ripening Merlot, the balance being mostly Cabernet Franc (also called Bouschet). The best white wines of Graves and Sauternes are made from the Sémillon and Sauvignon Blanc grapes.

The vine in Bordeaux is not allowed to grow wild; in fact, it is cut back close to the ground after the vintage, so that the winter appearance of a vineyard is that of a bare field dotted with an orderly series of stumps. The vines are not allowed to grow more than 2½ to 3½ feet high so that what strength they derive from the soil will go into producing grapes of quality.

There are more than thirty thousand vineyards in the Bordeaux wine region, most of which are called *château*, meaning "castle." In many cases the property boasts a medieval castle, but when the term is used as generally as it is in Bordeaux, the majority of these "castles" are simply farmhouses used only for pressing grapes and storing wine.

Bordeaux wine trade

Obviously, if each of the vineyard owners were to attempt to sell his wines directly to buyers from all over the world, there would be no end to the confusion. Hence there evolved many generations ago clearinghouses in the form of Bordeaux wine merchants, brokers who buy the wine from the different vineyard owners, sometimes bottled, but more often in larger quantities in the wood. The broker ships the wine as he receives it, or he blends it with wine from other vineyards and bottles it, not under the château or vineyard name, but under his own proprietary brand name. With few exceptions the vineyard owner never markets his own wines but depends on the wine merchant to do it for him.

The Bordeaux wine trade has developed five types of labels:

labeling

1. Château bottled
2. Château wine bottled by a cooperative or by a wine merchant
3. *Monopole* or trademark
4. Commune or regional
5. Varietal

There are two distinct types of labels used on château wines. The first, château bottled, indicates that the wine has been produced, cared for, and bottled at the vineyard property where the grapes were grown. It has on the label, or sometimes on the capsule, the phrase *mis en bouteille au château*, which means "bottled at the château." The vineyard owner delivers this wine, bottled, labeled, and cased, to the wine merchant or shipper. The cork is always branded with the château name and the vintage year. Examples are Château Lafite-Rothschild, Château Latour, and Château d'Yquem.

The second type of label, château wine bottled by the wine merchant, indicates that the wine has been produced at the château named on the label but has been purchased in the cask and bottled by the shipper in his Bordeaux cellars. The shipper's name appears on the label.

There are some châteaus that do not practice château bottling at all; they have found it more profitable to sell their wines in cask to the different wine merchants who bottle them. On these and other A.O.C. wines the following phrases may be found: *mis en bouteille à la propriété, mise d'origine,* and *mis en bouteille dan la région de . . .* , followed by the name of the specific region.

Whereas château bottling guarantees authenticity of origin, it does not have to guarantee quality. Because of changing vintage conditions, château-bottled wines vary in quality from year to year. This has a direct influence on the price governing each vintage and explains why a younger vintage will sometimes fetch a higher price than an older one of the same wine. A good example is the 1978 Château Lafite-Rothschild, which costs more than three times as much as the less desirable 1977.

In order to take care of his customer's needs in every part of the world, the Bordeaux shipper must always have a wide assortment of château wines. Although there is no wine "stock market" in Bordeaux, châteaux bottlings are traded in somewhat the same manner as stocks and bonds. Through the centuries the trade has evolved a system that is eminently fair and satisfactory, both to the vineyard owner and to the shipper.

Suppose, for instance, that the 1978 vintage of Château Latour totaled 300,000 bottles, all château bottled. Eight wine merchants agree to buy up the entire vintage and split it among themselves. Each of them would then have the same wine to offer to the trade, identical in every respect as to labeling, capsules, cases, and so forth, and their prices would be more or less the same. Along comes a ninth merchant who needs this wine for one of his customers. As the eight merchants have cornered the market on this wine, he must buy from one of the original purchasers and pay him a profit, and he must also make a profit for himself on the sale. Therefore, when buying château-bottled Bordeaux wines, shop for the lowest price, since it is all the same wine, assuming it has been properly stored.

The third type of label is the *monopole,* or private brand. A *monopole* wine is almost invariably a blend of various wines from different parts of a region that the shipper maintains year in and year out at the same standard of quality. It is a plentiful, everyday wine. There are many shippers who have these brands. Examples are: Grande Marque, Fonset-Lacour, La Cour Pavillon, and Mouton-Cadet.

The fourth label is the commune, district, or regional label. A bottle so labeled contains wine produced in the commune, district, or region named, for example, Médoc (wine in this bottle was produced in the Médoc district). This wine does not necessarily come from one vineyard but may be from several in the commune, district, or region named. It probably is a blended wine, bottled by the shipper at his Bordeaux cellars. For this reason it is possible to obtain wines of widely varying quality and price bearing identical place names and vintages from different shippers. One shipper may use better-quality wine in his blend, while another feels that price is more important than quality. The Bordeaux shipper, like any other businessman, tries to satisfy his customers'

TOP LEFT: Château-bottled wine. Note the phrase *mis en bouteille au château.*
TOP RIGHT: Monopole or trademark brand. Note the word *déposée*, meaning "registered brand."
BOTTOM LEFT: Varietal wine, bottled by the shipper.
BOTTOM RIGHT: Regional wine, bottled by the shipper.

needs. Beware of bargains, compare prices, and taste a bottle before you buy a case.

The varietal label is the fifth type. This term has been used in the United States to indicate that the grape variety named on the label predominates in the wine itself. The purpose was to break away from generic names that were not definitive and to identify more precisely the nature of a wine. This practice was formerly used only in Alsace, Switzerland, Italy, and a few other regions in Europe, but recently the shippers of Bordeaux, Burgundy, and the Loire have also used varietal labels. The French authorities require the use of 100 percent of the grapes named; the E.E.C. minimum is 85 percent, while the U.S. minimum is 75 percent. For France, this is a departure from the traditional style of winemaking, which usually uses more than one grape variety.

vintage   There seems to be some confusion as to the exact meaning of the word *vintage* in reference to wines, whether they are imported or produced in the United States. The word has two meanings:

1. *Vintage* means gathering the grapes, pressing them, and making wine. There is a vintage (harvest) every year.
2. The date (or *millésime*) on a bottle of wine signifies the year in which the grapes were harvested. Some vineyards bottle and date every year's production. Certain regions, such as Champagne, date only the wines of exceptional years. Since this is not done every year, the dated wines are known as vintage wines.

A vintage chart, judiciously used, can be helpful, but it is important to remember table wines change constantly. No two wines, even from the same district, develop at a constant rate. Furthermore, not all wines made in a great year are great, and not all wines made in a relatively poor year are poor. Sweeping generalities of this kind cannot be applied when one considers the thousands of vineyards involved. However, the chances are better for good wines when conditions are generally favorable, and with these reservations in mind, a vintage chart can be useful (see Appendix B).

CLASSIFIED GROWTHS

In 1855 a number of Bordeaux wines were to be established at the Exposition in Paris. There was some question about the order in which the wines should be shown as, inevitably, there was rivalry among the best-known vineyard owners as to who produced the finest wine. In order to settle the matter once and for all, a jury of wine brokers was selected to classify the outstanding clarets and Sauternes in order of merit. Although this was done over a century ago, for the most part these classifications still hold and are accepted the world over. ° Fifty-seven red wines of Médoc and one from Graves were chosen and classified in five classes or groups, while twenty Sauternes were grouped in two main classes, and one Sauternes was placed in a special class. After 1855 some vineyards were sold and subsequently divided. This accounts for the different number of classified châteaus found in different source books, depending on when the vineyards were counted, but at present the generally accepted number is sixty-one (see Appendix C). Below the fifth growth in the Médoc and the second growth in the Sauternes are further classifications: *grand crus bourgeois exceptionnel, grand crus bourgeois,* and *bourgeois.*

In 1953 the leading wines of Graves were officially classified. In 1959 the list was revised, and this time thirteen red and eight white wines were selected. In 1955 an official classification was made of the top clarets of Saint-Émilion. Twelve were chosen as first classified great growths (two rated "A" and ten rated "B") and seventy-two as great classified growths. Both of these classifications have been adopted by the *Institut National des Appellations d'Origine des Vins et Eaux-de-Vie* (see Appendix C). Because of the demand and the high prices of the great classified growths, more and more wines with regional labels and proprietary brands are being sold.

To differentiate between a classified claret and a *cru bourgeois* is easy. To tell the difference between a second and a third growth is very difficult. Most of the sixty-one vineyards produce excellent wines whose main differences lie in nuances of nose (bouquet), body, and delicacy apparent to the connoisseur, but not necessarily to the layman. However, certain basic, distinguishing marks are apparent in wines from different parishes or sections. For example, the wines of Pauillac (Château Lafite-Rothschild, Château Latour, Château Mouton-Rothschild, and so on) have more body than those of Margaux (Château Margaux), which have finesse and delicacy, while the red wines of the Graves (Château Haut-Brion, Château La Mission Haut Brion, and so on) are fuller than the Médoc wines mentioned. Even fuller and more fruity are the Pomerol (Château Pétrus) and Saint-Émilion (Château Ausone, Château Cheval Blanc, and so on).

the classified claret growths

CHÂTEAU LAFITE-ROTHSCHILD. Lafite is spelled with one *f* and one *t* and should not be confused with similar names such as Laffite or Laffitte. According to a document dated 1355, Château Lafite belonged to a certain Jean de Lafite. In 1868 Baron James de Rothschild acquired it at private auction for the reputed sum of 165,000 pounds, and it is still held by his heirs. In a good

° In 1787, sixty-eight years before the Bordeaux classification of 1855, Thomas Jefferson wrote, "The cantons in which the most celebrated wines of Bourdeaux are made are Medoc down the river, Grave adjoining the city, and the parishes next above; all on the same side of the river. . . . Of red wines, there are four vineyards of the first quality, *viz.,* 1. Château Margau, . . . 2. La Tour de Segur, . . . 3. Hautbrion, . . . 4. Château de la Fite. . . ."

year Château Lafite-Rothschild has a magnificent deep color, a softness and delicacy of flavor, and a violet bouquet.

CHÂTEAU LATOUR, also a first growth, takes its name from an ancient tower. This, according to legend, is the only remaining vestige of the original castle of Saint-Lambert, supposedly destroyed by Du Guesclin when the English were driven out of Gascony. The retiring English, say the ancient tales, left a vast fortune buried in or near the tower. But the fortune, as we well know, was buried not below but above the ground, for the great wines of Château Latour have more body and a more pronounced flavor than those of either Lafite or Margaux.

CHÂTEAU MARGAUX, in true medieval splendor, once boasted a stout fortress surrounded by moats a hundred feet wide, which were connected to the Gironde by canals so boats could sail up to its gates. In 1447 it was the property of Baron François de Montferrand. After him it passed through many hands until, in 1879, it came to Count Pillet-Will. Today it is owned by Mme. André Mentzelopoulos, widow of a financier. The wines of Château Margaux are generous without being too full bodied, are elegant, and have a delightfully fragrant bouquet. In one of the best parts of its vineyard a limited quantity of fine wine is produced from the Sémillon and Sauvignon Blanc grape varieties. It is labeled Pavillon Blanc due Château Margaux.

CHÂTEAU HAUT-BRION, in the parish of Pessac in the Graves, is the last of the original 1855 listing of first growths and the only wine of the sixty-one to be chosen from outside the Médoc. It is, in fact, in the suburbs of Bordeaux. Haut-Brion, pronounced *o-bree-ohn*, is, according to some chroniclers, the French spelling of O'Brien; this is possible, as there must have been some Irishmen in Gascony during the English period. As far back as the fourteenth century, at the court of Pope Clement V, these wines were highly regarded. Lacking the softness and lightness of their fellow first growths, these wines are renowned for their full, generous body and beautiful, deep color. This superb vineyard has been the property of the family of Clarence Dillon, the American financier, for a number of years.

CHÂTEAU MOUTON-ROTHSCHILD, whose owners were outspoken against the 1855 classification, did not accept tamely having their wine rated below the first four growths and as a result adopted this challenging motto:

Premier ne puis	First I cannot be
Second ne daigne	Second I do not deign to be
Mouton suis.	Mouton I am.

In 1973, after much work by Baron Philippe de Rothschild, the vineyard was classified in Bordeaux as a first growth. (The 1855 classification remains unchanged.) The Baron then wrote a new motto:

First, I am
Second, I was
But Mouton does not change.

Judging by the prices Mouton usually fetches, this move was more than justified. Over the years Mouton has consistently equaled the prices of the four first growths. Although the 1855 classification is still amazingly accurate, many inequities have developed however. On the basis of market prices, Château Pétrus of Pomerol and Château Cheval Blanc of Saint-Émilion, which were not included in the 1855 classification, are among the top clarets of Bordeaux.

Well-known second growths in the American market are the wines of Châteaus Léoville-Lascases, Léoville-Barton, Léoville-Poyferré, Gruaud-Larose, Ducru-Beaucaillou, Lascombes, Rausan-Ségla, Brane-Cantenac, Pichon-Longueville (Baron), Pichon-Longueville-Comtesse de Lalande, Cos d'Estournel, and Montrose.

Aerial view of the beautiful Château La Mission Haut Brion at Pessac, Graves. (*Courtesy Henri Woltner, Bordeaux*)

Among the third growths, Châteaus Giscours, Palmer, Kirwan, and Calon-Ségur are well known in America, while among the fourth growths, the wines of Châteaus Prieuré-Lichine, Talbot, and Beychevelle are often sold in the United States.

Finally, there are the fifth growths, of which the better known in the United States are Châteaus Pontet-Canet, Grand-Puy-Lacoste, Grand-Puy-Ducasse, Lynch-Bages, Mouton-Baron-Phillipe, and Batailley. There are too many people who turn up their noses at fifth growths, considering them poor or even inferior. What they forget or overlook is that fifth growths are still part of that special group of sixty-one wines that were selected from among thousands of the better red wines of Bordeaux. The fact is that they are still great wines, though perhaps not peers of the first growths.

Graves clarets   The fine clarets of the Graves region were not classifed officially in 1855. It was not until 1953, and again in 1959, that official classifications were at last made and published (see Appendix C). From the Graves come such outstanding wines as Châteaus La Mission Haut Brion, Pape-Clément, Haut-Bailly, Smith-Haut-Lafitte, Bouscaut, and Domaine de Chevalier. They are fuller bodied and not quite as delicate as the wines of the Médoc, but Graves clarets make up in richness what they lack in finesse.

Saint-Émilion   Politics or jealousy must have had something to do with the 1855 classifica-
and Pomerol   tion, as the wines of Châteaus Ausone and Cheval-Blanc in Saint-Émilion, and Pétrus, L'Évangile, and Vieux Château Certan in Pomerol, were not included. These wines, because of their high percentage of Merlot grapes, have a deep color, rich bouquet, and fullness of body. They also mature earlier than wines made with more Cabernet Sauvignon grapes. Because of all these factors, the wines made of Saint-Émilion and Pomerol are often called the Burgundies of Bordeaux. Ausone, whose average yield is quite small, Cheval Blanc, and Pétrus all produce magnificent wines that almost invariably command prices equal to the great Médoc clarets. Saint-Émilion clarets were finally classified in 1955 (see Appendix C). Still other wines of great repute are Châteaus Figeac, La Gaffelière, Canon, Magdelaine, Pavie, and Clos Fourtet in Saint-Émilion. In Pomerol famous wines include Petit-Village, La Fleur-Pétrus, Nenin, and Trotanoy.

WHITE WINES OF BORDEAUX

Graves   More white wine than red is made in the Graves (pronounced *grahv*). The white wines are clean, dry, and fresh and have a pleasant, fruity bouquet of their own.

Most of the Graves wines are shipped by the Bordeaux houses under private brand labels as standard blends, each house having several brands varying in quality and dryness in order to please the tastes of their several world markets. There are several outstanding château-bottled white Graves: Châteaus Olivier, Carbonnieux, and Laville Haut Brion. Of these, well known in this country is Château Olivier, from an estate whose castle and vineyards were renowned in the twelfth century. Here the Prince of Wales, known as Edward the Black Prince, had a hunting lodge during the time when Aquitaine was an English domain and he was governor general of Gascony.

The ancient legends of these old châteaus have the perfume and enchantment of the wines themselves. It is related of Château Carbonnieux that, in order to convince a certain sultan of Turkey of the merits of French wine (wine being prohibited to the Faithful by the Koran), Château Carbonnieux was shipped to him labeled "Mineral Water of Carbonnieux." So impressed was the Commander of the Faithful upon drinking the wine that he exclaimed, "When they have water that is so pure and so agreeable, how can the French drink wine?"

Other well-known white wines of the Graves are Châteaus Bouscaut, Domaine de Chevalier, and Haut-Brion Blanc.

The grape varieties in the Graves are the Sémillon and the Sauvignon Blanc. The Sémillon gives wine finesse, velvetiness, color, and aroma. The predominant Sauvignon Blanc produces a wine that is full and rich in bouquet. Sauvignon Blanc has the acidity to stand on its own as a varietal wine. Although the same grape varieties are used in the Graves as in the Sauternes, where the Sémillon predominates, the Graves produces a dry wine because the grapes are gathered when they are ripe. They are not left to hang on the vine until overripe, as is done in Sauternes, where climatic conditions are different.

There are five communes in the Sauternes area: Sauternes (which gives the regional name to the entire section), Barsac, Bommes, Fargues, and Preignac. Wine produced from grapes grown in any of these five communes is legally permitted to be called Sauternes. *Sauternes*

There is a pronounced difference in the way Sauternes are made as compared with the Graves. In fact, the wine originally resembled the Graves. But many years ago, it seems, the owner of a château in this district, reputedly Yquem, was away on a hunting trip. He was delayed and therefore did not return in time to order the gathering of the grapes when they were ripe. As his men had no authority to start this work, they waited for the master to appear some four weeks later. The grapes were overripe, shriveled, and covered with mold, but the owner decided to gather them nonetheless and see what could be done. To his own surprise as well as that of everyone else, the wine that developed from these overripe grapes was unlike anything they had tasted before. It was delicious—very rich, luscious, and highly perfumed.

Today we understand what happened. When the grapes reach a certain stage of maturity beyond the full stage of ripeness, a special mold settles upon them, known technically as *Botrytis cinerea*.

When gathering grapes in Sauternes, skilled workers do not begin until the sun is high, about half past eight in the morning, and they stop before the sun goes down because the dew washes off some *Botrytis cinerea*. The French call this condition of overripeness *pourriture noble,* meaning "noble rottenness." The grapes are not, of course, rotten, as rotten grapes are removed lest they spoil the wine; they are merely overripe. Only bunches in a perfect condition of overripeness are picked, and therefore a vineyard may be gone over as many as eight times before all the grapes are gathered, a procedure that naturally adds to the cost of production.

Leaving the grapes on the vine until they attain *pourriture noble* makes their skins become porous and the water in the grapes evaporates, thus concentrating the sugar, increasing glycerine, and reducing acidity. This gives a smaller yield of juice, or must, per acre, but it ensures richness. Sauternes, consequently, are always rich, sweet wines. There is no such thing as a dry Sauternes.

Because these wines are rich in sugar, it is difficult to keep them from refermenting during unseasonably warm weather. The only preventive is to sulfur the casks well before they are filled. The sulfur fumes sterilize the cask, destroying any bacteria that might be present, and, when the wine is poured in, the sulfur acts as a deterrent to the yeasts remaining in the wine, as they are ready to continue their fermentation job at the least provocation.

The wines of the five Sauternes communes are all very similar in character, and they are all sweet. Sweetness and dryness, of course, are relative qualities. Some Sauternes are sweeter and richer than others, but compared with white wines from the Graves or any other section of the Bordeaux wine region, they are much softer, sweeter, and fuller bodied.

Bordeaux Blanc   This does not mean that dry white wine cannot be produced. The Appellation of Origin law and its *Appellation Contrôlée* regulations do not prevent production of such a wine in Sauternes, but they forbid its being labeled Sauternes or Barsac. It can only be labeled Bordeaux Blanc.

Many châteaus in Sauternes are producing dry white wines from the Sauvignon Blanc grape alone. Since these are not in the famous sweet, rich style of Sauternes, they may not use the name of the château on the label. They are sometimes called "Bordeaux Sauvignon Sec."

the question of Barsac   Of the five communes entitled to use the regional term Sauternes, Barsac is the most enterprising. While the vintners in Sauternes, Bommes, Fargues, and Preignac are content to market their wines simply as Sauternes, those of Barsac prefer that their wines be known by the name of their commune. As far as sweetness is concerned, there is little difference between Barsac and the rest of Sauternes, at least when château-bottled wines are compared.

Château Olivier, with its moat, at Léognan, Graves. (*Courtesy Louis Eschenauer, Bordeaux*)

Famed Château d'Yquem, whose crenellated walls and towers enclose the residence, offices, winery, and cellars, in the heart of Sauternes. (*Courtesy Marquis Bertrand de Lur-Saluces, Bordeaux*)

However, comparing Sauternes and Barsac shipped under the label of a Bordeaux wine merchant is another story. These are blended wines, and when the shipper blends he can control the result. He can blend for sweetness, relative dryness, perfume, or body. He knows perfectly well that if his Sauternes and Barsac are identical, there is no reason to buy both wines. So he blends one wine for more sweetness, establishing two different wines. There is no consistency among shippers as to which of the two wines will be sweeter.

Haut Sauternes and Haut Barsac

Haut in French means "high," but it has no official significance for Sauternes and Barsac. The word is sometimes used on labels to denote the producer's level of quality. As a rule, these wines cost more than the simple Sauternes or Barsac. *Haut* has no geographical significance, as there is no region designated as Haut Barsac or Haut Sauternes.

the classified Sauternes growths

In the classification of 1855 the wines of the great Sauternes vineyards were classed in order of merit in the same manner of the clarets. This classification embraced twenty-one growths, but because of the split-up of several vineyards, the number today is twenty-seven (see Appendix C).

CHÂTEAU D'YQUEM.   In the fourteenth century when Edward II was king of England, his wine merchant and buyer in Bordeaux was Pierre Ayquem (also spelled *Eyquem*). It was he or one of his descendants who gave the family patronym to the vineyard whose storied wines have evoked more and greater hyperbole than almost any other wine since the celebrated Falernians of Roman times. A few of these are: "the extravagance of perfection," "a ray of sunshine concentrated in a glass," and "a ray more brilliant than the sun's."

In 1859 Grand Duke Constantine of Russia paid the fabulous sum of 20,000 gold francs for a tun (twelve hundred bottles) of the 1847 vintage. This was about $3.50 per bottle, an unheard-of price in those days.

There is no question about d'Yquem's wines being in a class by themselves, as demonstrated by their 1855 classification as Premier Cru Supérieur, and meriting the apparent exaggerations of poets intoxicated by such perfection. The finer vintages of Château d'Yquem combine richness of perfume, depth of vinosity, and fullness of body in perfect balance. There are differences among vintages and some are sweeter than others. D'Yquems will vary in their luscious richness, depending on their age and the vintage.

At Yquem, the usual proportion of grapes is 80 percent Sémillon and 20 percent Sauvignon Blanc. The Sémillon is allowed to hang on the vine until it is overripe, and has acquired the *Botrytis cinerea*. The Sauvignon Blanc is harvested at the usual time, to ensure that the wine has enough acidity.

CHÂTEAU LA TOUR-BLANCHE.   According to ancient documents, this fine vineyard was at one time the property of Jean Saint-Marc de La Tour-Blanche, treasurer general to the king. Sometime after the French Revolution its ownership passed to M. Osiris, who bequeathed the entire property to the state for a viticultural school. Its wines are elegant, full, and rich.

Note the spelling of *La Tour* as two words. Many people confuse Château La Tour-Blanche, the Sauternes, with Château Latour, the claret.

CHÂTEAU DE RAYNE-VIGNEAU.   Property for generations of the Vicomtes de Pontac, Rayne-Vigneau has had a glorious history. Its most notable exploit was defeating the best German wine in a blind tasting at the World's Fair of 1867 and being selected as the finest white wine of that age. The two wines in question were a Château Vigneau 1861 and a Rhine wine of the same vintage.

CHÂTEAU SUDUIRAUT,   bordering Château d'Yquem, was formerly controlled by the crown. Today its wine labels bear the legend *ancien cru du Roy* ("former property of the king"). The wine is vigorous, with a rich aroma, and commands very high prices.

CHÂTEAU GUIRAUD (formerly Bayle) is a beautiful property that includes a fine vineyard—about 150 acres in extent—a park of 350 acres, and a lovely old château. The wine of Château Guiraud is famed for its delicacy, perfume, and body.

CHÂTEAUS COUTET AND CLIMENS.   The wines of these vineyards, situated in the commune of Barsac, are first growths and possess the typical firmness and elegant bouquet of Sauternes. They are rich Sauternes like the other growths of Bommes, Fargues, Preignac, and Sauternes.

CHÂTEAUS LAFAURIE-PEYRAGUEY, CLOS HAUT-PEYRAGUEY, RIEUSSEC, RABAUD-PROMIS, AND SIGALAS-RABAUD.   These other first growths are all excellent wines that are sometimes available in the United States.

Among the second growths the best known on our market are Château Filhot, in the commune of Sauternes, and Château Myrat, in the commune of Barsac. Château Caillou, also from Barsac, ages gracefully. Although classed as second growths, they are nonetheless excellent wines possessing a fine, rich bouquet and body.

other white wines of Bordeaux

There are districts other than the major ones discussed previously that produce distinguished, useful, and usually less expensive wines. For example, Entre-deux-Mers, "between two seas," a large section lying between the Garonne and Dordogne rivers before they meet, produces a vast quantity of white wine, some dry and some sweet. Bourg and Blaye, across the Gironde from the Médoc, produce clean, dry white wines as well as robust, fruity red wines, some of exceptional quality.

See Appendix B for notes on the Bordeaux vintages, and Appendix C for the Classifications of Bordeaux.

2. BURGUNDY

"None other will I have," said Duke Philip the Good of Burgundy when he set his heart on marrying the beautiful Princess Isabella. This thoroughly typical phrase was adopted as the ducal motto of the House of Burgundy. It represents the attitude of Burgundians then and now, proud of their race, their lineage, and their wines. It was their wont to style themselves "Dukes of Burgundy and Lords of the finest wines in Christendom."

history The history of wine in Burgundy dates back to Caesar's conquest of Gaul and is almost as turbulent as the political story of the region. The Roman legions planted vines from Italy, and when the wine began competing with that of the mother country, Emperor Domitian ordered the vines uprooted and the fields planted in corn. This was in A.D. 96. Fortunately the edict was enforced only halfheartedly and was finally rescinded entirely by Emperor Probus in A.D. 278.

Long before the wine of the region was known by the regional term Burgundy, the Church—which here, as elsewhere, had a strong influence in the development of quality wines—had made famous among medieval gourmets the names of such vineyards as Clos de Bèze, Corton-Charlemagne, Romanée, Clos de Vougeot, Meursault, and Montrachet.

Wine from these vineyards—first known as wine of Auxerre, since the wine went to Paris and the outside world by boat down the Yonne River from the "port" of Auxerre, and later as wine of Beaune—did not acquire the name Burgundy until the sixteenth century. When Petrarch advised Pope Urban V to remove from Avignon to Rome, according to legend His Holiness demurred because his entourage complained, "There is no Beaune wine in Italy, and without Beaune wine how unhappy we would be." This difficulty seemingly was overcome during the pontificate of Gregory XII.

geography Wine has always been Burgundy's chief source of fame, but, unlike wine from other regions, Burgundy wines do not all come from a small, densely cultivated geographical locale. Because of the acquisitiveness of Burgundy's dukes, who reached out on all sides for more and more land, the area known as Burgundy was created by gradually adding small parcels of land. Wine produced in every part of the duchy became known simply as Burgundy. This wine-producing region includes vineyards in four different departments: Yonne, Côte d'Or, Saône-et-Loire, and Rhône.

First is the "true Burgundy," the Côte d'Or or "golden slope," divided into the Côte de Nuits and the Côte de Beaune. The Côte d'Or is a string of low-lying hills extending thirty-eight miles from Dijon in the north to Santenay in the south; the width of the vineyards is from 550 to 600 yards. Second, farther south lie the Côte Chalonnaise and the Mâconnais, in the Department of Saône-et-Loire. Beaujolais begins in the Saône-et-Loire but lies mainly in the Department of the Rhône. (This department should not be confused with the large, general wine-producing area called Côtes du Rhône, farther south). Last, about halfway between Dijon and Paris, north of the Côte d'Or, in the Department of the Yonne, there are thirteen hundred acres of vineyards around the town of Chablis that may be planted to produce that famous white wine.

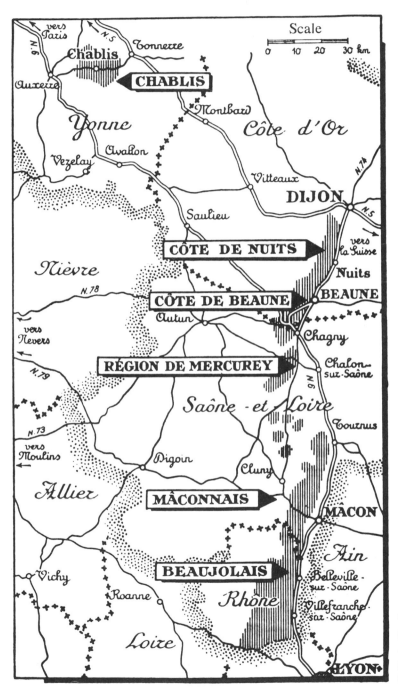

The wine regions of Burgundy. (*From Pierre Poupon and Pierre Forgeot,* The Wines of Burgundy, *courtesy Presses Universitaires de France*)

The soil of the Côte d'Or, rich in iron, is chalky, argillaceous (white clay), and rocky. The slopes are said to take their name from the burnished appearance they present in late fall when the leaves have turned golden.

grape varieties

The fine red wines come from the Pinot Noir grape, while the white wines of repute are produced from the Chardonnay. The Pinot Noir and Chardonnay are noble plants that produce quality but not quantity, and here as nowhere else is the *vigneron* tempted to increase his output at the sacrifice of quality.

The other red grape variety in Burgundy that predominates in the south is the Gamay, a more productive variety that gives a poor wine in the Côte d'Or but produces an extremely enjoyable red wine in the clay and granite soil of Mâcon and Beaujolais. The other white grape of Burgundy is the Aligoté, which is highly productive and makes a simple and short-lived white wine. Pinot Blanc, which used to be grown, has virtually disappeared. The label "Pinot Chardonnay Macon" is a misnomer, since the wine is not a blend of Pinot Blanc and Chardonnay, and Chardonnay is not even part of the Pinot family.

vineyards

The most famous vineyards are found on slopes with a southern exposure. They neither extend to the summit of the hills nor reach the lower plains. The fine vineyards form something like a wide, continuous ribbon laid along the gentle slopes, rarely dropping below the eight-hundred-foot elevation or rising above the thousand-foot level. The plain is seven hundred feet above sea level, and the higher hills are fifteen hundred feet.

It is on these slopes that the Pinot Noir seems to do best and the Gamay is rarely found. On the plains and summits, however, the Gamay is most in evidence. Wines from a mixture of the two varieties are known as Bourgogne Passe-Tout-Grains and contain at least one-third Pinot Noir grapes.

In Burgundy, as in other viticultural regions, *Phylloxera* did its devastating work, and today the vineyards have been replanted with American *Phylloxera*-resistant roots on which the native Chardonnay, Pinot Noir, Gamay, and other varieties have been grafted. The last native stocks were removed in the early 1950s.

The laws controlling the origin and labeling of wines limit the production of the vineyards that are capable of producing fine wines in order to ensure the highest quality possible, thus forcing the *vigneron* to prune his vines properly. As the quantity is strictly limited, he does everything in his power to aid the vine in giving quality.

The system of vineyard ownership in Burgundy is different from that in any other viticultural region of France and is duplicated to any extent only in Germany. To begin with, the vineyards are all very small. The largest, Clos de Vougeot, is only 126 acres, and Romanée is just about 2 acres, the average being under 25 acres. Not only are the vineyards extremely small, but with rare exceptions they are held by anywhere from three to sixty or more owners, each proprietor having title to a small parcel of the vineyard.

At Clos de Vougeot, for example, there are sixty-six owners who cultivate their individual parcels of the vineyard, gather the grapes from their own vines, press them, and vinify the resulting must. As the human element enters into production, it is understandable that, although the same Pinot variety is planted in the entire vineyard, and all the operations of making the wine take place at the same time, there may be sixty-six different wines produced, all legally entitled to the appellation Clos de Vougeot.

This may be contrasted with the system in Bordeaux, where even the largest and most famous châteaus are owned by just one person or corporation who controls the entire product that appears under the château's label.

Since Burgundy often has many owners of a vineyard, there cannot be château-bottled wines. However, "estate bottling" received great impetus after Repeal in the United States. American connoisseurs began to demand château-bottled Burgundies, and there simply was no such thing. Estate-bottled Burgundies have been grown, vinified, and bottled by a specific producer, whose name appears on the label, and are the equivalent of château-bottled Bordeaux. Estate-bottled wines are labeled *mis en bouteille au domaine.*

While this is good merchandising and benefits the consumer, since in theory the Burgundians would strive to offer only the very best quality, estate bottling guarantees only the authenticity of vineyard origin and that the wine comes from the grapes of a single producer and has not been blended with wines from any other producer or from any other vineyard. The practice of estate bottling has proliferated so since World War II that it is not uncommon today to see estate bottlings of wines labeled Gevrey-Chambertin, Chambolle-Musigny, Vosne-Romanée, and so forth, which contradicts the entire meaning and objective of the system. For example, a wine labeled Gevrey-Chambertin is a blend of wines produced in any part of the Gevrey-Chambertin commune. When the label also states it is estate bottled, the blend is made entirely of wines from the producer's vineyard holdings in Gevrey-Chambertin. These can be, although they are not necessarily, parcels in the great Le Chambertin and also from the most poorly rated vineyards in the commune. We believe that estate bottling should be reserved and practiced for only the unblended wine of the great vineyards that is bottled by the actual producer who is a proprietor, no matter how small his holding.

Not all of the growers ship their own wines, and if the shippers were to keep each grower's wines separate their lists would not only be interminable but also very confusing. For this reason it has been only natural for shippers to buy, say, Clos de Vougeot from several growers, blend these wines together, and offer them as their own (the shippers') quality of Clos de Vougeot. This also tends to equalize the price.

Wines that are not estate bottled may be labeled *mis en bouteille à la propriété* or *mise d'origine.*

labeling   The most famous Burgundy vineyards have their own appellations. Wines from vineyards that are less famous, but are from famous communes, will travel under the commune's appellation. If neither is well known, the wine will go forth as Côte de Nuits, Côte de Beaune, or simply red or white Burgundy. A Burgundy wine will always bear the best-known name to which it is entitled. (In Bordeaux, on the other hand, even the largest or most famous châteaus carry the appellation of their commune.)

For example, in the commune of Gevrey-Chambertin, wine from the famous Chambertin vineyard, which has its own appellation, will invariably be labeled Appellation Chambertin Contrôlée. Wine from a vineyard in the same commune whose name might be even less well known than the commune name, will be labeled Appellation Gevery-Chambertin Contrôlée, using the commune's appellation.

Wine from any vineyard in the communes of Comblanchien or Corgoloin will be labeled Côte de Nuits-Villages or simply Bourgogne Rouge, because neither the vineyards nor the communes are well known outside the district. Most of the red wines of the communes of Meursault, Puligny-Montrachet, and Chassagne-Montrachet suffer the same fate and are shipped as Côte de Beaune, as these communes, while world famous for their white wines, are not too well known for their reds.

The famous vineyards of the Côte de'Or have been classified by the *Appellation Contrôlée* authorities. A hierarchy of quality of Burgundy wines has been established based upon vineyard site and wines produced. The finest vineyards have been labeled Grands Crus, and their names have become controlled appellations. Premiers Crus vineyards are a notch below. Less famous vineyards may have their names on the label along with the commune name.

Probably the most expensive wine of Burgundy is that of Romanée-Conti, a rather small vineyard in the commune of Vosne-Romanée. Like all things, its price is governed by supply and demand, since the area planted in vines is a little less than $4\frac{1}{2}$ acres. In recent years, even larger vineyards in other communes that rival Romanée-Conti, such as Chambertin, Clos de Vougeot, and Musigny, also command very high prices, since actually the total amount of Burgundy produced is not enough to quench the thirst of the world.

CÔTE DE NUITS

The red wines of the Côte de Nuits are generous and full bodied and have a deep, fruity, unique bouquet that is the result of the combination of the Pinot Noir grape and the Burgundian soil. They develop less rapidly than the wines of the Côte de Beaune. In 1882 the commune of Musigny decided that the sale of all its wines would be increased if the commune were to adopt the name of its most famous vineyard, and therefore Chambolle became Chambolle-*Musigny*. This system has been adopted by the communes of Gevrey-*Chambertin*, Flagey-*Echézeaux*, Vosne-*Romanée*, Nuits-*Saint-Georges*, Aloxe-

Ancient Château du Clos de Vougeot, set in the very center of the vineyard, property of the Confrérie des Chevaliers du Tastevin, at Vougeot, Côte d'Or. (*Courtesy Confrérie des Chevaliers du Tastevin*)

Corton, Puligny-*Montrachet,* Chassagne-*Montrachet,* and others. The most important Grands Crus vineyards of the Côte de Nuits are discussed below:

CHAMBERTIN. Napoleon, so the story goes, would drink no other wine and planned all his great military and civil victories when warmed by the generous fire of Chambertin. But when he was before Moscow his supply ran out, resulting in his disastrous retreat from Russia. Knowing his penchant for Chambertin, the allies generously permitted that he be supplied with it at Saint Helena.

No one knows the date of origin for the vineyard of Chambertin, but like all ancient vineyards it is rich in legends. One story connected with it throws some light on the entire history of viticulture in Burgundy. In the year 630, according to the records, the Duc d'Amalgaire gave a parcel of vineyard, with an area of thirty-five acres, to the Abbey of Bèze. Henceforth the vineyard was known as Clos de Bèze, and in time its wines acquired much renown. Sometime later, but before 1219, when we have our next parchment record, a peasant named Bertin, who owned the field bordering Clos de Bèze, reasoned that if he planted the same grape varieties as grew in the famous Clos de Bèze vineyards, his wines would be good, too. The French word for field is *champ,* and the vineyard then must have been known as Champ de Bertin. This was finally contracted to the present Chambertin, and since 1219 the wines from the two vineyards have been confused and looked upon as one and the same. Today the total area of Chambertin and Chambertin-Clos de Bèze is sixty-seven acres. Chambertin-Clos de Bèze may be labeled either Chambertin-Clos de Bèze or simply Chambertin. Chambertin may not be labeled Chambertin-Clos de Bèze. Both wines are big, heady wines that acquire a firm roundness with age. See Appendix D for other Grands Crus vineyards in this commune.

LES MUSIGNY AND LES BONNES MARES. These two great rival vineyards lie in the commune of Chambolle-Musigny, but Les Bonnes Mares, which has 34 acres in Chambolle-Musigny, also has 4½ acres in the commune of Morey-Saint-Denis. Both wines are known for their finesse, suppleness, and elegance, but, although they are similar in character, Les Musigny, with only 14 acres, is the more famous of the two.

CLOS DE VOUGEOT. These are fruity wines, having rich flavor, color, body, bouquet, and infinite grace and character. The elegance of its wines has merited Clos de Vougeot, in the commune of Vougeot, an honor that is today traditional.

It is said that Napoleon, the Little Corporal and now all-powerful emperor, heard of the excellent wines made at Vougeot. He sent word to Dom Gobelet, the last clerical cellar-master at Clos de Vougeot, saying that it would please him to taste these superlative wines. "If he is that curious," replied the venerable Cistercian haughtily, "let him come to my house."

The beautiful, imposing Château du Clos de Vougeot is situated on the upper slopes in the very center of the vineyard. For many centuries it belonged to the Cistercian Abbey of Cîteaux. The earliest available records of the abbey vineyard ownership date back to 1110. The present château was begun in the thirteenth century and completed sometime in the sixteenth. Its primary function was to serve as the pressing house and cellars for the wine-production activities of the Cistercian Order, who owned it until the French Revolution, when it was secularized. Today the château is the property of the Confrérie des Chevaliers du Tastevin, the "brotherhood of gentlemen of the tasting cup." The great ceremonies, functions, and dinners of the Confrérie are held there.

ROMANÉE-CONTI, in Vosne-Romanée, is the generally accepted king of Burgundy, always having all the qualities of great wine: body, vinosity, bouquet, and character. The wines are rich and long lived.

ROMANÉE, ROMANÉE-SAINT-VIVANT, LE RICHEBOURG, AND LA TÂCHE. The commune richest in great vineyards is Vosne-Romanée. These vineyards vary in size from the bare two acres of Romanée, fifteen acres of La Tâche, and twenty acres of Le Richebourg, to almost twenty-four acres of Romanée-Saint-Vivant. The wines of these great growths differ, but it would take one long accustomed to drinking them to identify these differences. Suffice it to say that they all have beautiful color, a deep bouquet and flavor, body, and elegance.

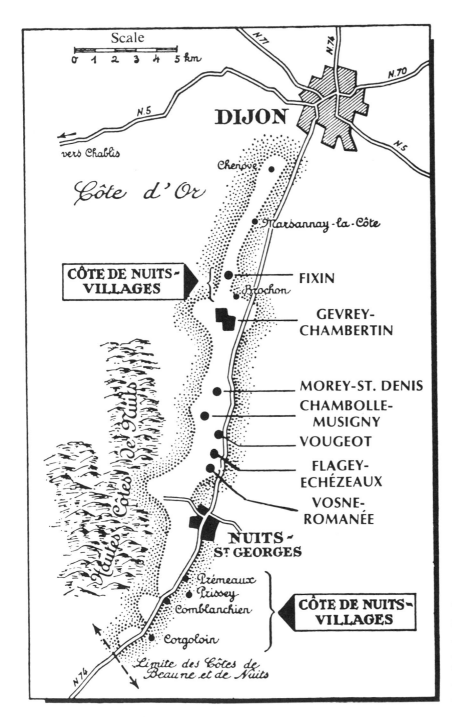

The communes of the Côte de Nuits. (*From Pierre Poupon and Pierre Forgeot*, The Wines of Burgundy, *courtesy Presses Universitaires de France*)

LES GRANDS ECHÉZEAUX AND ECHÉZEAUX. The former's twenty-three acres and the latter's seventy-four acres are neighbors to the west of Clos de Vougeot, and there is a close resemblance among all of these wines. While in the commune of Flagey-Echézeaux, these wines are usually considered with the wines of neighboring Vosne-Romanée, because Les Grands Echézeaux vineyard once belonged to the Abbey of Saint-Vivant, and today belongs almost entirely to the Société Civile du Domaine de la Romanée-Conti. The wines are softer and more delicate than the famed red wines of Vosne-Romanée.

CLOS DE TART, CLOS DE LA ROCHE, AND LES SAINT-GEORGES. The first two vineyards, with acreages of $17\frac{3}{4}$ and 38 respectively, lie in the commune of Morey-Saint-Georges. These three fine vineyards of the Côte de Nuits have rich wines, with color, body, and character, and in good years they are comparable to any of the great Côte de Nuits.

The most northerly commune of Côte de Nuits before Dijon is Fixin. Here the wines are similar to those of Gevrey-Chambertin and are sometimes their equal. La Perrière (not to be confused with Les Perrières of Meursault) and Clos-du-Chapitre produce good, strong Burgundy wines.

The appellation Côte de Nuits-Villages is restricted to the wines of the five communes of Fixin, Brochon, Prissey, Comblanchien, and Corgoloin.

CÔTE DE BEAUNE

The medieval city of Beaune is the headquarters of the Burgundy wine trade. Most of the great shipping houses have their cellars in the city itself and it is in Beaune that we find the world-famous Hospices de Beaune.

The red wines of the Côte de Beaune develop more rapidly and are ready for drinking sooner than those of the Côte de Nuits. They show a pleasant, fruity bouquet, softness, and finesse and are tenderly supple, which makes them most agreeable wines at all times.

HOSPICES DE BEAUNE. There are many well-preserved examples of Beaune's long history—churches, parts of the old city wall, and battlements—all still in use in one way or another; but her proudest monument is Les Hospices de Beaune, a charitable hospital built in 1443. It has rendered continuous and devoted service to the poor of the region for over five hundred years, wars and revolution notwithstanding.

The Hôtel-Dieu, or hospital, is an exquisite example of Flemish architectural style. It is a four-story-high, block-square building, surmounted by a slanting roof whose green, yellow, and black slates are arranged in a classic pattern. The cobblestone open central courtyard—the Court of Honor—was the original locale for the Hospices' annual wine auctions.

Central courtyard of fifteenth-century Hospices de Beaune, where the annual Hospices' wine auctions were formerly held. (*Courtesy Julius Wile Sons & Co., Inc., New York*)

Over the centuries modern improvements have been adopted in the care of the sick, but some of the original wards, kitchens, chapels, and the museum have been preserved in their original fifteenth-century state. The museum contains many works of art, including paintings of Nicolas Rolin and his wife, Guigone de Salins, and the magnificent altarpiece of the Last Judgment, all on wood, which she commissioned the Flemish painter Roger van der Weyden (1440–1464) to paint expressly for the Hospices de Beaune.

In 1441 Pope Eugene IV authorized the creation of the Hospices de Beaune as a hospital to care for the poor and indigent people of Beaune. Nicolas Rolin, tax collector during the reign of Louis XI, and his wife donated the property and erected the building. They also gave the Hospices several parcels of vineyards so that the Hospices might be supported by the sale of its wines.

The legend of the period has it that Nicolas Rolin could well afford to provide such a charity for the poor, as he had created so many of them. Whether or not that is true, the Hospices de Beaune has proved to be a remarkable institution. Its principal support has always come from the sale of wines produced from vineyards that devout Burgundians have willed to the Hospices. Today these comprise some thirty parcels that are known by the names of the donors (see Appendix D).

For over four centuries the Hospices' wines were sold privately, but since 1859 they have been sold at a festive public auction on the third Sunday of every November. All of the Hospices de Beaune vineyards are located in the Côte de Beaune, from Aloxe-Corton to Meursault, but because they represent the first real opportunity for buyers to taste the wines of each vintage, the prices fetched at the auction determine to a great extent the rating of the vintage for all Burgundy wines. Often the prices are more than the individual wines are really worth, but the factors of charity and publicity unquestionably influence the bidding.

LE CORTON, LE CLOS DU ROI, LES BRESSANDES, AND LES POUGETS. In the commune of Aloxe-Corton lie the famous vineyards of Le Corton with an area of 28 acres, Le Clos du Roi with 26 acres, Les Bressandes with 42 acres, and Les Pougets with 24½ acres. Le Corton is the only Grand Cru red wine of the Côte de Beaune. It is usually solid and robust. With bottle ripeness it expands and possesses a wealth of bouquet, roundness, body, and breed and can be compared with the great Côte de Nuits wines. Le Clos du Roi and Les Bressandes are also big wines, but they are more like Beaune wines in character. They have a lovely color, aroma, and finesse. The wines from Les Pougets vineyard are always very fine, with excellent color, flavor, and body.

ÎLE-DES-VERGELESSES AND LES BASSES-VERGELESSES. These vineyards have areas of twenty-three and forty-four acres, respectively, in the commune of Pernand, and their wines are renowned for their finesse and distinction.

LES FÈVES AND LES GRÈVES. These are the two outstanding examples from Beaune itself. Les Fèves, with 10½ acres, and Les Grèves, with 78½ acres, produce wines noted for their fine, rich softness and elegance.

LES RUGIENS AND LES ÉPENOTS. The commune name, Pommard, is probably the most famous Burgundy wine name. It is certainly far better known than that of its finest vineyard, Les Rugiens (33½ acres). For that reason most of its wine comes to our table labeled simply Pommard, and because of the demand its price is usually somewhat high. Should you come upon authentic and properly matured examples of Pommard-Rugiens of Les Épenots (27 acres), you will find them generally delicate, fruity, and well-rounded wines of character.

The red wines of the communes of Volnay and Monthélie are light red in color, elegant, and delightful. Those of the commune of Auxey-Duresses are somewhat like those of Pommard and Volnay, and the red wines of the commune of Chassagne-Montrachet have a richness and fullness that remind one of those of the Côte de Nuits.

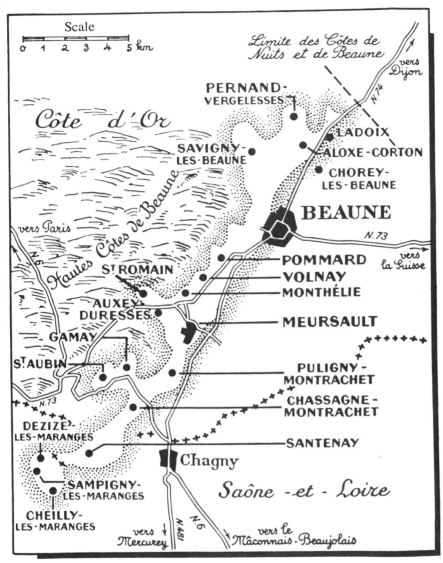

The communes of the Côte de Beaune. (*From Pierre Poupon and Pierre Forgeot,* The Wines of Burgundy, *courtesy Presses Universitaires de France*)

Santenay, at the southern end of the Côte de Beaune, produces firm red wines that can age nicely. These wines have recently come on the market as good values. Les Gravières is the best known vineyard.

The appellation Côte de Beaune-Villages applies to only red wine and is restricted to sixteen communes: Auxey-Duresses, Blagny, Chassagne-Montrachet, Cheilly-les-Maranges, Chorey-les-Beaune, Dezize-les-Maranges, Ladoix, Meursault, Monthélie, Pernand-Vergelesses, Puligny-Montrachet, Saint-Aubin, Saint-Romain, Sampigny-les-Maranges, Santenay, and Savigny-les-Beaune.

WHITE WINES OF BURGUNDY

All of the main subdivisions of the Burgundy wine region produce white wines, each of which is of an individual character and has its following. The Department of the Yonne gives us chablis. The Côte de Nuits sends us three unique white wines, although the majority of the great white wines of Burgundy come from the Côte de Beaune. Still farther south is Mâcon, which produces considerable quantities of crisp white wines, including Pouilly-Fuissé and Mâcon Blanc, which are great favorites in the United States. In neighboring Beaujolais a small amount of Beaujolais Blanc is produced.

grape varieties For making white wines the *plante noble* is the Chardonnay. Other varieties of grapes are used, but to a very minor degree, with the exception of the copious Aligoté, which produces large quantities of an agreeable but short-lived wine that is mostly consumed locally. This wine may be labeled varietally, as Bourgogne Aligoté, and it may have some Chardonnay or Pinot Blanc in it.

Chablis The wine the world knows as Chablis comes from the northernmost part of Burgundy. Its distinguishing characteristic, not to be found in every vintage, is an austere, flinty quality, much prized by those who have had the good fortune to encounter it. Chablis is, perhaps, the driest and palest of table wines. Its color should be a pale straw yellow.

The flinty quality is known as *pierre-a-fusil* ("gun flint"), and the taste is like a sharp, metallic tang. Added to this effect is the wine's delicate, fruity bouquet, and herein lies its cooling, refreshing quality. Although in good years Chablis is a long-lived wine, we prefer it young and fresh. Chablis is exceptional with oysters. They were made for each other, as you will discover if you try them together.

Chablis is classified, in descending order of quality, as follows: Chablis Grand Cru, Chablis Premier Cru, Chablis, and Petit Chablis. The best vineyards are crescent-shaped hillsides just north of the village of Chablis and make up the Grand Cru classification. They are Blanchots, Bougros, Les Clos, Grenouilles, Les Preuses, Valmur, and Vaudésir.

Chablis Premier Cru comes from twenty-nine vineyards, situated in ten communes, which are considered superior. Chablis is a blend of wine from several vineyards. Petit Chablis comes from the outskirts of the area. As with other wines of Burgundy, the reputation of the shipper is the best guarantee of quality. See Appendix D for a list of Premiers Crus vineyards.

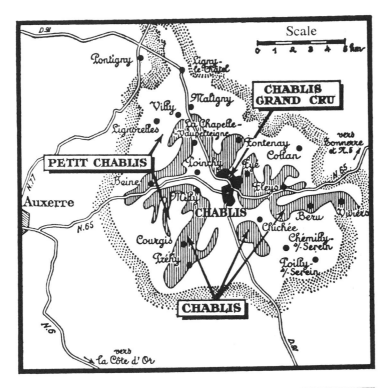

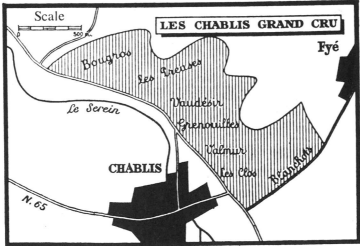

The Chablis region and its Grand Cru vineyards.
(*From Pierre Poupon and Pierre Forgeot,* The Wines of
Burgundy, *courtesy Presses Universitaires de France*)

Baskets of grapes in a Côte de Beaune vineyard. (*Courtesy Joseph E. Seagram & Sons, Inc., New York*)

Côte de Nuits   In the Côte de Nuits, at the famous Musigny vineyard in Chambolle-Musigny, about 100 cases of Musigny Blanc are produced by Comte Georges de Vogüé. To the south, next to the Château du Clos de Vougeot, famous for its red wines, are five acres planted with Chardonnay grapes from which 450 cases of Clos Blanc de Vougeot are made. In the commune of Nuits-Saint-Georges some 250 cases of Nuits-Saint-Georges Blanc are produced. These are distinguished wines, possessing full flavor and body.

Moving south to the Côte de Beaune we find the greatest white wines of   *Côte de Beaune*
Burgundy in the communes of Aloxe-Corton, Meursault, Puligny-Montrachet,
and Chassagne-Montrachet.

CORTON-CHARLEMAGNE. This renowned white wine is made in the commune of Aloxe-Corton, at the forty-two-acre Charlemagne vineyard, so
named in honor of the great emperor. It is a Grand Cru vineyard, making
Aloxe-Corton the only commune with both a white and a red Grand Cru
vineyard.

LES PERRIÈRES, LES GENEVRIÈRES, AND LES CHARMES. These famous
vineyards, with 42, 42, and 38¼ acres respectively, lie in the commune of
Meursault. The wines are full bodied and dry, with finesse and elegance. They
are said to have the perfume of hazelnuts.

At the southern end of the Côte de Beaune lie the communes of Puligny-
Montrachet and Chassagne-Montrachet. Like their counterparts in the Côte
de Nuits, they have affixed the name of their most famous vineyards, Le Montrachet, to their own names. Shippers' blends of wines from either of these
communes will usually be very good.

LE MONTRACHET. There is no question that this is one of the world's great
white wines. It is full bodied and robust yet possesses elegance, perfume, and
dignity that are hard to match. Coming from a rather small vineyard, only
18½ acres, half of which lies in the commune of Puligny and half in that of
Chassagne, the wines are in such demand that they usually fetch prices equal
to those of the great red growths of the Côte de Nuits. H. Warner Allen has
called Le Montrachet the Château d'Yquem of Burgundy.

CHEVALIER-MONTRACHET AND LE BÂTARD-MONTRACHET. Chevalier-
Montrachet has 15½ acres in the commune of Puligny-Montrachet, and Le
Bâtard-Montrachet, totaling 29¼ acres, is in both Puligny- and Chassagne-
Montrachet, as is Le Montrachet. The wines of these two vineyards are very
much like Le Montrachet, with a wealth of bouquet and finesse. They are never
inexpensive. Care must be taken not to confuse the vineyard wine Chevalier-
Montrachet with the commune wine of Chassagne-Montrachet.

CÔTE CHALONNAISE

The Côte Chalonnaise lies just south of the Côte de Beaune. The soil,
grapes, and wines of the Chalonnaise are quite similar to those of the Côte de
Beaune, but they do not often attain the same quality. The four communes
having appellations are Rully and Montagny, producing mostly white wines,
and Mercurey and Givry, producing mostly reds. A considerable amount of
sparkling wine is produced in Chalonnaise, especially in Rully.

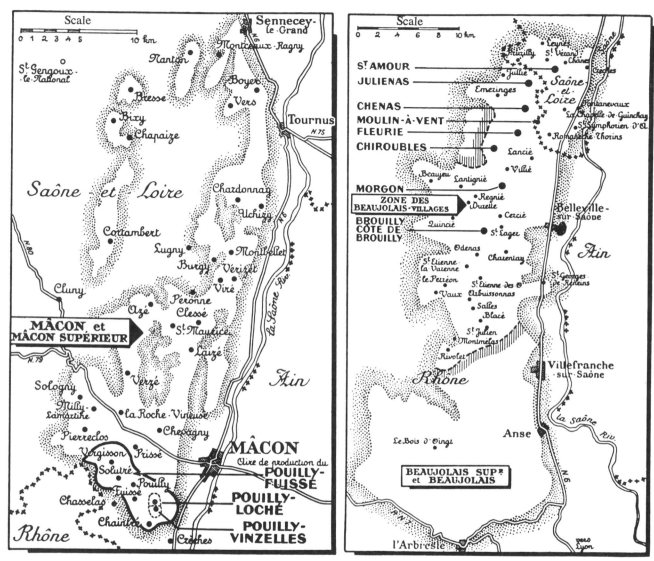

The wine regions of Mâcon and Beaujolais. (*From Pierre Poupon and Pierre Forgeot,* The Wines of Burgundy, *courtesy Presses Universitaires de France*)

MÂCONNAIS AND BEAUJOLAIS

On the rolling low hills south of the Côte d'Or lie the districts of Mâcon and Beaujolais. Although each makes both red and white wines, Mâcon is more famous for its white wines and Beaujolais is better known for its reds.

The most famous white wine of Mâcon is Pouilly-Fuissé, named for the twin towns of Pouilly and Fuissé where the vineyards lie. Nearby Pouilly-Loché and Pouilly Vinzelles also produce crisp white wines. Saint-Véran is the appellation for wines from villages that surround Pouilly-Fuissé. All of these wines are made from the Chardonnay grape. Wines that are Mâcon or Pinot-Chardonnay-Mâcon are made from the Chardonnay and Pinot Blanc grapes. They may be labeled as is, or Mâcon Supérieur, Mâcon-Villages, or Mâcon followed by the name of the community where it is produced, such as Lugny or Viré. No doubt more communes will apply for their own appellations as this wine increases in popularity. Red wines of Mâcon are made mainly from the Gamay grape, and are regionally named.

In Beaujolais the granitic soil brings out the best in the Gamay grape, which is not successful in the Côte d'Or. The best growth, or *crus*, in the north are limited to nine: Brouilly, Chénas, Chiroubles, Côte de Brouilly, Fleurie, Juliénas, Morgon, Moulin-à-Vent, and Saint-Amour. These may use the name Burgundy on their labels. The second classification is Beaujolais-Villages, which is limited to the wines of thirty-nine communes. Third comes Beaujolais-Supérieur, whose alcohol content is the same as Beaujolais-Villages, but which comes from a larger area; and, finally, enormous quantities of plain Beaujolais.

The wines of the region have a clear, brilliant red color and a fairly light body when compared with those of the Côte d'Or. Their primary characteristic is fresh fruitiness. They are most pleasant while in the fresh vigor of youth and for this reason should not be kept for many years. In France most of these wines are drunk before they are two or three years old.

For details on the Burgundy vintages, see Appendix B.

SPARKLING BURGUNDY

Sparkling wines may be made in Burgundy from red or white wines, but red sparkling wine is most usually seen. Because of the predominance of red juice, these wines are fuller bodied than the white counterparts, and are sometimes produced to be slightly sweeter.

At least 30 percent of the blend of sparkling Burgundy must be from Pinot Noir, Pinot Gris, Pinot Blanc, or Chardonnay grapes. The balance may be Aligoté, Melon, Sacy, and/or Gamay à Jus Blanc.

Sparkling Burgundies are made by the approved *méthode champenoise*, which will be explained in the following section on Champagne. All sparkling wines from Burgundy, whether red or white, must qualify under the appellation Crémant de Bourgogne. They may never be called Champagne.

3. CHAMPAGNE

The word *Champagne* is synonymous with happiness, gaiety, and laughter, for it is the joyous wine of festive occasions. "Champagne," said André L. Simon, "has always been, still is, and will ever be an extravagant wine and the most charming and fascinating of wines."

There is a difference between La Champagne and Le Champagne. The former is the name of the ancient French province, part of which is today the Department of the Marne; the latter is the sparkling wine produced in the delimited Champagne region, about the size of Washington, D.C., located ninety miles east of Paris.

Wine has been made in Champagne since early Roman times, when Caesar conquered Gaul. That early wine was a still wine, however, and even today a nonsparkling wine is made in the region under the appellation Côteaux Champenois. But the name Champagne is reserved for the sparkling wine of France whose qualities and unique characteristics result from climate, soil, subsoil, and grapes grown in the strictly delimited area of Champagne, from second fermentation within a tightly corked bottle, and from long aging in the cellars of Champagne.

history   The histories of the province and its wine are intertwined. The most important city, Reims, was named for Saint-Remi, one of its first archbishops, who in A.D. 496 converted the first Frankish king, Clovis, to Christianity and at the baptism presented Clovis with a cask of Champagne from his own vineyard.

It was not until the seventeenth century that the sparkling wine we associate with the name of Champagne came into use. Some say that Dom Pérignon (1639–1715), a blind Bénédictine monk who was treasurer and cellarer of the Abbey of Hautvillers near Épernay, is the man who put the bubbles in champagne.

Actually, the bubbles occurred naturally. Champagne is the most northerly wine-producing region of France, and the early arrival of winter often slowed down or halted fermentation before it was complete. After the wine was bottled, the arrival of warm spring weather would start a second fermentation inside the bottle. Carbon dioxide was released inside the closed bottle, which made the wine sparkle.

It was Dom Pérignon who was the first to use the bark of the cork tree as a stopper for Champagne bottles. Although cork bark had been used in other wine regions, Dom Pérignon introduced it in the Champagne region to replace the bits of tow soaked in oil that were used as stoppers, making it possible to retain the sparkle within the wine for long periods of time. Being an excellent taster, he soon observed that the wines of one vineyard were consistently dry, those of another richer and fuller bodied, while those of a third possessed more finesse. He decided to try blending these wines to produce a more balanced wine with a completeness that the component wines could not show individually. The result was that he made better wines than had been produced before, and to this day the system is followed to obtain a wine of uniformly high quality and distinctive house style.

With all this development in the bottle, there was the problem of removing sediment that had collected so the wine would be clear. Removing the sediment was time consuming, and effervescence was lost in the process. It wasn't until the nineteenth century that the system of *remuage*, which is still used today, was developed.

From 1927 to 1937 the *Appellation Contrôlée* laws were being developed in France. A separate clause dealing with Champagne processes defined the *méthode champenoise*, making Champagne one of the most rigorously controlled and most carefully made wines in the world.

geography The Champagne growing area today consists of 65,000 acres, which will be increased to 72,000 acres over the next few years. The vineyards are planted in 250 different villages, most of which are clustered around the cities of Reims and Épernay. The Marne River, which flows from east to west, forms an important line of division. North of the Marne mainly black grapes are grown, around the towns of Ay and Hautvillers and in the Montagne ("moun-

REIMS

Sillery
Rilly-La-Montagne
Verzenay
Verzy
PETITE MONTAGNE DE REIMS
MONTAGNE DE REIMS
Trepail
Bouzy
Ambonnay
VALLÉE DE LA MARNE
CHÂTEAU THIERRY
Venteuil
Hautvillers
Dizy
Ay
Marne R.
Boursault
EPERNAY
Marne R.
CÔTE DES BLANCS
Cramant
Avize
Oger
Le Mesnil
Vertus

REGION OF CHAMPAGNE

〰〰 Vineyard areas

tain") de Reims section at Mailly, Verzy, Verzenay, Bouzy, and Ambonnay. South of the river lies the Côte des Blancs, where white grapes are grown around the towns of Cramant, Avize, Oger, Le Mesnil, and Vertus.

soil   Chalk is important to the Champagne region, both for growing the vines and for aging the wine in the deep chalk cellars. A thin top layer of earth covers a chalky, porous subsoil that extends down for hundreds of feet. The porosity allows excess water to drain, while maintaining the proper amount of moisture necessary for growth of the vines.

grape varieties   The three grape varieties from which Champagne may be made are the red Pinot Noir and Pinot Meunier and the white Chardonnary. The Montagne de Reims vineyards are planted mainly in Pinot Noir, the grape that gives full flavor and body to the wine. Pinot Noir and Pinot Meunier are grown in the valley of the Marne. The Côte des Blancs, or "white slope," is so named because it is planted with Chardonnay. This grape contributes freshness, lightness, and elegance to the final blend.

All Champagne vineyards are rated for quality. The best vineyards or *crus* are rated 100 percent with the remainder anywhere down to 80 percent, dependent on such factors as exposure, drainage, microclimate, etc. When the grapes are harvested, the price for that vintage is agreed on, and the vineyards rated 100 percent get paid 100 percent of the price, and the other vineyards are compensated proportionately. The well-known Champagne houses usually buy the grapes from the vineyards rated between 90 and 100 percent.

THE CHAMPAGNE METHOD (MÉTHODE CHAMPENOISE)

The art of making Champagne really begins with the selection of grapes. Most of the important Champagne houses own vineyards, but to meet their needs all of them must also buy additional grapes from fourteen thousand small growers in Champagne's main vineyard areas. The vineyards are primarily family holdings averaging 3½ acres. Since Champagne is a blend of twenty to thirty still wines made from grapes grown in a number of different vineyards, no vineyard name appears on the label; consequently the name of the blender or producer, which is always there, takes on importance.

the harvest   Harvesting the grapes begins at the end of September or in early October, one hundred days after the vines flower. The exact time is determined by the *Comité Interprofessionnel du Vin de Champagne* (C.I.V.C.) after the laboratory tests of grape sugar content and acidity have been made and the grapes are fully ripe. Within ten days an army of seventy thousand workers does the harvesting.

The ripe grapes are gathered in baskets, called *paniers*. When a *panier* is

The *épluchage*. Highly skilled workers select only perfect bunches (culling out any imperfect grapes) before the *caques* are trucked to the wine press. (*Courtesy C.I.V.C., Épernay*)

Typical Champagne hydraulic press. (*Courtesy C.I.V.C., Épernay*)

full it is taken to the side of the road, where experienced sorters cull out any green, overripe, or defective grapes to ensure that only perfect, sound fruit goes to the press. This selection process is called *épluchage* and is only practiced by the leading producers. After the *épluchage* the grapes are placed in *caques* or *clayettes* ("large baskets") and carried to nearby pressing houses.

pressing The press may belong to a Champagne firm, to the local village, to a cooperative of vineyard owners, or to brokers or middlemen. To avoid coloration of the juice, wide but shallow hydraulic presses that hold eighty-eight hundred pounds are used. Each basket is weighed and marked to ensure the exact quantity being placed in the press. The amount of grapes that makes one loading of a press is called a *marc*. From each *marc* four pressings of juice are obtained, known as *cuvée, première taille, deuxième taille,* and *rebêche*.

Pressure is applied twice for the *cuvée,* and after each pressure the grapes are worked toward the center of the press with wooden shovels. For the *première* and *deuxième tailles* pressure is applied only once. For the *rebêche* the *marc* is removed to a smaller press. The finest houses, or *Grandes Marques,* which pride themselves on the quality of their wines, use only the *cuvée* and *première taille* pressings and sell the wine resulting from the *deuxième taille* in cask. *Rebêche* wine cannot be used for Champagne; it is used for distillation.

As the juice is pressed from the grapes, it gushes out from the bottom of the press through a channel and is gathered in a cistern below the presses, whence it is transferred at once into vats or casks and carefully labeled with the name of the vineyard where the grapes were grown.

first fermentation The first fermentation, as with all other white wines, starts out vigorously and gradually slows down during the second week. Fermentation may take place in traditional oak barrels, glass-lined tanks, or stainless steel tanks. With modern equipment, the temperature is maintained around 70 degrees Fahrenheit for the three weeks necessary to complete fermentation.

The new wine is racked to remove large particles that have settled to the bottom, and it is now chilled. This used to be accomplished by opening the winery doors to the cold winter air. Now modern refrigeration methods are used. This chilling causes the soluble tartrates to form insoluble bitartrates, which precipitate out, leaving the wine clear and stable.

By spring the *chef de cave,* or "cellar-master," will know whether he is making vintage or nonvintage Champagne. If nonvintage, he must decide which wines, from which vineyards and in what proportions, should be married to older reserve wines to produce the characteristic house style of Champagne with the desired quality, aroma, elegance, and durability.

The new wines are then pumped, in the proper proportions, into large blending vats where they are thoroughly combined.

Highly skilled workman deftly performing the *remuage* operation of shaking the sediment down onto the inner surface of the cork. (*Courtesy Champagne News and Information Bureau, New York*)

A small amount of sugar dissolved in old wine, together with special yeasts, is added to the blend to ensure uniform secondary fermentation. This is called the *liqueur de tirage* or *dosage de tirage*. The quantity of sugar varies from year to year, depending on the natural sugar the new wine contains. The wine is then bottled and corked. The corks are secured by either metal clips known as *agrafes* or crown caps such as those used on soft drink bottles.

The bottles are stacked on their sides in the cellars that are hewn out of the solid chalk subsoil of the region. The yeasts discover the sugar and go to work, creating additional alcohol and carbon dioxide gas. Since the gas cannot escape it becomes a component of the wine.

During the first couple of years in the chalk cellars the stacks of bottles are examined for breakage—which is inevitable, as there are bound to be a few imperfect bottles that cannot stand the strain of about 90 pounds per square inch pressure developed by the newly created gas. In the early days the percentage of breakage was very high (sometimes as much as every other bottle), but today, with improved methods of bottle manufacture and the scientific use of the saccharometer to measure the exact sugar content of the wine, breakage has been reduced to less than 1 percent.

remuage

The action of fermentation is like a fire, and where there is fire, there are ashes. As a result of the secondary fermentation that has taken place in the bottle, "ashes," or dead yeast cells, hae been left in the form of a sediment that must be removed to achieve a clear and brilliant wine. Removing the sediment is not easy, however. In this long, hard, tedious job the bottles are placed in specially built racks, called *pupitres*. At first the bottles are set at a forty-five-degree angle, and the angle is gradually increased until the bottles are standing perpendicularly, head down. A workman grasps each bottle, gives it a shake, a slight turn, and an increased tilt (*remuage*, or "riddling"), and lets it fall back into its slot on the rack with a small jolt. This is repeated every three days for each bottle. The object of this *remuage* is to move the sediment down onto the cork in a spiral movement. This operation takes about six to eight weeks. A skilled *remueur* can handle from thirty thousand to fifty thousand bottles a day.

When the wine is perfectly clear, the bottles are removed from the *pupitre* in preparation for the removal of sediment.

Since this is a very costly and time-consuming process, it stands to reason that attempts would be made to do this riddling automatically. After many years of testing, an acceptable machine has been developed, and some of the houses in Champagne are now using it.

dégorgement

Dégorgement is the process of removing the collected sediment from the corked bottle. The neck of the bottle is dipped into a very cold brine or glycol solution that freezes a little wine on the cork into a sludge with the sediment. Traditionally, a skilled workman, wearing a leather apron and often a wire-covered mask to protect his face in case of a bursting bottle, grasps the bottle. Standing opposite a barrel and protected by a shield, he releases the *agrafe* with a pair of pliers or removes the crown cap and at the same time turns the bottle right side up. The cork flies out, taking the frozen bit of sediment with it. He gives the neck of the bottle two sharp raps to loosen any bit of sediment that may have adhered to it. A small amount of the wine foams out. He examines this foam to be sure the wine has a perfectly clean bouquet, and then he hands the bottle to another workman sitting nearby, who adds the *liqueur d'expédition,* or *dosage.*

Today the disgorging process is automated in many houses.

liqueur d'expédition

The wine that has been lost during the *dégorgement* must be replaced. This is done by adding wine from previously disgorged bottles. Simultaneously some sweetening liqueur is added, the amount varying with the desired sweetness of the final product. This *liqueur d'expédition,* or *dosage,* is a concentrated solution of the finest sugar, dissolved in mature wine.

The shipping cork, which must say *Champagne,* is now driven in by machine and tightly wired down. During disgorgement some of the gas is lost, and the final pressure after recorking is reduced to about seventy-five pounds per square inch. The bottle goes back to the cellars for further rest before the labels and the plastic or lead-foil capsules are put on. When this is accomplished, the Champagne is ready to start its journey to our tables.

Because tastes vary, and some people prefer a dry and others a sweet *labeling* Champagne, shippers have adopted a simple system of labeling to indicate how sweet the wine in the bottle is. The following list should serve as a general guide to denote the varying degrees of sweetness. All shippers use these descriptive terms. There is, however, some variation. Thus, while a Brut is always drier than an Extra Sec, one shipper's Brut may be slightly drier than another's.

TYPE	DESCRIPTION	SUGAR CONTENT/LITER
Brut	very, very dry	less than 15 grams
Extra Dry	somewhat sweeter but fairly dry	from 12 to 20 grams
Sec or Dry	medium sweet	from 17 to 35 grams
Demi Sec	quite sweet	from 33 to 50 grams

As in other wine-producing regions, the quality of Champagne grapes and the resultant wine varies greatly according to summer weather conditions. Two qualities of vintage are possible: fairly good wines, which can be enhanced by blending with wines of a previous vintage; and fine, well-balanced wines that need no assistance and can stand on their own merit. The latter happens two, three, or possibly four times in a decade, and bottles of wine in this category are dated with the year in which the grapes that produced them were grown. These are known as vintage wines. Vintage wines are usually Brut. Wines in the first category, blends of several vintages, are not dated and are known as nonvintage wines.

The minimum standards specified under the existing *Appellation Contrôlée* regulations establish that nonvintage Champagne must be matured in bottle one and one-half years, and vintage Champagnes three years. Leading producers usually age their wines longer before they are shipped, especially the *tête de cuvée* wines, which are considered by the house to be their best.

A Champagne label carries a vintage year only when the *chef de cave* feels *vintage* it is warranted. This decision is made by the individual house, based on the *Champagne* merits of the harvest. Fine old vintage Champagne is one of the most delicate of all wines, and keeping vintage Champagne longer than ten years is risky. A fine vintage develops and matures nobly with the years if it is properly stored and undisturbed, but it becomes oxidized with age. On the other hand, young wines have a light, fruity freshness that is their most charming characteristic. Late-disgorged Champagnes are the only exception to these general comments. Many of the fine French Champagne producers store small quantities of various vintages undisgorged in their cellars for their personal use on great occasions. The House of Bollinger, however, has marketed late-disgorged Champagne labeled *R.D., Récemment Dégorgé* ("recently disgorged"). The label shows both the vintage date and the date of disgorgement. Late-disgorged Champagnes not only retain all their qualities but also benefit considerably from greater maturity.

Tête de cuvée, cuvée speciale, or prestige *cuvée* is a top-of-the-line Champagne that accounts for about 15 percent of Champagne sales in the United States, with about twenty different producers represented. While not specifically defined by the *Appellation Contrôlée* regulations, these Champagnes are made with the first pressings of grapes grown in the top-rated villages in vintage years, are aged longer on the yeasts than standard Champagnes, and are frequently bottled in replicas of antique bottles. They are very expensive.

nonvintage Champagne

Champagne is produced every year. In a vintage year, no more than 80 percent of the harvest may be sold, so that there will be sufficient reserve wines to blend with wines produced in lesser years. Nonvintage Champagne has no date on the label, and is always less expensive than vintage. This does not mean that the quality is necessarily less. These are the Champagne house's standard wines, and most houses will readily agree to be judged on the basis of their nonvintage bottlings.

English market

The first Champagne salesman was the Marquis de Sillery, of the seventeenth century. He was one of the richest vineyard owners of the region and in great favor at court. He introduced sparkling Champagne there and was the first to ship it to England.

What the Marquis de Sillery did for sparkling Champagne in France, Saint Evremond did in London. Soldier, writer, philosopher, and courtier, he was last but not least a gourmet and a connoisseur. Having incurred the displeasure of his king, he left France and settled in London, where he became one of the brightest lights of London society. He made it the fashion to drink Champagne, and the English ever since have been recognized as the most discriminating connoisseurs of fine Champagne and are the region's best customers outside France.

In those early days Champagnes were generally sweet to appeal to the tastes of the period. In the nineteenth century, however, Veuve Pommery reasoned that the sweetness masked the lively, delicate taste of Champagne and that Champagne might prove more enjoyable if the *dosage* was reduced. Her experiments led her to dry and extra dry Champagnes, which she introduced commercially. These became especially popular in London, and the term *English market* has since come to mean very dry Champagnes.

Recently, Americans have developed a taste for very dry Champagnes as well. Not only has the United States become the most important export market for Champagne, but about two-thirds of the Champagne shipped to this country is Brut. There are some Champagnes on the market that have no *dosage* at all.

A unique development in Champagne production was established by Pierre Taittinger, who felt that many people would prefer a light and more delicate Champagne. Knowing that Chardonnay grapes could impart these qualities to the *cuvée*, he departed from the usual proportions of two-thirds red grapes and one-third white, which is the traditional *cuvée*. Pierre Taittinger made a wine of 100 percent Chardonnay grapes from extensive holdings in vineyards south of Épernay in the Côte des Blancs. This Champagne is marketed as Blanc de Blancs and is dry, elegant, and expensive. Many houses produce this style of Champagne today.

Blanc de Blancs

Several firms offer Rosé or Pink Champagne, a wine that that is currently in vogue. It is usually produced by adding the desired proportion of still red table wine from the Champagne district, generally from the villages of Bouzy or Ambonnay, at the time of assembling the *cuvée* or just before the second fermentation in the bottle. It can be obtained in nonvintage, vintage, and *tête de cuvée* bottlings. It is usually quite dry.

Rosé Champagne— Pink Champagne

When the pressure in the bottle is between 3–4 atmospheres, rather than 5–6 atmospheres in a bottle of Champagne, the wine is called *crémant*, a Champagne with a light foam. Few houses export this quality, particularly since the sparkling wine taxes levied by the U.S. government are the same as for the product with higher pressure. Mumm's exports a *crémant* from the 100 percent village of Cramant.

crémant

Since 1975, French laws allows the word *crémant* on *vins mousseux* from other regions, *i.e.*, Crémant de Bourgogne, Crémant d'Alsace, and Crémant de Loire. These are full pressure sparkling wines, but should not be confused with those produced in the delimited Champagne region, even if made by the Champagne method.

Côteaux Champenois is an appellation under which still wines of Champagne may be shipped. The wines are made from the same grapes, under the same regulations as Champagne, but they do not go through the blending, aging, or second fermentation in the bottle. This explains why they may not be called Champagne. Bollinger, Laurent-Perrier, and Moët & Chandon, among others, export these fresh, dry wines.

Côteaux Champenois

Once a bottle of Champagne is uncorked, it generally should be consumed in its entirety. A Champagne recorker, however, will help to preserve the bubbles for about forty-eight hours, especially if the Champagne is kept very cold.

bottle sizes   For convenience, Champagne producers bottle their wine in various sizes. The following are permitted in the U.S. under metric bottling regulations:

NAME	SIZE	
	Metric standard (liters)	U.S. measure (fluid ounces)
Split	0.187	6.3
Half-bottle	0.375	12.7
Bottle	0.75	25.4
Magnum (2 bottles)	1.5	50.7
Jeroboam (4 bottles)	3.0	101.4
Methuselah (8 bottles)	6.0	204.8
Salmanazar (12 bottles)	9.0	307.2

Champagne, as is the case with most wines, develops better in a large container than in a small one, but it is important to know that the shippers rarely develop their Champagnes in sizes other than the half-bottles, bottles, magnums, and sometimes jeroboams. Methuselahs and Salmanazars are filled by decanting from bottles under pressure. While those are very festive for large parties, they should not be held too long in one's wine cellar. The magnum is the best practical size to use, followed by the bottle.

uses of Champagne   Champagne is one of the most delicate and delightful of all wines, but because it takes so long and is so costly to produce, it can never be cheap. This puts it in a class by itself as the "glamor" wine. It is indispensable at weddings, receptions, and formal banquets, but it is not limited to special occasions. Champagne is just as much at home with oysters as it is with ham or dessert, if a Champagne of the proper sweetness is chosen. Most people would not enjoy an extremely dry Brut with strawberry mousse, but a Demi Sec would be very pleasant. A chilled glass of Champagne makes a delightful aperitif to a wine-accompanied meal. Champagne also has its uses in the kitchen.

evaluating Champagnes   We have already spoken on page 16 about the general guidelines for tasting wines, noting the appearance, the bouquet, the taste, and the aftertaste. When one evaluates Champagne, however, there is an additional factor to be considered—and that is the bubbles. What is desired is an indication of good bonding of gas to liquid, and that is demonstrated by the presence of numerous, long lasting bubbles. Small-size bubbles are more desirable than larger bubbles for the same reason. Incidentally, a glass with a bowl that comes to a point, such as a flute or a tulip, will produce better bubbles than a saucer glass.

vin mousseux   *Vin mousseux* refers to all sparkling wines, although the name Champagne may be used only for sparkling wine made in the delimited district of Champagne. Almost every wine region of France produces a *vin mousseux*. In addition to Champagne, there are only sixteen other French *vins mousseux* that are entitled to carry an *Appellation Contrôlée*.

The finer producers of *vin mousseux* use the *méthode champenoise*, although other methods of production may be used.

Vin Mousseux-Produit en Cuve Close is the designation for sparkling wines made by the Charmat or bulk process (see Chapter 11).

4. ALSACE

The vineyards of Alsace are the most northern of France, extending from Strasbourg south to the border of Switzerland. The Vosges Mountains create a protective western border, with the Rhine River completing the boundaries to the east. Since it was easy to travel between France and Germany across the Rhine River, Alsace was often caught in a struggle between the two countries.

Despite the use of grape varieties more common to Germany, the people of Alsace, their grapes, and their wines are proudly French, producing bone dry wines, often vinified in oak, that offer contrast to neighboring German wines.

history

Alsace has been an important wine-producing region since the Roman conquerors occupied the valley of the Rhine. Undoubtedly they planted the vine in Alsace before they did in Germany. The vines they brought from Italy were not the same as those that flourish there today, but the records do not show when the change occurred. During the half-century of German authority, the Alsatian identity of these fine wines was submerged, and while much wine was made, it was all consumed in Germany or used for blending purposes. Quantity rather than quality was the order.

". . . a fertile country," wrote Julius Wile, "fields and valleys waving with grain, hillsides covered with symmetric rows of vines marching up and up until they merge with the orchards, bearers of the fruits from which are distilled the famous *eaux-de-vie d'Alsace*, Quetsch and Mirabelle [plum brandies] and Kirsch [cherry brandy]; and the orchards finally give way to the mighty forests which top the hills and cover the Vosges Mountains. . . .

"There is an atmosphere in Alsace—one of close alliance between man and soil, an aura of maturity combined with a freshness of spirit, of physical youngness that one finds even in the aged, of a people that has known the past, lives in the present, and does not fear the future."

Growing the vine and harvesting in Alsace do not differ radically from other white-wine regions in France except that, because of Alsace's more northerly location and cooler climate, the vines are trained high and allowed to reach for the sun. The grape varieties do not ripen at the same time, and since many vineyards are planted with three, four, or more varieties they must be picked over several times during the vintage.

geography   From the north southward the towns whose surrounding vineyards are famous are:

BARR. This is the home of the famous Clos Gaensbroennel ("little goose fountain") vineyard.

RIBEAUVILLÉ AND RIQUEWIHR. Located in the center of the region, they have long enjoyed a reputation for producing excellent Alsatian wines.

AMMERSCHWIHR. The important vineyard here is Kaefferkopf.

GUEBWILLER AND THANN. Almost in the shadows of Switzerland, these are the southernmost towns of the region. There is a hill at Guebwiller called Kitterle, or "leg cutter." These leg-cutter wines are said to have been among Napoleon's favorites.

grape varieties   The grapes permitted in the production of *Appellation Contrôlée* Vin d'Alsace are Riesling, Gewürztraminer, Sylvaner, Muscat d'Alsace, Pinot Gris (Tokay d'Alsace), Pinot Blanc (Klevner), and Pinot Noir. When these grapes appear on the label, there must be 100 percent of the variety used to make the wine.

The Riesling is considered the most notable of the grapes of Alsace, making wines that are rich, dry, and austere. The Gewürztraminer has a unique, spicy and flowery bouquet, with full flavor and a dry finish. In some very ripe years the Riesling and Gewürztraminer are affected by the "noble rot," and the wines produced are rich and luscious. The Pinot Noir, incidentally, makes a light rosé wine in Alsace.

labeling   In Alsace, the name of the wine is usually the name of the grape from which it is produced, sometimes in conjunction with the name of a village. For many years, the names of famous vineyards were seen on labels, such as Clos Ste. Hune and Clos Gaensbroennel. Since many of these vineyards date back to the fourteenth century, their names were permitted to be used.

New regulations now state that the term *Grand Cru* may be used on labels with vineyard or vineyard-area designations if the wines have come from classified vineyards, have been produced from Riesling, Gewürztraminer, Pinot Gris, or Muscat d'Alsace, and have been approved by a tasting panel. If the panel rejects the wine, the vineyard name may not be used—only the grape name.

Vineyard areas are being defined and classified. These place names are called *Lieu-Dit*. Fifteen vineyard areas have been listed so far. Phrases such as *Grande Réserve* or *Réserve Exceptionnelle* are no longer allowed.

The phrase *Vendange Tardive* is used for late-harvest wines. The rich, ripe wines, incidentally, need longer aging than the normally harvested wines.

Wines from Alsace also appear on the market under a shipper's trademark name, and are usually blends of grapes. These have generally replaced Edelzwicker. No grape name or classified place name will be on the label. The

WINE REGIONS OF ALSACE

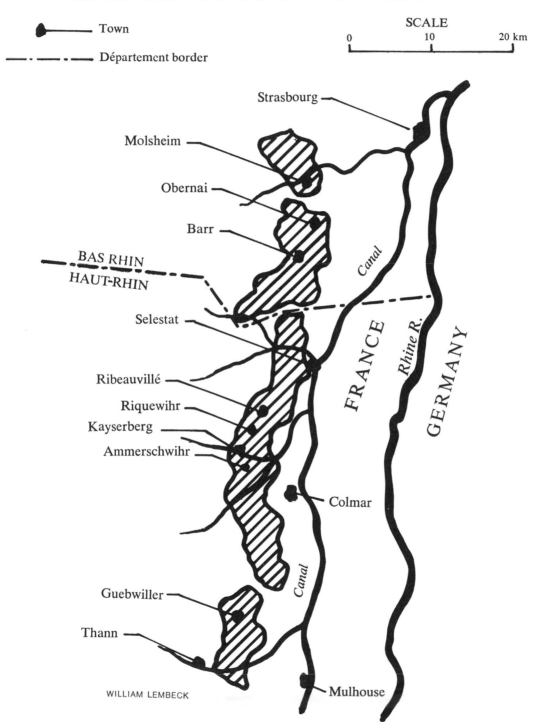

Town

Département border

SCALE

0   10   20 km

Strasbourg

Molsheim

Obernai

Barr

BAS RHIN
HAUT-RHIN

Canal

Selestat

FRANCE

Rhine R.

GERMANY

Ribeauvillé

Riquewihr

Kayserberg

Ammerschwihr

Colmar

Guebwiller

Canal

Thann

WILLIAM LEMBECK

Mulhouse

Typical wine village in Alsace. High above this carefully preserved town lie the sloping hills and the vineyards. (*Courtesy Alsace Wine Information Bureau, New York*)

shipper's name is of utmost importance, since is usually a wine grower and winemaker as well. As in Champagne, grapes are purchased to supplement the grower's own vineyards to create the final blend.

All Alsace wines must be bottled in the green Alsace flute, which is a tall, slim bottle. The wines must be bottled in the region and cannot be shipped in casks.

Sparkling wine is also produced in Alsace, carrying the *Appellation Contrôlée* designation of *Crémant d'Alsace*. White sparkling wines may be produced from white or black grapes. Rosé sparkling wines may only be produced from Pinot Noir.

5. RHÔNE WINES

The viticultural Rhône Valley stretches 130 miles, from the gastronomic center of Lyon to the ancient and historic city of Avignon. Here northern and southern vineyards produce two different styles of wines.

history

The Rhône River has been a means of transportation and communication, and the area has had historical and religious importance. South of Lyon, near the ancient Roman city of Vienne and across the river from Condrieu, lie the vineyards of the Côte Rôtie ("roasted slope"). The wines from this district were highly praised by Pliny the Younger, Plutarch, and Columella.

Thirty miles south of Côte Rôtie on the left bank of the Rhône near Tain, the renowned hill of Hermitage rises up majestically. Sir Gaspard de Sterimberg, a Crusader returning from the Albigensian Crusade, in southern France, decided to settle on these heights in 1209 and live the contemplative life of a hermit at the Chapel of Saint-Christophe at Hermitage. From the south he had brought a vine cutting, which he planted on the hill. According to legend it was the first Syrah brought to the Rhône. He tended his vine patiently and eventually it bore fruit, from which he made a fine wine that, ironically, brought him fame.

For seventy-two years, 1305-1377, the papacy was occupied by Frenchmen, who, fearful of the perils of Rome, maintained the Holy See at Avignon, to the south. This period is sometimes called the Babylonian Captivity of the popes. The first of the Avignon popes was Clement V, who, as a native of Bordeaux and archbishop of Bordeaux, was familiar with viticulture and left us the legacy of that grand Graves claret—Château Pape-Clément, the vineyard which he is said to have owned.

When Clement V decided to settle the Holy See at Avignon, he built a fortress-palace just outside the town. This edifice was dubbed the new château of the pope, Châteauneuf-du-Pape. Since wine is important to a man from Bordeaux, Clement had vines planted, and they still produce the wine that is known as Châteauneuf-du-Pape.

geography

Flowing southward, the turbulent Rhône River cuts its swath to the Mediterranean. Along its route there are two widely separated sections that produce red, rosé, and white wines of repute.

The northern part has terraced cliffs, giving the vines good exposure to the sun. The soil contains granite and shale. The southern part is covered with large round stones that hold the heat, and the climate is more typically Mediterranean. Throughout the Rhône Valley the growing season is long and hot, creating robust, alcoholic wines that take time to develop.

grape varieties The principal red grape variety of the Côtes du Rhône is the Syrah (sometimes called Sirah, Sirrac, or Sérine). While some true Syrah is also grown in California, it is unrelated to California's Petite Sirah. The Syrah is the only red grape permitted in Côte Rôtie and Hermitage. Of twenty-three grapes grown in the area, other important red grapes are the Grenache, Clairette, Bourboulenc, Mourvèdre, Cinsaut, and Carignan. White grapes include the Viognier, Roussanne, Marsanne, and Picpoul. These are used both for making white wines and for softening some red wines.

At Châteauneuf-du-Pape the wine may be the result of judicious blending of as many as thirteen grape varieties. Baron P. Le Roy Boiseaumarié, president of the Syndicate of Vineyard Owners of Châteauneuf-du-Pape and proprietor of Château Fortia, stated in 1932 that the choice of grapes to produce a perfect Châteauneuf-du-Pape was as follows (percentages and grape varieties vary today, with Grenache predominating):

1st group	For warmth, richness, and roundness	Grenache and Cinsaut	20 percent
2nd group	For solidity, keeping power, color, and the right flavor	Mourvèdre and Syrah	40 percent
3rd group	For vinosity, agreeableness, freshness, and bouquet	Counoise and Picpoul	30 percent
4th group	For finesse, fire, brilliance	Clairette and Bourboulenc	10 percent

vineyards The red wines of Châteaunef-du-Pape traditionally have been big and slow to develop. After a brief period where the wines were vinified to be drinkable sooner, winemakers have now returned to the traditional fuller style. Some white wine is also produced at Châteauneuf-du-Pape. It has good body, flavor, and character, although not as fine as the red.

The wines of Côte Rôtie are very deep in color and have a rich headiness and a roughness that takes some years to throw off. The wines spend three years in wood before bottling. As they grow older they lose some of their color, throw a rather heavy deposit, and rid themselves of their youthful harshness. Twelve to fifteen years is the youngest at which Côte Rôtie should be drunk.

Some white wine is produced at nearby Condrieu and at Château Grillet from the Viognier grape. Production from both is very small and it is rare to find these wines in commerce. If you are fortunate enough to come across any

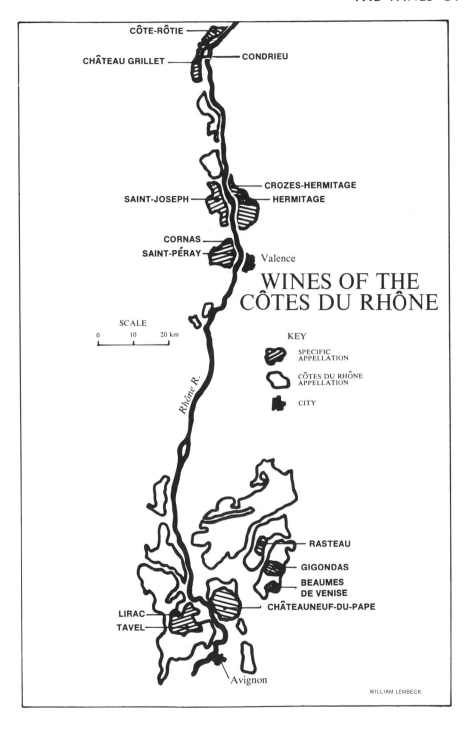

CÔTE-RÔTIE

CHÂTEAU GRILLET — — CONDRIEU

CROZES-HERMITAGE

SAINT-JOSEPH — — HERMITAGE

CORNAS
SAINT-PÉRAY

Valence

WINES OF THE
CÔTES DU RHÔNE

SCALE
0   10   20 km

KEY

SPECIFIC
APPELLATION

CÔTES DU RHÔNE
APPELLATION

CITY

Rhône R.

RASTEAU

GIGONDAS

BEAUMES
DE VENISE

LIRAC

TAVEL

CHÂTEAUNEUF-DU-PAPE

Avignon

WILLIAM LEMBECK

Château Grillet, you will find it to be pale in color and medium bodied, but with a wealth of character and a magnificent bouquet. It will be expensive. Château Grillet is one of France's smallest *Appellation Contrôlée* areas.

The vineyards of Hermitage are fewer than four hundred acres and produce both red and white wines. The red wines, which Professor Saintsbury called the "manliest of wines," are big, full bodied, strong, and deep colored and have marvelous keeping qualities. The white wines are full and medium dry and have a deep bouquet. When mature they have an amber gold color and a lovely mellowness.

The appellation Crozes-Hermitage has been in effect since 1952; it applies to wines produced in eleven townships around the famous hillside of Hermitage. They are similar to Hermitage wines but have somewhat less character. Cornas and Saint-Joseph are not as well known but are enjoyable and well priced.

The Côtes-du-Rhône appellation applies to wines made in over one hundred communes, which can be white, rosé, or red. Much of this wine is made in large cooperatives. Côtes-du-Rhône Villages, a more recent appellation, applies to wines made from the best seventeen communes, whose name may appear on the label. Beaumes de Venise, one of these communes, produces both dry red wines, labeled Côtes-du-Rhône Beaumes de Venise, and sweet Muscat wines, labeled simply Beaumes de Venise.

Tavel Rosé   Across the river from Avignon is the town of Tavel, which gives its name to one of the most delightful of all the rosé wines. Tavel combines the dryness of a red wine with the fresh lightness of a white. Several grapes are used, including not more than 60 percent Grenache and at least 15 percent Cinsault. It has a delightful coral color; is clean, fresh, and dry; and usually has a lovely, fruity bouquet and flavor. Tavel is best when young, no more than five years old. Neighboring Lirac also produces rosé wines that are similar to Tavel. They are coral in color; clean, fresh, and very dry. They should be drunk young. Rosé wines from the Rhône are usually shipped in clear, flute bottles.

Rhône wines, both red and white, are bottled in the same type of bottle used in Burgundy. They are more like Burgundy in character than any other wines. For these reasons many people have been confused, and on many a wine card Châteauneuf-du-Pape is erroneously listed as a Burgundy.

HOW AND WHEN TO SERVE
BORDEAUX, BURGUNDY, RHÔNE, AND ALSATIAN WINES

The place on the menu of any wine is a matter of personal taste and opinion. Fortunately, most wines lend themselves to many foods, and personal preference is the deciding factor.

In general, red wines go well with almost all foods except those from the *Bordeaux* sea. Experience has shown that a perfectly dry wine, one completely lacking in sugar, will taste better with foods that are not sweet. Of course you can drink a claret with fish and it will do you no physical harm, but you will enjoy the wine much more if it accompanies a meat dish. This is especially true if the claret is a fine old château bottling.

The white, crisp, dry Graves, on the other hand, is more versatile and may be served with all foods. It shines its brightest in the company of fish and does nobly with fowl and white meats.

Sauternes is a wine that people enjoy at the end of a meal. Since the wine is sweet and has a rich perfume, it does not seem appealing with dry-tasting foods. It is lovely with a dessert such as honeydew melon. Sauternes also go well with blue-veined cheese and with pâté de foie gras.

Red Burgundies, being perfectly dry like clarets, are also somewhat unsat- *Burgundy* isfactory with fish. They are good with high-protein foods. Game, red meat, or ripe cheese shows them off to the best advantage. Being rounder and softer than classical clarets, they often follow them at a formal dinner.

White wines are at home with all foods, but a good, crisp Chablis or a fresh Pouilly-Fuissé with just-opened oysters is food for the gods. When ordering wine, it is a good rule to match the dish that will show it off best, and it is our experience that fish brings out the best qualities of white Burgundies.

The red wines of the Rhône, being full bodied and related to red Burgun- *Rhône* dies in character, may be served with the same type of food: roasts, game, or cheese. Hermitage and venison are classic companions.

The white wines are at home with most foods but are best with fish, white meats, or fowl.

A chilled bottle of dry Tavel is a delightful luncheon wine with most dishes and is a good choice on a summer evening when the weather calls for a wine that is refreshing.

Since they are fragrant, full, and dry, Alsace wines may be served with *Alsace* almost all foods, as they are in their native Alsace. The wines should be served well chilled. They are, of course, ideal summer wines.

Alsace wines are generally bottled when very young, in the spring or summer, following the vintage. They are at their best when relatively young since freshness is one of their most pleasant characteristics. Occasionally, how- ever, some of the better wines, such as Vendange Tardive wines, are capable of attaining great age (ten to twenty years) while retaining their fruit and vigor.

6. THE LOIRE VALLEY

The château country of the tourist folder—issued by the *Commissariat National du Tourisme*—is not, as you might suppose, the Bordeaux wine region, but the part of France that inspired enchanting and exciting novels. Because of the proximity of the Loire Valley to Paris, the people of fashion in the time of the several Louises had to have châteaux there. The wines of the region were pleasant, and the courtiers at the royal court vied with one another showing off the wines from their Lorie properties, thus making them popular in court circles.

Almost the entire length of the valley of the Loire River, about six hundred miles, is a series of wine-producing areas from which come a variety of pleasant wines. Muscadet from the west and Pouilly-Fumé and Sancerre from the east are dry white wines, while from the middle, around Anjou and Vouvray, the wines have a touch of sweetness, may be still or sparkling, and can be red, rosé, or white. Aside from Muscadet, whose name is the same as the grape variety from which it is made, the wines of the Loire are named for the districts in which they are grown. From east to west, as the river flows, they are:

POUILLY-SUR-LOIRE AND POUILLY-FUMÉ. South of Paris the town of Pouilly-sur-Loire lies on the right bank of the Loire. The vineyards about Pouilly are planted with Sauvignon Blanc, known locally as the Blanc Fumé, and the Chasselas. For the wine to be called Pouilly-Fumé, it must be made from the Sauvignon Blanc grape only. If the wine is made from Chasselas, with or without any Sauvignon Blanc, then it is named for the town and is called Pouilly-sur-Loire. Pouilly-Fumé is a delicate, soft, dry white wine, and the best examples have a slightly smoky quality to the bouquet. Pouilly-sur-Loire is less delicate than Pouilly-Fumé but is attractive when drunk young. Do not confuse Pouilly-Fumé of the Loire with the Pouilly-Fuissé of Burgundy; they are completely dissimilar.

SANCERRE. On the left bank of the river, almost opposite Pouilly, we find Sancerre. As in Pouilly, white wines are also made from the Sauvignon Blanc grape. The wines of Sancerre are very fruity, and their acidity is more pronounced than the wines from Pouilly. Some red wine is made from the Pinot Noir grape, but little is exported.

VOUVRAY AND SAUMUR. These are wine districts around the city of Tours. Vouvray produces both still and sparkling white wines. The principal grape is the Pineau de la Loire or Chenin Blanc, which grows in chalky soil. Saumur produces white and rosé medium-dry sparkling wines. The grape varieties used are distinguished by their ability to produce effervescence. In addition to Chenin Blanc, other white grapes permitted in small amounts are Chardonnay and Sauvignon Blanc. Black grapes include Cabernet Franc, Cabernet Sauvignon, Gamay, Pineau d'Aunis, and Pinot Noir. Sparkling or *mousseux* wine is

WINE REGIONS OF THE LOIRE

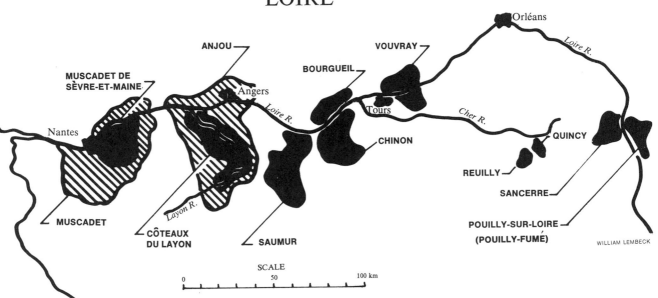

also made in the Côteaux de Touraine. The leading producers make their sparkling wines by the *méthode champenoise,* and wines from either Saumur or Touraine may use the appellation Crémant de Loire. Sparkling Vouvray remains Vouvray Mousseux.

CHINON AND BOURGUEIL. These districts produce two similiar red wines in the style of Beaujolais, made from mostly Cabérnet Franc grapes. Chinon was the home of Rabelais, lover of the good life, who consumed Chinon in vast amounts and praised it lavishly. The wine is pleasing and satisfying. Both wines should be drunk young, and may be cooled.

ANJOU. This region, near the city of Angers, produces large quantities of white and rosé wines. Some of the most popular rosé wines in the United States are the Anjou rosés, unquestionably because of their touch of sweetness and attractive pink color. Both still and sparkling white wines are made from the Chenin Blanc grape. Rosé de'Anjou is produced mainly from the Cabernet Franc, Cabernet Sauvignon, Gamay, and Pineau d'Aunis grapes. South of Angers, the Chenin Blanc grape, which in Anjou usually produces sweeter wines, makes a dry, rich wine called Savennières.

CÔTEAUX DU LAYON. The vineyards along the Layon River, a tributary of the Loire, are planted with Chenin Blanc grapes that make uncommonly good sweet wines. In this area, both Bonnezeaux and Quarts de Chaume have their own appellations for this style of sweet, rich dessert wines.

MUSCADET. On both banks of the Loire, as it flows into the Atlantic near Nantes, the vineyards are planted with Melon grapes, locally known as Muscadet. The light, gentle, bone-dry wine is called Muscadet. The best is from Sèvre-et-Maine, the heartland of the region, and is called Muscadet de Sèvre-et-Maine. When labeled *sur lie,* the wine has been bottled shortly after it was made, without having been racked. Muscadet is the most popular white wine of the Loire. Gros Plant, a more acid wine, comes from the Pays Nantais.

7. OTHER WINES OF FRANCE

CÔTES DE PROVENCE

Although red and white wines are made in this region, some of the smoothest, freshest rosés come from the Côtes de Provence. This region runs from Nice to Marseille, although the vinicultural heart lies between Saint-Raphaël and Aix-en-Provence. When the wines are young they have a delightful bouquet; older, they lose some bouquet but gain in softness. Other areas of the Côtes de Provence include Cassis, famous for its whites; Bandol, famous for reds, as is Palette; and Bellet, near Nice, which produces reds, whites, and rosés. Wines from Côtes de Provence were elevated to *Appellation Contrôlée* status in 1977, having previously been in the next lower V.D.Q.S. category.

MIDI

West of the Côtes de Provence, along the Mediterranean, lies a huge plain that extends down to the Spanish border. This area, called the Midi, produces immense quantities of ordinary table wines. The better wines of the area are the reds from Corbières, Minervois, and Roussillon. Sweet dessert wines are also made in this area. The most famous are Muscat de Frontignan and Banyuls. Most Midi wines are from the V.D.Q.S. category.

JURA

This region near Switzerland was famous in the past for its wines, but today only the Rosé d'Arbois and the wines of Château-Châlon retain some fame. The latter two are interesting in a special way.

At Château-Châlon the Savagnin grapes (considered the same as the Gewürztraminer grown elsewhere) are picked as late as possible, sometimes in December, and fermentation takes place in vats that have been cut out of the rock. Because of the late vintage, fermentation is rather slow. Some wines are then racked into very old casks that have held many previous vintages, and they remain in partially filled, sealed casks for a minimum of six years before they are ready for bottling. This wine will be a *vin jaune*, or yellow wine.

During this period a yeast film forms on the surface of the wine in the cask and performs its miraculous work. This is one of few wines in which this phenomenon occurs. An exception is sherry from Jerez, in which the *flor* is commonplace. As a result, Château-Châlon develops an alcohol content, usually about 15 percent, that gives extraordinary keeping qualities. It is said to live for decades and to have an austere dryness coupled with a delicate, nutty flavor, such as one encounters in a very old, dry sherry.

A few miles west of Château-Châlon lies one of the oldest vineyards known, Château d'Arlay, which produces wine similar to Château-Châlon, as well as red and white table wines. But it is the white, or rather straw-colored, *vin de paille*° that is most distinguished. Only wines of better-than-average-quality vintages are bottled. The twenty acres that compose the vineyard can produce upward of thirty thousand bottles, but the quantity is usually less.

BÉARN

In the Pyrénées and a former part of the Royaume de Navarre are the vineyards of Jurançon, which produce a rich, sweet wine of breed and character. Around Pau, the capital, Rosé de Béarn, a fine pink wine, is produced.

OTHER WINES OF THE SOUTHWEST

Near Bordeaux, from the Dordogne River to the Pyrénées, are some less famous areas that produce attractive wines. Cahors is a dark red wine, made mainly from the Malbec or Cot grape, which is highly tannic. This wine requires a great deal of bottle age to smooth out.

Bergerac, another region of the southwest, produces both red and white wines. Its most famous wine is Monbazillac, a rich dessert wine that reminds one of Sauternes, made from the same grapes.

°The term comes from the fact that the grapes are spread upon straw (*paille*) to dry for a period of time before pressing.

Castello della Sala in the heart of the Orvieto wine region. (*Courtesy Julius Wile Sons & Co., Inc., New York*)

6
THE WINES OF ITALY

The length of the Via Latina was once dotted with statues of Bacchus that were destroyed as pagan idols with the march of Christianity. The cult of Dionysus, during the Golden Age of Greece, taught man the contemplation of his own divinity, and wine was an important part of the cult's ritual. All Hellas honored the vine and spread the cult to Rome and Asia Minor. Plato records that Socrates drank unbelievable quantities of wine but was never intoxicated.

It is unquestionable that we owe to the Romans the spread of the vinification of the grape. Martial speaks of *"immortale Falernum"* with a reverence that borders on idolatry, referring to the merits of two-hundred year old wines that were said to remain drinkable.

The Romans had capable winemakers who understood the need for better storage of their wines. From the Greeks they took the method of lining their *amphorae, dolia,* and sometimes barrels with pitch or resin, for these containers were porous. While an improvement, storage was still far from ideal, and it was necessary to create wines of high alcohol and concentrated flavors to keep them from deteriorating.

Roman winemakers, therefore, made wines of great alcoholic strength, concentrated to the consistency of jelly, and served only after dilution with water. The wines were spiced and preserved with such substances as aloes, myrrh, resin, pitch, seawater, marble dust, perfumes, spices, and herbs.

After the fall of the Roman Empire, the Church took up the work of cultivating the vine, and the barons, under the sway of the Church, cooperated, for "mighty was the thirst of the Templar."

In the fourteenth and fifteenth centuries it became fashionable to live well, even if one had to live dangerously. The literature of the Renaissance is full of references to wines and vines. The banquets of the Medicis and the Barberinis were supreme exhibitions of aesthetic magnificence, with wines served in golden goblets and toasts sung in immortal rhymes.

From birth the Italian absorbs the love of the vine with no conscious effort. Wine is the common drink—inexpensive, natural, and sound. Because no germs harmful to man can live in wine, it was a safer drink than water, which in years past was often polluted with typhoid bacteria. As a result the annual per capita consumption of wine in Italy has been high, about 26 gallons, as compared with about 2 gallons in the United States.

The vine grows everywhere in Italy, profusely, as though displaying the bounty of nature through the fertility of her soil. In fact, Italy is one vast vineyard, from the snow-covered Alpine borders in the north to the volcanic southern tip of the boot.

Italy has often been called the vineyard of the world. Where nature is so bountiful, man is prone to leave things in the lap of the gods. Vines were permitted to luxuriate over fertile plains, to climb at will over fence and tree, and to grow in festoons. Viticulture was sometimes careless in Italy, although there were many producers who had always maintained strict standards. Over the last twenty years, economic realities, particularly Common Market trade policies, have necessitated the disciplining of all those Italian vineyards that had not previously maintained such high standards.

On the whole, the attitude of the Italian winemaker today has changed, being receptive both to the needs of the home market and to the market abroad. Italy shows us many facets: from top-quality estate wines to everyday quaffing wines, and also bulk wines for blending. Although much wine is imported to the United States, it is not always realized how much wine is also sold to France and Germany.

THE WINE LAW OF 1963

Much of the stimulus behind the modernization of the Italian wine industry came from a government and industry policy of tighter control of all aspects of wine production. The Wine Law of 1963, passed after thirty years of preliminary thought and effort, consolidated and defined all legal aspects with which the wine industry must comply. Its basic aims have been to protect the name of origin and the sources of musts and wines and to provide measures for the prevention of fraud and unfair competition. For example, chaptalization (a process sometimes used in northern countries with short, cool growing seasons whereby sugar is added to the must to increase the alcohol content of the wine) is forbidden by law in Italy. This can be enforced because the government distributes sugar.

The 1963 law delimits zones of production so that the same type of natural environment is provided for the production of grapes for a specific type of wine. There are three different denominations, graded as follows:

1. *Vino da Tavola* ("Table Wine") and/or *Vino Tipico* ("Typical Wine") is the Common Market category replacing *Denominazione Semplice,* the original first level of government regulated wines. This is a simple statement describing a wine with few restrictions on area, percent of alcohol, etc. These wines sometimes state the name of the region, such as *Vino da Tavola di Tuscana* or *Barbera del Piemonte.*

2. *Denominazione di Origine Controllata* ("Controlled Denomination of Origin") is an appellation reserved for wines that have met stipulated standards of quality. The label must state the area of origin. Natural conditions of the locality, such as soil type and geography, determine the traditional varieties of grapes permitted to be grown. Production practices must conform to approved methods of planting, cultivating, fertilizing, and other viticultural practices, and the maximum yield is controlled. Bottling specifications and minimum alcohol content and aging requirements are also controlled. Documents on these wines and on their sales are subject to inspection. All vineyards producing such wines are listed in an official register, and their wines carry the D.O.C. label.

3. *Denominazione di Origine Controllata e Garantita* ("Controlled and Guaranteed Denomination of Origin") encompasses all of the requirements of D.O.C. wines but is even more stringent. The wine must be bottled and sealed with a government seal by the producer, which may not be removed without breaking it. A government inspector can test and analyze the wine at any time, both in the laboratory and organoleptically. The label of such a wine must state that its origin, as well as the net contents of the bottle, the name of the grower and bottler, the place of bottling, and the alcoholic strength, is controlled and guaranteed by the Italian government. Containers may not be larger than five liter capacity.

Wine submitted by any producer which does not meet the required D.O.C.G. quality standards at any time during production, will be declassified to Table Wine, and will lose the right to use its official name.

The upgrading of D.O.C. to D.O.C.G. does not occur automatically, but only when a certain number of procedures of a given D.O.C. wine apply for the designation. Remaining producers may still maintain their D.O.C. status.

Any wine that is exported must comply with the 1963 law. In addition, the wine is tested by the *Istituto Commercio Estero* (formerly called the *Istituto Nazionale Esportazione*), which grants the red I.N.E. seal, mandatory on all bottles shipped to the United States, Canada, and Mexico. This seal indicates that the wine has met the standards of the export laws applicable to these countries and ensures the wine's authenticity.

See Appendix E for a listing of D.O.C. wine areas and D.O.C.G. wines.

labeling

If an Italian wine qualifies under D.O.C. laws, the words *Denominazione di Origine Controllata* appear on the label, below the name of the wine and the denomination of origin. The producer and bottler are indicated as well. Whether any further descriptive words can be used on a given label depends on the individual D.O.C. rules for each type of wine.

Some of the more common words that appear on Italian wine labels, whether D.O.C. wines or not, are the following:

Classico	Classic—may be used by any producer to describe his wine. In certain regions, such as Chianti, it means that the wine has come from a specific central area
Imbottigliato all'origine	Estate bottled
Riserva	Reserve—indicates extra aging in cask or bottle, the number of years varying with the D.O.C. requirements for different areas
Riserva Speciale	Special Reserve—wine is aged longer than Riserva
Superiore	Superior—wine has slightly higher alcohol content and sometimes greater age than a wine that does not have this designation
Vecchio	Old—a term found in Italy, but not permitted on U.S. labels. Vecchio wines are aged longer than Superiore but not as long as Riserva.

Vineyards planted in the more traditional style of Italy, with trellised vines. (*Courtesy Fratelli Folonari, Brescia*)

Vintages may be given on either the main label or the neck label. *Annata* means "year," and *vendemmia* means "vintage." Other descriptive terms are:

Amaro	tart, dry	*Rosato*	rosé
Secco	dry	*Chiaretto*	light red
Abboccato	semidry	*Rosso*	red
Amabile	semisweet	*Nero*	deep red
Dolce	sweet	*Frizzante*	crackling
Bianco	white	*Spumante*	sparkling

Extra and *Fine* may not be used

A growers' regional organization may add another seal guaranteeing authenticity, and the seal may provide additional information. The *Consorzio Vino Chianti Classico*, for example, surrounds its black rooster symbol with different colored borders, which indicate a Chianti Classico (black border) or a Chianti Classico Riserva (black and gold borders.) As the D.O.C. regulations become more generally effective, however, the use of seals is diminishing in some regions, and some of the best-known shippers are discontinuing their memberships and use of the local seals.

The same grape variety is often grown in several districts. Wine made from grapes grown in the mountainous northern region where the soil is watered by glacier-fed rivers, however, is distinctively different from that produced from the same grape grown in volcanic soil containing a great many minerals. That is why a varietal wine labeled with the name of the grape always lists the area where it was grown on the label as well. Sometimes the grape gives its local name to the wine; in other cases the wine may take its name from the town or village around which the grapes were grown.

Any D.O.C. wine, however, has a place name, whether the wine is named for a grape or has a fantasy name like Est! Est!! Est!!! Brand names, even if *Vino da Tavola*, mention regions as well. Non-D.O.C. wines in the *Vino Tipico* category may be labeled varietally with a place name, if the grape named comprises 85 percent of the wine in the bottle, and 85 percent of the wine comes from the region stated on the label.

geography

A map of the world shows that Italy lies in the same latitude as Canada and New England; Naples is in the same latitude as New York. The entire Italian peninsula is covered with mountains. In the west and north lie the majestic, snow-capped Alps; toward the east are the Venetian Alps—the picturesque needles of the Dolomites. Despite the handicaps of weather, snow, ice, erosion, and avalanche, the vine thrives because the valleys are fertile and the people are hard-working. Some of the finest vines are grown on forbidding ledges, which must be carefully terraced and tended.

The peninsula is split by the Apennine Mountains, which run from the Po River in the north to the very tip of Calabria in the south. While the Apennines are not as forbidding as the Alps, they are rocky and bleak and submit only to the constant struggle of industrious peasants whose forebears have fought the elements for over two thousand years.

The northern part of Italy is often foggy and rainy; the eternal snows on the Alpine peaks cool the warm sirocco from the south. Southern Italy has a semitropical Mediterranean climate, sunny and dry, with little rainfall. Sicily is the island of perpetual sunshine. The vine grows profusely in all of Italy, yet so varied are the climatic conditions, the soil, the methods of cultivation, and the varieties of vines used that Italian wine probably can satisfy the most discriminating requirements of any connoisseur.

grape varieties

From the Po River down to the Vesuvius region, with its hot, sandy, volcanic soil, Italy runs the entire gamut of varieties of grapes. There are so many types of vines that it is next to impossible to make an accurate estimate of their numbers, but counts run as high as three hundred varieties. The Common Market regulates which grapes can be grown in member countries. Italy has the highest approved number. The fifty most important of these are listed in Appendix E with the areas in which they are grown and the wines in which they are used.

red grapes

The noble grape of Italy is the Nebbiolo, a red-wine grape producing the rich, full wines of Piedmont and northern Lombardy. Barbera, Grignolino, and Dolcetto are also grown in Piedmont, but the latter two produce softer, lighter wines. The Sangiovese grape varieties are grown in several regions, but they are best known as the principal grapes of Chianti and Brunello di Montalcino. Some of the many varieties of Lambrusco grape make the popular wine of the same name in Emilia-Romagna. In the Veneto the Corvina Veronese grape produces both Bardolino and Valpolicella. Grapes discussed previously in Chapter 5, the Cabernet Sauvignon, Merlot, and Pinot Nero (Pinot Noir), are grown successfully in the northern regions that border on Switzerland and Austria: Lombardy, Trentino–Alto Adige, and Friuli-Venezia-Giulia. The Aglianico grape makes sturdy red wines in the region of Campania.

white grapes

One of the most widely planted white grapes, the Trebbiano, grows in the north and central parts of Italy. Trebbiano is in such famous wines as Soave, Lugana, Orvieto, Frascati, and Est! Est!! Est!!!, and a small amount is even used in Chianti to soften the blend of red grapes. Piedmont is the home of the Cortese Bianco grape. The Verdicchio grape produces, in the Marches, the varietally named Verdicchio wine. Pinot Bianco, Chardonnay, Pinot Grigio, Sauvignon Blanc, Riesling, Traminer, Müller-Thurgau, and Tocai grapes are seen elsewhere in Europe and make charming white wines in the northern

SWITZERLAND

AUSTRIA

TRENTINO–
ALTO
ADIGE

Sondrio

FRIULI–
VENEZIA
GIULIA

VALLE
D'AOSTA

LOMBARDY

*Lake
Garda*

VENETO

Adda R.

Brescia

Verona

Trieste

Venice

YUGOSLAVIA

Po R.

Milan

Pavia

Adige R.

Turin

Asti

Alba

EMILIA-ROMAGNA

PIEDMONT

Bologna

LIGURIA

Florence

SAN
MARINO

MARCHES

TUSCANY

Siena

ADRIATIC SEA

Montepulciano

Perugia

Montalcino

UMBRIA

Piceno

ELBA

Orvieto

Montefiascone

T Y R R H E N I A N   S E A

Tiber R.

ABRUZZI
AND MOLISE

Rome

LATIUM

Foggia

CAMPANIA

APULIA

SARDINIA

Naples

Bosa

ISCHIA

CAPRI

BASILICATA

WINE REGIONS
OF
ITALY

Cagliari

CALABRIA

Palermo

*MOUNT
ETNA*

Marsala

SICILY

WILLIAM LEMBECK

region of Friuli-Venezia-Giulia, Trentino–Alto Adige, and Veneto—the three regions historically known as the Tre Venezie. Many varieties of Malvasia grapes are planted throughout Italy, and they appear in various table wines. Assorted varieties of Moscatos produce sweet dessert wines from Piedmont in the north to Sicily in the south, as well as on the island of Sardinia.

PIEDMONT

Piedmont produces the majority of Italy's most regal red wines, while being one of the most austere regions in the country. From the glaciers of the Alpine banks the land descends in a series of charming valleys and fertile plains to the Po River, from which it again rises gradually to the hills of Monferrato, where the vine is cultivated with religious fervor. Piedmont's name is derived from *"a pie del monti,"* meaning "at the foot of the mountains." The famous red wines are full, rich, travel well, and improve with age. They include Barolo, Barbaresco, and Gattinara.

The region is ruled by Turin (Torino), the home of vermouth and the center of industry. It is the richest market for wines in the region. The Piedmontese are tenacious, industrious, and faithful to their land. Their vineyards are neat and symmetrical.

Barolo is the name of a town as well as the name of the surrounding area fully planted to its limits with over two thousand acres under vine. The area is situated on a hill of porous rock, which undoubtedly is an extinct volcano. On this hill Nebbiolo grapes grow best, and they give one of the finest and most justly celebrated red wines Italy has, also called Barolo. The proud growers call it the wine of kings and king of wines. In good years Barolo is a big, full-bodied wine, with a ruby-red color that takes on a brownish shade as it ages. It is generous yet austere, rich in alcohol, but, with age, always soft and velvety, with an unmistakable violet bouquet. All Barolos must spend at least two years in barrels of oak or chestnut. Barolo must be at least three years old before release, Barolo Riserva four years, and Barolo Riserva Speciale five years of age.

Northeast of Barolo is the town and district of Barbaresco, which produces Barbaresco wines. The hillside vineyards surround the old red-towered remnant of Barbaresco Castle on the crest of the hill, overlooking the stone houses below. The hills are also planted with Nebbiolo vines, but different soils create different wines. Barbaresco's minimum age is two years, with the Riserva aged for three, and the Riserva Speciale aged four. Both Barolo and Barbaresco have been granted D.O.C.G. status.

It is interesting to note that in Julius Caesar's *Commentaries* there is a reference to these wines, which he greatly appreciated and wanted to introduce to Rome. The particular wine to which he referred came from the little village of Morra (Murra). "From Murra," he wrote, "we brought the best wine to our city of Rome."

An aging cellar in the Nizza Monferrato in Piedmont. (*Courtesy Joseph E. Seagram & Sons, Inc., New York*)

The third most important red wine from Piedmont is Gattinara, principally made from the Nebbiolo grape, with some Bonarda permitted. Gattinara is a small D.O.C. area, with about eighty acres under vine, in the northeast part of Piedmont that borders on Lombardy. The Sesia River flows through Gattinara. The wine is aged at least four years, after which it begins to get a velvet quality.

Adjoining the D.O.C. area of Gattinara, are vineyards planted with the same grapes, often producing similar styles of wine, but without the D.O.C. classification. The wine is named for the colloquial name of the Nebbiolo grape, which is "Spanna."

Nebbiolo also appears as a varietal wine, when the place names of either Alba or Carema appear on the label.

The most widely planted grape in Piedmont is the Barbera, producing 50 percent of the red wines of this region. These varietally labeled wines always have a place name affixed to the grape name, such as Barbera d'Alba, Barbera d'Asti, Barbera dei Colli Tortonesi, and Barbera del Monferrato. The wine is usually drunk young, but can take moderate aging.

Many of the premium red wines mentioned thus far from Piedmont are now appearing on the market with single vineyard designations.

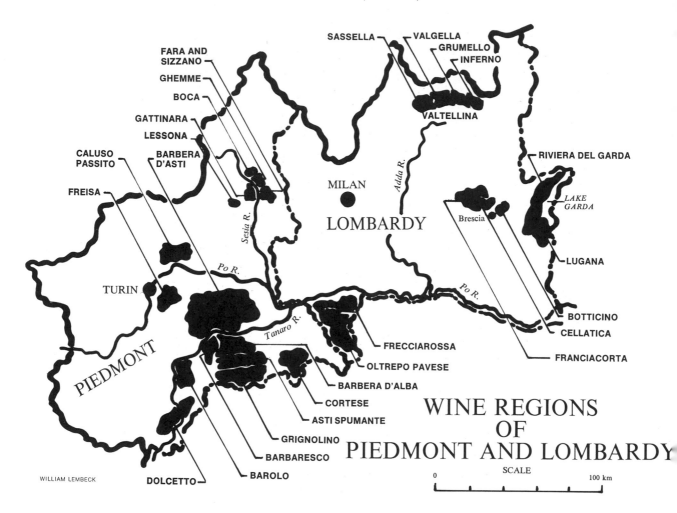

WINE REGIONS
OF
PIEDMONT AND LOMBARDY

WILLIAM LEMBECK

Grignolino, made from the grape of the same name, is a light, fruity, rather dry wine that sometimes has a slight natural effervescence. Dolcetto is another varietal red wine that is light and makes an excellent carafe wine. Another grape variety, Freisa, is so named for its raspberry bouquet. It makes both a dry red wine and a sweet, slightly sparkling, or "crackling," wine. Grignolino, Dolcetto, and Freisa have a place name after the grape variety name.

Boca, Fara, Ghemme, Lessona, and Sizzano are five other red wines made from the Nebbiolo, Vespolina, and Bonarda grapes. These are good red wines with limited production.

From the Cortese Bianco grape is produced Cortese, usually a delicate, straw-colored wine with a greenish cast, and a pleasant, fresh aroma. Cortese produced around the town of Gavi, however, is quite distinctive, and has been granted D.O.C. classification.

Asti, the sparkling wine center of Italy and the home of the famous sparkling Asti Spumante, is a town with a great historical background. Bismarck showed such predilection for it that he exclaimed: "I want one good bottle for each of my officers. It will serve to keep their heavy heads awake."

The actual production zone of Asti Spumante lies south of the town. The vineyards of San Stefano along the rugged banks of the Belbo River, and vineyards around Canelli produce the most highly prized Moscato Bianco grapes, which go into making this sparkling wine of Asti.

Asti Spumante is the most popular Italian sparkling wine. It is a delicious wine with a pleasant, decidedly sweet Muscat flavor and low alcohol (7.5 to 9 percent) that gives it a lovely, fresh fruitiness. Most of the shippers have changed over from bottle fermentation to Charmat fermentation (see Chapter 11). Aside from the time and expense savings, the fragrance of the Muscat grape is captured much better by this method. Some of the Italian sparkling wine producers do use the *méthode champenoise* in years of exceptional heat and sugar content. A sparkling wine that used to be made in Piedmont was Lacrima Christi, but this is no longer permitted. The wine is now made in Campania, the best coming from the province of Avellino. It may or may not be sparkling.

A sweet dessert wine, Caluso Passito, is produced north of Turin from the white Erbaluce grape in the area of Caluso. These grapes undergo a drying process (Passito) that raisins them and leaves them rich in sugar. When the wine is lightly fortified, it becomes a Passito Liquoroso.

LOMBARDY

Lombardy has three main wine regions: the northern lake region framed by the Swiss Alps with breathtaking beauty, the southwestern portion next to Piedmont, and the eastern sections separated from the western half by the Adda River, which borders on the Veneto. The Po River, Italy's longest river, flows through the southern part of the region. Milan, Italy's industrial capital, is situated in central Lombardy.

Some of the best wines of Lombardy come from an area known as the Valtellina, in the northernmost province of Sondrio on the Swiss border. The vineyards are carved out of the mountains and are tended by hardy individuals. Both red and white wines are made, but the Sassella, Grumello, Inferno, and Valgella reds are the most famous and are made from at least 95 percent Nebbiolo grapes, known locally as Chiavennasca. Differences in soil and altitude give these wines a different character from the Nebbiolo wines of Piedmont. A wine labeled Valtellina may come from any of the four named areas, and must be aged for one year minimum. With two years of aging it may be called Valtellina Superiore, and Riservas must have a minimum of four years age. A unique, high-alcohol, rich red wine, made with semidried grapes, is called Sforsato (Sfursat), which means "forced" in Italian.

In southwest Lombardy, the Oltrepò Pavese area, once part of Piedmont, is considered by many to be an excellent wine-producing district. Many good, inexpensive wines are made for local consumption, as well as for export, primarily from the Barbera and Bonarda grapes. One proprietary brand, Frecciarossa, is produced by the Odero family, whose château bottling dates back to the last century. Frecciarossa is made from different grape varieties, many brought from France, and appears as red, white, and rosé wine.

Many of the spumante producers buy grapes from this area, especially Pinot Bianco and Pinot Nero. Some white wines are produced from the Riesling, Cortese, and Pinot Bianco, and a rosé is made from Pinot Nero.

In the east, near charming Lake Garda, is produced a pleasant, light white wine called Lugana, made from the Trebbiano grape. It is most enjoyable when young, especially so with a freshly caught trout from Lake Garda. The most famous wine from this area is the Riviera del Garda Rosé. Called Chiaretto, which means "light red," it is a ruby-hued rosé with a gentle flavor, soft texture, and a hint of bitterness.

Slightly to the west of Lake Garda is the province of Brescia, where wines are produced in the Franciacorta zone. Light, flavorful reds are made from a mixture of Cabernet Franc, Barbera, Nebbiolo, and Merlot grapes, as are the red Cellatica and Botticino. The white Franciacorta Pinot Bianco makes fine dry still and sparkling wines, and some Pinot Grigio is also produced.

VENETO

The morning sun rising above the Adriatic gilds the peaks of the Dolomites in the north long before it touches the golden cupolas of San Marco in Venice. The land drops precipitously from rugged mountains. Cutting across southern Veneto, the Adige River passes through romantic Verona, where you can visit the houses of the Montagues and Capulets. There also stands majestically the Palazzo Scaglieri, where Cangrande toasted his guests with Vernaccia and where Dante Alighieri found refuge and protection.

Here along the eastern shores of Lake Garda, near Verona, are produced bright red Bardolino; Bianco di Custoza, a flowery white; and again, dry white Lugana. The long narrow valley running north from Verona is where the Corvina, Rondinella, and other grape varieties are blended to produce one of Italy's fruitiest red table wines—Valpolicella. Valpolicella is a fine, ruby-colored wine of delicate bouquet and with a pleasant crisp finish. Both Bardolino and Valpolicella may be lightly cooled and consumed as a young, fresh wine.

WINE REGIONS OF
NORTHEAST
ITALY

LAGREIN

SANTA
MADDALENA

CALDARO

TRENTINO–

GAMBELLARA

ALTO ADIGE

SOAVE

VALPOLICELLA
AND RECIOTO
VALPOLICELLA

BARDOLINO &
BIANCO DI CUSTOZA

LAKE GARDA

LUGANA

Verona

Adige R.

VENETO

Adige R.

Po R.

FRIULI-

VENEZIA-

COLLI ORIENTALE
DEL FRIULI

COLLI GRAVE
DEL FRIULI

COLLI
GORIZIANO

GIULIA

Trieste

CONEGLIANO-
VALDOBBIADENE

RABOSO

Venice

BREGANZE

LAMBRUSCO

EMILIA-
ROMAGNA

SCALE

0   100 km

WILLIAM LEMBECK

A special Valpolicella produced in limited quantities is called Recioto della Valpolicella-Amarone. It used to be made entirely with the ripest grapes taken from the upper part of the bunch. To the imaginative person these grapes represent the "ears" of the bunch, ergo *Recioto*, which means "ears." Today, whole bunches that are the best of the vineyard are selected. The grapes are then dried on reed trays in a shed for three months and are vinified. The high sugar concentration ferments to a rich, dry wine with a high alcohol content. Amarone actually refers to this process or style of winemaking. *Amaro* is the Venetian equivalent of "slightly bitter," which has a pleasant connotation to it and signifies that the wine was vinified to complete dryness.

From the vineyards around the ancient walled city of Soave, the Garganega and ubiquitous Trebbiano grapes produce Soave. It is a really suave white wine, medium body, fairly dry, with a pleasant, subtle bouquet, and a bit of piquant bitter undertone.

Soave, Bardolino, and Valpolicella are available as Classico wines, with a more defined zone of production, and the best are Classico Superiore.

A wine made to the east of Soave, the Garganega di Gambellara, is produced as a dry white, a sweet white, and a sparkling wine.

Other excellent white wines, such as the Bianco, made from 85 percent Tocai grapes; the Pinot Grigio Superiore, made from Pinot Bianco and Pinot Grigio grapes; and the Vespaiolo, made from 100 percent Vespaiolo grapes, are found in the Breganze area in the province of Vicenza. Good red wines from this area are being made from such classic varieties as Merlot, Pinot Nero, and Cabernet.

Further east in the province of Treviso, are the communes of Conegliano and Valdobbiadene. Here the best known wine is vinified from the Prosecco grape, as a still, *frizzante*, or *spumante* wine. Other white wines from Treviso include Tocai di Lison, Verduzzo, Pinot Grigio, and Pinot Bianco. In addition to Raboso, a local red, Cabernet and Merlot are also grown.

TRENTINO–ALTO ADIGE

Italy's northernmost region, bordering on Austria, is Trentino–Alto Adige. It produces many red and white wines using the traditional grapes grown in France and Germany. Some varietal red wines are Trentino-Cabernet, Trentino-Merlot, and Trentino–Pinot Nero, which use 100 percent of the grapes named. Among the white are Trentino-Riesling, Trentino-Pinot, and Trentino–Traminer Aromatico. These wines are similar to those made in the grapes' homelands. This area is known for its fine dry sparkling wines, thanks to advanced technology, and the availability of traditional sparkling wine grapes.

The province of Bolzano (Upper Adige) produces a wide variety of quality wines, but the best known are Santa Maddalena, Teroldego Rotaliano, and Caldaro—dry, red wines—and Lagrein—a dry, fresh rosé made from the Lagrein grape.

FRIULI–VENEZIA–GIULIA

Nestled between Veneto, Austria, and Yugoslavia is the individualistic region of Friuli-Venezia-Giulia. Some areas, such as Trieste, have been part of both Yugoslavia and Italy at different times and have developed cultures encompassing those of both countries. The wines come from three main areas: Colli Orientale del Friuli (Eastern Friuli Hills), Colli Grave del Friuli (Western Friuli Hills), and Colli Goriziano (Gorizia Hills). Three lesser areas are Isonzo, Aquileia, and Latisana. Some grapes used are the Pinot Nero, Cabernet, Merlot, and Refosco, which produce full, rich reds. Pinot Bianco, Pinot

Vineyards grow right up to the remains of the medieval fortress and battlements that protected the ancient city of Soave, near Verona. (*Courtesy Fratelli Folonari, Brescia*)

Grigio, Tocai, Sauvignon, Traminer, Riesling Renano, and Riesling Italico produce characteristic white wines. The Verduzzo grape, grown in the eastern and western hills, makes a full bodied and slightly tannic white wine called Verduzzo. Picolot, a rare grape grown in the Colli Orientali, makes a prized, delicate sweet wine.

While this area has its roots far back in history, much of it was destroyed during World War II. This has resulted in new plantings, coupled with modern equipment and advanced technology. Because of this, it can be considered a new wine area, producing high quality wines with worldwide acceptance.

EMILIA–ROMAGNA

We now come to the richest and most fertile region of the Po Valley. Surrounding the famed gastronomic center of Italy, which is Bologna, are the three main wine-producing areas. To the northwest are the Piacenza Hills, where Gutturnio, a dry, full-bodied red wine is made from Barbera and Bonarda grapes.

The central area around Modena and Parma, famous for Parma hams and Parmesan cheese, is the site of several different Lambrusco grape varieties. These grapes make the popular Lambrusco wine; lively, *frizzante*, semidry red wine that can be served chilled. (A dry version is also made, but it is consumed locally.) While this red wine has a D.O.C. classification, the same Lambrusco grapes are fermented off the skins to make both Bianco (white) and Rosato (rosé), with a similar flavor and effervescence to the red wine. Because of the difference in vinification, however, the Bianco and Rosato may not carry the D.O.C. on their labels. This has not affected their extreme popularity in the United States.

In the southeast corner of this region is the third wine-producing area, historically known as Romagna. It encompasses the provinces of Forli, Ravenna, and Bologna. The full red varietal Sangiovese di Romagna dominates premium wine production in Emilia-Romagna, and ranks third in volume behind Chianti and Soave among Italy's D.O.C. wines.

The white wines of this area are the dry, light Trebbiano di Romagna, and the Albana di Romagna, which varies from dry to semisweet, and from still to sparkling. Albana di Romagna is the first white wine to apply for D.O.C.G. classification.

TUSCANY

To the poets this region is Arcady—the home of Dante, Boccaccio, the Borgias, Saint Francis of Assisi, Saint Catherine of Siena. It bears the marks of the orgies and extravaganzas of its sinners and the pious virtues of its saints.

To most people Tuscany is the home of Italian wines, for it is the home of Chianti, the wine of the typical straw-covered flask (*fiasco*) originally used for breakage-free shipping. Of all containers for wine, it is the most picturesque, but difficult to fill, hard to stack, susceptible to mildew, and expensive to produce today.

The Chianti area is subdivided into seven districts, all of which lie on the beautiful rolling hillsides around and between Florence (Firenze) and Siena (see map on page 107). Wines produced from the center of the Chianti zone may be called Chianti Classico.

The proud and independent Tuscans followed many historical winemaking traditions, whether or not they were the best viticultural and enological methods. To Barone Bettino Ricasoli must go the credit for having brought Piedmontese viticultural methods into Tuscany by the nineteenth century. The work of improvement in vinification as well has set an example that other vineyard owners have followed.

Chianti has been clearly defined and regulated by the D.O.C. laws, regarding area, grapes, and methods of production. Since many Chianti Classico producers have requested and received D.O.C.G. status, the regulations have changed somewhat.

Chianti is made from several different grape varieties. The principal grape is the Sangiovese, which accounts for from 50 to 80 percent of the must; the Canaiolo Nero from 10 to 30 percent of the must; and the white Trebbiano Tuscano and Malvasia del Chianti, which can also account for 10 to 30 percent of the must. Other local grapes can provide up to 5 percent of the blend. The actual proportions vary with the vintage year and the style of Chianti being made.

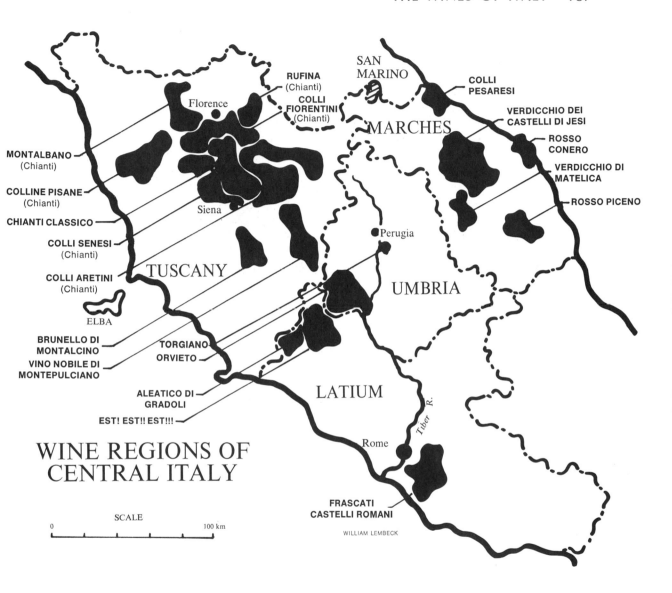

MONTALBANO
(Chianti)

COLLINE PISANE
(Chianti)

CHIANTI CLASSICO

COLLI SENESI
(Chianti)

COLLI ARETINI
(Chianti)

ELBA

BRUNELLO DI
MONTALCINO
VINO NOBILE DI
MONTEPULCIANO

ALEATICO DI
GRADOLI

EST! EST!! EST!!!

RUFINA
(Chianti)

COLLI
FIORENTINI
(Chianti)

Florence

SAN
MARINO

COLLI
PESARESI

VERDICCHIO DEI
CASTELLI DI JESI

ROSSO
CONERO

VERDICCHIO DI
MATELICA

ROSSO PICENO

MARCHES

Siena

TUSCANY

Perugia

UMBRIA

TORGIANO
ORVIETO

LATIUM

Tiber R.

Rome

WINE REGIONS OF
CENTRAL ITALY

FRASCATI
CASTELLI ROMANI

SCALE

0   100 km

WILLIAM LEMBECK

D.O.C.G. Chianti Classicos use less white grapes in the must, with only 8 to 10 percent permitted. In addition, the maximum yield per hectare has been decreased to ensure higher quality.

Three types of Chianti are generally produced: the wine for early consumption, light in color and body; a better quality, which comprises the largest quantity of all Chiantis produced and whose tannins soften after a year or so of aging; and the best quality, which requires longer aging to round out the increased alcohol, higher acids, and tannins.

For Chiantis meant to be drunk young, a process called *governo* is used in Tuscany. It consists of setting aside a small percentage of the harvest on mats to become raisins. These are added to the large vats of new Chianti. A slow, second fermentation takes place that softens the acids and makes the wine drinkable six months after this fermentation; it is lively, with a slight sparkle. This wine is called Chianti Governato, and it used to be shipped in the raffia-covered *fiaschi*. Since the *fiaschi* are expensive, as well as impractical, some producers are using the *Chiantiagiona* bottle or other exclusively designed bottles. The middle style of Chianti is found in either the *Chiantiagiona* or the claret-style bottle. The best quality Chianti is always found in the claret-style bottle, since the wine must develop in the bottle for a few years. Such Chianti will be a splendid, soft, rounded, and mellow wine of great character.

Young Chianti may be sold within a year of the harvest, but not before March 1. There is a two-year minimum-age Chianti called *Vecchio,* but it is not permitted in this country since U.S. laws do not permit words like *vecchio* ("old") on wine labels. Chianti Classico Riserva must be aged three years, and must also have an alcohol content of 12.5 percent, as opposed to 12 percent for Chianti Classico and 11.5 percent for Chianti.

Young Chianti is ideal to drink with rich, well-seasoned, oily foods because its tartness is just the thing to help digest these foods. Older aged Chiantis and Riservas have more elegance and can accompany more subtle dishes.

Southwest of Siena the hill town of Montalcino produces a noble red varietal wine called Brunello di Montalcino, made exclusively from a clone of the Sangiovese Grosso grape, locally called Brunello. This wine has attained international fame because of its limited production, high quality, ability to keep for a long time, and length of time before its initial release because of the high tannins and full body. Italy does not have the tradition of aging wine in most of its regions as it does here. D.O.C. regulations state that Brunello must spend at least four years in oak casks, and if it is labeled Riserva, it must spend five years in wood. The law stipulates that the Bordeaux-shaped bottle be used.

Brunello was the first wine to be declared D.O.C.G. in November 1980. One reason for its having been declared a D.O.C.G. first, was that of all the red wines applying for D.O.C.G. at that time, Brunello required the longest aging before release. Other red wines have subsequently been approved in order of aging requirements, so that five D.O.C.G. red wines will all appear on the market in 1985.

We have already mentioned Barolo and Barbaresco from Piedmont, and Brunello and Chianti Classico from Tuscany. It now remains to discuss Vino Nobile di Montepulciano, the last of this initial group of red D.O.C.G. wines.

Traveling due east from Montalcino, we arrive at the town of Montepulciano, near Siena. This is where Vino Nobile di Montepulciano is produced—so named because it was originally made by noblemen. The four major permitted grapes are the same as those permitted in Chianti, but the small amounts of local grapes vary, and are one reason that Vino Nobile di

Montepulciano is different from Chianti. In making this wine, the *governo* method may not be used, and two years minimum time in oak is required. If the wine is labeled Riserva, aging is increased to three years. Riserva Speciale must be aged for four years before bottling.

A handful of independent producers are disqualifying themselves from D.O.C. classifications and are omitting white grapes altogether from their wines. Sometimes they are using Cabernet instead. Most notable examples are Antinori's Tignanello and Sassicaia.

white wines of Tuscany

White wine has always been made in Tuscany, since white grapes such as the Trebbiano and Malvasia are grown in abundance. It used to be shipped as White Chianti, but the D.O.C. laws defined Chianti as a red wine. Even though white wine is produced in the Chianti district, it now must be shipped as Vino Bianco Toscano ("White Tuscan Wine").

With percentages of white grapes to be used in Chianti being relaxed, producers are finding themselves with an excess of white grapes at a time when market pressures demand more white wines. They have created a wine with the fantasy name "Galestro," vinified with modern technology into a fresh, fruity, lower alcohol wine than the traditional Vino Bianco Tuscano. Galestro is in the category of Vino da Tavola, from the region of Tuscany.

On the southwestern border of the Chianti district, in the area surrounding the ancient hill town of San Gimignano, a full-bodied and complex wine is produced from the Vernaccia grape. It is called Vernaccia di San Gimignano. If aged for one year it may be called Riserva. It became Italy's first D.O.C. wine in 1966.

A traditional white wine that has added to Tuscany's fame is Vin (Vino) Santo, a rich, generous, sometimes sweet dessert wine with a Muscat flavor and high alcohol content. Practically all winemakers in the region produce some. The white Trebbiano and Malvasia grapes are gathered when fully ripened and the bunches are strung on poles that are suspended under the attic-roof of the house. There they remain to dry until late December, when they are pressed; the rich juice ferments very slowly during the cold winter months, and the wine remains in casks for some time before bottling.

The historic island of Elba off the coast of Tuscany provides clean, pleasant, dry white, red, and rosé wines. The Trebbiano is the most important vine but there is some Sangiovese as well. A trace of iron ore in the soil gives these wines distinction.

MARCHES AND UMBRIA

The region of Marches on the Adriatic side of the peninsula is very hilly and exposed to the north wind. Several good wines are grown in this region. One in particular demands attention: the fine, light white wine Verdicchio dei Castelli di Jesi. It is one of Italy's distinguished white wines and the most

Trebbiano grapes hanging from the attic rafters to dry out before being pressed for making Vin Santo. (*Courtesy Ricasoli, Florence*)

crisply dry. It has a pale greenish cast, a delicate bouquet and flavor, a slightly tart aftertaste, and is customarily shipped in a green amphoralike bottle.

Another very similar wine, not as well known, is the Verdicchio di Matelica. The same grapes are used as for the first Verdicchio, but in different blending proportions. In general, the reds of Marches are good, ordinary wines. The best known are Rosso Piceno, Rosso Conero, and Sangiovese dei Colli Pesaresi.

Farther southwest is the region Umbria, where the beautiful cities of Assisi, Perugia, and Orvieto are located. It is a land of temperate climate and rolling hills through which flows the Tiber (Tevere) River. The well-drained soil is especially suited to growing grapes for fine white wines.

Traditionally, Orvieto wines have been bottled in a long-necked *fiasco* called *pulcinella*, but fortunately, the D.O.C. laws permit a more practically shaped bottle, which does not have the expensive straw wrappings.

The white wines of Orvieto are both *secco* ("dry") and *abboccato* ("semi-dry"). The grapes for *abboccato* are sometimes affected by "noble rot," called *muffa nobile* in Italy. Both are light straw-colored and have a fruity freshness, with a lingering aftertaste. The premium Orvieto wines are labeled Classico.

In the center of the region around the small town of Torgiano, the Lungarotti family holds court. Vineyard owners, winemakers, and museum curators, they produce about 85 percent of the region's wines. The reds are called Rubesco and Rubesco Riserva, the Riserva having no specified aging requirements, simply the winemaker's best. Grapes and blending proportions are similar to those in Chianti, but without the white grapes. A fresh, drinkable white of the area is Torre di Giano.

LATIUM

Latium was the home of Horace, and his poetry tells of Tusculum (now called Frascati), of the vines that he grew, and of the trees that he loved.

The proud Romans left the shores of the Tiber for the pleasures of the countryside, and on the hills adjacent to Rome they built their villas. Hence the wines produced on these estates are called Vini dei Castelli Romani.

Chiefly white wines are made, as the conditions of soil and climate are more favorable for them, but some good reds are made also.

In Rome every restaurant offers the light white Frascati, the whites of Marino, and other Castelli Romani wines from the hills around Rome. These wines are most enjoyable when young and fresh.

A little farther north around the ancient town of Montefiascone on Lake Bolsena is produced a brilliant, straw-yellow dry wine with a fruity and fresh bouquet, poetically named Est! Est!! Est!!! While the wine is very good per se, the manner in which it got its name is most interesting.

As the story goes, a long time ago—perhaps four or five centuries—a German bishop named Johannes de Fuger was on his way to the Vatican to pay his respects to the Holy Father. Being a man of taste and discrimination, he sent his secretary-valet ahead to find suitable accommodations. Where the food, and especially the wine, was good, the valet was to write with chalk the word *Est* on the wall of the inn. When this good man tasted the wines at Montefiascone he could not describe them truthfully with just one "It is," so he chalked on the wall of the inn *Est! Est!! Est!!!* ("It is! It is!! It is!!!"). When the bishop arrived he agreed with his valet's judgment. In fact, he tarried so long and drank so freely that he finally died at Montefiascone, without ever reaching Rome.

We wished to verify this story, and on our last visit to Italy we made a special trip to Montefiascone to find the bishop's tomb. It is there, just within the entrance to the Basilica of Saint Flaviano. The inscription is almost illegible from the thousands of feet that have trod the marble slab through the centuries, but one can still make out the words: *Est, Est, Est et propter nimium est, Johannes de Fuger, dominus meus, mortuus est,* which means, "It is, it is, it is, and through too much it is, my master, Johannes de Fuger, dead is."

The sequel to the story is that the grateful winemakers of Montefiascone who produce Est! Est!! Est!!! commemorate the anniversary of Bishop de Fuger's demise by spilling a barrel of Est! Est!! Est!!! wine over his tomb.

In the same area the sweet Aleatico di Gradoli is produced from the Aleatico (Moscato Nero) grape; it achieves a high alcohol content.

A bottle label of Est! Est!! Est!!! shows the Bishop de Fuger's arrival at the Montefiascone Inn.

CAMPANIA AND BASILICATA

Campania, dominated by Mount Vesuvius to the east of Naples, is one of the most unique spots on earth. The pumice of the volcano spreads over the land and enriches it. Hot springs and fissures evidence the volcanic nature of the soil. The climate is ideal and vegetation is luxuriant—three crops a year are rotated on farms. The vine is cultivated intensely, for the area is limited and the demand worldwide. Falernum, prized by the Romans, has fallen from popularity, and in its stead rules Lacryma Christi.

The still Lacryma Christi, made near Vesuvius, is a golden wine, not too dry, with a softness, delicacy, and somewhat aromatic bouquet that it gets from the hot volcanic soil. Some red and rosé Lacryma Christi is also made.

As does Umbria, this area has one predominant winemaking family that goes back for many generations. In Campania, it is the Mastroberardinos, who have added modern technology to the traditionally made wines of their forefathers. Grapes, such as Greco and Aglianico were introduced by the ancient Greeks. They achieve a special perfume in the mineral-rich volcanic soil.

In addition to the white Lacryma Christi, white wines include the dry Greco di Tufo and the almond-scented Fiano di Avellino. The red Taurasi, made from the historic Aglianico grape, benefits from wood aging and must be at least three years old before release; Taurasi Riserva must have four.

Off Campania's coast, surrounded by blue waters, lies Capri. Little original Capri wine is available, and most of it is used by the islanders themselves. More often than not, what we get is wine from the neighboring island of Ischia, where Ischia Rosso and Ischia Bianco are produced.

Basilicata is nestled in the arch of Italy's boot and offers just one D.O.C. wine from its meager resources. The Aglianico del Vulture is produced on the volcanic slopes of Monte Vulture, and when young is a pleasant, dry, red table wine. When aged, especially for the five years required to make it a *riserva,* it becomes deep, full, and can last for a decade or more.

APULIA AND ABRUZZI

One of the most prolific wine-growing regions is Apulia, or Puglia in Italian. Geographically it is the heel of Italy's boot, stretching from Molise and Campania in the north, along the Adriatic Sea, and dipping its peninsular heel in the Ionian Sea.

It produces generous, alcoholic wines because of the great amount of sunshine that bathes the land. This region is known as the wine cellar of Italy, for the wines are commonly shipped to northern Europe for blending with wines with lower alcohol content. As much wine is produced in Apulia as in Piedmont and Lombardy combined. Although there are eighteen D.O.C. wines from Apulia, these wines comprise only 2 percent of its total wine production.

The ever-present Aleatica grape makes wine throughout the region, labeled Aleatica di Puglia. The majority of the red wines are dark in color and high in alcohol, but they often lack acid. A few areas do produce better balanced wines, notably Castel del Monte and San Severo, which are available in red, white, and the particularly popular rosé. The Castel del Monte red and rosé are made from various blends of Uva di Troia, Bombino Nero, Montepulciano, and Sangiovese grapes, while the Bianco is made from mainly Pampanuto and Pampanino grapes with some Trebbiano varieties. San Severo red and rosé are mostly Montepulciano grapes, while the white is mainly Trebbiano Toscano. Locorotondo, a light, still or sparkling wine from the province of Taranto, blends local Verdeca and Bianco d'Alessano grapes for its dry delicate flavor.

Santo Stefano and Torre Quarto, made in the northern province of Foggia from a variety of grapes, are very big red wines that can take years of aging.

The Primitivo, believed to be the ancestor of the United States' Zinfandel, makes multistyled red wines called Primitivo di Manduria.

Experimentation is burgeoning now that Apulia is no longer just exporting nameless wine. Non-local grape varieties, such as Cabernet Franc, Pinot Nero, and Pinot Bianco, have added to Apulia's palette in developing new wines.

To the north of Apulia, the diverse region of Abruzzi follows the Adriatic coastline. Like its people, the wines of Abruzzi are uncomplicated, offering only two types: Montepulciano d'Abruzzo, which includes a big red of the same name and a cherry-colored Cerasuolo, and Trebbiano d'Abruzzo, a white wine well suited to fish. It should be noted that here, as well as in neighboring Apulia, "Montepulciano" is the name of a grape, while in Tuscany it is the name of a town.

CALABRIA

Here, in a wild country of bare, high mountains and fertile valleys, a country of contrasts, of chilly winds and tropical shores, the vine is cultivated extensively. It produces good local wines of rather high alcohol content. Much *vino da tavola* comes from this section, produced by growers' cooperatives.

The best wine of the region is the Cirò. The white is made from the Greco grape, and the red and rosé from the Gaglioppo grape. The red can be aged. The Gaglioppo grape can also be found in the red wines labeled Donnici and Lamezia.

SICILY

Homer speaks of Sicily as the land where "spontaneous wine from weighty clusters flows." "The Sicilians," said Plato, "build as if they were always to live, and sup as if they never were to sup again." The first to appreciate the enchanting beauty of the island were the English, who practically monopolized the output of Marsala, which produced Lord Nelson's favorite wine.

The most famous geographic feature of Sicily is the sometimes active Mount Etna in the east. Etna wines are produced in the province of Catania, on the slopes of the volcano. Etna Bianco is dry and straw-colored, with medium body. When it comes from the commune of Milo, it may be labeled *superiore* if it achieves a higher minimum alcohol. Etna Rosso is made from red Nerello varieties, and may have up to 10 percent white grapes added to the must. It is dry and full-bodied. Etna Rosato is a lighter, fresher version, a rosé made from the same grapes as Etna Rosso.

One of the famous wines of Italy is Corvo, which has spearheaded the acceptance of Sicilian table wines in the rest of the world. It comes from Casteldaccia, near Palermo in western Sicily. This wine is a development of Duca Salaparuta, whose desire to improve viticulture in Sicily has been achieved. Corvo is a fine dry wine, both red and white, with much character of the fire of Sicily.

From the province of Ragusa comes a full-bodied red, Cerasuolo di Vittorio. It is dry and has at least 13 percent alcohol.

Bianco d'Alcamo, produced in the northwest in the province of Trapani is a dry, fresh white wine.

New cooperatives in the major wine areas are enjoying modern technology in both viticulture and winemaking practices, and are producing many light, fresh table wines for contemporary tastes.

Sicily is famous for Marsala. Marsala is a fortified wine obtained from the Catarrato, Grillo, and Inzolia grapes. It comes from the provinces of Trapani, Palermo, and Agrigento. Concentrates are used to vary the style, which can be dry, semidry, sweet, or very sweet. Volcanic soil gives Marsala an acid undertone that is similar to Madeira.

Many sweet dessert wines are made in the western part of the island from the Zibibbo, which is a variety of the Moscato di Allessandria grape.

The Moscato Passito di Pantelleria, produced on the island of Pantelleria, has an amber color, rich bouquet, and sweet flavor. The minimum alcohol is 15 percent, and the wine is usually served chilled.

SARDINIA

The cork, the olive, and the vine grow well on the island of Sardinia. The wines are mostly heady, liquorous, and strong. Like nearby Sicily, Sardinia is well known for dessert wines, but modernization of the industry is creating good table wines.

Cannonau di Sardegna, a hearty red wine, is produced throughout the island. It is available in dry, semisweet, and/or sweet, and a good rosé may also be made from the same grapes. Monica di Sardegna is a lighter red wine, made from grapes of the same name throughout the island.

Nuragus di Cagliari is a straw-colored table wine. Vernaccia di Oristano, from the same grape found in Tuscany, is also a straw-colored wine, but with a hint of almond in the bouquet.

Moscato di Cagliari and Malvasia di Bosa are two white dessert wines with the characteristic flavor of the grape varieties from which they are made, while the Girò di Cagliari is a red dessert wine on the order of port.

GROWTH OF ITALIAN WINES IN THE U.S. MARKET

The wines of Italy run the gamut of the wines of the world. Many come from large cooperatives, and many more come from small producers. While sending over quaffing wines, there are others available to serious collectors.

Unlike French winemakers, whose exports heralded the glories of France, Italian producers kept their finest wines at home.

Beginning with the Lambrusco boom in 1974, interested consumers began to explore other Italian wines. Today there are more than fifty different brands of Barolo on the market, and over one hundred and fifty different brands of wine from Tuscany. Even Brunello di Montalcino, unheard of five years ago, and the most costly wine from Italy, has many brands available today.

The expanding Italian table wine market has carried along with it new interest in sparkling wine. In addition to the sweet Asti Spumante, there is new demand for the drier, elegant *bruts* from many areas.

The timely combination of new technology, D.O.C. regulations, which have bolstered consumer confidence, and the support of the Italian government, which has strengthened consumer knowledge, has made Italian wines the largest imported wine in the United States.

7
THE WINES OF
GERMANY

As one sails down the Rhine between its vine-clad hills, the orderly beauty makes a profound impression. But one rarely recalls that this is the result of centuries of unremitting toil. Considering the perfect weather conditions that are required to produce a good wine even in such temperate regions as Bordeaux and Burgundy, one must marvel at the courage and tenacity of the vineyard owners of the Rhine and Moselle valleys, the northernmost wine regions in Europe.

No grape grower has ever had a more discouraging or difficult task than have these Rhenish farmers, but they have triumphed magnificently over the tremendous obstacles nature has placed before them—lack of heat, a variable climate from year to year, precipitous hillsides to which the vines cling precariously, and natural diseases of the vine. Fortunately the growing season is long, with more frost-free days in Germany than in other vine-growing areas. This enables Germany to rank tenth among wine-producing countries, contributing some of the world's great wines.

The greatness of German wines is indicated by the fabulous prices they occasionally fetch. While it is still in cask, a great Trockenbeerenauslese may bring as much as $125 a bottle at auction. This sort of wine is available only on rare occasions, of course, and then only at the large estates, where never more than one-quarter cask, or four hundred bottles, of this quality can be made. Little of this wine reaches the channels of commerce; it is generally purchased by private connoisseurs.

history   In Germany, as in France, the traditions of wine are intertwined with the roots of the country's history. As far back as the time of Charlemagne (A.D. 800) the vineyards of the Rhine, probably planted by the Romans of Caesar's time, enjoyed great fame. During the eighteenth century most of the Rhine wine shipped to England was labeled Hochheimer. The English found this word difficult to pronounce and promptly shortened it to Hock. Today in all English-speaking countries the term *Hock*, or *Hocks*, means Rhine wine. This, of course, does not include the wines of the Moselle or those from Franconia.

The monastic orders of the Church in Germany did much to develop viticulture. Johannisberg takes its name from the Chapel of Saint John, erected in A.D. 853 by the Bénédictine monks of Saint Alban's of Mainz. On this hill is the castle (*Schloss*) whose vineyard produces very fine Rhine wines.

GERMAN WINE LAW

The German government published a new wine law that became effective on July 19, 1971. It defined and controlled more strictly the different types of wine being made in Germany by the selective picking method. It also aligned the old German law with laws in other wine-producing countries of the European Economic Community (EEC), or Common Market. The Common Market has separated wine-producing regions of its members into zones, based on growing temperatures. All of Germany is in zone "A" except for Baden, which is in zone "B."

Under this 1971 wine law, amended in 1982, there are four broad categories of German wines: Deutscher Tafelwein, Deutscher Landwein, Qualitätswein, and Qualitätswein mit Prädikat. Tafelwein is an ordinary wine that must have a minimum alcoholic strength of 44 *Öchsle* in zone "A" and 50 *Öchsle* in the warmer zone "B." It must be made from certain grape varieties grown in Germany in any of four Tafelwein regions: Rhein/Mosel (which has two subregions, Rhein and Mosel), Bayern, Neckar, and Oberrhein. The region must be on the label with the German spelling. A smaller community within the region may be mentioned on the label, but not the name of a vineyard. The name of the bottler (*Abfüller*) must appear, and brand names may be used. Deutscher Landwein is a new category of wines that are dry and uncomplicated, with more body than Tafelwein.

Qualitätswein and Qualitätswein mit Prädikat are wines made from permitted grape varieties, fermented in their areas of production. They have to obtain a minimum must weight and pass an official taste test and laboratory analysis in order to receive a control number to be printed on their labels. They must come from one of eleven regions, each of which is called a *Gebiet*, and their taste has to be characteristic of wines produced in that region. The next smaller geographic area from which the wines may come is a subregion known as a *Bereich*, or district. The subdistrict is called a *Grosslage* and is made up of several vineyard properties where the grapes are similar in taste. The smallest division is the *Lage*, or individual vineyard. The name of the region is always on the label of a Qualitätswein or a Qualitätswein mit Prädikat. The name of the *Bereich*, *Grosslage*, or *Lage* precedes or follows the local village name.

If the labels on these wines specify a grape variety, there must be at least 85 percent of that grape used, and the taste of the wine must be characteristic of the grape. If the labels carry a vintage year, the year specified must constitute 85 percent of the wines in the blend, and the taste must be characteristic of that year.

The inspection control number as it appears on the label of a bottle of German wine. (*Courtesy German Wine Information Bureau, New York*)

Tafelwein and Qualitätswein are sugared before fermentation to bring up the alcohol content of the wine (this is also permitted in Burgundy and Bordeaux when required), but Qualitätswein mit Prädikat cannot have any sugar added to the must. Qualitätswein mit Prädikat wines include Kabinett, Spätlese, Auslese, Beerenauslese, Trockenbeerenauslese, and Eiswein. Each level of these Prädikat wines has a minimum *Öchsle* that varies with the region where the wine is produced and the grape varieties used. (For conversion of *Öchsle* to alcohol see Appendix I). *Öchsle* is a measure of the amount of sugar in the must.

Kabinett wines must be made from ripe grapes whose minimum must weight ranges from 70 to 81, averaging about 75, to yield a wine with about 10 percent alcohol, depending on the region, the grape, and the method of vinification.

Spätlese wines must be made from fully ripened grapes usually gathered after the general harvest; the minimum must weight is usually around 80 *Öchsle*, but, for example, it is 76 *Öchsle* if the grape is Riesling, and the regions are Ahr, Mosel, and Mittelrhein.

Auslese wines are made from fully ripened bunches of grapes gathered selectively for their ripeness at any time during the harvest; minimum must weight is about 90 *Öchsle*, depending on the region.

Beerenauslese wines must be made from individually selected ripe grapes; minimum must weight is about 120 *Öchsle*, depending on the region.

Trockenbeerenauslese wines must be made from individually selected, overripe, shrunken grapes that are attacked by the *Edelfäule* mold; minimum must weight is 150 *Öchsle* in every region.

Eiswein is a sixth distinct Prädikat, limited to wines made from grapes that have a sugar equivalent of Beerenauslese, but are caught in a deep frost, harvested frozen, and then crushed before thawing. Eiswein previously could be used in conjunction with any of the other quality designations.

Rather than arresting fermentation and leaving some residual sugar in the wine, the sweetness in German wines is a result of the addition of some unfermented grape juice to the finished wine before bottling. This sweetness balances the often rather high acidity of German wines. The grape juice must be of the same wine as the one fermented, or of equally high quality and the same area as the fermented wine.

Qualitätswein and Qualitätswein mit Prädikat, which include all of the above wines, must be made solely from permitted grape varieties. When sold, they must specify whether they are Qualitätswein or Qualitätswein mit Prädikat and carry a control number. As a further guarantee of quality, the German wine law has special provisions for listing the name of the producer, the person responsible for the wine. Every quality wine has to list the bottler (*Abfüller*) on the label. If the wine is bottled by the producer, the person who owns the vineyard, then the label states *Erzeugerabfüllung* ("bottled by the producer") or *aus eigenem Lesegut* ("from his own grapes"), both of which are similar to estate bottling in France. If a shipper bottles a wine coming from an estate, he can indicate this on the label by stating *aus dem Lesegut von* and the name of the estate. This means literally "out of the harvest of. . . ."

Trocken describes a wine that is extremely dry. These bone-dry wines are not typical of German wines in general and are more suitable to being served with food than they are to being served by themselves. Trocken has been permitted on labels since 1976. Halbtrocken describes a wine that is semi-dry, in between a Trocken and a Kabinett.

Germany's wine quality control occurs in three stages:

1. During the harvest a wine grower must officially register the category of wines he intends to produce, such as Spätlese or Auslese. Thus the government controls the quality of both the grapes and the must.

2. When bottling begins, the wine is analyzed by an officially designated wine laboratory.

German wine-tasting panel of experts deciding whether the official certification number will be awarded. (*Courtesy German Wine Information Bureau, New York*)

3. Finally, the wine is tasted by a panel of experts. Clarity, bouquet, color, and flavor are checked on a standard point system. An official certification number, awarded only when the necessary points are recorded, must be on the label of all bottles containing the specific approved wine. The tasting commission retains sealed samples of the wine in case of consumer complaints.

The eleven specified regions of Qualitätswein and Qualitätswein mit Prädikat are different from the four regions of Tafelwein (see page 117). The eleven are Ahr, Mittelrhein, Mosel-Saar-Ruwer, Nahe, Rheingau, Rheinhessen, Rheinpfalz, Hessische Bergstrasse, Franken, Baden, and Württemberg.

labeling   The following designations are found on German wine labels:
Qualitätswein bestimmter Anbaugebiete—Q.b.A.—("quality wine of specified regions"). A quality wine bears the control number assigned by the tasting panel. It can be labeled by region (*Gebiet*), district (*Bereich*), subdistrict (*Grosslage*), or vineyard (*Lage*). The label usually bears the name of the village where the vineyards are located.

Qualitätswein mit Prädikat ("quality wine with distinction"). Wines in this category are divided, in ascending order, into Kabinett, Spätlese, Auslese, Beerenauslese, and Trockenbeerenauslese; sometimes with Eiswein, as described previously.

It is customary for each fine wine to bear the branded cork of its producer; the cork must also have the official number of the bottler.

The new German wine law has consolidated vineyards. Germany had fifty thousand individual vineyards that the government consolidated in the two years before the 1971 law went into effect. No vineyard can now be less than 12½ acres. As in Burgundy, these vineyards have many owners tending their own rows of vines and making their own wines.

geography   German viticulture is found in the Rhine Valley and the valleys of its tributaries, the Nahe and the Main, and in the Moselle Valley, with the valleys of its tributaries, the Saar and the Ruwer. The other important area is Baden, which is along the Rhine from Lake Constance to above Baden-Baden opposite Alsace. The smaller Württemberg area includes vineyards on both sides of the Neckar River.

The Rhine Valley, like all Gaul, is divided into three parts: the Rheingau, which embraces the right bank of the river from above Lorch to and including Hochheim on the Main; the Rheinhessen, which includes the land on the left bank of the river from Worms to Bingen and that lying between the Nahe and the Rhine; and the Rheinpfalz, or Palatinate, a triangle formed by the Rhine, the Harz Mountains, and the French border.

Rising in the Vosges Mountains, the Moselle River wanders through Lorraine, becomes part of the Franco-German border, continues northward to form the border between Luxembourg and Germany, and enters Germany

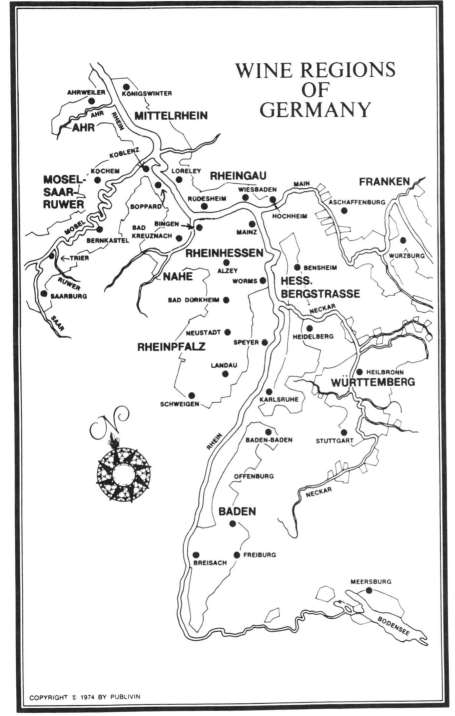

(From Fritz [S. F.] Hallgarten, A Guide to Vineyards, Estates, and Wines of Germany, *edited by Michel Roux, courtesy Publivin Publishing Company, Dallas, Texas)*

proper, where it is joined by the Saar and a little farther along by the Ruwer, from which point it winds and twists through its picturesque course until it reaches the Rhine at Koblenz.

Viticulturally, the Moselle Valley is divided into five *Bereiche*. They are the *Bereich* Zell, also called the Untermosel or Lower Moselle in the north from Zell to Koblenz; the *Bereich* Bernkastel or Mittel Mosel; the *Bereich* Saar-Ruwer; the *Bereich* Obermosel or Upper Moselle; and the *Bereich* Moseltor to the south.

The most famous vineyards lie in the *Bereich* Bernkastel or Mittel Mosel, and in the *Bereich* Saar-Ruwer. The *Bereich* Obermosel produces a few excellent wines, and the extremes of the river, the Moseltor and the *Bereich* Zell, produce little of note.

Along the Main River, the most famous city in Franken is Würzburg. The wines of this region are sold as Frankenwein and bottled in the distinctive *Bocksbeutel.*

Baden was the largest wine-producing region of Germany from the Middle Ages to the 1800's, with 66,000 acres of vineyards. A steady decline brought that number to only 15,000 acres by the 1950's, when a reversal of that trend began to reestablish Baden once again as an important wine-producing area. It is now third largest in Germany, with 33,500 acres.

soil   As in other wine regions of the world, the soil is most forbidding, suited to no other crop. The land is extremely rocky with a predominance of slate in the Moselle, where the vineyards are planted along steep, terraced slopes of the hills. The terraces are very narrow and require skillful hand labor. In the past thirty years, however, a change called *Flurbereinung* has resulted in greater vineyard efficiency since whole vineyards have been uprooted and hillsides leveled to allow for tractors and even some mechanical harvesting. Almost half of the vineyards in Rheinhessen and Rheinpfalz were mechanically harvested.

grape varieties   The Riesling accounts for 20 percent of total plantings.

The Müller-Thurgau grape, a cross between two clones of Riesling, is the biggest producer, and 27 percent of all German grapes are Müller-Thurgau. It is grown in all districts, with the least amount in the Rheingau and Mittelrhein. It ripens earlier than other varieties, producing very pleasant, highly aromatic, and light-bodied wines.

The Silvaner accounts for 11 percent of total plantings, and is grown in the Rheinhessen, the Rheinpfalz, Baden, Nahe, and Franconia.

The Gewürztraminer is grown mainly in Baden, the Palatinate, and Rheinhessen. It makes a very spicy wine.

The Ruländer, or Pinot Gris of Burgundy, is one of the most widely grown varieties in Baden. It can and does produce some charming wines with full aroma and flavor.

A complete list of all the grape varieties and the regions in which they are planted appears in Appendix F. New strains are being developed which produce greater yields with higher sugar content. These new grapes will mean more Qualitätswein mit Prädikat wines in the future at reasonable prices, but the wines will not have the longevity of wines made from classical varieties.

The Blauer Spätburgunder is the Pinot Noir of Burgundy and Champagne fame and, along with the Portugieser grape, is used to produce the few red wines of the Rheinpfalz, Ahr Valley, Baden, Württemberg, and Rheinhessen. It is not her red wines, however, which on the whole are rather thin and commonplace, on which Germany's vinicultural fame rests, but the magnificence of her white wines.

vintage

When the summer has been sunny, with at least 100 days of sun between May and October, there will be a good wine; if there are 120 days of sun there will be a great wine. The day of the general harvest is set by each village and is subject to strict regulations. If the sun holds, the grower picks only part of his crop right away and leaves the rest to be picked later, allowing the remaining grapes to become even riper. This means a sacrifice of quantity. The grapes that are picked later are made into wines designated as Spätlese, Auslese, Beerenauslese, and Trockenbeerenauslese.

If the must weight qualifies, Spätlese (*Spät*—"late," *lese*—"picking") takes place. Only fully ripened bunches are gathered, sometimes even before the general harvest. Auslese (*Aus*—"selected," *lese*—"picking") means that each bunch of grapes is gathered selectively as it ripens, any time during the harvest. Auslese wines are sweeter, richer, and fuller than Spätlese wines; these designations are strictly controlled by the specific density of the must.

Often *Edelfäule* can be discerned in great Spätlese and Auslese wines. *Edelfäule*, a mold that forms on the skin of the grape, reducing its moisture and concentrating its richness, occurs in great years, producing a full and luscious wine. The mold, *Botrytis cinerea*, is also known as "noble rot" in English and *pourriture noble* in French. It is usually present in Beerenauslese (*Beeren*—"berry," *auslese*—"selected picking"), a top-designated wine made from individually selected berries. If all the individual grapes are dried and shriveled as a result of *Edelfäule*, then Trockenbeerenauslese (*Trocken*—"dry," *beeren-auslese*—"selected berry picking"), the highest-designated wine, is made. It is very rich, luscious, elegant, and costly.

The wines are bottled very young—usually from six to nine months, having spent the time prior to bottling in stainless steel. If the wine has been in wood, it is older wood lined with tartrates and has little effect on the wine. A few growers on the Moselle bottle single casks, but that is not the usual practice.

Harvesting grapes near the ruins of Castle Ehrenfels at Rüdesheim on the Rhine. (*Courtesy German Wine Information Bureau, New York*)

WINES OF THE RHEINGAU

On the right bank of the Rhine, from above Lorch to Hochheim, is the celebrated Rheingau, one of the most famous viticultural regions in the world. Compared with other wine-growing regions of Germany, this is one of the smallest—but its wines are famous, many of them unsurpassed anywhere. Among the better-known villages in the Rheingau that have become famous over the years on wine labels are:

Eltville	Johannisberg
Erbach	Kiedrich
Geisenheim	Oestrich
Hallgarten	Rauenthal
Hattenheim	Rüdesheim
Hochheim	Winkel

In this area are the well-known estates of Schloss Johannisberg, Schloss Vollrads, Schloss Eltz, Schloss Schönborn, and Schloss Reinhartshausen, the last belonging to the Prinz zu Preussen. The most famous vineyards of this area are Steinberger, the largest single vineyard under one ownership in this region, belonging to the state government and bearing a German eagle on its label; Schloss Johannisberg; and Erbacher Marcobrunn. Marcobrunn is traditionally translated as "spring of Saint Marcus," as *Brunn* means "spring," and many German locations are named after saints. But the inscription on the arch over the spring is *Gemarkung*, which means "boundary" or "marking." As the spring is on the boundary between the towns of Hattenheim and Erbach, Marcobrunn is also taken to mean "boundary or marking spring."

Charlemagne is supposed to have selected the site for Schloss Johannisberg, although it is more than likely that wines from the Johannisberg hill vineyards already existed in his time. During the French Revolution the vineyard and castle on the crest of the hill came into the possession of William, Prince of Orange, from whom it was confiscated by Napoleon after the Battle of Jena. Napoleon presented the prize to Marshall Kellermann, Duke of Valmy, whose name, appropriately enough, means "cellarman."

After the Battle of Waterloo the vineyard again changed hands, passing to the Austrian emperor Franz I, who, in gratitude for services rendered, presented the castle and vineyards in perpetuity to his great chancellor, Prince von Metternich-Winneburg, whose decendants still own it.

The wines of all these vineyards combine every attribute of greatness in a good year. They have bouquet, body, flavor, character, and breed. The Rheingau wines generally have an austere fruitiness and a certain hardness, in which lies their character. They are the longest lived of all German wines.

WINES OF THE RHEINHESSEN

Rheinhessen is Germany's second-largest wine-producing region. Wines from here are softer and fuller than those of the Rheingau. The main villages producing fine wines are:

Bingen	Nackenheim
Bodenheim	Nierstein
Dienheim	Oppenheim
Laubenheim	Worms
Mettenheim	

At the southern border of the Rheinhessen is the rather dull, smoky, gray town of Worms. Neither dull nor gray are the legends about Worms, however, for it is the locale of the ancient story of the Nibelungs, of Siegfried's marriage to Brünhilde and his death by treachery.

Within the city limits of Worms stands the *Liebfrauenkirche* ("Church of Our Beloved Lady"). Surrounding it is a vineyard that has produced wines of some renown for many centuries—first under monastic or ecclesiastic control, but since secularization at the beginning of the nineteenth century as the private property of a number of people. The vineyard is called Liebfrauen-stift-Kirchenstück and is now owned by two shippers, Langenbach and Valckenberg.

The wines from this site (*Lage*) or vineyard are nearly always estate bottled and the labels normally read Wormser Liebfrauenstift-Kirchenstück. The word or name *Liebfraumilch* does not appear on the label. The wines are pleasant and good but somewhat lighter in body and character than those from the better Hessian vineyards of Nierstein and Oppenheim.

Liebfraumilch   Liebfraumilch is without question the best-known German wine name. Liebfraumilch is not a vineyard or a district, but rather a collective name for wines from the Rhine, just as Moselblümchen is for wines from the Moselle.

Tradition has it that the name derives from the *Liebfrauenkirche* of Worms. Who invented and first used the name is not clear, but it has been in use since 1744. From 1910 to 1971 "Liebfraumilch" could apply only to Rheinhessen wines. From 1971 to 1982, there were four permitted regions, but since 1982, the name "Liebfraumilch" may only apply to Qualitätswein from Nahe, Rheinhessen, or Rheinpfalz. The regions may not be blended together, and the region name must appear on the label.

In most cases Liebfraumilch is a blended wine. The better, more responsible shippers employ mostly the finer Hessian wines for their Liebfraumilch blends. To distinguish their individual blends, they identify their Liebfraumilch with an added registered trademark. Examples are Black Tower, Blue Nun, Crown of Crowns, Glockenspiel, Hanns Christof, Madrigal, Seagull, and Wedding Veil.

Liebfraumilch is an all-purpose German wine, usually of consistent quality from vintage to vintage.

WINES OF THE NAHE

One of the less well-known areas of Germany is that surrounding the Nahe, a stream that lies between the Moselle and the Rhine, into which it flows at historic Bingen. The wines harmoniously blend the hearty, masculine quality of good Rhines with the light tingle of Moselles. They are not as sturdy as the one, not as light as the other. Growing and shipping are both centered in Bad Kreuznach, where the wizard Professor Dr. Faustus once taught. The best-known villages producing fine wines are:

Kreuznach	Rüdesheim (not to be confused with
Langenlonsheim	the Rüdesheim in the Rheingau)
Niederhausen an der Nahe	Schloss Böckelheim
Norheim	

WINES OF THE RHEINPFALZ

The Palatinate (Rheinpfalz region) is the largest wine-producing area in Germany. The Upper Palatinate (südlicher Weinstrasse) produces the largest amount of table wine in Germany, the wine that is the daily diet in the German *weinstube*. In addition to several good white wines, this area produces 25 percent of all German red wines, most of which are drunk locally and seldom exported. Palatinate wines are known for their earthiness and full body.

The area best known for wines of great quality is the Mittelhaardt in the Palatinate, which has larger plantings of Riesling than the Rheingau. The wines are long lived. The finest communities producing wines in the Rheinpfalz are:

Bad Dürkheim	Königsbach
Deidesheim	Mussbach
Edenkoben	Neustadt
Forst	Ruppertsberg
Hambach	Wachenheim
Kallstadt	

Workers in the vineyards of the Rheinhessen district. (*Courtesy German Wine Information Bureau, New York*)

WINES OF THE MOSELLE

Moselle wines have a charming lightness, delicacy, fruity bouquet, elegance, and dryness that is most pleasing. But their most appealing quality is their spritz, or tingling sharpness, as though they were trying to be sparkling wines—and almost succeeding. The quality disappears after a few years, so Moselles are best when young because they are livelier and racier.

The soil of the Moselle Valley is, if such is possible, more forbidding than that in any other region, and harvesting is proportionately more difficult. The vineyard owners carry up the steep slopes pieces of slate that have been washed down the hillsides by the spring freshets, and as they go through the vineyards they laboriously arrange and rearrange the bits of slate so that they will preserve the warmth of the sun during the cool nights and help the development of the roots. It is to this backbreaking toil and infinite patience that we owe an exquisite glass of wine.

Moselle wines are the lightest fine wines made. They are very low in alcohol content, between 8 and 10 percent by volume, which is part of their charm.

There are two ways of recognizing the difference between Rhine and Moselle wines without opening the tall, flute-shaped bottle or tasting the wine. One is the color of the bottle, as Rhine wines always come in brown bottles, and the Moselle bottles are always dark green. The other is by the township name. The towns along the Rhine as a rule end in *heim*, while those of the Moselle do not. (There are, however, exceptions to this rule.)

It is simple to detect the differences in character in the wines of the Rheingau, Rheinhessen, and Rheinpfalz, but we have never found anyone who can make a similar claim about the wines of the Moselle, Saar, and Ruwer. They are all equally pleasant and intriguing, so it is not a matter of great importance.

One of the most famous vineyards of the Moselle is the Doctor at Bernkastel. In the year 1360, according to legend, Boemund II, Archbishop of Trier, fell ill with a fever while on a visit to Bernkastel. The doctors of the region did not know what to do for him. but Ritter von Holstein, whom the bishop had helped, recalled that he had cured himself of a similar ailment. He brought his finest Bernkastel wine to the bishop and told him, "Drink this and it will cure you." The bishop did so and fell into a sound sleep. The next day he awoke to find the fever gone. "This wine!" he cried. "This splendid doctor has cured me!" Since that day, over six hundred years ago, the vineyard has been known as the Doctor vineyard.

Acording to the records, the Bernkasteler Doctor *Lage* was the property of the Grafs von Hunolstein until the middle of the seventeenth century, when it passed to the Grafs von der Leyen, who held possession until 1804, when it was acquired by Anton Cetto, the mayor of Bernkastel, from whom it was eventually inherited by his nephew, Nikolaus Lauerburg. In 1882 the Lauerburgs sold a part of the vineyard to the Thanisch family and in 1900 they sold another portion to the Deinhards of Koblenz. The portion of the vineyard that Karl and Walter Lauerburg own today is planted with the original, ungrafted Riesling vines.

Because of the fame of the vineyard, the demand always exceeds the supply and, like Château d'Yquem, the wine fetches considerably higher prices than its neighbors.

Another famous vineyard in the Mittel Moselle is Wehlener Sonnenuhr ("the sundial of Wehlen"), and its wine commands almost as high a price in the marketplace as Bernkasteler Doctor.

The sundial at Wehlen on the Moselle. (*Courtesy Joh. Jos. Prüm, Wehlen*)

The villages that produce excellent wines are:

MOSELLE	SAAR
Bernkastel	Ayl
Brauneberg	Oberemmel
Dhron	Ockfen
Erden	Wiltingen
Graach	
Kröv	RUWER
Piesport	Eitelsbach
Traben-Trarbach	Maximin Grünhaus
Trittenheim	Waldrach
Ürzig	
Wehlen	
Zell	
Zeltingen	

Other well-known vineyards that produce superb wines in the Mittel Moselle are Trittenheimer Apotheke, Dhroner Hofberg, Piesporter Goldtröpfchen, Graacher Himmelreich, Josephshöfer, (the property of the Kesselstatt family), Zeltinger Himmelreich, Zeltinger Sonnenuhr, Erdener Treppchen, and Brauneberger Juffer. Two fine vineyards on the Saar are Scharzhofberger and Ockfener Bockstein.

Moselblümchen ("little flower of the Moselle") is a name used for a blended Moselle made of wines coming from anywhere in the region. It is a pleasant little wine, which may be either Tafelwein or Qualitätswein.

WINES OF BADEN

Baden has been a wine-producing area since the Middle Ages. Political divisions from then to now have created distinct areas which while they could be considered as one area viticulturally, have to be listed separately. The northeastern subregion of *Bereich* Badisches Frankenland, for example, borders on Franconia, and the wines are similar—yet they are considered as two regions. The *Bereich* Badische Bergstrasse, a small region bordering Heidelberg, has been split by the political borders of Hessen and Baden. Kraichgau, the central portion of Baden, produces 78 percent of the wine of the whole region. It is bordered by the Black Forest mountains on the west, and the Vosges mountains on the east, and contains four *Bereiche:* Ortenau, Kaiserstuhl-Tuniberg, which is dominated by an extinct volcano, Breisgau, and Markgräflerland. The last region of Baden is the small *Bereich* Bodensee on Lake Konstanz, of only 760 acres. Almost all wines of Baden are marketed under *Bereiche* or *Grosslagen* labels, produced by large cooperatives.

Since so much of Baden was replanted in the 1950's, modern technology has been coupled with careful selection of grape varieties and advanced vineyard management. About 20 percent of the plantings are in red grapes, the Pinot Noir or Spätburgunder being the most important, used especially for Weissherbst, a rosé wine of the region. Of the 80 percent white grapes, over one-third is Müller-Thurgau, followed by Ruländer (the French Pinot Gris), Gutedel (the Swiss Chasselas or Fendent), Riesling, and small amounts of Silvaner, Weissburgunder (Pinot Blanc), Gewürztraminer, and Nobling. Baden is in the EEC's viticultural zone "B," requiring the minimum must weight to be higher for all of the Prädikat wines, since the grapes have less trouble achieving ripeness.

A few individual properties should be noted, despite the cooperatives:

> Gutsverwaltung Freiherr von Neveu, Durbach
> Gräflich Wolff Metternisch'sches Weingut, Durbach
> Markgräflich Badisches Weingut Schloss Staufenberg
> Versuchs-und Lehrgut für Weinbau Blankenhornsberg, Ihringen
> Weingüter Max Markgraf von Baden, Salem
> Staatliche Weingüter, Meersburg
> Staatliches Weinbauinstitut, Freiburg

LESSER WINE REGIONS OF GERMANY

Württemberg

Württemberg, which borders Baden, has seen its formerly large vineyard areas decline to a present 20,000 acres. Wine making is dominated by cooperatives, with only 10 percent produced as estate wines. Württemberg has almost half of its vineyards in red grapes, the Trollinger being dominant. Other red grapes include the Schwarzriesling (Pinot Meunier), Portugieser, and Spätburgunder. The most important white grape is the Riesling, producing elegant wines, followed by the Müller-Thurgau, Silvaner, Kerner, Ruländer, and Weissburgunder.

Franconia

Finally we come to Franconia and its squat, flasklike *Bocksbeutel*. Franconia's robust wines, made largely from Müller-Thurgau and Silvaner grapes, possess more body, hardness, and keeping qualities than the Rhine and Moselle wines. They also take longer to develop. The outstanding communities are Würzburg, Escherndorf, Iphofen, Randersacker, Rodelsee, Sommerach, Sommerhausen, and Thüngersheim. The outstanding vineyards are the Würzburger Stein and Würzburger Leiste, which are parceled out among a number of proprietors, including two public institutions—the Juliusspital and Burgerspital—and the Bavarian Staatliche Kellerei (the organization controlling the Bavarian state-owned vineyards).

All Franken wines are sold in the traditional *Bocksbeutel* (see page 7).

SEKT

West Germany is the world's largest producer and consumer of sparkling wine. Almost 280 million bottles are consumed annually there. (Worldwide consumption of Champagne from France averages over 200 million bottles yearly.) Most of this wine is labeled "Sekt," since the use of the word *Champagne* is forbidden in Germany by treaty with France for anything but true French Champagne.

Sekt is made almost always by the tank process or *Cuvée close* method. The wines used in Sekt are not necessarily German. Most of them are either French, from the Loire Valley, or Italian. Only wines bearing a German designation of origin, such as Rheingau Sekt or Sparkling Moselle, are made entirely from German wines. This is usually the case, as well, when a Sekt is given a grape designation, such as Riesling. Sekts vary from Brut to Extra Dry. In Germany, Extra Dry is called "Trocken."

German vintages   Vintage years are usually judged by the amount of Prädikat wines produced, even though most of the wines exported from Germany are Qualitätswein. Not only are there variations in quality from year to year, but in quantity as well. The good Prädikat wines in the last decade have been 1971, 1975, 1976, and 1979. The good years for Qualitätswein have been 1978, 1980, and 1981. A vintage chart for German wines appears in Appendix B.

to sum up   It is not true that a wine must bear a famous name to be good. Much excellent, clean, pleasant wine comes to us labeled simply with the township name, such as Bernkastel, Piesport, Brauneberg, Rüdesheim, Hochheim, and Nierstein, or with a generic name, such as Moselblümchen or Liebfraumilch.

Most German wines, particularly the smaller ones, are at their best when the fresh bloom of youth is on them. In fact, we recommend that they be drunk when they are under ten years old, except for the very fine Auslese, Beerenauslese, and Trockenbeerenauslese wines.

HOW AND WHEN TO SERVE GERMAN WINES

White wines, light wines, fresh wines go well with almost all foods, particularly those that come from the sea. They are dry and sharp, without being acid, and when they are sweet they are not cloying. A well-chilled bottle of Moselle wine is the summer luncheon or dinner wine par excellence.

Another pleasant way to drink German wines is with soda water, mixed half and half. This produces a spritzer with a pleasing, flowery perfume.

German wines are often drunk by themselves after a meal instead of with the meal. In Germany they are commonly served at eleven A.M.—the equivalent of a U.S. coffee break.

8
THE WINES OF
SPAIN

The first records of Iberia tell of intrepid Phoenician sailors and merchants establishing trading posts. Before long the vine was planted, for nothing else would grow in the hard clay soil.

During the period of Rome's greatness the Iberian Peninsula did a thriving business with the Romans, as is indicated by the wine jars of Spanish make found among the ruins of Pompeii.

history

During the occupation by the Moors, which lasted for eight centuries, the vine flourished and prospered. In this era, the pot still was discovered, and the production of alcohol from grape juice, around A.D. 900, eventually led to the fortification of sherry with grape brandy. It was also discovered at that time that grapes left in the sun would become raisined, and their sugar could be concentrated.

1. SHERRY

It is Jerez de la Frontera and its renowned sherry wine that concern us most when we think of Spanish viniculture. Jerez has been a formally constituted trading post, town, and city for at least three thousand years. It was first a Phoenician outpost and town called Xera. During the Roman era it was called Seritium; later the Moorish kings and caliphs spelled it Scherris. Its present name, Jerez de la Frontera, was granted officially by King Don Juan I in his royal decree of April 21, 1380.

Throughout the centuries the region has produced wines that have always won high praise. But the history of sherry wine, as we know it today, began four centuries ago, when an enterprising wine merchant decided to take some wine to England, his vessel laden with casks branded:

VINO DE JEREZ
SACA

Arriving on the Thames, he discovered not only that the English could neither read nor speak Spanish but that they refused to try. If they had to use foreign words, and they did not take kindly to the idea, at least they would see that the words sounded as English as possible. The word *Jerez* (*heh-rehz*) they promply Anglicized to *jerries*, *sherries*, and finally to its present form, *sherry*.° *Saca*, after passing through several transmutations, became *sack*.† *Sherry* is, therefore, simply the English spelling of the Spanish *Jerez*.

Jerez de la Frontera is the city around which the sherry vineyards lie and the sherry trade revolves. The principal shippers have their *bodegas* ("ware-houses") there, and the vast reserves of wine that make possible sherry as we know it are kept in Jerez, Puerto de Santa María, and Sanlúcar de Barrameda.

Jerez de la Frontera is in the province of Andalucía, the southernmost part of Spain, and to understand the wine of the region one must know something about the Spaniard, particularly the Andaluz.

Spain is a confederation of the thirteen ancient kingdoms and peoples who have always inhabited the Iberian Peninsula. It has never been and perhaps never will be one people. Even today the Catalan from Barcelona speaks a different language from the Castilian of Madrid; he has different customs and, although he carries a Spanish passport, he will always, and with pride, call himself a Catalan—not a Spaniard. Most Spaniards, then, are regionally rather than nationally minded.

In Andalucía there is brilliant sunshine and the people are gay; they dress in flaming colors and worship objects of beauty, whether they be gardens, Arabian stallions, or the magnificent sherry wine. The Andaluz is romantic.

"Para los gustos, Dios hizo los colores" ("To please our tastes, God created colors"), say the Andalucíans, and this proverb applies most aptly to the wines of Jerez. For in sherry, as in a rainbow, almost any shade of color and taste may be found.

The greatest and best salesman sherry ever had was William Shakespeare. Sherry and sack crop up often in his plays, but most of all in *Henry IV*, in the words of Falstaff. "A good Sherris-sack," said the immortal rogue, "hath a two-fold operation in it. It ascends me into the brain; dries me there all the foolish and dull and crudy vapours which environ it; makes it apprehensive, quick, forgetive, full of nimble, fiery, and delectable shapes; which delivered o'er to the voice—the tongue—which is the birth, becomes excellent wit."

° Manuel Ma. González Gordon in his definitive *Jerez-Xerez-Scheris* attributes the present-day English spelling of *sherry* as "obviously a corruption of *Scherrisch*, the old Moorish name of the town."

† The word *sack* as a term meaning sherry is archaic. Its rightful use today is limited to the registered trademark of the sherry shippers Williams & Humbert.

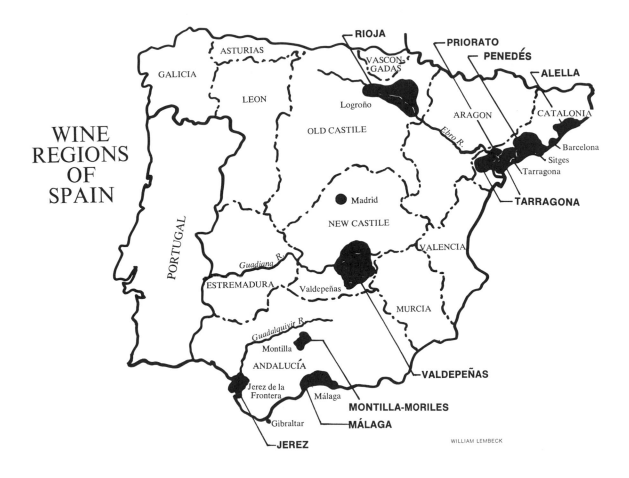

WINE
REGIONS
OF
SPAIN

WILLIAM LEMBECK

Andalucía, the most southern province of Spain, extends from the *geography*
Portuguese frontier on the west to the Mediterranean on the east. All sherry
vineyards are in a triangular growing area of 50,000 acres, delimited by the
Sherry Control Board, which also regulates all other aspects of sherry production and trade.

The sherry district lies between the Guadalquivir and the Guadalete
rivers, with the Atlantic seaboard on the west and a line paralleling the coast a
few miles north of Jerez on the east. Nature has endowed this little piece of
land with qualities that are unique, although a "sherry" is made wherever
grapes are grown. In this region all types of sherries are produced, from the
very driest to the sweetest.

soil   Three predominating types of soil divide the region into three sections. Around and a little to the north of Jerez itself is found the *albariza*—a soil composed primarily of chalk, magnesium, clay, and lime—from which the finest sherries are produced. Each producer must use grapes from the *albariza* zone for at least 40 percent of his production.

South of Jerez is the *barros* (clay). This reddish clay contains a great deal of iron. Both *barros* and *albariza* produce from 2½ to 3 butts (132-gallon casks) of wine per acre.

The *arenas* (sandy soil) is found toward the seashore and near the rivers. The *arenas* produces as much as six butts to the acre, but as quantity increases, quality decreases.

grape varieties   The Palomino is the classic and finest grape variety grown for making sherry wine. Ninety percent of the vines planted in the Jerez region are Palomino. The *albariza* vineyards are planted almost exclusively with it. The Mantúo Castellano, Mantúo de Pila, and Cañocazo are of secondary importance. Finally, there are the Pedro Ximenez (P.X.) and Moscotel used for making very sweet wines and for blending sherries, which are important to U.S. and Scottish distillers in making their blended whiskies.

All the Jerez vineyards were destroyed by *Phylloxera*, which invaded the region toward the end of the nineteenth century. Since then the traditional varieties have had to be grafted onto American *Phylloxera*-resistant rootstocks. This grafting resulted in a 20 percent increase in production.

vintage   The actual gathering of the grapes begins when they are fully ripened. This varies from year to year, from the last week of August to the second week of September, depending on the climatic conditions of the preceding summer months. However, the feast of the Nativity of the Virgin, which falls anywhere from September 8 to September 12, is the usual official commencement of the vintage.

Under the auspices of San Ginés de la Jara, patron saint of winemakers, the gay, very colorful *Fiesta de la Vendimia* ("Vintage Festival") is celebrated for four days. There is pageantry, fireworks, a horse show, a solemn *Te Deum*, the treading of a "first" butt of wine, and much happy singing and flamenco dancing.

After the *Te Deum*, a colorful ceremony takes place on the steps of the church before the image of San Ginés de la Jara. Baskets of Palomino grapes, borne by the vintage queen and her maids of honor, who are dressed in traditional local costumes, are blessed by the monsignor and then emptied into a specially erected *lagar*, or "pressing trough." Four treaders, who have won the honor, tread and press out this "first" butt of the new vintage.

As the juice begins to flow, hundreds of white pigeons are released into the bright sunlit sky from the church steps to announce the new sherry vintage.

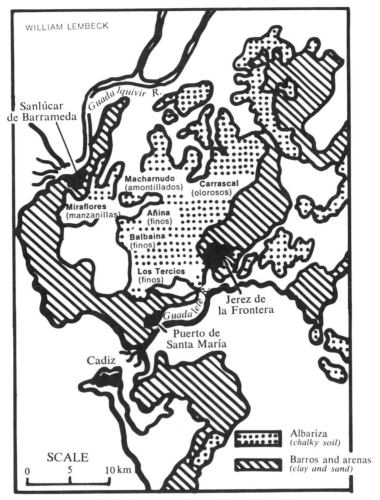

WILLIAM LEMBECK

Sanlúcar de Barrameda

Guadalquivir R.

Macharnudo (amontillados)

Carrascal (olorosos)

Miraflores (manzanillas)

Añina (finos)

Balbaina (finos)

Los Tercios (finos)

Jerez de la Frontera

Guadalete R.

Puerto de Santa María

Cadiz

SCALE
0   5   10 km

Albariza *(chalky soil)*

Barros and arenas *(clay and sand)*

DELIMITED SHERRY ZONE

Meanwhile, in the vineyards the work of the vintage goes on in all its intensity. The heavily laden rows of Palomino vines growing on the grayish white *albariza* soil of the best districts of Macharnudo, Balbaina, Carrascal, Añina, and Los Tercios are invaded by men with sharp knives. They cut the large bunches of grapes, placing them in containers, which are then trucked to mechanized press houses. Before being pressed, the grapes may be left in the sun, depending on the type of wine desired. Palomino grapes might be sunned for twelve to twenty-four hours for full olorosos, much less for finos. P.X. and Moscotel grapes are dried for one to three weeks to become raisins. The grapes are then destemmed, crushed, and pressed in modern presses.

Although rising labor costs have forced the sherry producers to develop new, automated methods, the traditional treading and pressing methods that have been used for so many generations, and are associated with sherry, bear describing. A few *bodegas* still maintain these procedures.

The traditional pressing hall is long and narrow, with *lagares* (wooden pressing troughs) lined along one side. They are sixteen to eighteen feet square and about two feet deep, and they are tilted forward from the wall to permit the juice to run freely through a doorlike opening. The *lagar* is raised three feet above the floor, and has a seven-foot screw post in the center. Sixty baskets, or fifteen hundred pounds, of golden Palomino grapes are the precise *marc* for each *lagar;* when treaded and pressed, the *marc* fills one butt.

Four men work each *lagar*. Wearing special hobnail shoes, they work the mass with a mincing sort of backward and forward step until the grapes are crushed into a pulp. The mass is then sprinkled with several handfuls of gypsum (calcium sulfate) to ensure an increased tartaric acid content in the wine. Then comes the pressing. Using wooden spades, the men pile the grape mass evenly around the center screw post, while wrapping an eighty-two-foot-long woven grass ribbon around the grape mass to hold it in place. A wooden block is slipped over the screw post, and above it is placed a threaded sleeve with two three-foot handles, which the men begin to turn. The remaining juice gushes forth, filtered through the grass ribbon, out of the *lagar,* and into the waiting butt.

All of the butts are made of American white oak, which has the ideal grain and porosity for sherry. This was actually observed after the time of Columbus, when trading began between Spain and North America.

The butts of freshly expressed must (juice) are trucked at once to the shippers' *bodegas* in Jerez, Puerto de Santa María, or Sanlúcar de Barrameda. They are placed in the fermenting warehouse to become wine. For the first week or so the fermentation process is violent. The must hisses, bubbles, and boils until most of the grape sugar has been converted. Fermentation then continues at a quieter, more leisurely pace through December, when the wine falls bright, which means that the insolubles have precipitated to form the lees and the wine has clarified itself. It is racked off into fresh butts, which are filled only to seven-eighths of their capacity to allow the *flor* to develop.

In the ordinary sense of winemaking the grape juice has by this time become wine; however, it is still called *mosto*, since it has not yet become sherry. For this to occur, the unique phenomenon of the *flor* ("flowering") must take place.

flowering   *Flowering* is the term used to describe the development and growth, sometimes to a thickness of over a quarter of an inch, of the yeast film on the

LEFT: Palomino grapes arriving at pressing house yard in traditional panniers and spread on *esparto* grass mats to dry.

BELOW: Older Jerez pressing house, showing treaders working ten *lagares*.

ABOVE: Grape mass being built up about the central post in the *lagar* ("pressing trough"). Note that the mass is held in place by a ribbon of woven *esparto* grass wrapped around it.

RIGHT: Hobnail Jerez treading shoes. (*Photos courtesy Julius Wile Sons & Co., Inc., New York*)

surface of the wine. It is a natural yeast associated with that which produced the original fermentation. The *flor* appears most strongly each spring and autumn. Along with matters of soil and climate, the *flor* contributes to sherry's distinctive characteristics, especially its delicacy, aroma, and nuttiness.

Flowering is peculiar to sherry. The only other wine-growing regions we know of where flowering has occurred naturally are South Africa, Russia, and in the Jura Mountains of France.

classifying   The new wine is carefully examined and classified. Sherry is the most *the new wines* unpredictable of all wines, and when the winemaker crushes his grapes, he has not the slightest idea of the type of sherry wine that will result. No two butts of must ferment into identical wines, even though the must has come from grapes of the same vineyard, was pressed at the same time, and has been treated identically. No one knows what causes this variation.

Some butts show signs of developing into the pale-colored, light, delicate fino type and have a thick *flor* layer; others have a deeper color and fuller body and a very thin layer of *flor*, indicating that they will become the oloroso type; while other butts develop coarsely and will be separated for distilling.

A simple system of chalk marks has evolved through the centuries to identify theses various qualities. The butts of the palest and finest wines are marked with one stroke / (*raya*); these are destined to be finos. The heavier wines receive two strokes // (*dos rayas*); these are destined to be olorosos. Lower-quality wines are marked with three strokes /// (*tres rayas*); ordinary wines to be used for seasoning and cleaning casks receive four strokes //// (*cuatro rayas*); and a grid ⧣ (*parilla*) marks the wines to be distilled or to be removed from the winery and turned into vinegar. These and the additional marks used in further classification vary somewhat from one sherry shipper to another.

At the time of the first classification the new wines are lightly fortified with brandy. The *rayas* have their alcohol content raised to 15 or $15\frac{1}{2}$ percent, and the *dos rayas* are fortified more strongly, to 17 percent. Since *flor* disappears at 16 percent, only the *rayas* continue to be affected by it during further development.

During the next year or two the *bodega* master, or *capataz*, continues the tasting and classification so that he can decide on the final type of wine that will develop and which *solera* it will eventually refresh.

He uses an instrument called the *venencia*, employed only in Jerez— a tall, narrow silver cup attached to the end of a long, springy whalebone handle. It is a tricky gadget, the use of which requires considerable skill. The cup is dipped deep into the butt through the bung in order to get a sample of clear wine. Then it is withdrawn and the wine is poured into a glass from a height, all in one motion. This looks simple until the uninitiated tries it, when he will discover that he is more likely to pour the wine down his sleeve than into the glass.

The original *rayas* are divided into *palmas*, one ⟋ , two ⟍ , three ⟋⟍ , and four ⟍⟍ , according to quality and age; these are true finos.

Manzanilla describes a fino made or matured in Sanlúcar de Barrameda, where the sea air imparts an echo of saltiness to the wine.

Amontillado is a *raya* that has become nuttier, fuller bodied, and darker than the finos.

Some original *dos rayas* develop fino characteristics and are divided into *palo cortado*, one ⟋, two ≠, three ⧣, and four ⧣ (cut sticks) according to quality. These are rather rare, however, and most of the *dos rayas* wines become olorosos.

An oloroso, in accordance with its name, has a characteristic aroma and also possesses more body than the finos. Cream sherry is a full oloroso.

The wines that develop body but not the proper finesse retain the original *raya* markings and are called either *raya* or *raya oloroso*.

The sherries are now ready to enter the *solera* system.

the solera system

The heart of the entire sherry trade is the *solera* system by which a uniform style, character, and quality are maintained year in and year out. Every sherry shipped from the Jerez region has gone through its *solera*. This system of aging and blending the wine has been in use since the 1800's.

Solera comes from the word *suelo* ("ground") and refers to the butts

Deft use of the *venencia*. Williams & Humbert's *capataz* ("*bodega* master") pouring a sample that he has just drawn from the Dry Sack *solera*. (*Courtesy Julius Wile Sons & Co., Inc., New York*)

FLOWLINE CHART OF A SOLERA SYSTEM

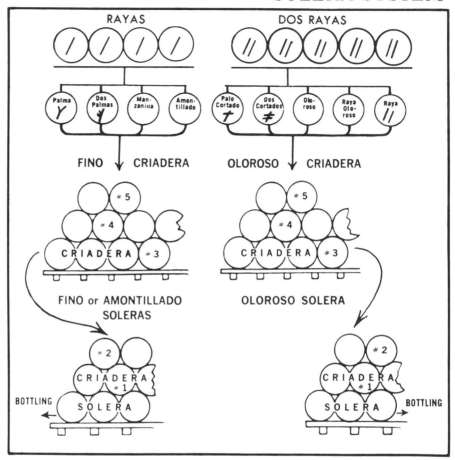

nearest the ground. It is created by laying down a number of butts of particularly fine-quality wine of a given style. The next year an equal number of butts of wine of the same style and character are placed above it to form a second tier, and the next year a third tier is placed above the second. Depending upon the needs and the desired quality of age, further lots of similar wine are set aside in succeeding years as additional tiers or scales to back up the original three.

All the tiers (scales) above the first one are called *criaderas* ("nursery reserves"). The number varies from one *solera* to another and one house to another. Each *criadera* tier is numbered. We have seen *soleras* that were backed up with six *criaderas* and others with as many as twelve. There is always a year's difference between each *criadera* number.

It is only when the shipper has established his full line of *criadera* tiers that he is ready to begin selling wine from the *solera*. He then draws wine from the original tier of butts, but not more than one-third of the wine may be drawn off in any one year. This wine is replaced with wine drawn from the next youngest *criadera* tier and so on. The wine from the youngest, or top row of butts is replaced with new wine that has been set aside for the particular *solera*. This wine will take from seven to ten years or longer to travel through the *solera* system before it reaches the bottle. By the time that this new wine has reached the bottom row, it has taken on the characteristics of the oldest wine in the *solera*. This complex and costly method of fractional blending, also known as "running the scales," produces the same type of sherry year in and year out, and a standard of quality can be maintained indefinitely.

Consequently, there is no such thing, commercially, as a vintage sherry. *Sherry is always a blended wine.* Occasionally a *solera* is dated, such as Solera 1870. This indicates the year when the *solera* was started, but it does not mean that the wine in the bottle is of the 1870 vintage. When you see a bottle labeled Vintage of 1900, you are being misled.

The sherry shipper can supply the finest shades of difference in color and taste by judicious and intelligent blending. Basically, all sherries are dry. The various degrees of sweetness are the result of the careful use of a special sweetening wine made from raisined Pedro Ximenez grapes, and the depth of color is obtained by blending in a small amount of color wine (*vino de color*).

Vino de color is made by boiling the must before fermentation begins. The result is a very dark, syrupy concentration of grape juice. If, in this process, the must is reduced to one-third of its original content, it is called *sancocho;* if down to one-fifth, *arrope.* To this are added eight or ten parts regular sherry wine of the same vintage, and the whole is known as *vino de color.* The color and sweetening wines are of great importance to the shipper, who maintains *soleras* of them. Since he uses small amounts in each blend of sherry, the quality must be on a par with the wine it is to color or sweeten. The final blending of the wine to be bottled includes the proper proportion of color wine.

It is interesting to note that, because of evaporation, the strength of the wine increases slightly, so that wine started out with 16 percent alcohol will have 18 percent or even more after a few years. This varies with the type of wine and with the shipper. Some shippers send their pale dry wines out with an alcohol content of 17 to 19 percent, while others fortify all of their wines up to 20½ percent.

The final step before bottling or shipping the wine is to fine it, in order to ensure clarity and brilliance. The best fining material for sherry is egg whites mixed with a small amount of wine (see page 28). In addition, some sherries are refrigerated for a period of time and then filtered. This procedure removes excess tartrates and stabilizes the wine.

SHERRY TYPES

All shippers produce the same general types of sherry. Each shipper, however, offers various qualities of each type, and in order to differentiate not only the various qualities but also his own brand from that of his competitors, the shipper has developed the custom of giving his *solera* a trade name.

The sherry shipper further subdivides the fino and oloroso styles as follows:

TYPE	DESCRIPTION
	FINOS
Manzanilla	Very dry, very pale, light body
Fino	Very dry, very pale, medium body
Amontillado	Dry, pale to light gold, full body, nutty
	OLOROSOS
Oloroso	Usually sweet, deep golden, full body, nutty
Cream	Sweet, deep golden, full body, nutty
Brown	Very sweet, dark brown, full body, nutty

Transferring wines in an outdoor *solera* system. Most *soleras* are inside the *bodegas*. (*Courtesy Julius Wile Sons & Co., Inc., New York*)

MANZANILLA. This is a very pale, very dry fino that has developed in the *bodegas* located at Sanlúcar de Barrameda, where the salt air of the Atlantic Ocean has a very definite influence and contributes to the wine's fragrance, lightness, and even slightly bitter tonic undertone. Must from the same vintage and vineyard developed in Jerez will become a fino without manzanilla characteristics. As a matter of fact, if a butt of manzanilla is moved to Jerez it loses its manzanilla character and turns into a typical Jerez fino.

FINO is the basic very pale, very dry, elegant wine of Jerez. It is a wine with a slight pungency.

AMONTILLADO is a deeper-colored fino that has developed considerable nuttiness and body. Usually it is a fairly dry wine, but some shippers blend their amontillados to be less dry.

OLOROSO is a deeper golden wine, which can be quite dry but generally is fairly sweet. It has a full body and is nutty. The term *amoroso* was formerly used for a somewhat sweet and velvety oloroso.

CREAM is a rich, golden, sweet, soft wine of full body. Cream wines are from old, extensive oloroso and color wine *soleras*.

BROWN is always a very dark walnut brown sweet wine of full-bodied nuttiness. This type is very popular in England and Scotland, but it has lost much of its appeal in the United States, where it has been replaced by the cream type.

Note: These sherry styles are the basic types shipped today. Each shipper varies his final blends according to what he believes will have the widest appeal. Some ship younger wines, while others use older wines.

PEDRO XIMENEZ

According to legend, the Pedro Ximenez grape was brought to Jerez from Germany by a man named Peter Siemens, whose name was Hispanicized to Pedro Ximenez.

In addition to the use of this grape for sweetening and coloring, a finished wine is also made from these grapes after they have been dried in the sun. The must that is obtained is not allowed to ferment because it is so syrupy that fermentation would be slow and arduous. Instead the must is run into butts containing a small amount of brandy so that all the natural sugar remains in the wine. P.X. wines go through their own *soleras*.

Obviously, this is an expensive wine to produce. In Spain and Latin America, Pedro Ximenez wine is popular, but its main use is to lend richness and softness to the blends of rich oloroso and brown sherries.

SHIPPERS

Sherry shipping firms do not spring up overnight. It takes years to form the *soleras,* and unless a firm can purchase a complete *bodega,* it takes many years to become established. That is why most of the well-known firms have been in existence for over a hundred years. As a firm does not stay in business unless it gives quality and deals fairly with its customers, the people managing these old firms handle fine wines and have solid reputations. In many cases the directors of these firms are direct descendants of the founders and are well aware of their responsibility to maintain the reputation of the firm on the same high plane as that of their forebears.

For this reason, and because sherry is always a blended wine, the shipper's name is of paramount importance in selecting a sherry. Every bottle bearing his label carries the shipper's assurance of honesty, ability, skill, and reputation for shipping wines of consistently high quality.

Every shipper, of course, handles both fine wines and inexpensive wines. Do not compare one shipper's fine wine with another's less expensive wine in trying to establish their relative merits as shippers.

HOW AND WHEN TO SERVE SHERRIES

Sherry is an ideal wine of hospitality, and, because of the variety of types, can be served before, during, and after meals, or any time during the morning, afternoon, or evening.

Manzanilla and fino sherries, served chilled, are ideal apéritifs. They go well with hors d'oeuvres and soups. In their native Spain, for example, they are served with the local *tapas:* olives, spicy meats, sausages, shrimps, and nuts.

Amontillados and dry olorosos may be served at room temperature or on the rocks. They add to the enjoyment of soups and cheeses, and are perfect for between-meal sipping. They are suitable when just one type of sherry is served.

The richer oloroso and cream sherries are better served at room temperature. They are satisfying as a dessert wine with fruit or pastry, or after a meal with coffee and nuts.

Because sherry is fortified and has a higher percentage of alcohol than table wines, it is a wine whose flavor is not impaired by smoking. It is sturdy, does not suffer from travel, and therefore is an ideal wine to take traveling or on a picnic. Furthermore, it is an economical wine, as once a bottle is opened, especially an oloroso, it will keep in the bottle or a decanter.

Manzanillas and finos do deteriorate in the bottle, because they are more delicate. Their color deepens and they lose their freshness. Some finos are now available in half-bottles for this reason. Finos should not be kept for more than a year, but may be conveniently stored in the refrigerator, since they are customarily served chilled anyway.

Sherry has many virtues. It can be used in mixed drinks, such as coolers, cobblers, and flips, and it is indispensable in the kitchen.

OTHER FORTIFIED WINES OF SPAIN

Another wine was shipped for generations from Jerez, although it was *Montilla-* produced near Córdoba, over a hundred miles inland from the sherry region. *Moriles* This wine is named Montilla because it is made in the Montilla Mountains, where the soil is chalky, as in the *albariza* district of Jerez. It is made much the same as the wine in Jerez, except it is fermented in enormous earthenware jars, called *tinajas,* instead of in oak butts. The wine is later transferred to oak butts for maturation in the *solera.* Montilla wines average 15½ to 16 percent alcohol and are made primarily from Pedro Ximenez grapes, though they are not put in the sun for concentration.

Montilla wines develop a dry, nutty character and are primarily apertifs. It is from this basic wine that the word and type of sherry wine called amontillado is obtained. *Amontillado* means "in the style of Montilla."

Because the Jerez houses shipped the wines of Montilla for many, many years, we came to accept them as sherry wines. Today Spanish wine laws delimit the Montilla-Moriles region, and its wines can no longer be classified as sherries.

An important sweet wine region for many centuries has been the province *Málaga* of Málaga on the southern Mediterranean coast.

A dozen types of Málaga wine are made, ranging from medium sweet to very sweet and from 14 to 23 percent alcohol. Several varieties of grapes are used, but the two dominant ones are Pedro Ximenez and Muscat. To the juice is added brandy and *vino de color* to make a strong, dark wine. The grapes are often sun dried before crushing and have high sugar and low acid content. Many producers develop and mature their wines in the *solera* system. One style of Málaga is called *Lagrimas* ("tears"), and is made from free-run juice only.

The highly individualistic region of Catalonia (Cataluña), with its beauti- *Tarragona* ful capital, Barcelona, produces interesting fortified wines of Tarragona and Sitges. Tarragona port is a sweet, red wine made similarly to that in Portugal. Priorato, a delimited area named for the mountainous district near Tarragona, makes strong, dry red wines.

Tarragona also produces white fortified wines from the Malvasia, Muscat, and Macabeo grapes for use as altar or sacramental wines.

Farther north, but still south of Barcelona, around the seaport of Sitges in the Penadés region, are produced the most famous Moscatel wines of Spain. These are prepared in the same manner as the Pedro Ximenez wines. They are light golden in color, have a pronounced Muscat flavor, and are very rich and soft. As a rule, they have an alcoholic strength of 16 to 18 percent.

2. TABLE WINES OF SPAIN

Spain's annual production of wine exceeds one billion gallons and gives work to about 15 percent of the population. The bulk of this production is not sherry but light, fresh table wine, most of which is consumed locally. However, certain regions of Spain export quality wines.

Besides Jerez, there are twenty-seven other controlled regions of Spain regulated by the *Instituto Nacional de Denominaciones de Origen* (I.N.D.O.). These regions produce mainly table wines and enhance Spain's position in the world market. The most important of these are Rioja, Catalonia, and Valdepeñas.

Rioja   The name with the most prestige among dry table wines of Spain is unquestionably Rioja. In the northern province of Logroño, in Navarre, about two hundred miles south of Bordeaux, lies the triangular basin of the Rio Oja, a tributary of the Ebro River. The two rivers join at Haro, the center of the Rioja wine industry, and site of its Viticultural Station. Most of the Rioja (contraction of Rio Oja) vineyards are planted in this basin, with some vineyards planted in the provinces of Alava and Navarre.

The Rioja region has three wine-growing districts. The Rioja Alta, on the south bank of the Ebro River, has the highest elevation and produces wines with high acidity. The Rioja Alavesa, on the north bank of the Ebro, has south-facing vineyards that receive a lot of sun and produce fruity wines. Both of these districts are influenced by the Atlantic Ocean. The third, and hottest, district, influenced by of the Mediterranean, is the Rioja Baja, producing wines of high alcohol. Rioja wines are traditionally blends of all three districts.

The grapes of Rioja are native Spanish varieties. For red wines, the most important grape is the Tempranillo, which is often blended with Garnacha Tinta (Grenache), Graciano, and Mazuelo. The principal grape for white wines is the Viura, which is blended with the Garnacha Blanca and Malvasia.

While newer wineries in Rioja ferment their wines in temperature-controlled stainless steel tanks, the wines still get much of their character from long aging in American oak barrels, even though the minimum time has been reduced to one year. Additional bottle aging follows before the wines are released, to attain more mellowness and character.

Recently, many white wines have been made in a fresher style, with more emphasis on stainless steel and less on wood for fermentation and aging. In addition, Rueda, to the west of Rioja, is becoming known as a white wine area.

Wines from the Rioja zone may carry the small square symbol of origin if they meet all of the regulations set forth by the Consejo Regulador. Since 1981 wines labeled Reserva must have two years in barrel and one year in bottle. Gran Reserva wines spend three years in barrel and two years in bottle or two years in barrel and four years in bottle. *Consecha* ("harvest") followed by a year indicates the vintage. Other words that might be found on a label are *tinto* ("red"), *clarete* ("light red"), *blanco* ("white"), *rosado* ("rosé"), *seco* ("dry"), *dulce* ("sweet"), and *embotellado en origen* ("estate-bottled").

Older Reservas and Gran Reservas can be laid down for many years, and will increase in complexity as the bottle bouquet develops.

In the northeastern corner of Spain, some excellent wines, both still and *Catalonia* sparkling, are made in the province of Catalonia. These accompany the excellent local fish. North of Barcelona, in Alella, light, dry table wines are produced, which are shipped in long, flute-shaped bottles. Granite in the soil gives the wines good acidity.

South of Barcelona is the delimited areas of Penedés, which has three distinct regions. The Bajo Penedés, along the Mediterranean coast, is the warmest of the three, growing mostly red grapes: Cariñena (Carignan), Garnacha (Grenache), Ull de Llebre (Tempranillo in Rioja), and Monastrell. White grapes that can tolerate the heat are Parellada (Xarel-lo) and Macabeo (the Viura of Rioja). The Medio Penedés, in the heartland of the area, has some of these grapes growing in its most important wine towns of Villafranca del Penedés and San Sadurni de Noya. The Alto Penedés, on the foothills of the Montserrat Mountains, is much cooler. It is here, recently, especially in the town of Pontóns, that the noble grapes of Europe are being grown successfully. Whites include the Chardonnay, Sauvignon Blanc, Riesling, Gewürztraminer, and Muscat d'Alsace; the reds are Cabernet Sauvignon, Cabernet Franc, and Pinot Noir.

For the past ten years, these table wines have become significant on the world market, especially with the use of cold fermentation and stainless steel for white wines, and small oak cooperage, both American and French, for reds.

Even more important is the large amount of quality sparkling wine being produced around San Sadurni de Noya, using the *Méthode Champenoise*. To distinguish these sparkling wines from Champagne, they are labeled *Cava*. Native grapes used are the red Monastrell, and the white Parellada and Macabeo. Many producers are using automatic riddling and other modern advances. The corks, of course, are from Spain. These sparkling wines offer excellent value.

In the central area of Spain, around Madrid, Valdepeñas wine is produced *Valdepeñas* on the plains of La Mancha, bordering Andalucía. While these wines, both red and white, are less delicate than the wines of the north, they are especially popular as carafe wines in Madrid. Grapes are the white Airen and the red Cencibel. White Valdepeñas is dry and full-bodied, with a lot of character and flavor. The reds are more like dark rosés, with high alcohol and good fruit. The wines of Valdepeñas are most enjoyable when young, and are usually exported when they arc still fresh and vigorous. Some of this wine is being shipped to this country with a brand name, rather than a regional name.

9
THE WINES OF PORTUGAL

1. PORTO

The sweet, warming wine of Portugal has been considered an English wine, for it was the English who changed it from a natural wine to the rich, fortified wine it is today, the English who created the markets for it, and the English who controlled the trade of this wine in Portugal. The English, in fact, enjoy Porto more than the Portuguese themselves. They prefer the light table wines of their country, which are better suited to the warm climate.

history   In Roman times Portus Cale, the harbor at the mouth of the Douro River, was the most important center of life and trade of ancient Lusitania. It eventually gave its name to the country, modernized to Portugal, and retained for itself the simple title of Oporto, "the port." In ancient days it was customary to close the port each night to prevent pirates from coming in. This was done by swinging heavy chains from one bank to the other because the harbor, called a *bar,* had a narrow mouth.

The history of the port wine trade, like that of Burgundy, is wrapped up in politics and wars. Although port has been sold in England since the fourteenth century, it was not until the Methuen Treaty, signed in 1703, that the wine trade began to develop. English merchants had first settled in Lisbon and Oporto in the sixteenth century, after the discovery of Brazil led to increased trading possibilities. When the crews of English boats began stopping there, as the years went on, England gradually became acquainted with the Portuguese wines.

In 1703 Queen Anne's forces were at war with France. As a blow against the French wine trade, Queen Anne had the English ambassador, John Methuen, draw up a commercial treaty with Don Pedro II whereby, in exchange for free entry of English woolens, port wine was given an advantageous preferential duty over all other wines coming into England.

150

At first the wine, despite its low price, was not popular, being both harsh and sharp. After long experimentation, however, the enterprising English wine merchants in Oporto discovered that by adding brandy to the wine before all the sugar had been fermented out, they had a wine suited to the English taste and climate. It won ready acceptance at home, and the port trade was established on a firm foundation.

Like so many of our great wines, port takes its name from the place whence it was first shipped. It is defined by the Anglo-Portuguese Treaty of 1916 as a "fortified wine produced in the delimited Douro region and exported through the Bar of Oporto."

Because of the Douro farmers' desire for a greater share of the profits in the sale of their product, however, an experimental government declaration was initiated in 1978. This allowed a shipping company to be set up in the Douro itself, permitting the growers to cellar and stockpile *Vinho Generoso* (not called Porto), and eventually to sell it directly to the world without going through either the Bar of Oporto or the lodges of the traditional shippers. Since the growers have little experience in world marketing, this plan may or may not succeed.

In the United States, ports are produced and sold that appear with American prefixes, such as California Port or New York State Port.

In 1968, however, it was legally established, with the concurrence of Portuguese and U.S. authorities, that the fortified wine that is produced and bottled in Portugal must be called Porto or Vinho do Porto in the United States. Wines bottled after 1968 and shipped to the United States must conform to this ruling.

The controlling body for Porto is the Instituto do Vinho do Porto.

grape varieties

The Douro region, one of the most beautiful wine countries in the world, is a rough, mountainous district, with a river winding, twisting, and turning between steep slopes of striated rock. The vineyards, known as *quintas* ("farms"), are planted in terraces so that the vines cannot be washed down into the river.

There are many varieties of grapes grown in the Douro Valley, but only two types are essential to making Porto. The first, including such *plantes nobles* as the Touriga, Mourisco, and Bastardo, produces a juice lacking in color, fairly light bodied, but giving the wine character and finesse. The second type of vines includes the Tinta Cão, Tinta Francisca, and Souzão, which contribute some balance and color to the must.

It is usual for a *quinta* to be planted with anywhere from ten to fifteen grape varieties, which are all gathered and pressed together, each contributing its individual character to produce a balanced wine.

The principal grape varieties employed in making white Porto are the Rabigato, Moscatel Branco, Malvasia Fina, and Verdelho.

vintage   The vintage begins at the end of September or the beginning of October, depending on the weather. Men and women gather the grapes, carrying them in single file down the mountain in huge baskets on their backs, supported by a head harness, balancing themselves with a crooked stick. The grapes may also be piled in squeaking, two-wheeled, oxen-drawn carts, and it is amazing to watch these lumbering beasts cart the grapes down the steep, narrow roads to the pressing house without accident.

While vintage time in Portugal has always had a festival spirit, mechanization is replacing treading of the grapes, except for small, specific batches. Not all of the grapes are destemmed before fermentation, as some stems are needed to assist the juice in draining. During fermentation, the wine is pumped over a great deal, to replace the skin contact that would have been accomplished with the treading of an earlier day.

fermentation   Fermentation begins almost at once and is allowed to continue for from two to three days. The difference between Porto and other wines occurs at this stage, and, therefore, the fermentation is carefully watched. The sugar content of the must is measured periodically with a mustimeter, and when just the requisite amount of sugar remains unfermented, the must is run off into pipes (138-gallon casks), which contain sufficient brandy, distilled from wines of the district, to raise the alcohol content to approximately 20 percent. This stops fermentation, and the unfermented grape sugar remains in the wine as sweetening. Because of this, Porto is always a sweet wine. The amount of sweetness varies with the choice of each vineyard owner, usually around 8 percent.

After the free-run juice has been run into pipes, the balance of the must is pressed to express the last drops of juice. The wine made from this pressing sometimes becomes Porto, but usually brandy is distilled from it to be used in fortifying the Porto wines.

The new wines are kept at the *quintas* until the following spring, when they are racked off into fresh pipes and traditionally sent down the Douro to the shippers' wine lodges in Oporto or Vila Nova de Gaia, twin cities on opposite banks at the mouth of the river. The wines used to be shipped down the Douro aboard picturesque sailboats, called *rabelos*, but are now shipped by truck or railroad. Today one *rabelo* remains at anchor in Oporto as a symbol of the past. At the wine lodges the wine is carefully stored until it is decided whether it will be shipped as Vintage, Ruby, or Tawny Porto.

PORTO TYPES

Vintage Porto   Vintage Porto is wine of any exceptional year, when weather, rain, sun, and soil cooperate to produce a big wine with character, bouquet, and balanced flavor. It is bottled within two years of the vintage. On the average, the shippers are able to ship about three such vintages in every decade.

Table wines of Portugal ripen, mature, and are at their best in two to ten years, as in other wine-producing countries, but the richly fortified Vintage Portos require upward of ten years to reach their prime. The wine must rest for a considerable period of time, varying with different vintages; but at least eight to ten years are required for it to mature, and it will continue to develop for many more years.

A generous, full wine such as Vintage Porto throws a heavy deposit as it matures, consisting of tartrates, coloring matter, and other tannins, which settle as a leafy crust in the bottle. Once this deposit begins to form, the bottles must be handled carefully, since the crust is easily disturbed and clouds the wine. The wine will then need some time, standing upright, for the deposit to recollect around the punt (depression) in the bottom of the bottle before it can be decanted.

In his *Romance of Wine* H. Warner Allen tells a story about his great-grandfather's uncle, who was greatly addicted to Porto: ". . . and when gout and old age at last drove him to bed, his old servant explained to his nephew how he was nursing his master: 'I keeps a-turning of his Worship 'cause you see, Sir, he's got that much Port in his inside, he'd be bound to get crusted, if I let 'un stop too long on one side.'"

Gathering the grapes at a typical Upper Douro *quinta* during the vintage. (*Courtesy Casa de Portugal, New York*)

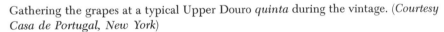

Vintage Porto has the deepest ruby color, the fruitiest bouquet, and the most body of all styles of Porto. Until fully matured it is quite rough. Thus, it has been customary for the English to lay down a considerable quantity of a Vintage Port, purchased when it first appears on the market at the opening price, permitting it to mature and increase in value in twenty-odd years. Often the Vintage Porto is purchased to celebrate a child's birth, and later, his maturity when the bottles are opened.

Vintage Porto must be bottled in Portugal, and may not be exported in bulk for bottling elsewhere. The cork and the label must have the vintage date, and the label may also have the bottling date.

See Appendix B for notes on Porto vintages.

Ruby and Tawny Portos

Ruby and Tawny Portos are generally blended wines that are matured in wood, opposed to the bottle maturation of Vintage Portos. In fact, they are sometimes referred to as Wooded Portos. The blending, or vatting, is done in the Porto lodges to ensure that a definite style and standard of quality is maintained for each brand that the shipper offers. The shipper may use as many as thirty or more wines in his blend. Some contribute the attributes of different years, some contribute finesse and delicacy, and others contribute body.

Ruby Porto is a bright, ruby-colored blend of young Portos that have spent some time in wood. It is very fruity, with the sweetness of the wine still in evidence. It must be at least three years old before being shipped, and can be drunk when bottled.

Tawny Porto is ideally a blend of well-matured wooded Portos, even though the minimum legal age before release is only three years. Since the tawniness comes from repeated finings, it stands to reason that Tawny Portos need more time to achieve their character.

While the wine is maturing in the pipe, it throws a deposit (crust) just as it does in the bottle. Some of the deposit is not heavy enough to precipitate and remains in suspension, causing the wine to have a dull, or "blind," appearance. This is overcome by fining. Experience has proved that wines develop best if kept in a good, brilliant condition. They are therefore fined on an average of twice a year. The material used may be a commercial fining material, but for better wines the shippers generally use whites of eggs.

As the film formed by the fining process settles, it carries down with it not only the sediment of fliers that were floating in the wine, but also a certain amount of the coloring matter. As a result, the longer a wine is kept in wood, the greater the number of times it is fined, and the less color it retains. An old wooded Porto, consequently, is paler in color than a young wine.

The quality of paleness is called tawniness because as the wine loses redness, both from repeated finings and from oxidation during wood storage, a tawny amber glint appears. As it increases in tawniness, a Porto becomes

Historical photo of Douro *rabelo* laden with pipes of new wine destined for the shippers' lodges at Oporto or Vila Nova de Gaia. (*Courtesy Casa de Portugal, New York*)

drier, so that an old Tawny will be drier than a young Tawny. The word *dry* is used, in this case, in a relative sense.

Most Tawny Portos do not have any age statements on the label. Older Tawny Portos from a single year used to appear as "Port of the Vintage," a label that is no longer allowed. Sometimes older Tawnies are bottled "with an indication of age." This value will be an average.

Late-Bottled Vintage (LBV) is Tawny Porto from a single good year that remains in cask and is not blended. The wine matures faster in cask than it does in the bottle, and is thus readier sooner than true Vintage Porto. Also, most of the sediment or crust is left behind in the cask, so that LBV Portos do not require decanting. They do, of course, have a vintage date on the label, but are less expensive than Vintage Portos.

White Porto is another type of wine produced in the Douro region. Except for the fact that white grapes are used exclusively, it is made in the same manner as red Porto. It is matured in wood and is generally quite soft, pleasant, and a shade drier than other Portos. Sometimes it is blended with less expensive Tawny Portos to make them paler and softer in a shorter time. It is very popular in France where it is consumed as an apéritif.

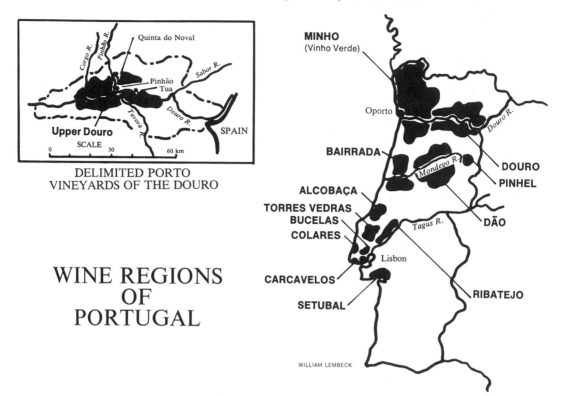

DELIMITED PORTO
VINEYARDS OF THE DOURO

WINE REGIONS
OF
PORTUGAL

Crusted Porto Crusted Porto has virtually disappeared, but it used to be a close relative of Vintage Porto in that it was usually wine of a single year. Sometimes, however, it was a blend of vintage wines from several vintages. Because it did not quite come up to vintage standard in quality, it was sold without any date. It resembled Vintage Porto in character and deposited a crust.

HOW AND WHEN TO SERVE PORTO

Porto wine may be served at the end of a meal with dessert or coffee, and is traditional with Stilton or cheddar for the cheese course. Cigars may also be enjoyed along with Porto. Porto has many uses in the kitchen: in sauces, Porto wine jellies, and fruit cups, and for plumping up dried fruits.

OTHER FORTIFIED WINES OF PORTUGAL

Carcavelos and Moscatel de Setúbal As previously stated, it is illegal to call a wine Porto unless it has been produced in the delimited Upper Douro region, yet sweet, fortified wines such as Carcavelos and Moscatel de Setúbal are made in other parts of Portugal, primarily on the Tagus River and in the Estremadura region.

Carcavelos, located at the mouth of the Tagus River, just west of Lisbon, is most famous for its white fortified wine known since the thirteenth century. The climate favors the production of must of higher quality because the breezes blow away the humidity that would otherwise adversely affect the grapes producing the must. A first-class Carcavelos wine has an alcohol content of 19 percent and is good as an aperitif or dessert wine, depending on the sweetness. It has a pleasant bouquet, is smooth to the taste, and ages well.

Moscatel de Setúbal, a wine with several royal charters, is produced in Setúbal, a beautiful area south of Lisbon. It owes its perfumed scent and flavor to the distinguishing characteristics of Muscat grapes and long aging in oak. It is golden in color, very sweet, and, like Carcavelos, improves with age.

2. TABLE WINES OF PORTUGAL

The Setúbal district is also well known for its good-quality table wines, the majority of which are red and are made from the Periquita grape.

Bucelas and Colares

Of Lisbon's local wines, the two best are Bucelas, a pleasant, fresh, dry white, and Colares, a dry red wine.

Bucelas is a town just north of Lisbon where the wine is made primarily from the Arinto grape. Dry, with a recognizable aroma and characteristic straw-yellow color, it has a fine bouquet that increases with age.

Colares is a small town on the Atlantic, west of Lisbon. The vineyards of the region are planted with the Ramisco grape, which produces a clean, full-bodied, ruby-red beverage wine. Grown in sandy soil, this grape is not attacked by *Phylloxera*, which ravaged European vineyards in the last century, as *Phylloxera* cannot exist in sand. The very deep roots of the vines may go down nine or ten feet through the sand to a clay layer below. Colares and Periquita are wines drunk today made from the same vines as those that produced wines thousands of years ago. Although the very early history of Colares wine is unknown, it is known that in 1385 it enjoyed a flourishing trade. Very little of the local Lisbon wine is exported to this country.

Dão

The Dão region is named for the Dão River, a tributary of the Mondego River, which flows midway between Oporto and Lisbon. Only a small amount of the land is under vine because of the rocky, granitic soil. The red wines are characterized by a ruby-red color, rich bouquet, smooth taste, and woody flavor that comes from two years minimum aging in oak. The wine can age well, and older wines are known as *vinho maduro*. The Tourigo, Alvarelhão, Bastardo, and Tinta Pinheira grapes impart the principal characteristics to red Dão wines. The Dão red is considered the best of the Portuguese red table wines, with the best of them being labeled *garrafeira*. The white wines are dry, full, and aromatic, with a woody undertone. They are produced mostly from the Arinto grape. Genuine Dão wines are guaranteed by the Federation of Dão Viniculturists.

Vinho Verde   One of the most pleasant and simple wines of Portugal is the Vinho Verde, produced in the northern province of Entre-Douro-e-Minho. The literal translation of *vinho verde* is "green wine," but the term really means "young wine," as opposed to *vinho madura*. It is not green, but white, red, or rosé. It is always a light, somewhat acid, refreshing, slightly *pétillant*, and fragrant wine with an alcohol content of 8 to 11 percent. The various grapes used are high in malic acid and low in sugar, because the vines are trained up high, providing a canopy of shade for the fruit, while avoiding the radiating heat from the ground. A malolactic fermentation provides the *pétillance*. Being light, pleasant, and thirst quenching, it is a wine that is generally drunk in large drafts, not sipped. Vinho Verde should be drunk young, while it is fresh; it may oxidize after two years. We recall a particularly delightful luncheon at a waterfront bistro, the main dish of which was huge platters of roasted, crunchy shrimp, washed down with goblets of white Vinho Verde. When the host ordered a bottle per person, we thought it was too much, but we found it was insufficient and more wine had to be served.

other table wines   Other districts yielding Portuguese table wines include Pinhel, which gives a pleasant, light wine; Bairrada, producing mostly red table wines that have body with good flavor and some white wines held in high esteem; Alcobaça, whose fame dates from the twelfth century and whose fine wines are tantalizingly aromatic; Torres Vedras, producing mostly red wines with body and a high percentage of tannin, as well as some good white wines that are alcoholic, aromatic, and flavorful; and Ribatejo, where alcoholic white wines with little acidity are produced, as well as red wines, dark in color and full bodied, with a high percentage of alcohol.

rosé wines   By far the greatest volume of Portuguese wines that come to the United States are the rosé wines. Originally these wines were slightly carbonated to appeal to the American taste, but the current preference is for still, non-carbonated wines. While the majority of these wines come to the market as trade-marked brands, the Portuguese government is trying to establish the geographic origins of the wines with regional designations on the labels. These wines are clean, sound, and moderately sweet, and are served chilled with almost any food.

sparkling wines   There are some bottle-fermented sparkling wines made in Bairrada and Lamego, but they have not been shipped to the United States.

3. MADEIRA

Madeira is an island in the Atlantic Ocean that belongs to Portugal, but is 535 miles south by southwest of Lisbon and 360 miles off the North African coast. The oldest grape, Malvasia Candiae, was originally from Crete, known as Candia in the thirteenth century. The wines from Crete enjoyed a brisk trade with England, despite political domination by Venice at that time. Once similar wines became available in Madeira, however, the English quickly began trading with that Portuguese island, and strong ties developed.

There is some question as to whether it was Prince Henry or one of his *history* captains, João Gonçalves, surnamed Zarco, who discovered Madeira, in 1418 or 1420. Whoever it was, Zarco was named Captain of Madeira, and he founded a settlement there on the Bay of Funchal. The name of the island, which was covered with dense forest from mountaintop to seashore, meant "wooded island." When Zarco arrived with his family and a group of colonists, he found Madeira uninhabited and untillable because of the heavy forest. Being a man of action and having little manpower, he did not attempt to cut the timber but fired it instead. It is said to have burned for seven years, but when, at length, the fire went out, there was added to the volcanic quality of the soil, and the accumulation of centuries of leaf mold, the potash of the burned forest, which made Madeira one of the most fertile of all islands.

Before long sugarcane and grapevines were planted, and Portugal had a rich colony. The grapevines were brought primarily from Candia and were of the Malvasia variety that is still grown on the island. Today both bananas and sugarcane are competitive crops to grapes on this lush, subtropical island.

By the end of the fifteenth century Madeira was exporting wines to Europe; these wines found favor both in France and in England. Shakespeare mentions Madeira in several of his plays, notably in *Henry IV* where Poins greets Falstaff: "Jack! how agrees the devil and thee about thy soul, that thou soldest him on Good Friday last for a cup of Madeira and a cold capon's leg?"

By 1754 there were thirteen small wine-exporting businesses established, with several more coming into being in the 1800s. The sailing vessels of the American colonies and English ships sailing to America made it a practice to stop at Madeira for water and provisions. Here they invariably loaded a few pipes (138-gallon casks) of Madeira wine, and it became the fashionable wine of the American colonies, a fashion that remained until the turn of the twentieth century.

During the early decades of the nineteenth century Madeira wines were often known by the names of the great shipping families of the Atlantic seaboard whose ship captains brought pipes of wine to their owners. There were famous Madeiras shipped to Boston, New York, Philadelphia, New Orleans, Charleston, and Savannah, and especially Baltimore.

When the vineyards were almost destroyed by *Phylloxera* and *oïdium*, exports were sharply curtailed, and Madeira lost its standing at fashionable tables. The Madeira Wine Institute, founded in 1979, is now trying to correct this.

grape varieties

The principal grape varieties grown on this steep and rocky island are the Sercial, Verdelho, Bual or Boal, and Malvasia. Most of the grapes grow on small, hand-tended plots, due to the rugged terrain. Sercial, which is actually a Riesling, grows best at 800 meters. At this height, maturation comes later, and sugars are lower than the other varieties. The Verdelho, which makes up two-thirds of the planted vines, grows at 500 meters. Bual and Malmsey grow on lower slopes, and are richer, with higher sugars. The original Malmsey was produced in Greece in Monemvasia, and in the Middle Ages red and white Malmseys were shipped all over the world. Later this wine was produced not only in Madeira but in Italy, Spain, and the Canary Islands. The name Monemvasia becomes Malvasia in Italy, Malvoisie in France, and Malmsey in England. The Malvasia grape requires a very dry soil and intense heat and is not gathered until it is shriveled and raisinlike.

The Tinta Negra Mole, a black grape from Portugal with Pinot Noir origins, is very sweet and nutty when ripe. Up to 15 percent may be used in the blends. A cross developed at the National Agronomical Station, producing wine similar to the Negra Mole, is the Complexa or Malvasia Tinta.

In the larger vineyards the various kinds of grapes, especially the Verdelho, Sercial, Bual, and Malvasia varieties, are pressed separately and the must from each is kept separate.

Smaller vineyards are planted with several varieties of vines. The cultivator does not bother to separate the different species before pressing them. As a result, there is a rich and somewhat deep-colored wine from the admixture of black grapes.

vintage

The system of viticulture in Madeira differs in some ways from that of other wine regions. Most of the land is cultivated under the old feudal system of small tenant farmers, known as *caseiros*. The *caseiro* pays half of his grape crop as rent.

Every inch of ground on the island of Madeira is utilized. The hillsides are so steep that one can hardly find foothold, yet they are made up into tiny terraces, each complete with water channels for irrigation.

Madeira has not sufficient rainfall for its needs, and the land depends on irrigation for its moisture. The water is brought down from the hills in shallow channels that usually run by the roadside. The network of these channels covers the entire island, and the water is managed by committees appointed by the *caseiros*. A farmer may be entitled to so many hours of water every fifteen days and at a given hour—whether it be three o'clock in the morning or three o'clock in the afternoon—he is advised, "It is your turn to get water." The stream is turned into his farm, and at the end of his time it is shunted to the next farm. This organization is extraordinarily efficient.

The Madeira farmer knows little of modern implements or scientific methods and does all his cultivating with the primitive *enchada*, a cross between a pick and a hoe. The hillsides are so steep that not even wheelbarrows can be used, and everything is carted in baskets carried on the head or shoulders.

The vines are not carefully pruned as on the Continent, as it has been found more practical, because of the luxuriant growth, to grow them on trellises four to six feet high, with vines fifteen to twenty feet long.

It is the custom on the island for merchants and shippers to buy the produce of the vineyard while the grapes are still on the vine. Their agents watch to see that grape picking is not begun until the proper time, and they supervise the work up to the time that the must is delivered to the shippers' cellars.

As only the ripest grapes are picked, it is often necessary to go over the vineyard as many as four times.

The grapes used to be emptied into large wooden *lagares*, to be trodden by workmen. The juice was then hand carried down from the hills in heavy goatskin sacks to the shippers' lodges. Mechanized presses and trucks have now replaced the more primitive crushing and transportation efforts.

The grape juice ferments for two to four weeks. When making the sweeter wines, fermentation is stopped by adding grape alcohol. Drier wines are fermented to completion. The wine is now known as Vinho Claro.

Madeiras are treated in a manner peculiar to the island. They are matured in *estufas* or "hothouses," lined with hot water pipes. The *estufas* vary in temperature from 95 to 120 degrees Farenheit (35–50 degrees C.), according

VINEYARDS OF MADEIRA

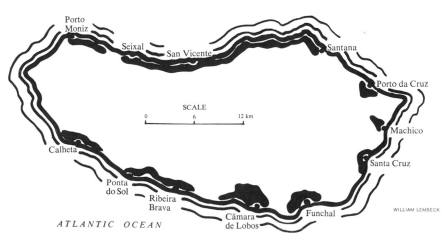

Model of an old wooden Madeira wine press. (*Courtesy Casa de Portugal, New York*)

to the length of time the wine is to be heated. If it is to be kept for six months in the *estufa*, the temperature is 95 degrees, but if it is going to be kept only three months, then a higher temperature is used. During this treatment wines that enter a deep purple color undergo a change and emerge amber colored.

This method of maturing the wine is costly, as there is a loss through evaporation, but a well-matured wine is safe against after-fermentation. All of the work is carried out under government regulations. When the wine comes from the *estufa* it is known as Vinho Estufado. It is allowed to rest for a period of time and is then racked into fresh casks, becoming Vinho Trasfugado.

The heating process originated many years ago, when it was discovered that Madeira wine was greatly improved by a long voyage in the hold of a ship. At one time, indeed, it was a regular practice to send wine in the hold of sailing vessels bound for India and thence back to Europe or America, where it was known as East India Madeira. Whether it was the intense heat of the tropical seas through which the wine sailed or the motion of the ship that matured the wine, no one knew. In any case, Madeira merchants have learned that the *estufas* produce the same result.

It used to be customary in America for famous shipping families to keep a cask of Madeira slung in a rocking cradle that was placed in the entrance hall of the shipping office. It was the duty of every person who passed through the hall to give the cradle a shove. In this way the wine was kept in motion from morning until night. Of all wines madeira is the only one that enjoys motion, and there is none that is a better sailor.

The Vinho Trasfugado is additionally fortified to bring it up to an alcoholic strength of around 20 percent, and it then becomes known as Vinho Generoso. After this it is blended with other wines of similar character and matured for a number of years.

MADEIRA TYPES

There are four main types of Madeira, corresponding to the noble grapes mentioned before. They range from very dry to very sweet. Wines made from a mixture of grapes are shipped under trade names. All Madeiras reflect the mineral-laden volcanic soil with a particular tangy flavor.

SERCIAL, the driest wine of Madeira, can be pale or golden, delicate, with a refreshing acid undertone. It is a perfect apertif but is suitable for any occasion. One Sercial that was extraordinarily dry was described by the late André L. Simon as "so soft and refined that it has no body, no sugar, no color left, and yet it has bouquet and power; the sort of wine that Rabelais, had he known it, would have called 'A Soul with a Nose.'"

VERDELHO is a medium-rich, golden wine with a dry finish. It is a good all-purpose wine and can be enjoyed before or after meals.

BUAL OR BOAL is a golden wine, fragrant and slightly less sweet than Malmsey. It is distinctly a dessert wine.

MALMSEY is a full-bodied, soft-textured, very fragrant, dark brown wine. It is the sweetest of all Madeira wines. In fact, it is of an almost liqueurlike sweetness.

Rainwater

Some wine historians credit the name of Rainwater to a Madeira enthusiast, Mr. Habisham of Savannah. He employed a secret fining process that made the wine paler in color without impairing its bouquet or character.

Rainwater Madeira is now a blend of Sercial, Verdelho, and/or Bual. It is a golden, medium-dry wine suitable for almost every occasion.

Madeira is one of the most long-lived of all wines, and even one-hundred-year-old wines are magnificent and continue to improve as do no other choice wines. In the past it was customary to keep the vintages separate, and the wines were sold as vintage wines. Since *Phylloxera* devastated the vineyards nearly a century ago, however, the old vintage wines have been used to improve the new *soleras*. As a result, true old Madeiras are difficult to obtain today, although a few wine merchants have offered such prize bottles as 1898 Verdelho, 1864 Sercial, 1891 Bual, and 1885 Malmsey.

labeling   *Vintage* on the label means that the wine has come from the nobel varieties, and has spent twenty years in cask and two years more in bottle.

Old Reserve or *Very Old* wines have a minimum age of ten years.

Reserve, Old, or *Vieux* wines are aged for a minimum of five years.

Selected, Choice, or *Finest* wines have three years minimum age.

Soleras for Madeiras are based on the same principles as those in Spain, but the regulations vary. The wines must be a minimum of five years before bottling, and no more than 10 percent may be withdrawn at any time. No more than ten additions may be made to the *solera*, after which the entire balance may be bottled at one time. If the *solera* has a vintage date, it is the date of the based wine.

Superior may only be used in conjunction with varietal names, such as "Bual Superior," or "Superior Malmsey."

No vintage dates may be used except on wines made from the noble grapes. All must be a minimum of five years old, with the exception of Sercial, which must be at least seven years old.

If the wines are for export, they must show their Portuguese origin with "Produce of Madeira (Portugal)" or simply, "Produce of Portugal."

HOW AND WHEN TO SERVE MADEIRA

Madeira is especially versatile, because of its different types. Sercial and Verdelho, being dry, make fine, chilled apértifs. They may also be served with the soup course in formal dinners. The sweeter Bual may be sipped with desserts or cheeses. The very rich Malmsey makes a splendid after-dinner drink. Madeiras may also be served by themselves in the afternoon or evening. It is rich in phosphates, iron, and minerals, and thus is also useful as a tonic.

Madeira is one of the most useful of all wines in the kitchen. It may be used in soups, sauces (such as Sauce Madère), or desserts and can be used in place of sherry or Porto in most recipes. The largest export market for Madeira is France, where it is used almost exclusively in Sauce Madère and other culinary preparations.

10
OTHER WINES
OF EUROPE

1. AUSTRIA

Although Austria's history of winemaking goes back to Roman times, the golden age of viniculture took place shortly after the Turks occupied neighboring Hungary in the 1500s, as Hungary ceased to produce wine during that period. Vine plantings increased greatly in Austria, and it is estimated that the total vineyards acreage was five to ten times what it is now.

One law, passed during Maria Theresa's (d. 1780) reign, led to a tradition that still prevails today. The winemaker was allowed to sell his own wine without having to pay any taxes on it. A hanging branch above his doorway signified to passersby that the owner had new wine to sell. This started the tradition of the *Heurige*, which occurs every year in the countryside around Vienna. Both local residents and tourists rush to purchase the new wine.

There are many wine regions in the eastern part of Austria, but the ones that are seen in this country are Wachau, Vienna, Südbahn, Burgenland, and Styria.

The vast Wachau region is northwest of Vienna, with vineyards along the Danube River, south of the Alpine ranges. This cool area, coupled with minerals in the soil, produces wines that are high in acid, crisp and elegant. The best resemble the Rieslings of Germany. Schluck is the important wine from the Sylvaner. The main towns are Krems, Dürnstein, Stein, and Loiben.

Vienna is the smallest wine growing region in Austria, producing mainly white wine, from the Grüner Veltliner and Neuberger grapes. The most famous wine producing suburbs are Grinzing, Nussdorf, and Klosterneuburg.

South of Vienna is the Südbahn region, where the famous Gumpoldskirchner vineyards lie. Baden and Vöslau are two other towns in this region, the latter producing a red table wine called Vöslau Rotwein.

Farther to the south and to the east is the Burgenland district, with extensive plantings around a large lake, the Neusiedler See. Some wines are produced from the Furmint grape, which also grows in neighboring Hungary. The towns of Rust and Oggau produce red and white wines, with late-harvest wines a specialty of Rust. Since there is sandy soil that is not hospitable to *Phylloxera*, many of these wines are made from ungrafted vines.

Finally, the southern region of Styria, which borders Yugoslavia, is warm, and has a dry, clay soil. The wines are mostly white, and consumed locally.

grape varieties and wines

Austrian grapes are a combination of native *vinifera* vines, the Furmint of Hungary, the Kadarka of the Balkan countries, and other, more famous, varieties that have taken Austrian names. Of the native varieties the Grüner Veltliner and Neuberger produce white wines, while the Rotgipfler is used for both white and red wines. Of the more familiar varieties, the Rheinriesling (Riesling), Traminer, Sylvaner, Müller-Thurgau, Wälschriesling, Ruländer (Pinot Gris), and Muskat-Ottonel are used to make the majority of white wines, which amount to 90 percent of the total production.

The Blauburgunder, or Spätburgunder (Pinot Noir), Blaufränkisch (Gamay), Blauer Portugieser, and Muskat Saint Laurent are the principal grapes used to make red wines.

Although Austria is a large producer of wine, averaging 80 million gallons annually, the per capita consumption is also very large, 9½ gallons, and Austria does not produce enough wine for its needs and must import large quantities, mostly red wines. Some of the more famous whites, however, are exported in small quantities. These include Gumpoldskirchner, Kremser, Klosterneuburger, and Ruster.

WINE REGIONS OF AUSTRIA

WILLIAM LEMBECK

WINE REGIONS OF BULGARIA

ROMANIA

Danube R.

Shumen:
SYLVANER
CHARDONNAY

YUGOSLAVIA

Suhindol:
GAMZA
CABERNET

Karlova:
MISKET

Sofia

BLACK
SEA

DIMIAT
RKATSITELI
RIESLING

Maritsa
Valley

Maritsa R.

TURKEY

MELNIK

GREECE

PAMID
MAVRUD
CABERNET

WILLIAM LEMBECK

2. BULGARIA

Bulgaria, like the other Balkan countries, is a large wine producer, ranking nineteenth in world production. In some years over 100 million gallons of red and white wines are produced in this small country.

history

The earliest references to Bulgarian viticulture appear with those of northern Greece. As in Austria, winemaking in Bulgarian territory came to a halt when it was under Turkish rule. Because of suitable climate and soil, grape growing gradually returned to this Balkan country after World War I. Except for a brief pause during and immediately after World War II, Bulgaria's wine industry has continued to grow. Today the collective farms of this Communist country have become mechanized, and the advanced technology is responsible for their large production. Most of the wine is exported, primarily to the U.S.S.R., but also to other communist and noncommunist countries.

wine regions

There are three main viticultural areas in Bulgaria. The Danube River, which separates Bulgaria from Romania, has a 250-mile-long valley with vineyards along its entire length. This region includes Shumen in the east, known for fine white wines, and Suhindol, more central, known for reds. The second region, Maritza Valley, is further south, and protected by the Balkan mountains. The third region, contiguous to the first two, is to the east, along the Black Sea.

grape varieties and wines

Bulgaria's wine grapes are a mixture of local and foreign varieties. White wines produced range from dry, light, acidic wines to the sweet types typical of the Maritsa Valley. The reds range from light, fruity types to full, dark wines that need aging.

The ubiquitous Dimiat, Bulgaria's native white-wine grape, is usually vinified dry and has a crisp, fruity taste. Grapes from the Muscat family are also common and appear in some wines, as the semidry Misket Karlova, for example, whose label indicates both grape and region; or the sweet Hemus, which is a brand name. Hungary's Furmint grape makes a dry white wine named Bulgarian Sun, and Russia's Rkatsiteli grape makes a fruity white wine named Sunshine Coast. Riesling, Sylvaner, and Chardonnay are also grown in fair quantities and produce good examples of their famous counterparts.

Traditional red-wine grape varieties, such as the Melnik and Mavrud, produce full-bodied, dark red wines. Other traditional varieties, such as Pamid and Gamza (Kadarka), make fresh, light wines that are best when drunk young. Blending is an accomplished art in Bulgaria, and both locally consumed and exported wines are blends of several grape varieties. Recent plantings of the noble varieties of Cabernet Sauvignon and Merlot have resulted in some fine red wines.

3. CZECHOSLOVAKIA

Czechoslovakia, unlike its other central European neighbors, is not a large wine producer, nor is it as avid a wine consumer, although some wine must be imported to meet its needs. This may be because Czechoslovakia's more northerly geographic position, corresponding approximately to the latitude of the wine regions of Germany, limits the grape varieties that can be grown successfully. Wine production has increased to thirty-seven million gallons, but it is not enough for local consumption. Czech wines are rarely exported.

wine regions

Czechoslovakia's wine production centers around three major regions: Bohemia, Moravia, and Slovakia. Bohemia, the most westerly region, borders Germany and Austria. Most of its vineyard area lies just north of the capital city of Prague. Moravia, in central Czechoslovakia, touches Poland in the north and Austria in the south. The major vineyards are along the southern border, just south of Brno. Slovakia, to the east, produces the bulk of the wine of this country. The most famous area of Slovakia is just north of Hungary's Tokaj region, around the town of Malá Trňa, but the biggest vineyard concentration is just north of Bratislava.

grape varieties and wines

Bohemian wines, because they are produced so close to Germany, are similar to those of the Rhine. The Riesling, Sylvaner, and Traminer grapes produce good white table wines with fruitiness and a touch of sweetness. Some red wines are also produced in this area from grape varieties seen also in Austria: the Blauburgunder, Blauer Portugieser, and Muskat Saint Laurent.

Moravian vineyards account for one-third of the wine of Czechoslovakia. The countryside surrounding the towns of Znojmo, Hustopeče, and Mikulov, at the Austrian border, grows the Austrian Grüner Veltliner, as well as the Rhine Riesling and Italian Riesling varieties. Only white wines are produced in this section, and these are light, dry, and crisp, with perhaps a touch too much acidity.

Slovakia, producing almost two-thirds of the country's wine, makes the majority of its wines, which are consumed locally, in the Modra and Pezinok countryside, north of the border where Austria and Hungary meet Czechoslovakia. The most famous wine made by the Slavs is their version of Tokay, produced near Hungary's famous Tokaj wine region; it is sometimes exported. Like Hungary's Tokay, the Czech Tokay is made mainly from the Furmint grape, with a little of a Muscat variety for added fragrance.

WINE REGIONS OF CZECHOSLOVAKIA

POLAND

Prague

BOHEMIA

MORAVIA

Brno

GERMANY

Znojmo

Mikulov

Hustopeče

SLOVAKIA

U.S.S.R.

Malá Trňa

AUSTRIA

Bratislava

HUNGARY

Modra

Pezinok

WILLIAM LEMBECK

4. ENGLAND

England's main contribution to the wine world has been the encouragement and development of wine areas in countries other than its own: Bordeaux, Jerez de la Frontera, Oporto, and Madeira. While winemaking in England has been enthusiastically embraced, there has been little commercial production.

While vineyards flourished during the Middle Ages, the English business of world commerce led to the importing of wines to the English taste, and the decline of local winemaking. From the first serious new vineyard in 1951, to two hundred new wineries by 1981, acreage, viticultural research, and quality have all increased. The formation of the English Vineyards Association in 1967 has spearheaded these efforts.

The vineyards are mostly concentrated in the southeastern part of the country, especially in Kent, East Sussex, West Sussex, Hampshire, Suffolk, Norfolk, Surrey, Somerset, Berkshire, Wiltshire, Avon, and Gloucester. The Gulf Stream moderates the climate despite the northerly latitude.

grape varieties and wines Most of the grapes are white, with both *viniferas* and French-American hybrids being grown. German varieties, such as Müller-Thurgau and Reichensteiner, are the most successful, with Riesling less so. Of the hybrids, Seyval Blanc predominates. Of the noble *viniferas*, Chardonnay and Pinot Noir are being planted in experimental lots.

Cider from apples, perry from pears, and mead from honey are also produced.

5. GREECE

The Greeks have long cultivated the vine, and their efforts have been praised in prose and poetry by all the ancient poets. Today the Greeks still produce wine in large enough quantities to place Greece eleventh in world production, with an annual production rate of 150 million gallons. The Greeks love to drink wine, and their consumption is a hearty 12 gallons per capita.

Apparently the natural flavor of the grape itself was too bland for the sophisticated Greek palate, so they stored their wines in *amphorae* ("large jars") pitched with tar. This imparted a resinous flavor to the wine, and, as if this were not enough, bags containing spices and aromatic gums were suspended in the wine to ensure its "preservation" and improved flavor. Present-day Greeks still prefer a resinated wine to a natural wine, a taste that must be acquired, as the harsh, pungent turpentine bouquet and flavor shock the unaccustomed palate. The resinated white wines are labeled Retsina while the resinated red wine is called Kokkineli.

The peninsula of Peloponnesus, which is virtually a huge island, since it is connected to the mainland only by a thin strip of land at Corinth, is the most important wine-producing area of Greece.

On the mainland a native grape variety that grows in the vineyards around Corinth, the Savatiano, is used to make all types of white wines, including the local favorite, Retsina.

The Greek islands of Chios, Coo, Corfu, Crete, Cyclades, Lesbos, Limín, Rhodes, Samos, and Santorini all produce wine today, although their products do not enjoy the majestic reputation they had when the Hellenes were masters of the known world.

Everyone in Greece drinks wine, and most of the cultivated area is devoted to vineyards, although the climate is not suitable for the best grapes for making table wine. The ancient Greeks—like those of today—preferred rich, sweet wines.

The grape varieties cultivated are those that have grown there for ages.

wine regions

grape varieties and wines

WILLIAM LEMBECK

WINE REGIONS OF GREECE

The most famous of these is the Malvasia, which originated in the region of Monemvasia, a small town in the Peloponnesian peninsula, and which is grown today in almost every wine region of the world, but most notably in Crete and Madeira (where it produces Malmsey).

The Mavrodaphne, grown in vineyards around the town of Patras along the Gulf of Corinth, is also the name of one of the most popular wines in Greece. This grape was discovered about a century ago by a viticulturist named Gustave Clauss. Because the berry reminded him of the laurel berry, he named it Mavrodaphne ("black laurel"). The wine is sweet, red, and portlike in character. It has an alcohol content varying from 15½ to 20 percent, depending on the quality of the must and the amount of brandy used for fortifying.

The Muscat is grown all over Greece, but most successfully on the island of Samos, close to Turkey. Muscat of Samos, a favorite of Lord Byron, is a pleasant, sweet, fortified white wine.

Not all Greek wine is resinated or sweet and fortified. There are many dry, light red wines, such as Demestica, Pendeli, and the dry rosé Rhoditys, made from the grape of the same name.

The dry whites are more prevalent, and these include Hymettus, named after the famous mountain near Athens, Mantinia, Kantza, Santa Helena, and the white wine of Demestica.

A big red wine from the region of Náousa is made in the northern Macedonian section of Greece from native varieties. Plantings of Cabernet Sauvignon, under the direction of French viticulturists, have also been successful in the northern region along the coastline of the Aegean Sea.

6. HUNGARY

TOKAY

When we think of Hungary and wine, we think first of Tokay.° For generations only royalty could obtain the few bottles of Tokay produced each year, so it came to be known as a royal wine. The finest vineyards in the heart of the district belonged to the royal household, and Emperor Franz Joseph made the princely gesture of sending Queen Victoria a gift of Tokay every year on her birthday, a dozen bottles for each year of her age. Year by year, as the queen grew older, the present augmented in size, until on her eighty-first birthday, in 1900, the emperor sent 972 bottles of that rare wine, Tokaji Aszú,

° Tokay is the name of an American dessert wine. However, it has come to be the Americanized name of the wines from the Tokaj area in Hungary. Because the use of Tokay with regard to Hungarian wines has become so widespread, we bow to that common usage, and henceforth in this section the wines of Tokaj will be called Tokay.

The letter *i* affixed to the name of a town means "from." For example, an Aszú wine from Tokaj would be labeled Tokaji Aszú.

which Professor Saintsbury called "no more a wine but a prince of liqueurs."

The wines commonly called Tokay derive their name from the small village of Tokaj in the Hegyalja country (northeastern Hungary) at the foot of the Carpathian Mountains. The delimited Tokaj district is a small plateau, less than half the size of New York City, around which rise the Carpathians. Although this district is fifteen hundred feet above sea level, the protecting mountains produce a special condition that makes possible extremes of weather highly beneficial to growing the grape. These climates vary from bitterly cold winters, accompanied by howling winds, to cool, dry weather in the spring, to very hot summer weather. The rains of early fall give way to a fine, dry Indian summer, important for the grapes, which are left hanging on the vine for extra maturing. The soil is rich in iron and contains some lime. It is of volcanic origin, and the dominant rock of the region is trachyte.

The most important grape in Tokay is the Furmint. Young Furmint grapes are quite thick skinned, but as they ripen the skin becomes thinner and more transparent. The sun penetrates it, evaporating most of the water in the juice, with a consequent concentration of the natural sugar. Sometimes the grapes that ripen earliest are so full of juice that the skin bursts and some of the juice runs out. Oddly enough, a new skin forms over the crack and the grapes do not rot, as would normally happen. The grapes are allowed to hang on the vine until they develop *pourriture noble.* They are called Trockenbeeren.

The combination of the grapes, which may also include Hárslevelü and the Muskotály, the minerals in the soil, the climatic conditions, and the special manner in which the grapes are treated is unique to the Hungarian Tokaj-Hegyalja. For this reason no other wine-producing region has been able to imitate Tokay. (Tokay grapes, said to have originated in Algeria, are no relation to the Furmint but are table grapes that are sometimes used to make a rather characterless wine that has no relation to the Tokay of Hungary.)

To make Tokay, the grapes are gathered in wooden vessels known as *puttonos,* which hold about 30 quarts. The universal measure in the Hegyalja is the *gönci hordó,* or "cask from Gönc," which holds 120 to 140 liters (about 30 to 35 gallons). It is the number of *puttonos* of overripe Furmint grapes per *gönc* cask that determines the quality and richness of the Tokay.

There are three main types of Tokay: Szamorodni, Aszú, and Eszencia. *making the wine*

SZAMORODNI. This wine is made in much the same way as any other white wine, in the lower sections of the plateau where the grapes do not shrivel and in those years when weather conditions have not been favorable for the Trockenbeeren. Szamorodni is an excellent dry wine, with a "fresh-bread-crust" flavor. It is a full-blown wine, with an alcoholic strength of 14 percent. In years when there are not enough Trockenbeeren to make a commercial quantity of Aszú, they are pressed with the other grapes and a sweet Szamorodni results.

Aszú. When one considers that the average yield of all the vines in the Tokaj-Hegyalja is only 2,650,000 gallons and that Aszú wine represents less than 1 percent, it is apparent that this wine is extremely rare.

In making Aszú (very rich Tokay), the Trockenbeeren are first kneaded into a pulp in a trough. Then the proper proportion of must, pressed from ordinarily ripened grapes, is poured over the pulp, and the mixture is stirred at intervals. The wine is racked after twelve to forty-eight hours of fermentation. In the *gönc* cask, where the bung hole is not tightly closed, a slow fermentation-oxidation proceeds for several years in cool surroundings.

It is the number of *puttonos* of Trockenbeeren (overripe Furmint) that determines the quality of the wine. The wines are labeled three, four, or five *puttonos* in accordance with the number of *puttonos* of overripe Furmint grapes added to the must. Three Puttonos contains about 30 percent Trockenbeeren; Four Puttonos contains about 40 percent; and Five Puttonos, the richest and finest quality that we see in this country, contains about 50 percent Trockenbeeren. Aszú wines are not made every year, only when the vintage is moderately successful.

P. Morton Shand relates Robert Druitt as saying that "Tokay has a flavor of green tea, but an amalgam of the scents of meadow-sweet, acacia-blossom, and the lime-tree in flower, rendered perceptible to the palate . . . is possibly somewhere nearer the mark. No wine possesses such a tremendous force and volume of flavor."

It is the natural sweetness and natural high alcohol content, often exceeding 14 percent, that raise Tokaji Aszú wine so high in the estimation of wine lovers.

ESZENCIA, ESSENZ, OR ESSENCE. In exceptionally successful and plentiful years only Trockenbeeren are put in a cask. The juice that collects without any pressure other than the weight of the Trockenbeeren is allowed to ferment apart and is called Eszencia. This is a fabulous wine that takes years to develop and will live for centuries. There were Eszencias, notably in Poland, over 200 years old. A newspaper account of the marriage of the president of Poland in 1933 reported that toasts were made with 250-year-old wine: "The wine, if good, could only have been Essence of Tokay, and the centuries-old friendship between Poland and Hungary would seem to support this conclusion."

Very little Eszencia is ever made. It is rare and almost unprocurable, as what little is produced is used mostly for enriching the Aszús of poorer years.

HOW AND WHEN TO SERVE TOKAY

Dry Szamorodni should be served well chilled. With its full-bodied dryness it makes an excellent aperitif or all-around table wine.

Sweet Szamorodni may be served at room temperature or cooled. It can be used as any sweet white wine is, but it is more properly a dessert wine.

Aszús have a ripe, luscious quality and should be slightly cooled. They are dessert wines of the first order, but they are more often enjoyed by themselves. A small glass is often one of the most tonic and wholesome restoratives one can take.

Tokay wines spend three or four years in cask, and can develop even further in the bottle. They usually appear as vintage wines, with the number of *puttonos* stated on the label. While the traditional one-half-liter (500 ml, 17 ounce) long-necked bottle is used throughout the world, the U.S. laws now require the wine to be in a 750 ml bottle.

OTHER HUNGARIAN TABLE WINES

Winemaking is an important part of Hungarian agriculture, as wine is produced in fifty of her sixty-three *Megye* ("counties"). Most of this wine is drunk locally, but Hungary also produces some very fine *Vörös* ("red") and *Feher* ("white") table wines whose quality is known and appreciated worldwide. The wines are labeled with the name of the town first, followed by either the name of the grape used or the type of wine.

There are five main wine producing regions. The first four are rough and mountainous, with topsoil of volcanic origin, contributing to the fiery character of many of these wines. The Tokaj-Hegyalja region, in the northeast, has

wine regions

WINE REGIONS
OF
HUNGARY

WILLIAM LEMBECK

already been discussed. To the west, lies the Northern Hungarian wine region, centered around the towns of Eger and Debrö. Even further west is the Northern Transdanubia region, whose main towns include Somló and Sopron. In this region lies the largest lake in Europe, Lake Balaton. On the northern shore, where the water moderates the climate, is Badacsony, center of the vineyards producing the best quality white table wines. The fourth main region, the Southern Transdanubian, bordering Yugoslavia, contains the towns of Villány-Pècs and Szekszárd, where both red and white table wines are produced.

Finally we come to the Great Plain region, where the soil is sandy, and which produces many wines that are less famous. Magyar Riesling, however, offers good value. The capitol city of Budapest is here.

grape varieties

Grape varieties grown today can be considered native species. Chief among these for white wines are Furmint, Hárslevelü, Kéknyelü, Leányka, and Muskotaly (Muscat). The Kadarka is an important native red-wine grape. In addition to native varieties, a number of European varieties are grown. Some whites are Olaszrizling (Italian Riesling), Szilvani (Sylvaner), and Szürkebarát (Pinot Gris). Reds are Cabernet, Pinot Noir, and Médoc Noir (Merlot).

white wines

Typical Hungarian wines and descriptions of their taste are:

TOKAJI FURMINT. A complex sweet wine with a dry finish, made in the same district as the Tokaji wines mentioned previously. This wine differs from other Tokaji wines since it uses only Furmint.

SOMLÓI FURMINT. A fragrant wine that resembles the Tokaji Furmint.

BADACSONYI KÉKNYELÜ. From the Badacsony district on the north shore along Lake Balaton comes this gold-green, medium-dry wine, with a bouquet reminiscent of new-mown hay. Kéknyelü is the name of the vine and it means "blue-stalked."

BADACSONYI SZÜRKEBARÁT. A medium-dry, golden table wine from Badacsony. The vine is named Szürkebarát, which translates as "gray friar"; it is the Pinot Gris of France. The wine derives its distinctive flavor from the volcanic soil of Mount Badacsony.

BADACSONYI RIZLING. A dry, crisp wine with a spicy fragrance.

DEBRÖI HÁRSLEVELÜ. A medium-sweet wine with a pleasing perfume from the small wine district of Debrö in northern Hungary, near the town of Eger. It is produced from the Hárslevelü grape, whose name means "linden-leaf."

LEÁNYKA. A light table wine from the traditional vine-growing mountain villages around the city of Eger. The name, meaning "young girl," refers to the softness and delicacy of the wine.

MUSKOTALY. One of the lightest and most highly perfumed wines of Hungary, with a pronounced Muscat flavor. Made in various districts, it is always a pleasant wine, although not one of the finest.

EGRI BIKAVÉR. Because of its deep, red color, it is called Bikavér, or "bull's blood," and is probably the best-known Hungarian red wine. It is supposed to have fortified the inhabitants of Eger, enabling them to withstand the siege by the Turks in the sixteenth century. Today it is much lighter and fruitier.

SZEKSZÁRDI VÖRÖS. A dry red wine from the town of Szekszárd, south of Lake Balaton. This is one of the oldest wine regions of Hungary, dating from Roman times. The wine is made from the Kadarka grape and is dry and well balanced. It was a favorite wine of Franz Liszt. It sometimes appears as "Magyar Vörös."

NEMES KADAR. The name means "noble Kadar," and the wine is made from the Kadarka grape. It has a very bright red color and is light bodied with some sweetness.

VILLÁNYI BURGUNDI. This is the best-known red wine from this southern area. It is fruity, dry, and spicy.

VILLÁNYI MERLOT. This wine is dark red and very rich, with good acidity.

Some sparkling wines are also made in Hungary, using the Champagne method and the Charmat process. They are vinified both dry and slightly sweet.

Typical Hungarian vintage scene. Gathering grapes to produce the red Egri Bikavér at Eger, Hungary.

7. LUXEMBOURG

history   Vines have been grown in Luxembourg since Roman times. Until World War II, however, the wines were mostly consumed within the duchy, and many of them were blended with German wines. After World War II a brief effort was made to promote Luxembourg wines outside the country, but the combination of French and German competition and a large internal demand for wine made this effort fail.

Luxembourg is a small wine producer, ranking forty-third in world production, with an annual yield that has declined to one and one-third million gallons. The residents of Luxembourg rank sixth in consumption, however, at thirteen gallons per capita, necessitating imports from France and Italy.

wine regions   This inland duchy, which is 999 square miles in area, is surrounded by Belgium on the west and north, France on the south, and Germany on the east. Luxembourg is separated from Germany by the Moselle River, and it is along the Moselle that Luxembourg's vineyards lie.

The Moselle River actually begins in France, but before it reaches the famous Moselle wine region in Germany it cuts through Luxembourg, with vineyards along its western bank. This gives the vineyards an eastern slope and exposure to the morning sun.

The best wine-producing villages are Wormeldange, Remich, Wintringen, Ehnen, Grevenmacher, and Wasserbillig. Each main town has cooperatives made up of many small vineyards.

grape varieties and wines   As in Germany, the finest grape grown is the Riesling. Pinot varieties include Pinot Blanc, Ruländer (Pinot Gris), and Auxerrois. The Sylvaner, Müller-Thurgau, Traminer, Elbling, and Muscat Ottonel round out the list.

Luxembourg wines are light and not as flowery as their German counterparts, although they do have a touch of sweetness. They appear in Moselle-style green fluted bottles. Wines bottled under government supervision have the words *Marque Nationale* on a neck label.

8. ROMANIA

Catching up with the country's demand, Romanian wine production has reached the point where a large quantity is finding its way into the export market, with some entering the United States. Romania has always been a large producer and a big consumer as well. On an international scale this relatively small country ranks eighth in production, with an average 220 million gallons produced annually, and twelfth in consumption, averaging almost 8 gallons per capita.

Romania has always been the most important wine producer of the Balkan nations (Albania, Bulgaria, Romania, and Yugoslavia), with archaeologists claiming that vines were planted six thousand years ago. Romania's war-torn history has alternately enlarged and diminished its land area, depending on its alliance with a conqueror nation or a conquered nation. Before World War I the country consisted of a narrow, curved strip of land encompassing Moldavia and Wallachia. These lands were in the prime viticultural belt that passed through France's Bordeaux and Burgundy vineyards, as well as Italy's Piedmont region. Between 1919 and 1945 Romania's borders expanded to include Transylvania, acquired from Hungary, and Bessarabia, from the Russian Empire. This meant that large areas of vineyards came under Romanian rule. After World War II the loss of Bessarabia and some of Moldavia to the U.S.S.R. cut Romania's production by about 40 percent. Continued plantings, both private and cooperative, have now increased its output to a prodigious amount.

history

Although the Carpathian mountain range covers a major portion of this country, the foothills provide sunny slopes over large areas. Wine-growing areas stretch southward from the northeast to the Black Sea and then curve westward to the western part of the country.

wine regions

WILLIAM LEMBECK

The many wine regions include the Moldavia area which borders on the U.S.S.R. This area includes the vineyards of Cotnari in the northeast; south of Cotnari are the vineyards of Focşani, composed of Odobesti, Panciu, and Nicoresti. The Murfatlar vineyards along the Black Sea are in the southeast. The Dealul Mare vineyards are inland from the Black Sea, near the city of Ploeşti, nestled in the southeastern Carpathian foothills. The Tîrnave vineyards, the most important in Romania, are in the heart of Transylvania, and spread along the Tîrnave River in the center of Romania. The Drăgăşani and Segarcea vineyards are in the southern plains, bordering on Bulgaria. The Tirol and Minis vineyards are located in the most westerly part of the country, in the province of Banat.

white grapes   RIESLING. Grown extensively throughout Romania, Riesling is often used as the major grape in a blend to produce such wines as Perla de Tîrnave. In addition to these aromatic and often slightly sweet wines, Riesling produces varietal wines with regional designations, such as Riesling de Tîrnave or Riesling de Dealul Mare.

FETEASCĂ. This is a native variety that is suitable to many regions of the country. It is used in blends from such regions as Cotnari, Tîrnave, and Focşani. Its wine also appears under a varietal label, such as Fetească de Tîrnave.

CHARDONNAY. This noble grape takes on a different character when grown in the Murfatlar vineyards. It makes a dessert wine, rich and honeylike, and not the usual wine that comes from Chardonnay in the rest of the world.

GRASĂ. Grown in Cotnari, this grape often gets some "noble rot," making wine with a honeyed aroma and a full, rich taste.

ITALIAN RIESLING, FURMINT, MUSCAT OTTONEL, AND TRAMINER are other white grapes used throughout Romania.

red grapes   CABERNET SAUVIGNON. This noble grape is found in many of the quality red wines of Romania, notably those from the Murfatlar, Dealul-Mare, and Focşani regions.

PINOT NOIR. This grape is planted in the same regions as the Cabernet Sauvignon. The wines from this grape are full bodied and improve with age.

KADARKA. This Balkan grape is used to make the popular Kadarka de Banat, a big red wine with a rich aroma.

BĂBEASCĂ. This native variety is notable for a wine it produces in the Focşani region called Băbească de Nicoreşti.

Romanian wines that are exported have the letters V.S.O. for wines with an appellation of origin, and are of high quality. The letters V.S.O.C. are the same as V.S.O., with the addition of a numerical quality grade, with number 1 being the best.

Vines growing on terraced ground above Visperterminen, Valais. (*Courtesy Swiss Tourist Bureau, New York*)

9. SWITZERLAND

Surrounded by major wine-producing countries, Switzerland is intensely wine conscious. It is both a producer (about thirty million gallons in good years) and a consumer (about twelve gallons per capita) and imports a great deal of wine from Italy, France, and Spain, among other countries. Most of this is red wine, since two-thirds of the wine produced in nineteen of Switzerland's twenty-two cantons is white.

history

Swiss vineyards date back to Roman times, when vines were first cultivated around Lakes Neuchâtel, Morat, and Bienne. In the Swiss mountains, passes, such as the Simplon and Saint Gotthard, led to France, Austria, Germany, and Italy and thus became the highroads of the Middle Ages.

geography

The Alps are an important influence on Swiss viticulture. They shield the Valais area from winds and storms, for example, resulting in a temperate climate in summer, even though winters are cold.

Many vineyards are at high altitudes, carefully terraced. Visperterminen, which is at an altitude of four thousand feet, is the highest vineyard in Europe. Because of the cold climate and high altitude, most vineyards face south over lakes and rivers to benefit from both direct and reflected sunlight.

Much of the thirty thousand acres under vine is irrigated with water from melting glaciers through a system of canals.

grape varieties

While some ancient Roman vines are still grown, such as the Arvine, Amigne, Humagne, and Rèze, the invading dukes of Burgundy brought European varieties with them, and it is these grapes that are grown in Switzerland today. The early indigenous grapes have been replaced, for the most part, by Chasselas, Pinot Noir, and Gamay.

white grapes

The Chasselas is the most important white-wine grape, and it appears under several names in different parts of Switzerland. In Valais it is called the Fendant, in Vaud it is the Dorin, near Geneva it is the Perlan, and in the German cantons it is the Gutedel. In Neuchâtel it is called the Chasselas.

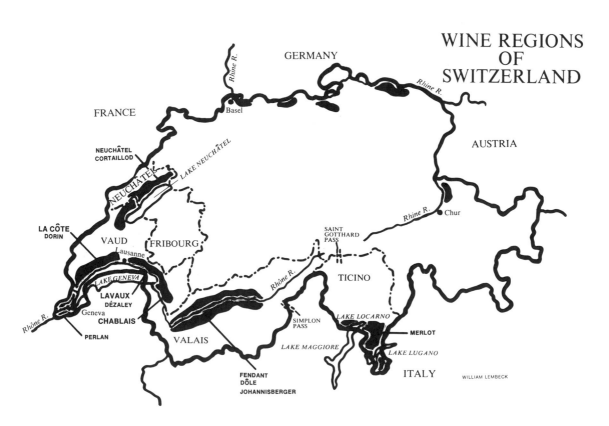

WINE REGIONS
OF
SWITZERLAND

WILLIAM LEMBECK

The Sylvaner grape appears in Valais, Vaud, and Geneva, while a cross between Riesling and Sylvaner is grown in the German cantons. The Traminer grape in Valais is sometimes called the Savagnin.

Red wine grapes of French origin are the Pinot Noir and Gamay of Burgundy and the Merlot of Bordeaux. In the German cantons the Pinot Noir is known as the Blauburgunder and the Clevner. The Gamay, in Valais, is called the Goron. The Merlot, a newer vine to Switzerland, grows in Ticino, an Italian region, along with the Italian varieties Nebbiolo and Bondolo. *red grapes*

The Italian and French cantons of Ticino, Valais, Vaud, Geneva, Neuchâtel, and Fribourg produce 90 percent of the wine in Switzerland. *wine regions and wines*

On the southwestern frontiers of Switzerland is the Lake Geneva region, which is subdivided into smaller regions. Chablais, southeast of Lake Geneva, produces good reds and pleasant whites. East of Lausanne is Lavaux, where one of the finest white wines, Dézaley, is produced from the Chasselas grape. West of Lausanne is La Côte, producing a fresh white wine called Dorin. On the tip of the lake is Geneva itself, the third largest producer. Red wines are produced in Vaud from the Gamay and Pinot Noir grapes, and are labeled Salvagnin.

The Valais, a long valley along the Rhône River, is third largest in area and first in wine production. This canton is favored with good soil and climate. The best wine is Fendant, and some wine called Johannisberger is produced from the Sylvaner. Dôle, considered the best red wine of Switzerland, is made from 60 percent Pinot Noir, the balance being Gamay.

The Seeland area, which includes Lakes Neuchâtel, Morat, and Bienne, has a chalky soil rich in limestone and makes especially good white wines. North of Lausanne, on the north shore of Lake Neuchâtel, is the home of the clean, fresh white wine called Neuchâtel. It is made from the Chasselas grape and undergoes a second fermentation in the bottle. The wine has a slight *pétillance* because of this and is most refreshing. A light red and a "partridge-eye" rosé are produced from the Pinot Noir in the Seeland area. The best red wine is called Cortaillod, named for the village where it is made.

Ticino (Tessin), an Italian region on the other side of the Saint Gotthard Pass from Valais, is on the southern slopes of the Alps. There are ten thousand growers around Lakes Locarno, Lugano, and Maggiore. The climate is temperate, and the Merlot has been expanded from two thousand to thirty thousand acres in the past twenty-five years. Merlot produces eight million gallons annually, and the best is labeled *Viti*, for the appellation Vino Ticinese, if it passes government inspection.

Along the Rhine River, from Chur to Basel, are the German cantons, which produce about 10 percent of Swiss wines. Here red wine, which is 80 percent of the local production, is made from the Pinot Noir.

10. U.S.S.R.

The U.S.S.R. is the fourth largest wine-producing country in the world, ranking after Italy, France, and Spain with an estimated production of 850 million gallons. One would not expect such large production from a country whose severe winters are legendary, but in the southeastern region, where grapes are planted, the winters are actually mild and can be tolerated by the vine. It is the Black Sea that has this moderating effect on the climate. Viticultural techniques, such as insulating the vines for the winter under blankets of dirt, also account for successful wine production.

Wine consumption in Russia is 4 gallons per capita, and most of this is in sweet wines. There is a decided preference for wines on the sweet side; dry still and sparkling wines are in the minority.

WINE REGIONS
OF THE
U.S.S.R.

wine regions

There are three main regions of wine production and a few other, less important, ones. The three major regions are Moldavia, Crimea, and the republics of Georgia, Armenia, and Azerbaijan (Azerbaidzhan). Table and sparkling wines are also produced around Krasnodar and around the Don River, below Rostov.

Moldavia, north of the Black Sea, is one of the smallest Soviet republics, yet it produces the greatest quantity of wine. Production from this region accounts for one-fourth of the total amount of wine produced in the U.S.S.R. The wines are similar in style to the wines of neighboring Romania and Bulgaria. In fact, Moldavia was part of Romania until 1940 and was known as Bessarabia. Both red and white table and fortified wines are produced here.

Crimea produces the highest-quality wines of the U.S.S.R. The area is a peninsula that extends far into the Black Sea and eastward across the Straits of Kerch into the Kuban Valley below the western Caucasus. Table, dessert, and sparkling wines, as well as some brandy, are produced here. Massandra is the location of the largest combine of Crimean wine collectives.

Farther east, along the southern slopes of the Caucasus Mountains, are the republics of Georgia, Armenia, and Azerbaijan, bordering Turkey. Georgia produces fine table wines, but it is fortified and dessert wines for which the republics are most famous.

grape varieties

In Russia there are *vinifera* varieties, local grapes, and hybrids. In the Moldavian region there is Cabernet Sauvignon, Aligoté, Riesling, and Traminer. One of the local grapes, which makes a dry white wine, is Fetyaska. East of Moldavia, in the Ukraine, many hybrids had been planted, but these vineyards are being converted to *vinifera* varieties.

The Crimean region has the same grapes as Moldavia, but there is also a great deal of Muscat planted, which is used in dessert wines.

Georgia, Armenia, and Azerbaijan grow local grapes that include Saperavi and Mzvane, which produce red wines, and Rkatsiteli, a white-wine grape. Rkatsiteli has been grown successfully in the Livermore Valley in California, where it was planted experimentally in 1969 by the Concannons as part of an exchange of vines.

11. YUGOSLAVIA

history

The vine has always flourished wherever the ancient Greeks and Romans had their influence. Yugoslavia was doubly blessed in this matter, with its southern vineyards neighboring Greece and its northern vineyards under the Roman influence.

This state of affairs continued until the Turks took over and decreed that the vines be uprooted. From then viticulture ceased until the 1800s. It was only in the north, in the lands that belonged to Austria, that vines continued to grow, and these wines continue to show the Austrian influence.

Yugoslavia as we know it today was formed after World War I from Slovenia, Croatia, Serbia, Bosnia-Herzegovina, Montenegro, and northern Macedonia. Wine production in Yogoslavia is about 175 million gallons annually, and wine has become Yugoslavia's second largest export, with 20 percent going to East and West Germany, Switzerland, Russia, Canada, Japan, the United Kingdom, and the United States. Local consumption is 7¼ gallons per capita.

wine regions   The wine regions of Yugoslavia have maintained the identities they had when they were separate states under the Austro-Hungarian Empire: Slovenia, Croatia, Serbia, and Macedonia.

WINE REGIONS OF YUGOSLAVIA

WILLIAM LEMBECK

Vintage in vineyards near Belgrade. (*Courtesy Yugoslav Information Center, New York*)

Slovenia, in the northwest, has two wine districts. One is in the valleys of the Sava and Drava rivers, near Austria, and the other is along a short stretch of the Adriatic Sea, near Trieste at the Italian border.

Croatia produces varied styles of wines in three main sections. In the north, near Slovenia, the vineyards also come under the influence of the Sava and Drava rivers. Light white wines are produced here, similar to those of Slovenia. The Istrian Peninsula, in the north near Trieste, projects into the Adriatic Sea. The vines are protected by the tempering influence of this large body of water.

Dalmatia, also in Croatia, is a coastal region, stretching for almost 150 miles along the Adriatic Sea. It produces mostly red wines, in one of the largest cooperatives.

The Serbian region is the largest wine-producing area, contributing 35 percent of Yugoslavia's total wine output. It adjoins Romania and Bulgaria.

This inland area makes mostly white wines, with a few reds and rosés, all primarily from the Prokupac grape.

Macedonia is the southernmost region of Yugoslavia, with Albania to the west, Bulgaria to the east, and Greece, which has been the major influence on Macedonian viticulture, to the south.

grape varieties

All types of vines are grown in Yugoslavia. There are European *vinifera*, some native varieties, and hybrids that were planted at the time of *Phylloxera* intrusion.

White wine grapes include Traminac (Traminer), Beli Burgundac (Pinot Blanc), Sauvignon, Sémillon, Malvasia, several varieties of Rizlings, as well as the native Sipon, Zilavka, and Smedervka.

Red *vinifera* are represented by Burgundac (Pinot Noir), Bogonja (Gamay), Cabernet, and Merlot. Native grapes are Teran, Plavac, Skadarka, Babic, Plavina, Začinak, and the ubiquitous Prokupac.

wines

Yugoslavia produces table, sparkling, and dessert wines. They are either varietal wines labeled with a regional suffix or blended wines labeled with a regional name. Most vintages of different years are blended, and vintage labeling is not so important.

Wine production in Yugoslavia is dominated by large cooperatives that have thousands of members. Since there is such great interest in the export market, great care is taken with quality. New classifications are being developed for different levels of wines.

Slovenia, which once belonged to Austria, produces wines in an Austrian and German style. These wines are, however, higher in alcohol, and some subtlety is exchanged for more fullness. The most famous wine is Ljutomer, which is named after the town of that name.

Croatia's inland white wines are similar to those of Slovenia, with some of the same character and perfume. Istria and Dalmatia, on the Adriatic coast, produce red wines in a robust Italian style. These wines are big and full, with high alcohol and tannin content. Opol is a famous rosé wine of Dalmatia.

Serbian wines are mostly of the carafe, or jug, type and are named for the district of origin.

Macedonia, less influenced by other European countries, produces wines of a more native style. This region, with new plantings, is becoming more important.

11
THE WINES OF THE UNITED STATES

history

America is one of the richest countries in the world in viticultural natural resources. More than half of the known species of grapevines (*Vitis*) are indigenous to our continent. According to popular legend a band of Norse Vikings reached the eastern shores of America and found a profusion of wild grapes growing in the forests. They were so impressed by the abundant grapevines that they named the new land Vineland the Good, and so it was known in Icelandic sagas for centuries. The truth is that the Norsemen never came as far south as the grape country, and we know now that they mistook mountain cranberries for grapes. But had they traveled far enough south they would have found a land rich in vines after all.

The Indians used grapes as a staple fruit, and in early settlers' narrations the grape is found in the list of resources and treasures of the newfound continent that indeed proved to be a natural vineyard.

The winemaker's life is never an easy one, and in the United States it was more discouraging than in other lands. Our earliest settlers on the eastern seaboard made wine from the native grapes, but the wines were unlike those of Europe; the settlers wanted wines similar to the European types with which they were familiar. Since the native vines grew so luxuriantly, the settlers reasoned that their tastes could be easily satisfied by planting European (*Vitis vinifera*) varieties. In Mexico, the missionary priests did much the same thing and had great success. In the East, however, the settlers' efforts were doomed to failure.

Phylloxera

The reasons for the miserable failure of the eastern attempt to grow *Vitis vinifera* grapes were many, but the most immediate cause was the presence of native fungus diseases, such as powdery mildew (*oïdium*), downy mildew, black rot, and Pierce's Disease. After those came the scourge of the grapevine, *Phylloxera vastatrix*.

Phylloxera vastatrix is, to the best of our knowledge, native to North America. It is a plant pest of the louse family that lives on the sweet, soft roots of the grapevine. *Phylloxera* attacks the roots very slowly, over a period of years, and the results are always ruinous. This dreaded plant louse probably did not actually do much damage to the early American plantings of *vinifera* varieties, since those were destroyed by diseases before they would have been killed by *Phylloxera*.

Sometime between 1858 and 1863, Europe imported many American vines for experimental purposes. It is practically certain that the deadly *Phylloxera* was brought in on these American rootstocks, which also carried native American fungus diseases. The proximity of the European vineyards to one another facilitated the spread of *Phylloxera*. Within a few years it had become a true scourge, and from 1865 to 1890 *Phylloxera* devastated the vineyards of Europe eastward from France to Russia and northward from Spain to Germany; eventually the pest even appeared in Australia. In the United States it seriously damaged most of the vineyards of California in 1880, when, ironically, it was brought in on contaminated European vinestocks.

It is impossible today to estimate the actual pecuniary loss, but in 1888 M. Lalande, president of the Chamber of Commerce of Bordeaux, calculated that the loss to France alone amounted to $2 billion, or twice the indemnity paid to Germany in 1871 after the Franco-Prussian War.

Phylloxera subsists on the sap of the vine, which it obtains by piercing the bark of the root with its sharp proboscis. One solitary louse can do very little damage, but each lays many eggs that hatch in six to ten days. When only a few days old, the young attach themselves to the root and within three weeks they become adults that lay more eggs. It has been estimated that a single female that lays a batch of eggs in March and then dies would have twenty-five million descendants by October.

Every known method of combating diseases of the vine was employed but with little success. It was not until the European viticulturists discovered that the native American rootstocks were hardier—and immune to *Phylloxera*—that they found that the solution to their problem was to graft the European vines onto resistant American rootstocks. Even then it took many years of viticultural investigation to find the best rootstocks that were suitably resistant yet compatible with European vines.

During the frantic search for a solution to the problem, many nurseries and grape specialists worldwide started an intensive program of hybridization between *Vitis vinifera* varieties and native American varieties to produce new selections with the *Phylloxera* resistance of the American parents and the wine characteristics of the *vinifera* parents.

The United States has radically and vitally influenced European and world viticulture and wine. Yet even though American rootstocks are in fairly general use in Europe, there has been no significant change in the basic character of the various grape varieties that have been grafted onto them and form the vines themselves. The wines made from these grapes are essentially the same as before grafting.

To the best of our knowledge Chilean vineyards have hardly been infested by *Phylloxera*. There are also certain scattered vineyard areas with sandy soil, such as Colares in Portugal, that are *Phylloxera*-free. But every other non-American vineyard region of the world has been invaded and devastated by this louse, and all have had to graft their *Vitis vinifera* vines onto American *Phylloxera*-resistant rootstocks.

Even in California, where European varieties of grapes are grown almost exclusively, it is usually necessary to use certain resistant American rootstocks as a defense against the ever present *Phylloxera*, so truly surnamed *vastatrix* ("devastating"). Some plantings, notably in Monterey County, have been made with European varieties on their own roots. The growers took this calculated risk (which saved time and money when the vineyards were being established) since *Phylloxera* requires heavy soil, and the soil in Monterey County is granitic, very light, and sandy. The risk was also reduced because grapes had never been planted in that region before.

Prohibition

Near the end of the nineteenth century the U.S. wine industry was producing wines fine enough to win some medals and gain recognition in expositions in France. In fact, there are many strong indications that American wines were well on their way to becoming firmly established when another and more fatal blight was visited upon the vineyards—national Prohibition.

There was consternation among the winemakers in 1919. What were they going to do with the grapes, which were good only for making wine? Smaller and less sweet than table or raisin grapes, they were poor travelers because of their thin, easily bruised skins. The inevitable happened—many vineyards were uprooted and replanted with more salable types of grapes, and in some cases with other fruits.

Amateur winemaking—perfectly legal during Prohibition—flourished during this period. The true wine grapes from California, in addition to not shipping well, did not look as plump as some of the raisin and table varieties, and many of the new, inexperienced winemakers did not know enough to buy the better grapes. As a result, wine grapes were replaced by the less useful table varieties that the amateurs demanded. By the end of Prohibition amateur winemakers were producing ninety million gallons of wine per year, and the grape acreage was close to 35 percent greater than that in 1919. Only in 1975 did California acreage return to Prohibition levels.

The legacy of Prohibition, however, was a country almost bereft of fine wine grapes and a few scattered wineries that could still produce quality wine. The country had to rebuild its reputation for quality while it suffered from the added disadvantage of supplying quantity for a thirsty public.

MAKING THE WINE

At the time of Repeal American winemakers faced many problems. During Prohibition nearly all their vineyards had been replanted with other crops or with table and raisin grapes. Repeal came suddenly. Ipso facto, on December 5, 1933, the day of Repeal, the winemaker was expected to have wine ready even though until then it was illegal to make wine commercially. Regardless of what cold-storage grapes were used, it still took time to crush the grapes, ferment the must, and allow the wine to develop.

The first few post-Repeal years were very difficult for American wine producers, but they diligently set about resolving their production bottlenecks. New methods were tried. Some were discarded, but many were adopted and have become standard practice not only in the United States but in most wine regions of the world today.

The method of making wine in the United States varies, of course, from vineyard to vineyard and region to region. It also depends to some extent on the size of the vineyard. Even the smaller vineyards in the coastal parts of California in the counties surrounding San Francisco Bay tend to follow modern methods, from gathering the grapes to bottling the wine. In the small vineyards of Europe usually one type of wine is produced, not only in a single vineyard, but in an entire region. Very often the grower is a small farmer who makes, in some instances, only a few hogsheads of wine.

In the United States, however, where individual vineyards may run to thousands of acres and, in nearly all cases, produce several types and classes of wines, large-scale production is inevitable. Where the vineyards are extensive, and enormous quantities of grapes ripen at the same time, it becomes impossible to follow the small-scale European methods, and new, modern ones must be employed.

table wines   The grapes are trucked to the winery as soon as they are picked. After being examined, weighed, and sugars checked, they are dumped onto conveyors that carry them to a power-driven destemmer and crusher. This breaks the grape skins without breaking the seeds, allows the juice to run freely, and, finally, separates and throws out the stems.

As in Europe, in making red wines the grapes and juice are conveyed directly to the fermenting vats, while in making white wines, the juice is separated from the skins before fermentation. In large production wineries a juicer extracts even more liquid from the fruit before pressing.

To ensure normal fermentation, wild yeasts are inhibited by the addition of sulfur dioxide (SO_2), and smooth fermentation is carried out by SO_2-acclimated culture yeasts—*Saccharomyces ellipsoideus*. Since fermenting wine generates heat, the wine must be carefully watched. Temperatures are controlled and the fermenting must is never permitted to go above 90 degrees Fahrenheit for red wines and 70 degrees Fahrenheit for whites (sometimes not

A modern method for planting a vineyard. Five rows of new vines are planted simultaneously at Pinnacles vineyard. (*Courtesy Paul Masson Vineyard, Saratoga, California*)

Boxes are scattered through this California vineyard, ready to be filled with the rich grapes as they are picked. The full boxes are then taken to the winery where the grape juice is transformed into wine. (*Courtesy Wine Institute, San Francisco, California*)

Outdoor fermenting tanks at Paul Masson Vineyards, northern California. (*Courtesy Paul Masson Vineyards, Saratoga, California*)

above 55 degrees). Higher temperatures tend to arrest fermentation and contribute to loss of bouquet. White wines especially benefit from a long, cool fermentation that retains the fruity character of the grape. A cool fermentation can be achieved by using double-jacketed stainless steel fermenting tanks that have a cooling liquid pumped between the inner and outer walls.

For certain varieties some winemakers prefer to ferment in small oak barrels. While this fermentation is more difficult to control, certain wood flavors are extracted as alcohol is produced, adding complexity to the wine.

The first, or violent, fermentation phase takes about a week, after which the still-fermenting must is run off into closed oak or California redwood vats or stainless steel tanks to complete fermentation. In some other wineries coated concrete tanks are employed. The total fermentation period takes about two weeks for red and three weeks for white wines in the cooler areas, but often less than one week for red in the warmer areas, since fermentation may be run at a higher temperature. After fermentation the new wine is placed in storage cooperage of various sizes to begin clarification, racking, and aging. Some wineries maintain air conditioning, which ensures dry, clean, mold-free cellars and precise and continuous temperature and humidity control.

Generally speaking, at the majority of wineries the most modern and improved methods of treating wines are in use, such as refrigeration, to ensure a perfectly bright, stable wine, a healthy wine free of heavy sediment.

Wine, table wine in particular, is constantly developing, with minute changes taking place. This occurs because of the action of the yeasts that may remain in the wine and because of the acids, the solids, and the other components of the wine that act and react, some with, and others against, one another. The result is a state of continual change. One of the natural phenomena of the development of a wine is the formation of cream of tartar, which settles in the form of crystalline sediment. This can be hastened if the wine is held at a low temperature for a short period of time. This is called cold stabilization and ensures that the wine, after filtering, will be less likely to throw any further deposit.

These modern Wilmes presses gently extract as much juice as possible from crushed grapes without breaking the seeds. The press on the right stands ready for loading with doors removed. A rubber bag in the center of the press is inflated to gently squeeze the grapes against the press' inside walls. A continuous screw conveyor brings the grape must from the crusher. These presses are typical of the modern equipment used in California's wineries. (*Courtesy Wine Institute, San Francisco, California*)

Since the consuming public has become accustomed to seeing so much brilliant, sediment-free wine, it has come to believe that a wine that has a natural sediment or deposit is not in good condition for serving. By the same token too many retail merchants, rather than explain the facts to their customers, take the easier path and request from the supplier a refund for or replacement of the "unsalable" wine.

dessert wines   In the production of dessert wines such as sherry, port, Muscatel, and Angelica, fermentation is arrested before all of the natural sugar of the must has been converted. The alcohol content is brought up to about 20 percent by the addition of fortification brandy, which in many cases is distilled by the brandy distillery associated with the winery itself. The wines are stored in large vats or casks and are treated in the same manner as are similar wines all over the world. They are racked periodically, so the wine will not remain on its lees, and then fined and filtered as necessary.

sherry*   Sherry in the United States is a generic wine, produced to resemble the wine made in Jerez, Spain. The essential difference in the method of producing this wine between the United States and Spain lies in the "flowering," described on page 140, that occurs in Jerez. A few California winemakers, trying to duplicate this process, have had success with film yeast, using the "submerged-*flor*" process, which has given them some unusually fine *rancio-* or nutty-flavored sherries.

Generally in California, the wine is "baked" to impart the characteristic sherry flavor. This is done by racking the wine into large tanks or vats located in cellars where the temperature is carefully maintained. The wine is kept in these baking cellars anywhere from two to six months at temperatures that vary from 100 degrees to 140 degrees Fahrenheit, depending on the length of time the wine is baked. Wine kept for only two months is held at a higher temperature and wine kept for a longer time is held at a lower temperature, similar to the baking process in Madeira. Each producer has his own formula for the method that gives the best results. The vats are heated, in some cases by hot water coils in the vat itself, while in other cases the entire cellar room is heated to the desired controlled temperature.

The baking process causes the color to deepen somewhat, gives the wine the desired tang, and develops the typical nutty flavor of California sherries.

Upon completion of the baking process, the wine is allowed to cool slowly to cellar temperature. It is then stored for aging and treated as other dessert wines to acquire mellowness, to be blended with older wines.

° The U.S. government considers all sherries to be dessert wines.

These winery workers are racking a tank of wine into smaller wooden casks where the wine will age and develop smoothness before it is bottled. Racking, or transferring by pump from a larger to a smaller container, also helps clear the wine of any deposits acquired during fermentation to ensure that the wine is brilliantly clear when it reaches the consumer. (*Courtesy Wine Institute, San Francisco, California*)

Some New York State winemakers have developed their own methods of producing sherry. One method is the Tressler process. Niagara, Concord, Dutchess, and other eastern grapes are used to produce a wine that is then fortified. These wines are stored in special vats at a temperature of 140 degrees Fahrenheit for four to six weeks. During this time oxygen is bubbled through the wine. This oxidation develops the sherry character, and when the desired flavor is obtained, the wine is fined, filtered, and aged in other barrels for months or years.

In other wineries a weathering process is used in which fortified wines of sherry character, in uncharred fifty-gallon barrels, are stored on the roof of the winery and left exposed to the sun and elements for four years. After the wines have developed the desired nuttiness and mellowness, they are blended, filtered, and bottled.

A few wineries in the United States, both in the East and in the West, have *solera* systems, begun several years ago. The sherries are aged in a way similar to the aging that is done in Spain. Some wineries even use sherry barrels imported from Spain. In this method older wines are systemically blended with younger wines.

Vermouth and the other aromatized appetizer wines are produced according to the traditional methods to be described in Chapter 15.

sparkling wines

Champagne that is produced in the United States is a generic sparkling wine, the best of which being produced in the same manner as those of Champagne, France, with a secondary fermentation in the bottle.

Because of the problems of removing the sediment from the bottles, the transfer system has been introduced into this country. This is an attempt to retain the advantages of the Champagne method, with the second fermentation in bottles, while eliminating the disadvantages of costly riddling to remove sediment. The bottles are chilled, but not frozen, standing up, rather than tilting downward. The corks are withdrawn and the wine is emptied, under pressure, into a large tank. The sparkling wine is then filtered into another pressure tank under refrigeration. Finally, it is filtered, still under pressure, into clean bottles. Wines produced in this way are often labeled "naturally fermented in *the* bottle," as distinguished from those using the Champagne method, often labeled "naturally fermented in *this* bottle."

Sparkling wines made by the Champagne method or the transfer process each have the advantage of a second fermentation in the bottle, which gives a small volume of liquid intimate contact with the yeast. Newer collaborative efforts between large houses in Champagne, France, and California have resulted in an increase of Champagne method-produced sparkling wine in California, and a decrease of generic labeling. Some of those California wineries are now using automatic riddling (see pages 71–72), which has recently been allowed in Champagne, France.

In New York State, almost all of the sparkling wine production centers around the Finger Lakes, and the transfer method predominates.

Sparkling wines are also made where the second fermentation takes place in large tanks before being bottled under pressure. This method is known as bulk process or Charmat process (named after the inventor) and must be so labeled.

Bulk process fermentation saves several years and a great deal of labor in making the wine available for market, and consequently, it is much less costly to produce. Improvements in this method, which include ways of continually stirring the wine so that it will have good contact with the yeast, have made bulk process sparkling wines good values, if somewhat less inspired than those made by the Champagne method, since both bulk process and transfer process have an additional filtration.

There is still another type of sparkling wine that is artificially carbonated by adding carbon dioxide gas in much the same way in which soft drinks are made. It cannot be called or labeled Champagne; it must be labeled carbonated wine.

Taylor and Great Western New York State Champagnes are produced by the transfer process, which allows for fermentation and aging in the bottle. (*Courtesy Taylor Wine Company, Hammondsport, New York*)

Transfer method of Champagne production in New York State. Champagne and yeast sediments are removed from bottles after secondary fermentation by the injection of nitrogen, a substance that has no effect on the taste, aroma, or carbonation of the wine. (*Courtesy Taylor Wine Company, Hammondsport, New York*)

WINE TYPES

U.S. wines fall into three types: generic,° varietal, and proprietary. Generics are merely generalized wine types with borrowed names, whose geographic origins have lost their significance, such as Chablis, claret, and Burgundy from France, and Rhine from Germany. When these names are used domestically, the place of production must also appear on the label, such as California Chablis.

A varietally labeled wine is one bearing the name of the grape variety from which the wine was made. A *vinifera* wine must have at least 75 percent of the grapes of the variety on the label used in the wine. Examples are Cabernet Sauvignon, Chardonnay, and White Riesling. *Labruscana* varieties need only have 51 percent. Examples are Concord, Dutchess, and Catawba. Blends of varietals, where no grape exceeds 75 percent, must have all grapes listed with the percentages of each, unless the wine has been given a proprietary name.

° The correct term in the U.S. regulations is *semigeneric* because of the regional designation on the label, but *generic* is popularly used.

Proprietary labeling is another way that wineries can point to the uniqueness of their wines. A proprietary name is one created by the winery that no other winery may use. Often these names invoke an image or describe the wine itself. Many wineries are developing proprietary or trademarked brand names for their specialty blends and/or everyday wines.

federal labeling laws   Both federal and state laws require specific labeling for wines. State laws, often varying from state to state, may be more stringent than those decreed by the federal government. Historically, it has been the careful winemaker who has been responsible for the increasingly high standards for U.S. wines. The consumer should study these phrases to understand what is in the bottle:

State or county designation—75 percent of the grapes must come from the area

Adjoining states (two or more)—must have percentages of wine from each state

Viticultural area (approved appellation)—85 percent of the grapes grown in the area

Vintage wine—95 percent of the grapes must come from that year

Proprietor grown or *Vintner grown*—100 percent of the grapes must come from vineyards owned or controlled by the bottler, with no area requirement

Estate bottled—100 percent of the grapes must come from an approved viticultural area, from the winery's vineyards, or from those that are controlled by the winery. All winemaking steps, including bottling, must be done at a single winery, even if an estate has more than one winery.

Produced and bottled by—75 percent of the grapes must be crushed and fermented at the winery

Made and bottled by—no minimum percent of grapes crushed and fermented at the winery

Bottled by—wines purchased and then bottled at the winery

Cellared and bottled by—wines purchased, blended, and then bottled at the winery

Alcohol content—Table wines by law must contain not less than 7 percent alcohol and not more than 14 percent alcohol. Federal regulations allow up to $1\frac{1}{2}$ percent variation in either direction for table wines, stopping at 14 percent. Thus a wine labeled $11\frac{1}{2}$ percent means that the wine could have anywhere from 10 to 13 percent alcohol by volume. Dessert wines have alcohol in excess of 14 percent but not more than 21 percent. The allowable leeway on the label is 1 percent in either direction.

Sugar content—for wines labeled Late Harvest or Late Picked the sugar content of the grapes and juice used to make the wine, as well as the residual sugar of the finished wine, must be stated on the label. It is also customary to state the percent of alcohol in these wines.

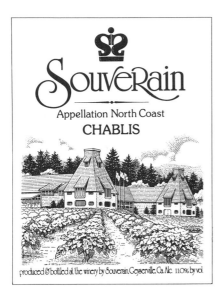

Four common types of American labels.
TOP LEFT: Generic label with a state designation.
TOP RIGHT: Varietal label with a regional designation.
BOTTOM LEFT: Varietal label with generic description.
BOTTOM RIGHT: Proprietary label.

The wines of the United States have fallen into two categories: western states, which is mainly California, and the states east of the Rocky Mountains, of which New York is the most significant.

A wine designated as the product of a state must contain a minimum percentage of grapes grown in that state, and the percentage may vary. New York, for example, requires 75 percent (the federal minimum), while California requires 100 percent.

The term *American* is also seen on labels when the producer has blended wines from two or more states, California and New York, for example, and chooses this labeling over a regional designation, which would require specific minimum percentages of grapes used.

California wines produced from *Vitis vinifera* grapes have much in common with European wines while still exhibiting their own distinct regional personalities. Eastern wines are made from several types of vines: the indigenous varieties of American grapes that are mainly American hybrids, developed in the early stages of the eastern wine industry, and some *Vitis rotundifolia;* the French hybrids, which were developed to combat the devastation from *Phylloxera*; and, with increased viticultural knowledge, *Vitis vinifera* grapes. (All of these vine types will be discussed later in this chapter.)

No specific United States wineries are mentioned in this chapter except when they are of historical significance. A list of U.S. wineries appears in Appendix G.

1. CALIFORNIA AND WESTERN WINES

history The records show that in 1518 Cortés, the Spanish conqueror and overlord of Mexico, ordered the establishment of a wine industry in the New World, obliging holders of land grants to plant one thousand vines per year for five years, for every hundred Indians living on the land. This agricultural program proved so successful that Spain, fearing harm to her own wine industry, ordered winemaking stopped and decreed that wine not imported from Spain should be considered contraband. The decree failed in its purpose; the vines, once planted, continued to bear fruit and wine was made surreptitiously.

Eventually the Spanish colonizers pushed west and then north, into what is today California. This movement was led by the missionaries, whose primary object was the propagation of the Faith.

Beautiful mountain setting for Inglenook, a northern California vineyard. (*Courtesy Wine Institute, San Francisco, California*)

It was only natural when the Church established its missions with their surrounding settlements that vines should be planted. The Franciscan padres, led by Padre Junipero Serra, planted grapes in California as early as 1769 at the San Diego Mission and for the first time found soil in North America in which the European vine would prosper and produce good wine. The arid lands of northern Mexico and Baja California did not lend themselves graciously to viticulture.

The Franciscan missionaries built twenty-one missions, reaching as far north as Sonoma, the northern terminus of *El Camino Real* ("King's Highway"). Descendants of the vines planted at these missions are still growing. The missionaries' largest winery was at the Mission of San Gabriel, near present-day Los Angeles, and the original adobe winery building, where the Indians trod the grapes, still exists with its three wine presses. There, too, the famous Trinity vine, planted by the Franciscans, flourished and bore grapes for over 170 years.

Until 1824 the Franciscans were the only wine producers in California. They did not attempt commercial production but confined their efforts to their own sacramental and table needs. At that time Joseph Chapman, an American, settled near Los Angeles and planted four thousand vines. He was followed in 1831 by a Bordeaux Frenchman, Jean Louis Vignes, who soon began producing very excellent wine and brandy. In 1832, a substantial vineyard was established in Sonoma by an Indian who grew grapes for sacramental wine for the northernmost of the missions—San Francisco de Solano. Vignes, in the meantime, was so successful that by 1840 he was chartering vessels to ship his wine and brandy to the ports of Santa Barbara, Monterey, and San Francisco. The trade, however, was still small. Then came the Gold Rush of 1849 and with it a boom in all activities. The widening of the market made it financially possible for still another and most important change in California wines.

The vines the missionaries planted came from those varieties originally brought to Mexico from Spain during the preceding three centuries. While they were true *vinifera* vines, their value for winemaking was limited. As a matter of fact, one of these vines, which had been known as the Criolla grape, lost its original European varietal identity, and is today known and classified as the Mission grape.

Because the soil and climate of California were so hospitable to the European *Vitis vinifera* family of vines, no serious attempt has been made to cultivate native American varieties in California, and all grapes grown there commercially, whether for wine, table, or raisin use, are from *vinifera* vines.

Vignes brought over choice *vinifera* cuttings from France that prospered in his vineyard, and others did likewise, but it was not until after the arrival of that amazing gentleman, Count Agoston Haraszthy, in 1849—a Johnny Appleseed to the California grapevine—that a real wine industry was developed.

The tireless and farsighted Haraszthy convinced John G. Downey, the governor of California, of the important part the wine industry could play in the development of the economy of the new state. As a result, he was sent to Europe in 1861 to select and bring back the widest possible selection of European (*vinifera*) grape varieties. He returned with over 100,000 cuttings of some 300 varieties, and in the space of a few short years he had a vineyard in the Sonoma Valley with 85,000 vines developed from imported stocks and a nursery of 460,000 vines. With this effort he set the course for commercial winemaking from which those who have followed him have benefited.

Haraszthy experimented at his Sonoma Valley vineyard and nursery, selecting those vines that showed greatest promise. These were then sold or distributed in all sections of the state. Although at first the wines obtained were rather indifferent, it was not long before the winemakers learned to improve their product and were obtaining some good, sound, drinkable wine that improved in quality each year. By 1875 California was producing four million gallons of wine a year.

Around the same time some vineyards whose names we know today were also being established: Paul Masson, Almadén, Mirassou, Charles Krug, Schramsberg, Beringer Brothers, and Inglenook.

California wines began to acquire characteristics of their own, and the custom of estate bottling was practiced at some of the best vineyards. In 1895 fifteen million gallons of wine were made, and most of it was shipped to other parts of the United States, Mexico, Central America, and Asia.

Gaining confidence in their early success, the winemakers began to compete with the European producers and by 1900 they had won gold, silver, and bronze medals, a few blue ribbons, and even grand prizes at international expositions. Many of the great names associated with the development of California and the Pacific Coast were actively engaged in the wine industry as vineyard owners: Leland Stanford, George Hearst, James G. Fair, Elias "Lucky" Baldwin, John Sutter, and Lawrence Marshall, to mention only a few.

setbacks

The vineyards of California were and are no more immune to the ravages of the elements, disease, and countless other enemies than those of other wine regions of the world. One day in 1874 a vineyard in Sonoma County was found to be withering from an unknown ailment. Soon other vineyards became similarly affected, and in less than five years the vineyards of Sonoma, Napa, Yolo, El Dorado, and Placer counties were being ravaged by the same blight. The villain turned out to be the American *Phylloxera* (grape louse). We had quite innocently exported it to Europe on American rootstocks and then reimported it into California on the European cuttings.

Another plague struck at Anaheim, southeast of Los Angeles, where a group of winemakers of German background had founded a vineyard colony.

In 1884, a bacteria spread by insects caused dried and scorched leaves on the vines. Since new growth after a vine has contracted the disease is stunted and yellowed, the vineyards of Anaheim, which had been producing over a million gallons of quality wine annually, were never replanted. This ailment has become known as Pierce's Disease.

In order to learn the cause of and find the remedy for these blights, the California State Board of Viticultural Commissioners was set up in 1880. This agency not only helped to conquer the plant diseases but also did much to improve wine quality and production practices. It also sponsored an experimental station for grape growing and wine production under the auspices of the College of Agriculture of the University of California. This station, located today at Davis, California, seventy-five miles northeast of San Francisco, has continued its research work and the teaching of viticulture and enology. It is one of the leading research establishments in its field and is visited by students and scientists from all wine regions in the world.

One of the university's important contributions to the American wine industry was recommending the use of various types of disease-resistant rootstocks, such as *rupestris* Saint George, Richter 99, and Ganzin 1. Developed abroad but tested extensively in California by the University of California at Davis, some of these resistant rootstocks have become the basic rootstocks of all the world's great vineyards.

The plagues visited upon the vineyards by nature were nothing compared with the man-made blight that befell the vines as a result of the Eighteenth or Prohibition Amendment to the U.S. Constitution, which went into effect on January 1, 1919.

Thousands upon thousands of acres of vineyards that had been laboriously planted to fine wine-producing varieties that were unsuited for any other use had to be uprooted and replanted with table grape varieties or other crops. In 1934, after Repeal, the whole process began a slow reversal and the vineyards were replanted with wine-producing varieties.

Since it takes time for new vines to come into production, and the immediate post-Repeal demand far exceeded supply, many of the first wines produced and shipped from California were of indifferent quality. However, this has long since changed. In ever increasing numbers fine wines of outstanding quality are being produced, and it is generally accepted that present-day wines are, on the whole, far superior to those California produced before 1919. This is the result in great part of the efforts made by the wine producers themselves and of the severe regulations° governing standards of quality that have been adopted.

° Title 17, California Administrative Code.

WINE REGIONS
OF
CALIFORNIA

MENDOCINO

LAKE

YUBA

PLACER

SONOMA

YOLO

NAPA

SACRA-
MENTO

AMADOR

SIERRA
FOOTHILLS

GREAT
CENTRAL
VALLEY

MARIN

SOLANO

SAN
JOAQUIN

NORTH
COAST
DISTRICT

ALAMEDA

SANTA
CLARA

STANISLAUS

SANTA
CRUZ

MERCED

NORTH
CENTRAL
COAST
DISTRICT

SAN
BENITO

MADERA

FRESNO

MONTEREY

KINGS

TULARE

ACIFIC OCEAN

SAN
LUIS
OBISPO

KERN

SCALE

0   50   100   150   200 mi

SANTA
BARBARA

SOUTH
CENTRAL
COAST
DISTRICT

WILLIAM LEMBECK

SAN BERNARDINO

RIVERSIDE

SOUTHERN
CALIFORNIA
DISTRICT

SAN DIEGO

RANCHO/TEMECULA DISTRICT

recovery   The studies and research of men such as Dr. Maynard A. Amerine, Harold H. Berg, Dr. William V. Cruess, Dr. M. A. Joslyn, Dr. Harold P. Olmo, Dr. Albert J. Winkler, Dr. A. D. Webb, and other great enologists of the University of California at Davis have caused a revolution in viti-viniculture. The effect of their work on commercial wine production has been invaluable for both the winemaker and consumer.

The increased demand for wine in America began in the mid-1960s when there were 477,400 acres of vines under cultivation, only 30 percent of which were wine grapes. By 1980 there were over 660,000 acres planted, half of which produced wine grapes. Furthermore, increased technology, such as development of drip irrigation, and better insight into microclimates, combined with greater demand for land, has led to hillside plantings that would not have been considered a mere decade ago. The knowledge that microclimates, or small areas whose climates are different from the broader surrounding area, have led to plantings in regions hitherto thought unfit for wine grapes.

California faces new problems, brought about, in part, by this increased prosperity and greater production and sales. Urbanization is a constant threat to agricultural areas, and vineyards are no exception. Land is scarce and expensive, and the water available for irrigation is diminishing. Threats of pollution of both air and soil (for example, grapevines are especially susceptible to weed killers) and escalating costs for labor, materials, and interest on capital, can be deterrents to new entries into this field.

Those who are established, however, are enjoying increased sales of both the popular and inexpensive jug wines and the highly individual premium varietal wines. No longer wishing to produce wines in the shadow of Europe, winemakers have been developing their own styles, which are today enjoyed both locally and in Europe. There is no question that California has been recognized as one of the world's premier wine-growing regions.

geography   In California the climate and soil can approximate almost every viticultural region in the world, for the seven hundred miles of vineyard extend over mountain slopes, irrigated deserts, lush inland valley floors, and the moist plains of the coast. The winemaker has little difficulty obtaining a fine red wine from the Cabernet Sauvignon grape when it is grown in one of the cool coastal counties, or a jug wine from a warmer inland region. The entire spectrum of wines is covered in California.

Viticulturally, California has two great regions: the cool Coastal Counties, extending from Mendocino, north of San Francisco, all the way south to San Diego, which produce 15 percent of California's wines; and the Great Central Valley, starting at Sacramento and ending above Bakersfield in Kern County, which produces 85 percent of the wines. These two regions encompass many smaller subregions.

The Great Central Valley produces over 300 million gallons of wines that are of consistent quality year after year because of the even climate. The Coastal regions produce 57 million gallons of fine table wines. There the climate is not predictable, and vintage differences, which reflect years of drought, extreme heat, etc., are reflected in the wines.

It is a common misconception that north means cool and south means hot. California's temperatures do not depend on latitude but on an area's proximity to the coast. There are parts of southern California, around San Diego, that are cooler than the Sacramento Valley in northern California.

It is this uniqueness of area that has prompted grape growers and winemakers to try to analyze their region and set forth the characteristics that make them different from surrounding areas, and then to receive government recognition that this is so. This unique area of origin is known as "appellation" and encompasses the combination of soil and microclimates that exist within certain boundaries, which provides the wine produced there with a distinctive and identifiable character. Setting the boundaries of various regions can be filled with controversy, particularly where the economic stakes are high.

Coastal Counties

The Coastal Counties can be divided into the North Coast District, which includes, from north to south, Mendocino, Lake, Sonoma, Napa, and Solano counties; and the Central Coast District, which includes Contra Costa, Alameda, Santa Clara, Santa Cruz, San Benito, Monterey, San Luis Obispo, and Santa Barbara counties. The counties that are on the Pacific Ocean have maritime influences, which include cool nights and some fog.

MENDOCINO COUNTY,   one hundred to one hundred and fifty miles north of San Francisco, has had new wineries in the Anderson Valley, joining older, established wineries, along the Russian River, just north of the Sonoma County line. The terrain is mountainous, with grape growing concentrated in the valleys. The most famous is the Anderson Valley, west of Ukiah. The 700-acre McDowell Valley has been granted a viticultural appellation, one reason being the gravelly soil.

LAKE COUNTY,   east of Mendocino, has most of its vineyards in the southern part, around Clear Lake and Lake Berryessa. Guenoc Valley has received an appellation of single vineyard/single proprietor. The valley floor is two miles long, 300 to 700 yards wide, and at a 1,000-foot elevation.

SONOMA COUNTY,   forty to one hundred miles north of San Francisco, can be divided into two areas. Many northerly vineyards are clustered along or near the Russian River, mainly in the Alexander Valley. The more southerly vineyards are clustered in the Sonoma Valley, also known as the "Valley of the Moon." The Sonoma Valley has been given a viticultural appellation. In addition to these two valleys, many wineries are scattered throughout the county—from Carneros district in the south to the town of Cloverdale in the north.

NAPA COUNTY, about fifty to ninety miles northeast of San Francisco, boasts many wineries dating back to the beginning of northern California commercial viticulture, established along the thirty-five mile Napa Valley. The contour of the land and the area that could be cultivated led to relatively small vineyards, with newer wineries going up into the Mayacamas Mountains to the west and the inland Howle Mountains. The climate is variable, with both coastal and inland influences. The Carneros district, mentioned above in Sonoma, extends into the southern part of Napa, and is distinguished by its cool temperatures and gently rolling hills. In the northern part of the valley, near Calistoga, the influence of the Pacific is lessened, and the climate warms to Region III. Napa Valley is a viticultural appellation.

LIVERMORE VALLEY, in Alameda County, is just east of San Francisco. The valley, surrounded by arid hills, has a gravelly soil like that of the Graves district of Bordeaux. This soil releases heat at night and maintains a more constant temperature around the vines, as well as providing good drainage. The valley is only fifteen miles long and ten miles wide, but its east-west orientation allows the breezes from the Pacific Ocean to flow through easily.

SANTA CLARA, SAN BENITO, AND SANTA CRUZ COUNTIES. Santa Clara County stretches from thirty to seventy miles southeast of San Francisco, and includes the Santa Clara Valley as well as the foothills of the Santa Cruz Mountains. San Benito, south of Santa Clara has three times as much grape acreage planted. Santa Cruz, directly on the Pacific has only about one hundred acres under vine, but Santa Cruz Mountains is a viticultural appellation.

Mechanical grape harvesters can predictably do the work of from 40 to 100 pickers. L-shaped trellises, which enable wine grapes to hang freely, will enable 90 percent of the grapes to be picked without being bruised or injured. (*Courtesy Wine Institute, San Francisco, California*)

Skilled hands of a vineyard worker gather a ripe cluster of Cabernet Sauvignon grapes during harvest season. (*Courtesy Wine Institute, San Francisco, California*)

Ukiah

MENDOCINO

Cloverdale
Geyserville

Healdsburg

Russian R.

Santa Rosa

SONOMA

Sonoma

MARIN

PACIFIC OCEAN

NAPA VALLEY

NAPA

Calistoga
Saint Helena
Rutherford
Oakville
Yountville

Napa

CARNEROS VALLEY

SCALE

0   10   20   30   40 mi

ALEXANDER VALLEY

SONOMA VALLEY

SAN FRANCISCO BAY

CONTRA COSTA

San Francisco

ALAMEDA

LIVERMORE VALLEY

SAN MATEO

SANTA CLARA

SANTA CLARA VALLEY

Saratoga

Los Gatos

SANTA CRUZ MOUNTAINS

San Martin

SANTA CRUZ

WINE
REGIONS
OF THE
COASTAL
COUNTIES
(CALIFORNIA)

Paicines

SAN BENITO

Salinas

MONTEREY

MONTEREY VALLEY

Soledad

WILLIAM LEMBECK

MONTEREY COUNTY became an important viticultural area in the 1970s when some row crops and cattle ranges were displaced by grapes. The temperature of the area had been classified as suitable for grape growing in the 1930s, but nothing had been done until the increased demand for production required it. The fact that this area had never had grapes meant that there was no *Phylloxera*, and ungrafted vines were planted. The growing season is exceptionally long and cool. Monterey ranks fourth in wine grape production among California counties.

SAN LUIS OBISPO AND SANTA BARBARA are newer areas with cool enough microclimates to grow premium varieties. San Luis Obispo boasts viticultural appellations for the Santa Maria Valley and the Edna Valley. Santa Barbara's most important wine area is around the Santa Ynez Valley.

Great Central Valley

The winemaking regions of the Great Central Valley, which follow along the San Joaquin River, are hot and must be irrigated. They are naturally suited for the production of dessert wines, but with increased consumption of table wines the emphasis has shifted toward production of table wines. Many new inexpensive, good-quality varietal wines have appeared on the wine scene and are becoming known as "valley varietals."

The districts of the Great Central Valley are:

SACRAMENTO VALLEY, inland from the Coastal Counties, is the northernmost section of the Central Valley District. It is comprised of Butte, Colusa, Glenn, Sacramento, Sutter, Tehama, Yolo, and Yuba counties. New wineries are appearing in this valley, which is the coolest sector of the otherwise hot Central Valley, producing both table and dessert wines.

SIERRA FOOTHILLS, east of Sacramento, is a very old viticultural area that includes Amador, Calaveras, El Dorado, Nevada, and Placer counties, but it is Amador that has achieved viticultural distinction today. The Shenandoah Valley, a microclimate in Amador, is especially known for its very old Zinfandel vines, although other varieties are grown there also.

MODESTO. To the south, around the city of Modesto, encompassing southern San Joaquin, Stanislaus, and Merced counties, are the largest wineries in the United States, producing about 30 percent of all California wine.

CENTRAL SAN JOAQUIN VALLEY. The counties of Fresno, Madera, and Kings are hotter than other regions and are better suited for dessert wines. This area also provides about 30 percent of California wine production, with more dessert wines than any other area.

SOUTHERN SAN JOAQUIN VALLEY. Kern, Tulare, and San Luis Obispo counties make up this region and produce about 11 percent of California's wines. Production is divided between table and dessert wines.

SOUTHERN CALIFORNIA includes San Bernardino, Riverside, and San Diego, but acreage has dropped drastically due to urban encroachment. Temecula is a microclimate for premium wines in the county of San Diego.

Picturesque courtyard of a winery in the Alexander Valley. (*Courtesy Souverain*)

heat summation   Different wines are produced in the coastal and central regions because of the differences in climate. The amount of accumulated heat affects the ripening of the grapes. This total heat has been measured by a system called heat summation, developed by researchers at the University of California at Davis. Climate zones, corresponding to five categories of total heat summation, were established throughout California, enabling growers to determine which regions would be best for which grapes. Monterey County, for example, had not been a grape-growing area until the 1970s, when this research was applied. There are now thirty-three thousand acres under vine there.

Total heat summation for each region is found in the following way: between April 1 and October 31 (the growing season) each day's average temperature is determined. If the average temperature is above 50 degrees Fahrenheit, the difference between 50 degrees and the average temperature is the number of degree-days for that day. For example, if the average temperature for a given day is 70 degrees Fahrenheit, then the 20 degrees above 50 degrees would be the number of degree-days for that day. The next day's average temperature above 50 degrees would be added to the total thus far, and so on. The total number of degree-days for the growing season determines the climate zone as follows:

REGION I.   2,500 or fewer degree-days (very cool). Examples are Sonoma (Sonoma County), Oakville (Napa), and Salinas (Monterey). Fine varietals do well; similar to Germany and in Beaune, France.

REGION II.   2,501 to 3,000 degree-days (cool). Examples are Saint Helena (Napa), Healdsburg (Sonoma), and Ukiah (Mendocino). Table wine grapes do best here; similar to Bordeaux and Piedmont.

REGION III.   3,001 to 3,500 degree-days (moderate). Examples are Livermore (Alameda), Asti (Sonoma), and Calistoga (Napa). Table wine grapes and dessert wine grapes are grown here; similar to that of the Rhône.

REGION IV.   3,501 to 4,000 degree-days (warm). Examples are Lodi (San Joaquin) and Modesto (Stanislaus). The University of California has developed grapes so that table wines with sufficient acidity can be made despite the heat; similar to Tuscany, Italy.

REGION V.   4,000 or more degree-days (very warm). An example is most of the central and southern San Joaquin Valley. Dessert wine and brandy grapes as well as table and raisin varieties are grown here; similar to that of North Africa.

Since the development of this system more variables are being studied and tabulated. Climatic factors under present investigation include duration of sunlight (as opposed to amounts of heat), fog, humidity, and rainfall.

The slope and lay of the land also affects these values. Many microclimates have been identified due to local information.

GRAPE VARIETIES

Grapes are classed as wine, table, or raisin grapes. The wine grapes whose acreage is recorded by California's Department of Agriculture are the following:

TO PRODUCE RED WINES

Aleatico	Gamay Noir	Pinot Saint George
Alicante Bouschet	(Napa Gamay)	(not a Pinot variety)
Aramon	Grand Noir	Refosco
Barbera	Grenache	(Mondeuse)
Beclan	Grignolino	Royalty°
Black Malvoisie	Malbec	Rubired°
Cabernet Franc	Mataro (Mourvèdre)	Ruby Cabernet°
Cabernet Sauvignon	Merlot	(part Cabernet
Carignane	Meunier	Sauvignon parentage)
Carnelian°	(strain of Pinot Noir)	Saint-Macaire
Centurion°	Mission	Salvador
Charbono	Muscat Hamburg	Souzão
(Corbeau)	Nebbiolo	Syrah French
Early Burgundy	Perelli 101°	Tinta Madeira
(Portuguese Blue)	Petite Sirah (Durif)	Valdepeñas
Gamay Beaujolais	Pinot Noir	Zinfandel
(strain of Pinot Noir)		

Of the above varieties, the ones with the greatest acreage as of 1980 were:†

GRAPE	TOTAL ACREAGE	% COASTAL COUNTIES ACREAGE	% CENTRAL VALLEY ACREAGE
Zinfandel	29,148	44	56
Carignane	25,293	15	85
Cabernet Sauvignon	22,811	86	14
Barbera	19,305	1	99
Grenache	17,560	5	95
Ruby Cabernet	16,935	2	98
Petite Sirah	11,254	48	52
Rubired	10,658	—	100
Pinot Noir	9,402	99	1

° These grapes originated in the California breeding program under the supervision of Dr. H. P. Olmo of the University of California at Davis.

† *California Grape Acreage 1980*, California Crop and Livestock Reporting Service.

TO PRODUCE WHITE WINES

Burger
Chardonnay
  (not a Pinot variety)
Chenin Blanc
  (Pineau de la Loire,
  White Pinot, but
  not a Pinot variety)
Emerald Riesling°
  (not a true Riesling)
Feher Szagos
Flora°
Folle Blanche
French Colombard
Gewürztraminer
Gray Riesling
  (not a true Riesling)

Green Hungarian
Malvasia Bianca
Muscadelle
Muscadelle du Bordelais
Muscat Blanc
  (Muscat de Frontignan,
  Muscat Canelli)
Palomino
  (Golden Chasselas,
  but not a Chasselas)
Pedro Ximenes
Peverella
Pinot Blanc
  (Pinot Blanc Vrai)
Red Veltliner
  (called Traminer,

but not Traminer)
Saint-Émilion
  (Ugni Blanc,
  Trebbiano)
Sauvignon Blanc
Sauvignon Vert
Sémillon
Sylvaner
  (Franken Riesling,
  but not Riesling)
White Riesling
  (Johannisberg Ries-
  ling, the only
  true Riesling)

Of the above varieties, the ones with the greatest acreage as of 1980 were:†

GRAPE	TOTAL ACREAGE	% COASTAL COUNTIES ACREAGE	% CENTRAL VALLEY ACREAGE
French Colombard	44,252	9	91
Chenin Blanc	32,279	28	72
Chardonnay	17,033	94	6
White Riesling	10,186	90	10
Sauvignon Blanc	7,269	77	23

Thompson Seedless and Muscat of Alexandria are large table and dessert wine producers, but since they are classed as raisin grapes, they are not on this list. Thompson Seedless is planted in an astounding 259,513 acres; Muscat of Alexandria in 10,658 acres.

Tokay, Emperor, and White Malaga are also large wine producers, but they are classed as table grapes, and do not appear on this list either.

A glance at the above percentages of grapes and where they are planted tells quickly which grapes are better suited for the coastal regions, and which are better suited to the Central Valley. Some varieties succeed in both areas.

° These grapes originated in the California breeding program under the supervision of Dr. H. P. Olmo of the University of California at Davis.

† *California Grape Acreage 1980*, California Crop and Livestock Reporting Service.

TO PRODUCE DESSERT WINES

GRAPE	WINE PRODUCED
Alicante Bouschet	port
Carignane	port
Grenache	sherry, port
Mission	cream sherry, Angelica
Palomino	sherry
Royalty	port
Rubired	port
Salvador	port, color wine
Souzão	port
Tinta Madeira	port
Zinfandel	port

Dessert wines are blends of any and all grape varieties that are available. Any of the previously listed varieties can and have been used for fortified dessert wines; table and raisin grapes are also used. The grape's contribution is not so much varietal character as it is yield per acre. Exceptions are a small amount of sherry and port production and some special Muscat wines. Most of the above grapes for dessert wines are grown in the Central Valley. Sherries and ports are generic wines.

Vineyards have benefited from careful research. Scientists at both the University of California at Davis and California State University at Fresno have developed disease-free rootstocks and virus-free vines. Specialists in grape cultivation and breeding have developed grape varieties, such as Ruby Cabernet, Carnelian, Centurion, and Emerald Riesling, that yield good table wines in the warm interior valley. They have also determined that some of the traditional wine grapes, such as Barbera, Zinfandel, French Colombard, and Chenin Blanc, make good wine in the warmer growing areas as well. Symphony, the newest grape from UC/Davis, is a white Muscat-type with very high yields.

types

There are three types of California wines: generic, varietal, and proprietary; these terms have been discussed on pages 199–202. In the past generic wines were the most salable because their names, being those of other famous wine districts, were familiar to the public. But as both winemakers and consumers have become more sophisticated, producers have slowly turned from generic labeling toward varietal and proprietary labeling.

Varietal labeling, especially, is an effort to show the unique nature of California wines, rather than presenting them as European copies. Varietal wines are named for the grape varieties from which they are made, such as Cabernet Sauvignon, Zinfandel, and Gewürztraminer. Under California regulations a wine bearing a varietal name on the label must be produced from at least 75 percent of the named variety. In many cases it comes closer to 100 percent of the designated grape variety, allowing for some judicious blending with other grapes to enhance the varietal character. All wines are under close federal and state inspection to guarantee that the wine is labeled accurately.

Proprietary labeling puts emphasis on a producer's style, rather than on creating a European copy, or a wine with specific varietal character.

classes California is rich in a variety of soils and climates. Many important species of European grapes (*Vitis vinifera*) may be found, and consequently almost every wine type is made. The classes and types of California wines have been defined by the Wine Institute of California. Wines are divided into five main classes: red table wines, white table wines, appetizer wines, sweet dessert wines, and sparkling wines. Table wines are those whose alcohol content range from 7 to 14 percent. The majority range between 11 and 13½ percent, and "light" or "soft" wines from 7 to 10 percent. Many of the latter have reduced calories.

RED TABLE WINES

varietal wines CABERNET SAUVIGNON. A fine red wine made in the cool regions of California from the principal claret grape of Bordeaux. The wine is astringent when young but develops complexity and depth as it matures.

MERLOT. A soft wine that tastes like Cabernet Sauvignon but with less tannin and astringency. It is often used to soften Cabernet Sauvignon in California, as it does in Bordeaux. It ages more rapidly than Cabernet Sauvignon.

PINOT NOIR. A wine made from the noble grape of Burgundy, which is difficult to cultivate and vinify in California and which needs a very special microclimate. When properly grown and vinified, the wine can be excellent.

ZINFANDEL. A claret-type wine, with a spicy, berrylike aroma and taste. The grape's origins are unknown, but it is most widely cultivated in California. The latest research, however, suggests that this grape was introduced into California from New England, where it was grown as a hothouse grape. It may be vinified in varying styles, from a *vin ordinaire*, which should be drunk cool, to a rich, full wine that should be aged.

GAMAY. A fresh, sprightly wine previously thought to be made from the grape of the Beaujolais area, in California called Gamay Noir or Napa Gamay.

GAMAY BEAUJOLAIS. A medium- to full-bodied wine with a fruity aroma, but not resembling the French Beaujolais. Its grape has been identified as a strain of the Pinot Noir and should not be confused with the Gamay.

PETITE SIRAH. This wine has a deep red color and is sometimes exceptionally full and tannic, with a spicy nose.

BARBERA. A dark, sometimes robust, full-bodied wine that has a pleasant tartness. The grape, which originated in Piedmont, Italy, has enough acidity to do well in the warmer central regions.

Other varietal wines are made, but in limited quantities. Examples are Carignane, Charbono, Grignolino, and Syrah.

CALIFORNIA BURGUNDY. A full-bodied wine that is soft and smooth on the palate, with medium to deep red color. It is bottled in the traditional Burgundy-shaped bottle, but does not resemble Burgundy from France.

CALIFORNIA CLARET. A dry, tart wine with medium body and medium color. This wine is not nearly as prevalent as California Burgundy.

CALIFORNIA CHIANTI. A full, dry wine without any of the rough character associated with some of the *fiaschi* types.

generic wines

These generic types vary from one winery to another. Burgundies from two different wineries may be entirely different.

ROSÉ WINES

It is important to remember that wine that contains *any* red coloring (which is obtained from the grape skins that are allowed to remain in contact with the must during fermentation) is classified as a red wine. There are only two colors in wine—white and red—and red wines vary in color from the very pale pink-hued rosés to the very deep, inky reds of some Barberas.

In a generic rosé, emphasis is on pigmentation and not on varietal character. In a varietal rosé specific character is there, but reduced because the must is removed from the skins after only twelve to sixteen hours. Because some rosé wines are made from fine varietals, innovative winemakers have begun drawing off the pigmented must to make the rosé wine, and adding the remaining skins, which are still rich in pigment and tannin, to working red wine fermenting tanks of the same grape. This creates a bonus of very rich, concentrated red wines, while making some elegant and fruity rosés.

CABERNET ROSÉ. Has a more distinctive flavor and is best made in the cooler regions.

GAMAY BEAUJOLAIS ROSÉ. Full wine with a deep rose color and good fruitiness.

GAMAY ROSÉ. A fine, delicate rosé with a good fruity character.

GRENACHE ROSÉ. A slightly sweet popular wine with orange tones. The grape is used extensively because of its high yield.

PINOT NOIR ROSÉ. Has a pale, partridge-eye or *oeil deperdrix* (tea rose) color and delicate flavor. It spends a very short time on the skins.

ZINFANDEL ROSÉ. Has some of the bramble character of the grape, with a moderately deep color.

varietal wines

CALIFORNIA ROSÉ. Usually a commercial wine with some sweetness and light body; refreshing as a summer wine.

generic wine

WHITE TABLE WINES

Although white table wines are described as white, no wine is colorless. White wines can vary from a very pale straw yellow to a very dark brown. In taste they vary from bone dry to very sweet.

varietal wines   CHARDONNAY.   A dry and full wine, with complexity, that can take some bottle aging, as well as aging in wood. Sometimes erroneously called Pinot Chardonnay, this wine is made from the grape of Burgundy and Champagne and produces some of the finest wines of the coastal regions of California.

WHITE RIESLING OR JOHANNISBERG RIESLING.   A fruity wine, with a distinctive perfume and often a touch of sweetness, from the fine grape of Germany and Alsace. In some areas and only in some years, cool, humid weather causes the grapes to get *Botrytis cinerea,* "noble rot." Grapes are sometimes left in the vineyards for later picking, when the sugars are concentrated. Rich, exquisite, and expensive sweet wines are then made.

SAUVIGNON BLANC.   A wine of considerable character, from the grape of Bordeaux, sometimes labeled Fumé Blanc. This wine may also be aged in oak and can develop character in the bottle.

CHENIN BLANC.   Also called Pineau de la Loire, this fragrant wine can range from dry to semisweet, as it does when produced along the Loire River. In humid microclimates grapes with "noble rot" make a very sweet wine.

GEWÜRZTRAMINER.   Often slightly sweet, with spiciness, this wine, which is from the grape of Alsace, has a highly aromatic bouquet and a distinctive character.

OTHER RIESLINGS.   The grape that makes Gray Riesling produces a wine in California that is soft and mildly spicy. Wine made from the Franken Riesling, or Sylvaner, grape, which has German origins, is delicate and pleasant. The Emerald Riesling grape is a cross between White Riesling and Muscadelle, developed at the University of California. This variety is often used in blends.

There are other white varietal wines produced, but in smaller quantities. The Pinot Blanc (Melon) is probably the finest of these. Other attractive varietal wines are French Colombard and Green Hungarian, but these usually lack distinctive varietal character.

generic wines   CALIFORNIA CHABLIS.   This is the most common of the California white generic table wines and comes closest to being an all-purpose medium to dry white wine. It is straw colored, with medium body, and is generally made from the Chenin Blanc, French Colombard, Burger, Palomino, Green Hungarian, and other varieties growing anywhere in California.

CALIFORNIA SAUTERNE. (note spelling without final *s*).   This is usually a light, golden, pleasant wine. It is soft without noticeable acidity. When dry, it is sometimes labeled Dry Sauterne, clearly a contradiction in terms.

CALIFORNIA RHINE AND MOSELLE. These wines have a pale color and medium body and acidity. They should have the fruity character of the Riesling varieties and usually have a slight sweetness. When the wine is made from grapes such as the Grey Riesling and the Franken Riesling, which are not true Rieslings, it can be labeled Riesling, but this designation is being replaced with the name Rhine or, less commonly, Moselle.

APPETIZER WINES*

Appetizer wines are those that, as the class name implies, are popularly used before meals as appetite sharpeners. They include sherry (more often the drier types), vermouth, and apertif wines.

CALIFORNIA DRY VERMOUTH (French type). A straw-colored, herb-flavored wine with a minimum of 15 percent alcohol and some vermouth character. Light Dry Vermouth is lighter in color, aroma, and flavor, with less character, and was developed for cocktail use.

CALIFORNIA SWEET VERMOUTH (Italian type). This is used as an appetizer wine despite its high sugar content. It is dark amber, with a pronounced herb character, and may have a Muscat aroma.

California vermouth is not marketed just as vermouth, but rather under the distinctive brand of the producer. This is because the aromatizing formula used by the producer is his very distinctive secret.

CALIFORNIA DRY, OR COCKTAIL, SHERRY. This is the type produced by baking (see page 196). It is pale amber, with a nutty character, and is light bodied and smooth. It is sometimes sold as Pale Sherry.

CALIFORNIA MEDIUM SHERRY. This is also sold as simply California Sherry. It is medium amber in color, full bodied, rich, developed, nutty, and well balanced.

CALIFORNIA DRY FLOR SHERRY. This is the type produced with an aldehyde-producing yeast, and there is no baked character. Hence it has a less pronounced nuttiness. The color is light amber, and the wine is light bodied. It is sometimes sold as Flor Fino Sherry.

CALIFORNIA MEDIUM FLOR SHERRY. This wine is light amber in color and medium bodied and has some *flor* character.

California Sherry and Flor Sherry have 17 percent minimum alcohol.

DESSERT WINES

California dessert wines include all the rich, sweet, full-bodied wines that were formerly known in the trade as sweet wines. Their alcohol content is usually under 20 percent, the minimum being 17 percent for sherries and 18

---

*The U.S. government classifies appetizer wines as dessert wines.

A terraced California vineyard nestled high in the foothills. California is blessed with ideal growing conditions for many of the world's finest wine grapes. (*Courtesy Wine Institute, San Francisco, California*)

Information recorded on each carved cask of wine aging in this California winery cellar is carefully checked by a worker. (*Courtesy Wine Institute, San Francisco, California*)

percent for port, Madeira, Muscatel, and Angelica, the upper limit being 21 percent. They range in taste from medium to very sweet and include both white and red wines. If the wine name is preceded by the word *light*, the alcohol content can be as low as 14 percent.

CALIFORNIA PORT.   This is rightfully one of the more popular dessert wines. The color can range from medium to deep ruby red, and the wine is made from grape varieties known for their high pigmentation, such as Carignane, Salvador, Rubired, Zinfandel, and Alicante Bouschet. Tinta Madeira and Souzão have enough quality and aroma to make varietally labeled ports.

CALIFORNIA TAWNEY PORT.   This wine has a reddish brown or tawny color that comes from aging or baking. Tawny Ports are produced either from grapes that are not so rich in color or by blending white port with ruby port to reduce the pigmentation.

CALIFORNIA WHITE PORT.   This wine ranges from light straw yellow to pale gold and has a mellow taste. It is generally produced from the Thompson Seedless grape.

All California port is very sweet in taste, having as much as 10 to 15 percent unfermented natural grape sugar.

CALIFORNIA SWEET SHERRY.   This is the baked-type sherry and is also known as Cream or Mellow. It is dark amber colored, with full body and a rich, nutty flavor. When it is baked in the absence of air, the color is lighter.

CALIFORNIA ANGELICA.   Originating in California and produced mostly from Mission grapes, this wine is usually very sweet, having 10 to 15 percent unfermented sugar and low acidity. It is full bodied, fruity, and smooth.

CALIFORNIA TOKAY.   Do not confuse this wine with the Tokay of Hungary; the only connection is the name. Nor does this wine get its name from the Flame Tokay grape, which may or may not be used in the production of California Tokay. This wine is always a blend, with port, sherry, and Angelica used in the production. A slightly nutty flavor comes from the sherry in this amber-colored blend.

CALIFORNIA MALAGA, MADEIRA, AND MARSALA.   These wines are rarely produced in this country anymore. Malaga is a blend, similar to Angelica. Madeira and Marsala are produced like the sweeter sherries.

CALIFORNIA MUSCAT WINE.   Muscat is sometimes called Muscatel when produced from the white Muscat of Alexandria. Wines labeled Muscat Canelli or Muscat de Frontignan are made from the White Muscat grape, which originated in Frontignan, France, and Canelli, Italy. Red Muscat and Black Muscat are obtained from the Aleatico and Muscat Hamburg grapes. All Muscat wines have a distinctive Muscat fragrance.

Dessert wines are generally considered fortified wines, and the term *fortified* has long been and is still used to describe wines that have brandy added to them for the purpose of arresting fermentation, or simply to increase the alcohol content above the level at which wines will normally ferment out.

"fortified" wines

Fortified cannot, however, legally be used in the United States. The regulations include the statement that no advertisement for wine, label, wrapper, container, and so on, can contain: "any statement, design, device, or representation which relates to alcoholic content, or which tends to create the impression that the wine has been 'fortified.'"

SPARKLING WINES

California sparkling wines include champagne, sparkling burgundy, pink champagne or sparkling rosé, and sparkling moscato. They are produced by the traditional French bottle-fermented method, the Charmat process, and the transfer process, as described on page 198.

CALIFORNIA CHAMPAGNE. This can be pale straw yellow to light gold color. The wines are marketed in varying degrees of sweetness, following French Champagne labeling practices: Natural, Brut, Extra Dry, and Sec. California champagne is made from a number of grape varieties, such as Chenin Blanc, French Colombard, Folle Blanche, Sémillon, some Riesling varieties, and Burger. Pinot Blanc, Pinot Noir, and Chardonnay are used in the finer champagnes, which have limited production. Chardonnay is sometimes specifically named on the label. Additional information has begun to appear on some labels, such as Blanc de Blancs for a wine made of only white grapes, Blanc de Noir for a wine made of only black grapes, and Oeil de Perdrix for a pale Rosé champagne.

CALIFORNIA SPARKLING BURGUNDY. This sparkling wine is produced in the same way as California champagne, which is either bottle fermented or bulk fermented. It is made with red wine instead of white and has some sweetness.

CALIFORNIA PINK CHAMPAGNE. Also called sparkling rosé, it is light pink in color and is produced in the same manner as California champagne, except that it is made with pink or rosé wine.

COLD DUCK.° A combination of champagne and sparkling burgundy, it is usually semisweet or sweet. These wines have a distinct Concord taste that comes from concentrate of Concord grapes shipped in from Washington State.

CALIFORNIA SPARKLING MUSCAT. A sparkling wine usually made from the Muscat of Alexandria grape, with strong Muscat bouquet. It is generally sold as Moscato Champagne or Spumante.

CARBONATED WINES. Sparkling wines that are made effervescent by artificial carbonation, somewhat less expensive than naturally sparkling wines. Both red and white and dry and sweet wines are produced.

° Cold Duck is a combination of white sparkling wine and sparkling Burgundy and has a sweet taste. It is supposed to have originated in Bavaria among the hunting set, where it was customary to drink Champagne before starting off. Much of it was left in the open bottles, and when the hunters returned, rather than waste it, they mixed it with cold sparkling Burgundy and called it *Kalte Ende*—"cold end." Before long the *Ende* became *Ente*, and the Americans translated it literally into "Cold Duck."

2. NORTHWEST WINES

Wine production in the northwest corner of the United States centers around Washington, Oregon, and Idaho. Although not nearly as developed as California, this viticultural area is emerging with its own style, and increased production will eventually play a role in satisfying future demand for wine.

In the 1870s, almost one hundred years after the Franciscan missionaries *history* planted grapes in California, the beginnings of viticulture in Washington and Oregon were tied to the early settlers' western migrations over the Oregon Trail. The first known wineries in Oregon were established by Ernest Reater in 1880 and Adolph Doerner in 1890. In Washington, Lambert B. Evans planted the first vines in 1872, in the southern part of the Puget Sound area—a location that is now reduced to about one hundred acres because of sudden, damaging rains. Plantings continued sporadically until 1906, when irrigation from the Cascade watershed, which separated the cool, rainy western part of Washington from the dry eastern section, opened up the arid Yakima Valley in the east. During Prohibition only sacramental wines were produced. Repeal brought new winery development along the Columbia River, between Washington and Oregon, with the biggest areas around Seattle and the Yakima Valley. Many fruit wines were produced, as were table and dessert wines.

There were also vineyards in Idaho before Prohibition, with some wines winning prizes at the 1898 Chicago World's Fair. Growing was active after Repeal, in spite of winter temperatures that can fall to well below zero.

WINE REGIONS OF THE
NORTHWESTERN UNITED STATES

The biggest advance in fine winemaking in this area did not come until André Tchelistcheff came to Washington in 1967 and instructed the American Wine Growers on grape growing and vinifying procedures. The results led to varietal wines being produced in the Yakima Valley, as well as in the Willamette and Tualatin valleys in Oregon. In 1969 grape planting spread to neighboring Idaho. Permission in Idaho in 1971 to sell wine in food stores and not just in state monopoly stores encouraged planting even more.

grape varieties and wines

The choice of grapes first planted in Washington and Oregon was governed by the harsh winter temperatures and consisted of hardy eastern grape varieties, such as Concord, Delaware, Diamond, and Campbell Early. An interesting development of these early plantings was the discovery of Island Belle, a grape very similar to Campbell Early that was suited to areas of high rainfall, while its counterpart thrived in dry areas. Both Campbell Early and Island Belle are grown to make sweet table wine as well as grape juice, jams, and jellies. The wines are marketed under the more familiar name of Concord.

While these cool growing areas have produced excellent *vinifera* wines, the majority of acreage is still in *labruscanas*. The market for these grapes is Cold Duck and sweet sacramental wines, with the balance being used for juice, jams and jellies. Some French hybrids are also grown in small quantities.

The most important *viniferas* currently planted include the more hardy White Riesling, Gewürztraminer, and Pinot Noir; the moderately hardy Chardonnay, Semillon, Chenin Blanc, Pinot Blanc, and Merlot; and the least hardy Cabernet Sauvignon and Sauvignon Blanc. This hardiness is dependent not only on environment but on cultural practices as well. White Riesling, Gewürztraminer, and Chenin Blanc, incidentally, are sometimes affected by *Botrytis*, and are made into sweet wines. Pinot Noir is used for sparkling wines.

Washington State

Winemaking in Washington is concentrated in the south-central part of the state, where rain is blocked by the Cascade Mountains. Irrigation is a necessity. The *Phylloxera*-free sandy loam soil has permitted the use of carefully selected, virus-free ungrafted vines, planted on south-facing slopes to utilize as much of the sun's energy as possible. The climate in this region around Grandview-Sunnyside, in the lower Yakima Valley, is the equivalent of California's Regions I and II, 2,300 to 2,800 degree-days. Coolness at night, coupled with an average of over seventeen hours of daylight, due to the northern latitude, retains the acidity necessary for good sugar-acid balance.

Of the 26,500 acres of wine grapes, 4,500 are in *vinifera* vines. Mechanical harvesting is desirable, since here the grape harvest coincides with the apple harvest and picking crews are scarce. Traditional fruit wines are still made in large quantities, using berries, cherries, apricots, and rhubarb. Fruits are often frozen and made into wines later on in the year, after grape-wine operations have been completed. Thus, equipment can be used all year long and is not idle most of the time.

Oregon has 1,200 acres under cultivation in three areas: the southwest part *Oregon* of the state, near the northern California border in the Rogue River Valley; north of the Rogue River in the Umpqua Valley; and the Willamette and Tualatin valleys thirty miles west of Portland in the northwest part of the state. Yamhill County, in this northwest region, averages 1,950 degree-days.

Oregon's laws for *vinifera* wines require 90 percent for varietal wines, except for Cabernet Sauvignon, which may have 75 percent if the balance is comprised of other red Bordeaux grapes. Wines must have appellations of origin on the label, and grapes used must be limited to those areas. Some wineries use grapes from Washington state and this is also indicated on the label. No generic wines are permitted. *Labruscana* and fruit wines are not subject to these regulations.

Idaho's grape plantings have progressed from Concords to French hybrids *Idaho* to *vinifera* varieties. There are 300 acres planted, mainly in the southwestern part of the state, near the Oregon border, and north of the Snake River. White Riesling and Chardonnay have been especially successful.

Winemakers in these states, unencumbered by precedent, have explored new techniques dictated by their unique location and climate. A combined potential of 300,000 acres that could be planted in premium varietals may make this area even more important than it has already become.

3. EASTERN WINES

Early travelers and colonists left records of the wealth of wild grapes *history* found in many sections along the eastern seaboard. In 1565 Captain John Hawkins spoke of the grapes he found in the Spanish settlements in Florida and mentioned that the Spaniards had made twenty hogsheads of wine from the wild grapes—probably *Vitis rotundifolia* (Muscadines), best represented by the Scuppernong, found along the Atlantic seaboard from Maryland to Florida. Still later, Thomas Hariot, writing of the advisability of establishing colonies in America, mentioned grapes that were of two kinds; one was small and sour, the size of the European grape, while the other was larger, sweeter, and more luscious.

In the early 1600s colonizer Captain John Smith wrote in greater detail. "Of vines," he said, "great abundance in many parts, that climbe the toppes of highest trees in some places, but these beare but few grapes except by the rivers and savage habitations, where they are overshadowed from the sunne; they are covered with fruit though never prunned nor manured. Of these hedge grapes we made neere twentie gallons of wine, which was like our British wine, but certainly they would prove good were they well manured. There is another sort of grape neere as great as cherry, this they [Indians] call messamins; they be fatte and juyce thicks, neither doth the taste so well please when these be made in wine."

It is understandable that the newly arrived colonists should find the wines made from native grapes with their strange, wild taste a shock to their palates. Instead of recognizing the merits of the new wine, however, they insisted that it be like the old, with which they were familiar. If these early settlers had attempted to adapt to native wines, it is possible that succeeding generations would have accepted them.

It was Lord Delaware, governor of Virginia, who first suggested that a wine industry be established in America, when he wrote to the London Company in 1616. The idea was enthusiastically approved, and expert French vine dressers and a wide assortment of the finest European vine cuttings were sent to this country. But because of the easy culture and high price of tobacco, most settlers failed to grow European vines.

Even so, over the years many attempts were made, vine dressers changed, vines varied, but all to no avail. For two centuries after Lord Delaware's first efforts, a few winemakers stubbornly continued their efforts to grow the foreign vine, and it was not until the nineteenth century, when they understood the devastation wrought by the endemic pests on foreign vines, that they gave up their efforts. Finally the native grapes east of the Rockies were permitted to stand on their own.

Grapevines grow and sometimes prosper in almost every state east of the Rockies. Climatic variations from place to place and year to year mean that grape varieties that do well in one place may fail just a short distance away. The annual variations make the growers' job risky, and it may take decades to learn how to cope with these risks and produce the best grapes possible. Local grape growers and winemakers are very dedicated, however, and may make this eastern area very important viticulturally after all.

Recent farm winery legislation in such states as New York, Pennsylvania, and Connecticut have eased the restrictions and financial burdens for small wineries, and have provided technical information on grape and wine research. The formation of such groups as the Association of American Vintners and various state and wine and grape associations show a new pride in eastern wines and an eagerness to promote them outside of their region of production.

REGIONS

When discussing eastern wine-producing areas, we feel that it is better to discuss geographic areas of similar climate and geology than to group areas by states. Many wine-producing areas cross political boundaries. The Chautauqua area of western New York, for example, lies in New York State, but the wines realistically should be grouped with those around neighboring Lake Erie.°

° See Appendix G for a list of commercially important eastern wineries.

WINE REGIONS
OF THE
EASTERN
UNITED STATES

MINNESOTA

WISCONSIN

L. MICHIGAN

MICHIGAN

IOWA

ILLINOIS

INDIANA

OHIO

L. ONTARIO

L. ERIE

VERMONT

NEW YORK

FINGER LAKES

Hudson R.

NEW HAMPSHIRE

MASSACHUSETTS

RHODE ISLAND
CONNECTICUT
Long Island

PENNSYLVANIA

NEW JERSEY

EGG HARBOR

Ohio R.

WEST VIRGINIA

VIRGINIA

MARYLAND

MISSOURI

KENTUCKY

ARKANSAS

TENNESSEE

NORTH CAROLINA

Mississippi R.

MISSISSIPPI

ALABAMA

GEORGIA

SOUTH CAROLINA

FLORIDA

KEY

Six or more wineries

Individual wineries:

less than 50,000 gal.

50,000 to 1 million gal.

over 1 million gal.

SCALE

0   100   200   300   400 mi

WILLIAM LEMBECK

Finger Lakes   The oldest and most important wine-producing region of the East is the Finger Lakes region of New York. As early as 1867 the Pleasant Valley Wine Company, which made both sparkling and still wine, produced American champagne of such excellent quality that it won a gold medal at the Paris Exposition. Gold Seal Vineyards, known then as Urbana Wine Company, also produced both wine types and received awards in Vienna in 1873 and in Paris in 1878.

The Finger Lakes region is a beautiful countryside of rolling hills, dotted with lakes. The center of the region is Lake Keuka, with Hammondsport at one end, Penn Yan at the other, and Naples nearby to the northwest. Lake Seneca, just east of Lake Keuka, and enjoying a slightly milder microclimate, has recently been planted with the more delicate *vinifera* vines.

The climate, soil, and drainage bear a striking resemblance to the Champagne district of France, and it is not surprising that this area has been known for its sparkling wine production. Recently, however, with the modernization of equipment of the older wineries, the hiring of winemakers who have the latest technical training, and the springing up of new wineries, the area is becoming known for classic table wines.

Hudson Valley   The Hudson River Valley is one of the nation's oldest wine-producing districts. Steep slopes with striking views of the Hudson River make this area, which is very close to New York City, a popular day-trip destination for visitors to both large and small wineries. Marlboro is at the center of the region, which extends from Washingtonville in the south to Kingston in the north, and from Walker Valley to the west and Amenia and Millerton to the east.

Long Island   South and further east of the Hudson Valley, grapes are being grown on the northeastern tip of Long Island, where the combination of Great South Bay, Long Island Sound, and the Atlantic Ocean moderates the eastern winter climate.

New England   New England has commercially producing wineries in New Hampshire, in Rhode Island along Rhode Island Sound, in Connecticut, and in Massachusetts, including Martha's Vineyard, an island off Cape Cod.

Lake Erie   Lake Erie is bordered on its eastern and southern shores by vineyards that are in Pennsylvania, western New York, and Ohio. The Pennsylvania wineries are mostly around the city of North East. The New York wineries are south of Buffalo in the Chautauqua area. The Ohio wineries range from the eastern border around Conneaut, westward past Cleveland to Sandusky. Wines labeled "Lake Erie" may have grapes from these three states, and represent a viticultural area rather than a political area, which would be bounded by state lines. (See page 200 for regulations).

As is Lake Erie, Lake Michigan is bordered by several states. These are *Lake Michigan* Michigan, Indiana, Illinois, and Wisconsin. Michigan's wineries have the most favorable sites, including the eastern shore of the lake, where Fennville to the south, and Leelanau Peninsula to the north, have been declared approved appellations. Lake Michigan moderates the extreme climate, and in winter provides the prevailing westerly winds with moisture to create a snow cover that protects the vines from any severe low temperatures that may occur.

In addition to the Ohio wineries that border on Lake Erie, there are many *Ohio Valley* wineries in southwestern Ohio, along the Ohio River. This district is also shared by a few wineries in southern Indiana and Kentucky. The history of this area goes back more than 150 years to Nicholas Longworth, who founded the Ohio wine industry around Cincinnati. His death, along with a disease that affected the vines, caused a decline in the Ohio River Valley wine industry, which did not resume again until after Repeal. Near Columbus and Springfield, the Ohio Central wine region is also developing.

The Middle Atlantic states include New Jersey, which is the third largest *Middle* state in wine production, eastern Pennsylvania, Maryland, and Virginia. The *Atlantic* wine industry in new Jersey centers around Egg Harbor. In eastern Pennsylva- *States* nia wineries are clustered around the Main Line and Lancaster areas. Maryland's vineyards range from Baltimore northwest to Hagerstown. Its viticultural history began with Lord Baltimore's directive to plant vines in 1662. Modern history has been made with Philip and Jocelyn Wagner, who established a winery in the 1940s and supplied vine stock from their nursery to other growers. Grape growing in Virginia predates that of Maryland, since Lord Delaware planted grapes there in 1619. Today there are wineries in the Washington, D.C., area, from Middleburg to Culpeper, and in the central part of the state, near Charlottesville.

The central states of Iowa, Missouri, and Arkansas have had established *Midwestern* wineries for many years. In Iowa the wineries are in the Amana area, about *States* eighty miles west of the Mississippi River. In Missouri the wineries mostly border along the Missouri River, west of where it meets the Mississippi River. Augusta was the United States' first approved appellation. Arkansas' wineries are in the western part of the state near Altus, in the valley of the Arkansas River. Texas, to the south, also boasts several premium wineries.

Actually, almost every state in the continental United States has at least one bonded winery. Some regions are thriving while others are struggling. The only eastern regions where commercial grape growing shows no current promise are the northern plains of the Dakotas, the Mississippi Delta, and other Gulf regions.

INDIGENOUS GRAPE VARIETIES

Of the many grape species native to our country, only a few are important to wine production. Wines made from the native *Vitis labrusca* are most important in terms of volume. Some viticulture experts now believe that essentially all of the *labrusca* varieties grown commercially are actually crosses with *vinifera* or other species of grapes. Many of these crosses probably occurred during the eighteenth and nineteenth centuries when *vinifera* and other species of grapes were grown near the native *labrusca* varieties. These experts are proposing that these commercial native varieties be called *Vitis labruscana* to denote this mixed parentage.

The wines made from our native American grapes have a distinctive flavor unlike those of any other part of the world. As the grapes grew wild the early settlers attributed the strong, strange taste to the fact that the grapes were not cultivated or domesticated, and so called the taste wild or "foxy." The term *foxy* has been greatly misunderstood. It's original meaning is "strangeness, wildness," referring to the general character of the wines, different from the familiar (European) wines. In recent years enologists have analysed the complex bouquet and taste of *labruscanas* and have found compounds that contribute floral, animal, grapey, and candy-like fragrances. Methyl anthranilate, the ester that produces the grapey flavor, is used as an index of *labrusca* character since it is easy to determine the concentration of this highly odorous ester analytically, and the average person can detect as little as one part ester in ten million parts wine.

High acids and low sugars are other characteristics of *labruscana* grapes that pose challenges to eastern winemakers, but adaptability and resistance to disease are boons.

The *labruscana* grapes used by winemakers are:

white grapes   DIAMOND.   Originated by Jacob Moore in 1870, from Concord and Iona parents. It resembles the Niagara, but is less commercially important because of lower yields. Sparkling wine producers like its dry, distinctive qualities.

DUTCHESS.   Originated by A. J. Caywood of Marlboro from a white Concord seedling pollinated by mixed pollen of Delaware and Walter in 1868. It is pale yellow-green, and has good flavor. It would be more widely planted if it were not so susceptible to fungus and cold.

ELVIRA.   Originated by Jacob Rommel of Missouri in 1863, its low sugar and high acid make it good for sparkling wines. It is very resistant to *Phylloxera*.

NIAGARA.   Originated by C. L. Hoag and B. W. Clark of Niagara County in 1868. It is the most abundant green grape, produced from Concord fertilized by Cassady. High production and early ripening make it very popular.

NOAH.   Similar to Elvira but more foxy. Used also as a stock for grafting.

CONCORD.   Horace Greeley called it "the grape for the millions." It is the *black grapes*
most widely grown native American hybrid, adaptable to many soils, highly
fruitful, and a virile parent of many other grapes when crossbred. It was
introduced by Ephraim Wales Bull of Concord, Massachusetts, in 1854. All of
the commercial grape juice that is produced in the United States is from the
Concord, as well as grape jelly and preserves. It is used for making kosher
wine, but must be heavily sugared to obtain the necessary amount of alcohol.
It makes a foxy wine.

CYNTHIANA.   A more southern grape, it is popular along the Missouri
River, having originated in Arkansas. It is vigorous and makes distinctive,
non-foxy wine. It was grown and admired in France where it was planted after
the *Phylloxera* devastation and ensuing vineyard reconstruction.

STEUBEN.   Ripens shortly after the Concord, and has vigorous and productive vines. The fruit is sweet and slightly spicy.

The only other black grapes of note are Isabella and Lenoir. Isabella is
planted in more different regions of the world than any other grape, but has
been replaced commercially by Concord. Lenoir is one of the oldest varieties,
but when planted in the proper location, still makes a distinctive wine.

DELAWARE.   Popularized by Abram Thompson of Delaware, Ohio, about *red grapes*
1850, this light red, thin-skinned, and very sweet grape was an immediate
success as an ornamental as well as a table and wine grape. It is used for white
still and sparkling wines. It is early ripening.

CATAWBA.   Introduced by John Adlum of the District of Columbia in
1823, it was thought to have originated in North Carolina. It has been considered the first great American grape. With high sugars and high acids, it makes
a dry and spicy white or pinkish still wine, but is used, with Delaware, for
sparkling wines.

The Catawba attained its greatest fame because of the energy of Nicholas *Catawba*
Longworth. As a hobby Mr. Longworth made a sparkling Catawba that was so *history*
good and so popular that it won gold medals in foreign competitions. He used
to sell upward of 100,000 bottles a year, produced at his vineyards near Cincinnati, Ohio. Among his papers is a letter Mr. Longworth wrote to the members of the Cincinnati Horticultural Society, dated September 10, 1825, which
is particularly interesting because it indicated the progress wines had made
and their bright future. It read in part:

The day is not distant when the Ohio River will rival the Rhine in the quantity
and quality of this wine. I give the Catawba the preference over all other grapes for a
general crop for wine. Sugar was formerly added. The Germans have taught us better.
Where the fruit is well-ripened, sugar will injure it where intended for long keeping;
where the grapes do not ripen well, I should still add from 6 to 10 oz. of sugar to the
gallon of must. It rivals the best Hock and makes a superior Champagne. . . .

If we intend cultivating the grape for wine, we must rely on our native grapes and new varieties raised from their seed.

If I could get my lease of life renewed for 20 or 30 years, I would devote my attention to the subject, and I would cross our best native varieties with the best table and wine grapes of Europe. We live in a great age. Discoveries are daily made that confound us, and we know not where we shall stop.

Muscadines   There is another group of native American grapes called the Muscadines, of the specie *Vitis rotundifolia*. They grow in the southeastern United States, from the Potomac River down to Florida and west to the eastern part of Texas. Of the dozen or so varieties being grown, the Scuppernong is the oldest and best known. It is a bronze-colored grape that grows profusely south of the Mason-Dixon line, particularly in Virginia, the Carolinas, Tennessee, Georgia, and Florida. The fresh fruit is sold locally, since it deteriorates rapidly. Much is used for pies and jellies, as well as wine. Carlos is one of the newer varieties that is now of more commercial interest than some of the older wine varieties like Creek. One compound isolated from the smells of Muscadines has also been found in roses.

HYBRIDS AND NEW VARIETIES

Considerable work has been done to develop new wine-grape varieties by crossbreeding *vinifera* varieties with native American ones. Curiously enough the outstanding hybrids have been developed in France because of the search for fungus- and *Phylloxera*-resistant vines, combined with the less pronounced flavor of the *vinifera* vines. These French hybrids were made available to eastern winemakers by Philip Wagner, who grew them in his Boordy Vineyard at Riderwood, Maryland, and eventually sold them to other growers from his nursery.

The first leading French hybridizer was Louis Seibel. Out of the more than thirty thousand hybrids he grew, only a few—less than one in a thousand—have proved satisfactory. Other well-known French hybridizers have been Seyve-Villard, Ravat, Landot, Baco, Bertille-Seyve, Joannès-Seyve, Burdin, Couderc, Galibert, and Kuhlmann. Their hybrids usually bear their name with a number, and, if they become commercially successful, they get a more popular given name.

Some of the grapes used with considerable success are:

TO PRODUCE WHITE WINES

Aurore (Seibel 5279)	Verdelet (Seibel 9110)
Ravat Blanc (Ravat 6)	Vidal Blanc (Vidal 256)
Rayon d'Or (Seibel 4986)	Vignoles (Ravat 51)
Seyval (Seyve-Villard 5-276)	Villard Blanc (Seyve-Villard 12-375)

Vineyards need year-round care. Here workers prune vines in winter. (*Courtesy the Taylor Wine Company, Hammondsport, New York*)

TO PRODUCE RED WINES

Baco Noir (Baco No. 1)	De Chaunac (Seibel 9549)
Cascade (Seibel 13053)	Landot Noir (Landot 4511)
Chambourcin (Johannès-Seyve 26-205)	Léon Millot (Kuhlmann 194-2)
Chancellor (Seibel 7053)	Maréchal Foch (Kuhlmann 188-2)
Chelois (Seibel 10878)	Villard Noir (Seyve-Villard 18-315)

The New York State Agricultural Experiment Station at Geneva dates back to 1882. The current grape breeding program is designed to supply the wine industry with varieties that will produce European-type wines and supplement the traditional wine types produced in New York. Parents are selected for wine quality and resistance to disease, insects, pollution, and cold. One successful grape has been Cayuga White (G.W. 3). Other scientific research is being done on flavor chemistry, microbiology, and biochemistry as related to wines.

The planting of French-American hybrids in the eastern United States is of immense importance if the total number of vineyards, rather than the total acreage, is considered. More and more amateur winemakers are planting their own grapevines to ensure a continuous supply of raw material for their hobby, and these vines are mostly French hybrids. Out of the ranks of these amateur winemakers have sprung the small wineries in the East. Because the hybrids are hardy and relatively disease resistant, the vineyards and wineries are not limited to any perfect viticultural region.

VINIFERA VARIETIES

Possibly one of the most important developments in the New York State wine industry occurred in the early 1950s when Charles Fournier of Gold Seal Vineyards, who always dreamed of growing *vinifera* vines in New York State, met Dr. Konstantin Frank at the Geneva Experiment Station. Dr. Frank had great experience in growing *vinifera* grapes in the Ukraine and persuaded Charles Fournier that it could be done here, too. Fournier set aside a piece of land for Dr. Frank to work and the experiments began.

Dr. Frank's success and enthusiasm have since stirred many people to start vineyards of their own using *vinifera* varieties. At first these followers searched out microclimates in areas near the Finger Lakes region of New York, but eventually the distances increased to include vineyards around Lake Erie in Pennsylvania and Ohio and around Lake Michigan in Michigan, Indiana, and Illinois. Today *vinifera* vines are grown in such diverse areas as New England and Long Island, Maryland and Virginia, Arkansas and Texas, and, most recently, Colorado, Utah, Arizona, and New Mexico. Since the Northeast can expect severe winter setbacks in about two years out of ten, with far-reaching aftereffects, production of *vinifera* there is a brave choice.

The Chardonnay, White Riesling (which is sometimes affected by *Botrytis cinerea*), and Gewürztraminer, because of their relative winter hardiness, are being grown commercially on a limited basis. They require the best sites, the least temperature extremes, and expert viticultural care against winter damage. The red Cabernet Sauvignon, Pinot Noir, and Zinfandel are even more troublesome to produce. A few wineries have produced wines equal to those of Europe and California, but in very small amounts. It will probably be well into the next century before the commercial viability of these premium grapes in the Northeast can be determined.

EASTERN WINE TYPES*

Eastern wineries produce all classes and types of wines. While eastern wineries have long been famous for sparkling and dessert wines, table wines with consumer appeal now occupy the attention of both large and small wineries. Varietals, proprietaries, and generics are all being produced.

Sherries and ports are still important, and some wineries have their own *soleras* for blending and aging. Some apéritif wines are also produced.

The eastern producers have been better known for their white wines. However, because red-black French hybrid grapes have been planted, red wines produced from them are beginning to appear on the American market.

The care exercised in the vineyards while the grapes are maturing and at vintage time is very much the same as in European wine regions. Winery operations include the best of the old-fashioned methods to which the most modern advances have been adapted.

*For a review of the descriptions of wine types, see pages 199–202.

Original entrance to Great Western's Champagne cellar, the oldest cellar in continuous use in the United States. (*Courtesy Pleasant Valley Wine Company, Hammondsport, New York*)

American champagne

Eastern winemakers have made a name for themselves with the production of sparkling wines. The two most important native grape varieties used are the Catawba and the Delaware. Since these are both red grapes, it is necessary to remove the juice from the skins as soon as it is pressed in order to produce a white sparkling wine. White hybrid grapes are now being used more and more in the sparkling wine cuvées, usually in conjunction with the *labruscana* varieties, but sometimes with *vinifera* grapes. Some sparkling wine made from all Chardonnay grapes is produced in small quantities. The major American champagne districts east of the Rockies are located in the Finger Lakes region of New York, and in the area around Sandusky, Ohio, on Lake Erie. Some fruit-flavored champagnes and Cold Duck, made from the plentiful supply of *labruscana* grapes, round out the sparkling wine picture.

kosher wines

Kosher wines, especially those produced in the eastern United States, are generally classed as Concord grape wines, sweetened with syrup. Kosher wines must be made under rabbinical supervision and meet all Talmudic stipulations for making pure, unmixed wine. For example, employees who handle the wine must be orthodox Jews, and nonkosher food may not be brought into the plant. This is not to say that all kosher wines are sweet. There are many kosher European table wines that are imported from Israel, France, Italy, and Germany that are dry.

Eastern kosher wines are of high quality, and their sweetness has made them readily acceptible to the public. That, along with intensive advertising done by the two or three principal firms that specialize in the production of these wines, has given them wide appeal. The consumer who is unfamiliar with dry table wines finds the pleasant, fruity, grapey taste and rich sweetness easy to like. The familiar taste of grape juice is reassuring to a new wine consumer.

Although eastern producers of kosher wines offer a wide assortment of sparkling, table, and fruit wines, the biggest seller is the wine made from the Concord grape. Often this wine is made from concentrates, which enables the wines to be made at wineries far from the vineyards. It also allows production throughout the year, not just at harvest time. Monarch Wine Company, for example, has vineyards in upstate New York, in the Finger Lakes, and in Chautauqua, near Lake Erie. At harvest time the grapes are pressed into juice and frozen in bulk at plants in Dunkirk and Fredonia. The winery itself is in Brooklyn, New York.

Other states producing kosher wine besides New York are New Jersey, Michigan, Washington, and California.

Certainly the consumption of kosher wines is no longer confined to people of one religious faith. Many kosher wines sell more at Christmas than they do at Jewish holidays. One of the biggest markets for kosher wines is Puerto Rico. They are also shipped to other major cities in the world, including Bangkok, Tokyo, and Hong Kong. The United States' production used to be sufficient to supply these markets, but sweet wines from Israel are also being shipped now to satisfy the demand.

fruit wines   In addition to producing wines from native, hybrid, and *vinifera* grapes, wines are also produced from fruits, such as apples, pears, cherries, nectarines, peaches, plums, and assorted berries. Oranges have been used in the southeast. Some are vinified to taste like dry table wines, with no specific fruit flavor, and others are produced to resemble the fruit from which they are made. Fruits are often obtained from states other than the winery's state. Wines made from fruits always have the name of the fruit on the label.

THE DEVELOPMENT OF
THE WINE INDUSTRY IN THE UNITED STATES

Before 1919 the American wine industry was making slow but steady progress. Repeal, in 1933, brought with it a legacy of lesser grape varieties, loss of winemaking expertise, and loss of a public palate for fine wines. Growth was also slowed by severe control measures set up by many states. The hodge-podge of local laws governing the production and sale of wines still remains, and these barriers are only slowly being removed.

The steady, healthy progress of wine consumption in this country has snowballed during the last few decades, beginning with servicemen returning from duty in Europe after World War II, who had sampled local wines. The economic boom following the war gave rise to tourism abroad, where Americans could observe how Europeans used wine as a regular part of their diet. Following this example, they began to enjoy a glass of wine with meals after their return home.

Another factor that accounted for increased interest in wine was the wealth of advertising that has appeared in the press and on radio and television, originally necessitated by the fact that there was no strong wine drinking tradition in this country before Prohibition and Repeal.

New wineries in California and other states during the last decade have further stimulated the demand, and the states with the highest consumption are usually also states where wines are locally produced. California and New York are in the lead, followed by Florida, Illinois, Massachusetts, Michigan, New Jersey, Ohio, Pennsylvania, and Texas. It is probable that wine consumption will develop a broader base as more states develop a local wine industry.

The Wine Institute, founded in California after Repeal, has united many California producers in their common goal of consumption of quality California wines. Over 400 members subscribe to the self-regulation that has produced excellent results. In addition to free distribution of booklets to the trade, the press, and the public, the Wine Institute has also succeeded in obtaining much of the wine legislation that has been passed in several states, and in preventing legislation that many feel would set the industry back.

A new phenomenon of large corporations entering the wine arena with no prior experience in wines has also led to new, favorable legislation, since they had not been brought up with the idea that wine legislation was inviolate. These large corporations have also brought a new look to wine merchandising.

Lately, we have observed new European influences, ranging from foreign ownership of vineyards and wineries, to actual European collaboration on the wines produced. This began with the sparkling wine producers, but has extended to premium table wines. France, Germany, and Switzerland are the most involved.

It is possible to buy wine in food stores in several states, but not in two of the most populous, New York and Pennsylvania. As it is now, wine must be retailed either by specially franchised outlets, which by law cannot engage in any other business, or, as in Pennsylvania, by the state itself. The most important way that naturally fermented wines should be used is with food, and we shall not think of light wine as a food until we can buy it in a food store.

If and when wine is classified as a food and relieved of its present tax burden, now levied at almost every step that wine takes, from the vineyard to the consumer's table, prices may be lower, and, more important, wine will not have the "luxury" status now conferred upon it. Realistically speaking, higher costs for bottles, corks, labels, foils, and other packaging, as well as labor, would probably use up any savings, but would, at least, keep wine competitively priced and ensure the continuous growth of consumption.

12
OTHER WINES OF
THE AMERICAS

1. CANADA

The vineyards of Canada can be considered extensions of the vineyards of the northern United States because the areas where grapes can be grown successfully in Canada are contiguous to American regions.

Canada is a very small producer, making about as much wine as the island of Cyprus, or about fifteen million gallons annually.

history   Canada's first vineyard and winery were established in 1811 by John Schiller in Ontario province. Generally, Canada's winemaking history parallels that of the United States, with a period of Prohibition for each country at about the same time. Both countries also planted experimental grapevines at about the same time.

geography   In the eastern regions of Canada grapes are planted on the southwest shore of Lake Ontario and the northern shore of Lake Erie, in the Niagara Peninsula, which is in the province of Ontario. The mitigating effects of Lakes Erie and Ontario on the climate temper the winters and cool the summers. *Labruscana* grape varieties such as Concord, Niagara, Elvira, Agawam, Fredonia, and Catawba are planted, as are French hybrids such as De Chaunac, Maréchal Foch, and Baco Noir. Some *vinifera* grapes have been successful in small amounts; these include Chardonnay, Riesling, Gewürztraminer, Gamay Beaujolais, and Pinot Noir. Seventy-five percent of all Canadian wine is made in this area of the Great Lakes.

In the western part of the country the Okanagan Valley, in the province of British Columbia, produces the balance of Canada's wines. The seventy-five-mile-long Okanagan Lake lessens the effects of the low winter temperatures. Even so, it is Concord and Thompson Seedless grapes that are planted in large quantities. Hardy Rieslings and other *vinifera* varieties are little more than experimental plantings. Much wine made in this region is blended with wine made from grapes that are harvested in California and trucked north for vinification.

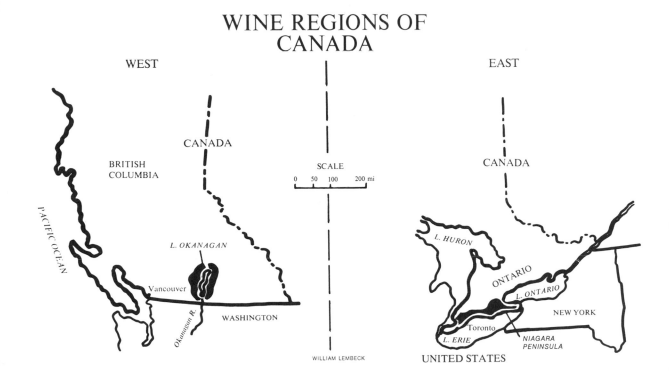

WINE REGIONS OF CANADA

Both eastern and western Canadian wineries produce table wines, baked *wines* and *flor* sherries, ports, and Tokays. Some wines are not vintage dated because of the need to blend for uniformity and quality.

Wine practices are controlled by individual provinces. The only way wines may be purchased anywhere in Canada is in a government-owned liquor store or in a restaurant. A small amount of wine is exported; most is consumed locally.

2. LATIN AMERICA

South of the Río Grande wines are produced in a number of Latin American countries, but of these only wines from Argentina and Chile find their way into the United States. Brazil, Peru, and Uruguay produce wines for home consumption. Two-thirds of South America lies in the tropics and is not as hospitable to the vine as North America.

ARGENTINA

Argentina is the largest producer of wine in the Western Hemisphere, ranking fifth among world producers. Only Italy, France, Spain, and the U.S.S.R.° outrank it. The country's vineyard acreage is over 750,000, about 15 percent more than that of California, but because the average yield per acre is almost double that of California, Argentina ranks much higher in total production, which is over 700 million gallons per year.

history   The earliest known vineyards in Argentina were planted in 1556 by the Jesuit Father Cedron in the Mendoza region. The variety planted was the Mission grape, called the *Criollo de vino* in Argentina. The later missionaries who brought the grape to South America belonged to the same religious order as those who brought the grape to California.

It was the Italian immigrants, arriving in Argentina during the latter part of the nineteenth century, who established the present wine-producing areas, methods, and grape varieties. Like their relatives who went to California, they worked hard, irrigated the land, and converted arid areas into magnificent grape- and fruit-producing regions. Finding that the grape had been cultivated with success since the establishment of the missions by the Spanish explorers, these settlers naturally paid attention to the expansion of vineyards and the production of wine. This activity, coupled with the Buenos Aires–Mendoza railway link, completed in 1884, turned winemaking into a viable industry.

geography   The three principal wine regions of Argentina, all lying in the South Temperate Zone, are in the provinces of Mendoza, San Juan, and Río Negro. Here spring is from October to December, summer is from January to March, fall is from April to June, and winter is from July to September.

Mendoza lies in the west, on the Chilean border, and is the "California Great Central Valley" of Argentina. It is only in the last hundred years that the province has been developed. Mendoza was a vast, arid, sandy desert, showing green patches only along the banks of the several rivers that cut through in draining off the melting Andean snows. Today Mendoza accounts for 70 percent of Argentina's total annual wine production and 90 percent of its table wine production.

The province of San Juan lies immediately north of Mendoza and has similar soil conditions, irrigation being always necessary. Because climatic conditions are on the whole somewhat hotter, the San Juan vineyards are the source of dessert wines, wines for vermouth production, and almost all the table or eating grapes, as well as the magnificent raisins that are available in

---

° Since production varies from year to year, there are some years when Argentina produces more wine than the U.S.S.R., and it then moves to fourth place in world production.

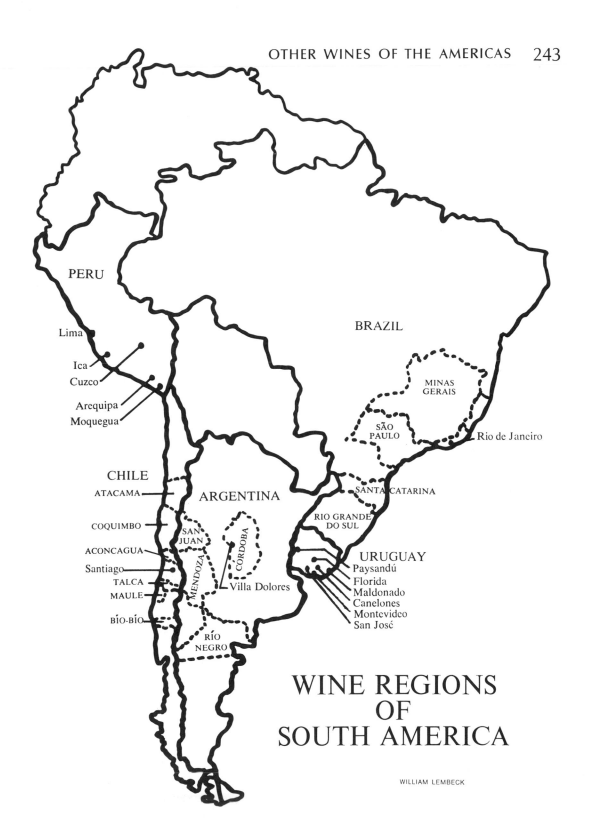

PERU

Lima
Ica
Cuzco
Arequipa
Moquegua

BRAZIL

MINAS
GERAIS

SÃO
PAULO

Rio de Janeiro

CHILE

ATACAMA

ARGENTINA

SANTA CATARINA

COQUIMBO

SAN
JUAN

CÓRDOBA

RIO GRANDE
DO SUL

ACONCAGUA

Santiago

TALCA

MAULE

MENDOZA

Villa Dolores

URUGUAY
Paysandú
Florida
Maldonado
Canelones
Montevideo
San José

BÍO-BÍO

RÍO
NEGRO

WINE REGIONS
OF
SOUTH AMERICA

WILLIAM LEMBECK

such profusion in Argentina's public markets. San Juan also produces some very pleasant table wines that enjoy wide popularity. This province produces about 20 percent of Argentina's wine.

In the province of Río Negro, south of Mendoza, the climate is comparable to the Champagne and German wine regions of Europe. Here are produced some of Argentina's best white table and sparkling wines. The quantities produced are small, from 3 to 5 percent of the country's total production. Very little, if any, irrigation is required in Río Negro, and the soil is less sandy, being more argillaceous and containing sections that are quite chalky in character.

While some wine is produced in practically every province of Argentina, all that is produced outside the three principal provinces does not amount to more than 5 percent of the country's total annual production. In the mountainous Córdoba province there is a small region around Villa Dolores where interesting wine is produced. The quantity is small but both the red and the white are uniformly good—fruity, full bodied, and well balanced. They are wines of character.

Argentina's vineyards, like those of other wine regions, have suffered from and been subjected to attack from various diseases, such as downy mildew, oïdium ("powdery mildew"), and Phylloxera, which have ravaged vineyards, particularly in Mendoza and San Juan.

In Mendoza and San Juan the wines generally are made on a mass-production basis similar to the methods used in the large wineries of California. A dozen or so giants of the wine industry control about a quarter of the annual production. Some of the largest wineries and wine cellars in the world are found in Mendoza.

The viticultural and vinicultural experiment station that forms part of the University of Cuyo at Mendoza has made significant contributions to the advances and modernization of winemaking in Argentina.

grape varieties   The vinifera varieties are cultivated exclusively for commercial wine production and are controlled by government regulation. Varieties permitted for red table wines are the Criolla, Malbec, Cabernet Sauvignon, Barbera, Petite Sirah, Pinot Noir, Tempranilla, Merlot, Sangiovese, and Lambrusco. For white table wines permitted grapes are the Criolla, Sauvignon Blanc, Sémillon, Chardonnay, Pinot Blanc, Riesling, and Trebbiano. Fortified and dessert wines are made from the Pedro Ximenez, Muscat of Alexandria, and Malvasia varieties.

The Criolla grape is the most widely planted grape in Argentina, and it is used for both red and white wines.

wines   All classes and types of wines are produced in Argentina, and almost all of them are consumed there. The largest portion of the market is wines made from a blend of the wines of the Criolla, Malbec, and Barbera grapes.

Premium wines are emerging both for local consumption and for export. Labels indicating varietal wines, such as Cabernet Sauvignon, and labels indicating age, such as Gran Reserve or Viejo ("old"), are appearing on the market, with the definition of some of these terms being up to the producer. Aging often takes place in French oak casks.

A number of the leading wine houses also produce sparkling wines by all the methods known in the wine trade. Argentine Champagne may be made by the traditional bottle-fermented method; by the transfer process; by the Charmat, or bulk-fermentation, process; or by artificial carbonation. Sparkling rosé is also produced, generally by the Charmat method. Champagnes are labeled Brut, Extra Brut, Sec, Demi Sec, and Dulce, in ascending order of sweetness. The Argentines prefer the sweeter types. Pinot Noir, Chardonnay, Chenin Blanc, and Ugni Blanc are the most common varieties used to make the *cuvée*.

Sherry and port wines of very satisfactory quality are offered, but the Muscatels of San Juan are of superior quality—comparable, in fact, to the Muscatel wines of the Mediterranean islands. These wines do not contain more than 16 percent alcohol.

Argentina is one of the largest consumers of vermouth, where one brand alone markets over 2 million cases a year of the $3\frac{1}{2}$ million sold. Vermouth is consumed almost entirely as an aperitif, served on the rocks or with a dash of soda and a dash or two of Italian-style bitters.

Argentine table wines are well made, and most compare favorably with everyday drinking wines produced elsewhere. In Argentina wine is part of the diet. In every restaurant, whether it be the finest luxury establishment or a simple workers' eating place, there is wine on every table, while in the home it is always found on the host's table as well as the servants'. It is served as a matter of course, as coffee or soft drinks are served in the United States. The people of Argentina drink over twenty gallons of wine per capita each year.

There has been little Argentine wine for export, but a few importers have begun to bring in the finer premium wines from Mendoza. The local preference has always been for soft, well-matured, nonacid wines; but the Argentine drive for greater acceptance in the world market has caused producers to modify their winemaking techniques and produce a bouquet and taste more similar to the fresher, drier wines preferred in Europe and America.

BRAZIL

Viticulture is relatively new to the Brazilians, as grapes were not planted there until after World War I, by Italians. Even though the Portuguese originally colonized Brazil, the wines reflect this Italian influence, as well as a strong German influence. The French have also established modern wineries in Brazil and have brought over their own technologists.

history

geography   While Brazil is the largest South American country, most of it is too tropical for grape growing, and there are only 170,000 acres under vine in the most southern area. Winemaking activity is centered from about 15 degrees to 30 degrees latitude, in the South Temperate Zone, where the seasons are reversed. The biggest and southernmost area is Rio Grande do Sul, on the Atlantic. Rio de Janeiro and Minas Gerais are more northerly states where grapes are also grown. São Paulo has some vines, and it vinifies its own wines as well as makes wine from grapes of the adjoining Santa Catarina region.

grape varieties and wines   Because of the tropical humidity, the most successful grapes are hybrids and non-*vinifera* types. Most prominent are the Isabella and the Herbemont. Others include Dutchess, Majara, Concord, Cintiana, Gothe, Muscat, and Malvasia. Barbera, Shiraz, and Trebbiano are examples of European grapes that can succeed in the warmer temperatures.

Some noble grape varieties, such as Cabernet, Merlot, Pinot Noir, Sémillon, and Riesling, have been successful in small quantities.

Both generic and varietal wines are made in Brazil, and the types include table, fortified, and sparkling wines. The Italian influence is apparent with the production of vermouths and bitter aperitifs. The fifty to sixty million gallons produced annually are consumed locally, and some wine is imported from neighboring South American countries to augment local production.

CHILE

By comparison with Argentina across the Andes, Chile is a small country both in area and in population. From the standpoint of fine wines, however, Chile is very important, as the finest wines of South America are produced there.

history   Chile is endowed with a delightfully sunny climate, ideal soil conditions, and, above all, practically disease-free vineyards. The Chilean vines have never had a serious plague such as mildew or *Phylloxera* because of the country's fortunate terrain, climate, and location, as well as the relentless precautions taken by agricultural inspectors at the borders. Such diseases as the vines suffer are not serious; probably the worst worry the vineyard owner has is that of late spring or early summer hailstorms, which are, on occasion, quite devastating.

The vine has been cultivated in Chile since the beginning of Spanish colonization in the sixteenth century, when the early missionaries, as they did elsewhere, planted the vine for the production of wine for the Sacrament. Because of the propitious volcanic soil, it was not long before these vineyards were producing wines for more mundane purposes. It is presumed that the first vines planted in Chile were cuttings brought down from Cuzco, the ancient capital of the Incas. This must have been before 1551, because in letters of that date Don Pedro de Valdivia, one of Chile's early leaders, mentions eating locally grown grapes, and several years later he comments on the wine produced near the city of Santiago.

Cultivation of the vine and production of wine were rather haphazardly pursued in Chile for three centuries. Then in 1851 Don Silvestre Ochagavia contracted the services of M. Bertrand, a French viticulturer who brought with him the first cuttings of Cabernets, Pinots, and other grapes, and with his arrival began the modernization and vast expansion of wine production, consumption, and appreciation in Chile. During the century that has followed, M. Bertrand has been succeeded by a long series of eminent French viticulturists and enologists, such as Gaston Canu, Georges Guyot de Granmaison, Leopold Gamerre, O. Brard, and Paul Pacottet. As is evident, Chilean viniculture has developed primarily along French lines.

geography

Chile is a rather long and narrow strip of land that begins at the southern border of Peru and extends twenty-eight hundred miles south to icy Tierra del Fuego and the Straits of Magellan. At its back lies the ever present and imposing massif of the snow-covered Andes range, including the twenty-three-thousand-foot-high Mount Aconcagua, the tallest peak in the Western Hemisphere. Washing Chile's long shoreline is the equally impressive Pacific Ocean and its cold Humboldt Current. The fresh breezes striking the high wall of the mountain backdrop produce the ideal climatic conditions that have such a marked effect on all the fruits of Chile's soil. Whether they are grapes, peaches, raspberries, pears, melons, lentils, onions, or garlic, they are rich in perfume, flavor, and character. The country's wines are no exception.

From Coquimbo, about 30 degrees south latitude, south to Temuco, 40 degrees south latitude—some six hundred miles of land, including about 275,000 acres of vineyards—wine is made.

wine regions

There are three principal wine-producing regions in Chile. In the provinces of Atacama and Coquimbo in the north the wines are high in alcohol content and are mainly sweet, fortified types. The central provinces, from Aconcagua to Talca, produce the best table wines of Chile. The southern provinces, from Maule to Bío-Bío, produce the bulk wines of the country.

grape varieties and wines

The principal *vinifera* varieties are cultivated for wine production, as are table grapes and raisins. Most of the original cuttings were brought from the various European wine regions, but in recent years cuttings have also been imported from California. For white wines the varieties most used are the Sauvignon Blanc, Sémillon, Pinot Blanc, Chardonnay, Trebbiano, Riesling, Traminer, and the Chilean native variety known as the Loca Blanca. For red wines producers use primarily the Cabernet Sauvignon, Cabernet Franc, Malbec, Petit Verdot, Merlot, and Pinot Noir. The table and raisin varieties tend to be the Muscat of Alexandria, Malvasia, Malaga, and seedless varieties such as the Corinth and Thompson, of which thousands of boxes are exported annually to the American market.

Wine production in Chile follows European methods in all respects. Fermentation takes place in vats and the new wine is racked into small or medium-size cooperage for its development. The wines are generally bottled after one to one and a half years for white wines, and two and a half years for red wines.

All classes and types of wines can be and are produced in Chile, but consumption of wines other than red and white table wines is negligible by comparison. Good but rather sweetish sparkling wine is produced, mostly by bulk process. Some sherry and port types are also made, as well as vermouth.

The largest volume of wine sold in Chile is labeled simply Tinto or Blanco ("red" or "white"); it is sold generally in grocery stores, in a typically Chilean wicker-covered demijohn of five to ten liters, called a *chuico*. The customer leaves a deposit for the container that is refunded when he returns it.

In clubs, restaurants, hotels, and fine groceries, premium wines, which are abundant, are offered in the traditional European bottles. These wines, sometimes bearing vintage dates and resembling quite closely their namesakes, are labeled Cabernet, Borgoña (Burgundy), Pommard, Pinot, Riesling, Rhine, Chablis, Sauvignon, Sémillon, Sauternes, and so on. In addition, the labels bear the name of the vineyard and one of the following phrases, in order of quality (the first being the best): Gran Vino para Banquetes ("great wine for banquets"), Gran Vino, or Reservado.

With few exceptions Riesling and Rhine wines are bottled, for sale in Chile, in the *Bocksbeutel* of Steinwein of Franconia fame.

Grape growing in Chile is a very important agricultural endeavor and one that is of great concern to the people as a whole and to the government—particularly the Internal Revenue Department, which is charged with controlling every step of the wine's progress, from planting the grape until its final service on the consumer's table. Strict supervision of labeling, quality standards, and so forth, is maintained.

As a temperance measure the Chilean legislature passed a law limiting the amount of wine that can be sold within the country to 60 liters (15.85 gallons) per capita. The average consumption is actually less than this, amounting to 10.6 gallons per capita. In supervising strict compliance with this law, the Internal Revenue Department establishes quotas governing new plantings, wine production, and marketing. This does not mean that production is limited to the 60-liter-per-capita consumption figure. Any wine produced in excess of the statutory limit must be either exported, distilled into brandy or alcohol for fuel purposes, or dumped. Since under the law only 85 to 90 million gallons can be marketed internally, and Chile's production approaches 150 million gallons annually, the industry has to find a continually expanding export market if it wishes to progress and prosper. Some wine leaders have developed excellent markets for premium wines, exported in bottles to this country and the other American countries, and for standard quality wines shipped in bulk to a number of European markets, notably Belgium, Holland, the Scandinavian countries, Switzerland, Germany, and France. A much greater volume of exports is made to European countries than to the American nations.

Chilean wines have justifiably found a very ready acceptance wherever they have been offered. In the United States, where they are very moderately priced, they represent some of the best wine values available.

MEXICO

The history of wine in Mexico has been an interesting paradox. This area *history* was the portal of Spain's introduction to viticulture and viniculture to the Americas—to California, Peru, Chile, Argentina, and the rest of South America. Yet despite determined and intermittent efforts, Mexico's total production of table wine is only 4 million gallons a year; the per capita consumption is about $7\frac{1}{2}$ ounces.

Wines have been made in Mexico ever since Hernando Cortés had cuttings from Spain planted between 1521 and 1527. After that vines were planted by traveling missionaries. In 1593 and 1626 the first two commercial wineries were established four hundred miles north of Mexico City.

During three centuries of Spanish rule, vines were uprooted and could not be replanted, in order to protect the Spanish wine monopoly. After Mexico achieved independence in the early 1800s vines again were planted, but the wines produced were of low quality. The very large Bodegas de Santo Tomás was established in 1888 in Baja California, the long peninsula stretching south from California.

The history of Mexican wines is filled with names well known to California. From 1889 to 1904 John Concannon sent cuttings of the better French grape varieties from his property in Livermore. This was the first effort to replace the ubiquitous Mission, or Criolla, grape, which gave a high yield of low-grade wine.

Antonio Perelli-Minetti later planted nine hundred acres between 1910 and 1916 with Zinfandel, Petite Sirah, Malaga, and Flame Tokay grapes, managing to protect his vineyards during the Mexican Revolution.

Fifty years later Dmitri Tchelistcheff became the technical director of Santo Tomás. During a ten-year period he replanted vineyards with noble varieties and other varieties suitable to the climate and introduced sound winemaking techniques, such as cold fermentation of white wines, barrel and bottle aging for red wines, making *flor*-process sherries, making bulk-process and bottle-fermented Champagnes, and even producing a pot-still brandy.

Nazario Ortiz Garza, who became Mexico's secretary of agriculture, built

WINE REGIONS
OF
MEXICO

Valle Redondo
Tañama
Guadalupe
Ensenada
Rancho Viejo
Santo Tomás

BAJA
CALIFORNIA

SONORA

Hermosillo

CHIHUAHUA

Delicias ●

COAHUILA

Torreón *Parras*

Saltillo

DURANGO

AGUASCALIENTES

QUERÉTARO

Guadalajara

San Juan del Río

Mexico City ●

SCALE

0   200   400   600 km

WILLIAM LEMBECK

four wineries between 1929 and 1966. The first was at Saltillo and is now about two hundred acres; the second in Mexico City, supplied with grapes from farther north; the third at Aguascalientes, comprising eight thousand acres; and the last at Torreón. Also at Torreón the Mexican government established a vineyard supplied with rootstocks from the University of California at Davis to propagate and supply virus-free vines.

The Mexican Winegrowers' Association has launched a strong effort to increase the use of table wines by the Mexican people. Some highly rated European producers have built modern facilities to make table wine, vermouth, and brandy in Mexico. With all this activity, vineyard acreage has increased from 4,000 in 1939 to over 100,000 in 1977. Wine production has also increased to about forty million gallons a year, but most of it is distilled into brandy. Most of this increase has taken place in the last ten years.

wine regions   Most of the vineyards are in northern Mexico, where mile-high elevations provide cooler temperatures. One problem is a lack of water, and many areas must be irrigated.

The most important wine region is that of northern Baja California, which is within one hundred miles of the California border and is cooled by the moist ocean breezes of the Pacific. The most important valleys are Santo Tomás, Rancho Viejo, Guadalupe, Valle Redondo, and Tañama.

In northwest Mexico, south of Arizona, is the semitropical Hermosillo district in the state of Sonora. In north-central Mexico, south of Texas, is the Delicias district in the state of Chihuahua. Parras and Saltillo, in the state of Coahuila, also south of Texas, is five thousand feet above sea level. Parras was the site of the first winery, built in 1593, and is said to be the cradle of viniculture of the Americas. Another viticultural region is Torreón, at the border of the states of Coahuila and Durango. Aguascalientes, northeast of Guadalajara, and San Juan del Río, in Querétaro, complete the main grape-growing areas in Mexico. San Juan del Río is the most southern, only one hundred miles north of Mexico City, but its high altitude of sixty-one hundred feet means cool growing conditions, despite its being so far south.

The best table wines are from the Ensenada area of Baja California. These wines are made from Cabernet Sauvignon, Pinot Noir, Barbera, Zinfandel, Riesling, Chardonnay, Sémillon, Chenin Blanc, and Aligoté grapes. The San Juan del Río area also has been successful with noble grape varieties. *grape varieties and wines*

Wines are named for the grape varieties used, and many wineries are establishing proprietary names as well. Vermouths and fortified wines, such as baked sherry, are popular. The Chenin Blanc is being used to make a good sparkling wine.

PERU

The vine has been growing in Peru for almost five hundred years, having been planted there in the 1500s. Production is small—about two million gallons a year—and all the wine is consumed locally. *history*

The vineyards of Peru stretch from Lima, the capital, south to Moquegua, along the Pacific Coast. There are twenty thousand acres around Ica, which is south of Lima. Cuzco, somewhat inland, and Arequipa, a cathedral town near the Pacific, are also vineyard sites. *wine regions*

European Mission grape varieties are grown in Peru, producing red and white table wines resembling the Mediterranean style. Some fortified wines, similar to sherry, port, and Madeira, are also produced. The Muscat grape produces the famous Pisco brandy. *grape varieties and wines*

URUGUAY

Uruguay's vineyards were not established until the 1890s, so the viticultural attitudes are very modern. Since it was discovered that the mild climate was hospitable to the vine, the University of Uruguay has been working to develop the winemaking industry, even sending students to Italy and France for further study. *history wine regions* Uruguay is the smallest wine-producing South American country, but it has fifty thousand acres under vine and produces 24 million gallons a year. Since it has a relatively high annual per capita consumption of 6.6 gallons, the wines produced remain in Uruguay.

The earliest cultivated area was around Montevideo, the southernmost city. Vineyards extend to neighboring Canelones, San José, and Maldonado, along the Río de la Plata. Paysandú to the north, next to Argentina, and Florida in south-central Uruguay are other grape-growing districts. The climate is mild, tempered by ocean breezes, with a high of 70 degrees Fahrenheit in summer (January and February) and a low of 50 degrees Fahrenheit in winter (July and August). Rainfall is generally adequate, but in some years there are droughts.

grape varieties and wines Most of the grapes have European origins: the Cabernet and Sémillon of Bordeaux, the Pinot Blanc of Burgundy, and the Barbera and Nebbiolo from Italy. The most widely planted grape is the Harriague, originally from the Pyrénées. Some hybrids and *labruscana* types are also grown. Table, fortified, aromatized, and sparkling wines are all produced, mostly under local names.

13
THE WINES OF THE MIDDLE EAST AND AFRICA

The lands of the Middle East and North Africa share many common traditions. The most pervasive of these, the Islamic religion, forbids the use of alcoholic beverages. This religious prohibition is the major reason for the very slow development of winemaking in this potentially lush viticultural region. It is ironic that this huge area should rank so low in world production and consumption, since it is generally acknowledged to be the fountainhead of the stream of wine.

According to the Persians, their country (present-day Iran) was the birthplace of winemaking. Persia has given us many riches in philosophy, art, and poetry, but it has also bequeathed us a vine that has since prospered in many regions of the world—the Shiraz and the Syrrah of the Rhône (the descendants of which are the Petite Sirah of California). Shiraz and its wine must have been in the mind of Omar Khayyam when he wrote:

> I sometimes wonder what the vintner buys
> One half so precious as the stuff he sells?

In *A Book of Other Wines* P. Morton Shand recounts the Persian version of the discovery of wine. The Shah Jamshid always had a dish of grapes by his bedside, and one day, observing that some of the overripe berries were fermented, he ordered them to be thrown away, thinking them poisonous. A discarded favorite from his harem seized the grapes and drank the juice to put an end to her sorrow. This she achieved, but not in the way she had expected. When the surprised shah found her, mildly intoxicated but far from melancholy, she revealed the delightful secret of the grapes, and through her discovery of wine she recaptured the devotion of the shah.

This chapter follows the development of wines throughout the Middle East and North Africa and ends with a leap to South Africa. Although South Africa is the newest of the countries to enter into winemaking, it is the second largest producer on the African continent, ranking behind Algeria.

1. THE MIDDLE EAST

CYPRUS

history   Cyprus today is an independent nation. Even though it was long held by England, it has maintained its viticultural ties to Greece, which had controlled it previously. Mythology calls this island the home of the goddess Aphrodite, and a dry white wine with a high alcohol content bears her name. The English Crusaders took over the island from Greece in the twelfth century and ruled until 1571, when the Ottoman Empire annexed Cyprus to its vast domain. During the English reign the Knights Templar glorified the rich and sweet Commandaria wine and established its use at English banquets.

Under Turkish rule the vine continued to flourish in quantity, but it declined in quality. From 1878 to 1960 England again took control of the island and rebuilt the wine industry to its present status.

geography   Cyprus lies off the southern coast of Turkey and the western shores of Syria, no more than seventy-five miles from either mainland country. A hilly terrain, which provides many southern exposures, combined with the moderating effect on temperature of the surrounding Mediterranean Sea, provides this island with excellent conditions for 100,000 acres of vineyards.

WINE REGIONS OF
CYPRUS AND TURKEY

All types of table, sparkling, and fortified wines are produced. A great deal is exported, traditionally to the United Kingdom, but not in the same quantities as when Cyprus was under English control. The native black Mavron grape is used to produce red wines, as well as the nonresinated Cypriot version of the resinated Greek Kokkineli wine. On Cyprus, however, the Kokkineli is a deep rosé, not a red. The most famous dry red wines are Othello and Afames.

grape varieties and wines

The indigenous white Xynisteri grape produces all of the white wines, which account for only a small percentage of the total production.

Cypriot winemakers are planting *vinifera* varieties on an experimental basis, hoping for success with varieties from Spain and southern France.

Of all Cypriot wines, Commanderia is the most famous. It is made from a blend of Mavron and Xynisteri grapes that have been raisined for a few days, leaving a high residual sugar content after fermentation. The wines mature in a modified *solera* system. Commanderia is a sweet, dark red port-like dessert wine.

Cyprus also boasts many other styles of sherry-type dessert wines. These traditionally have been exported to Great Britain.

ISRAEL

According to Genesis, as soon as Noah emerged from his ark he planted a vineyard. Wine production flourished until the Muslim occupation, when vines were uprooted because the Koran forbade wine drinking. Except for a small amount made for religious ceremonies, no wine was made commercially.

history

The modern wine industry began in 1870, when the first agricultural school was established in Mikve near Jaffa. Baron Edmond de Rothschild, an owner of Château Mouton-Rothschild, later sent a team of specialists who helped with the planting of *vinifera* vines. They also helped with the construction of two large wineries at Richon Le Zion and Zichron Jacob, with wine produced under the supervision of the baron's winemaker. The *Société Coopérative Vigneronne des Grandes Caves* was formed in 1906 by the farmers, who have continually updated viticultural practices. Israeli winemakers have glass-lined storage tanks with a combined capacity for several million gallons, and they use mechanized bottling facilities.

Vineyards are spread over a large area in Galilee, Shomron, the slopes of Mount Carmel, and the Judean Hills toward Jerusalem.

wine regions and grape varieties

Red wines are produced from the Cabernet Sauvignon, Alicante Grenache, Carignane, and, in the last twenty years, the Israeli Concord grapes. These are all used for varietal wines. Other red grapes are Bouschet and Ruby Royal.

White varietal wines are made from the Sémillon, Sauvignon Blanc, Chenin Blanc, and French Colombard. Other white grapes include the Clairette, Muscat of Alexandria, Muscat de Frontignan, and Dabouki, a local grape.

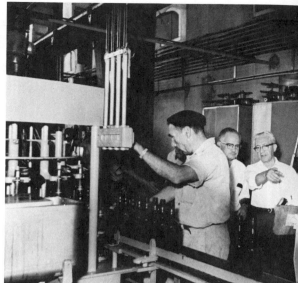

LEFT: Carignane grapes from the slopes of Mount Carmel in the crusher at Richon le Zion, in Israel. (*Courtesy Carmel Wine Company, Inc., New York*) RIGHT: Fully automated bottling plant at Richon le Zion. (*Photo by Photo-Emka Ltd., courtesy Carmel Wine Company, Inc., New York*)

WINE REGIONS OF ISRAEL

SCALE
0 10 20 30 40 50 km

LEBANON

SHOMRON VINEYARDS

SYRIA

MOUNT CARMEL VINEYARDS

GALILEE VINEYARDS

ZICHRON JACOB WINERY AND VINEYARDS

JORDAN

MEDITERRANEAN SEA

Tel Aviv

RICHON LE ZION—WINERY AND VINEYARDS

Rehovat Wine Institute

Jordan R.

Jerusalem

JUDEAN VINEYARDS

DEAD SEA

WILLIAM LEMBECK

EGYPT

Red, white, and rosé table and sparkling wines in all degrees of sweetness are produced. Dessert wines and sweet and dry vermouth are also made. All wines are kosher and are acceptable for religious ceremonies as well as for table use throughout the world.

Until 1961 many wines were generically named. When Israel signed the Madrid Pact, however, agreeing not to use territorial names outside its borders, new Hebrew names were adopted, identifying their Israeli origins:

NAME	DESCRIPTION
Adom Atic	dry, red, Burgundy type
Avdat Red	dry, red
Avdat White	dry, light white
Château Richon	semidry, golden, Sauternes type
Kadmon	sweet, amber, Madeira type
Partom	sweet, red, port type
Sharir	semidry, golden, sherry type
Topaz	sweet, golden, Tokay type

TURKEY

history

Although wine has been produced in Turkey on both sides of the Dardanelles for many centuries, it has never been an important enterprise, for, while Turkey possesses great vineyard acreage, the Islamic influence has limited winemaking to a small percentage of the total grape harvest.

Modern cultural changes, combined with a relaxation of traditional religious strictures, have greatly increased the vinicultural pursuits of this country. The government produces virtually all wines and spirits through state-owned wineries and distilleries. A few private concerns still make wine, but only for local consumption.

wine regions and wines

The best viticultural areas lie in the western part of Turkey's vast Anatolian peninsula, but there are a number of highly productive vineyards on the hilly slopes of Thrace in the European part of Turkey.

The wines of Turkey are produced from native grapes. Although very few wines are exported, some do appear on the wine lists of Turkish restaurants around the world. The red wines Adabag, Kalebag, and Buzbag, from Anatolia, and the white or red Trakya from Thrace are the most famous table wines. There are several good Turkish dessert wines, but few are exported.

Table wines are served mainly at dinnertime in Turkey, and consumption amounts to only one gallon per capita. The main alcoholic beverage is the anise-flavored spirit Raki, which is consumed, mainly by men, at all times of the day. Raki has a licoricelike flavor and a milky, pearlescent color when mixed with water.

2. NORTH AFRICA

ALGERIA

history   The Koran forbids the Faithful to drink alcoholic beverages, but the followers of Muhammad have always tended the vine wherever it would grow because they liked to eat the fruit. It was not until the early nineteenth century, when France colonized Algeria, that winemaking was begun in earnest. The devastation by *Phylloxera* in France during this period drove many French viticulturists to Algeria. Along with their knowledge of winemaking, the French brought their native vines—some, unfortunately, infested with the grape louse that later consumed the Algerian vineyards. Despite the scourge, the French succeeded in developing enormous vineyards on the slopes of sun-bathed hills, in the plains several miles inland, and along the coasts.

Before Algeria won its independence in 1962, this African country produced 400 million gallons annually. Most of these wines, as in other countries with hot climates, were quite full, deep red, and rich in alcohol. They were perfect blending wines for the thin bulk wines of France's Midi and were good base wines for some of the French proprietary wines, red table wines, and aperitifs. The colonial trade relationship allowed France to concentrate on producing quality wines for export and to supply its people with low-priced

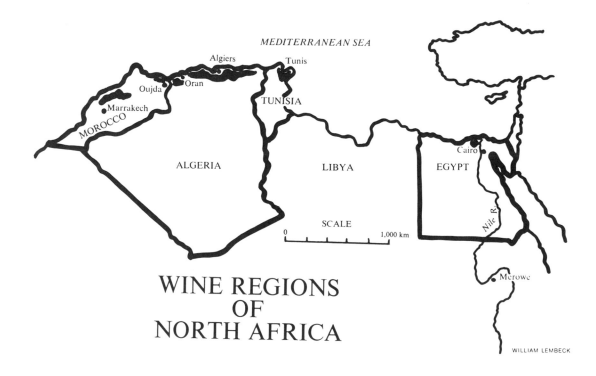

WINE REGIONS
OF
NORTH AFRICA

WILLIAM LEMBECK

Algerian quaffing wines, while establishing a strong economic base for the people of Algeria. After 1962, when the French winemakers were forced to leave Algeria, the demand for Algerian wines diminished because French growers insisted that the importation of cheap Algerian wine be stopped. Algeria has thus slipped from a major wine producer to a declining one, falling from ninth in worldwide production in 1974 to eighteenth in 1980.

wine regions and grape varieties

The vineyards of Algeria are located along the entire northern portion of the country, but the two departments of Algiers and Oran produce the majority of the wine. The Atlas mountain range separates the arable vineyard land from the vast nonarable interior. On the plains are produced light wines that mature quickly, while the hilly slopes and mountains are the source of fuller, more fragrant, and longer-lasting wines.

The vines cultivated are mostly those of the Midi: Carignane, Mourvèdre, and Cinsault for the reds and Clairette, Ugni Blanc, and Muscat for the whites. In better soils and more favorable exposures along the slopes the better varieties of Cabernet, Pinot Noir, Gamay, Chasselas, and Grenache are grown.

EGYPT

Although Egypt is in North Africa, it is closely allied with the Arab countries of the Middle East. Because of its Muslim heritage, Egypt is neither a large producer nor a large consumer of wine.

history

Historical references indicate that wine was made 6,000 years ago, as far south as the city of Merowe in the Upper Nile. This region is now part of Sudan. Presently, vineyards extend from Cairo to Alexandria, where the Nile empties into the Mediterranean Sea.

wine regions

Although the vineyards lie along the northern coast, they are as close to the Equator as they could be without suffering from the absence of the cooler altitudes provided by a mountain chain. Through a fortunate combination of soil, grape variety, and microclimate, Egypt has built up a wine industry since the start of this century that produces about two million gallons per year. Although more than one-third of it is exported, none has yet commercially reached the United States.

MOROCCO

history

The history of Morocco's wine industry is very similar to that of Algeria's, except for the period after Morocco's independence from France in 1956. The Moroccan people gained their independence in an orderly transition without the uprisings and war that racked Algeria. Regulations and controls were laid down by the Moroccan ministry along lines already established by the French, and a channel of commerce was established with the Common Market countries to absorb Morocco's surplus production.

wine regions and grape varieties

Morocco's vineyards stretch from Marrakech in the west to Oujda in the east, bordering on the Algerian vineyards around Oran. These vineyards all lie between the coast and the northern slopes of the Middle Atlas mountain chain.

As in Algeria, the grape varieties are the popular ones found along the Mediterranean basin, producing red and white wines. Carignane, Cinsault, Grenache, and Clairette are the major varieties. The red wines they produce are generally alcoholic and fiery, with a tendency toward heaviness. They are sound, drinkable wines with no claim to greatness. They are often blended with thin, light wines, to which they give body and life. Their white wines are pleasant when young and fresh and are consumed locally.

TUNISIA

history

The wine industry in Tunisia is confined to a small area around the Gulf of Tunis, where vineyards once flourished around the ancient city of Carthage. This winemaking area has remained confined because of centuries of Muslim influence. After France took control of the country, as in Morocco and Algeria, Tunisia's production soared until *Phylloxera* attacked the vineyards in the 1930s. A twenty-year program of uprooting and replanting on grafted stocks has restored the Tunisian wine trade. Tunisia now produces eighteen million gallons a year. The establishment of specific appellations in the 1940s helped this country maintain the high quality of its wines at a time when large quantities of bulk wine were needed in Europe. Tunisia's independence in 1956 did not affect its export market, which consisted mainly of France. After supplying domestic needs, Tunisia has no trouble selling its large surplus of wines on the international market.

grape varieties and wines

The familiar Mediterranean grapes are grown in Tunisian vineyards. Carignane, Cinsault, Alicante Bouschet, Mourvèdre, Clairette, and Ugni Blanc are some of the traditional varieties, but other *vinifera* grapes such as Pedro Ximenez, Sémillon, and Sauvignon Blanc have been planted to improve the white wines, which oxidize quickly in this hot climate. Muscat wines, produced from several varieties, are an important category and enjoy a special appellation, indicative of Tunisia's pride in these sweet wines.

While Tunisians consume a scant three-quarters of a gallon per capita, it still exceeds the wine consumption of Algeria and Morocco.

3. SOUTH AFRICA

Although South Africa's wine industry goes back more than three hundred   *history*
years, it is only since the early 1900s that wines were vinified and marketed to
the rest of the world. Today South Africa ranks ninth in production with 200
million gallons, but approximately half of this is distilled into brandy. Consumption of wine is about $2\frac{1}{2}$ gallons per capita.

The first vines arrived on a ship from the Dutch East India Company in
1655. They were planted by Johan van Riebeeck, and the first Cape wine was
produced four years later. The second Dutch governor, Simon van der Stel,
established an important vineyard at Constantia. With the arrival of French
Huguenots in 1688, vineyards were extended and wines were improved. By
1826 exports to Britain were increasing, and this continued until 1861, when
shipments were reduced because the tariff advantage to the Commonwealth
was eliminated. By 1885, when *Phylloxera* destroyed the vineyards of the
Cape, the wine industry was almost in ruins. By grafting their vines onto
American rootstocks, which were resistant to *Phylloxera*, winemaking resumed, and it reached a point where there was a troublesome surplus.

To help solve this production-consumption problem, the *Ko-operative
Wijnbouwers Vereniging (K.W.V.)* or Cooperative Winegrowers Association
was established, and today it has over seventy members. They set prices for
wines, standardized wine for export, and distilled any excess wine. The resulting brandy was improved by double distillation in pot stills and wood aging.

Although the cooperatives crush 85 percent of the entire South African
wine harvest and distill half of it, they are by no means the largest marketers
of alcoholic beverages. A registered group of producing merchants (*Produse-
rende Groothandelaars*) buys most of the wine from the cooperatives for bottling—either by itself or blended with wines they have produced themselves
or purchased from "Estates," which they then market under their own labels.
These merchants actually sell the bulk of wines and spirits consumed in South
Africa. One merchant, in fact, Cape Wines & Distillers, controls over 75 percent of the market.

The "Estates" (*Geregistreerde Landgoedere*) are individual wine producers
who produce the balance of the wines and bottle them under their own labels.

A system of guaranteeing the area of origin and the grape was put into   *areas of*
effect in 1973. A simple Wines of Origin (W.O.) seal appears on the capsule if   *origin laws*
the wine has a vintage date and contains at least 80 percent of wine from the
area on the label and is made from specified grape varieties.

Regarding grape restrictions, at least 75 percent of the wine must be made
from a specific grape variety (*cultivar*). If the grape is a noble variety, which
might be in short supply, a special provision allows the wine to contain only
50 percent of that grape until 1983. After that the wine will have to contain

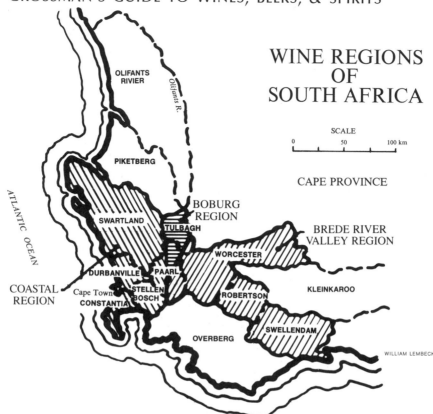

WINE REGIONS
OF
SOUTH AFRICA

SCALE

CAPE PROVINCE

WILLIAM LEMBECK

75 percent of the grape named on the label. If the grape used is in good supply, then the wine currently must contain 75 percent of the grape.

The highest level of guaranteed quality wine is the Wines of Origin Superior (W.O.S.) gold seal. This seal is awarded to a wine that accumulates more than the specified number of points when it is entered for certification by the local control board.

wine regions   The areas from which these certified wines may originate are called *Geproklameerde Gebiede van Oorsprong* (Proclaimed Areas of Origin). There are three main regions, which are subdivided into nine smaller districts, along with eight other districts located outside of the three main regions. These districts may be further divided into individual wards. The present official areas are as follows (see map above): The Brede River Valley Region, whose districts include Worcester, Robertson, Swellendam, and part of Tulbagh; the Boberg Region, which contains the balance of Tulbagh and part of Paarl; and the Coastal Region, which has the districts of Stellenbosch, Swartland, Durbanville, Constantia, and the rest of Paarl. The eight other districts are: Kleinkaroo, Olifantsrivier, Benede-Oranje, Piketberg, Overberg, Douglas, Cedarberg, and Vaalharts.

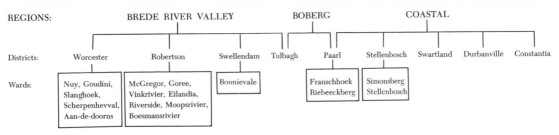

Other districts: Kleinkaroo, Olifantsrivier, Benede-Oranje, Piketberg, Overberg, Douglas, Vaalharts, Cedarberg

Actually, South Africa can be divided into two main wine areas: vineyards located along the coast or slightly inland, and others that are further inland, nestled in protective valleys. The best wines come from the Coastal Region, which is under the influence of the Atlantic Ocean. It gets 25 inches of rain per year, most of it in the winter when the vines are dormant. The more interior parts of the Brede River Valley, the Kleinkaroo, and the very interior Vaalharts, Douglas, and Benede-Oranje districts, produce more ordinary table wines and also fortified wines.

Included in the Coastal Region is the well-known Stellenbosch district, named for Governor de Stel, where one of the largest wineries in the world is located. Paarl, another important region, is on an equivalent latitude south as is Jerez, Spain, in the north, and sherries have been made in Paarl since the 1930s. Paarl also produces excellent table wines. South of Cape Town, the Constantia vineyards produce good red and white table wines, although it was a sweet Muscat wine that brought them fame in the past century. Tulbagh, 32 miles north of Paarl, is especially known for its white wines, some of which are late harvested.

Almost all of the individual Estate wineries are clustered in the Stellenbosch, Paarl, Tulbagh, Robertson, and Worcester districts, comprising the heartland of the fine wine industry.

grape varieties

South Africa grows many different vines, some that are familiar European varieties, and some that are native crossings. One important red-wine grape is the Pinotage, a cross between the Hermitage (an old synonym for the Cinsaut vine) and Pinot Noir.

Since the grapes are growing in the Southern Hemisphere, not only are the seasons reversed from the Northern Hemisphere, but so are the grapes' growing requirements. The whites do best on the cooler southern slopes, and the reds prefer the warmer northern slopes that face the sun.

Red grapes grown in the coastal region include Cinsaut (Cinsault), Pinotage, Cabernet Sauvignon, Shiraz, and Gamay.

White grapes of the coastal region are Steen (Chenin Blanc), Witfrans (Palomino), Kaapse Riesling and Ryn Riesling, Colombar (Colombard), Gewürztraminer, and Clairette Blanche. Both Steen and the Rieslings are vinified in the German style, and sweet wines are often produced from those grapes during a late harvest.

In the warmer interior districts, grapes that can tolerate the heat are more successful. Cinsaut is the most commonly grown red, although Cabernet Sauvignon and Pinotage are more important for the better wines. Dessert wine grapes, such as Witfrans (Palomino), Hanepoot (Muscat of Alexandria), Sultana (Thompson Seedless), and Steen (Chenin Blanc) complete the list of white grapes. Four grapes—Steen (Chenin Blanc), Witfrans (Palomino), Cinsaut, and Hanepoot (Muscat of Alexandria) comprise 68 percent of all grapes planted. Steen (Chenin Blanc) alone accounts for 27 percent.

wines   All types of wines are produced in South Africa. The coastal region is known for its table wines and some sherries and ports. Red table wines are vinified for aging in both wood and bottle. The most famous ones are produced in Paarl, Stellenbosch, Durbanville, and Constantia.

White wines have a freshness that comes from cool fermentation. The best whites come from Tulbagh, Paarl, and Stellenbosch. Since 1973 the winery at Nederburg, in the Stellenbosch district, has made a *Botrytised* wine every year called *Edelkeur*.

In 1980 the South African wine industry adopted regulations for amounts of allowable residual sugar, including three types of Late Harvest wines. While patterned after the German wine laws, these are more specific regarding residual sugar and alcohol in the finished wine, and are not only concerned with the weight of sugar in the must (Balling) at harvest.

Extra Dry Wine	Residual sugar no more than .25%
Dry Wine	Residual sugar no more than .4%
Semi Dry Wine	Residual sugar between .4 and 1.2%
Semi Sweet White	Residual sugar between .4 and 3.0%
Late Harvest Wine	Residual sugar between 2.0 and 3.0%
Special Late Harvest Wine	Residual sugar between 2.0 and 5.0%
Noble Late Harvest Wine	Residual sugar more than 5.0%

Late Harvest wines may not be fortified and no sweetening agents may be used.

Dessert wines, especially sherries, are made at Paarl and Stellenbosch. Traditional *flor* yeasts occur naturally here (see Chapter 8) and both *flor* and *solera* sherries are produced. With proper aging they are considered to be quite good. As in Jerez, the Palomino grape is used, but the best sherries produced in South Africa are made from the Steen (Chenin Blanc). Other popular sweet and fortified wines are produced in the districts of Constantia, Worcester, Robertson, and several areas located in Kleinkaroo.

Both bottle- and tank-fermented sparkling wines are made from the Riesling and Clairette Blanche grapes. They range in sweetness from extra dry to sweet. A carbonated *Perlwine* is also popular.

14
WINES OF AUSTRALIA, NEW ZEALAND, AND THE FAR EAST

1.   AUSTRALIA

rape cultivation in Australia began with Captain Arthur Phillip, who *history*
brought vine cuttings with his first fleet of eleven ships, when he arrived
to found the penal colony of New South Wales in 1788. His cuttings
came from Rio de Janeiro and the Cape of Good Hope, which had been stops
along the way. Unfortunately his three acres of vineyards were attacked by
fungus.

Three other pioneers made their mark on Australian winemaking during
the nineteenth century. They were Gregory Blaxland, John MacArthur, and
James Busby.

In 1816 Blaxland planted red-wine grapes, which he had obtained from the
Cape of Good Hope, on his farm in Parramatta Valley.

John MacArthur and his two sons planted a commercially successful vineyard near Penrith in New South Wales and were producing twenty thousand
gallons of wine annually by 1827.

James Busby, often called the father of Australian viticulture, arrived in
Australia in 1824 from his native Scotland. He was given a grant to teach
viticulture and to organize an agricultural institute. His main contributions
were writing two treatises on planting vines and on making wine and collecting and planting 678 varieties of vines from France, Luxembourg, England,
and Spain.

Many other *vignerons* planted in the 1800s, with their growing areas widespread throughout southern Australia. The first development was in the
Hunter Valley in New South Wales, closely followed by South Australia, and
Victoria. From the late 1800s to the 1960s, most wines produced were fortified
for home consumption and export to the United Kingdom. Table wine production was isolated, and it was mainly red wine.

During the last twenty years or so, there has been an era of growth and
change unknown in Australia's earlier viticultural history. This was due to

several factors. The first was the postwar migration of people from many European countries, bringing with them a taste for table wine. As affluence increased in Australia, and travel abroad became more available, there was even more exposure to European lifestyles. This, coupled with increased technology that could produce fresher, lighter wines, created a new interest in wines, especially whites. Today, these are the clear-cut preference for the Australian public.

AUSTRALIAN STATES

Australian wine areas are spread across the southern part of the continent, for twenty-five hundred miles. These areas vary from warm districts that require irrigation to cooler, high altitude (1500' to 2000') regions. The warm areas are warmer and dryer than those of Europe. During the summer, dry conditions help to ensure disease-free crops.

South Australia

South Australia is the premier wine-producing state, providing 60 percent of all wines in the country. The Barossa Valley is the best known winemaking area in Australia. It was originally planted by German settlers, and still shows their influence. Connawarra, in the southeast part of the state, is especially known for its premium red wines. The Riverland district provides much of the bulk wines of the country, and is one of the biggest wine-producing areas. Southern Vales and Clare-Watervale are historic areas that have made a significant contribution to the reputation of South Australia's wines.

New South Wales

New South Wales was the first state to produce grapes. The famous Hunter Valley actually produces only 1 percent of Australia's wines, but they are of premium varieties. The Murrumbidgee Irrigation Area (M.I.A.) or "Riverina" supplies about 20 percent of Australia's total vintage. Mudgee is another region in this state, and it is benefiting from new technology. Cowra, still another region, is typical of the newly emerging districts, and is acquiring a reputation as one of Australia's premium Chardonnay areas.

Victoria

Victoria has recently enjoyed an influx of new winemakers and greatly increased production. The Yarra Valley has become known for many small, limited production wineries. North-east Victoria is well known for its fortified muscat and port wines, although good table wines are also produced there. The Goulburn Valley, with Tabilk at its center, has an excellent reputation for its table wines. The central Victorian district has also seen an increase in new wineries, primarily among the smaller winemaking operations. Great Western is the home of one of Australia's major sparkling wine producers, but is also renowned for its long-lived dry red wines. Mildura, in the northwest, produces a great volume of bulk wines.

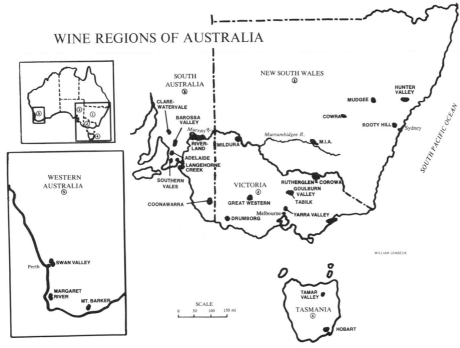

WINE REGIONS OF AUSTRALIA

The Swan Valley, around the city of Perth, has a long history of winemaking. This small enclave on the west coast of Australia, gets a great deal of sunshine, which helps to produce grapes that are rich in sugar and low in acid. Here, again, the area is benefiting from new technology, which has achieved significant refining of table wines. In the southwestern part, the areas around the Margaret River and Mount Barker have a cool climate that imparts strong varietal flavor. They are part of important new wine areas to emerge during the last decade.

Western Australia

In addition, Tasmania, off the coast of Australia, is south enough of the equator to make its location comparable to fine wine areas of Europe. This area has begun to flourish, with a number of small wineries starting to produce some very fine Rhine Rieslings and Cabernet Sauvignons.

Tasmania

There is so much experimentation of both technology and planting of various grape varieties in different microclimates, in this growing and expanding industry, that the producers are not ready yet for regulations on appellations. Many producers, in fact, buy grapes from different regions for their blends. The wine trade, at this point, is self-regulating. There are over three hundred wineries in Australia that produce 100 million gallons of wine annually for a 4 gallon per capita consumption.

For export, strict government and industry regulations ensure the highest possible quality. Wines and brandies are inspected by officers of the Department of Customs and Excise, as well as by inspectors appointed by the Australian Wine and Brandy Corporation.

GRAPE VARIETIES

There are many different grape varieties grown, all from *vinifera* stock. If a wine is varietally labeled, there must be a minimum of 80 percent of the named grape in the wine. The most prominent grapes are:

red wine varieties

SHIRAZ. This grape is the most widely planted grape for the production of red table wines and fortified wines. In Australia there are over twenty thousand acres of Shiraz grown in virtually all districts. It is sometimes blended with other varieties, notably Cabernet Sauvignon.

CABERNET SAUVIGNON. As in Bordeaux and California, this is Australia's most sought-after grape. Its acreage has increased dramatically, and there are now over 10,000 acres under cultivation. The Cabernets from Coonawarra have been traditionally highly regarded, but there is competition from newly emerging areas.

MERLOT AND PINOT NOIR. These French grapes are not yet planted in large amounts, but they will increase in importance as winemakers learn more about growing and vinifying them.

GRENACHE. This grape is used in the commercial, bulk wines, but is diminishing in importance. Still second to Shiraz, it has now decreased to 13,000 acres.

white wine varieties

SEMILLON. This premium variety is widely planted, with over 6,000 acres. It is usually vinified as a full, dry wine, and is sometimes known as the "poor man's Chardonnay."

RHINE RIESLING. The Rhine Riesling is the true Riesling of Germany or California. It makes a fruity wine with good acidity in the cooler regions, and a smoother wine with more glycerine in the warmer areas. In some years and areas, it is late picked, sometimes affected by *Botrytis*. It then produces intensely flavored sweet wines.

CHARDONNAY. This variety has emerged in the last fifteen years as a premium varietal. It is vinified in either a full, rich style, often aged in oak, or a lighter, fruitier style that is ready to drink sooner.

SULTANA AND MUSCAT GORDO BLANCO. The Sultana is the Thompson Seedless of California (a table grape) with 45,000 acres planted. It is used for commercial table wines, fortified wines, and for distillation. The Muscat Gordo Blanco is the Muscat of Alexandria. It is used a great deal for cream sherry, but can be fermented dry for table wines. It is grown in over 10,000 acres, and is also used as a table and raisin grape.

TRAMINER (GEWÜRZTRAMINER), SAUVIGNON BLANC, AND CHENIN BLANC. These grapes round out Australia's white table wine production, and will most likely emerge as important varietals.

DORADILLO, PALOMINO, AND PEDRO XIMENEZ.   These grapes used to be important in fortified wine production, but with consumption patterns changing towards lighter, table wines, they are much less useful than before, and acreage is decreasing.

All classes and types of wines are produced in Australia. The wine industry shows great diversity with its fine table and sparkling wines, as well as its impressive fortified wines. The constant experimentation on the part of new winemakers is producing many wine styles.

High technology, combined with low taxes on alcoholic beverages, is creating affordable wines of good quality. Labeling is clear and explicit, and the implication of the various wine districts is becoming clearer to the public.

While many wineries used to use predominantly generic names, such as claret, Burgundy, Chablis, sherry, Sauternes, port, Moselle, etc., now many wines are marketed under district names, such as Barossa, Hunter Valley, Coonawarra—as well as varietal names, such as Cabernet Sauvignon, Shiraz, Pinot Noir, Rhine Riesling, and Chardonnay.

The patterns of production and consumption have been surprisingly similar to those of the United States, and there is a similar "pioneer" spirit as well, in the exploration and development of new wine regions.

2 . N E W Z E A L A N D

The wine industry in New Zealand can be traced directly to Australia in the 1800s, with European influences not appearing until the early 1900s. New Zealand's first winemaker was James Busby, British Resident to Waitangi in 1838. Before that appointment, Busby had already established vineyards in Australia. *history*

Romeo Bragatto, a graduate of Italy's school of viticulture in Conegliano, became New Zealand's first official head of viticulture in the Department of Agriculture in 1902. He urged research on the proper choice of vines for the different regions, and struggled against *Phylloxera*, disease, and mildew. At the same time, Yugoslavian immigrants from Dalmatia entered the wine business. In fact, New Zealand's largest winery, Montana, means "mountain" in Yugoslavian.

Efforts to use resistant varieties led to the changing of *vinifera* varieties to *labruscana* and hybrid varieties, with a consequent reduction in wine quality. This, coupled with new efforts by prohibitionists caused New Zealand's wine industry to dwindle to a few small wineries and home winemakers.

After World War II grape acreage and wine production began to increase, and in 1957 restaurateurs and retailers were licensed to sell single bottles of wine rather than two-gallon lots. From a mere 600 acres in 1940, acreage now stands at 12,000, and 10 million gallons of wine are produced annually. Table

WINE REGIONS
OF
NEW ZEALAND

AUCKLAND

WAIKATO

NORTH
ISLAND

GISBORNE

HAWKES BAY

SCALE

0   50   100   150 mi

SOUTH
ISLAND

MARLBOROUGH

WILLIAM LEMBECK

wines account for 72 percent, and by 1980 *vinifera* varieties had climbed back up to 85 percent, and hybrids accounted for only 15 percent.

wine regions   New Zealand is made up of two large islands, North and South. Winemaking in New Zealand began in the warmer north, but the search for good microclimates for various grape varieties has led to large plantings in the cooler south. The newest wine-growing area, Marlborough, is, in fact, at the north end of South Island. The value of this area for grapes was determined after a thorough survey of the islands in the early 1970s. The Wairau Valley in Marlborough has the highest sunshine hours, low rainfall, temperate climate, and good soil types. These conditions are especially good for crisp, white wines.

On North Island, the most important areas are Poverty Bay in Gisborne and Hawkes Bay, both on the east coast. Auckland, which used to be the largest growing area, has dropped in importance because of high humidity and urban development. Waikato, south of Auckland, is last in acreage.

grape varieties   In an effort to combat *Phylloxera* and continue growing *vinifera* varieties,
and wines   wines are increasingly being grafted onto resistant rootstock.

White grape varieties account for more than 80 percent of the total plantings. The Riesling-Sylvaner (Müller-Thurgau) accounts for about 30 percent of this. Chardonnay, Gewürztraminer, Sauvignon Blanc, Rhine (Johannisberg) Riesling, Dr. Hogg Muscat, and some Siebel hybrids complete the list.

Red varieties include Cabernet Sauvignon, Pinot Noir, and Pinotage (a cross between Pinot Noir and Cinsaut), and Shiraz.

Fortified wines have declined to 28 percent, and the thrust is for premium varietals.

3. CHINA

The first vines in China came from the Arabs in Turkestan in the late second century B.C. By the seventh century A.D. vines were widespread. One major setback came in 1322, when vines were uprooted by order of the emperor so that cereals and grains could be planted. Even though some vines were replanted, to this day more beer and rice wine is produced and consumed than grape wine. Recently, however, some agricultural experimental stations have been studying the vine, and cooperative vineyards are becoming more important. *history*

Grapes are grown in the region around old Turkestan, called Turfan. They are also grown north of the Yangtze River and south of the Great Wall. Five provinces along the Yellow River—Shantung, Honan, Kiangsu, Hopeh, and Shansi—are growing grapes successfully. Some vines are also planted around Beijing (Peking). *wine regions*

WINE REGIONS OF CHINA

WILLIAM LEMBECK

grape varieties and wines   The grapes that grow in China include some native Asian stock, such as the early ripening Kashikar and the late ripening Koumiss, and some *labruscanas*. *Vinifera* varieties include Muscat, the Dimiat of Bulgaria, Riesling, and Sylvaner. Grapes are used for wine, table grapes and raisins, and medicine.

White, rosé, and red wines (*p'u t'ao chiu*) that go up to 16 percent alcohol are produced. A sweet wine called Chefoo is available in red and white. A dry wine called Tsingtao is also available in red and white from the Shantung province in northern China. Sparkling wines (*ba-xiangpin-chiu*) are also made. In addition to grapes, sweet wines are made from plums and litchis. Shaohsing and Hua Tian are dry rice wines.

4. JAPAN

history   The wine industry is small in Japan, with production averaging 6 million gallons a year. Native varieties of grapes, the Koshu and Jaraku, have been planted since the twelfth century. They are believed to have European origins that go very far back. In the nineteenth century Americans and Europeans brought in *labruscana* grapes, such as Concord, Delaware, Campbell Early, and Baily A, a Muscat hybrid. Some *vinifera* grapes were also introduced, including Sémillon, Chardonnay, Riesling, Cabernet Sauvignon, and Merlot.

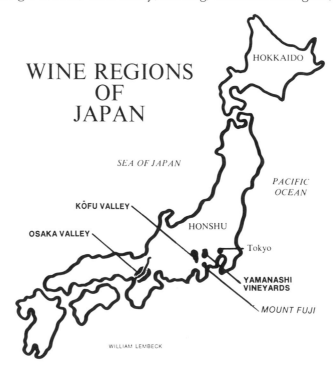

WINE REGIONS OF JAPAN

HOKKAIDO

SEA OF JAPAN

PACIFIC OCEAN

KÔFU VALLEY

OSAKA VALLEY

HONSHU

Tokyo

YAMANASHI VINEYARDS

MOUNT FUJI

WILLIAM LEMBECK

Two women pick grapes for the production of wine in the Yamanashi Vineyard, the largest vineyard in the Orient, located near the foot of Mount Fuji. (*Courtesy Suntory International*)

wine regions

The main island of Honshu contains the two most important wine-growing regions, although grapes are grown to the north and to the south. The main regions are the Kōfu Valley and the Osaka Valley, and the acreage equals more than half of Japan's total acreage under vine. Japan is generally quite humid, but on Honshu Island the humidity is lower and the grapes have a better chance against fungus, *oïdium*, and mildew.

Other wines are produced on the island of Hokkaido in the north and at Katsunuma in Yamanashi province west of Tokyo.

wines

As in China, wines are made from native, *labruscana*, and *vinifera* grapes. Problems with humidity and with acid soil, however, produce wines that are astringent and unbalanced. Torrential rains around harvest time point up the need for early-ripening varieties. Sugaring wines is quite common, and many more sweet and fortified wines are produced than table wines.

Because the most popular imported wines are French reds and German whites, the finest Japanese *vinifera* wines have French or German labels. Phrases such as *Vin Blanc, Vin Rouge,* or *Mise au Château* are not uncommon.

15
AROMATIZED
WINES

Man first learned to make his wine aromatic," said the late André L.
Simon, "when he discovered that by adding honey or sage or some
herb to his sour wine, it became more palatable." Since that day
great strides have been made in the science of producing aromatized wines.

The ancient Greeks preferred pitched or resinated to natural wine, as do
many Greeks of the present day. The Romans liked to flavor their wines with
such interesting materials as pepper, spikenard, cypress, wormwood, myrrh,
poppy, tar, pitch, bitumen, aloe, chalk, mastic gum, boiled seawater, and
asafetida. Is it strange that one ancient Roman writer said of wine, "It biteth
like a serpent"?

Aromatized wine is the fourth classification of wines, the others being still,
sparkling, and fortified. It is a fortified wine in which herbs, roots, flowers,
barks, and other flavoring ingredients have been steeped in order to change
the natural flavor of the wine.

Aromatized wines include both dry (French origin) and sweet (Italian origin) vermouths and the quinined or other apéritif wines of various countries,
such as Spain, Portugal, United States, Australia, Argentina, and South Africa.
All, including vermouths, are apéritifs, from the Latin *aperio*, meaning "to
open." That is exactly what they are supposed to do. They open—whet the
appetite pleasantly.

VERMOUTH

The term *vermouth* comes from the German *wermut* ("wormwood") but
was first used commercially in 1786 by Antonio Benedetto Carpano of Torino,
Italy, who may be called the founder of the vermouth industry. He used the
white Piedmont wines nearest at hand, especially the fine Canelli Muscats,
and produced a bittersweet vermouth.

In 1800 Joseph Noilly of Lyon, France, independently invented a somewhat drier vermouth by using the thin Hérault wines of the Midi. Thus, the
dry type has come to be referred to as French and the sweet type as Italian.
Today, however, the Italian producers also make vast quantities of the dry,
while the French producers also make the sweet type. In fact, great quantities
of both types are made outside Italy and France. These are either local prod-

ucts for local consumption or famous brands that are licensed to be made outside of their original homes, with strict adherence to the original recipes.

More sweet vermouth is drunk throughout the world than the dry, except in the United States, where consumption of sweet and dry are about equal. The highest per capita consumption of vermouth in the world is in Argentina.

The French type is the dry vermouth. According to French law, a vermouth must consist of at least 80 percent wine, which must have an alcoholic strength of at least 10 percent. Alcohol may be added later in order to raise the strength of the wine to up to 19 percent. Sugar, too, may be added in order to soften the bitterness.

dry or French vermouth

The wines used for making French vermouth are produced in the Midi in the Department of the Hérault, which produces more wine than any other province of France. They are light, thin, and rather characterless wines, made from the Picpoul and Clairette grapes.

The process of maturing the wines plays a very important part in making French vermouth. The dryness of the vermouth is a perfectly natural development, since Clairette and Picpoul wines become very dry as they mature. In fact, to prevent too much dryness they are mixed with the less dry Grenache in a proportion of three to one. The wines are fortified with grape brandy, and are aged at least one year in large 25,000- to 35,000-liter oak vats. They are then transferred for an additional year of aging to smaller oak casks of about 600 liters, called *demi-muids*. Part of the storage by some producers takes place in the courtyard of the establishment, where the wines can receive the benefits of the sun's rays during the day and of the coolness at night. This daily variation in temperature ages the wines more rapidly, but loses 8 percent due to evaporation.

To give the vermouth its softness, the better houses use *mistelle* or *vin de liqueur* in place of sugar. The *mistelle* is made from sweet grape juice that has had enough alcohol added to it to prevent or stop fermentation. Because the grape sugar has not been allowed to convert to alcohol, the *mistelle* remains sweet. In making vermouth, *mistelles* of Grenache and Muscat are used. They are aged separately for the same length of time as the other wines.

Incidentally, in some parts of the world, *mistelles* in themselves are apéritif wines without any additional flavorings. While they are not aromatized wines, they are mentioned in this chapter because of similarities in their production to aromatized wines. In Champagne, France, the local *mistelle* is called *ratafia*. One *ratafia* made the same way, but in California, is called "Panache." In Cognac, France, the local *mistelle* has Cognac in it and is called *Pineau des Charentes*. The most famous brand in this country is Reynac.

After the wines are matured, they are blended in a proportion of 80 percent Hérault wine and 20 percent *mistelle*. This is known as basic wine. The basic wine is then flavored by an infusion obtained by steeping the special

Casks of maturing wine stored in an open courtyard, exposed to the elements, before being made into dry vermouth. (*Courtesy Noilly Prat & Cie., Marseille*)

flavoring agents in the wine, according to a duly tested formula, which is the prized secret of each producing house. This brings out the characteristic vermouth bouquet, in which a complex aroma is blended in the most attractive manner.

Anywhere from thirty to fifty different types of herbs, plants, roots, leaves, peels, seeds, and flowers may go into a single formula for making French vermouth. Some of these are nutmeg, coriander seeds, cloves, cinnamon, rose leaves from Bengal, Peruvian quinine bark, hyssop, marjoram, angelica root, wormwood, bitter orange peel, camomile, linden tea, centaury, gentian, and flowers of elder.

All the plants are put in a large tank. The basic wine is poured in and left in contact with the plants from three weeks to one month; then this wine, which has taken on flavor from the plants, is drawn off and new basic wine is added in its place. This is repeated several times before the flavor of the plants is exhausted. The flavored basic wines are then blended, and the resulting mixture is known as the infusion. The infusion is mixed in a proportion of one to five with other basic wine, and brandy is added to raise the alcoholic strength of the wine to up to 19 percent.

This mixture is put into glass-lined vats where the wines are brought down to a temperature of nearly freezing and are stirred constantly by giant paddles to ensure perfect blending. The refrigeration has a purpose. Vermouth, like all wine, contains some tartaric acid, which is a natural element in the composition of wine. It is invisible, but in time it crystallizes and forms a deposit known as cream of tartar. The formation of the deposit can be forced by abruptly lowering the temperature of the wine.

It takes three and a half to four years to mature, age, and prepare a true French vermouth. This means that enormous reserve supplies must always be kept on hand and that large sums of money are invested in these stocks for a great many years. For this reason only well-established, financially sound houses can afford to finance the aging process that ensures the wines will acquire the properties of perfect maturity. In addition, the French vermouth business must be conducted on a mass-production scale; otherwise it would not be economically feasible.

sweet or Italian vermouth

The Italian vermouth is the sweet type, made from white wines. This sweetness results from the fact that the basic wine used for making Italian vermouth is sweeter and fuller than the thin white Hérault wine of the Midi and because sweetening is added later on in the production. The law in Italy specifies that vermouth be made from wines that are at least one year old. Between infusion and final filtering another year passes, so it takes approximately two years to produce an Italian vermouth.

Most of the wines used in making Italian vermouth are those from Apulia, although some Moscato di Canelli is always blended in for flavor and sweetness. These rather bland wines are infused with various herbs, roots, seeds, and a little quinine. They are allowed to mature, and as soon as they have absorbed a sufficient amount of flavor they are drawn off, fortified, and filtered, and some sugar and coloring matter are added. The brown color is obtained by adding caramel.

There is a reason for the use of quinine. When the European countries started colonizing the tropics they encountered malaria, and the best medicine for this was quinine, which has an extremely bitter taste. To get the soldiers to take their medicine, an ingenious physician gave them quinine in sweetened wine. Thus was born the taste for *quinquina* ("quinined wine"), the apéritif wines for which the French and Italians have never lost their taste.

domestic vermouths

Vermouth production is quite streamlined in the United States. For dry vermouth, a base wine is prepared from any neutral and inexpensive white wine that has been stabilized and acid-adjusted. Wine spirits are used to increase the alcohol to under 24 percent. Infusions of herbs are prepared by different flavor houses to keep the formulas secret. Imported flavors are used. About 0.3 percent of this infusion is added, along with some liquid sugar, and water to reduce the alcohol to about 20 percent. There is no aging, to keep the color light.

For sweet vermouth, the base wine is a blend of one- or two-year-old wines, including red and white port, cream sherry, and Muscatel, with some caramel for color correction. The base wine has an alchohol content of 19 percent, and the sugar is about 7 percent. An infusion of herbs and spices from Italy is added. Infusions from U.S. flavor houses may be used as well. Along with more sugar, the vermouth is allowed to "marry" in stainless steel tanks for four to six months. The finished wine has an alcohol level of about 18 percent, and the sugar is now around 10 percent. It is pleasant and aromatic, with a slight bitterness in the aftertaste.

OTHER AROMATIZED WINES

The apéritif wines are made in almost all European wine-producing countries in the same manner as French vermouth, except that the proportion of *mistelle* is generally greater, making the wines sweeter.

Apéritif wines are usually quinined wines. When the apéritif is white, the basic wine used is white; when red, the basic wine is red. The variation in taste—the sweetness, bitterness, or aromatic flavor—results from the use of different formulas, which are trade secrets of each producing house.

The principal apéritif wines sold in this market are the French Dubonnet (red and white), Byrrh (red), Lillet (red and white), and St. Raphaël (red and white, but only the red is sold in the United States). From Italy comes Campari, Cynar, Blackberry Julep, and Punt é Mes. Cynar's name and principal flavor, incidentally, are derived from the artichoke. The ancient Romans felt that the *cynara* ("artichoke") helped "keep the liver young."

HOW AND WHEN TO SERVE VERMOUTHS AND APÉRITIF WINES

In America we think of vermouths as wines to be used in preparing cocktails—Martini (dry vermouth) and Manhattan (sweet vermouth)—and that is the principal use made of them. Apéritif wines, however, are increasing in popularity in the United States. Since spirits before dinner tend to dull the palate, many people have found that a wine apéritif is the best prelude to a wine-accompanied dinner. With increased interest in fine foods, Americans are now enjoying apéritifs beforehand.

Vermouths are always served well chilled. The classic ways to drink them are neat, on the rocks, or with a splash of soda and a twist of lemon peel. Lillet, however, is enhanced by a strip of orange peel. Both sweet and dry vermouths are often mixed together, half and half. (See Chapter 26 for recipes using vermouths and apéritif wines.)

Since these apéritif wines are used chilled, they may be stored in the refrigerator. They will thus be ready for drinking neat, or for use in cocktails,
without being diluted by melting ice, and the aromatic flavors will maintain
their freshness longer.

These wines may also be used in cooking, since they combine wines and
flavorful herbs. Vermouths provide an easy-to-use blend of some of the world's
most prized seasonings. Dry vermouth, for example, can often be substituted
for dry white wine in recipes, and the amount of herbs indicated can be
reduced.

Making vermouth at Cinzano. The still, called *alambicco* in Italian, is used to
transform spices into extract. (*Courtesy Cinzano*)

16
SPECIALTY
WINES

1. WINES FROM FRUITS OTHER THAN THE GRAPE

Thus far we have discussed wines that have been made from grapes, but wine can be made from the juice of other fruits as well. Apples, pears, cherries, berries, and plums are some of the fruits that yield very attractive wines.

CIDER AND PERRY, APPLE AND PEAR WINE

Cider, or *sidra* in Spanish, comes from the Hebrew word *shekhar,* meaning "strong drink." Cider and perry are obtained by fermenting the freshly expressed juice of apples and pears, respectively. Their alcohol content varies from 2 to 8 percent and is sometimes slightly higher. This, of course, is the cider that in the United States is called hard cider, as opposed to the nonalcoholic sweet cider.

Both cider and perry are rather sweet beverages that are wholesome and have the pronounced flavor of the fruit. Just as good eating grapes are poor wine varieties, so apples and pears that are good to eat are poor for making cider or perry.

Normandy, in northwest France, is the apple- and pear-growing region of the nation. There cider, and not wine, is the table beverage.

In the United States, apple and pear wines are made in Pennsylvania and Massachusetts. They may or may not be sweetened.

In Spain and England, a secondary fermentation may be induced in the bottle or in bulk, producing a wine called Champagne Cider. All Spanish cider is treated in this manner. The fermentation is produced by adding a small amount of sugar syrup, the carbon dioxide thus created being retained. In Latin America vast quantities of it are sold as the poor man's Champagne, because it is about half as expensive as Champagne. It is somewhat sweet and has a pleasant apple flavor. It is also useful in making punch.

BERRY WINES

Berry wines include wines made from blackberries, raspberries, strawberries, elderberries, loganberries, boysenberries, and currants. All are very sweet and fruity, and each has its individual flavor appeal.

In Europe these wines are made from freshly expressed fruit juices. In the United States they are often made from fresh frozen fruit or concentrated fruit juice, although some dried fruit may also be added. For example, a good blueberry wine is made in Massachusetts from the frozen concentrate of Maine blueberries.

In all cases it is necessary to add water and sugar. The fruit musts have to be ameliorated with sugar to balance their high acid content. For example, the acid content of blackberry must is about 1 percent, principally isocitric acid, which gives the wine its distinctive character. In order to maintain color and fresh flavor, berry wines are not aged very long.

Most of the commercial fruit wines are marketed at 10 to $12\frac{1}{2}$ percent alcohol, but some are fortified to up to 20 percent. Berry wines have been imported to the United States from Czechoslovakia, Israel, Holland, Japan, Poland, and Yugoslavia.

CHERRY WINES

Cherry wines are made in Europe from sour cherries. Denmark, which is an important producer of these wines, uses the small black native Langeskov cherries.

When the wines are being made some of the cherry pits are crushed and left in to give a subtle almond flavor. If more than 10 percent of the stones are used, however, the flavor of the stones dominates the flavor of the cherries. Like berry wines, cherry wines cannot be aged too long.

The wines are fortified, being shipped with an alcohol content of $17\frac{1}{2}$ to $19\frac{1}{2}$ percent. They are rich in fruitiness and quite sweet—a good reason for their popularity. They are most pleasant if served well chilled or in mixed drinks, and the cherry wine is finding wide use in the kitchen to give a delightful dash of cherry flavor to fruits and desserts.

PLUM WINES

Wines are made from different varieties of plums in Europe, the Far East, and California. Japan, especially, has a humid climate where the plum thrives. In California the plums are grown in the Santa Clara area.

These wines are seen in two styles, either with the natural plum flavor or with a slight almond flavor resulting from the presence of the stones during fermentation. It is not as easy to make a wine from a pulpy fruit as it is to make wine from a berry, but the plum wines on the market are all quite successful. In California an apricot wine is also made, and in the northeast, plum, nectarine, and peach wines are produced in small quantities. A litchi wine comes from China. These are all made similarly to plum wines.

PINEAPPLE WINE

Pineapple wine is made in Hawaii and Puerto Rico. In Hawaii the wine is made from juice obtained from pineapple processing plants. It is then fermented at the winery and, when completed, does not have a strong pineapple taste. Some sparkling pineapple wine is also made.

A very fruity pineapple wine is made in Puerto Rico from the red Spanish pineapple. It is fortified with pineapply brandy and has a beautiful golden color and tart pineapple character.

CITRUS WINES

Some citrus wines, usually fortified and tasting like sherry, are made in Florida.

WINES MADE FROM DRIED FRUITS

Wines can be made from dried fruits, such as figs, dates, and raisins. The fruit is shredded and then steeped in hot water. This liquid becomes the fermenting must. Dried apricots and dried peaches become too gummy to be used successfully.

HONEY WINE / MEAD

Mead dates back to biblical times. Mead, or honey wine, is not really a fruit product but a fruit-related product, since much honey comes from the flowers of fruit trees.

Mild-flavored honey is better than strong honey for making honey wine. After the honey has fermented it may be sweetened with either sugar or more honey. It also may be fortified to 18 to 20 percent by adding brandy to the partially fermented must.

Honey wine is made in California and is also imported from England and Poland; a kosher mead is made in New York State.

HOW AND WHEN TO SERVE FRUIT WINES

Fruit wines can be drunk chilled, either neat or on the rocks. With soda they make a fine spritzer. They are delicious poured over fresh fruits or ice cream for dessert. In the kitchen they can be used in glazes for ham and as sauce ingredients for game birds.

2. SPECIAL
NATURAL WINES

In 1954 a law was passed in the United States permitting a new wine type—special natural wines. By 1975 almost 57 million gallons were being made, but by 1981 the amount had dropped to $31\frac{1}{2}$ million gallons.

Special natural wines are flavored wines that resemble vermouths, but they are not vermouths. They are natural wines, lightly flavored with herbs, spices, fruit juices, essences, aromatics, and other natural flavorings, such as citrus or exotic tropical fruits. All flavorings must be approved by the government. While these wines cannot resemble natural fruit wines, lemon flavor may be used, for example, since there is no lemon wine on the market.

Special natural wines may be sweetened with sugar. If they are made in California, they must be designated as American, since California state law does not permit sugaring of its wines.

When these wines first appeared around 1960 they were fortified to 18 to 19 percent. With the trend toward lightness, however, they are now below 14 percent, and many have a slight amount of carbonation for even more freshness. Some examples are Annie Green Springs, Ripple, and Bali Hai.

With the trend toward a return to "natural" things, the category of "natural wines" in the 1980s implies less of flavored wines, and is now more associated with the new light, low calorie wines.

3. SACRAMENTAL WINES

From the beginning, there has been a close alliance between wine and religion. Even during Prohibition in the United States wine for religious purposes was permitted. Almost all Western religions use wine in their rituals, the two most important and frequent users being Roman Catholics and Jews.

USE OF WINE IN THE MASS

Originally the wine used in the Eucharistic Sacrifice had to be pure grape juice that had been completely fermented. The Congregation of Sacraments, on July 31, 1890, said, "Provided that the alcohol has been extracted from the fruit of the grape, and the quantity added, together with that which the wine to be treated naturally possesses, does not exceed the proportion of 12 percent, there is no obstacle in the way of using such wine in the Holy Sacrifice of the Mass." This means that the alcohol contained in the juice from the grape itself, plus that added from an outside source, could not exceed 12 percent.

Since extra-sweet wines were subject to refermentation, the Holy Office amended the ruling on August 5, 1896, to allow the addition of alcohol so that the wine was not to exceed 18 percent alcohol, provided that such addition be made before fermentation was completed.

Sour wine is invalid for use in the Mass, and no chemical process, such as the use of tartrate or potassium, may be used to correct the natural tartness of the wine. In addition, the Sacred Congregation of the Holy Office declared that sugar could not be added to the wine. The wine may be either red or white.°

Wine is also used for the Communion service by many Protestant denominations.

USE OF WINE IN THE SYNAGOGUE

Rabbi A. Hyman kindly furnished the information on the use of wine in the synagogue and in the homes of pious Jews.

In order to be used for ritual purposes, the wine must be made according to the rabbinical law and must be a pure, natural wine, unmixed and sound. It may be either red or white. If it becomes sour, or has impurities from the lees, it cannot be used. There is no such thing as a sanctified wine in the sense that a special wine is used in the synagogue. The same wine may be used in the temple as is used in the home.

Wine is used both at the incoming prayer of the Sabbath, Friday evening, and at the outgoing prayer at the end of the Sabbath, Saturday evening. It is also part of the services on the eve of festivals and on holy days. At wedding ceremonies the bride and bridegroom must share a glass of wine. The most widespread use of wine is on the two Seder nights of Passover, when it is obligatory for each person to drink four glasses of wine.

In the synagogue and at home the amount of wine served at services, according to ancient ritual, should equal "an egg and a half full"—about two and a half ounces—and more than half of it must be drunk.

Most sacramental wine is made primarily from the Concord grape, grown in the central and eastern states, which seems to fit in with the need for a mellow, rich wine.

The Concord wine is rich, sweet, and deep purple in color. After the wine has fermented out naturally, sugar is added to counteract the natural acidity of the grape and to balance the pronounced flavor.

For a discussion of New York State kosher wines, see pages 237–38.

Kosher dry table wines are also available. Imports include varietal wines from Israel, Soave and Asti Spumante from Italy, and some petit château wines from Bordeaux. An excellent kosher Riesling is made in the Napa Valley in California.

° References: Tanguerey, *De Sacramentis in Geneve*, p. 80; Wuest Mullaney, *Matters Liturgical*, p. 56; McHugh and Collan, *Catechism of the Council of Trent*, pp. 221–223.

17
BEERS AND ALES

Until now we have discussed wines, which are produced from grapes or other fruits rich in sugar. Living yeast cells, by the process known as fermentation, convert this sugar into alcohol. No matter what variations there are—white wines or red wines, indoors or outdoors, Europe or the United States—the basic chemistry is the conversion of sugar into alcohol and carbon dioxide.

But what if fruits are not readily available as a source of sugar? Can sugar be obtained from something else? In this chapter we shall look at alcoholic beverages made from grains rich in starch, instead of from fruits rich in sugar. Starch cannot be converted directly into alcohol. But with the help of nature, man can convert starch into sugar. Once this step has occurred the sugar can then be converted into alcohol by the familiar process of fermentation.

In order for starch to be converted into sugar, the grain that contains the starch must be germinated—dampened with warm water so it can sprout. A by-product of this sprouting is the formation of a vegetable enzyme called amylase. In the 1830s, when this phenomenon was beginning to be understood, this substance was called diastase, from the Greek word meaning "separation." Separation is significant because starch exists in long chains, each fragment of which is $C_6H_{10}O_5$. The enzyme amylase, in a water solution, acts to separate this long chain into double fragments and, at the same time, adds a water molecule (H_2O) to each, forming a maltose sugar molecule, $C_{12}H_{22}O_{11}$.

enzymatic action

To this day, in the alcoholic beverage industry the words *amylase* and *diastase* are used interchangeably. Other enzymes play a part later in the brewing and fermenting processes. Among those that may be either formed or added by the brewer are the proteases and zymase. The proteases act on insoluble protein matter, helping to make the finished beverage clear and free of haze. Zymase, a yeast by-product, converts sugar into alcohol.

history   In Germany in the early part of the present century, excavators discovered a jug whose contents proved to be beer mash that had been made sixteen centuries ago—probably the oldest bottle of beer in existence. And yet that mash had been made when the beer industry was already thousands of years old, for the history of brewing is as old as recorded history—over seven thousand years.

Archaeologists have found hieroglyphics that represent brewing. They have found jugs that were used for beer, and chemical analysis has proved that barley was used. They have even found some of the yeast cells by which beer was fermented. In ancient days the brewmaster and the baker were the same man. The nobility and the priesthood were interested in brewing, and there was a close association between religious ceremonies and beer.

According to Pliny, the Egyptians made beer from corn. The Greeks learned the art of preparing beer from the Egyptians. Through the ages, in every country from Egypt to the New World, the existence of beer has been recorded in all languages. Medieval history is replete with references to brewing and its importance to the development of civilization. The Kaffir peoples of Africa made, and still make, a kind of beer from millet, while the natives of Nubia, Abyssinia, and other parts of Africa prepared a fermented beverage that they called *bousa*.

The Russian *quass* or *kvass* from black bread (rye), the Chinese *samshu*, and the Japanese *saké* from rice are all beers of ancient origin.

Had it not been for the lack of beer and food, the Pilgrims on the *Mayflower* would have continued their journey to Virginia, where they had intended to make their home. Instead they landed at Plymouth Rock because, as recorded in their journal, "we could not now take time for further search or considerations, our victuals being spent, especially our beer."

Although the Pilgrims called their brew beer, what they drank was really ale, as the Germans did not introduce lager beer to America until 1840. Although most colonial households brewed their own beer, records show that a brewery was in operation by 1637. William Penn, founder of Pennsylvania, was probably the first to operate a large commercial brewery, at Pennsbury in Bucks County. Another early brewery belonged to the Dutch brewer Jacobus, whose first brewery and beer garden was located at what is now the corner of Pearl Street and Old Slip in New York City.

Among the early Americans who were brewers or who had financial interests in breweries were George Washington, James Oglethorpe, Israel Putnam, Samuel Adams, and Thomas Chittenden, the first governor of Vermont. They were all men of integrity and standing, so the industry started in America under excellent auspices.

definitions   BEER is a brewed and fermented beverage made from malted barley and other starchy cereals, flavored with hops. During fermentation the yeast sinks to the bottom; hence beer is a *bottom-fermentation* brew. *Beer* is also the generic term for all malt beverages.

LAGER is a bright, clear, light-bodied beer that is sparkling and effervescent, brewed from malt—and in some cases from prepared cereals such as corn grits or cracked rice—hops, and water. The resultant wort is fermented and lagered (stored) for aging and sedimentation. After this period it is kräusened, or carbonated. All American beers are the lager type.

PILSNER is a term employed universally on labels of light beers. The original and most famous is the Pilsner Urquell from Pilsen, Czechoslovakia. By labeling their beers Pilsner other brewers wish to convey the impression that their beer is similar to that of Pilsen. All Pilsners are bright, light, lagered beers, but none comes close to duplicating the original. Pilsner is not a separate type of beer, as bock beer is.

BOCK BEER, OR BOCKBIER, is a special brew of heavy beer, usually somewhat darker and sweeter than regular beer. It was originally brewed in the spring, but it no longer has any seasonal significance. Some people think the name is a corruption of *Einbecker Bier,* from the town of Einbeck in Germany. There is no legal definition for bock beer, and it varies with the brand.

MALT LIQUOR is a malt beverage, brewed like beer, that usually has a higher alcohol content than beers, the percentages of alcohol being regulated by each state, but is usually between 6 and 7 percent. In Ohio, the range may be from 3.2 to 7 percent by weight, and in Oregon, for example, it may vary from 4 to 8 percent by weight. The color is usually light and pale.

ALE is an aromatic brew made of malt or malt and cereal and is usually fuller bodied and more bitter than beer. Ale is fermented at a higher temperature than beer, and most of the yeast rises to the top of the brew; hence ale is a *top-fermentation* brew.

PORTER is the predecessor of stout and is lower in alcohol, with a dark color and bittersweet taste. As its producers increased its alcohol content it was referred to as an "extra stout" porter, and stout soon became a separate product.

STOUT is a very dark ale that is malty and slightly bitter, flavored and colored by the addition of roasted barley to the brew.

SAKÉ is a refermented brew of high alcohol content produced mostly in Japan from rice.

BREWING PROCESS

In brewing beer, as in preparing a fine dish in the kitchen, the result is as good as its ingredients. These are much the same whether you wish to produce a light lager beer or a full-bodied creamy ale; the only difference is the way the ingredients are treated—how long the malt is dried and roasted, the quantities used, the yeasts used, and the time and temperature of fermentation.

raw materials   WATER. Although the quality of each ingredient is important, none is more so than the quality of the water, not only because it forms 85 to 90 percent of the finished beer, but because it is used in every step of the brewing operation and has a great deal to do with the character of the beer. The first consideration, therefore, is the quality and type of water. This explains why the great brewing centers of the world developed around suitable sources of water. Furthermore, water that was good for ale was not necessarily good for lager-type beer, and vice versa.

Most waters used for brewing today, however, can have their pH adjusted with either calcium carbonate or citric acid, followed by filtration. Since waters can be analyzed and then corrected in this manner, finding the "ideal" source is no longer as important as it once was. Brewing water, by the way, is called *liquor.*

YEAST. The fermenting agent, the pedigreed brewer's yeast, converts the wort into beer. This unicellular, microscopic plant is protected more carefully in a brewery than any other ingredient, for once the particular strain has been selected it must not be changed or the character of the beer changes with it. It is not merely that the yeast causes the sugars to become alcohol—another yeast would do that—but it performs other functions that probably influence the character of the beer more than the alcohol does. It is these secondary products of fermentation that vary with the types of yeast. The yeast for lager-type beer is *Saccharomyces Carlsbergensis,* named for the place where it was discovered. Ale yeast is *Saccharomyces cerevisiae,* the same kind that is used for bread.

MALT. Brewers use only the finest barley malt. As a general rule the breweries do not do their own malting but buy malt from specialists, although the manner in which the malt is treated is specified by the brewmaster when ordering. The exact amount of kilning and the degree to which the barley is roasted are important in obtaining the amount of dryness or sweetness of the final beer or ale and in whether it will be a light beer or a dark beer.

OTHER CEREALS. These can be either raw, such as corn and rice, or in varying stages of preparation, such as corn grits (cracked corn) and hominy, or they may even be like the breakfast cereal corn flakes. Certain types of sugars or corn syrups may be used. These are called malt adjuncts, and their use lowers costs, and results in a lighter product.

HOPS. Hops did not come into general use until the fourteenth century, and for a while there were laws in Europe forbidding their use in brewing. Up to that time other substances had been used to give the brews bitterness and character, but it did not take long for people to realize that hops were the best. Hops come from Czechoslovakia, Germany, and England, and each has different characteristics. In the United States, hops are grown in California, Oregon, Washington, and Idaho. Some American brewers use both domestic and imported hops. Only the flower of the female hop vine is used, which is like a small pine cone with very soft petals. It must be picked at just the right time, as under- or overripeness is detrimental to the brew. The hop is picked free of leaves and stems and is dried carefully to conserve the delicate, fine aroma essential to choice brewing. At the breweries the hops are stored in clean, air-conditioned cold-storage chambers at a temperature of 35 to 40 degrees Fahrenheit.

Rather than simply judging hops by their appearance, as was formerly done, hops today are chemically analyzed to determine the exact amount of humulone and lupulin (alpha and beta resins, respectively) they contain, because of the flavor these resins impart. Bitterness oils are measured in International Bitterness Units. Hops also provide an antiseptic action that prevents the development of wild bacteria, which might contaminate the wort.

With the ingredients and the proper plant equipment the brewer is ready to make beer. The first step is malting the barley, which, as mentioned previously, is done by specialists to the brewmaster's specifications if it is not done by the brewmaster himself. *steps in making beer*

In general, the malting procedure is as follows. The barley goes to the barley-receiving room, where it is dressed, that is, sieved, or passed over screens so that small and inferior grain will be eliminated. The best grain is then steeped or soaked in water for two days until it is thoroughly softened. It then goes into germinating compartments, where the temperature and moisture levels are controlled, for about three weeks, during which time the grain begins to germinate, or sprout.

When the sprouts are about three-quarters of an inch long, the water is turned off and the grain is known as green malt. It is already malt, for malt is germinated grain. During this germination process a chemical change occurs in the grain that is important to its future function in the brewing process. The enzyme amylase has been produced, and it has the property of converting the balance of the starch into sugars—maltose and dextrin—which are fermentable, whereas the starch in its original state is not.

To stop further growth of the sprouts, the green malt is placed in a kiln and dried. The temperature and length of time the malt is roasted determine the color and sweetness of the final product. Roasting proceeds until either light, dark, or black malt is produced.

The kilned malt is now screened to remove the culm, or dried sprouts, after which it goes to the mill room, where it is ground into meal, or grist.

The next step is mashing. The ground malt first goes through a hopper into a mash tun. This is a horizontal or vertical cylindrical copper or stainless steel vessel with a turbine or ribbon mixer unit. It contains a heating device and a set of temperature controls.

When a raw cereal is used, it is cooked in a cooker, a vessel similar to a mash tun, to gelatinize or liquefy the starch. Prepared or precooked cereals do not require heating. The malt, the cereals, and the proper amount of hot water are thoroughly mixed and are left to stand or are cooked as long as is necessary to obtain the maximum extraction of soluble materials. It is during this mashing operation that the brewmaster can determine the composition of the finished beer, for it is the temperature and the length of time at which the mash is maintained at a given temperature that determine the amount of fermentable and nonfermentable substances the wort will contain. It is the nonfermentable substances that give body to the brew. With modern equipment all of these operations are scientifically controlled, and the beer from a given brewery is uniform. After the cooker mash is added to the main mash in the mash tun, the starch is converted into fermentable sugars. Then the total mash is pumped into a lauter tun. This is a circular copper or stainless steel vessel containing a false slotted bottom and a series of movable rakes.

When the stirring is stopped the solids are allowed to settle. What has been going on is predigestion. Compounds have been broken down and made digestible; insoluble substances have been made soluble. The solids, which settle on the bottom, form the filter bed. The liquid, which is now wort, flows through this natural filter and passes into the brewing kettle. In order to ensure that every bit of goodness has been obtained from the grain, the solids are sparged (rinsed) with water. This rinse from the sparging is added to the wort. In the kettle, hops are added to the wort, which is then boiled for two to two and a half hours. This accomplishes the following:

1. The wort is sterilized.
2. Some excess water evaporates.
3. Certain volatile materials from the hops and malt that are not needed are lost through evaporation.
4. Some of the insoluble substances in the wort are made soluble by the high heat. The brewer calls this the hot break.
5. Because of a small amount of caramelization, a certain amount of darkening of color occurs.

After the hot break and the completed work of the hops, the wort runs from the kettle through a hop strainer, or hop-jack. There the hops are passed over a screen and the wort, which is now called hot wort, runs through, leaving the spent hops behind. The hot wort is cooled down and goes into the fermenting vat.

The temperature to which the wort is cooled depends on whether the brewer is making beer or ale. In the case of beer, fermentation takes place at a very low temperature—between 37 and 49 degrees Fahrenheit. Ale, on the other hand, is fermented at a higher temperature, between 50 and 70 degrees Fahrenheit. This is one difference. Another is that the yeast used in fermenting ale is different from that used for beer.

To start the fermentation, yeast is added at this point. There is as much

difference between brewer's yeast and ordinary yeast as there is between a
Derby winner and a truck horse. The secret of the flavor in many world-
famous beers is the result, unquestionably, of the strain of yeast used. The
difference between lager beer yeast and ale yeast is that lager beer yeast
settles to the bottom and does its work there during fermentation and after.
Beer is the result of bottom fermentation.

In the case of ale, the yeasts, in multiplying, have a tendency to stick
together, creating more of a surface, and do their work after rising to the top
of the liquid. Ale is the result of top fermentation. This is partly because of the
higher temperature at which ale is fermented and partly because of the different type of yeast used. Beer fermentation takes longer than ale fermentation—eight to eleven days being the fermenting time for beer, while five to six
days are usually sufficient for ale.

Beer usually has a lower alcohol content than ale, while ale has a stronger
hop flavor than beer.

Beer in fermentation in open fermenting vats. (*Courtesy United States Brewers Association Washington, D.C.*)

During fermentation the carbon dioxide gas (CO_2) that is given off is gathered and stored to be added back later, in part, to the beer. After the principal fermentation is over and most of the yeast has settled down, the young beer is run off into glass-lined or otherwise protected storage vats, where it is kept at a very low temperature, close to the freezing point, so that the yeast and other solids that would give it a cloudy appearance may precipitate by the natural process of sedimentation. Sometimes beechwood chips are added to attract the impurities and promote clarification. During this resting period (*ruh*), a slow, secondary fermentation takes place that develops the immature beer, and increases carbonation. The beer throws off its roughness and, as it matures, it becomes mellower and more pleasing. This is the lagering, and it usually takes from two weeks to two months.

Finally the beer is carbonated to make it effervescent and refreshing. The carbon dioxide gas that was released by the wort during fermentation is added, after having been compressed. Another popular method used for the carbonation of beer, known as kräusening, is accomplished by adding about 15 percent of the fermenting wort, or kräusen, to the beer in storage; a short additional

1. Barley grain is cleaned, graded, and stored before start of malting process.
2. Barley is soaked (steeped) in warm water to soften the grain.
3. Softened barley remains in scientifically humidity- and temperature-controlled compartments where it germinates.
4. The germinated barley, now green malt, is placed in kilns where it is dried out with heated air.
5. After kilning, the malt is cleaned and stored for aging.
6. Matured malt is ground into a meal.
7. Ground malt and corn grits, in proper proportion.
8. and 9. Separately, the malt and the corn grits are mixed with hot water and cooked briefly.
10. The mashing or starch liquefaction and conversion to maltose and dextrin. The liquid is now wort.
11. The wort is filtered through the lauter tun, which separates the wort from the grain solids, which in turn are processed for cattle feed.
12. The filtered wort is flavored with hops in the brew kettle, where it is boiled for several hours.
13. Spent hops are separated from the wort when the brew kettle is emptied.
14. Wort cools in wort-collecting tank.
15. Refrigerated wort cooler.
16. Pure yeast culture is added to the wort.
17. The wort remains in the starting tank only long enough for fermentation to begin.
18. Now beer, it is filled into the fermenters, where the process takes seven days. The CO_2 produced is gathered, compressed, and stored, to be added back to the beer later.
19. The new beer is put into storage tanks. Some young, unfermented (kräusen) beer is added to ferment slowly at a low temperature, under pressure, to give the beer its zest.
20. After several months at low-temperature storage, the mellowed beer is filtered, has a small amount of CO_2 added back, and is finally kegged, bottled, or canned.

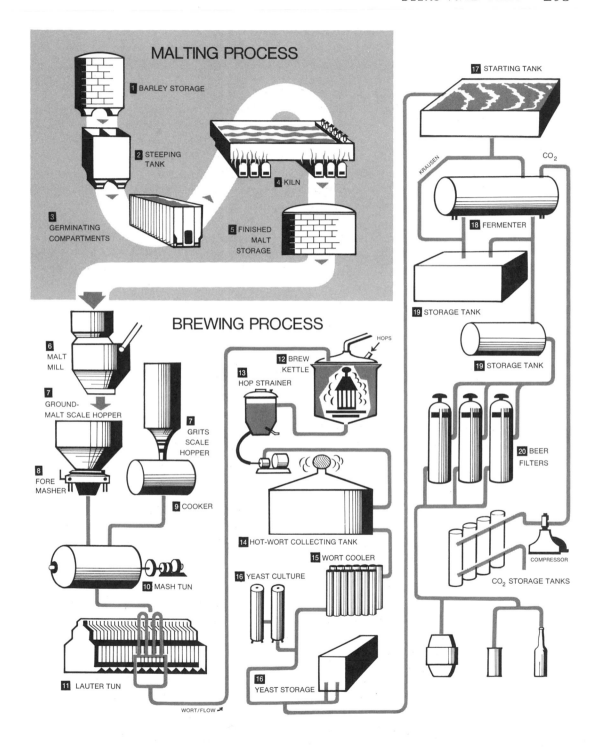

MALTING PROCESS

1 BARLEY STORAGE

2 STEEPING TANK

3 GERMINATING COMPARTMENTS

4 KILN

5 FINISHED MALT STORAGE

BREWING PROCESS

6 MALT MILL

7 GROUND-MALT SCALE HOPPER

7 GRITS SCALE HOPPER

8 FORE MASHER

9 COOKER

10 MASH TUN

11 LAUTER TUN

WORT/FLOW

12 BREW KETTLE

HOPS

13 HOP STRAINER

14 HOT-WORT COLLECTING TANK

15 WORT COOLER

16 YEAST CULTURE

16 YEAST STORAGE

17 STARTING TANK

KRÄUSEN

CO_2

18 FERMENTER

19 STORAGE TANK

19 STORAGE TANK

20 BEER FILTERS

COMPRESSOR

CO_2 STORAGE TANKS

fermentation increases the carbonation of the product, making it lively. Regardless of the method used, once the beer is carbonated it is refrigerated, it may be centrifuged, and it is then filtered. The product is now ready for packaging.

The three forms of packaging beer are kegs or barrels, bottles, and cans. The beer, under pressure, passes through closed pipelines into the containers.

Beer cannot be kept or stored in direct contact with wood, as it will take on an unpleasant woody flavor. Previously, barrels made from wood were lined with pitch, which was tasteless, did not dissolve in the beer, and kept it from touching the wood. Metal kegs of aluminum or stainless steel are used today almost exclusively. These kegs are built to withstand a much greater pressure than is usually found in beer. Wooden cooperage can stand a pressure of 45 pounds per square inch, while metal kegs can stand about 300 pounds.

As these containers are safe against additional pressure that might be created by additional fermentation, beer so packaged is not pasteurized but is kept under refrigeration. Beer packaged in bottles or cans is likely to remain in the package longer and to be shipped farther away from the brewery than that in kegs, so in order to protect the package this beer is pasteurized, making it sterile and killing any yeast that might still be active. If this were not done, additional carbon dioxide gas could form and perhaps burst the bottle or can. This is the principal object in pasteurizing bottled or canned beer. Pasteurization takes place at 150 to 160 degrees Fahrenheit, at which temperature the beer is kept for about ten to fifteen minutes. It is then cooled rapidly. Flash pasteurization is sometimes used. This is a faster process whereby the beer is kept at 180 to 185 degrees Fahrenheit for one minute only.

As with milk, the pasteurization of beer in the bottle slows down but does not halt the ravages of time. The peak quality of pasteurized packaged beer is not indefinite. In cans it is four months, while in bottles it is six months.

As also with milk, the pasteurization of beer does, in some small measure, alter the taste. The principal difference between draft beer and bottled beer is that pasteurization diminishes the fresh flavor, although it does contribute to the beer's stability.

All bottled and canned beers were once pasteurized. Today, with the advent of microporous materials that filter out yeast cells, unpasteurized beer can be packaged in bottles and cans with assurance of a safe shelf life for this sterile-filtered beer, permitting it to retain its "draft" taste.

According to U.S. government regulations, the words *draft beer* on the labels and advertising of both keg beer and bottled or canned beer may be used as follows:

1. Beer in containers of one gallon or more, the contents of which are drawn off through a tap or spigot, may be described as draft beer whether the beer has been pasteurized or sterile filtered or is unpasteurized.

2. Bottled or canned beer may be described as draft beer if it is unpasteurized or has been sterile filtered.

3. Bottled or canned beer may not be described as draft beer if it has been pasteurized, but the use of such terms as *draft brewed, draft beer flavor,* and *old-time on-tap* taste is permitted as long as the label or advertisement conspicuously states that the beer has been pasteurized.

Beers and ales are complex food products. They contain:

the finished product

Water	85 to 90 percent by weight
Alcohol	3.2 to 8 percent by weight
Carbohydrates (sugars)	3 to 6 percent by weight
Protein	0.3 to 0.5 percent by weight
Calories	10 to 17 per ounce

As can be seen, the largest part of beer is water. This explains why, historically, areas with good water supplies were so important.

The alcohol content of beers varies from 3.2 percent to 4 percent by weight, while the specialized beer marketed as malt liquor varies from 3.2 to 8 percent by weight. Ales average 4.5 percent by weight, and fuller ales, such as stout, average 6 percent by weight. In Scandinavian countries there is a "motorist" beer that contains only 2.8 percent alcohol by weight. A few imports have the alcohol removed at the end of the brewing process, so that it has no alcohol at all yet retains the character of a malt beverage. The alcohol content of U.S. malt beverages is regulated by individual states and varies from state to state; states have held this right since Repeal. This explains why the same brand of beer may taste different in different parts of the country. The consumer does not know the alcohol content because the government forbids the mention of alcohol on the label.

The calories in beers and ales vary, naturally, with the alcohol and carbohydrate contents of the individual brands. The average U.S. beer has 12½ calories per ounce. Bock beer, malt liquor, special ales, stout, and porter have a higher caloric value. Low-carbohydrate beers, which have one-half to two-thirds the calories of regular beers, are available.

There is a great demand for lower calorie and lower carbohydrate beers, and several of the major brands on the market have light beers as part of their line. These beers have about one-third fewer calories than standard beers.

One way of reducing carbohydrates, and therefore calories, is by the elimination of any unfermented sugars in the finished beer. This can be done by using more malt adjuncts, which give a more complete conversion than straight barley malt, during fermentation. A more complete conversion can also be accomplished by the use of additional dextrin-fermenting enzymes added to the brewing process.

A less satisfactory way to reduce calories is simply to dilute the beer with carbonated water. Sometimes all these methods are combined to lower the calories in the light beers. These beers have a shorter shelf life.

SUGGESTIONS for KEEPING and SERVING
"BEER AT ITS BEST"

SITUATION	CAUSE / EFFECT and REMEDY	SITUATION	CAUSE / EFFECT and REMEDY
If Your Beer Is WILD SECTION 1	*Temperature too high* Keep temperature in storage box 45° F. or lower. Also refer to Section 4. Coil boxes should be properly iced in both upper and lower box and ice kept broken up, preferably by a small stick used with a stirring motion, to prevent the arching of the ice. Do not beat ice down with a club as this is apt to flatten out pipes or kink them. *Keg has been agitated* This disturbs the carbonic gas. Allow kegs to rest several hours after delivery. Don't move them about roughly. *Pressure too high* Causes turbulent beer and excessive foaming. Decrease pressure as described in Section 3. *Pitch or sediment in tap rod holes* Prevents free flow and gives turbulent beer. Clean holes before tapping. Don't ram the rod into the bottom—it might damage both rod and barrel lining. *Uninsulated beer pipe line* Heats up the beer in warm weather.—See also Section 4. *Kinks or dents in coils or beer pipe line* Have such kinks or dents removed; results in turbulent beer. Repairs must be effected. *Holding glass too far from faucet* Results in excessive foaming. Try holding glass closer to faucet. *"Cracking faucet"* (Faucet partly open) Causes artificial foam and destroys part of the quality. Open faucet wide as fast as possible when drawing beer.	**If Your Beer Is TOO WARM or TOO COLD** SECTION 4	*Pre-cooling too great or insufficient* Kegs on tap as well as in reserve should be kept cool. However, the temperature of the cooling compartment should be so controlled that it permits serving the beer at between 40° and 45° F. Unless this temperature is regulated to suit the rate of drawing beer, it is apt to run too cold or too warm at times. *Cooling in coil box too great or insufficient* If considerable time elapses between servings, the beer in the line may be cooled too far, even to the point of being chilled, thus losing its fine flavor. Similarly, if the beer is drawn very fast, it may not have time to get cool enough. Control the refrigeration in the coil box accordingly. *Uninsulated pipe lines* All exposed lines must be well insulated otherwise variations in the atmospheric temperature may have a considerable influence upon the temperature of the beer drawn. *Too much or too little equipment* Dispensing equipment cannot be oversized. In case of too little equipment the beer is drawn too fast and may run warm, while excessive equipment, standing idle much of the time, may result in chilled beer.
If Your Beer Is CLOUDY SECTION 2	*Old, defective beer hose* Beer hose has a limited life. Old hose is likely to be the cause of contamination no matter how often it is cleaned. *Sagging beer pipe line* The resulting pockets harbor slime and bacteria which are difficult to remove. Check lines for straightness. *Beer chilled in coils* Beer, left in lines over night, usually becomes chilled, losing flavor and color, appearing cloudy. It should be discarded before serving in the morning. *Coils not properly cleaned* Merely going through a cleaning procedure is not enough unless it is performed in an approved manner, preferably by a reliable and experienced expert on this type of work. It is poor economy to do the cleaning cheaply but poorly and thus spoil beer and lose trade, worth many times the saving on cleaners. *"Cracking faucet"* (Faucet partly open) This practice is harmful to the beer, having the effect of de-gassing, which sometimes leaves a cloudy appearance.	**If Your Beer Is FLAT** SECTION 5	*Temperature too low* Chilled beer appears flat and loses its flavor. Maintain 40°-45° F.—See also Section 4. *Insufficient pressure* Will not allow beer to flow freely. Note little or no foam. Increase pressure. *Leaky pressure line* Leaks allow the gas to escape and must be located to remedy. *Pressure shut off during night* This allows the carbonic gas to separate from the beer. Once a keg is tapped, the pressure must be left on continuously until emptied. *Loose bung or tap connections* May be caused by rough handling and result in loss of the gas same as through any other leak. Check carefully and tighten. *Kegs stored in non-refrigerated compartment* Storage in a warm, dry place causes wooden kegs to dry out and spring leaks. *Greasy glasses* Any fatty substance makes beer go flat instantly. Wash glasses in hot water *without* soap. Rinse in pure cold water. Do not dry glass before using.
If You Have PRESSURE PROBLEMS SECTION 3	*Too long beer pipe line* A long pipe line causes a lot of friction, which is harmful to the beer and makes it almost impossible to draw a good glass. The keg should be as close as possible to the bar. *Gauge and regulator away from bar* These devices should be installed at the bar so that they are readily accessible and under continuous control of the operator. *Defective gauge or regulator* Should be checked occasionally to make sure that they function correctly. *Air-bound coils* Results in unsteady flow. Put on extra pressure for a moment while faucet is wide open to clear the line. *Pressure off during night* Apply pressure immediately upon tapping keg and never shut off until empty.—See also Section 5. *Pressure leaks* Whether gas or compressed air is used, the loss due to leaks is considerable. All lines should be checked regularly. *Air compressor system* Extreme care must be taken to prevent oil from entering beer line.—See also Section 6. *Correct pressure* Depends entirely on:—1. distance between keg and bar;—2. condition and temperature of beer in keg;—3. whether vertical or horizontal beer line;—4. length of coil;—5. whether beer is drawn fast or slowly;—6. number of barrels tapped at one time.—Each installation has its own characteristics and it is therefore up to the operator to establish the most effective pressure. If using more than one beer be sure pressure is correctly adjusted for each beer on tap inasmuch as different pressure may be necessary.	**If Your Beer Is UNPALATABLE** SECTION 6	*Unsanitary conditions at bar or in cellar* Remove empty kegs from refrigerating compartment as soon as possible. Clear lines every morning of beer that has been standing in them over night. Observe strict sanitation everywhere. *Sagging beer pipe line* Forms pockets for accumulation of bacteria and slime, which is difficult to remove. *Uninsulated beer pipe line* Guard against the ill effects of possible high temperature by insulating all exposed lines. *Old, defective beer hose* Replace defective hose at regular intervals—its life is limited and can be the cause of unpalatable beer.—See also Section 2. *Coils not cleaned properly* This is a common cause of trouble. Should be cleaned by specialists at least once every week. Use compound made for purpose, never strong chemical solutions.—Also note Section 2. *Rods and bungs* These must be cleaned regularly, and when not in use, hang on wall of box. *Coil box* Any mud deposit which may collect in the bottom of the coil box should be removed, as this mud forms an insulation which prevents the full refrigerating effect of ice for which you pay. *Air compressor location* If compressor is used, see that intake is extending to outside to draw fresh air. Should be equipped with an effective filtering device.—See also Section 3. *Foul air line or air tank* Check lines and tank for possible accumulation of oil, dust or water. Clean out occasionally. Drain tank regularly of condensed water. *Unclean faucet* Take apart occasionally, thoroughly remove all deposits and then sterilize.

NOTE:

1—Place beer in storage box immediately when delivered.
2—A rubber emergency bung and extra wooden bungs should be kept on hand in case a bung is accidentally split.

3—Always use a wooden mallet...never one of metal...in tapping.
4—When removing bung and rod from keg, tap the bung lightly on each side, alternately, until loose. Never use the rod as a lever, as this may bend it and cause it to become useless.
5—Don't have more barrels on tap than requirements call for.

Federal Regulations require revenue stamp to be defaced when tapping barrel by driving rod through stamp

Suggestions for keeping and serving beer. (*Courtesy the F. & M. Schaefer Brewing Company, reprinted by permission of A. O. Smith Corporation*)

DISPENSING DRAFT BEER

The three cardinal points of beer service are cleanliness, temperature, and pressure.

Beer is one of the most delicate and perishable food products a restaurant handles. It is highly susceptible to extraneous odors, to bacteria in the air, and to strong light. It should be stored by itself in a spotless room that is well ventilated and in which a constant temperature of 40 degrees Fahrenheit is maintained.

cleanliness

The dispensing equipment should be checked and thoroughly cleaned as often as possible, but at least once a week. If an establishment wishes to serve perfect beer, no detail is too small to be overlooked, no precaution too great, in maintaining and ensuring cleanliness of beer service.

One of the main causes for flat beer is the American tendency to serve it too cold. The ideal temperature is 45 degrees Fahrenheit for beer and 50 degrees Fahrenheit for ale, although it is customary to chill as low as 40 degrees for lager and 45 degrees for ale. Do not chill below 40 degrees; the nearer the beer is to 45 degrees, the better it tastes.

temperature

Imported beers should be served at 48 to 50 degrees Fahrenheit and English ale or Irish stout at 55 degrees.

Beer that is too cold is flat and cloudy. If it is too warm, the gas breaks away from the liquid and there is too much gas. Beer in this condition is called wild beer. Do not take any chances. Maintain a constant and uniform temperature. Use a thermometer and store the barrels as close to the dispensing unit or units as possible.

To maintain an even flow of beer from the tap, the pressure must be carefully watched and controlled. Since some of the natural pressure of the carbon dioxide gas is bound to be lost between the time the barrel is opened and the time the last glass of beer is drawn, additional pressure must be supplied. Some people prefer air and others carbon dioxide. Carbon dioxide, while more expensive, ensures a more even supply of gas from the first to the last glass and eliminates the possibility of foul air being drawn into the system, as may happen when air pressure is used. Just as the gasoline gauge on the dashboard of an automobile permits the driver to check his supply at a glance, so the gas pressure gauge should be at the bar where the operator may check and control the pressure.

pressure

Final operation in a brewery—filling the aluminum kegs. (*Courtesy the F. & M. Schaefer Brewing Company.*)

As bottles of beer move along conveyor belts, inspectors make sure each bottle is properly filled. (*Courtesy Jos. Schlitz Brewing Company*)

HANDLING PACKAGED BEER

Bottled beer should be stored in a dark, cool place. Beer exposed to the direct rays of the sun in a shop window for display cannot be used, as beer is extremely sensitive to light and will, after only a few moments, take on a strange odor and flavor commonly called skunky. It may also become cloudy. This is caused by a substance in the hops that is light sensitive. If the hops are treated with hydrogen, the skunky-producing elements will be eliminated.

Beer in cans is not affected by light, but it should be kept in a cool place. In the home beer should be stored in the lowest, coolest part of the refrigerator. Storing bottled or canned beer in the door shelf of a refrigerator is risky because the constant jostling and the drafts of warm air from the kitchen could hasten the beer's deterioration.

serving

When serving bottled or canned beer, allow the glass to remain on the table in an upright position. Pour the beer so that the stream flows straight into the center of the glass. Do not tilt the glass and pour down its side because you will not release enough carbon dioxide. U.S. beers are usually more heavily carbonated than European beers, and they, especially, should be poured in a forceful stream.

IMPORTANT SERVING NOTE. Glasses or containers to be used for serving beer or ale must never be washed with soap or soapy water. The soap leaves a fatty film on the inner surface of the glass that will break down the bubbles of carbon dioxide, thus destroying the desired collar of foam. Nonsoapy detergents may be employed, but always make sure that the glass is rinsed well before it is used. Glasses should be "beer clean."

UNITED STATES BEERS

The United States is the world's largest producer of malt beverages, producing all types of beers and ales. Most of the twenty-two gallons per capita consumed in this country is the nationally produced, light-colored, light-bodied beer. Large breweries, with nationwide distribution, brew toward a taste level that is pleasing to all areas of the country. The biggest breweries in the United States, in order of barrels shipped, are Anheuser-Busch, Miller, Schlitz, Heilemann, Pabst, Coors, and Stroh. Most have breweries in many different cities.

Of the more than seven hundred breweries in the United States that sprang up after Prohibition, there are now only about seventy left. For small, local breweries costs are high and volume is low. They do, however, produce fine beers and fill a special need, brewing to local tastes. The beers are not mass produced, and the brewmaster can take time with each step, giving the brew extra aging. Since the beers are drunk near the breweries, they are fresher than those that are shipped great distances.

There are many fine producers dotted throughout the United States. Here is a partial list of cities with local breweries; there are, of course, many other local favorites.

Allentown, PA	Horlacher
Chicago, IL	Peter Hand
Cincinnati, OH	Wiedermann's, Schoenling
Cold Spring City, MN	Cold Spring Export
Louisville, KY	Falls City, Drummond Brothers
Philadelphia, PA	Ortlieb's, Prior
New York, NY	Old New York Beer
St. Mary's, PA	Straub's
San Antonio, TX	Pearl, Lone Star
San Francisco, CA	Anchor Steam Beer
Sonoma, CA	New Albion
Wilkes-Barre, PA	Stegmaier

BEERS OF OTHER LANDS

The beers of Europe that are most popular in America are the light brews, best exemplified by the famous Bohemian Pilsner Urquell of Pilsen, Czechoslovakia. Most of the German, Danish, and Dutch beers are similar to the Pilsner. They are very pale-colored, light, hop-tasting beers. From Munich, Germany, also come some much-favored darker-colored, richer, and slightly maltier-tasting beers.

England and Ireland have long supplied the American market with their famous ales and stouts. These brews are much darker, richer, and more bitter than those of the Continent.

In the Americas, Canada and Mexico have been the principal suppliers because of their proximity to the United States. Canadian beers and ales are very light, and enjoy the position of being imports, even though they are very similar to domestic beers. Mexican beers are light and tart and complement spicy foods quite well.

Usually imported beers are aged longer than the average American beer and are fuller bodied, with more character. Some have a higher alcohol content than those produced in the United States. Beer devotees feel that the fuller beers are for sipping, while the lighter ones are for quaffing.

There are many famous beers and ales produced in the world. Each has its own individual character. A partial list of imported beers includes:

Australia	Foster
Canada	Labatt's Ale, Molson, Moosehead
China	Tsingtao
Czechoslovakia	Pilsner Urquell
Denmark	Carlsberg
England	Bass Ale, Mackeson's Stout, Whitbread Ale
France	Brassin de Garde, Fischer, Kronenbourg
Germany	Beck's, Dortmunder Union, St. Pauli Girl, Würzburger
Holland	Amstel, Heineken
India	Eagle
Ireland	Guinness Stout, Harp
Italy	Perroni, Raffo
Japan	Asahi, Kirin, Saporo
Mexico	Carta Blanca, Dos Equis, Superior
Norway	Ringness
Philippines	San Miguel
Sweden	Kalback, Pripps

Many of the beers mentioned above are available both light and dark.

Note: Denmark's Tuborg and Germany's Löwenbräu are now being made in the United States according to their original recipes. These are domestic beers, but are often priced with imports.

HOW AND WHEN TO SERVE BEER

Beer is one of the healthiest beverages one can consume. The alcohol and carbohydrates, with their food value, furnish energy. The proteins help assimilate food. The carbon dioxide gas, which gives the beer its head, or collar, helps create the cooling or refreshing effect that makes beer so popular in the summertime. The bitter hops stimulate the appetite.

Beer may be served at almost any hour and is appropriate during any season of the year. It blends with almost all foods, except heavy cream-sauce dishes and whipped-cream desserts. The characteristic sharp tang of beer adapts it to highly flavored or spicy dishes and to such foods as hamburger, steak, corned beef and cabbage, Irish stew, sausage, cold cuts, all pork dishes, fried dishes, curries, and broiled lobster, to mention only a few. All the sharper cheeses go well with either beer or ale.

The uses of beer in cooking are legion. Since many colonial recipes call for beer as an ingredient, it seems that the early Americans often depended on beer to give their dishes tang and character. A Yard of Flannel is a warm ale drink, and is said to be an especially good cold remedy (see page 409).

SAKÉ

The word *saké* means "the essence of the spirit of rice." Saké, made from rice, is a specialized form of beer. Saké is produced in Japan, and a small amount is made in Hawaii and California. It is not a spirit; it is not a wine. Because of its high alcohol content, and because it looks like wine, many people call it Japanese rice wine.[*] Unlike beer, as we know it, saké is almost colorless and quite still. It has none of the carbon dioxide that is in creamy beers.

The preparation of saké is unique to brewing. Polished rice is soaked in water for about twelve hours, and then steamed in a *koshiki*, a rice-steaming tub. Some steamed rice is treated with a culture of a special spore, *Aspergillus oryzae*, which produces an enzyme that converts the starch in the rice to sugar. This step takes about thirty-five hours and produces a culture called *koji* that is rich in this enzyme.

In order to develop the fermenting yeast culture, some *koji* is added to a thin paste of steamed rice and water, with a small amount of yeast starter. The yeast begins to multiply slowly, feeding on the sugar produced by the *koji*. After two to three weeks, the mash becomes a fully ripened *moto*.

Finally, the *moto*, more *koji*, and water are slowly added to freshly steamed rice, and alcoholic fermentation begins. The quality of finished saké, by the way, is determined by the amount that the rice has been polished down in size, getting closer to the heart of the kernel. The finest saké is made from rice that has been polished down to 50 percent of its original size. Most sakés are made from 70 percent rice. A combined process of two conversions, starch-to-sugar and sugar-to-alcohol, now occurs in a single vat. Sakés are generally fermented at 60 degrees Fahrenheit for about three weeks. The best sakés are fermented for about four weeks, at 50 degrees Fahrenheit. When fermentation is complete, the liquor, now saké, is drawn off, filtered, allowed to settle, and then run into casks to mature for a short period. Finally the saké is pasteurized before being bottled or casked. While sakés are graded as Special, First-, and Second-Grade, this grade does not appear on export labels.

Saké is quite strong for a brewed beverage, usually having 14 to 16 percent alcohol by volume. It has a slightly sweet first taste and a dry aftertaste. Traditionally, saké is served warm because heating releases its heady bouquet.

To warm saké, place the opened bottle in a pot of boiling water. Remove it when the saké is about 100 to 105 degrees Fahrenheit. To serve saké in the Japanese manner, decant the warm saké into small ceramic bottles, called *tokkuri*, and then pour it into tiny porcelain bowls, called *sakazuki*, which hold a little more than an ounce. Saké should be sipped from these bowls.

Saké may also be drunk at room temperature, chilled, or on the rocks, with assorted mixers. It can be used to replace the vermouth in Martinis.

---

[*] The U.S. Government, in the Standards of Identity for Wine, lists saké in Class 6, wine from other agricultural products.

18
DISTILLED SPIRITS
IN GENERAL

I t is poetic to call the secret of distillation a gift of the gods, but it is more reasonable to suppose that it was discovered by some long-forgotten alchemist.

The essence of the principle of distillation is this: alcohol vaporizes—becomes a gas—at a lower temperature than water. The boiling point of water at sea level is 212 degrees Fahrenheit, when it vaporizes and becomes steam, while that of ethyl alcohol is 173 degrees Fahrenheit. Therefore, if heat is applied to a liquid that contains alcohol, and the temperature is kept below 212 degrees Fahrenheit, the alcohol may be separated from the original liquid. If, at the same time, an apparatus is used whereby the alcohol vapors are gathered and not allowed to escape into the air, it is possible to recondense them into liquid form. The result is an alcohol of high purity. This sounds simple and so it is, if one wishes to produce alcohol, but if one is trying to produce a potable alcoholic beverage, the problem is more difficult and, if the product is to be a fine one, more delicate.

Apparently the science of distillation was known to the ancient Egyptians and Chaldeans. Long before the Christian era the Chinese obtained a spirit from rice beer, and arak has been distilled from sugarcane and rice in the East Indies since 800 B.C. Later Aristotle (384–322 B.C.), the great Greek philosopher, stated in his *Meteorology* that "seawater can be made potable by distillation; wine and other liquids can be submitted to the same process." There are many such references to distilled spirits in ancient writings. Even Captain Cook, on his voyage of discovery to the South Pacific, found the natives of the islands familiar with the distillation process.

For practical purposes, however, the modern history of distillation may be said to have originated with the Arabs or Saracens. They gave us the words *alcohol* and *alembic;* the latter word means "a still" and is used in all but

history

303

English-speaking countries. The first mention of distillation is attributed to an Arabian alchemist of the tenth century, one Albukassen; later in the thirteenth century a Majorcan chemist and philosopher, Raymond Lully, described the process. Even before his time the Celts of Eire and Scotia, unaware of the efforts of the Arabs, were producing a potable spirit that they called *uisgebeatha* or *uisgebaugh* ("water of life").

Distilled liquids are called ardent spirits. The word *ardent* comes from the Latin *ardere*, which means "to burn" and hence to distill. Although modern science has grown more and more efficient, the apparatus used for distilling many spirits is still much the same, as the one used by the original distillers many centuries ago. Such an apparatus is known as a pot still. Reduced to its two essential parts, it consists of a still and a worm condenser. The still is a copper pot with a broad, rounded bottom and a long, tapered neck. The worm condenser is a spiral copper tube that is connected to the still by a copper pipe. The worm passes through a jacket that contains cold water to assist in a rapid condensation of the vapors. Pot stills produce spirits in individual batches and are used to a large extent in the distillation of brandies, Scotch and Irish whiskies, some rums, and some liqueurs.

In 1826 Robert Stein, of a famous Scotch whisky-distilling family, invented the continuous still. This was later perfected by Aeneas Coffey, whose patent replaced Stein's and whose name has come down to us in connection with this type of still, which is known as a Coffey, or patent, still. Patent stills are used to distill lighter, grain whiskies.

spirits So far in this book we have discussed wines, which are the result of the natural processes of fermentation of the sugar contained in the grape juice, and beers, which are the result of the fermentation of grain. Now we are about to study what happens when the essence of the previously discussed wines or beers is distilled out to create alcoholic beverages. There are many of these, and while we shall consider each type in separate chapters, it is important to classify and define them.

BRANDY is a potable spirit, often aged in wood, obtained by distilling wine or a fermented mash of fruit. Examples are Cognac and Armagnac from France and grape brandies from the United States, Mexico, Spain, Greece, and Israel. Fruit brandies include Kirsch or Kirschwasser (from cherries), Calvados or Applejack (from apples), and Slivovitz, Mirabelle, and Quetsch (from plums).

WHISKY is a spirit, suitably aged in wood, usually oak, obtained from the distillation of a fermented mash of grain. Examples are Scotch whisky, Irish whiskey, Canadian whisky, rye whisky, and Bourbon whisky.

RUM is a potable spirit, suitably aged in wood, obtained from the distillation of a fermented mash of sugarcane juice or molasses. Examples are Jamaican rum, Demeraran rum, Barbados rum, Martinique rhum, Cuban ron, Puerto Rican ron, Haitian rhum, Philippine ron, Batavia arak, and others.

GIN is a flavored beverage obtained by redistilling a high-proof neutral spirit in the presence of juniper berries and other flavoring agents. Examples are English and American gins (London Dry type), Dutch gins (Genever, Schiedam, or Hollands), and fruit-flavored gins. Compound gin is made by adding essential oils of juniper and other flavorings to neutral spirits.

VODKA, made in America, is neutral spirits so distilled, or so treated after distillation with charcoal or other material, as to be without distinctive character, aroma, taste, or color. If any flavoring material is added to the distillate, the vodka is usually characterized with the name of the flavoring material used. Vodka made elsewhere may have some color, flavor, or aroma.

LIQUEURS AND CORDIALS are flavored beverages whose flavor is obtained either by infusion or by distillation of the flavoring agent, to which is then added simple syrup for sweetening. They may be artificially colored, if so stated on the label. All cordials or liqueurs are sweet. For tariff and taxation purposes, the regulations specify that a cordial or liqueur must have in excess of 2½ percent sugar by volume. Examples are amaretto, apricot liqueur, Bénédictine, blackberry liqueur, Chartreuse, Cointreau, cream liqueurs, créme de cacao, créme de cassis, créme de menthe, Grand Marnier, and Triple Sec.

Other spirits are obtained by distilling various fermented starchy or sugar-containing products. They include Tequila, Aquavit, Okolehao, and bitters.

Potable spirits, obtained from a given basic material, have different trade names. But the factors that make them different from one another are the matters, aside from alcohol, that are necessarily distilled out with the alcohol: the flavoring elements; the small amounts of alcohols other than ethyl; and the solids and minerals, which differ in fruits, grains, and sugarcane.

If in distillation the separation could be carried out where only the alcohol is removed, the resultant spirit would be pure, or absolute, alcohol of 200 proof. Commercial distillation results in a "constantly boiling mixture" that never goes above 194 proof, or 97 percent. To achieve 200 proof, or 100 percent, alcohol, a dehydration procedure would have to be carried out in the laboratory. Such a spirit would be the same, whether obtained from fruit, grain, or molasses, and would have no character whatsoever. We are not concerned here with such a pure spirit—in fact, for all practical purposes a spirit of 190 proof is sufficiently neutral for blending, and such spirits are used by the trade daily. The trade term for them is *neutral spirits* or *cologne spirits*.

Newly distilled spirits, whether obtained from fruit, grain, molasses, or other raw materials, are colorless, have little character, and are quite similar. They have a sharp, biting aroma and taste. When they have been matured for a certain length of time in wood, however, congeners, or "impurities," which are extracted from the wood, change the spirits' aroma, taste, and character

The various congeners in spirits consist of acids, esters, aldehydes, furfural, traces of fusel oils, extracts of mineral salts, and solids in minute quantities.

Fusel oils are a complex mixture of higher alcohols, mainly propyl, butyl, amyl, hexyl, heptyl, and the dialcohols, trialcohols, and their reaction products.

Acids found in spirits vary, but they include propionic, butyric, tartaric, lactic, succinic, and others.

Esters, produced by the chemical combination of the acids and the alcohols, are the volatile substances that give the aroma to the spirit.

Aldehydes are produced by the combination of the alcohols and air and are a contributing factor in giving a distinctive character to the spirit.

Furfural is an aldehyde. It is mostly obtained during distillation and partly extracted from the oak casks in which spirits are matured.

When the freshly distilled spirit flows from the still it is colorless and has a sharp, pungent alcoholic aroma and sharp taste. If distilled out at 180 proof or above, it is difficult for all but the most experienced distillers to distinguish whether the source of the distillate is grain, fruit, or cane. When the spirit is distilled out at a lower proof, it contains more congeners and has more character of the original source. Such flavorful spirits are usually matured in wood.

Once in wood, there is constant change that develops the flavor and character of the spirit. Oxidation through this porous container causes the esters to increase materially, the aldehydes to increase slowly, while the fusel oils remain practically the same. Furthermore, the spirit absorbs some tannin and coloring matter from the wood container, and becomes less harsh. In time, some spirit evaporates and the proof changes, depending on the surrounding conditions of humidity and temperature. After the spirit is bottled and sealed against the air, no matter how long, no further change will take place.

proof Before making distilled spirits became a science, the primitive distillers had a very simple method for determining the potable strength of the distillate. Equal quantities of spirit and gunpowder were mixed and a flame applied. If the gunpowder failed to burn, the spirit was to weak; if it burned too brightly, it was too strong. But if the mixture burned evenly, with a blue flame, it was said to have been proved.

Today we know that this potable mean was approximately 50 percent alcohol by volume, and we have adopted the term *proof* to describe the strength of alcoholic beverages. In the United States a 100-proof spirit is a spirit containing 50 percent alcohol by volume at a temperature of 60 degrees Fahrenheit. This is an arbitrary measurement. One proof gallon is equal to one measured wine gallon at 100 proof. Each degree of proof is equal to $\frac{1}{2}$ percent alcohol. Therefore, a spirit of 90 proof contains 45 percent alcohol, and one gallon at 90 proof would equal 0.9 proof gallons. A spirit of 150 proof contains 75 percent alcohol, and one gallon at 150 proof would equal 1.5 proof gallons.

The trade term for a spirit of more than 100 proof is an *overproof* spirit.

A tax gallon is the gallonage on which duties and revenue taxes are paid. When the duties and taxes are determined, the tax gallons are equivalent to proof gallons at 100 proof or higher. See Appendix O for British "Sikes" and metric "Gay-Lussac" tables.

What is rectifying? Theoretically it means to purify or improve, but practically it means anything that changes the character of a spirit. A rectification tax of $0.30 per tax gallon applies to most rectified spirits. Rectifying must be performed in a distilled spirits plant.

rectified spirits

What constitutes taxable rectification?

1. Blending two different spirits.
2. Blending two different whiskies, that is, whiskies distilled in different distilleries or in different seasons of the year.
3. Blending whisky with neutral spirits.
4. Redistilling whisky that has been stored in a barrel.
5. Adding coloring, flavoring, or anything except water to distilled spirits.
6. Redistilling neutral spirits for potable purposes.

Automated barrel-filling at Schenley's Bernheim Distillery in Louisville, Kentucky. (*Courtesy Schenley Industries, Inc., New York*)

7. Distilling neutral spirits over a flavoring agent.

8. Compounding spirits, essential oils, or other flavors and sugar to make cordials, liqueurs, and gin.

The following do *not* constitute taxable rectification and consequently are not subject to the rectification tax:

1. Blending whiskies that are four or more years old.

2. Blending rums that are two or more years old.

3. Making gin by original distillation or redistillation of spirits with juniper and other flavors.

4. Reducing the proof with water only.

THERAPEUTIC VALUE OF SPIRITS

The question of drinking, unhappily, has been invested with so much mumbo jumbo, loudly proclaimed by badly informed zealots of reform, that the quieter, more restrained voices of the scientific investigators have been drowned out. There is room for a balanced judgment that can recognize the beneficial qualities of alcoholic beverages and also be aware of their faults.

Alcohol is a compound of several elements—carbon, hydrogen, and oxygen—and in itself it not only is not harmful to man but is a necessary constitutent of his bloodstream. The normal alcohol content of the average person's blood is 0.003 percent; the lethal limit is around 0.7 percent.

Alcohol is the only food taken into the system that is unaffected by the digestive system. The stomach and intestines pass it into the bloodstream, unchanged, and it is diffused so rapidly that within a few minutes after being swallowed it has reached every part of the body. In the bloodstream it is carried to the liver, where most of it is filtered out, then to the heart, to the lungs, back to the heart, then through the aorta into the arteries, and throughout the body, finally coming to the brain and the higher nerve centers. This is where it has its most pronounced effect.

The popular idea is that alcohol is a stimulant. Pathologically that is not true. There is a false sense of stimulation because of the loss of control of the inhibitory nerve centers that control heartbeat, thus increasing the heartbeat and causing a sensation of warmth. Actually, the effect is relaxing rather than stimulating.

In regard to this sensation of warmth, alcohol dilates the peripheral blood vessels, increasing the flow of blood to the skin. It is actually only the surface of the body that is warmed, and in reality more heat is given off by the body than is supplied by the alcohol. As a matter of fact, alcohol is an excellent way of reducing body heat rapidly. This is why so much rum is drunk in the tropics; it is more cooling than ice water.

For the cardiac patient, the dilation of the blood vessels brings blood to the oxygen-starved heart muscles and to the rest of the body, helping the patient overcome shortness of breath at the same time. Alcohol provides energy and acts as a sedative to the brain, relaxing the patient.

All investigations made on the toxic effects of alcohol have been based on large doses of alcohol. These effects are materially reduced as dilution is increased, and when alcohol is a small part of other liquids, such as wine or beer, its intoxicating quality is reduced further.

A book that has done much to correct the misconceptions about the properties of alcohol is Morris E. Chafetz's *Liquor: The Servant of Man*, which states the following points:

Alcohol is actually manufactured in the human body, but is less toxic than most of the other natural secretions, such as thyroid, pituitary, adrenal, pancreas and bile.

Alcohol, if taken in anything remotely approaching customary amounts, is harmless to the body and in many cases beneficial.

Alcohol is one of the most valuable medicines in the world, both as a sedative and as a food, is useful for these and other reasons in many disease conditions, and is almost always indicated in old age.

Alcohol, to indulge in an understatement, has had a conspicuous position in the history of the race. It fathered religion and science and agriculture, provided more human confidence, and promoted good will toward men. It is the most efficient and practical relaxer of the driving force in the brain; it offers an immediate method of personal enjoyment; it is the greatest medium known for the purpose of permitting man to forget, at least for a little while, the shortness of life and the ludicrously helpless and infinitesimal part he plays in the functions of the universe.

Temperate alcohol use does not physically damage the nervous system or any of the healthy, important organs of the body, such as the heart, liver, kidneys, stomach, or brain.

points to remember about alcohol

Alcohol produces energy without making the body work because it is taken into the bloodstream in its original state. Alcohol itself does not produce fat. Other foods, which would normally produce the energy needed by the body, are stored, as an energy reserve, in the form of fat by those who drink regularly in substantial amounts.

The part of the body most quickly and directly affected by alcohol is the brain, and the effect is relaxing, not stimulating.

Once absorbed, excess alcohol cannot be "worked off" except by oxidation and excretion. The normal rate of elimination is about ten cubic centimeters° per hour, and this remains constant whether you lie in bed, walk around in the open, or sit in a Turkish bath.

° This is one-third of an ounce of absolute alcohol.

The best insulation against the effects of overindulgence is food to line the walls of the stomach. The best food is the fat of milk. In the order of their protective value, the foods you can take are cream, whole milk, butter, meat fats, olive oil, and meat.

The heart of a hangover is the accumulation of residual lactic acid in the muscles. Lactic acid normally occurs in the body as a waste product of energy production. Excess alcohol produces excess lactic acid in the body, which can be eliminated only by the blood and the kidneys. This process cannot be hastened, and the only cure is rest and time.

There is no evidence that alcohol in itself causes any disease. The principal danger of too much alcohol is social. One who is drunk, whether from imbibing one or ten drinks, has a narcotized brain—one that is not awake. In a moment of crisis, when a quick decision is necessary, the part of the brain that reasons may be awake, while the part that commands the muscles may be asleep, or vice versa. The result in either case is trouble.

Alcohol is prescribed in many ailments but is contraindicated in some for which the layman believes it most valuable. These are shock, snake bite, and fatigue. In the first two the blood pressure is lowered, and the additional lowering of blood pressure by alcohol is unnecessary. Fatigue means that you already have too much lactic acid in the system, and alcohol adds to it.

The conclusion one reaches is that alcoholic beverages in themselves are not damaging or harmful to man physically. When taken temperately, they are beneficial.

We do not advocate that anyone drink for the "kick." Drinking should be done for pleasure, relaxation, and the release to which the beverage contributes; it should be a part of the good life.

19
BRANDIES

Brandy is a potable spirit, suitably aged in wood, that is obtained from the distillation of wine or a fermented mash of fruit. An alcoholic beverage answering this description may be produced in any part of the world.

1. BRANDIES OF FRANCE

The art of distillation, although known to the ancients, was not applied to wine commercially until the sixteenth century, when the brandy trade began. Supposedly, a brisk trade in wine existed between the port of La Rochelle, on the Charente River in France, and Holland. All of this trade was carried on by sea, and the perils of war placed a premium on shipping.

Casks of wine take up quite a lot of space, particularly on small sailing vessels. The story is told of one very bright Dutch shipmaster who hit upon the idea of concentrating the wine—eliminating the water—and transporting the spirit, or the "soul," of the wine to Holland, where the water could be put back. In his thrifty mind he figured that he could save an enormous amount on the freight charges.

When this enterprising man arrived in Holland, however, with his "concentrated wine," his Dutch friends tasted it and liked it as it was. It would be a waste of water, they decided, to try to make it wine again. And thus the brandy trade had its inception. The Dutch called the new product *brandewijn* ("burned wine"), presumably because fire, or heat, is used in the process of distillation. In time this term was Anglicized to the present-day word—*brandy*.

COGNAC

When we say brandy, we usually mean the delightful "soul" of wine. There is one brandy that the world has accepted and recognized as superior to all

311

all others: Cognac. It is important to understand that all Cognac is brandy, but all brandies are not Cognac. Cognac is a brandy distilled from wines made of grapes grown within the legal limits of the Charente and Charente-Maritime departments of France.

The ancient city of Cognac, on the Charente River, is in the heart of the district that produces the brandies that have carried its fame throughout the world. In fact, they have done the job so well that *Cognac* is one of the best-known French words in the world.

The quality that makes Cognac superior to all other brandies is not only the special process of distillation that has been used in this district for centuries, but also the combination of ideal soil, climate, and other conditions. While it might be possible for another section to reproduce one or two of these essentials, the combination of all the factors cannot be achieved elsewhere.

The Charentais, or Cognac district, has seven subdivisions, or *crus*, but the last two are often combined. This explains why some references list only six.

SUBDIVISION	RANK	ACRES UNDER CULTIVATION
Grande Champagne (Grande Fine Champagne)	1st *Cru*	32,250
Petite Champagne (Petite Fine Champagne)	2nd *Cru*	40,310
Borderies	3rd *Cru*	10,200
Fins Bois	4th *Cru*	94,230
Bons Bois	5th *Cru*	44,630
Bois Ordinaires } Bois Communs	6th *Cru*	7,380

The entire Cognac region was delimited by law in 1909; the seven subdivisions, in 1936. The Grande Champagne is a small district that is the kernel of the region. In it lies the town of Cognac, around which everything centers: the territory, the commerce, and the fame of the product. Almost completely surrounding it is the Petite Champagne. To the north, and situated at about the point where the encirclement of the Grande Champagne is incomplete, is the smallest district, the Borderies. Completely surrounding these first three districts are the Fins Bois. Around all these are the Bons Bois, and advancing from the Bons Bois to the Atlantic Ocean in the west are the Bois Ordinaires and the Bois Communs or "Bois Communs dit a Terroir."

Actually, in 1918 two maps were drawn to define the region. One map was done by local geologists, and the other by a committee of tasters. Both maps came out the same, confirming the significance of the soil.

In Cognac the small farmer may have his own still. Big shippers very often own a vineyard or two but they cannot possibly own the amount of vineyard land they would need to take care of the worldwide demand for their brands.

It is the custom in Cognac, therefore, for all shippers to buy the brandy from the farmer. Each farmer has his little vineyard, gathers his grapes, makes his wine, and distills it as soon as it falls bright or has it distilled for him by one of the regional distillers. Distillation of brandy in France, and especially in Cognac, is supervised by government inspectors. At vintage time the inspectors visit each farm, measure the wine, and thereafter control the amount of brandy that each farmer may distill.

The subsoil in Cognac is chalky, and the more chalk, the more suitable are the wines produced for making Cognac. The two Champagne heartland regions have the highest amounts of chalk. Outside the Champagne area the chalky layer becomes shallower, while the earthy top layer becomes deeper. The Bois are so named because they used to be covered with woods, whose life cycle added to the soil layer. The Atlantic Ocean and the Gironde River modify the variations in temperature and help maintain humidity levels favorable to the production of Cognac.

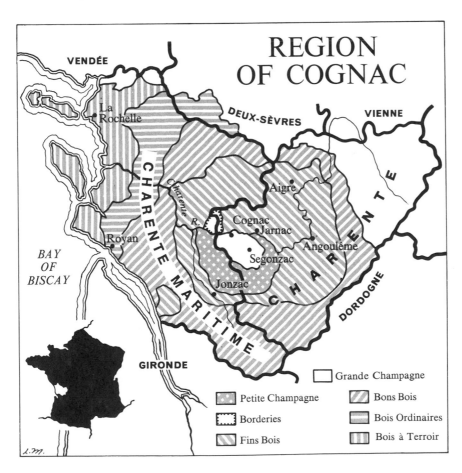

In 1936 French law decreed that wines that produce Cognac should be made from Folle Blanche, Saint-Émilion, and Colombard grapes, with up to 10 percent permitted to be made from other white grapes. Since then, Saint-Émilion, also known as Ugni Blanc, has emerged as the predominant variety because of its high yield of wines that are low in alcohol, about 8 percent, and high in acid. It is this type of wine, thin and unpleasant to drink, that produces the best Cognac. Cognac, by law, may be produced only from white grapes.

production   The grapes are picked, pressed, and allowed to ferment; skins, pips, and all are necessary to give the full character to the brandy.

The wine is brought to the distilleries in modern tankers. This wine often contains the lees of fermentation. Some producers allow the wine to settle before it enters the still to remove the lees; others prefer to leave a small amount of lees for extra flavor. The stills are old-fashioned, copper pot stills, or alembics. Copper is used because it is resistant to the lengthy contact with acid wine. There are no patent stills permitted in Cognac.

Distillation begins in a simple boiler, heated directly by a coal or wood fire. On top of the boiler is a metal hood to collect the vapors produced from an initial batch of wine put into the boiler. These vapors travel through a thin, curved tube, which leads them to a preheating chamber, known as the *chauffe-vin*. Remaining in the tube, the hot vapors preheat the wine, placed in the *chauffe-vin*, which is to be distilled. From the *chauffe-vin* this warmed wine now enters the boiler. The vapors, having given up some of their heat in the *chauffe-vin*, give up the rest of their heat in a condensing coil, which is surrounded by cold water. The vapors have now become a liquid, and it trickles out into a receiving pan. All of the metal used in a still of this type is pure copper.

The conversion of the wine into *eau-de-vie de Charente* is accomplished in two operations, the *première chauffe* and the *bonne chauffe*, which are ingeniously connected. In the *première chauffe* the first vapors that are distilled from the boiling wine are the heads, and they are collected separately, to be added back to a subsequent *première chauffe*. The middle distillate, or *brouillis*, is collected for use in the second distillation, known as the *bonne chauffe*. The alcohol content of the *brouillis* is 24 to 32 percent. What remains in the boiler, and what comes off with little alcohol, is called the tails. This, like the heads, is put back into the next *première chauffe* with a new lot of wine.

When enough *brouillis* have been collected, the *bonne chauffe* distillation begins. As before, the first vapors to come off, the heads, are collected separately and added back to the *première chauffe*. The middle-range vapors, or heart, will become Cognac. These vapors are condensed at an average of 70 percent alcohol. The next distillate, now called seconds, varies in alcoholic strength from 50 percent to around 5 percent. This is put back in the *bonne chauffe* with additional *brouillis* for further distillation. The last part, from 5

Cognac still room showing the traditional alembics—copper pot stills—used for generations. (*Courtesy Cognac Information Bureau, New York*)

percent to no alcohol at all, is again known as tails, and goes back into a *première chauffe*.

Hand regulation of all steps is the key to traditional Cognac production. Most important are uniform procedures, evenness of heating, and precise control of the separation of distillates and the quantities produced. The alembics work continuously, twenty-four hours a day, seven days a week, during the distilling season, which starts in November and lasts from three to five months—perhaps six months if there is a large harvest. All distilling must be completed by April 30.

With so many different people carrying out this process of distillation, it stands to reason that some sell directly to various shippers, who examine and taste the new brandy. Others are part of a large cooperative that buys either grapes or wine from the farmers, and then distills and matures it.

Right out of the still, the distillate is colorless and has a sharp, but fruity, coppery bouquet and taste. The coppery character, *gout de cuivre*, passes after the brandy has been in wood for a year.

Cognac is aged in casks made of Limousin oak obtained from the forest near Limoges. After the first year the brandy is transferred from new casks to old ones to prevent the brandy from absorbing too much tannin from the wood. The cooperage must stand up for forty to fifty years. The casks are laid away in many cellars or warehouses to guard against fire loss.

In the cask the Cognac changes by action of the wood and by contact with the oxygen in the air that enters through the pores of the wood. In the same way that the air enters, the brandy evaporates.

There is a continual yearly loss in volume that amounts to 15 percent of the world's annual consumption. As the alcohol evaporates more rapidly than the water and other constituents of the brandy in the humid atmosphere around Cognac, there is a corresponding diminution of strength. It is rapid during the first few years and becomes more gradual after that, the average being about 2 percent a year. This loss of proof is considered essential to the proper development of Cognac. During this time the brandy gradually changes from a colorless state, taking on a beautiful amber tone, and the taste and perfume are changed, so that what finally results is a finished Cognac, a delicate mellow essence with a natural bouquet of grapes.

Today the demand is for a standard of quality that remains the same year in and year out. This requires large stocks being held by the brandy merchant as well as judicious and exact blending.

This *coupage*, or blending, is done many months before bottling. The various brandies are put into tremendous oak vats and are brought down to shipping strength—40 to 43 percent alcohol as required—by the addition of distilled water or diluted brandy. Coloring matter (caramel) is added to ensure uniform color in every bottle. Inside these vats wooden propellerlike paddles rotate from time to time, mixing the brandies. After several months the blend, thoroughly "married," is put in bottles, cased, and is ready for market.

The French government has passed laws to protect the public as to what is and is not Cognac. Every consignment travels with a certificate, called an *Acquit Régional Jaune d'Or*, which guarantees that the product comes from Cognac; it has nothing to do with age.

labeling   The various qualities of Cognacs are often indicated by stars: one, two, or three, in ascending quality. Wine people are superstitious. One of their firmest beliefs is that comet years produce fine wines. The legend is that in the comet year of 1811, when a superb brandy was produced, one of the shippers decided to designate the brandy of that year with a star. An equally excellent brandy was produced in the following year and this he designated by two stars. By this time he had acquired the habit, but fortunately he stopped when he reached five stars. The firm of Hennessy claims to have originated the system. Each house blends its brandies for uniformity of quality, which is maintained year in and year out. The standards represented by the stars vary with the different houses, but since 1975 French law has decreed that a three-star Cognac, the youngest blend on the market, must have spent at least two and a half years in wood. Most Cognacs average three to five years. In order to enter the United States, Cognac must be at least two and one-half years old. No age statements are permitted on the labels of Cognacs brought into the United States, so beware of so-called vintage Cognacs you may see in your foreign travels.

Better-quality brandies are sometimes identified by letters to indicate quality. The letters, oddly enough, represent not French words but English, because of the traditional importance of the English market. They represent the following:

C means Cognac	*P* means Pale
E means Extra or Especial	*S* means Superior
F means Fine	*V* means Very
O means Old	*X* means Extra

These words used to apear on the label at the discretion of the producer. Since 1955 certain combinations of letters have had age significance. For instance the letters *VO* or *VSOP* not only mean Very Old or Very Superior Old Pale, respectively, but they also mean, as does the word *Réserve*, that the Cognac has been aged in wood at least four and a half years. In reality, VSOP Cognacs are usually aged seven to ten years.

Since Cognac by and large is a business of brands, many houses have abandoned the stars and letters and identify their various qualities either by proprietary names or by the district of origin.

Some other words producers use to describe their best Cognacs are now also regulated by French law. Extra, Napoléon, and Vieille Réserve require that the Cognac has been in cask for a minimum of $6\frac{1}{2}$ years. The romantic nonsense about the 80- and 104-year-old so-called Napoléon brandies is nothing but a ploy for the unknowing buyer.

Cognac improves in wood for roughly fifty to fifty-five years. The cost of aging the brandy for this length of time is very high, as the losses through evaporation and the risk of aging too long are considerable and make the ultimate selling prices excessive. Once the Cognac is bottled, it neither varies nor improves. A Cognac bottled in 1900 will taste exactly the same today as it did the day it was placed in the glass. Yet the question naturally arises: What is the best age for Cognac? It is at its best between the ages of twenty-five and forty.

From the consumer's point of view there are several other questions that are frequently asked.

What is Fine Champagne? This means that the brandies have been made from grapes grown in either the Grande or Petite Champagne, with at least 50 percent of the grapes coming from the Grande Champagne region. Consequently, a Fine Champagne Cognac should be very good.

What is *Fine*? Legally, a *Fine* is a Cognac. In France, however, every restaurant includes among its list of brandies a *Fine de la Maison,* which is bar brandy. More than likely, if you just order a *Fine* (pronounced *feen*), you will get a good French brandy, even though you should be getting a Cognac. It is wiser to ask for Fine Champagne Cognac, if that is what you want.

Cognacs should be examined with the nose before actually being tasted. The best way is to put one's nose on the rim of the glass, and not too deeply into the glass. The alcohol is quite strong for the nose. For this reason, many prefer small chimney glasses or tulips to large snifters. The glass should never be larger than one is capable of holding and warming in one hand, but the one-ounce pony or cordial glass should be avoided. When evaluating Cognacs, a few drops on the tongue is all that is necessary. Good Cognacs should be light.

Since distilled spirits do not change once they are bottled, old bottles mean nothing. Large magnum bottles should be avoided, since once the Cognac is started, it may remain partly full for a long time. Then, both evaporation and oxidation will make the Cognac deteriorate. While a bottle of cognac need not be consumed at one sitting, ideally, it should not be left open for more than six months.

A good test of a fine Cognac is to smell a glass that has had some Cognac poured into it. Hours after it has been consumed, the glass should retain its delicious aroma. A good long drink, by the way, is Cognac with ginger ale.

ARMAGNAC

Second only to Cognac is the Armagnac brandy produced predominantly in the Department of Gers, southeast of Bordeaux in the heart of Gascony. The center of the trade is the city of Condom. There are three subregions: Bas-Armagnac, the most westerly growing area, Tenareze in the center, and Haut-Armagnac to the east. These areas were defined by the *Appellation Contrôlée* authorities in 1936. Brandies from any of these subregions are so named on the label. Armagnac by itself on a label means that the liquid is a blend of brandies from two or three subregions.

Only white grapes are permitted in making the wines for distillation into Armagnac. The predominant grape is the Saint-Émilion (Ugni Blanc), which, as in Cognac, is replacing the Folle Blanche in importance. Other varieties permitted are the Colombard, Meslier, Jurançon, and a few others. The hybrid Baco 22A has been planted in the sandier areas of the Bas-Armagnac. Armagnac has chalk in the soil, but less chalk than in Cognac.

A major difference in the systems of distilling Armagnac and Cognac is that in Armagnac the original and redistillation operations are continuous, whereas in Cognac they are two separate batch operations. Another difference lies in the fact that the Armagnac aging casks are made of black oak from the Monlezun Forest, instead of the Limousin oak used in Cognac.

Armagnac is regulated and labeled similarly to Cognac, with the same age requirements for three-star, VSOP, and so on. Age statements may appear on the label, and must be the age of the youngest component of the blend. Armagnac is often seen at ten years old, and *Hors d'Age* is more than ten years old.

Armagnac has a pungent bouquet, but a dry and surprisingly smooth taste.

MARC

Brandies distilled from the grape pomace of the wine press are called *eaux-de-vie de Marc* (pronounced *mar*) and are obtained in various parts of France, but notably in Burgundy. They have a strawlike, woody taste and rustic character appreciated by some devotees.

OTHER FRENCH BRANDIES

Substantial quantities of good brandy, not necessarily made from pomace, are distilled in various parts of France, outside the delimited Cognac and Armagnac regions. They are, generally speaking, good, clean, pleasant brandies that do not pretend to have the character or quality of Cognac. Their production is less restricted, and they are less costly.

2. BRANDIES OF OTHER LANDS

CALIFORNIA BRANDY

"California Brandy" is a controlled appellation applied only to beverage brandy distilled entirely from California grapes. Production is at almost nineteen million gallons, and California brandy comprises 75 percent of all brandy consumed in the United States. In addition, about thirty-five million gallons of high-proof brandy is produced for use in fortified wines and cordials.

California brandy is produced mainly from Thompson Seedless and Flame Tokay grapes, with some Colombard, Ugni Blanc, and Folle Blanche used at times. Most grapes are grown in the San Joachin Valley, from Lodi to Fresno.

The continuous still (also known as patent and Coffey) is preferred in California because it yields an extremely clean distillate and at the same time retains the highly desired congeners of the wine, when distillation is performed at appropriate proof. It is very efficient and produces a uniform product.

The pot still is used in 20 percent of California's distilleries. Some of this product is used to enhance blends. Other producers are developing stocks to produce only pot still brandies. A major Cognac company has even joined one Napa Valley producer to make California brandy in the French tradition.

Fifty-gallon white oak barrels from Tennessee and Arkansas are used for storage and aging, during which time the wood imparts the characteristic oak flavor and golden color. Some producers use previously aged whisky barrels that are charred inside and routed. By law, California brandy must be aged two years in oak, although it usually is not released until four years. Some eight-year-old brandies are available both as straights and blends.

Ample stocks of sound, mature American brandy—forty-five million tax gallons—have now been accumulated, despite the fact that the industry was compelled to restart from scratch in 1933, when Prohibition ended.

Typical California brandies are light and mellow, with a pronounced grape flavor. They vary widely in degree of dryness to sweetness.

GERMAN BRANDY

From Germany comes a soft grape brandy with characteristic mellow taste and fine aroma and bouquet. It is blended from especially selected distillates of wines from Germany, as well as from other countries, and is matured in oak. It has a great deal of finesse.

GREEK BRANDY

A great deal of brandy is distilled in Greece and much of it is exported. Greek brandy is becoming more popular. It usually has a clean flavor, with a touch of sweetness from the caramel used to give it color. The most popular Greek brandy in the United States, Metaxa, is technically a liqueur since it has been sweetened to the minimum level of a liqueur to give it wider appeal.

Cyprus is an independent country today, but it cannot separate itself from its Greek heritage. Cypriot brandies are good and very similar to those of Greece.

ISRAELI BRANDY

Good, sound, clean grape and other fruit brandies have been distilled in the Holy Land for many years, but it is only since the State of Israel came into being that any serious efforts have been made to export them. Israeli brandy is always kosher.

ITALIAN BRANDY

Italy produces an excellent, clean grape brandy whose foreign market popularity increases every year. It is a good, all-purpose brandy that has a touch of sweetness. Grappa brandy, like Marc, is distilled from grape pomace. Grappa is usually unaged and sharp in taste, and it has its devoted following.

MEXICAN BRANDY

Brandy was not produced in Mexico in any quantity before 1950, but in the past twenty-five years it has become the national drink, surpassing rum and Tequila. Many brandies are made in the Spanish style, following the Spanish methods of *solera* blending and aging in white oak barrels, after local wines have been distilled. Some brandies are produced in pot stills and may have Limousin oak aging, in the French style.

PERUVIAN BRANDY

The brandy of Peru is Pisco, which takes its name from the port in southern Peru whence it is shipped. This brandy is distilled from Muscat wines produced in the Ica Valley, near Pisco. Pisco is matured in clay jars and is consumed in Peru quite young.

Pisco Punch, which is really a sour, is the most popular cocktail in Peru and also in Chile. It is a delightfully pleasant drink.

Muscat brandies are also produced in both Chile and Argentina.

SPANISH BRANDY

Very little Spanish brandy is distilled from sherry wine. Spanish brandies are distilled from wines of other wine regions of Spain, mostly from Valdepeñas. They are developed, aged, and marketed by many sherry shippers. In fact, there is slightly more brandy shipped from Jerez than sherry. Spanish brandy has a distinctive aroma and flavor and is different from Cognac or Armagnac. It is a sweeter brandy with an earthy character.

This list would not be complete without mentioning that brandy is made in Portugal, Yugoslavia, South Africa, Australia, and all other wine-producing countries in both hemispheres.

3. FRUIT BRANDIES

The fermented mash of fruits other than grapes is the source of a wide variety of unique brandies. They form three broad categories: brandies made with apples and pears; brandies made with stone fruits, such as cherries, plums, and apricots; and brandies made from berries, such as raspberries, strawberries, blackberries, and elderberries. These brandies come from Switzerland, France, Germany, Hungary, Israel, Yugoslavia, and the United States. Some of these fruits and the brandies they produce are as follows:

FRUIT	BRANDY
Apple	Apple brandy
	Applejack or apple jack
	Calvados
Apricot	Apricot brandy
	Barack Palinka
Blackberry	Blackberry brandy
Cherry	Kirsch
	Kirschwasser
Elderberry	Elderberry brandy
Pear	Pear brandy
	Eau-de-vie de poire
Pineapple	Pineapple brandy
Plum	Slivovitz
	Mirabelle
	Quetsch
	Prunelle
	Pflümli
Raspberry	Framboise
Strawberry	Fraise

APPLE BRANDY

The two principal sources of apple brandy are the United States and France. In the United States it is commonly called applejack, while in France the most famous is called Calvados, from the Department of Calvados in Normandy, center of apple and cider production in France. In France Calvados is also made in other parts of Normandy and in Brittany and Maine.

The production of Calvados begins with the juice of only sound, ripe cider apples. The juice is allowed to ferment for at least a month until no sugar remains, and it is then distilled. The best Calvados, with the appellation

Calvados du Pays d'Auge, is distilled only in pot stills. Pot or continuous stills are used to produce brandies with the appellation Reglementees Calvados. Ordinary French apple brandy is called *eaux-de-vie-de-cidre de Normandie, . . . de Bretagne,* or *. . . du Maine.*

The Calvados du Pays d'Auge is double distilled, similar to the way Cognac is made. The first, or low, wines are redistilled to obtain the high wines, or brandy. These spirits are drawn off at around 140 proof and then aged in Limousin oak barrels, where they pick up color as they mature. Calvados may be aged up to forty years, when it can acquire the finesse of Cognac. Aged Calvados has a very pronounced apple flavor, and its bouquet combines wood and fruit. It is bottled at 80 to 84 proof. Age phrases are similar to Cognac and Armagnac.

Applejack is made in a manner similar to Calvados. The legal U.S. minimum age for applejack is two years in wood, but most is aged longer. Applejack is bottled as a straight brandy at 100 proof, aged brandy at 80 proof, or it may be blended with neutral spirits and bottled at 80 proof as a blended applejack. *Applejack* and *apple brandy* are synonymous terms.

PEAR BRANDY

Pear brandy, or *eau-de-vie de poire,* is made in both France and Switzerland. It is distilled from the Williams pear, which is the Bartlett pear of the United States. Pear brandy is unaged and colorless, with a distinct aroma. The production is similar to other colorless fruit brandies.

OTHER FRUIT BRANDIES

After apple brandy the most widely produced fruit brandies are distilled from cherries and plums. All are produced in a similar fashion, except that only some are aged.

Those that are aged in wood and have a golden brown color are the plum brandies of central Europe (Hungary, Romania, Yugoslavia), known as Slivovitz; the apricot brandy of Hungary, called Barack Palinka; and some blackberry brandy, whose color is enhanced by the addition of some dark-colored juice to the matured spirit.

The brandies that are unaged are always colorless and are genally referred to as white alcohols. They include those distilled from a fermented mash of cherries, from varieties of plums, from raspberries, from strawberries, as well as from Williams pears.

The source of the finest Kirschwasser (cherry brandy) is the small black wild cherry from the valley of the Rhine. Because of geopolitics, however, the three best sources are in three different countries: Switzerland, where the Rhine starts on its way to the sea; Alsace, on the French side of the Rhine; and the Black Forest, on the opposite side of the Rhine in Germany. One can always find those who will claim that the Kirschwasser of one of these three sources is superior to the others, but they are all excellent.

Fruit brandies are made in the following manner. The fully ripened fruit is gathered and thoroughly mixed or mashed with wooden paddles in a wooden tub, where it is allowed to ferment—stones and all. After six weeks, when fermentation is complete, the entire contents of the t b are placed in a pot still and distilled twice. A small amount of oil from the stones is distilled over with the spirit. This oil imparts the characteristic bitter almond flavor usually found in good Kirschwasser or Slivovitz.

All of these white brandies are distilled off at a fairly low proof, usually around 100 proof or slightly less. In this way the maximum fruit aroma and flavor are retained. Since this is their most attractive and desired characteristic, they are bottled promptly, without any further reduction, so they will not lose any of their fragrance, or else they are stored in either glass-lined casks or earthenware containers. If aged in plain oak they would take on color, which is not desirable. Slivovitz, however, is preferred with color, so it is matured in wood.

So much fruit is required to obtain these essences that white alcohols are very expensive and luxurious.

HOW AND WHEN TO SERVE BRANDIES

Aside from their medicinal uses, which are well established, all brandies, those obtained from wine in particular, find their primary use as after-dinner drinks. They are most attractive when served neat, although brandy and soda is a pleasant drink after dinner or at any time when a refreshing and relaxing long drink is desired. Since brandy was considered a sort of wine concentrate, it has traditionally been drunk with water also, either mixed into the brandy or on the side. Brandy is also excellent in coffee.

Brandies have many uses in the kitchen. They may be flamed, which leaves a concentration of flavor after the alcohol burns off.

Kirsch, or one of the other white alcohols, is a delightful addition to any fresh fruit cup and as one of the flavorings in the delicious French dish Crêpes au Kirsch. The intensity of the white alcohols makes it possible to impart flavor with very small amounts. They are especially good as flavorings in desserts, puddings, cakes, and ice creams. Unlike other brandies, the white alcohols are most enjoyable when served ice cold.

All brandies, both aged and unaged, may be used in making mixed drinks of all kinds.

When a palate cleanser is called for around the middle of a formal dinner, a small glass of Calvados may be served. This is known as a *Trou Normand* and is said to aid digestion.

20
WHISKIES

After the process of distillation was discovered, it was inevitable that man should use the product closest at hand, easiest to obtain, and least expensive for distillation. As a result, where there is an abundance of grain, whisky is distilled.

the word whisky— its origin

The word *whisky* comes from the Celtic *uisgebeatha* or *uisgebaugh* (pronounced *whis-geh-BAW*), the Scottish and Irish words, respectively, for "water of life." Whether it was the Scots or the Irish who first used the word or first distilled whisky is a source of never-ending argument between them.

The English found the Celtic word too difficult and too long, so they shortened and Anglicized it to *whisky*. The Canadians and the Scottish use the same spelling, without the *e;* the Irish keep the *e*. The United States used to use the *e*, but it now omits it in the Standards of Identity but permits its use in a traditional context.

SCOTCH WHISKY

In the beginning every Highland laird had his own still, and the spirits he obtained were rough and harsh, with a smoky pungency appreciated only by the Caledonians. The whiskies were distilled freely and their distillers paid no taxes. In 1814 distillation from all stills of less than five hundred gallons' capacity was prohibited in Scotland, and the law almost caused a revolution. The British government continued to tax whisky throughout the 1800's, and illicit distillation and smuggling were prevalent right up to 1823. A similar situation prevailed in Ireland at the same time.

Four regions of Scotland produce malt whisky: the Highlands, the Lowlands, Campbeltown, and Islay (pronounced *I-lay*). Each produces a whisky with an individual character.

making Scotch malt whisky

Scotch whisky is obtained primarily from barley from East Anglia, England, since Scotland cannot produce enough barley for its distilling purposes.

There are five main stages in making Scotch: malting, mashing, fermenting, distilling, and maturing and blending.

On arrival at the distillery the barley goes into the barley-receiving room, where it is dressed, that is, sieved, or passed over screens so that small and inferior grain will be eliminated, after which the best grain is stored. When required for use, it is placed in tanks, called steeps, where it is soaked in water until thoroughly softened. It then used to be spread out on the floor of the malting house for about three weeks. Today this is rarely done. This traditional method has been replaced by mechanical drum maltings. The barley is turned regularly to control temperature and rate of germination, or sprouting. This is done by hand using wooden shovels, known as shields.

When the sprouts are about three-quarters of an inch long, the grain is known as green malt. It is already malt, for malt is germinated grain. During this germination process a chemical change occurs in the grain, as explained on page 289, that is important in its future function of producing whisky. The enzyme amylase, traditionally called diastase in the beverage industry, is produced and has the property of converting the starch into sugars—maltose and dextrin—which are fermentable, whereas the starch in its original state is not.

The green malt is transferred to a kiln, where it rests on a screen directly above a peat° fire. Like green wood, peat gives off a much more acrid and oilier smoke than soft coal. This swirls around the grain, which becomes impregnated with the aroma of the smoke. Drying is then completed by burning coke or anthracite. The length of time that the peat is burned determines the smokiness of the malt and, eventually, of the whisky.

The kilning, or drying, process is very important, as it is here that the malt acquires a good part of its character, and a variation occurs here in the various regions. The malt in the Lowlands is kilned less than that in the Highlands, whereas the Campbeltown and Islay grains are more heavily roasted.

The kilned malt is now screened to remove the culm, or dried sprouts, after which it goes to the mill room, where it is ground into meal, or grist.

The next step is mashing. The ground malt is thoroughly mixed with warm water in a mash tun, also referred to as a mash tub, where it soaks until the water has liquefied all of the starches and the diastase has converted them into sugar. When the water has absorbed all of the goodness from the grain, it is drawn off, cooled, and is known as wort.

The wort now passes into the fermenting vats, where a small quantity of carefully cultivated pure yeast is added and fermentation takes place. The yeast acts upon the sugars in the wort in the same manner as the natural yeasts act upon the sugars in grape juice, producing alcohol and carbon dioxide gas.

°Peat is coal in its primary stage and consists of partially carbonized vegetable material, usually heather, found in bogs. Pressed and dried peat is used for fuel.

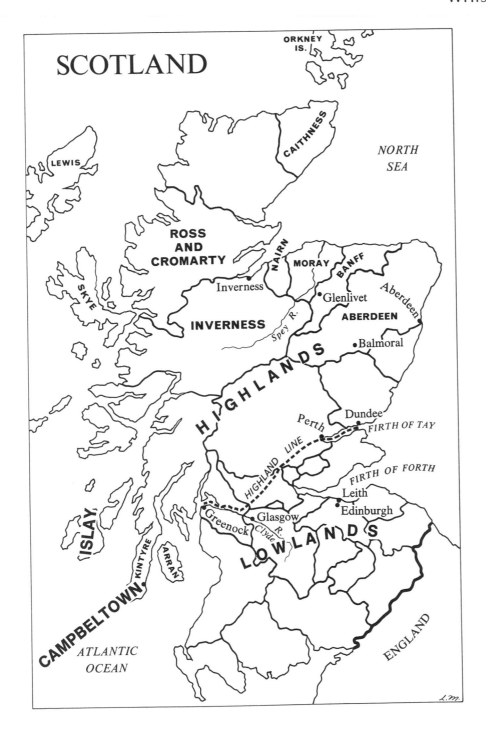

SCOTLAND

ORKNEY IS.

CAITHNESS

NORTH SEA

LEWIS

ROSS AND CROMARTY

NAIRN

MORAY

BANFF

Inverness

Glenlivet

Aberdeen

SKYE

INVERNESS

ABERDEEN

Spey R.

Balmoral

HIGHLANDS

Dundee

Perth

FIRTH OF TAY

HIGHLAND LINE

FIRTH OF FORTH

Leith

Edinburgh

Glasgow

Greenock

Clyde R.

LOWLANDS

ISLAY

KINTYRE

ARRAN

CAMPBELTOWN

ATLANTIC OCEAN

ENGLAND

L.m.

When fermentation is completed, the liquid is known as beer, or wash. To this point the process is identical with that of brewing ales and beers, except for the omission of hops.

The beer now goes into a pot still, which is known as the wash still. The result of the first distillation is a distillate of low alcoholic strength, which is known as low wines. The low wines pass into the spirit pot still where they are redistilled. The first part of the distillation, "foreshots," and the last part, "feints," are gathered separately from the middle portion, which is the useful part of the distillation. At the beginning and at the end of the distillation operation too high a percentage of impurities is carried over with the spirit, which, if used, would impair the flavor of the spirit when matured. The feints, however, contain a substantial quantity of useful alcohol and are returned to the spirit still with the next charge of low wines, and the alcohol is distilled out. The impurities are disposed of with the residual slop from the spirit still operation, that is, the waste material that is thrown out.

The useful spirit, distilled off at between 140 and 142 proof, flows into a spirit vat from where it is put into casks. It is now called "plain British spirits," but after three years of aging, it may be called "whisky." These casks, generally made of American white oak, vary in size from the 34-gallon quarter cask to the 132-gallon butt. The different sizes are used for convenience. They may be new or old, and very often they are casks that have previously been used for maturing whisky, or in which sherry has been shipped. The choice of cask affects the flavor, and whiskies matured in sherry casks are sweeter and fuller.

At the time of barreling the whisky is reduced in proof to 124 to 126.8 by the addition of water. According to Dr. P. Schidrowitz, whose notes are quoted by Peter Valaer in his excellent paper on Scotch whisky, "It is held that the best water is that which has its origin as a spring served with water which has passed through a red granite formation, and which, after rising from its source, passes through peaty country. Such waters are generally very soft and possess certain qualities which are apparently due to the peaty soil or heather-clad moor through or over which the water passes on its way to the distillery."

blended Scotch whisky   Until 1853 Scotch whiskies were either straight malt or straight grain whiskies, but at that time the firm of Andrew Usher & Company, and later other companies, began the practice of blending malt whiskies with grain whiskies. These grain whiskies, produced primarily from corn with a small amount of barley malt, came from distilleries in lower Scotland and were distilled in the patent still. Grain whisky in Scotland is *whisky* and not neutral spirits, as some people believe. The Scotch grain whiskies are distilled out at slightly over 180 proof. They are reduced to 124 proof when barreled in seasoned sherry or Bourbon casks for aging. (See pages 334–36 for a description of how grain whisky is made.)

Line-up of modern wash and low-wine spirit copper pot stills, Tormore Distillery at Advie, Grantown-on-Spey, Morayshire, Scottish Highlands. (*Courtesy Long John Distilleries, Ltd., Glasgow*)

Before this time the taste for Scotch had been confined to Scotland, but after blending became a general practice, Scotch whisky became popular in England and throughout the rest of the world. Blending grain whiskies with malt whiskies produced a drink that people generally liked.

The blending is done after the whiskies are three to four years old. A master blender examines them and indicates the exact proportions of Highland, Lowland, Campbeltown, and Islay malts of various ages and of grain whisky that are to be married. This is accomplished by placing the whiskies in a large vat where they are thoroughly mixed both by rotating paddles and by compressed air blown up from the bottom. The whisky is then returned to the sherry or Bourbon casks for a further period of maturing (marrying) before bottling or shipping in bulk.

The usual Scotch blend contains 20 to 50 percent malt whisky, the balance being grain whisky. The original object of using grain whiskies, which are always distilled in patent stills, was to reduce the cost, but in doing so a lighter whisky was produced that appealed much more to the other peoples of the world than had the fuller, smokier Scotch whiskies previously made.

The essential difference between blends is the proportions used of different single malts. Of these, the Highland malts are considered the finest and are always the most costly. They are fairly light in body and flavor and do not have too much smoke. The finest Highland section is Banffshire, and within it the Glen Livet and Speyside regions are considered the best. Next in importance is Moray. Lowland malts are also light in body, but not as smoky in flavor. Almost all of the grain whisky distilleries are in the Lowlands. Campbeltown malts are very full in body and quite smoky. The Islay malts are also very full, smoky, and pungent. In each category, however, malts can vary tremendously, some being much heavier than others.

In the last analysis, the reasons for blending are to obtain a smoother, more balanced product than any of the blend's single components and to ensure uniform continuity of a given brand. In this way the consumer can expect the same character, flavor, taste, and quality year in and year out. A Scotch whisky blend can very easily be the result of a marriage of as many as thirty or forty malt whiskies, together with five or more grain whiskies.

The ages of the individual whiskies at the time of blending may vary widely, since no single whisky is employed before it has reached its proper maturity. The number of years required for this is governed by the character of the whisky itself and the climatic conditions under which it is matured. The fuller-bodied malts of Islay and Campbeltown take much longer, sometimes ten to twelve years, while the Highland and Lowland malts may be ready in six to eight years, and the grain whiskies may require only four years. The greater the climatic dampness, the slower the aging process.

The secret of fine Scotch whisky, therefore, lies in the art of the blender. On his unique ability depend the polish, smoothness, and uniformity of the whisky. There are 130 distilleries in Scotland (95 Highland malt, 11 Lowland malt, 8 Islay malt, 2 Campbeltown malt, and 14 grain whisky distilleries) producing about 150 internationally marketed blends and single malts, and about 1,000 more private label and lesser brands. As we have already indicated, there are many reasons why Scotch whisky from one area differs from Scotches of other areas. Local conditions, such as water, peat, and climate, and traditional distilling practices of individual distilleries are all contributing factors. But to understand fully the Scotch picture, it is important to remember that there are many distilleries, each one turning out a whisky that has its own individual characteristics. By combining the full-flavored malt whiskies with gentler grain whiskies, the blenders obtain the individuality of character and quality that distinguishes their brands. Blends may also be tailored to producers' interpretations of consumer preferences, even to having different blends produced for various countries under the same label. The United States consumes about one-third of all the Scotch whisky sold each year. Thus, the Scotch whisky blender tries to supply what appeals most to the important American customer.

There has been an unquestioned trend in the United States toward light- *light Scotch*
ness of flavor and body in most of the beverages Americans consume. An *whisky*
indication is the continuing, enormous increase of the share of the market in
the United States held by "white goods" (gin, vodka, rum, and Tequila).

Those brands of Scotch whisky that have been blended for lightness by
judicious selection of light-bodied, lighter-flavored malts are among the largest-selling brands in the United States. The American public has come to associate paleness or lack of color with lightness and dryness. This is nonsense, since
the depth of color in a Scotch whisky as shipped is governed by the amount
of caramel (burned sugar) used in all blends to ensure color uniformity.

Even though more than 99 percent of the Scotch whisky consumed outside *all-malt whisky*
Scotland is blended whisky, there are also marketed in small quantities
straight, unblended Highland malt whiskies, as well as blends of only malt
whiskies, known as vatted malts, in which no grain whisky has been used. Such
whiskies are much fuller bodied and usually are of very fine quality.

A liqueur Scotch whisky is one that, through proper aging and blending, *liqueur Scotch*
has acquired a mellow softness both in the bouquet and on the palate. The
word *liqueur,* when used with Scotch whisky, applies to older, finer whiskies,
particularly the premium or deluxe brands, and should not be confused with a
sweetened cordial or liqueur. These whiskies are rare and expensive.

The high regard for age statements in the United States may frequently *age in Scotch*
lead us astray. A Scotch whisky with a ten-year-old age statement on the label *whisky*
is not necessarily a better whisky than one with no age statement at all. Naturally aging is important in making a Scotch (or any other whisky) mellow and
more palatable, but the quality of the whisky and the skill of the blender's
hand must be there first. Some fully aged Scotch is laid away in casks, after it
has been blended, for marrying for periods of up to one year. The law stipulates an aging period of at least three years for Scotch whisky, and none can
enter the United States under four years of age. Practically all Scotch malts
remain in their casks for a minimum of five years. Blends with higher percentages of malt whiskies are usually aged longer than those with more grain
whiskies. Thus, when a brand is marketed with different age statements, it is
not simply the same whisky aged for different lengths of time. The whisky
indicating the oldest age was fuller to begin with, and always required more
time in cask to mellow.

Before 1979 the duty and Internal Revenue tax on imported distilled spir- *Scotland versus*
its was assessed on total gallonage, at 100 proof, even if a case of Scotch *U.S. bottled*
whisky, for example, was only 86 proof. It was economical, therefore, to import Scotch in bulk at 100 proof, and to reduce it to 86 proof with distilled or

deionized water after it arrived in the United States, for a 14 percent duty and tax saving. Since 1979 both domestic and foreign producers are taxed on proof-gallons, based on the amount of alcohol rather than the volume of liquid. The price advantage of Scotch whisky imported in bulk over bottled-in-Scotland whisky now comes solely from savings in freight and handling.

There is no difference in flavor between the two, since distilled or deionized water is used universally to bring whisky down to bottling proof. In 1982 bulk imports accounted for 41 percent of all Scotch imports.

IRISH WHISKEY

There is a common belief that Irish whiskey is a potato whiskey. This is not true at all. No doubt the misconception stems from the fact that the Irish refer to illicitly distilled whiskey as *poteen,* a term derived from the pot still in which it has traditionally been distilled.

Whiskey in Ireland is distilled from a fermented mash of grains, namely, malted barley, unmalted barley, corn, rye, wheat, and oats, similar to the mash used in Scotland.

The barley malt is dried in a kiln that has a solid floor. Even when peat was used as a fuel the smoke could not come in contact with the malt. Now peat has been replaced by smokeless anthracite, and the malt is not smoke cured, as is the case in Scotland.

Much Irish whiskey is distilled in the pot still. There are three distinct distilling operations. The wash is first distilled in a large wash still, yielding the low wines. These low wines are then distilled in a smaller pot still, producing strong and weak feints, which are collected separately. Thus far the process is similar to the distillation of Scotch malt whisky. The distillation of Irish whiskey differs from Scotch whisky, however, in that a third pot still is used to obtain the final whiskey from the distillation of the strongest feints. That is why Irish whiskey is said to be triple distilled.

Some houses distill grain whiskey in column, or patent, stills. These are blended with pot-still whiskies to produce lighter-bodied and lighter-flavored whiskies, mostly for export.

Irish whiskies must be aged in seasoned cooperage for at least four years, but usually they are aged seven to eight years before being shipped.

Irish is a particularly smooth whiskey, with medium body and a clean, unique flavor. It is consumed in the same manner as Scotch whisky and also is popularly used in Irish Coffee.

AMERICAN WHISKY

history   Early American settlers brought spirituous liquors with them, as they were considered essential in withstanding the hardships of an ocean voyage and a

Average proportions of grain used in producing Bourbon. In practice, proportions vary with the distiller's formula. LEFT TO RIGHT: Corn, 51 to 79 percent; rye, 2 to 37 percent; barley malt, approximately 10 percent. The bins in the rear contain the grains shown in the glass. (*Courtesy Bourbon Institute*)

medicine in cases of illness in the new, savage land. For a long time spirits had to be imported from Europe.

The first commercially distilled spirit in what is the present-day United States was New England rum. Distilling whisky on a commercial scale began over a century later.

There is a record of distilling on Staten Island in New York in 1640, but it was not until the early eighteenth century that whisky distilling began to develop. The grains used along the eastern seaboard were rye and barley. As the settlements began extending westward, however, it became apparent that transporting newly grown grain back to the populous seaboard cities was difficult for the settlers, particularly those in western Pennsylvania. They found it was simpler to distill their grain, both rye and corn, into whisky. It not only kept longer, but it was easier to transport to the cities. Whisky and furs, indeed, became the best means of exchange, particularly during the Revolutionary War, when Continental currency was worth less than five cents on the dollar.

Whisky played a prominent part in early U.S. history, in determining the right and ability to be a self-governed nation. Whisky had always been distilled in small, family-owned distilleries without legal interference from any government. In 1791, money being a crying need for the new nation and an excise tax was levied on whisky.

The independent Pennsylvania distillers resented the tax on their product, and the tax collectors in some cases were even tarred and feathered. There were riots and stormy scenes in these "western" communities, and President

Washington, in great haste, sent a force of militia to quell the insurrection. It was done without bloodshed and accomplished its object. While in itself the insurrection was of minor importance, it was of tremendous significance to the future of the federal government and is still known as the Whiskey Rebellion.

Many of the disgruntled Dutch, Scottish, and Irish farmer-distillers decided to move out of reach of the tax collector, which meant going farther west into Indian territory. They found the proper water for distilling in southern Indiana and Kentucky.

The first whisky distilled in Kentucky is generally attributed to the Reverend Elijah Craig at Georgetown, in Bourbon County. The grain he employed was corn (maize), as it was more plentiful than rye. His product became known as Bourbon County whisky, and the name Bourbon has remained as the designation of whiskies distilled from a corn mash.

The important whisky-distilling areas in the United States are not located where they are by pure chance but because of the most important factor in making whisky—the quality of the water. It comes from springs that pass up through layer on layer of limestone rock. The limestone mantle runs along western Pennsylvania and cuts across southern Indiana over into Kentucky. There is another isolated limestone region in Maryland around Baltimore.

With the advancement of science and the development of inexpensive water technology the distiller has been freed from the necessity of locating his

Flow diagram showing entire modern grain distillery operation from the arrival of the grain to the barreling of whisky and grain neutral spirits and the processing of the spent grain into various types of fodder. (*Courtesy Joseph E. Seagram & Sons, Inc., New York*)

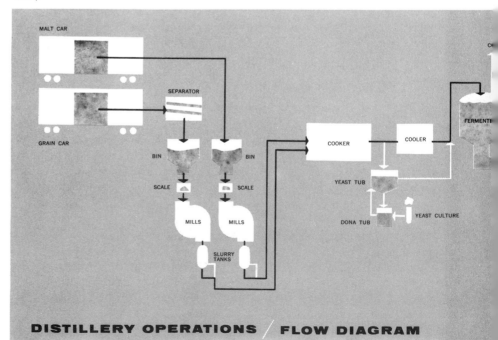

DISTILLERY OPERATIONS / FLOW DIAGRAM

production at or near these limestone mantle outcroppings. Today he can and does distill whisky in many other parts of the United States.

grain whisky production

The early distillers used very crude and primitive equipment. Fermentation was carried on in open mash tubs, the yeast being the wild varieties the air afforded. Since that day tremendous changes have taken place.

Briefly the steps in making whisky are as follows:

1. Upon arrival at the distillery the grain is carefully inspected and cleaned of all dust.

2. It is ground in the gristmill to a meal.

3. The meal is first cooked to release starch from its tough cellular coating, then malt is added to convert the starches.

4. Pure cultured yeast is propagated in increasingly large containers—a flask in the laboratory, a dona tub in the yeast room, the yeast tub in the distillery.

5. The cooled wort is yeasted with the propagated yeast and goes to the fermenting vats to become beer.

6. The beer goes into a patent, or double-column, still. The result is whisky, which is distilled out at below 160 proof. It is then reduced in proof to 105 to 110 by adding deionized (demineralized) water.

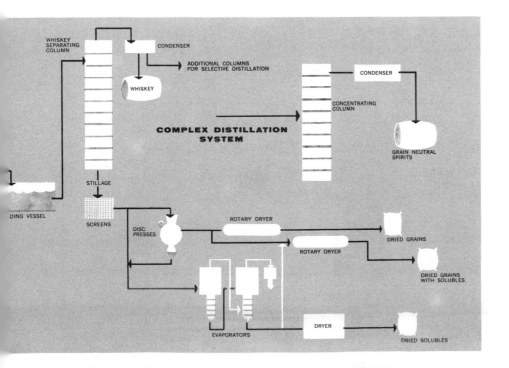

All new whisky (except corn whisky and light whisky) is placed in *new* charred white oak barrels to mature in bonded warehouses, under the custody of the distiller. Taxes are paid, based on proof, at the time that the whisky is shipped.

proof changes through aging

Spirits are generally matured in porous containers so the air can seep in to oxidize and mellow the alcohol. The most common container is made of wood (generally oak). Wood is a porous substance, and when liquid is stored in a wooden barrel, even though it be tightly closed, some of it seeps through, that is, evaporates or escapes through the pores of the wood.

Aged spirits, such as brandy, rum, and Scotch whisky, are barreled for aging at proofs varying from 124 to 150 proof. These spirits lose some alcoholic strength as they mature because they are stored under humid conditions.

American whiskies, on the other hand, are barreled at 105 to 110 proof ($52\frac{1}{2}$ to 55 percent alcohol), and as they mature their alcoholic strength increases because of the warm, dry conditions under which they are stored.

To illustrate this point, after four years of aging, a fifty-gallon barrel of new whisky at a hypothetical 100 proof (twenty-five gallons of alcohol and twenty-five gallons of water) has lost ten gallons of liquid, but the alcoholic strength is 110 proof. This means that 55 percent of the forty gallons remaining is alcohol (twenty-two gallons) and the remaining eighteen gallons are water.

Newly distilled Bourbon (LEFT) and samples at one, two, four, six, and eight years of age. Note how Bourbon whisky picks up color year by year as it matures in new charred oak barrels. Evaporation also takes place, reducing the amount of whisky in a 50-gallon barrel by as much as $1\frac{1}{2}$ gallons per year. (*Photograph by Marty Cobin, courtesy Joseph E. Seagram & Sons, Inc., New York*)

NEW   1   2   4   6   8

No one knows exactly how the advantage of charring barrels was learned. One legend is that as a result of a fire in a warehouse in Jamaica some barrels of rum were heavily charred. After some time it was learned that the rum in the charred barrels had acquired both color and quality it had lacked before.

origin of charring barrels

Another explanation is that in order to bend the barrel staves into the proper shape for the barrel, the early Kentuckians heated them before an open fire, and often they became charred. Discovering that the more charred the staves the more palatable the whisky, charring became an accepted practice. Kentuckians were also said to have burned out the inside of used barrels so that the whisky would not pick up off-flavors. It is likely that none of these stories is true, as it is probable that the virtues of charring the barrels in which whisky was to be stored were stumbled upon quite by accident. Staves average one inch in thickness, and one-eighth-inch depth of char is most common.

There are two yeasting processes used in America—the sweet-mash, or yeast-mash process, and the sour-mash, or yeasting-back process. The sour-mash process is used primarily in making Bourbon whisky.

sweet and sour mash

A sweet mash is produced by adding all or almost all freshly developed yeast to the mash, that is, no stillage (liquid recovered after the alcohols have been distilled off) from a previous distillation is mixed with the fresh mash to adjust the acidity. It is allowed to ferment from thirty-six to fifty hours and the fermenter can be, and usually is, refilled almost immediately when empty.

Sour mash means that at least one-quarter of the fermenting mash must be stillage, or spent beer, from a previous distillation, along with the fresh mash. The mash is allowed to ferment from seventy-two to ninety-six hours. Fermentation generally takes place in open fermenting vats at low temperatures. When emptied, the fermenters are sterilized, aerated, and allowed to "sweeten" for twenty-four hours before being used again.

Sour mash offers a favorable pH for yeast growth and inhibits bacterial contamination. Sweet mash is more difficult to control and must be done above 80 degrees Fahrenheit to end quickly and avoid contamination.

There are three main categories of whiskies produced in America: straights, blends, and light whiskies. Each one has several subcategories. Because these products are often blended together, a whisky may appear in more than one category.

A straight whisky, under federal regulations, is one that has been distilled off at a proof not exceeding 160, aged in new, charred white oak barrels for at least two years, and reduced by the addition of water at the time of bottling to no lower than 80 proof, from a minimum of 51 percent of a grain. Nothing may be added other than the water. Straights include Bourbon, Tennessee, rye, corn, and wheat whiskies.

straight whisky

The higher the proof at which a spirit is distilled out, the lighter it will be in character, flavor, and body. This is because more and more of the congeners (flavor and body components) are eliminated as the proof of the spirit is increased.

Under U.S. regulations the theoretical critical point is reached at 190 proof (95 percent alcohol). Any spirit distilled out at 190 proof or higher is called a neutral spirit and should not possess any noticeable aroma, flavor, or character. Conversely, the lower the proof of distillation the greater the amount of congeners that will be distilled over and become a part of the distillate to give character, aroma, flavor, and body. Since straight whisky by regulation cannot be distilled out at a strength exceeding 160 proof, it possesses very definite aroma, flavor, and body characteristics when suitably aged in wood.

The predominant grain used in the mash formula determines the final designation under which the whisky is labeled and marketed. If 51 percent or more of the grain is corn, it is straight Bourbon; 51 percent or more rye grain makes it a straight rye; 51 percent wheat, straight wheat whisky; 51 percent barley malt or rye malt, straight malt whisky or straight rye malt whisky; 80 percent or more corn, aged in uncharred oak barrels or reused charred oak barrels, is designated straight corn whisky.

Tennessee whisky is a straight whisky that must be distilled in Tennessee from a fermented mash containing 51 percent or more of *any* grain. Even though there is no grain criteria, corn is usually used. This is a Bourbon-type whisky, but it is very full-bodied since it is treated with maple wood charcoal to remove the lighter flavors.

Barrels of Bourbon whisky aging in a modern temperature- and humidity-controlled warehouse in Kentucky. In the background the operator is ricking a barrel. (*Courtesy Schenley Industries, Inc., New York*)

Straight whiskies may be mixed, provided the mixture is made up of whiskies of the same distilling period and from the same distillery. Such whiskies do not lose their straight whisky designation.

Straight whiskies of different distilling periods and from different distilleries may also be mixed or blended, but they must be labeled blended Bourbon whisky, blended rye whisky, and so on. When straight whiskies that are homogeneous are mixed, the mixture carries the age of the youngest whisky it contains. Most straight whiskies on the market greatly exceed the minimum age requirement because each distiller attempts to age his product until he feels his whisky has reached the ripeness or maturity that is ideal for that particular whisky. Most authorities agree that the average Bourbon attains this stage in about six years, but this varies with the flavor intensity of the initial distillate.

Two-thirds of the American-distilled whisky consumed in the United States is straight whisky or blends of straight whiskies.

The term *bottled in bond* is generally misunderstood, not only by the public but too often by people in the retail liquor trade itself. The term is *not* a guarantee of quality; it refers only to the Internal Revenue tax. Only straight whiskies are bottled in bond.

bottled in bond

The Bottled in Bond Act of 1894 permitted distillers to bottle whisky (or other distilled spirits) without paying the excise taxes, provided the whisky was at least four years old, distilled at one plant by the same proprietor, and bottled at 100 proof, under the supervision of the U.S. Treasury Department. After bottling, the whisky remained in the bonded warehouse until the distiller was ready to sell it, at which time the tax was to be paid or determined, before withdrawing the whisky from bond.

In 1980 the All-In-Bond system was put into use. This created an atmosphere of joint custody between the proprietor and the U.S. government. The proprietor now has full custody of spirits whose production must be fully documented. So long as there are complete records, it is no longer necessary for a government inspector to be in the plant every day, and no strip stamps are required on the bottles. No taxes have to be paid until the whiskies are shipped.

Bottled in bond spirits still have the same meaning as before, which is that they have been distilled out below 160 proof, are straight, are four or more years old, and are bottled at 100 proof. In addition to whiskies, other products may include rum and grape and apple brandies.

Bottled in bond is not a guarantee of purity or quality of spirits, and the government assumes no responsibility with respect to claims by dealers when advertising these spirits in this connection.

blended whisky   Nearly half of the American-produced whisky consumed in the United States is blended whisky. The blender devotes his art to mixing carefully selected, full-bodied, straight whiskies with grain spirits and/or light whiskies to produce a lighter, more harmoniously balanced whole and to duplicate, day in and day out, an identical, uniform product. The straight whiskies contribute aroma, flavor, and body, while the grain spirits and/or light whiskies give the final product lightness and smoothness without sacrificing character.

To be a blended whisky, at least 20 percent of the blend must be straight whisky. The balance may be grain neutral spirits, grain spirits, and/or light whiskies. Grain neutral spirits are spirits that are distilled out at over 190 proof and have no recognizable aroma or flavor. Grain spirits are neutral spirits that have been aged in reused oak barrels to give them a delicate flavor and soft mellowness. It is important that the barrel be compatible with the flavor intensity of the grain neutral spirits, since the woody character of a new barrel would overwhelm the light flavor of the grain neutral spirits. Light whiskies, the newest category, have become an important component for the blender.

Regulations also permit the use of certain blending materials in blended whiskies, up to $2\frac{1}{2}$ percent by volume. Those most often employed are sherry wine and prune or peach juice.

There is an unending discussion as to the merits and demerits of blended whisky in comparison to straight whisky. Both usually are fine, very drinkable products. The one you enjoy more—the one that pleases your palate—is the one you should choose. It is absurd to consider one inferior to the other; they are simply different. The straight whisky is full bodied and full flavored, while the blended whisky is comparatively light bodied and light in flavor.

Curiously, many people in the northeastern states refer to blended whisky as rye. It is not. While this is probably the result of the long tradition of using a great deal of rye in making whisky in that area, true rye whisky contains at least 51 percent of that grain and has a pronounced rye flavor. If someone unknowingly gets a true rye whisky, the strong flavor and full body may shock his palate.

light whisky   Light whisky is whisky that has been distilled in the United States at more than 160 proof and less than 190 proof and stored in seasoned, charred oak containers. This whisky is permitted to be entered for storage at proofs higher than 125. The Standard of Identity for light whisky became effective in 1972.

The primary purpose for this category was to permit the production of light distillates that could be aged in seasoned oak casks—that is, reused cooperage—which are more compatible in developing the lower flavor intensities found in this type of whisky.

One of the newest and most modern distilleries in the nation, at Lawrenceburg, Indiana, showing the towering distilling columns and the complex control panel by which precise temperatures and distilling proofs can be maintained scientifically. (*Courtesy Schenley Distillers, Inc., New York*)

In general, the techniques used in the production of straight whisky and grain neutral spirits are followed in making light whisky. The proportions and types of cereal grains used in the formula are left entirely to the discretion of the distiller, but most distillers use corn (up to 90 percent) as the major portion of their formula. The main emphasis in this process is on distillation techniques. The higher proof requirements permit the use of more sophisticated distillation systems, such as those used in distilling grain spirits. The distiller also has a wide range of proofs in which to work. At 161 proof the whisky is still flavorful; at 189 proof it is extremely light in flavor and character. At almost every level of proof in between, a changing relative amount of flavor components is left in the distillate to affect the body, flavor, and character of the whisky. The distiller can distill his light whisky out at any of these proofs and achieve different weights of flavor. He can mix different batches of different proofs for his final product.

Typical distillery tasting room at Lawrenceburg, Indiana, where tasters evaluate samples. (*Courtesy Schenley Distillers, Inc., New York*)

The age of light whisky as it is withdrawn for bottling affects its final character. As with America's straight whiskies and imported whiskies, a major factor in the character of the light whisky brands is their maturity.

It had been hoped that this category would be enjoyed by the segment of the population that enjoys "white goods," but this has failed to materialize. The biggest use for light whiskies has been in blends, as a replacement for grain neutral spirits, which even if they were aged, could not show an age statement. Light whisky is available in three ways:

1. As light whisky, in the bottle as distilled and reduced in proof, and including mixtures of these distillates.

2. As blended light whisky, a mixture of less than 20 percent straight whisky at 100 proof with light whisky.

3. In the traditional blended whisky, with the light whisky portion unidentified in a mixture with 20 percent or more straight whisky at 100 proof.

For more precise information about these whiskies, refer to the Standards of Identity for distilled spirits in Appendix P.

CANADIAN WHISKY

According to U.S. federal regulations, "Canadian whisky is a distinctive product of Canada, manufactured in Canada in compliance with laws of the Dominion of Canada . . . containing no distilled spirits less than three years old . . . such whisky is blended Canadian whisky. Canadian whisky shall not be designated as straight."

According to Canadian law, Canadian whisky must be produced from cereal grain only. While the Canadian Excise Tax Bureau exercises the customary controls to ensure proper collection of the tax, the government sets no other limitation as to grain formulas, distilling proofs, or special type of aging cooperage. It believes the distillers are better judges than the government of what the public, both at home and abroad, wants in a Canadian whisky.

Many people believe that Canadian whisky is a rye whisky, which it is not. Corn, rye, wheat, and barley malt are the grains generally used, and none can be more than 50 percent. The proportions of grains used are the trade secrets of the individual distillers.

The methods of production are similar but the procedures of maturing differ somewhat from U.S. standards and practices. For example, any loss from evaporation may be made up by adding new whisky to replace the amount lost.

The distillers have developed a whisky with a delicate flavor and light body. They obtain these characteristics with mash formulas designed to produce lightness and delicacy and by distilling out at varying strengths, ranging from 140 to 180 proof. Practically all Canadian whisky is six years old or older when marketed. If it is less than four years old (it may be bottled when it is three years old), its age must be listed on the label.

More than half of the Canadian whisky coming to the United States is in bulk.

JAPANESE WHISKY

The Japanese wine and spirits industry is an old one, going back into antiquity. However, until relatively recent times (about 1870) it was in large part devoted to such traditional beverages as saké, Umeshu (a Japanese plum wine made by infusion), and Umechu (a Japanese medicinal wine). With the advent of Westernizing influences in Japan, distillation was also introduced. Since then products such as Japanese whisky, liqueurs, brandies, and Sochu (a neutral spirit made from grain or sweet potatoes) have become part of the Japanese culture.

Although historically much of the technique of distillation was learned from the West, especially Scotland and France, the Japanese adapted the methods to their own economy. For example, their whisky is primarily a blended whisky made up of varying percentages of fuller-bodied whiskies produced in pot stills and lighter-bodied whiskies produced by continuous distillation using column stills, many of which were adapted from French designs. While the original Japanese whiskies were an attempt to duplicate Scotch whisky, the grains employed in these whiskies were different from those used in Scotland. Japan now produces a whisky different from any currently made in the United States and from any of the other imported whiskies entering the United States.

Many of the fuller-bodied whiskies are made from malted barley, some small portion of which is cured over peat. Most of the whisky used in blended Japanese whisky is made from millet, corn, Indian corn, some small quantities of rice, and other grains in varying proportions in their mash bill (formula). Wheat and rye are seldom used. The milling and fermentation procedure is similar to that of the Western methods. The saccharification method differs, however, in that most of the lighter whisky uses the Japanese *koji* enzyme, an enzyme similar to that used in making saké (see page 302) to convert the starch to sugar.

The proofs of the whiskies, when removed from the stills, vary from about 130 proof for the fuller-bodied whiskies to about 180 proof for the lighter-bodied whiskies. The whiskies are aged separately in used charred oak barrels before blending. Blending, the subsequent marrying period, and further aging last from months to years, depending on the quality of the whisky. The laws of Japan define various classes of whisky primarily for Japanese tax purposes and regulate the aging and handling of whisky.

OTHER WHISKIES

Whisky types are also produced in Holland, Germany, Denmark, and Australia. In Australia the Scotch method—first producing malt whisky and then a blend of malts and grains—is followed. Although made on the Scotch pattern, Australian whisky has a distinctive character.

TASTE OF WHISKIES

The principal taste distinction of Scotch whisky is its smoky peat flavor, whereas Irish whiskey has a similar barley-malt whisky character without the smoky flavor. Both are somewhat lighter in body than American straight whiskies because high proof, very light-bodied grain whiskies are used for blending. Also, because Scotch and Irish whiskies are matured in old, previously used cooperage they require a longer aging period. This is usually seven to eight years, and up to twelve for the heavier distillates, which require more time to smooth out.

Rye and Bourbon whiskies have the distinctive tastes and characters of the rye and corn grains used respectively. Because of the different methods of mashing and the lower proofs at which they are distilled out, which give them a higher congeneric content, they are both sweeter and fuller bodied than Scotch or Irish. Furthermore, aging in new charred oak cooperage makes it possible for the American whiskies to reach maturity sooner.

With the trend towards lightness in American taste, American blended whisky and Canadian whisky are quite popular.

HOW AND WHEN TO SERVE WHISKIES

Aside from their most common use as a straight drink or on the rocks, whiskies may be used in innumerable cocktails, punches, and other mixed drinks. They are also very popular in long drinks, such as highballs and coolers (see Chapter 26).

21
VODKAS

When this book first appeared in 1940, only half a page was devoted to vodka. In the short space of four decades this most neutral of spirits has risen from its "also ran" listing among the "other spirits" to a degree of popularity that has made it the largest-selling individual type of spirits in the United States, replacing Bourbon and blended whisky. It was not until 1950 tht vodka was separately reported in trade statistics. In 1955 it represented only 3.4 percent of the total distilled spirits market, and by 1982 it had risen to 22 percent.

history The word *vodka* is a diminutive of the Russian word for "water," *voda*, and it was the Russians who originated this particular "water of life." In Russia, Finland, Czechoslovakia, Poland, and elsewhere in northern and eastern Europe, spirits have long been distilled to a very high proof, resulting in a minimum of flavor.

According to many historians vodka was first produced in Russia in the fourteenth century. The vast Smirnoff distilleries in Moscow, dating from 1818, passed out of the family's control with the 1917 revolution. The formula was brought to America in the 1930s via Paris, and Smirnoff was the first and only American-made vodka for many years. It alone can be given credit for generating a new fashion of drinking in the United States.

how vodka Vodka has always been distilled from the most plentiful and least expen-
is made sive materials available to the distiller, wherever he might be. Vodka is made from potatoes and various grains, principally corn, with some wheat added. The best export vodkas, and all those produced in the United States, are made from grain.

Vodka, like whisky, is an alcoholic distillate from a fermented mash. Whisky, however, is distilled at low proof to retain flavor. Vodka is distilled at high proof and then processed still further, if required, to extract all congeners.

346

In a sense vodka is like gin, but with one big difference. Both are made from neutral spirits; neither has to be aged. But in making American gin, as will be described in Chapter 22, the neutral spirits are delicately flavored with juniper and aromatics. In making vodka nothing is added to the neutral spirits; instead all character is absent, leaving the spirits colorless and without distinctive odor or taste.

Vodka is made neutral by either of two processes. In the first, neutral spirits flow continuously through tanks containing no less than one and a half pounds of vegetable charcoal for each gallon of spirits, so that the spirits are in intimate contact with the charcoal for a minimum of eight hours. At least 10 percent of the charcoal is replaced after each forty hours of operation. In the second method spirits are agitated for a minimum of eight hours in contact with no less than six pounds of new vegetable charcoal for every one hundred gallons of spirits. Vodka can also be made by purifying or refining the spirits by any other method that the government finds will result in a product without distinctive character, aroma, or taste. American vodka is bottled at proofs ranging from 80 to 100, the majority of sales being at the lower figure. (See Appendix P for the U.S. Standards of Identity for vodka.)

Inspecting activated charcoal used for filtering vodka. (*Courtesy Ste. Pierre Smirnoff Fls., Hartford, Connecticut*)

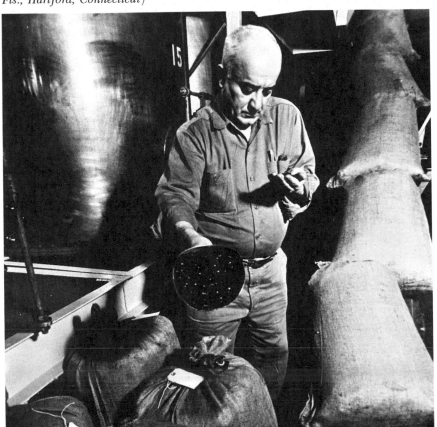

IMPORTED VODKAS

The most significant and prestigious imported vodkas are those from the original Russian, Finnish, and Polish sources. With vodka's increasing popularity, however, an increased flow has come from England, France, Holland, Czechoslovakia, Turkey, and China. There is a kosher vodka from Israel.

FLAVORED VODKAS

Flavored varieties of vodka are popular, particularly in Poland and Russia, where infusions and mixtures with herbs, grasses, leaves, spices, and seeds are involved. Some of these vodkas are colored and, as vodka-based liqueurs, are sweetened and fruit flavored. The most common of the flavored vodkas, which range from 70 proof up, are:

ZUBROWKA. Flavored with a type of grass found only in the forests of eastern Poland. These grasslands are the breeding grounds for a particular species of bison indigenous to Poland, and the zubrowka ("bison grass vodka") has a slightly yellowish tinge and an aromatic bouquet. The FDA, however, has questioned the effects of bison grass on the human body.

STÁRKA ("old"). Vodka ages for about ten years in special oak casks previously used for fine-quality wines. This maturing imparts an amber color and flavor to Stárka, which is a vodka for brandy lovers.

YUBILEYNEYA OSOBAYA ("jubilee vodka"). Contains brandy, honey, and other ingredients.

PERTSOVKA. A dark brown Russian pepper vodka with a pleasant aroma and burning taste. It is prepared from an infusion of capsicum, cayenne, and cubeb. History records that Czar Peter the Great seasoned his vodka with pepper, and numerous Russians apparently continue to enjoy its sharp bite.

OKHOTNICHYA ("hunter's vodka"). A spirit flavored with many herbs; has a scent that suggests heather honey.

Russian vodka makers produce about thirty other vodkas with a wide range of flavors, some of which are available in the United States.

Fruit-flavored vodka is made in the United States. There are orange, lemon, cherry, and other flavors that must be stated on the label. U.S. flavored vodka is a product of rectification, and pays the $.30-per-gallon rectification tax.

HOW AND WHEN TO SERVE VODKA

In the middle of the twentieth century general consumption of vodka was confined almost entirely to Russia, Poland, and the Baltic states. Vodka has been produced in the United States since 1933, but until 1948 it was an exotic specialty consumed by a few people of eastern European origin. It was drunk straight, ice cold, in a small, one-ounce glass, at one gulp, and almost always with a sharp-tasting appetizer. Drinking vodka in this way, however, did not have much appeal for Americans, and it would have remained little known except for an accident of chance—an accident that had nothing to do with vodka.

After World War II a Hollywood restaurant owner found himself with a large and unsalable stock of ginger beer. Realizing that he had to find a new use for it or take a heavy loss, he tried mixing it with any number of products without success, until he used vodka. He added half a lime, served it in a copper mug, and named it the Moscow Mule. The Mule caught on, and other distillers made vodka and created new drinks. From Hollywood the vodka fashion swept across the country.

Because it has no flavor of its own, vodka was quickly recognized as the most versatile of all mixers. It combines exceedingly well with fruit juices and flavors of all types. This fact, perhaps more than any other, accounts for the remarkable growth of vodka's popularity. The Screwdriver (vodka and orange juice) was one of the earliest drinks specially created. The most significant vodka drink, which has become part of the American scene, is the Bloody Mary (vodka and tomato juice). Vodka and Tonic is also enormously popular, and vodka is substituted freely for gin in the Martini and other drinks.

America has also begun to enjoy vodka straight—chilled in the refrigerator or freezer—particularly with spicy appetizers, smoked salmon, and caviar. Vodka is often served on the rocks.

22
GINS

history Gin is one of the few liquors in whose production man plays a more important part than nature. In the wines and spirits studied so far, we have seen that natural forces age and develop the liquor. But here man has manufactured the whole product. Gin did not happen by chance; it was created quite intentionally for a specific purpose. Credit for this belongs to Franciscus de la Boe (1614–1672), also known as Doctor Sylvius, a seventeenth-century physician and professor of medicine at Holland's famed University of Leyden.

Doctor Sylvius was not thinking of a beverage spirit, much less a Dry Martini. His objective was medicinal in the purest sense. Knowing the diuretic properties of the oil of the juniper berry (*Juniperus communis*), he felt that by redistilling a pure alcohol with the juniper berry he could obtain its therapeutic oil in a form that would provide an inexpensive medicine. And he succeeded. Within a few years all Holland found itself suffering from ills that could be cured only by Dr. Sylvius's medicine. He named it Genièvre, the French name for the juniper berry. The Dutch called it Genever, which they still do, and today it is also known in the Netherlands as Hollands and Schiedam (a gin-distilling center near Rotterdam). The English shortened and Anglicized it to gin.

The popularity of gin in England came about as the result of a demand for distilled spirits that were palatable and also inexpensive. During the reign of Queen Anne (1702–1714) the only way distillers knew how to satisfy this demand was to take the lees of wine or beer and distill out the alcohol. Such seventeenth-century spirits did not possess a very pleasant flavor, and something had to be done about it. The solution was found in gin.

English soldiers returning from the seventeenth-century wars on the Continent brought back a taste for "Dutch Courage," as they dubbed the beverage. In no time at all gin became the national drink of England, as it has remained ever since. (Contrary to the general belief, the popularity of Scotch whisky among the English is quite recent, only a little more than a century old.)

Queen Anne helped matters along by raising the duties and taxes on French wines and brandies and at the same time lowering the excise tax on English distilled spirits. Naturally the production of this new, inexpensive beverage flourished. In fact, gin was so cheap for a time in England that one innkeeper put up a sign that read:

> Drunk for a penny,
> Dead drunk for twopence,
> Clean straw for nothing!

This gives a mild idea of the kind of gin that was made, although it is unlikely it was much worse than the kind many people drank in America during the bathtub gin era of the twenties.

During the course of the years tremendous improvements have been made in production methods. Today making gin is a highly refined science, with very precise quality controls to ensure continuous uniformity. This does not mean that all gins are identical. Each distiller has his own closely guarded secret formula and method of making gin.

There are only two basic styles or types of gin: Dutch—Hollands, Genever, or Schiedam gin; and Dry—English or American gin, often called London Dry.

Dutch gins are very full flavored and full bodied and possess a complex, malty aroma and taste.

English and American gins are quite light in flavor and body by comparison. They are more aromatic and flavorful

HOLLANDS GIN

In the Netherlands gin is generally made in the following manner:

1. A grain formula of approximately equal parts of barley malt, corn, and rye is mashed, cooked, and fermented into a beer.

2. The resulting beer is distilled in a pot still and the distillate may be redistilled once or twice. The final spirits, known as malt wine, are distilled off higher than the first distillates, but still at a very low proof, between 100 and 110.

3. The malt wine is then redistilled, together with juniper berries, in another pot still. The first gin is distilled off at between 94 and 98 proof. (Other botanicals are included with the juniper berries, but not in the quantity or variety employed in England and the United States.)

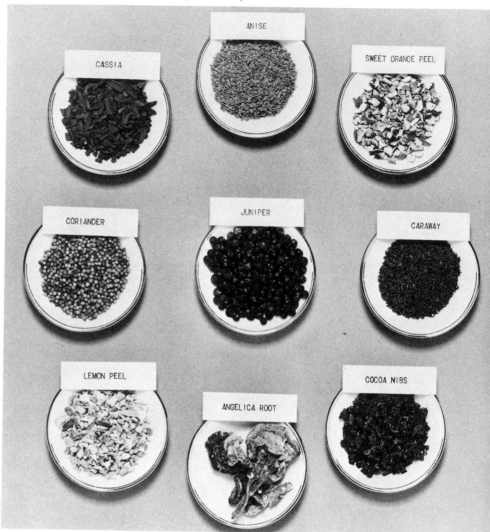

Some of the botanicals used to impart distinctive flavor to gin. (*Courtesy Joseph E. Seagram & Sons, Inc., New York*)

Because of the low proof at which it is distilled, Hollands, Genever, or Schiedam is a very full-bodied gin with a clean but pronounced malty aroma and flavor. Dutch gin cannot be mixed with other ingredients to make cocktails because its own definite taste will predominate and overshadow whatever other wine or spirit it is mixed with, but a dash of bitters is pleasant.

DRY GIN—ENGLISH

Originally the term *London Dry Gin* signified gin produced in or near London, where most English gin has always been distilled, but today the term has been adopted by American gin distillers as well as gin producers in other countries. Therefore it has lost its geographical significance. The term *dry* does not have much meaning either, since all English, American, and Dutch gins are equally dry.

English and American gins are very different in character from Dutch gins. This is the result of the different production methods used.

In England making gin begins with a grain formula made up of 75 percent corn, 15 percent barley malt, and 10 percent other grains. This is mashed, cooked, and fermented, much the same as the mash is handled for the production of whisky. After fermentation is completed, the wort, or beer, is distilled and rectified in a column still to obtain a rather pure spirit above 190 proof. This is reduced to 120 proof by the addition of distilled water. The reduced spirit is placed in a gin still, which is usually a pot still, and redistilled in the presence of the flavoring agents, primarily juniper berries. However, other flavoring materials, known as botanicals, are used in rather small quantities to add flavor nuances to the gin. Among those generally used are dried lemon and orange peel, cardamom and coriander seeds, bitter almonds, angelica and orris root, as well as anise, caraway, fennel, licorice, and so on. The precise formula is always a secret. There is also a variation in the method of distilling. Some producers mix the botanicals with the spirit and distill the entire mash, while others place the botanicals on wire mesh trays that are suspended above the spirit in the still, so that the alcohol vapors, upon rising, will pass through and around the botanicals, thus becoming impregnated with the aromatic flavoring oils they contain.

The resulting spirit comes off the gin still at 150 to 170 proof and is recovered as gin. Character can be influenced by adjusting the cutoff in the run, since the aromatics are extracted in varying amounts during the process. Only the heart of the run is used, and it is reduced in proof to bottling strength—80 to 97 proof—and is ready to be marketed. If it is not to be bottled at once, it is stored in glass-lined or stainless steel tanks, since gin is generally not aged.

There is a difference in character between English and American gin, primarily because of the slightly lower proof of the spirits employed by English distillers. These spirits retain some character.

other English gins

While virtually the whole trade in gin in the British Isles is concerned with London Dry, there are some other varieties. The most important of these is Plymouth Gin. It is a heavier, more strongly flavored gin than the London Dry type.

A few English gin distillers still produce in small amounts a sweetened gin labeled Old Tom Gin. It is rarely sold today.

DRY GIN—AMERICAN

American gin is either distilled or compounded. Distilled gin can be made by adding the flavor ingredients as part of a continuous process, during which the alcohol is first distilled from the mash, or by redistilling distilled spirits.

In some cases the botanicals are suspended above the liquid so that the flavor is removed by the alcohol vapor. In other cases, when redistillation occurs, the ingredients may be put directly into the alcohol to be redistilled.

Compound gin is made by combining distilled spirits with essential oils or extracts of the botanicals. The main characteristic flavor must be from juniper berries, although many other ingredients are used, each according to the formula of the maker.

Grain alcohol passes into the still to be evaporated by the heat from a steam coil. In some instances botanicals are mixed with the spirits in the gin still and heated. The vapor, rich with the essence of the botanicals, passes to a condenser, through a tail box for control, and into the storage tank.

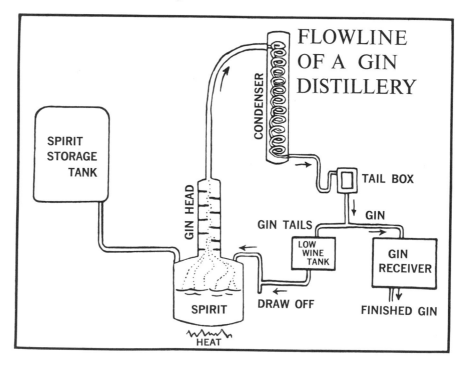

FLOWLINE OF A GIN DISTILLERY

Gin produced by original distillation or redistillation may be designated distilled. Compound gin needs no special designation. In every case the type of spirits used must be mentioned on the label.

To make a quality gin the producer must start with neutral spirits that are clean and free of any foreign flavor. The juniper berries and other botanicals must also be of the best grades. Because botanicals vary in flavor content each season, the distiller must continually adjust the proportions to maintain his brand's consistency.

As stated earlier, virtually all gins on the market use the word *dry* as descriptive of the brand. The label may read Dry Gin, Extra Dry Gin, Very Dry Gin, London Dry Gin, or English Dry Gin, but all express the same meaning—lacking in sweetness.

Dry gin is also produced in Germany, Italy, Israel, Norway, the Balkans, and Africa.

FRUIT-FLAVORED GINS

In all gin-producing countries there are people who enjoy a gin with a special flavor: orange, lemon, pineapple, mint, and so forth. These are gins to which the specific flavoring has been added and the name of the flavor put on the label. In the United States these are considered the product of rectification and pay the $0.30-per-gallon rectification tax.

For a product to be a gin the one requirement *sine qua non* is that its principal flavoring agent be juniper berries. There is one exception, however: sloe gin. Sloe gin is a gin in name only since it is a cordial; it will be discussed in Chapter 25.

AGING GIN

U.S. regulations do not permit any age claims to be made for gin. In fact, gin does not require aging to be smooth, palatable, and drinkable. It is ready for consumption when it comes off the gin still and has been reduced to potable strength. Some producers in the United States do age their gin in wood for short periods of time, which gives the gin a light golden color. This product is often called "Golden" gin, but the producers cannot advertise or make any age claims on the label.

There is a general misconception about Dutch gins being aged. In the Netherlands aging is not recognized by law, although it would still not be illegal to practice it. Whether labeled Hollands, Genever, or Schiedam, the gin is not aged. As it comes from the still it is stored for bottling, either in large, glazed earthenware vats or more often in glass-linked tanks. Any slight yellowish or golden color to be found in Dutch gin is the product of a slight amount of caramel coloring that has been added.

HOW AND WHEN TO SERVE GIN

Hollands gin should be drunk straight; in the East Indies, however, it is drunk with bitters. Take a regular whisky glass and add two dashes of bitters, roll the glass around until the inside of the glass is covered with the bitters, then throw out the rest. Fill with Hollands gin. It is a quick drink and a good aperitif.

The most popular dry gin cocktail by far is the Dry Martini, but it is only one of hundreds of gin cocktails, such as the Alexander, Negroni, Gibson, and Gimlet. Dry gin is also widely used in long drinks, such as the Gin and Tonic, Tom Collins, Gin Rickey, and Gin and Bitter Lemon, all especially refreshing in warm weather (see Chapter 26).

Because of the strong juniper flavor, gin may be used in cooking where recipes, such as those for game dishes, call for juniper berries.

23
RUMS

Rum,° the name of that multifaceted alcoholic beverage, conjures up pictures of Sir Henry Morgan, the Spanish explorers in the New World, and the smugglers, or rum runners, of Prohibition. Its career has been romantic, colorful, and replete with legends, some of which are doubtless apocryphal.

Rum has been in and out of fashion in the United States, but recently its popularity has soared. In fact, one single brand of rum has become the largest selling brand of *any* spirit in the United States. Rum, as a category, doubled from 1975 to 1982, and rum now has 7 percent of the spirits market.

Rum comes from a grass whose botanical name is *Saccharum officinarum,* *history* but it is more commonly known as sugarcane. The earliest mention we have of sugarcane dates back to 327 B.C., when Alexander the Great returned from his expedition to India. Whether sugarcane originated in the northeastern valleys of India or in the islands of the South Pacific we may never know, but it was finally brought to Europe by the Arabs after A.D. 636. Still, crystallized sugar was a costly rarity until Columbus took cane cuttings from the Canary Islands to the West Indies. It prospered so well there that sugar made from cane became inexpensive and could be enjoyed by everyone.

Almost at once, distillation of rum sprang up as a by-product of the sugar factory. Today it is made in all parts of the world, wherever sugarcane grows.

Rum is any alcoholic distillate or a mixture of distillates from the fermented juice of sugarcane, sugarcane molasses, or other sugarcane by-products distilled at less than 190 proof (whether or not such proof is further reduced before bottling to not less than 80 proof). The distillate must possess the taste, aroma, and characteristics generally attributed to rum.

°*Ron* (Spanish); *rhum* (French).

The early Spanish settlers of the West Indies noted that the residual molasses of their primitive sugar factories fermented easily, so it was natural that they experimented with distilling. The result was a pleasant-tasting alcoholic beverage. The freebooters of the period took the product back to Europe, where it found ready acceptance.

How rum got its name is a matter of conjecture. Its origin is lost among the legends of sixteenth-century swashbuckling pirates. Purists believe it is a shortened form of the Latin *saccharum,* which means "sugar." Another idea is that the wild lads of the Spanish Main first called the product *rumbullion* or *rumbustion.*

Still others credit the name to the English Navy. In 1745 Admiral Vernon discovered that his men were suffering from scurvy. Not knowing what to do about it, he cut the daily ration of beer from their diet and replaced it with the strange, new West Indian beverage, which conquered the scurvy problem and won him the lasting regard of his men, who referred to him affectionately as Old Rummy and in his honor called the new drink rum. (In eighteenth-century England the word *rum* was a slang expression used to describe people, things, or events that were very good, the very best. Thus, when the British sailors named the beverage rum it was the highest accolade they could bestow upon it.)

For over three hundred years rum has been made in the West Indies, but it is also produced in other sugarcane-growing sections of the world. It was made in New England, which imported molasses from the West Indies for this purpose. Many New England shipping families engaged in an infamous cycle of trade in the production of New England rum.

Rum, distilled in New England, was carried to Africa, perhaps with stops at Madeira, the Azores, or the Canaries, where some of it was sold. The remainder was exchanged for African blacks, who were brought back to the West Indies to become slaves, in exchange for molasses that was brought back to New England to be distilled into rum so that the cycle could begin all over again.

production   The production of rum begins with harvesting the cane. The freshly cut cane is brought to the sugar mills, where it is passed through enormous, very heavy crushing rollers that express the juice. The juice is boiled to concentrate the sugar and evaporate the water. Then it is clarified. The result is a heavy, thick syrup.

The syrup is pumped into high-speed centrifugal machines, whirling at over twenty-two hundred revolutions per minute, where the sugar in the syrup is crystallized and separated from the other solids. After the sugar is removed, what remains is molasses. Sometimes this still retains up to 5 percent sugar. The only economical way to recover, or not to lose, the residue of sugar is to ferment this molasses and distill it into rum.

Cutting sugarcane in Puerto Rico, the first step of many in making rum. (*Courtesy Bar Management, New York*)

There are four main classifications of rum: the first is the very dry, light-bodied rums, generally produced in the Spanish-speaking countries, of which Puerto Rican rum is today's outstanding example; the second is the medium-bodied rums; the third is the rich, full-bodied, pungent rums usually produced in the English-speaking islands and countries, the best example of which is Jamaican rum; and the fourth is the light-bodied but pungently aromatic East Indian Batavia arak rum from Java.

The rums of the various islands of the West Indies, as well as those from elsewhere, all have their own individual character. So we have Jamaican rum, Puerto Rican rum, and so forth. The B.A.T.F. declares that the word *type* cannot be used in identifying a rum, as is done in the case of many wines; rather a rum must carry the name of the locality from which it comes. Therefore there cannot be a Jamaica-type rum made in some other place.

Rums are mainly produced in the region of the Caribbean Sea, including the West Indies and the northern countries of South America. Light-bodied rums are produced in Puerto Rico, the Virgin Islands, the Bahamas, the Do-

Bacardi distillery at Palo Seco, San Juan—the world's largest rum plant. (*Courtesy Bacardi & Company, Ltd., Miami, Florida*)

minican Republic, Brazil, Colombia, Venezuela, Mexico, Spain, and Canada. Medium-bodied rums, which are more in the style of the light rums, include those from Haiti, Barbados, Trinidad, and Guyana (known as Demeraran rums). The full-bodied, pungent rums come primarily from Jamaica and Martinique. This does not mean that Puerto Rico produces only light-bodied and Jamaica only full-bodied rums. Both countries can produce both types, but they are better known for their own traditional type.

PUERTO RICAN RUM

The molasses is placed in large vats holding thousands of gallons. Water is added, together with a substantial proportion of mash from a previous distillation. Special yeast strains are added to a small amount of molasses in a test tube. Fermentation begins, and the mixture is transferred to successively larger containers until it reaches the fermenting tanks. Fermentation lasts two to four days.

After fermentation is completed, the fermented mash, containing about 7 percent alcohol, is pumped into a column still, where the spirit is distilled off at 160 proof or higher. Distilling at a high proof produces a spirit low in congeners, light in body, and fairly neutral in flavor.

Only the middle rum (middle part of the distillation), the *madilla*, also called *aguardiente* in the trade, is used for rum. It is aged in seasoned oak barrels, some charred and some uncharred, when color is not desired.

When the rum has matured—after a minimum of one year under Puerto Rican law to more than six years for some special aged rums—it is passed through a filtering and leaching vat. At this point rums are clear with a very light taste and lightness of body. These clear, more neutral rums are designated as White or Silver.

Deeper-colored and more flavored rums, designated as Amber or Gold, are aged a minimum of three years and have caramel added to give a deeper, more uniform color. In the case of rum, caramel does not affect the flavor because rum is a sugar-based product. Most of these rums are marketed at 80 proof.

The characteristic taste of the White and Gold Label rums is dry, with a very slight molasses flavor, the Gold Label being slightly mellower and having a more pronounced taste. A spiced and flavored Puerto Rican rum is available.

The older "liqueur" rums are usually shipped under brand names. While these rums are generally quite dry, they have a fine, mellow, rummy bouquet and flavor. Because of their dryness they can be likened to a fine old brandy. Puerto Rican producers now offer full-bodied rums in addition to the light. These may be labeled either Red Label or Heavy Dark, for Planter's Punch.

VIRGIN ISLANDS RUM

The Virgin Islands have always been known for three things: rum (the kind you drink), bay rum (the kind you put on your hair), and as pirate hangouts during the days of the Spanish Main.

Purchased by the United States in 1917, the Virgin Islands were subject to our Prohibition laws and had to confine their efforts to bay rum until 1933. The islands were in bad financial straits, and our Department of Insular Affairs decided to assist the islands by reestablishing the Virgin Islands rum industry. Eventually the first shipments of the new rum arrived amid the greatest fanfare of free publicity any liquor ever had. Virgin Islands rum is of the light-bodied type. The best rums are from the island of Saint Croix.

Since the Virgin Islands are part of the United States, much local rum, as well as other spirits, are brought back to the mainland duty-free by visiting American tourists.

OTHER LIGHT-BODIED RUMS

While Puerto Rico, the Virgin Islands, and Cuba are the principal areas that produce light-bodied rums, this type is also distilled in the Dominican Republic, Venezuela, Mexico, Brazil, Argentina, Peru, Paraguay, and more recently in Jamaica, Bermuda, and Guyana. Light-bodied rum is also made in Hawaii, the Philippines, and the continental United States.

MEDIUM RUMS

Among others in this group are rums from Haiti and Martinique that are made from sugarcane juice, rather than from the more usual molasses. They are made in pot stills, in the French brandy-making tradition, and develop a fine mellow bouquet.

DEMERARAN RUM

Demeraran rum is distilled from sugarcane molasses grown along the Demerara River in Guyana (formerly British Guiana), South America. The chief difference between Demeraran rum and fuller-bodied rum is the result of the variations in character of the sugarcane and the soil and the fact that Demeraran rum is distilled in column stills. Demeraran rum is much darker and not nearly as pungent as Jamaican rum.

Demeraran rum is obtainable in this market at 80, 86, and 151 proofs. The overproof rum is used in northern lumber camps, by the Grand Banks fishermen, and in Alaska. After exposure to intense cold, these outdoorsmen need a very strong bracer to thaw them out. The rum is generally consumed in the form of grog, that is, mixed half and half with very hot water, as well as in many fancy rum drinks.

When the Zombie became a popular drink, the 151-proof Demeraran rum found a new outlet.

JAMAICAN RUM

The typical Jamaican rum is a full-bodied rum, and its manufacture differs considerably from that of light-bodied rum.

To the molasses in the fermentation vats are added the skimmings from previous distillations—the dunder, known also as burned ale. The natural yeast spores in the air promptly settle on the surface of the liquid mass, multiply rapidly, and cause fermentation to begin.

Some call this wild fermentation and others spontaneous fermentation. The correct term is *natural* fermentation. In addition to the dunder, usually a certain amount of the residue from a previous fermentation is added. This natural free method of fermentation is slower, taking anywhere from five to twenty days, depending on the abundance of free yeast spores and climatic or temperature conditions at the time.

This also permits a larger amount of congeners to develop, which in turn are carried over in the distillation.

The fermented liquor is pumped into a pot still, where it is distilled, producing a low wine. This is then redistilled in another pot still. Only the middle rum, taken off after the heads and before the tails begin to come over, is used.

The new rum is taken off between 140 and 160 proof, sometimes lower. The result is a very full-bodied, very pungent rummy spirit.

The new rum, like all distillates, is colorless, but with time in oak puncheons (casks) it takes on a golden hue. The depth of color of Jamaican rum, however, is governed by the amount of caramel added. Jamaican rums are always blended, and being full bodied and rich in congeners they require more aging than lighter-bodied rums, anywhere from five to seven years and more. Some "liqueur" rums of Jamaica are aged fifteen years before bottling.

Dark mahogany-colored rums have become very popular because they give greater color to the drinks made with them. These darker rums are generally labeled "for Planter's Punch," as this is the drink in which they are used most often. The intense color is produced by adding caramel.

Jamaica's best market is Great Britain, where much of the rum is shipped for aging and blending. The damp climate is excellent for maturing rum. (Jamaican rums are usually shipped to Britain at their original high proof. They are reduced to potable strength at the time of bottling by adding only water.) Such rums, when they are stored and blended in bonded warehouses at the London docks, are known in the trade as London Dock rums.

Jamaican rums are usually marketed at 86 to 97 proof and occasionally at 151 proof. Traditional Jamaican rum is the most pungent of all alcoholic beverages. It has a unique, buttery molasses aroma and flavor. Recently some producers have installed column stills and are making light rums.

BATAVIA ARAK

Arak is a rum produced from molasses that comes from the sugar factories near Batavia (the former name of Djakarta), on the island of Java, in the Republic of Indonesia (formerly Dutch East Indies). Because of the special treatment given the molasses and the special quality of the river water used in fermentation, a dry, highly aromatic rum results. The quality of arak owes much, too, to the wild, uncultured yeast *Saccharomyces vordermanni* and to the little cakes of specially cooked and dried red Javanese rice that are placed in the fermenting tubs of molasses.

The arak is aged for three or four years in Java, after which it is shipped to

Holland, where it is aged for another four to six years, blended, and then bottled.

Arak is a brandylike rum of great pungency and rumminess and is used as is any other rum. In Sweden, however, its greatest use is for making Swedish Punsch.

NEW ENGLAND RUM

New England rum is now obsolete and was eliminated from the U.S. Standards of Identity in 1968. It was straight rum, distilled at less than 160 proof, with considerable body and pungency.

HOW AND WHEN TO SERVE RUM

In rum-producing countries rum is drunk straight, rather than in mixtures, and this is the best way to appreciate the qualities of a fine rum. In the United States the most popular ways of drinking rum are with cola, in Daiquiris (see page 392 for recipe), on the rocks, with water and other mixers, such as 7-Up, tonic, and orange juice, and as a substitute for gin in Martinis.

There has been a great change in the market in the last few years, and exotic drinks made with rum, while still consumed, particularly in Polynesian restaurants, have been overtaken by the more contemporary drinks, which are simpler to prepare.

Rums are used extensively in the kitchen for making sauces, for desserts, and in ice creams and candies.

Finally, rum, when it has been denatured to make it unsuitable for beverage purposes, and thus not subject to high consumption taxes, is one of the most widely used flavors in the tobacco industry.

24
OTHER SPIRITS

In all countries where spirits are produced, man has always used the most available and least costly basic material. Thus we find brandies where grapes and fruits are grown, whiskies where corn and barley are grown, and rum where sugarcane is grown.

This chapter will discuss some of the more interesting and popular spirits produced from, and occasionally flavored by, local products.

ANISE/LICORICE-FLAVORED SPIRITS

No alcoholic beverage has been less understood than absinthe, poetically described as "the water of the Star Wormwood—the Green Muse." It was supposed to be wicked, to drive the drinker insane, and to have killed many. In France its sale was prohibited before World War I because of the belief that it would cause a decrease in the birthrate. Possibly it could have done all these terrible things, as it was one of the most potent of all alcoholic beverages. It was not, however, because of the wormwood that it was so dangerous, but rather because of its alcoholic strength. Absinthe was generally shipped at a proof of 136 (68 percent alcohol). The sale of absinthe is prohibited in Switzerland, where it was invented, as well as in France, the United States, and most other countries.

Just what was this absinthe of which we heard so much and of which we know so little? The "elixir" absinthe was composed of aromatic plants, *Artemisia mayoris* and *vulgaris*, balm-mint, hyssop, fennel, star-anise, and a high-proof spirit. It was invented toward the end of the eighteenth century by a physician and pharmacist, Dr. Ordinaire, a French exile living in Couvet, Switzerland. In 1797 Henri-Louis Pernod acquired the recipe, and since that time the Pernod name has been so closely associated with absinthe that they have become synonymous.

365

The classic absinthe drink was the Absinthe Drip, which required a special two-piece glass. A jigger of absinthe was poured into the glass, then a cube of sugar placed over the drip hole of the upper section, which was then packed with cracked ice. Cold water was added to fill the dripper. When all of the water had dripped through, the drink was ready. Some people preferred a slightly sweeter drink, which was made by using one ounce of absinthe and one ounce of anisette. This drink was an excellent restorative in cases of sea-sickness, airsickness, and nausea. One was enough.

Since absinthe is prohibited in the United States and other countries, the Pernod firm produces, in France, an anise-flavored spirit of 90 proof that is reminiscent in flavor and character of absinthe. It has a light yellow-green color and a sharp, pronounced aroma, in which the dominant note is licorice. When it is mixed with water (as it always should be), it changes color, becoming streaked, then milky, and finally a cloudy opalescent color.

The highly concentrated natural essential oils that give the flavor to these products are more soluble in alcohol than in water. Therefore when water is added the oils precipitate, making the mixture cloudy. If a great deal of water is added, they become clear again. Since anise has a strong flavor, up to five parts water are added to these spirits for general consumption.

There are other anise products produced throughout the world. They vary one from another, but none is absinthe, since the formulas do not contain wormwood. They are popular drinks of the countries bordering the Mediterranean. The product is known in each country by its local name—thus in Spain it is Ojen; in France it is Pastis, the best-known brand of which is Ricard; in Italy it is Anesone; in Greece it is Ouzo and Mastikha; in Israel it is Arak; in Turkey it is Raki; and in the U.S. it is Herbsaint. They are rarely ever drunk neat but usually mixed with water, similarly to Pernod, producing a long opalescent cooler. They are served both as apéritifs and as refreshers.

AQUAVIT (AKVAVIT)

Aquavit literally means "water of life," since it has been considered a cure for various ailments since the 1500's. It is the national beverage of the Scandinavian countries.

The method of producing Aquavit is similar in Denmark (where it is called Akvavit), Norway, Sweden, and Iceland, although there are some variations, mainly in the proportions of flavorings.

Aquavit may be made from a fermented mash of either barley malt and grain or potatoes, depending on the time of the year. The potatoes have an especially high starch content, grown for this purpose. The principal flavoring is the caraway seed. Aquavit is first distilled as a neutral spirit at 190 proof, reduced with demineralized water to 120 proof, and then redistilled with flavorings, similar to the production of gin. In addition to caraway, other botanicals may be used, such as coriander, fennel, cinnamon, anise, cardamom, and other botanicals originally selected for their medicinal properties.

Aquavit is matured for about a year before bottling. It is colorless, with an alcoholic strength of 80 proof. There is also an Aquavit that is amber-colored, and 90 proof. This has a strong yellow-dill flavor in addition to the caraway.

Some compare Aquavit to the liqueur Kümmel (see page 375), because they both have a pronounced caraway flavor. Kümmel, however, is sweetened with syrup, and is only 70 to 80 proof. Aquavit, of course, is quite dry.

Aquavit is always served ice cold. While it may substitute for the gin or vodka in cocktails, it is usually taken neat with food—appetizers, small open sandwiches in the Scandinavian style, caviar, and smoked fish—often with a beer chaser. The usual portion of Aquavit is one ounce, not sipped, but taken at one swallow. It is traditionally drunk to this Scandinavian toast:

> *Skaal! Min skaal—din skaal,*
> *Alla vackra flickornas skaal!*

> Health! My health—your health,
> All the pretty girls' health!

BITTERS

Bitters consist of bitter and aromatic essences and flavors incorporated into an alcohol base. The flavors come from fruits, plants, seeds, flowers, leaves, bark, roots, and stems. Most bitters are made from closely guarded formulas, proprietary secrets handed down from generation to generation. These products are the result of infusion and distillation processes and their one common characteristic is bitterness.

Bitters are classified into two categories: fit for use as beverages and not fit for use as beverages. Those fit for beverages are subject to the Internal Revenue tax of $10.50 per tax gallon plus $0.50 per tax gallon duty if imported. Bitters not fit for beverage use made in the United States have a $1.00 per tax gallon Internal Revenue tax. If bitters are imported and are not fit for beverages, there is no Internal Revenue tax and the applicable duty is $0.94 per tax gallon.

Bitters not fit for beverages contain components of such nature or in such amounts that only small quantities of the bitters can be used as flavoring agents in cocktails and general cuisine. The best known of this type is Angostura Bitters, which is made in Trinidad. Other such bitters are Peychaud's from New Orleans, Underberg from Germany, and various orange bitters.

Bitters fit for beverages include stomachics or aids to digestion such as Fernet Branca and Unicum from Italy. Campari is a beverage bitter from Italy, where its consumption is so pervasive that premixed and bottled Campari and soda is sold everywhere.

OKOLEHAO

Hawaii has made several contributions to our way of life, but the most exotic offering is Okolehao, or Oke, as it is known on the islands.

According to the producer of Okolehao, it is distilled solely from fermented mash of the roots of the sacred ti plant of Hawaii (*Cordyline australis*).

Okolehao was first made by an Australian, William Stevenson, about 1790. He cooked the ti roots, which are rich in levulose (fructose), and allowed the mash to ferment in the bottom of a canoe. He then distilled the fermented mash in a still constructed from a ship's cooking pot, with an inverted calabash for a lid and a water-cooled gun barrel for a coil.

Today, of course, Okolehao is distilled in a modern distillery employing column stills and all the most advanced scientific mashing and distilling control techniques.

Okolehao is not aged. After distillation it is filtered through charcoal. Both a Crystal Clear and a Golden Oke are produced. It has an unusual and subtle flavor. Okolehao is marketed at 80 proof. It is drunk straight, on the rocks, in tall drinks, and in highballs, and it is employed in the preparation of a number of intriguingly named cocktails, such as Mahalo, which means "thank you" in Hawaiian, Ti A'A Sour, Scratch Me Lani, Okole-Wow, No-Mo-Pain, Aloha, and Coke and Oke.

PIMM'S CUP

Pimm's Cup is a drink that dates back more than a century. The story is that a bartender in a Pimm's restaurant in the London financial district invented the original gin sling many years ago, and the patrons liked it so much they used to ask that it be prepared for them in quantity so they could take it up to the country when they went on holiday. From the numerous requests of this nature, it was natural that the drink be prepared commercially. Today it is produced in England as Pimm's No. 1, at 67 proof. It is sweetened, and flavored with herbs, spices, and fruits. Pimm's is served over ice with soda and a twist of lemon or lime, for a satisfying, cooling thirst quencher.

TEQUILA AND PULQUE

Tequila is a descendant of the first alcoholic beverage produced in North America, the origins of which are interwoven with Aztec history. Before the Spaniards brought the art of distillation to Mexico in the early 1500s, the Aztecs were drinking a winelike liquid called pulque. Pulque is the fermented product of the mezcal plant, which belongs to the genus *agave* (which the Spanish referred to as *maguey*).

Pulque has a rather heavy flavor resembling sour milk, but it is much

Guillermo Freytag holds the 100 millionth *agave* head to be harvested at the Cuervo plantation, near the town of Tequila, in the state of Jalisco, Mexico. (*Courtesy Liquor Publications, Inc.*)

appreciated by the Mexicans because of its cooling, wholesome, and nutritional properties. Pulque is always consumed freshly made and is not readily available very far from its source.

When pulque is distilled it makes a *maguey* brandy, known as *vino mezcal.* The best *vino mezcal* is Tequila, which comes from the upland valleys surrounding the town of Tequila, northwest of Guadalajara, in the state of Jalisco, Mexico.

The Mexican government has decreed that only the superior *vino mezcal* from a carefully delineated section of Jalisco may be called Tequila, just as the French, for example, earlier declared that only brandies from the province of Charente could be called Cognac. There are about twenty-six Tequila distillers in the town of Tequila.

The best species of mezcal plant, grown near Tequila, is the *Agave tequileana* Weber, blue variety. There are hundreds of varieties of the proliferous mezcal *agave* plant, and their differences are marked enough that one makes a good Tequila and another does not. The blue *agave* is cultivated for Tequila production. Many people believe that the mezcal plant is a type of cactus, but technically it belongs to the amaryllis family (*Amarillydaceae*).

The mezcal plant takes ten to twelve years to reach proper maturity, at which time the sap flows to the base. When the plant reaches maturity, the outer leaves are removed and the base, resembling a pineapple but larger and heavier, weighing 75 to 150 pounds, is cut from the plant, leaving a stump.

These "pineapples," or heads of the plant, are heavy with sweet sap called *aguamiel* ("honey water"). When the matured *agave* heads arrive at the distillery, they are split open and placed in an oven, where they are steamed for nine to twenty-four hours at 200 degrees Fahrenheit. This causes a considerable amount of *aguamiel* to run off freely. The heads are then shredded and the remaining juice is expressed by mechanical means. The juices are placed in large vats to ferment, creating *madre pulque* ("mother pulque").

Because the mezcal plant takes ten to twelve years to mature fully, while consumption of Tequila has increased dramatically, the Mexican government now permits the addition of up to 49 percent of other sources of fermentable sugars to the must. Premium Tequilas may still be made from 100 percent blue *agave*.

To start fermentation and to ensure uniform character, a small amount of must from a previous fermentation is added to each new batch. Fermentation takes about two and a half days. The fermented product is distilled in copper pot stills, first to 28 proof, and then redistilled at 104 to 106 proof.

The Tequila shipped to this country as White is unaged. It is reduced in proof with demineralized water when it leaves the still, and bottled at 80 proof, although some Tequila is shipped to the United States in bulk and is bottled here. A few producers ship a Gold Tequila, which is purported to be aged in oak vats. Gold Tequila has no official government recognition and is aged and colored before bottling at the discretion of the producer. *Anejo* ("aged") Tequila, which has been aged for at least one year in seasoned oak, is recognized officially. *Anejo* Tequilas are often shipped at from 92 to 101 proof.

Tequila has a distinctive flavor, quite different from other spirits. Its flavor is assertive and reveals its herbaceous origins. Tequila has a natural affinity to lime juice and salt. The traditional method of drinking Tequila in Mexico is a ceremony in itself. The imbiber takes a wedge of lime or lemon, puts a pinch of salt on his thumbnail or on the back of his hand, and pours a chilled jigger of Tequila. He then bites the lime, licks the salt, and gulps down the Tequila.

Another way Mexicans enjoy Tequila is with Sangrita, a spicy tomato and citrus juice mixture that is held in one hand while the Tequila is held in the other. They are sipped alternately.

The Margarita, a Tequila cocktail developed in Los Angeles, was the springboard to Tequila consumption in this country. Since 1969, when Tequila imports were 770,000 gallons, or 0.2 percent of the total distilled spirits market, consumption has jumped to 8 million gallons in 1982, or 1.8 percent of the market. This is a remarkable increase of over 1,000 percent.

25
LIQUEURS AND CORDIALS

A closely sheltered room, a thin, ascetic individual wearing a black robe with flowing sleeves bending over strange vessels and retorts, stirring up a fire in search of gold and the everlasting life! This is a picture of the early distiller, the alchemist who was thought to be in communion with the devil. The medieval distiller was the magician of his day; he was trying to find the chemical secret of obtaining gold from baser metals—at which he failed—and an elixir that would prolong life beyond the normal span. If this medieval magician did not learn how to prolong life, at least he learned the secret of making it more interesting, for his experiments produced the first liqueurs.

Originally liqueurs were used as medicinal remedies, love potions, aphrodisiacs, and general cure-alls. It is unnecessary to explain the medicinal and therapeutic value of certain seeds, herbs, and roots that were used at that time, as most of them are found in a modern pharmacopoeia; caraway seed, coriander, angelica root, oil of orange, oil of lemon, and various herbs rich in iodine are but a few.

In his *Wines and Spirits* the late André L. Simon said: "In the making of wine . . . the art of man intervenes only to make the best use possible of Nature's own gift . . . but in the making of liqueurs, man has a much wider field wherein to exercise his ingenuity; he is at liberty to give to his liqueurs practically any shade or color he thinks best to attract the attention, raise the curiosity, and charm the eye; he also has at his command all the fruits of the earth from which to extract an almost unlimited variety of aromas and flavors, wherewith to please the most fastidious taste and flatter the most jaded palate."

By the same token it is theoretically possible to make any liqueur with equal success in any part of the world, but the theory works only up to a point. Certain countries have produced such excellent liqueurs that their products are recognized throughout the world as standards of quality. Foremost in this respect are France and Holland, although certain specialties of great repute are produced in other countries, such as Italy's Strega and Liquore Galliano;

Yugoslavian Maraschino; Germany's Gilka Kümmel and Danziger Goldwasser; Sweden's Swedish Punsch; Denmark's Peter Heering; and Spain's Anis del Mono.

Liqueurs and cordials have been known by many names and described at one time or another as balms, crémes, elixirs, oils, and so on. The terms *liqueur* and *cordial* are synonymous, with the former said to apply more to European products and the latter to American products. Liqueurs are alcoholic beverages prepared by mixing or redistilling various spirits (brandy, whisky, rum, gin, or other spirits) with certain flavoring materials. These materials can be fruits, flowers, herbs, seeds, barks, roots, peels, berries, juices, or other natural flavoring substances or extracts derived from them.

Liqueurs and cordials differ from all other spirits because they must contain at least 2½ percent sugar by weight. The sugar may be beet, maple, cane, honey, corn, or a combination of these. There are no hard rules. The United States has very white, stable sugar. Between the 2½ percent minimum and a 10 percent sugar content the product is still not very sweet, and it may include the word *dry* on the label. Most liqueurs and cordials contain up to 35 percent of a sweetening agent.

PRODUCTION OF LIQUEURS AND CORDIALS

There are two basic ways of extracting flavors when making liqueurs. They are, simply, the cold method and the hot method. The method chosen depends on the flavor to be made and the source of that flavor. Generally, fruit flavors are extracted by the cold method, and other plant products, such as seeds, peels, and flowers, have their flavors extracted by the hot method. Each method encompasses several processes, and each fruit or plant product is handled differently.

infusion or maceration

The cold method is used when the flavoring material is sensitive to heat and would be damaged by it. Cold extractions can take up to a year, but attempts to make the process go faster by using heat would destroy the flavor. One cold method can be either infusion or maceration and is very much like making tea. If crushed fruits are steeped in water, the process is called infusion. If the fruits are steeped in alcohol, such as 120- to 130-proof brandy, it is maceration. The water or brandy eventually absorbs almost all of the aroma, flavor, and color of the fruit or berry.

In some cases, when the stones (seeds) of the fruit are present, some of the oil from the stones is also extracted, which accounts for the slight bitter almond undertone sometimes found in such liqueurs as apricot and cherry.

When ready, the liquid is drawn off, allowed to rest for several days in a storage tank that will not impart any flavor (such as stainless steel), and then filtered.

The mass of remaining fruit still contains both useful alcohol and some essential flavorings. In order to recover them, the mass is placed in a still and the last drop of flavor is extracted by distillation. The resultant distillate may then be added to the original maceration in order to give it more character.

The finished maceration is then sweetened to the desired richness by adding sugar and/or other sweetening material in syrup form. The finished product is sometimes aged before bottling.

percolation

Another method of cold extraction is percolation, or brewing, which is somewhat like making coffee. The flavoring agent, in the form of leaves or herbs, is placed in the upper part of an apparatus, the principle of which is the same as that of a coffee percolator. Brandy or another spirit is in the lower part and is pumped up over the flavoring and allowed to percolate through it, extracting and carrying down the aroma and flavor. The pumping and percolation are repeated continuously for weeks or months until most of the flavor constituents have been obtained. The spirit-soaked flavoring agent is then distilled to obtain whatever flavor remains. This distillate may be mixed with the percolate, and the whole is filtered, sweetened with sugar syrup, and often bottled at once, although some plant liqueurs of this group are aged for a time.

distillation

The hot extraction method is used mostly for seeds and flowers, such as anise, caraway, orange peel, mint, roses, and violets. These materials can withstand some heat and benefit from a quicker extraction of flavor than the slower cold methods.

The distillation method is normally carried out in small to medium-size copper pot stills, in many cases similar to a gin still.

The normal procedure is to steep the flavoring agent—plant, seed, root, or herb—in alcohol for several hours, after which it is placed in the still with additional spirits and distilled. The heads and tails are either discarded or redistilled.

A variation of the distillation process is used on delicate flowers and herbs, such as mint, roses, and violets, whose flavors disappear soon after picking. These are distilled quickly and gently in an aqueous solution rather than in a spirit. A vacuum is created so that distillation can take place at a lower temperature, preserving more of the floral aroma.

The resultant distillate, always colorless, is sweetened with simple syrup and colored with natural vegetable coloring matter or approved food dyes. Thus the producer can give his Curaçao or crème de menthe whatever hue he wishes. We have seen crème de menthe colorless, as well as various shades of green, gold, red, and blue.

fruit and plant liqueurs

The liqueur family is divided into two main branches: the natural-colored, or fruit, liqueurs and the plant liqueurs, which are colorless. The principal fruit liqueurs marketed are apricot, blackberry, cherry, crème de cassis, maraschino, peach, and sloe gin. Leading examples of plant liqueurs are anisette, crème de cacao, crème de menthe, and Kümmel.

Some liqueurs fall into a borderline category because they are made from the peels or stones of a particular fruit, not from the fruit itself. Examples of these are Curaçao and Triple Sec, made from orange peels, and crème de noyaux, an almond-flavored liqueur made from pits of fruits such as peaches or cherries.

Whereas fruit liqueurs derive their color and flavor naturally from one informing fruit, plant liqueurs very often require more than one flavoring agent to balance or bring out the desired flavor. For example, vanilla is often part of the formula in crème de cacao. Plant liqueurs, such as Bénédictine, Chartreuse, or Drambuie, result from blending flavors obtained from many plants, seeds, roots, and herbs, as many as fifty different ones in some cases. Because these herb and spice liqueurs were originally made by monks, they are sometimes known as monastery types.

cream liqueurs   A recent development has been the combining of spirits and cream with other flavorings to create a low-proof cream liqueur. Originating in Ireland, fresh cream was blended with Irish whisky, and stabilized so that it did not have to be refrigerated. Bailey's, the first on the market, proved so popular that there are now cream liqueurs made with imported spirits that are mixed with American cream and bottled in the United States, and even cream liqueurs that are made with nondairy creamers. Proofs range from 32 to 40. While many new brands have been created, some traditional houses are adding creams to their lines. Examples are Myer's Original Rum and Crème de Grand Marnier liqueur.

GENERIC LIQUEURS AND CORDIALS SHIPPED BY MANY HOUSES

Many producers all over the world make and market a wide variety of liqueurs under generic or universally used names. In the following list are those shipped by most general liqueur producers, together with a description of their principal flavor and usual proof. Since many producers use different flavoring formulas, there are variations in brands of the same type of liqueur.

ADVOCAAT.   Sometimes called Egg Brandy, made in Holland from eggs, sugar, and brandy. It is creamy and thick, with an eggnog flavor. 30 proof.

AMARETTO.   Almond flavor comes from apricot stones. 40 to 56 proof.

ANESONE.   Anise/licorice-flavored liqueur made in Italy and the United States. 90 proof.

ANIS.   Spanish spelling of anisette, when made in Spain and Latin America. 78 to 96 proof.

ANISETTE.   Flavor is obtained principally from aniseed. 50 to 60 proof.

APRICOT LIQUEUR. Principal flavor is from apricots. Often shipped under a trade name such as Apry or Viennese Apricot. 60 to 70 proof.

BLACKBERRY LIQUEUR. Obtained from blackberries, but occasionally has a small amount of red wine or other fruit essences added. 60 proof.

CHERRY LIQUEUR. Flavor is generally obtained from small, wild black cherries. 48 to 60 proof.

COCONUT LIQUEUR. Flavor is obtained from fresh coconuts, with other flavors sometimes added, such as rum or chocolate. 42 to 60 proof.

COFFEE LIQUEUR. Based on coffee beans. Many sold under proprietary names. 53 to 60 proof.

CRANBERRY LIQUEUR. Made with fresh cranberry juice. 40 proof.

CRÈME DE BANANES. Artificial banana flavor. 50 to 60 proof.

CRÈME DE CACAO. Flavor is obtained from cacao and vanilla beans, produced either white or brown. The word *Chouao* often found on crème de cacao labels indicates that the beans come from the Chouao region of Venezuela—considered to produce the finest cacao beans in the world. 50 to 60 proof.

CRÈME DE CASSIS. Flavor is obtained primarily from black currants. 32 to 40 proof.

CRÈME DE MENTHE. Flavor is obtained from several varieties of mint but principally peppermint. Both white and green are usually shipped. The only difference is that the green has harmless certified coloring added. 60 proof.

CRÈME DE NOYAUX. Flavor is obtained primarily from fruit stones, resulting in a bitter almond flavor. 50 to 60 proof.

CRÈME DE ROSE. Flavor is obtained primarily from the essential oil of rose petals and vanilla. 60 proof.

CRÈME DE VANILLE. Flavor is obtained primarily from the finest Mexican vanilla beans. 60 proof.

CRÈME DE VIOLETTE. Flavor is obtained from essential oil of violets and green oranges from the island of Curaçao. Produced in orange, white, and blue colors. 54 to 80 proof.

CURAÇAO. Flavor is obtained primarily from the dried peel of the famous green oranges from the island of Curaçao, produced in orange, white, and blue colors. 54 to 80 proof.

GINGER. Flavor is obtained from ginger root. 70 proof.

KÜMMEL. Flavor is obtained principally from caraway seeds. If the Kümmel has crystallized sugar in it, it is sold as Kümmel Crystallizé. 70 to 82 proof.

MANDARINE. Flavor is obtained primarily from dried peel of mandarines (tangerines). 80 proof.

MARASCHINO. Flavor is obtained from the special Dalmatian Marasca cherry. 60 to 78 proof.

PEACH LIQUEUR. Flavor is obtained from fresh and dried peaches. 60 to 72 proof.

PEAR WILLIAM.   Made from fresh pears from France and Austria. 60 to 70 proof.

PEPPERMINT SCHNAPPS.   Mint liqueur, less sweet than crème de menthe. 40 to 100 proof.

PRUNELLE.   Flavor is obtained from European blackthorn or sloe plum. 60 to 80 proof.

RASPBERRY LIQUEUR.   Flavor is obtained from French raspberries. 33 to 40 proof.

ROCK AND RYE.   A liqueur with a rye whisky base, but including grain neutral spirits, rock candy syrup, and sometimes fruits—lemons, oranges, and cherries. 54 to 70 proof.

SAMBUCA.   Licorice flavor, obtained from the elderbush, whose Latin name is *sambucus.* 70 to 84 proof.

SLOE GIN.   Flavor is obtained from the sloe berry. 42 proof.

STRAWBERRY.   Flavor is obtained from strawberries. 40 to 60 proof.

TRIPLE SEC.   A white Curaçao (orange flavor). 60 to 80 proof.

WISHNIAK.   A wild cherry liqueur from Israel, Russia, Poland, and Czechoslovakia. 48 to 60 proof.

While generic liqueurs may be made by any producer, there are many that have trademarked names and that may be made only by a single producer. For example, anyone may make crème de menthe, but only Cusenier may make Freezomint. Similarly, any producer may make apricot liqueur, but only Garnier may make Abricotine and only Marie Brizard may make Apry.

fruit-flavored brandies   In most countries the word *brandy* is used very loosely in connection with liqueurs, and it is quite common to find these products labeled apricot brandy, cherry brandy, and so forth. Under these circumstances, apricot brandy and apricot liqueur would be the same thing. In the United States brandy must be a distillate obtained solely from the fermented juice, mash, or wine of fruit. Therefore, a liqueur made from fruit cannot be labeled or marketed as a brandy. True fruit brandies are marketed under specific designations such as Kirschwasser or Slivovitz. (See Chapter 19.)

This regulation caused some confusion for the public who believed apricot brandy and apricot liqueur were the same product (as they are in other countries). For this reason the U.S. government established a category of fruit-flavored brandies, which are the equivalent of the fruit brandies or fruit liqueurs seen abroad. These products must be made solely with a brandy base, be 70 proof (minimum), and contain more than $2\frac{1}{2}$ percent sugar by weight. To the best of our knowledge, all fruit-flavored brandies marketed in the United States are produced in this country; none is imported.

Most producers make some or all of the following: apricot-flavored brandy, blackberry-flavored brandy, cherry-flavored brandy, coffee-flavored brandy, ginger-flavored brandy, and peach-flavored brandy.

Battery of copper pot stills employed to distill the various herbs, flowers, and plants used to flavor Bénédictine liqueurs at Fécamp, France. (*Courtesy Julius Wile Sons & Co., Inc., New York*)

Stained glass window at Bénédictine Distillerie, Fécamp, France, showing Dom Bernardo Vincelli directing his brother Bénédictines in his medieval laboratory. (*Courtesy Julius Wile Sons & Co., Inc., New York*)

FAMOUS PROPRIETARY BRANDS

These are, in most cases, world-famous specialty liqueurs that are produced under closely guarded secret formulas and marketed under registered trademark brands. Every producer believes the formula he uses is unique and is his secret, and he goes to great lengths to guard it. These liqueurs are made in each case by only one house. Most of them have centuries of tradition behind them and have become household names.

BÉNÉDICTINE. To the best of our knowledge, the oldest liqueur is the world-famous D.O.M Bénédictine, which is still produced on the spot where its secret formula was developed in 1510.

If you should visit this corner of France, you would see the duplicate of the original Bénédictine Abbey of Fécamp, where Dom Bernardo Vincelli first gave his brother monks his new elixir to comfort them when they were fatigued or ill. D.O.M, which appears on every label, stands for the Latin words *Dio Optimo Maximo*, "To God, Most Good, Most Great."

Today Bénédictine has no connection with any religious order but is produced by a family-owned corporation founded by Alexandre Le Grand in 1863.

The formula for Bénédictine is one of the most closely guarded secrets in the world. Only three people ever know the complete details. It is a tribute to their ability to keep the secret inviolate that every attempt to imitate this liqueur—and attempts have been made in every part of the world—has failed. At the distillery at Fécamp they point to their *Salon de Contrefaçons* ("Hall of Counterfeits"), where the walls are lined with cabinets filled with examples of hundreds of attempted imitations. This is one liqueur of which can truly be said, "There is only one."

Bénédictine is a plant liqueur made from twenty-seven different herbs, plants, and peels on a fine Cognac brandy base. It is made in a number of operations; not all of the flavors are distilled out at the same time. They are obtained separately and are then skillfully blended. Bénédictine is aged for four years before being bottled.

In the 1930s the heads of the firm were convinced that a substantial amount of Bénédictine was drunk in the form of Bénédictine and brandy by people who preferred a drier liqueur. They therefore decided to prepare their own uniform B & B liqueur, D.O.M, which creates a drier Bénédictine. They are each 86 proof.

CHARTREUSE. The most famous liqueur still made by a religious order is Chartreuse. It is made from a secret formula given to Les Pères Chartreux (the Carthusian Fathers) of the convent of the Grande Chartreuse at Grenoble, France, in 1605 by the Maréchal d'Estrées. The original formula was slightly modified and perfected in 1737 by one of the monks, Brother Gérome Maubec, whom a writer of the period described as a "very clever apothecary."

LEFT: A monk working amid the Chartreuse distilling and blending tanks at Voiron. RIGHT: A monk removing residue from a Chartreuse pot still. (*Courtesy Chartreuse, Voiron, France*)

In 1903, because of a law against religious orders passed in France, the Carthusian Fathers were expelled from their monastery of the Grande Chartreuse. The clever fathers, who still had their secret formula, repaired to another monastery of their order in Tarragona, Spain, where they continued to produce their famous liqueur. The Spanish bottles bore two labels: the original label used before the expulsion from France and a second that carried the legend Liqueur Fabriquée à Tarragone par Les Pères Chartreux.

During the order's absence from France, the French government tried to duplicate the formula without success. By 1927, when the production company was bankrupt and the shares were selling for almost nothing, some local businessmen from Voiron bought the shares, thus gaining legal control of the company. They mailed these shares, as a gift, to the Carthusian Fathers in Tarragona. With the distillery back in their possession, the monks began their secret return to France. Although the Carthusians were in France illegally, the French government chose not to prosecute, and the monks were producing Chartreuse by 1929. When the distillery was destroyed by a mud slide after eleven days of heavy rains in 1935, the French government even sent army engineers to help rebuild (and relocate) the distillery. The new distillery was established in the town of Voiron, but rather than place it on its original site on a mountainside, it was located near the railroad station where the monks already had warehouses to store the Chartreuse before shipping.

After World War II the French government lifted the expulsion order making the monks legal residents once again of their own country.

Two types of Chartreuse—yellow (80 to 86 proof) and green (110 proof)—have been faithfully made according to the original formula. Both yellow and green Chartreuse are plant liqueurs with a spicy, aromatic flavor, made on a brandy base, the green being much drier and somewhat more aromatic than the yellow.

Occasionally, the Carthusian monks age a small amount of the yellow and green Chartreuse in oak casks for about twelve years. These are labeled Chartreuse V.E.P., and state the year that they were put into casks. This extra aging makes the liqueurs softer and paler, with slightly lower proofs.

CHÉRI-SUISSE is a chocolate-cherry liqueur from Switzerland. 60 proof.

CHOCOLAT SUISSE is a chocolate-flavored Swiss liqueur with miniature squares of chocolate floating in the bottle. 60 proof.

COINTREAU is a brand name for one of the finest Triple Secs. While the Cointreau family formerly made many flavors of liqueurs, the name Cointreau has come to be synonymous with orange liqueur, and the other flavors are now produced under the Regnier label. 80 proof.

CORDIAL MÉDOC is a cocktail of liqueurs—a blend of fine brandy, orange Curaçao, and crème de cacao—produced in Bordeaux, France. 80 proof.

DANZIGER GOLDWASSER. The flavor is obtained primarily from orange peel, anise, and various other spicy herbs and plants. It contains tiny flecks of genuine gold leaf that are harmless when consumed. 80 proof.

DRAMBUIE liqueur was originally made from a private recipe of Prince Charles Edward Stuart (Bonnie Prince Charles). When the prince arrived from France in 1745, one of his attendants brought with him the recipe of his master's favorite liqueur. After the battle of Culloden Moor, where the Scottish rebels were defeated, the prince was hunted and a price was put on his head. One of his Highland friends, Mackinnon of Strathaird, protected the prince and helped him escape back to France. In gratitude the prince presented Mackinnon with his secret recipe. Since then the Mackinnon family has been making this liqueur. It is made with old Highland malt Scotch whisky and heather honey. 80 proof.

FIOR D'ALPE ISOLABELLA is a spicy Italian liqueur bottled with an herb sprig inside the bottle and made with an excess of sugar that crystallizes on the sprig. The recipe for this liqueur is centuries old and involves the numerous herbs found in the Alps, such as juniper, mint, thyme, arnica, wild marjoram, and hyssop. 92 proof.

FORBIDDEN FRUIT is a liqueur made in America. It is made from a type of grapefruit, called the shaddock, steeped in fine brandy. 64 proof.

GILKA BERLINER KÜMMEL, made in Germany, has for almost a century been accepted as the standard of quality. The old firm of Bols in Holland, however, claims that their Bolskümmel was the original Kümmel, distilled by Erven Lucas Bols in 1575. This is said to have so impressed a Russian czar that he took the recipe back to Russia and eventually made Russia the principal producer and consumer of Kümmel. Kümmel is flavored principally with caraway seed and cumin seed. 86 proof.

GRAND MARNIER is one of the finest orange Curaçao liqueurs. It is made on a Cognac base, from small, green Curaçao oranges that are hand peeled. The peels are dried in the sun to concentrate the flavors and are then shipped to France for maceration and distillation. 80 proof.

IRISH MIST is a spicy Irish whiskey and heather honey liqueur from Tulloch Mhor. During an exodus of warriors in 1692, the recipe was lost. It was eventually located in Austria and returned to Ireland. 80 proof.

IZARRA is produced in two forms—green (100 proof) and yellow (86 proof). Its brandy base is flavored from plants grown in the French Pyrénées.

KAHLÚA is the popular coffee-flavored liqueur from Mexico. 53 proof.

LIQUEUR CREOLE SHRUBB, produced by the firm of Clément in Martinique, is made with orange peels and rum, according to the traditional local recipes. 80 proof.

LIQUORE GALLIANO was created in the late 1800s and was named after the Italian Major Giuseppe Galliano. It is made from herbs and flowers and is a golden, spicy, aromatic liqueur. 80 proof.

PASHA is a coffee liqueur from Turkey. 53 proof.

PETER HEERING, formerly known as Cherry Heering, is made in Copenhagen, Denmark, and is recognized as one of the finest cherry liqueurs in the world. 49 proof.

SABRA is a popular liqueur of Israel, made from a blend of Jaffa oranges and chocolate. 60 proof.

SOUTHERN COMFORT is an American specialty. It was known originally as Cuff and Buttons around 1875, when this phrase meant "white tie and tails." According to the legend it was Louis Herron, a bartender in St. Louis, Missouri, who gave it the very apt name of Southern Comfort. To Bourbon whisky is added a moderate quantity of peach liqueur and fresh peaches. The liqueur and fruit mellow the whisky, even though it is 100 proof.

STREGA is a famous spicy plant liqueur from Italy. 80 proof.

TIA MARIA from Jamaica is claimed to be the original coffee-flavored liqueur. It is made on a rum base with local Blue Mountain coffee. 63 proof.

VANDERMINT is a chocolate-mint liqueur from Holland. 60 proof.

VIEILLE CURE is an aromatic plant liqueur blended with Cognac and Armagnac and produced in Bordeaux. It is made both green and yellow. Each is 86 proof.

As has been noted, Peter Heering's cherry liqueur is considered the best cherry liqueur and Cointreau and Grand Marnier are considered the best orange-flavored liqueurs. There are a few generic liqueurs that have achieved proprietary status because of their quality and perfection. For example, Get's Pippermint crème de menthe is most highly regarded, as is Marie Brizard's anisette, which uses special green anise from Spain, rather than star anise.

HOW AND WHEN TO SERVE LIQUEURS AND CORDIALS

Liqueurs, being sweet and potent and containing certain beneficial, essential oils, are natural digestives. For this reason they are most popular as after-dinner drinks, their primary use today. During Prohibition, however, liqueurs came into wide use as cocktail ingredients because their rich sweetness was helpful in covering up the harsh bite of the spirits bootleggers supplied. Many cocktails invented during that period call for liqueurs as an important ingredient. In fact, many people have found that a dash of a liqueur in a cocktail gives it added smoothness, texture, and palatability.

In France certain liqueurs are used in various ways aside from their customary use as after-dinner drinks. Most of the crème de menthe used in France, for instance, is drunk in the form of highballs. Crème de cassis, made from black currants, is drunk mixed with French vermouth and soda or with white wine. A popular way of serving liqueurs is as frappés, which are made by filling a small glass with finely shaved ice and then pouring the liqueur into it. Liqueurs are compatible with sweet cream, other liqueurs, liquors, and mixers.

In addition to all these uses, liqueurs and syrups are used in cooking, in baking, to flavor ices and ice creams, in making sauces for puddings, in fruit dishes, and in desserts in general.

SPECIFIC GRAVITY OF LIQUEURS AND CORDIALS

In France a Pousse-Café is a brandy or cordial served to "push down the coffee." In the United States the Pousse-Café is a colorful combination of "floated" liqueurs. For those who want to prepare this delightful creation, we offer the following table of colors and specific gravities (densities) of some of the more popular liqueurs and cordials. Not all liqueur manufacturers use identical formulas and consequently the densities vary slightly among different shippers, but this should serve as a fairly good guide. To pour each layer of the Pousse-Café so that one colored liqueur will settle on another without disturbing the earlier ones in the glass, pour each liqueur over an inverted spoon. The heaviest liqueur goes on the bottom, and each lighter product floats on the denser one. Pousse-Cafés can be prepared ahead of time. They will keep for at least an hour in the refrigerator before the layers start to blend.

LIQUEUR OR CORDIAL	COLOR	SPECIFIC GRAVITY
Kirsch	Clear	0.940
Sloe gin	Red	1.040
B & B liqueur	Amber	1.045
Kümmel	Clear	1.055
Rock and Rye	Amber	1.065
Triple Sec	Clear	1.075
Peach-flavored brandy	Peach	1.085
Blackberry liqueur	Dark red	1.110
Blue Curaçao	Blue	1.120
Apricot liqueur	Apricot	1.125
Crème de cacao	Brown	1.150
	Clear	1.150
Crème de menthe	Green	1.160
	Clear	1.160
Crème de cassis	Deep purple	1.170
Crème de bananes	Yellow	1.180

N.B.: The higher the specific gravity, the heavier the liqueur.

Because of the rapidly expanding interest in liqueurs and cordials, many new brands and combinations of flavors are constantly entering the market. From 1975 to 1982, consumption of liqueurs and cordials has increased about 50 percent. In 1982 about 20 million cases of cordials and liqueurs were sold.

26
COCKTAILS
AND OTHER
MIXED DRINKS

The cocktail is a purely American institution, and there are almost as many versions of the origin of its name as there are legends about the beds George Washington is said to have slept in. Actually, the first cocktail was made by the first person who mixed his wine with a bit of honey or an herb or two to give it zest.

history

One story is that Betsy Flanagan, a spirited Irish lass who had a tavern near Yorktown, New York, was responsible for naming the cocktail. In 1779 Betsy's Tavern was a meeting place for the American and French officers of Washington's army. Here they came to relax and to fortify themselves for the rigors of the campaign with a concoction called a bracer. The officers used to tease Betsy about the fine chickens owned by a Tory neighbor, until one day she threatened to make them eat their words.

No true patriot would buy anything from a Tory, but Betsy arranged for the patrons of her tavern to have a Tory chicken feast, and when it was over they repaired to the bar to continue the celebration with bracers. To their amusement, they found each bottle of bracer decorated with a cock's tail from the Tory farmer's roost. A toast was called for, and one of the Frenchmen exclaimed: *"Vive le cock tail."* Thenceforth Betsy's concoctions were known as cocktails, a name that has prevailed to this day.

mixing guidelines

A cocktail is a fairly short drink made by mixing liquor and/or wine with fruit juices, eggs, and/or bitters, by either stirring or shaking in a bar glass. A mixed drink is liquor with a mixer, usually served in a tall glass over ice.

Cocktails made from liquor and wine are always stirred, except in a few private clubs, where traditionally they are shaken. Cocktails that include sugar or eggs are always shaken. Mixing in an electric blender gives the same effect as shaking.

383

The object of a cocktail is to mix two or more ingredients so that the result is a pleasant, palatable drink. No single ingredient should overshadow the rest. An unbalanced mixture produces an unsatisfying drink. Because cocktails are always mixed with ice, their strength varies with the length of time they remain in contact with the ice, which dilutes the liquor as it melts.

If you want to be sure that your cocktails are always the same, use a measure for the ingredients and always use exactly the same quantities. While experienced bartenders usually measure by eye, their drinks vary. This does not necessarily mean that they produce a good cocktail and then a bad one, but simply that at a large bar, where there are several bartenders, no two will make identical cocktails unless they all use a measuring jigger. Here are some important measurements:

> A jigger is $1\frac{1}{2}$ liquid ounces
> A pony is 1 liquid ounce
> A liquid ounce is 2 tablespoons
> A dash is $\frac{1}{6}$ teaspoon, or about 10 drops
> A teaspoon is $\frac{1}{6}$ ounce
> A wineglass is 4 ounces

Sometimes recipes are given in parts, as cocktail glasses vary greatly in size. Melting ice adds from $\frac{1}{2}$ to $\frac{3}{4}$ ounce liquid to a cocktail if it is shaken for ten seconds, and proportionately more if shaken longer.

basic rules   There are a few fundamentals that if followed with care will contribute to making pleasant, palatable mixed drinks.

1. Accuracy in the formula ensures uniformity. Follow recipes carefully.
2. Measure ingredients. Use a measuring jigger.
3. Mixed drinks are only as good as the ingredients used. Always use the best, whether it be liquor, fruit juice, or mixer.
4. Always use fresh, clean ice. Never rinse or reuse ice even for making a new batch of the same cocktail. Use ice cubes for long drinks and cocktails that are stirred. Use cracked ice for cocktails that are shaken. Shaved ice is too fine in a hand-shaken cocktail; it will melt and dilute before chilling the drink properly. When making drinks in a blender, however, shaved ice is the most practical to use.
5. To remove the snowy look on ice cubes, sprinkle them with lukewarm water.
6. Use only perfect, fresh fruit. Do not slice oranges or lemons too thinly; they will curl and appear to droop. Cover the sliced fruit with a damp napkin to keep it fresh and prevent it from drying out. When preparing orange or lemon peel for garnish, remove the white pithy underlining, as it is bitter. A

twist is a small strip of peel that is twisted over the glass to release its aromatic oils. It is then dropped into the drink.

7. Lemons and oranges give more juice if you first soak them in warm water.

8. Use only the best mixer, be it soda water,° tonic (or quinine water), ginger ale, or whatever. A mediocre or poor mixer will spoil the finest liquor.

9. For aromatic bitters† or other ingredients where the recipe usually specifies only a dash, use a special dasher stopper. This will ensure the proper dash, which is ⅙ teaspoon.

10. Whenever granulated sugar is called for, use superfine sugar, as it will dissolve more easily than the standard granulated sugar.

11. Use white of egg only for foaming cocktails.

12. When mixing the ingredients for a cocktail, always add the liquor last. For a mixed drink, put the liquor in first.

13. Stir briskly cocktails that should be stirred. These are generally mixtures of liquor and wine. Stir long enough to mix—approximately seven stirs.

14. Shake firmly (do not rock) cocktails that are shaken. These are usually cocktails that contain sugar, fruit juices, cordials, or cream.

15. To muddle ingredients, use a wooden muddler or the back of a spoon to crush solid pieces so they may be mixed with the liquid.

16. Glassware should sparkle.

17. Always strain cocktails before serving them.

18. Do not leave ice in the "dividend" remaining in the cocktail shaker. It will dilute the remains and produce a watery second round.

19. Serving a cocktail in a prechilled glass will keep it cold longer than serving it in a warm glass. If you wish to frost the rim of the cocktail glass, moisten the rim lightly and dip it in powdered sugar.

syrups

Sometimes recipes call for a syrup, three of which are described below. These may be either made or purchased.

SUGAR SYRUP may be prepared in advance and stored in the refrigerator. To make sugar syrup, dissolve 2 cups sugar in 1 cup water in a saucepan. Simmer for 5 to 10 minutes. Pour into a bottle or jar, cool, and cover. Larger amounts may be prepared for punches. Use wherever recipes call for sugar syrup or simple syrup.

GRENADINE is sweet and has a deep red color and the flavor of pomegranates. In fact, the French word for pomegranate is *grenadier.* Grenadine is available without alcohol or with very little alcohol, about 5 proof. It is an ingredient in certain mixed drinks, but it may also be used as a general sweetening agent.

° Wherever soda water is mentioned, it is used as a generic term that includes sparkling water, charged water, mineral water, seltzer, and club soda.

† Wherever aromatic bitters are mentioned, use Angostura or Peychaud's brand.

FALERNUM is a pleasant flavoring syrup, with a small amount of alcohol (6 percent), made up of simple syrup, lime, almond, ginger, cloves, and other spices and flavorings. It is milky colored.

Falernum was invented over two hundred years ago in Barbados, British West Indies, and was named after the ancient Falernian wine of Roman times. Aside from this, Falernum has no connection with wine or Italy, for it is made in the West Indies and the United States. Its principal use is as a flavoring and sweetening ingredient in rum drinks.

ORGEAT is a sweet, white, nonalcoholic, almond-flavored syrup.

types of mixed drinks

Mixed drinks have a very special nomenclature. The following list should be helpful in identifying the type of mixed drink, the glass in which it is served, and the ingredients of which it is made.

TYPES OF MIXED DRINKS

DRINK	GLASS°	INGREDIENTS	ICE
Apéritif	Wine or cocktail	Straight and mixed	Chill
	Old-fashioned		Cubes
Cobbler	Stemmed goblet	Whisky, sherry, or port; sugar; fruit	Cracked or shaved
Cocktail	Cocktail	According to recipe	Cracked—in shaker only
	Old-fashioned		Cubes
Collins	Collins	Liquor, lemon juice, sugar, soda water, fruit	Cracked
Cooler	Collins	Liquor, lemon juice, ginger ale or soda water, grenadine or sugar, bitters fruit if desired	Cracked
Crusta	Wine	Liquor, orange slice, lemon juice, maraschino, aromatic bitters (sugar rim of glass)	Cracked—in shaker only
Cup	Stem glass or cup (serve in pitcher or bowl)	Liquor, Curaçao, cucumber rind, brandy, fruit, mint	Cubes or block

° Glassware is described in Chapter 28.

DRINK	GLASS	INGREDIENTS	ICE
Daisy	Highball or metal stein	Liquor, grenadine, lemon juice, soda water, fruit	Shaved
Eggnog	Cup or old-fashioned	Liquor, egg, milk, sugar, nutmeg	Cracked—in shaker only
Fix	Highball	Liquor, lemon juice, sugar, water, fruit	Shaved
Fizz	Highball	Liquor, lemon juice, sugar, soda water	Cubes
Flip	Cocktail	Liquor, sugar, egg, nutmeg	Cracked—in shaker only
Frappé	Cocktail or saucer	Liqueur	Shaved
Highball	Highball	Liquor, ginger ale or soda water	Cubes
Hot But-tered Rum	Mug	Rum, sugar, hard butter, cinnamon, cloves, nutmeg	Boiling water
Julep	Tankard or Collins	Liquor, sugar, mint	Shaved
Puff	Collins	Brandy, fresh milk, tonic	Cubes
Punch	Cup, Collins, or tankard (serve in bowl)	According to recipe	Cubes or block
Rickey	Highball	Liquor, lime, soda water	Cubes
Sangaree	Highball	Liquor, sweetening, nutmeg	Cracked
Sling	Collins	Liquor, fruit juice, liqueurs, soda water, fruit	Cubes
Smash	Old-fashioned	Liquor, lump sugar, mint	Cubes
Sour	Sour	Liquor, lemon juice, sugar, fruit	Cracked—in shaker only
	Old-fashioned		Cubes

DRINK	GLASS	INGREDIENTS	ICE
Swizzle	Highball	Liquor, sweetening, soda water	Cubes
Toddy	Toddy (hot) Old-fashioned (cold)	Liquor, lemon, sugar, cloves, cinnamon	Boiling water Cubes

Martini

There is no standard recipe on which all professionals agree. Tastes change with time. The best example of this is the manner in which the fashion has changed for the Martini.

The Martini has always been the most popular cocktail. It is a dry, sharp, appetite-whetting drink, and it is simple to make, requiring less fuss and bother than many other mixtures. Consequently it is made more often in the home. Those who make this cocktail at home develop a taste for it and naturally order it when they go to a bar.

There is some question as to the origin of the Martini and how it got its name. The earliest recipe we have been able to find is for the Martinez Cocktail, which appeared in Professor Jerry Thomas's *Bon Vivant's Companion or How to Mix Drinks*, originally published in 1862. His recipe is a far cry from today's.

Through the years the cocktail became progressively drier. By the time it was referred to as a Martini it had become a mixture of equal parts gin and dry vermouth. Before World War I the accepted standard was two parts gin to one part dry vermouth, stirred briskly with large pieces of ice and strained into a cocktail glass. For twenty years after Repeal the standard recipe was four parts gin to one part dry vermouth. The ratio gradually crept up to fifteen to one, and eventually to the foolishness of chilled gin being called a Martini because it was served in a cocktail glass. When one of the basic ingredients of a recipe is totally eliminated, it is time to give the recipe a new name.

To give you a clearer picture of the development of the Dry Martini recipe, note the changes that have taken place over the past century.

MARTINEZ COCKTAIL
(Professor Jerry Thomas's original recipe)

1 dash bitters
2 dashes maraschino liqueur
1 pony Old Tom gin
1 wineglass vermouth
2 small lumps of ice

Shake up thoroughly and strain into a large cocktail glass. Put a quarter of a slice of lemon in the glass and serve. If the guest prefers it very sweet, add two dashes of gum syrup.

MARTINI COCKTAIL
(*Mauve Decade recipe*)

1 part gin
1 part dry vermouth

DRY MARTINI COCKTAIL
(*pre-Prohibition*)

2 parts gin
1 part dry vermouth
1 dash orange bitters

VERY DRY MARTINI COCKTAIL
(*pre-World War II*)

4 parts gin
1 part dry vermouth
1 dash orange bitters or
twist of lemon

MARTINI
(*post-World War II*)

15 parts gin
1 part dry vermouth
garnishes

NAKED MARTINI

gin on the rocks
garnishes

There appears to be a reversal taking place in Martini fashion. Some devotees who enjoy a not-so-dry Martini have reverted to the pre-World War II recipe of a four-to-one Martini. These ingredients are stirred in a mixing glass with ice, and in most bars a piece of lemon peel is twisted over the cocktail after it is strained into the glass to give the added zip of the oil from the peel. A Martini can also be served on the rocks and should be garnished with a small olive. If garnished with one or more pearl onions, the drink becomes a Gibson.

Some variations that have captured popular fancy are:

VODKA OR AQUAVIT MARTINI

7 parts vodka or aquavit
1 part dry vermouth

SAKÉ MARTINI (SAKINI)

3 parts gin
1 part saké
olive

COCKTAILS

The following are standard recipes for the most popular cocktails and long drinks. In addition to these, new cocktails are continuously being developed. Some are successful and endure, while others last only a short time.

ALEXANDER

½ ounce crème de cacao
½ ounce gin
½ ounce heavy cream

Shake well with cracked ice and strain into cocktail glass.

VARIATION: For a Brandy Alexander, substitute brandy for the gin.

AMERICANO

1½ ounces Campari
1½ ounces sweet vermouth

Pour over cracked ice in old-fashioned glass and stir. Add twist of lemon.

BACARDI

juice of ½ large or 1 small lime
½ teaspoon sugar
1 dash grenadine
1½ ounces Bacardi White Label rum

Shake lime juice, sugar, and grenadine with cracked ice until cold. Put in rum and shake until shaker frosts. Strain into cocktail glass.

BANSHEE

1 ounce cream
½ ounce simple syrup
¾ ounce white crème de cacao
¾ ounce crème de bananes°

Blend with shaved ice and strain into cocktail glass.

BETWEEN THE SHEETS

juice of ¼ lemon
½ ounce brandy
½ ounce Triple Sec or Cointreau
½ ounce light rum

Shake well with cracked ice and strain into cocktail glass.

° 1½ ounces chocolate banana liqueur may be substituted for the crème de cacao and crème de bananes.

BLACK RUSSIAN

1 ounce vodka
½ ounce Kahlúa

Pour over ice cubes in old-fashioned glass and stir.

VARIATION: For a White Russian, add ½ ounce cream.

BRANDY CRUSTA

Moisten the edge of a cocktail glass with lemon juice and dip in sugar. Cut the rind of half a lemon into a spiral and place in glass. To a bar glass add:

1 teaspoon lemon juice
1 teaspoon maraschino
¾ ounce Triple Sec
1½ ounces brandy
1 dash aromatic bitters

Shake well with cracked ice and strain into cocktail glass. Add slice of orange.

BRAVE BULL

1½ ounces Tequila
1 ounce Kahlúa

Pour over ice cubes in old-fashioned glass and stir. Add twist of lemon.

BRONX

In a mixing glass muddle several pieces of sliced orange that have a bit of the rind on them to give flavor. To this add:

½ ounce sweet vermouth
½ ounce dry vermouth
1 ounce gin

Shake well with cracked ice and strain into cocktail glass.

CHAMPAGNE COCKTAIL

Place 1 cube of sugar saturated with 1 dash of aromatic bitters in cocktail glass. Add cube of ice. Fill glass with chilled Champagne and add twist of lemon.

CLOVER CLUB

$\frac{3}{4}$ ounce lemon juice
white of 1 egg
$1\frac{1}{2}$ ounces gin
1 teaspoon grenadine

Shake well with cracked ice and strain into cocktail glass.

Daiquiri   This is the most popular cocktail made with light rum. The origin of the recipe is unknown, but the drink got its name shortly after the Spanish-American War of 1898, when a group of American engineers was invited to Santiago, Cuba, to help develop the Daiquiri iron mines. The job was hard, the climate was hot, and at the end of a long day's work the men needed a refreshing relaxer. It was made from the ingredients most readily available—rum, limes, ice, and sugar to balance the acidity of the lime juice. On weekends the engineers' headquarters in Santiago was the bar of the Venus Hotel, where the bartender would make this cocktail for them. On one such occasion, early in 1900, Jennings S. Cox, the chief engineer, suggested that the cocktail be named the Daiquiri after the mines, and so it has remained ever since.

Perhaps the biggest Daiquiri ever made was mixed right at the mines in honor of Charles M. Schwab, president of Bethlehem Steel Company, on one of his inspection trips. According to accounts, the hosts used half an oak barrel into which they emptied two big pails of ice, the juice of a hundred limes, a pound of sugar, and ten bottles of Bacardi Carta Blanca rum. This was stirred briskly with a wooden paddle and ladled out to Schwab and his entourage when they emerged from the mine pits.

If it is properly made, a Daiquiri is a most delightful and refreshing cocktail. It must never be made with lemon juice; only freshly squeezed lime juice will make a proper Daiquiri. You can also use the frozen Daiquiri mix, which contains lime juice. For the Daiquiri as it was prepared in the Floradida Bar in Havana, Cuba, add $\frac{1}{4}$ ounce maraschino.

DAIQUIRI

juice of $\frac{1}{2}$ lime, freshly squeezed
1 teaspoon sugar
$1\frac{1}{2}$ ounces light rum

Shake the lime juice and sugar with cracked ice until it gets cold. Add rum and shake until the shaker frosts. Strain into cocktail glass.

IMPORTANT: A Daiquiri should be drunk immediately because the rum, lime, and sugar tend to separate if the drink is allowed to stand.

FROZEN DAIQUIRI

For a Frozen Daiquiri, use the basic Daiquiri ingredients, with shaved ice instead of cracked ice, and mixed in a blender. Add ⅓ cup sliced strawberries to blender for a Frozen Strawberry Daiquiri.

DUBONNET COCKTAIL

½ ounce gin
1 ounce red Dubonnet

Stir well with cracked ice and strain into cocktail glass.

FRAPPÉ

Pour 1½ ounces of any liqueur into a cocktail or saucer glass filled with finely shaved ice. Serve with a straw.

GIMLET

½ ounce Rose's Lime Juice
1½ ounces gin

Stir with an ice cube and strain into cocktail glass or serve over ice cubes in old-fashioned glass. Garnish with a slice of lime.

VARIATION: For a Vodka Gimlet, substitute vodka for the gin, or white rum for a Rum & Rose's.

GODFATHER

1½ ounces Scotch whisky
1½ ounces amaretto

Pour over ice cubes in old-fashioned glass and stir.

GODMOTHER

1½ ounces vodka
1½ ounces amaretto

Pour over ice cubes in old-fashioned glass and stir. Some cream may be added.

GOLDEN CADILLAC

2 ounces light cream
¾ ounce Galliano liqueur
¾ ounce white crème de cacao

Shake well with cracked ice and strain into cocktail glass.

GRASSHOPPER

¾ ounce light cream
¾ ounce green crème de menthe
¾ ounce white crème de cacao

Shake well with cracked ice until very cold. Strain into cocktail glass.

HALF & HALF

2 ounces sweet vermouth
2 ounces dry vermouth

Pour over ice cubes in old-fashioned glass and stir. Add twist of lemon.

JACK ROSE

juice of ½ lime
1 teaspoon grenadine
1½ ounces applejack

Shake well with cracked ice and strain into cocktail glass.

MAI TAI

½ teaspoon sugar
½ ounce lime juice
1 ounce light rum
1 ounce dark rum
½ ounce Curaçao
½ ounce Orgeat
1 ounce grenadine

Shake well with cracked ice and strain into cocktail glass or serve over ice cubes in old-fashioned glass. Decorate with fresh pineapple and cocktail cherry.

MANHATTAN°	or	DRY MANHATTAN
1½ ounces rye or blended whisky		1½ ounces blended whisky
½ ounce sweet vermouth		½ ounce dry vermouth
1 dash aromatic bitters		1 dash aromatic bitters

Stir well with cracked ice and strain into cocktail glass. Decorate with cocktail cherry or twist of lemon.

° This was named after the Manhattan Club, which first mixed this drink in 1870.

MARGARITA

juice of ½ lime or lemon
1½ ounces Tequila
½ ounce Triple Sec

Shake well with cracked ice and strain into cocktail glass rimmed with salt.

NAVY GROG

½ ounce lime juice
½ ounce orange juice
½ ounce pineapple juice
½ ounce Falernum
2 ounces dark rum
1 ounce light rum
½ cup finely cracked ice

Blend all ingredients and pour into large old-fashioned glass half filled with shaved ice.

NEGRONI

1 ounce Campari
1 ounce sweet vermouth
1 ounce gin

Shake well with cracked ice and strain into cocktail glass.
VARIATION: For a tall drink pour over icecubes in highball glass and fill with soda water.

OLD FASHIONED

Place in an old-fashioned glass:
1 cube sugar muddled with ½ jigger water
1½ ounces whisky
3 dashes aromatic bitters

Add ice cubes and stir. Garnish with slice of orange and cocktail cherry. Add twist of lemon and serve with cocktail pick.

ORANGE BLOSSOM

1 ounce orange juice
1 teaspoon sugar, optional
1½ ounces gin

Shake well with cracked ice and strain into cocktail glass.

PINK LADY

1 egg white
juice of $\frac{1}{2}$ lemon
$1\frac{1}{2}$ ounces gin
$1\frac{1}{2}$ ounces applejack
$\frac{1}{2}$ ounce grenadine

Shake well with cracked ice and strain into cocktail glass.

PINK SQUIRREL

1 ounce light cream
1 ounce crème de noyaux (almond) or cherry liqueur
$\frac{1}{2}$ ounce white crème de cacao

Shake well with cracked ice and strain into cocktail glass.

PRESIDENTE

$1\frac{1}{2}$ ounces light rum
$\frac{3}{4}$ ounce dry vermouth
2 dashes Curacao
1 dash grenadine

Shake well with cracked ice and strain into cocktail glass.

ROB ROY   or   DRY ROB ROY

ROB ROY	DRY ROB ROY
$1\frac{1}{2}$ ounce Scotch whisky	$1\frac{1}{2}$ ounce Scotch whisky
$\frac{1}{2}$ ounce sweet vermouth	$\frac{1}{2}$ ounce dry vermouth
2 dashed aromatic bitters	2 dashes aromatic bitters

Shake well with cracked ice and strain into cocktail glass.

RUSTY NAIL

$\frac{1}{2}$ ounce Drambuie
$1\frac{1}{2}$ ounces Scotch whisky

Pour over ice cubes in old-fashioned glass and stir.

SALTY DOG

3 ounces grapefruit juice
$1\frac{1}{2}$ ounces gin
dash salt

Pour over ice cubes in old-fashioned glass and stir.
VARIATION: Substitute Tequila for the gin.

SAZEREC

1 cube sugar
1 teaspoon water
$\frac{1}{2}$ ounce Pernod, Ricard, or Herbsaint
1 dash aromatic bitters
1 dash Peychaud Bitters
2 ounces Bourbon whisky

Coat the inside of a chilled glass with the Pernod, Ricard, or Herbsaint. Discard any excess. Muddle the cube of sugar with the teaspoon of water and the 2 dashes of bitters. Add ice cubes. Pour in Bourbon and top with twist of lemon. If Peychaud Bitters are not available, use an extra dash of aromatic bitters.

SCARLETT O'HARA

2 ounces orange juice
1 ounce grenadine
$\frac{3}{4}$ ounce Southern Comfort

Pour over ice cubes in old-fashioned glass and stir.

SCOTCH MIST

Pour $1\frac{1}{2}$ ounces Scotch whisky into old-fashioned glass filled with shaved ice. Add twist of lemon.

VARIATION: For a Whisky Mist, substitute any whisky for the Scotch.

SHERRY FLIP

1 egg
1 teaspoon sugar
$1\frac{1}{2}$ ounces sweet sherry

Shake well and pour over ice cubes in old-fashioned glass. Sprinkle a little nutmeg on top.

VARIATIONS: Brandy, port, rum, or whisky may be substituted for the sherry.

SIDE CAR

$\frac{1}{2}$ ounce lemon juice
$\frac{1}{2}$ ounce Triple Sec
$\frac{1}{2}$ ounce brandy

Shake well with cracked ice and strain into cocktail glass.

STINGER

$\frac{3}{4}$ ounce brandy
$\frac{3}{4}$ ounce white crème de menthe

Shake well with cracked ice and strain into cocktail glass. Add twist of lemon.

TEQUILA SUNRISE

4 ounces orange juice
$1\frac{1}{2}$ ounces Tequila
$\frac{1}{2}$ to $\frac{3}{4}$ ounce grenadine

Pour orange juice and Tequila over ice cubes in old-fashioned glass and stir. Add grenadine and let it settle to the bottom. Stir very gently and watch the "sunrise."

WHISKY SMASH

1 cube sugar
1 ounce water
mint sprigs
$1\frac{1}{2}$ ounces whisky

Muddle sugar with water and a few sprigs of mint in old-fashioned glass. Add ice cubes. Pour in whisky and stir. Decorate with four or five sprigs of mint. Serve with soda water on the side.

WHISKY SOUR

$\frac{3}{4}$ ounce lemon or lime juice
1 teaspoon sugar
$1\frac{1}{2}$ ounces Bourbon or blended whisky

Shake well with cracked ice and strain into sour glass. When served over ice cubes, use old-fashioned glass. Add cocktail cherry and slice of orange.

VARIATIONS: Scotch, gin, brandy, rum, Tequila, or vodka may be substituted for the whisky. For an Apricot Sour, substitute apricot-flavored brandy for the whisky.

LONG DRINKS

APRICOT COOLER

juice of $\frac{1}{2}$ lemon or 1 lime
$1\frac{1}{2}$ ounces apricot-flavored brandy
2 dashes grenadine
soda water

Shake lemon or lime juice, apricot-flavored brandy, and grenadine well and pour over cracked ice in highball glass. Fill with soda water.

BLOODY MARY

3 ounces tomato juice
juice of $\frac{1}{2}$ lemon
$1\frac{1}{2}$ ounces vodka
2 dashes Worcestershire sauce
dash of salt and pepper

Shake well (shaking produces a superb drink) and pour over ice cubes in highball glass. This recipe makes an excellent Bloody Mary, particularly when Sacramento or another thick tomato juice is used. Some people use more Worcestershire sauce, some add a dash of Tabasco sauce, and some substitute gin for the vodka.

BULL SHOT

$1\frac{1}{2}$ ounces vodka
4 ounces beef bouillon
dash of salt and pepper

Pour over ice cubes in highball glass and stir.

COFFEE ROYALE

5 ounces very hot black coffee
1 sugar cube
$1\frac{1}{2}$ ounces brandy

Pour coffee into a cup. Place spoon across cup and pour some brandy into spoon with sugar cube. Pour balance of brandy into the coffee. Place before guest and ignite brandy in spoon. Stir when flame subsides and add twist of lemon.

CUBA LIBRE

$1\frac{1}{2}$ ounces light or dark rum
6 ounces cola

Pour over ice cubes in highball glass and stir. Some people squeeze and insert a wedge of a fresh lime.

FRENCH 75

juice of 1 lemon
1 teaspoon sugar
1½ ounces brandy
Champagne

Shake lemon juice, sugar, and brandy well and pour over ice cubes in highball glass. Fill with chilled Champagne.

GIN AND BITTER LEMON

1½ ounces gin
6 ounces bitter lemon

Pour over ice cubes in highball glass and stir. Add twist of lemon.

GIN DAISY

juice of ½ lemon
½ teaspoon sugar
1 teaspoon grenadine
1½ ounces gin
soda water

Shake lemon juice, sugar, grenadine, and gin well and pour over shaved ice in highball glass or metal stein. Add soda water as desired. Garnish with fruit.

VARIATIONS: Brandy, rum, vodka, or whisky may be substituted for the gin.

GIN FIX

juice of ¼ lemon
1 tablespoon sugar
1 ounce water
1½ ounces gin

Shake well and pour into highball glass filled with shaved ice. Garnish with lemon slice and other fruit.

VARIATIONS: Brandy, rum, or whisky may be substituted for the gin.

GIN FIZZ

juice of ½ lemon
1 teaspoon sugar
1½ ounces gin
soda water

Shake lemon juice, sugar, and gin well and pour over ice cubes in highball glass. Fill with soda water and add twist of lemon.

VARIATION: For a Silver Fizz, make as above but shake with 1 egg white.

GIN RICKEY

juice and rind of ½ lime
2 ounces gin
soda water

Pour lime juice and gin over ice cubes in highball glass and stir. Fill with soda water and drop lime rind into drink.

GIN AND TONIC

1½ ounces gin
6 ounces tonic

Pour over ice cubes in highball glass and stir. Squeeze lime wedge and drop into drink.

HARVEY WALLBANGER

1 ounce vodka
6 ounces orange juice
½ ounce Galliano liqueur

Pour vodka and orange juice over ice cubes in highball glass and stir. Float liqueur on top.

HIGHLAND COOLER

juice of ½ lemon
1 teaspoon sugar
1½ ounces Scotch whisky
2 dashes aromatic bitters
ginger ale

Shake lemon juice, powdered sugar, whisky, and bitters well and pour over ice cubes in Collins glass. Fill with ginger ale.

VARIATIONS: Gin, rum, or vodka may be substituted for the Scotch whisky.

HOT BUTTERED RUM

This is the classic warmer-upper of colonial days, and it is still popular today. It is guaranteed to take away cold stiffness if you have been skating, skiing, or out in the cold too long. We do not recommend it if you are going back out into the freezing cold weather.

1 teaspoon sugar
$1\frac{1}{2}$ ounces dark rum
5 ounces boiling water
1 pat hard butter
nutmeg or cloves
1 cinnamon stick

Rinse an 8-ounce mug or cup with hot water. Put in the sugar, rum, and boiling water. Float the pat of butter on the surface and sprinkle with nutmeg. Use the cinnamon stick as a stirrer. Inhale the wonderful aroma and drink while the mixture is good and hot.

IRISH COFFEE

This drink was made famous by the Buena Vista Café at San Francisco's Fisherman's Wharf shortly after World War II. It has since become popular all over the world.

1 teaspoon sugar
$1\frac{1}{2}$ ounces Irish whiskey
5 ounces very hot, strong black coffee
whipped cream

Rinse an 8-ounce stemmed goblet with very hot water. Place the sugar in the glass and pour in the Irish whiskey and coffee. Stir to dissolve sugar and top with whipped cream.

KIR

4 ounces chilled dry white Burgundy wine
$\frac{1}{2}$ ounce crème de cassis (or to taste)

Pour over ice cubes in wineglass or highball glass and stir.

MIMOSA

2 ounces orange juice
$6\frac{1}{2}$ ounces (a split) Champagne
1 teaspoon Grand Marnier (optional)

Pour over ice cubes in highball glass and stir.

MINT JULEP

In a Collins glass or pewter tankard, dissolve 1 teaspoon sugar in just enough water to cover it. Fill with shaved ice. Pour in Bourbon whisky to within a half-inch of the top. Stir until glass is thoroughly frosted. Decorate generously with fresh mint.

If you want a more pronounced mint flavor, crush a sprig of mint together with the sugar and water and leave it in the glass. Then pack with ice, add the Bourbon, stir, and decorate.

MOSCOW MULE

$1\frac{1}{2}$ ounces vodka
juice of $\frac{1}{2}$ lime
ginger beer

Pour vodka and lime juice over ice cubes in an 8-ounce copper mug and stir. Fill with ginger beer. Garnish with wedge of lime.

PIÑA COLADA

$1\frac{1}{2}$ ounces cream of coconut
3 ounces pineapple juice
3 ounces light rum

Blend with shaved ice and strain into Collins glass. Serve with a straw.

PLANTER'S PUNCH

1 ounce lime juice
1 teaspoon sugar
2 ounces Jamaican rum

Dissolve the sugar in the lime juice in a bar glass. Put in the rum and cracked ice and shake well. Strain into a highball glass that is half filled with finely cracked ice. Decorate with maraschino cherry, sliver of fresh pineapple, half a slice of orange, and sprig of mint. Serve with a straw.

PORT WINE SANGAREE

$2\frac{1}{4}$ ounces port wine
$\frac{1}{2}$ ounce simple syrup

Pour over ice cubes in highball glass and stir. Grate nutmeg on top.

RUM SWIZZLE

juice of 1 lime
1 teaspoon powdered sugar
1½ ounces light rum
2 dashes bitters
soda water

Shake lime juice, sugar, rum, and bitters well and pour over ice cubes in highball glass. Fill with soda water. Serve with swizzle stick.

VARIATIONS: Brandy, gin, or whisky may be substituted for the rum.

RUM TODDY

1 cube sugar
1½ ounces dark rum
boiling water
1 cinnamon stick
lemon slice
cloves

Place sugar cube and rum in toddy glass and fill with boiling water. Insert one small piece of cinnamon and one slice of lemon garnished with cloves. Stir. Serve with a spoon and a small pitcher of hot water on the side.

SCREWDRIVER

1½ ounces vodka
5 ounces orange juice

Pour over ice cubes in highball glass and stir.

SHERRY COBBLER

2 ounces sweet sherry
¾ ounce simple syrup

Pour over shaved ice in stemmed goblet and stir. Decorate with fresh fruits, cubed or slice, cocktail cherry, and sprig of mint. Serve with a straw.

VARIATIONS: Whisky or port may be substituted for the sherry.

SINGAPORE SLING

1 ounce lime juice
1 ounce cherry liqueur
2 ounces gin
soda water

Shake lime juice, cherry liqueur, and gin well and pour over ice cubes in Collins glass. Fill with soda water. Decorate with orange slice and sprig of mint. Then add through the middle with a dropper:

4 drops Bénédictine
4 drops brandy   (or 8 drops B & B)

This recipe is said to be the original from the Raffles Hotel in Singapore. Modern versions include bitters, grenadine, pineapple juice, and Cointreau.

SLOE GIN FIZZ

¾ ounce lemon juice
1 teaspoon sugar
1½ ounces sloe gin liqueur
soda water

Shake lemon juice, sugar, and sloe gin liqueur well and pour over ice cubes in highball glass. Fill with soda water.

TOM COLLINS

¾ ounce lemon juice
1 teaspoon sugar
1½ ounces gin
soda water

Shake lemon juice, sugar, and gin well and pour over ice cubes in Collins glass. Fill with soda water.

VARIATION: For a Vodka Collins, substitute vodka for the gin.

TOM AND JERRY

1 egg, separated
1 teaspoon sugar
1 ounce brandy
1 ounce dark rum
hot milk or boiling water

In an 8-ounce cup mix the yolk of the egg with the sugar. Pour in a brandy and rum. Stir thoroughly. Put in the beaten white of egg and, while stirring, pour in hot milk or boiling water to fill the cup. Sprinkle nutmeg on top.

VERMOUTH CASSIS

$1\frac{1}{2}$ ounces dry vermouth
$\frac{1}{2}$ ounce crème de cassis
soda water

Pour vermouth and crème de cassis over ice cubes in highball glass and stir. Fill with soda water.

WARD EIGHT

1 ounce lemon juice
$1\frac{1}{2}$ ounces whisky
1 teaspoon grenadine
soda water

Shake lemon juice, whisky, and grenadine well and pour over ice cubes in highball glass. Fill with soda water.

ZOMBIE°

$\frac{3}{4}$ ounce lime juice
$\frac{3}{4}$ ounce pineapple juice
1 teaspoon Falernum or simple syrup
1 ounce light rum
2 ounces medium rum
1 ounce Jamaican rum
$\frac{1}{2}$ ounce 151-proof Demeraran rum
$\frac{1}{2}$ ounce apricot liqueur

Shake well and pour into 14-ounce Zombie glass half-filled with shaved ice. Garnish with slice of orange and several sprigs of mint. Serve with a straw.

PUNCHES AND WINE CUPS

BRANDY MILK PUNCH

1 pint brandy
1 quart milk
4 teaspoons sugar

Stir together in a punch bowl. Add a small block of ice and dust top liberally with nutmeg. Serves twelve.

° The original recipe is supposedly still a closely guarded secret of Don the Beachcomber.

CHAMPAGNE CUP

1 tablespoon sugar
4 ounces brandy
2 ounces Curaçao
1 ounce maraschino
1 ounce Grand Marnier
1 bottle Champagne

Stir together in a pitcher or bowl. Add a small block of ice and decorate with slices of orange and pineapple, one piece of cucumber rind, and sprigs of mint. Serve in a stem glass or punch cup.

VARIATIONS: Claret, Rhine wine, or Sauternes may be substitued for the Champagne.

EGG NOG

12 eggs, separated
1 cup sugar
1 quart milk
1 quart heavy cream
1 quart rum, Bourbon, or brandy

Beat egg yolks until light and beat in sugar. Beat in milk and rum, Bourbon, or brandy. Chill. Whip cream until stiff and fold into mixture. Shortly before serving, beat egg whites until stiff and fold in. Sprinkle top with nutmeg.

FISH HOUSE PUNCH

$\frac{3}{4}$ pound loaf sugar
1 to 2 quarts water
1 quart lemon juice
2 quarts Jamaican rum
1 quart Cognac
4 ounces peach liqueur

Dissolve loaf sugar in the water in punch bowl. When entirely dissolved, add lemon juice, then all the other ingredients. Put a large piece of solid ice in the punch bowl and allow the mixture to steep for about two hours, stirring occasionally. In winter, when ice melts slowly, more water may be used; in summer, less. The melting ice dilutes the mixture sufficiently. This will make $1\frac{1}{2}$ gallons, depending on dilution.

This is the original Fish House Punch, made by the Fish House Club, now called the State in Schuylkill, founded in 1732. We are indebted to Anna Wetherill Reed, in whose *Philadelphia Cook Book of Town and Country* this recipe appears.

MAYWINE PUNCH

½ package Waldmeister
13 bottles German or Alsatian wine
1 bottle Champagne
2 ounces Bénédictine
2 ounces Cognac
¼ pound sugar
1 quart soda water

Soak Waldmeister (sweet-scented woodruff—a European woodland herb) six hours in 1 bottle of wine. Strain and mix with 12 remaining bottles. Add Champagne, Bénédictine, and Cognac. Dissolve sugar in soda water and add. Decorate with strawberries and fresh Waldmeister. When sufficiently cold, serve in wineglasses from a punch bowl. To keep the punch cold, place a pitcher full of shaved ice in the center of the bowl. This will serve approximately 100 cups of 3½ ounces each.

MULLED RED WINE

2 cups water
1 cup sugar
4 cinnamon sticks
4 cloves
2 lemons
1 bottle claret or Burgundy

Boil the water with the sugar, cinnamon, and cloves for five minutes. Then add the lemons sliced very thin, cover, and let stand for ten minutes. Add the wine and heat gradually, but do not allow to boil. Serve very hot in a pitcher or brown jug. A spoon placed in each glass will prevent it from cracking.

SANGRIA

Throughout the Spanish-speaking world one of the traditional ways of enjoying wine is in the form of a wine cup, the Sangria. The recipe given is more time-consuming than using bottled Sangria, but the fresh fruit flavor more than compensates.

¼ cup sugar (or to taste)
1 cup water
1 orange, thinly sliced
1 lime, thinly sliced
1 bottle red or white wine
6 ounces soda water

Dissolve sugar in water in large pitcher. Add fruit and wine, plus 12 or more ice cubes. Stir until cold. Add sparkling water. Serve, putting some of the fruit in each glass.

WASSAIL BOWL

2 cups water
1 teaspoon freshly ground nutmeg
2 teaspoons ground ginger
2-inch stick of cinnamon
6 whole cloves
6 allspice berries
4 coriander seeds
4 cardamom seeds
2 bottles cream sherry or Madeira
2 quarts ale
4 cups sugar
12 eggs, separated
1 cup Cognac or brandy
12 roasted slices of apples or 12 tiny roasted apples

Combine water and spices in a saucepan and simmer for 10 minutes. Add sherry and ale and stir in sugar. Heat, but do not boil. Beat 12 egg yolks until they are pale and thick; fold in 12 stiffly beaten egg whites. Strain half the ale and sherry mixture over the eggs. Turn into a warmed punch bowl. Bring the remaining ale and sherry to a boil and strain it into the punch bowl. Add Cognac and roasted apples or apple slices.

A YARD OF FLANNEL

1 quart ale
2 egg whites
4 egg yolks
4 tablespoons brown sugar
$\frac{1}{2}$ tablespoon nutmeg

Stir brown sugar and nutmeg into beaten egg yolks. Fold in beaten egg whites. Boil ale and gradually stir in egg-sugar-nutmeg mixture. Then pour it rapidly back and forth between two pans until the drink is smooth and finely frothed. Serve hot.

PREPARED COCKTAILS

Certain mixed drinks whose ingredients include wine and spirits can very easily be prepared in large quantities and stored and distributed in bottles and cans. These prepared cocktails are practical for those who do not have facilities in the home for mixing them fresh. They have the advantage of being uniform, and they can be put in the refrigerator until needed. Many come in convenient one- or two-portion containers.

The most popular varieties are Martinis, Manhattans, Sours, and Daiquiris. But prepared cocktails also include Tequila Sours, Margaritas, Vodka Martinis, Scotch Mists, Banana Daiquiris, Black Russians, Gin Collinses and Sours, Gimlets, Screwdrivers, Side Cars, Stingers, and many others. Bottled Sangria is probably the most widely sold wine cocktail.

The liquor industry had to overcome many obstacles in making prepared cocktails that would keep a long time. The aim was to make drinks that were uniform in quality, that would taste the same a week after the bottle was opened, and in which the sugar would not change flavor or crystallize. With the development of nondairy creamers that need no refrigeration, a new field of prepared drinks has opened up for the liquor industry. Prepared eggnogs, Brandy Alexanders, and Grasshoppers are examples of drinks that formerly had to be made with fresh cream but can now be purchased as finished beverages.

COCKTAIL MIXES

Cocktail mixes are expertly prepared cocktails with all the necessary ingredients except the liquor. To create a Manhattan, for example, add whisky to the appropriate mix.

There are two main types of cocktail mixes now on the market: liquid and dry powder. The liquid mix, to which you just add liquor to make the appropriate drink, has been in existence for decades, although the range of cocktails has increased tremendously. The dry mix is a powder to which water and liquor are added to dissolve the powder and create the drink. Recently freeze-dried fruit has been added to dry mixes, making for fresher flavor.

Frozen cocktail mixes offer the advantages of fresh-tasting fruit juices. The most popular is the frozen Daiquiri mix, which is made with fresh lime juice, and is approved by the Puerto Rican rum producers. Refrigerated egg nog mix, sold around the holiday season, needs only liquor and a dusting of nutmeg.

In addition to being convenient, mixes allow the home bartender to be creative. He can add Scotch to the Manhattan mix and get a Rob Roy. The Daiquiri mix is a starting point for a Planter's Punch, Pink Lady, Clover Club, Ward Eight, or Gin Fizz. In addition, of course, the host or hostess can choose which brands of liquor they want to use.

27
PREPARING
WINE LISTS
AND MENUS

In the Mauve Decade and the years before World War I, the art of wining and dining reached its height in this country, epitomized, perhaps, by the Waldorf-Astoria Hotel with its great Oscar as host to fashionable America. Prohibition brought a period of gastronomical and vinicultural depression. But since Repeal and the increasing sophistication, the country has recultivated the fine arts of good living, dining, wining, and stimulating conversation.

A new Waldorf-Astoria replaces the original, but no one can replace Oscar Tschirky, who was the Waldorf's banquet manager par excellence. The banquet manager serves an important function in a hotel. It is his job to know his menus and to know which dishes the chef prepares best for a small party and which for a large party. He must know his wines and how to sell them. He must be the epitome of tact, for it is his job to advise the host or hostess who consults him, suggest the wine or food the host should order, supervise the details of the gathering, and have insight into the tastes of the person he is advising. All in all, it is an imporant position requiring tact, intelligence, and ability.

The following menu is an example of an informal banquet dinner. A dry white wine can be served through the meal—a Burgundy such as Meursault, an Alsatian Riesling, or a California Chardonnay.

Consommé

Filet of Sea Bass, Bonne Femme

Roast Veal

Green Beans au Beurre

Pommes Anna

Green Salad Vinaigrette

Fresh Strawberries

Parfait Glacé à la Vanille

Petits Fours

Coffee

411

For a more formal banquet the following menu with its full complement of wines was served by the Waldorf-Astoria in the 1930s.

APÉRITIF	Les Canapés Russes
	Amuse-Bouche Gabriel
SHERRY	Le Fumet de Gombo
	Paillettes Dorées
	Céleri Amandes Salées Olives
POUILLY-FUISSÉ 1928	Les Crabes de Californie
	en Turban
CHÂTEAU LÉOVILLE-POYFERRÉ 1928	L'Entrecôte Grillée Vendôme
	Bouquetière de Légumes
	Pommes Colorette
	Salade de Floride
ERNEST IRROY CHAMPAGNE 1928	Feuillantine Nesselrode
	Son Sabayon
COGNAC	Moka
LIQUEURS	

(Courtesy the late Oscar Tschirky, The Waldorf-Astoria Hotel)

The great interest in wining and dining has been evidenced by the formation, in many metropolitan centers, of branches of the Wine and Food Society, an organization founded in London by the late André L. Simon, who devoted himself to increasing the enjoyment of the better things of life. The Wine and Food Society holds periodic tastings of wines, spirits, and foods and occasional dinners. The object of the society is to acquaint its members with the most interesting wines or foods, and it is educational in the truest sense.

Many similar groups exist, and each in its own way also contributes to the general interest in better eating and drinking. Some of these are the Confrérie des Chevaliers du Tastevin ("The Brotherhood of Gentlemen of the Tasting Cup"), devoted to a greater appreciation of the wines and food of Burgundy; Commanderie de Bordeaux, whose main interest is the wines and food of Bordeaux; and Confrérie de la Chaîne des Rôtisseurs ("The Fraternity of the Turners of the Roasting Spit"), who give their allegiance to good food, especially roasts, and the wines that complement them best. Other groups celebrate the wines of Alsace, Beaujolais, or Germany, and Les Amis du Vin conducts tastings of wines from all over the world.

OPPOSITE: Annual Induction Dinner of the Confrérie des Chevaliers du Tastevin, January 24, 1983, at the Hotel Pierre in New York.

ESCRITEAU

Chairman du Comités Gastronomique et Oenologique
WILLIAM ZECKENDORF

Offic er Commandeur Jack J. Frishman - Charge du Dîner

Comité Gastronomique

Grand Officier Thomas H. Ahrens
Officier Commandeur John E. Oxley
Commandeur Irwin Scherzer

Pour la Reception
Les Amuses Bouche du Japon
Les Huîtres Belon et Cotuit
Le Saumon Fumé de l'Ecosse
Les Langoustines d'Espagne

Champagne Perrier Jouët

Chassagne Montrachet 1977
Josepoh Drouhin

Le Dîner

Le Consommé St. Hubert

Les Quenelles de Saumon et de Sole
Sauces Mousseline et Nantua

Meursault-Poruzois 1978
Ropiteau Frères

Le Contrefilet de Charolais
Sauce Marchand de Vin

Choux Rouges a la Façon du Chef   Pommes Boulangeres

Beaune Clos des Mouches 1976
Joseph Drouhin

Les Haricots verts Primeur

Les Fromages de France

Musigny 1974
Comte Georges du Vogüé

Le Soufflé de Framboises

Comtes de Champagne Rosé 1975
Taittinger

Les Friandises

Le Café des Chevaliers

Director of Catering
Herbert Rose

Les Cadets de Bourgogne

Herbert L. Gould
Robert L. Keeney III
David Mishkin
Kirkpatrick MacDonald
Alexander C. McNally
Robert Tenny

Pour l'Intronisation
Bonnes Mares 1972
Comte Georges du Vogüé

Grand Officier Jules Bond - Consultante

Comité Oenologique

Grand Officier Charles S. Mueller
Officier Commandeur David S. Milligan
Officier Commandeur Morton Keifer
Commandeur Harold B. Barg
Commandeur Robert F. Fairchild
Commandeur Stanley H. Levy

Chef de Cuisine
Franz Klampfer

Maitre d' Hôtel
Guenther Noeth

"In Vino Veritas!"

*"Jamais en Vain
Toujours en Vin"*

For formal entertaining, where several wines are in order, the long-accepted order of service should be followed: dry sparkling wines; light, dry wines; full-bodies wines; and rich, sweet wines. Other suggestions for appropriate wine service are:

Do not serve a dry claret or Burgundy after a rich Sauternes—the red wines, being dry, would taste harsh on the sweetened palate.

When two vintages of the same type of wine are being served, the younger should precede the softer, mellower, older wine. The only exception is Champagne. In this case the older comes first, as it will seem to lack life and vigor if it follows a fresh, young wine.

When serving fine wines, it is advisable to avoid vinegar sauces.

When serving dry red or white wine, avoid dishes with sweet sauces. They will make the wine taste harsh.

Rich, well-seasoned food needs as full-bodied wine. Such food will interfere with the full enjoyment of a delicate wine, while a powerful, big wine will completely dominate any delicate, light dish. There should be harmony between them.

In printing menus for formal dinners of banquets, two forms are commonly used for listing the wines. One is to print the wines and spirits on the left side of the menu, listing each opposite the course with which it is to be served. The other is to list the wine or spirit (brandy or liqueurs) as part of the menu, putting each wine immediately below the course with which it is served. In listing wines on a formal dinner menu, full information as to name, vintage, and producer should be given. For example, Château Lafite-Rothschild 1961, or Corton-Pougets 1976, Louis Jadot, would be proper listings. If the wine is in magnum or an even larger-sized bottle, that should also be noted.

A home dinner today may consist of an appetizer, a main dish with its accompanying vegetables, salad, dessert, and coffee. With such a dinner one wine is sufficient. This may be either white or red, depending on the main course and on one's personal preference. When entertaining informally this menu may be expanded to include a soup, but one wine is still correct.

THE WINE LIST

The wine list is as important a silent salesman for wine as the menu is for food, and it should always be presented to a guest along with the menu.

It is not possible to prepare a wine list that would be equally useful in every establishment, as the wine list, like the menu, must reflect the character of a restaurant and therefore is prepared with a view to the taste of its patrons.

OPPOSITE: Menu for the first dinner of the New York chapter of Les Dames d'Escoffier, March 17, 1977, at the Carlyle Hotel in New York.

Le Premier Dîner
Les Dames d'Escoffier, New York

The Carlyle
March 27, 1977
Guest of Honor
Honorary Grande Dame Julia Child

Le Comité de la Bonne Bouche
Elayne Kleeman, Hôtesse
Cécile L. Cuming
Linda Downs
Grace Kent
Anna Muffoletto
Sylvia Schur
Jeanne Voltz
Robert Frédy ~ Directeur des Restaurants
Henri Thongs - Directeur de Cuisine

Chablis Les Preuses Grand Cru
Domaine de la Maladière 1974

Champagne Dom Ruinart Blanc de Blancs 1969

Château Figeac 1966

Muscat Ottonel Dr Konstantin Frank

Cognac and Liqueurs

La Réception
Les Huîtres de la Saison

La Matière
Mousse de Foie de Canard

Coquille Saint Jacques à la Nage

Selle d'Agneau Forestière

Asperges Sauce Moutarde

L'Apotéose
Soufflé Glacé à la Chartreuse

Mignardises

Café

While there is a similarity in certain price groups, each hotel or restaurant has to bear in mind its own clientele in preparing its wine list. A great hotel or fashionable restaurant will have an elaborate wine list, while a smaller establishment, whose atmosphere is simpler, will plan its list accordingly. It is not profitable to list a great number and variety of wines when experience shows that there is no demand for them.

The wine list should be simple and should list wines, spirits, beers, and mineral waters.

If there is enough space, it will add interest and invite a guest to peruse the entire wine list if short paragraphs describing each type of wine are included, such as a short account of Champagne or Bordeaux wines. Short descriptions of each wine, if there is room for them, assist a guest in selecting wine. Specific suggestions for wine and food combinations may be helpful.

In making up a wine list, check all spellings carefully, copying them from the labels on the bottles. Correct vintages should also be listed. Avoid repetition within classes of wine. For instance, one regional Graves is enough. There is no point in having three.

One of the most complete wine lists in the United States is that of the New York Hilton at Rockefeller Center. Listing two hundred wines, it is very extensive yet practical for the Hilton. It embodies all of the recommended points, and at one time or another the hotel's guests have ordered all of the wines listed.

There are no arbitrary rules for the order in which wines should appear on a wine list or as to whether cocktails and mixed drinks should appear on a left-hand or right-hand page when a large single-fold list is used.

Our preference is for the following order:

Champagnes	Red Bordeaux (Clarets)
U.S. Sparkling wines	Red Burgundy wines
Other Sparkling wines	Red Rhône wines
Apéritif wines	Red U.S. wines
Alsace wines	Red Italian wines
White Bordeaux wines	Wines from other countries
White Burgundy wines	Sherries
White U.S. wines	Portos
White Italian wines	Madeiras
White German wines	Special dessert wines
Cognacs and brandies	Rums
Whiskies	Miscellaneous spirits
Vodkas	Beers
Gins	

TURBACK'S OF ITHACA, NY

The "I L♥VE New York" Wine List

WHITE WINES

Hybrid Varieties

Seyval Blanc
Otter Springs, Hammondsport........9.95
Seyval Blanc
Johnson Estate, Westfield............7.95
Seyval Blanc
Wagner, Lodi.....................7.95
Seyval Blanc
Merritt Estate, Forestville...........7.95
Seyval Blanc
Bully Hill, Hammondsport...........10.95
Seyval Naturel
Bully Hill, Hammondsport...........12.95
Vidal Blanc
Bully Hill, Hammondsport...........10.95
Aurora
Heron Hill, Hammondsport..........8.95
Aurora Blanc
Johnson Estate, Westfield............7.95
Aurora Blanc
Bully Hill, Hammondsport...........8.95
White Blend
Bully Hill, Hammondsport...........8.95
Cayuga Natural
Lucas, Interlaken..................6.95
Cayuga
Wickham, Hector..................7.95
Cayuga
Glenora, Dundee...................8.95
Cayuga White
Chateau Esperanza, Bluff Point........8.95
Ravat
Heron Hill, Hammondsport..........8.95
Ravat Blanc
McGregor, Dundee.................8.95
Verdelet Blanc
Bully Hill, Hammondsport..........12.95
Verdelet Blanc
Great Western, Hammondsport........8.95
A Little White Wine
Cascade Mountain, Amenia..........5.00

Vinifera Varieties

Chenin Blanc
Four Chimneys, Himrod...........12.95
Gewurztraminer
Woodbury, Dunkirk...............12.00
Gewurztraminer
Gold Seal, Hammondsport..........16.00
Gewurztraminer
Hermann Wiemer, Dundee..........24.00
Gewurztraminer
Casa Larga, Fairport..............14.95

Chardonnay
Casa Larga, Fairport...............12.95
Chardonnay
Wagner, Lodi......................36.00
Chardonnay
Dr. Frank, Hammondsport...........14.95
Chardonnay (Robert Plane Vineyard)
Glenora, Dundee...................16.00
Chardonnay
Gold Seal, Hammondsport..........20.00
Chardonnay
Heron Hill, Hammondsport..........12.95
Chardonnay
Hermann Wiemer, Dundee..........18.00
Chardonnay
Chateau Esperanza, Bluff Point......20.00
Johannisberg Riesling (Ingle Vineyard)
Heron Hill, Hammondsport..........18.00
Johannisberg Riesling
Dr. Frank, Hammondsport...........14.95
Johannisberg Riesling
Hermann Wiemer, Dundee..........16.00
Johannisberg Riesling
Gold Seal, Hammondsport..........14.95
Johannisberg Riesling
Glenora, Dundee..................12.95
Johannisberg Riesling
Chateau Esperanza, Bluff Point......16.00

RED WINES

Hybrid Varieties

Le Hamburgér Red
Cascade Mountain, Amenia............5.00
DeChaunac
Wagner, Lodi.....................7.95
DeChaunac
Glenora, Dundee...................8.95
Baco Noir
DeMay, Hammondsport..............7.95
Baco Noir
Bully Hill, Hammondsport..........10.95
Marechal Foch
Bully Hill, Hammondsport..........10.95
Foch
Chateau Esperanza, Bluff Point........9.95
Leon Millot
Chateau Esperanza, Bluff Point......10.95
Clairet
Otter Springs, Hammondsport........9.95
Rougeon
Wagner, Lodi.....................6.95
Red Blend
Casa Larga, Fairport...............7.95
Red Blend
Chateau Esperanza, Bluff Point......10.95

Red Blend
Bully Hill, Hammondsport...........8.95
Glacier Ridge Red
Woodbury, Dunkirk.................6.95
Classic New Yorker
Chadwick Bay, Fredonia.............6.95
Chancellor Noir
Bully Hill, Hammondsport..........10.95
Chancellor Noir
Johnson Estate, Westfield............7.95

Vinifera Varieties

Pinot Noir
Casa Larga, Fairport...............16.00
Pinot Noir
McGregor, Dundee.................16.00
Cabernet Sauvignon
Casa Larga, Fairport...............18.00
Cabernet Sauvignon
Four Chimneys, Himrod...........20.00

ROSÉ WINES

Rosé of Iona
Barry, Conesus....................9.95
DeChaunac Rosé
Wagner, Lodi.....................6.95
Baco Noir Rosé
Glenora, Dundee...................7.95
Blended Rosé
Chateau Esperanza, Bluff Point........8.95
Vin Rosé
DeMay, Hammondsport..............5.95
Blended Rosé
Heron Hill, Hammondsport..........7.95
Military Rosé
Bully Hill, Hammondsport...........9.95
Space Shuttle Rosé
Bully Hill, Hammondsport..........10.95

SPARKLING WINES

Blanc de Blancs Champagne
Gold Seal, Hammondsport..........18.00
Blanc de Blancs Champagne (375 ml)
Gold Seal, Hammondsport............9.95
Naturel Champagne
Great Western, Hammondsport.......15.00
Champagne
DeMay, Hammondsport.............12.00
Brut Champagne
Gold Seal, Hammondsport..........12.00
Spumante
Woodbury, Dunkirk...............10.95
Seyval Blanc Champagne
Bully Hill, Hammondsport..........20.00

This Finger Lakes, New York restaurant offers wines only from New York State, especially from the Finger Lakes region. (*Courtesy Turback's of Ithaca, NY*)

We list Champagne first because it is an excellent apéritif wine and starts any dinner off on a festive note. One cannot deny that it is costly, but lower priced sparkling wines may also be selected. The rest of the list seems logical.

Obviously this list does not include all the possibilities; on the other hand, not every establishment need have every category. Where only one or two wines of a given class are stocked, two or more may be listed under one heading, such as Porto and Madeira wines.

Wine lists need not be complicated or very long, but they should be appropriate to the type of restaurant in which they are used. A good selection of five or ten wines is better than a poor selection of fifty. Wine lists should be up to date, and above all they should be available and used. A menu that has changes and deletions is not acceptable in a good restaurant. Therefore it follows that a wine list is not acceptable if it lists items that are out of stock or has many changes.

The wine list should be as clear and clean and presentable as the menu from which the diner selects his food. Enough information should be given on the list so the customer knows what he is ordering without having to ask questions. The type of wine, the name of the wine, its vintage if there is any, the name of the shipper, and the size of the bottle, are all important. Identifying each wine by a number may eliminate embarrassment in pronunciation.

In addition to the wine list many establishments with cocktail lounges find it profitable to print a small secondary list including the most popular bar drinks, such as cocktails, mixed drinks, and spirits. This is generally called the drink list. It should be printed on a card, which may be folded, and it may include a small selection of wines, particularly Champagnes.

Establishments doing a large banquet and function business often have a third list, called the banquet wine list, which includes a selection of the more popular mixed drinks, Champagnes, table wines, apéritif wines, spirits, and beers—in short, whatever experience shows is most frequently ordered at large functions. It is important for this list to contain a notation regarding corkage, which is customarily charged when guests bring their own beverages. In most cities this is $8 to $15 a bottle for Champagne and spirits and $5 to $10 for table wines.

Hotels often use a fourth kind of list, known as the Room Service List, which is an abbreviated list of wines and spirits that can be sent to a guest's room.

OPPOSITE: This wine list is unique for a steak house because of its great variety of California and other wines of the world. The menu is much shorter than the wine list. (*Courtesy Sparks Steak House, New York*)

WINE LIST

California

HOUSE WINES IN BOTTLE
CABERNET SAUVIGNON
100 Beaulieu Vineyards Rutherford 1978 12.95
MERLOT
101 Clos Du Bois 1978 12.95

ESTATE BOTTLED CALIFORNIA VARIETALS

CABERNET SAUVIGNON
102 Robert Mondavi 1978 21.50
103 Simi Special Reserve 1974 34.00
104 Chappellet 1974 Magnum 49.00
105 Rutherford Ranch 1978 19.00
106 Beringer Private Reserve 1978 24.00
107 Sterling Vineyards 1978 19.00
108 Inglenook Cask Bottling 1974 28.00
109 Joseph Phelps 1976 19.50
110 Sterling Vineyards 1976 Reserve 39.00
111 Jordan 1978 24.50
112 Mirassou Harvest Selection 1974 28.00
113 Silver Oaks Cellars 1977 35.00
114 Christian Brothers 1974 19.50
115 Clos Du Val Reserve 1977 29.00
116 Raymond 1978 19.50
117 Château Montelana 1976 26.00
118 Gundlach Bundschu Batto Ranch 1977 21.50
119 Stags Leap Cellars Lot 2 1976 39.00
120 Caymus Vineyards 1978 24.00
121 Franciscan Private Reserve 1975 21.50
122 Clos Du Bois Marlstone 1978 19.50
123 Ridge York Creek 1977 27.00
124 Ridge Montebello 1972 59.00
125 Mount Veeder 1976 23.00
126 Conn Creek Lot I 1978 24.00
127 Villa Mont Eden 1978 24.00
128 Beaulieu Vineyards Latour Reserve 1976 39.00
129 Charles Krug Vintage Selection 1974 29.50
130 Charles Krug Vintage Selection 1965 59.00
131 Burgess Cellars 1978 22.00
132 Shafer 1978 22.50
133 Robert Mondavi Special Reserve 1976 41.00
134 Robert Mondavi 1968 75.00
135 Heitz Cellars 1968 75.00
136 Heitz Cellars Nathan Fay 1975 39.00
137 Beaulieu Vineyards Latour Reserve 1973 39.00

PINOT NOIR
150 Sterling Vineyards 1974 15.50
152 Carneros Creek 1979 23.00
153 Kenwood Jack London 1978 20.50
154 Robert Mondavi 1978 19.50
155 Hoffman Mountain Ranch 1975 25.00
156 Acacia 1979 24.00
158 Rodney D. Strong 1977 18.50

ZINFANDEL
170 Granite Springs 1980 15.00
171 Sutter Home 1975 15.00
172 Rutherford Hill 1976 15.00
173 Burgess Cellars 1973 Magnum 29.50
174 Château Montelena 1978 18.00
175 Hoffman Mountain Ranch 1977 16.00
176 Mirassou Harvest Selection 1977 16.00
177 Carneros Creek 1976 15.50
178 Santino Fiddletown 1978 16.50
179 Preston Vineyards 1978 15.50
180 Ridge York Creek 1979 19.00
181 Montevina 1979 15.00
182 Grgich Hills 1979 19.50
183 Lytton Spring 1979 18.50
184 Clos Du Val 1979 18.50
185 Sonoma River West Old Vines 1977 18.00

PETITE SIRAH
190 Joseph Phelps–Syrah 1975 17.50
191 Concannon 1976 16.50
187 Stags Leap Cellars 1980 19.50
192 Mirassou Harvest Selection 1975 16.00
193 Burgess Cellars 1973 Magnum 30.00

MERLOT
194 Sterling Vineyards 1978 20.50
195 Duckhorn Vineyards 1980 22.50
188 Clos Du Val 1979 21.50
159 Rutherford Hill 1979 19.50
160 St. Francis 1980 19.50
161 Caparone 1980 19.00

GAMAY BEAUJOLAIS
196 Georges Duboeuf & Son 11.00
197 Robert Mondavi 11.00

BARBERA
189 Sebastiani Proprietor's Reserve 1976 14.00

CHARBONO 198 Franciscan 1974 17.00

ALICANTE BOSCHE 199 Angelo Papagni 1973 15.00

CALIFORNIA CHARDONNAY
205 Beaulieu Vineyards Beaufort 1981 17.50
206 Heitz Cellars 1979 24.00
207 Grgich Hills 1980 34.00
208 Dry Creek Vintner's Reserve 1980 25.00
210 Carneros Creek 1977 21.50
211 Robert Mondavi Reserve 1979 29.00
212 Spring Mountain 1980 23.00
213 Alexander Valley 1980 21.00
214 Raymond 1979 21.50
215 Jekel Vineyard 1979 20.50
216 Leeward 1981 20.00
217 Acacia 1981 23.00
218 Villa Mont Eden 1979 26.00
219 Château St. Jean 1980 23.00
220 Château Montelena 1979 29.50
221 Far Niente 1981 25.00
222 Zaca Mesa Special Selection 1980 21.50
223 Beringer Private Reserve 1980 21.50
224 Mark West 1979 21.50
225 Sterling Vineyards 1980 23.00
226 Stonegate Spaulding Vineyard 1979 24.00
227 Burgess Cellars 1979 23.00
228 St. Clement 1980 23.00
229 Château St. Jean Robert Young 1980 33.00
230 Iron Horse 1980 21.50
231 Ventana 1980 23.00
232 (Idaho) Ste. Chapelle Reserve 1980 29.00

CHENIN BLANC
241 Chappellet 14.50
242 Robert Mondavi 14.50

SAUVIGNON BLANC
250 Sterling Vineyards 17.00
251 Newton Vineyards 17.00
268 Joseph Phelps 17.50

FUME BLANC
252 Robert Mondavi Reserve 21.50
253 Château St. Jean 19.00
269 Vichon Cheurier Blanc 17.00

RIESLING
260 Riesling Trefethen 13.95
261 Riesling Callaway 13.95
262 Johannisberg Riesling Jekel 13.95
263 Johannisberg Riesling Gundlach Bundschu 13.95
264 Johannisberg Riesling Château St. Jean 13.95

GEWURZTRAMINER
265 Joseph Phelps 14.95
266 Gundlach Bundschu 14.95
267 Château St. Jean 14.95

DESSERT WINE

LATE HARVEST/RIESLING/GEWURZTRAMINER & OTHERS
M70 Freemark Abbey Johannisberg Riesling Sweet Select Bottle 22.00
M71 Freemark Abbey Edelwein Bottle 29.00
M72 Burgess Cellars Late Harvest Johannisberg Riesling Bottle 24.00
M73 Château St. Jean Late Harvest Johannisberg Riesling Bottle 24.00
M74 Joseph Phelps Late Harvest Johannisberg Riesling Bottle 24.00
M75 Callaway Santana White Riesling Bottle 18.00
M76 Moscato d'Oro Robert Mondavi 14.50
M77 Malvasia Bianca Stony Ridge 14.50
M78 Robert Mondavi Special Selection 24.00

VERY SPECIAL SELECT LATE HARVEST

JOHANNISBERG RIESLING AND GEWURZTRAMINER
M80 Robert Mondavi ½ Bottle 32.00
M81 Château St. Jean Late Harvest Johannisberg Riesling Belle Terre ½ Bottle 35.00
M82 Altera Vineyards ½ Bottle 39.00
M83 Raymond Johannisberg Riesling Late Harvest ½ Bottle 29.00
M84 Joseph Phelps Special Late Harvest Johannisberg Riesling ½ Bottle 26.00

GEWURZTRAMINER
M85 Château St. Jean Late Harvest Belle Terre ½ Bottle 25.00
M86 Joseph Phelps Special Late Harvest ½ Bottle 25.00

CALIFORNIA
Champagne
290 Schramsberg 28.00
291 Korbel Natural 21.50
292 Hanns Kornel Sehr Trocken 21.50
294 Domaine Chandon Blanc de Noir 23.00
295 Domaine Chandon Brut 23.00

Italian

HOUSE WINE IN BOTTLE
400 Melini Vino Mobile Di Montepeuliano 1970 15.00

340 Barbaresco Gaja 1971 39.00
345 Barbaresco Gaja 1961 79.00
300 Barbaresco De Forville 1971 26.00
301 Barolo Borgogno 1971 27.00
302 Barolo Borgogno 1964 42.00
303 Barolo Borgogno 1958 49.00
304 Barolo Borgogno 1955 65.00
305 Barolo Borgogno 1947 110.00
306 Barolo Fontanafredda La Rosa 1971 27.00
350 Barolo Gran Duca Special Reserve 1974 23.00
307 Barolo Fonchetta Ibrunate 1974 24.00
308 Gattinara Nervi 1971 21.50
342 Gattinara Monsecco 1968 32.00
349 Gattinara Monsecco 1958 47.00
309 Ghemme Ponti 1974 14.50
310 Fara Ferrando 1975 14.50
311 Amarone Reciotto della Valpolicella Amarone Classico 22.50
313 Amarone Tommasi 1964 39.00
314 Brunello di Montalcino Estate Bottled 1974 26.00
315 Brunello di Montalcino Fattoria Dei Barbi 1970 59.00
316 Brusco dei Barbi 1974 24.00
317 Grumello 1974 Rainoldi 14.50
318 Sassella 1971 Rainnoldi 14.50
319 Inferno Polatti 1975 14.50
320 Sfursat Late Harvest 1974 Rainoldi 18.00
321 Chianti Ruffino Riserva Ducale Gold Label 1971 26.00
341 Chianti Badia a Coltibuono Riserva 1968 30.00
347 Chianti Ruffino Riserva Ducale Gold Label 1958 41.00
348 Chianti Ruffino Riserva Ducale Gold Label 1955 55.00
344 Chianti Ruffino Riserva Ducale Gold Label 1947 160.00
322 Chianti Villa Antinori Riserva Marchese 1974 21.00
323 Villa Antinori Sassicaia 1976 29.50
325 Chianti Olivieri 1967 Riserva 25.00
326 Chianti Olivieri 1962 25.00
327 Tignanello Antinori 1978 26.00
328 Rubesco Riserva Lungarotti 1974 21.00
329 Carema Riserva 1964 Ferrando 39.00
330 Bricco del Drago 1976 17.50
331 Taurasi Mastroberardino 1968 49.00
346 Frecciarossa Grand Cru 1968 35.00
332 Spanna Traversagna 1967 26.00
334 Spanna Montalbano 1966 26.00
336 Spanna del Piemonte 1968 26.00

ITALIAN WHITE WINE
401 Orvieto Le Vellette 13.75
402 Est Est Est Antinori 13.75
403 Verdicchio Fazi Battaglia 13.75
404 Pinot Grigio Cavit 13.75
405 Frascati Fontana Candida 13.75
406 Corvo della Salaparuta 13.75
407 Bianco di Montagna Polatti 13.75
408 Vernaccia di San Giamignano Ponte A. Rondolino 15.00
409 Bianco del Beato Barbi 14.50
410 Fiano di Avellino Mastroberardino 22.00
411 Greco di Tufo Mastroberardino 18.50
412 Lacryma Christi Mastroberardino 18.50
413 Gavi Principessa 18.50
414 Tocai Friulano Livo Felluga 18.50
415 (Sparkling) Ferrari Brut (Methode Champenoise) 25.00
416 (Sparkling) Contratto Asti Spumante 24.00

Red Wines from Around The World
1014 Chile Marques de Casa Concha 11.50
1015 Argentina Cabernet Sauvignon Toso 11.00
1001 Hungary Egri Bikaver 11.50
1002 Provence France Bandol Dom. Tempier 19.50
1003 Australia Château Clare 14.50
1017 Australia Cabernet Sauvignon Taltarni 15.50
1004 Spain Marques de Riscal 1966 39.00
1005 Spain Vega Sicilia 1966 39.00
1006 Spain Jean Leon Cabernet Sauvignon 1974 16.50
1007 Spain Bilbainas Vina Pomal 1969 19.00
1008 Spain Bilbainas Vendemia Especial 1969 19.00
1009 Spain Cune Reserva 1970 18.50
1010 Spain Cune Reserva 1966 18.50
1011 Spain Olerra Reserva 1970 16.50
1019 Spain Marques de Caceres 1970 16.50
1012 Portugal Periquita 1970 13.50
1013 Portugal Garrafeira 1966 15.50
1018 Lebanon Château Musar 16.50

Champagne
A900 Louis Roederer Cristal Bottle 89.00
A901 Dom Perignon Bottle 89.00 Magnum 179.00
A902 Veuve Clicquot Brut Vintage 44.00
A903 Möet & Chandon White Star 34.00 (½ Bottle 18.00)
A904 Laurent Perrier Grand Siecle 69.00
A905 Perrier Jouet Fleur de Champagne 75.00
A906 A. Charbaut (Rose) Brut 39.00

ITALIAN SPARKLING
415 Ferrari Brut (Methode Champenoise) 25.00
416 Contratto Asti Spumante 24.00

Bordeaux

HOUSE WINE IN BOTTLE
900 St. Julien Château Lagarance 1976 19.00

800 Pauillac Château Lafite Rothschild 1976 79.00
801 Margaux Château Margaux 1976 69.00
802 Pauillac Château Mouton Rothschild 1971 89.00
803 Pauillac Château Latour 1971 89.00
804 Graves Château Haut Brion 1976 69.00
805 St. Emilion Château Chevel Blanc 1971 89.00
806 St. Estèphe Cos d'Estournel 1971 41.00
807 Margaux Château Giscours 1976 28.00
808 Pauillac Château Grand Puy Lacoste 1976 27.00
809 St. Emilion Château Pavie 1971 41.00
810 St. Julien Château Talbot 1970 44.00
811 Margaux Château Dufort Vivens 1970 44.00
812 St. Emilion Château Grand Pontet 1976 24.00
813 Haut-Medoc Château Lagune 1976 30.00
814 Graves Château Bouscaut 1970 44.00
815 Pauillac Château Croizet Bages 1970 45.00
816 Pomerol Château Petrus 1976 85.00
817 Pomerol Château Trotanoy 1976 47.00
818 Margaux Château Brane Cantenac 1970 45.00
819 St. Julien Château Gloria 1970 41.00
820 Pauillac Château Pichon Lalande 1971 44.00
821 Pomerol Château Beauregard 1970 44.00
822 St. Julien Château Ducru Beaucaillou 1976 30.00
823 St. Julien Château Leoville Poyferre 1966 61.00
824 St. Julien Château Gruaud Larose 1961 98.00
825 St. Emilion Château Chevel Blanc 1955 200.00
826 St. Julien Château Talbot 1961 98.00
827 Margaux Château Giscours 1966 69.00
828 Pauillac Château Lynch Bages 1961 105.00
829 St. Julien Château Talbot 1949 115.00
830 Sauternes Château d'Yquem ½ Bottle 1976 45.00
831 Sauternes Château d'Yquem Bottle 1967 175.00
832 Sauternes Château Coutet 1971 42.00

MAGNUMS
A833 St. Estèphe Cos d'Estournel 1971 Magnum 85.00
A834 Pauillac Château Croizet Bages 1970 Magnum 85.00
A835 Graves Château Picque Caillou 1966 Magnum 69.00
A836 St. Julien Château Beychevelle 1971 Magnum 95.00
A837 Margaux Château Giscours 1976 55.00
A838 St. Emilion Château Clos Fourtet 1971 69.00
A839 Pauillac Château Latour 1971 Magnum 190.00
A840 Margaux Château Dufort Vivens 1971 Magnum 79.00
A841 Pauillac Château Lafite Rothschild 1971 Magnum 195.00
A842 St. Julien Château Talbot 1970 Magnum 95.00
A843 Graves Château Haut-Bailly 1971 72.00
A845 St. Julien Château Talbot 1952 Magnum 185.00
A846 St. Julien Château Talbot 1945 Magnum 300.00
A847 Pomerol Château Nenin 1959 Magnum 195.00
A848 Pauillac Château Lafite Rothschild 1966 Magnum 275.00

Burgundy
500 Beaujolais Moulin-A-Vent Louis Latour 1978 17.50
501 Beaujolais Brouilly Château des Tours 1979 17.00
502 Pommard Dom. La Posse D'or 1979 34.00
503 Nutis St. Georges La Boure Roi 1976 33.00
504 Vosne Romanee Clos Frantin 1978 31.00
505 Corton Clos Des Miex 1976 41.00
506 Morey Saint Denis Clos des Ormes 1978 33.00
507 Clos Vougeot Château De La Tour 1976 47.00
508 Chambolle Musigny Faiveley Taste Vine 1971 61.00
509 Clos de Tart Mommessin 1978 47.00
510 Musigny Faiveley 1964 65.00
511 Clos de la Roche Domaine Ponsot 1976 47.00
512 Santenay R. Chapelle 1978 23.00
513 Mercurey Faiveley 1976 28.00
514 Clos De La Roche Faiveley 1971 54.00
515 Romaneè St. Vivant Dom Del La Romaneè Conti 1972 69.00
516 Romaneè Conti Dom Del La Romaneè Conti 1972 145.00

WHITE BURGUNDY
615 Pouilly Fuisse Bouchard 1980 23.00
600 Chablis Grand Cru Valmur J. Moreau 1979 25.00
601 Meursault Charmes Rougeot 1979 37.00
602 Puligny Montrachet Premier Cru Louis Latour 1979 36.00
603 Chassagne Montrachet Jacques Colin 1979 36.00
604 Batard Montrachet . . . . Bottle Presented 59.00
605 Clos Blanc de Vougeot . . . . Bottle Presented 48.00
606 Corton Charlemagne . . . . Bottle Presented 48.00
607 Clos Des Mouches Blanc Joseph Drouhin 1979 56.00
608 Le Montrachet Pierre Morey 1979 120.00
609 Mercury Blanc Clos Rochette Faiveley 1978 22.00
610 Pouilly Fume (Loire) 15.50
619 Lodoucette (Loire) 1979 24.00
611 Hermitage Blanc (Rhone) Jaboulet 25.00
612 White Châteuneuf du Pape (Rhone) 23.00
613 Condrieu (White Rhone) 1979 42.00
616 (Alsace) Clos St. Landelin Riesling (DRY) 1978 15.00
614 (Bordeaux) Château Margaux Blanc 1979 43.00

RHONE WINE
700 Châteauneuf du Pape Beaucastel 21.50
702 Gigondas Paul Jaboulet 1973 21.00
703 Hermitage Paul Jaboulet 1973 23.00
704 Côte Rôtie A. Drevon 1978 23.00

Four Seasons wine policy

One of the first restaurants in New York to respond to the increased demand for a broad spectrum of wines at fair prices was the Four Seasons. It now has at least four hundred wines available, all chosen as very good examples of their class. The list includes a large selection of American wines, as well as those from France, Italy, Spain, Germany, and other countries.

The price of the wine to the dinner guest is determined carefully, with lower-priced wines marked up to three times the restuarant's cost and higher-priced wines marked up two and a half times the cost. This brings the price to about double that in a retail store, which is fair to the consumer and which includes a reasonable amount for the restaurant for service.

The Four Seasons offers Champagne by the glass, which makes it possible to have a glass of Champagne when others are having cocktails. In the less formal Bar Room, at dinner, five or six different red and white wines from France and California are offered by the glass. These wines are served as if the patron had ordered a whole bottle, with the bottle being presented to the guest, and the wine poured at the table.

tasting with the winemaker

Lavin's Restaurant in New York not only offers a wide range of wines by the glass, but also hosts many visiting winemakers. Patrons are introduced to the winemaker when they enter for lunch or dinner, and a glass of the winemaker's wine is poured at no charge. The winemaker circulates during the meal, and talks to the patrons. Any additional glasses of wine are charged for.

Other New York restaurants that are notable for their extensive selections of wines at fair prices are Sparks Steak House, Windows on the World, and, especially for an excellent list of over sixty American white wines, the Oyster Bar in Grand Central Station.

Century Plaza wine and spirits policy

In Los Angeles, the Century Plaza Hotel has innovative policies regarding both wines and spirits. Since its opening in 1966, the room service policy on bottled spirits has been to price them at retail, without the high markups that are often charged. Furthermore, the spirits are delivered to a guest's room with the necessary ice and glasses. Small folded signs in the rooms notify guests of this policy.

The wine list of the Vineyard Restaurant in the Century Plaza Hotel is on computer, along with information for the sommelier and for the director of food and beverage, such as inventory, wholesale prices, and bin numbers. Guests see only the name of the wine, its vintage, and its price. The twelve-page list can be easily kept up to date, since printouts are made twice a week.

Enlightened restaurateurs have learned that a smaller profit per bottle generates greater volume and encourages diners to explore different wines with different dishes.

HOW TO USE THE WINE LIST

Although the wine list is a silent salesman, it cannot perform its selling job unless it receives some assistance from the restaurant's selling staff.

First, the waiter who takes the food order should present the wine list together with the menu.

Second, if the guest or host of a party fails to order a beverage when ordering his meal, he should be asked, "Do you care to order something to drink now?"

Third, to sell you must tell; to tell you must know. It is the duty of the management to have and to impart to the service staff complete information about the wines in stock. This can be done at the regular meetings all well-organized restaurants hold periodically to instruct the staff on house policies and service, deportment, and so forth. This is important, as we have never known anyone who could sell a product successfully without knowing anything about it.

As most waiters depend on tips for a considerable portion of their income, it should not be difficult to point out to them that they will make more money (through larger tips) when they sell a bottle of wine or some other alcoholic beverage to a guest.

The restaurant has everything to gain and nothing to lose by its wine sales. Wine sales are plus sales because they are often made at a time when the guest would normally not drink any other alcoholic beverage, and they are sold at no additional overhead to the restaurant.

While there are no set rules about what drinks should be served with specific dishes, there are some traditional customs that are observed because they are practical.

We do not agree with the theory that cocktails should not be served before a dinner at which wine is to be served. If a cocktail whets the appetite, then one should drink it. However, too many drinks on an empty stomach take away the desire for food instead of stimulating it, because the alcohol supplies food value and the system may be satisfied before the meal is begun.

28
BEVERAGE
SERVICE

1. GLASSWARE

The first wineglass is said to have been made from a bubble of seafoam cut in half by Aphrodite as she came forth from the sea—a pretty myth and one that has a point: the wineglass should be crystal clear.

Undoubtedly, the first cup man used was his hand. As he became more civilized and acquired tools with which to fashion implements, he made himself a drinking vessel. The earliest one was fashioned from a dried gourd. Later on he experimented with wood, shells, and metals, and finally, when he learned how to work with glass, he made the first of our present-day containers. The origin of glass is credited both to the early Assyrians and to the Egyptians. The examples of early glass drinking cups that survive today are misshapen and not very transparent, but even so they were useful and a great improvement on other containers of potables.

As time went on and the art of glassblowing was improved, much beauty and perfection of line were blown into wine bottles and goblets. Later the art of glass cutting further enhanced the elegance and beauty of the container.

The most famous glassmakers were the Venetians and Bohemians. They had a secret for coloring their glass that no one else possessed, and up to the end of the last century colored glasses for wine were still the fashion. There was a definite reason for color in wineglasses. More often than not the wine was not perfectly clear. It had sediment in it and was dull and uninteresting to look at. Today wines are perfectly brilliant when shipped, and advances in technology and sanitation ensure their clarity—therefore colored wineglasses are no longer necessary.

The enjoyment of beverages, and wine in particular, calls for using three senses: sight, smell, and taste. Before we smell or taste a wine, we see it. There is pleasure in the bright red of a claret, the deep ruby of a Burgundy, and the mellow, golden hue of a Sauternes, to say nothing of the dancing brightness of Champagne. The sight of wine shimmering in a transparent, delicately stemmed glass increases the pleasure of anticipation. A colored glass deprives us of this pleasure.

GLASSWARE FOR THE HOME

The glassware needed for a well-appointed house and that required for a hotel are two different requirements. For the home it is unnecessary to have many different shapes and sizes. Many beverages may be served in the same size glass.

A complete set of glassware for a household that entertains up to twelve guests at a dinner should include:

> 12 old-fashioned or on-the-rocks glasses (8 ounces)
> 12 cocktail glasses (4 or 4½ ounces)
> 12 highball glasses (10 ounces)
> 12 Champagne tulip glasses (8 ounces)
> 12 all-purpose wineglasses (9 ounces)
> 12 sherry or dessert wineglasses (6 ounces)
> 12 brandy snifters marked at 2 ounces

In their desire to be of service, the glassware people have done much to frighten the American public away from wine by advocating the use of a different glass for every type of wine. The number of types of glasses necessary and some difference of opinion as to what type of glass should be used with certain wines have prevented many people from serving wine at all.

The ideal, all-purpose wineglass (one that is quite proper for red and white table wines and all sparkling wines) should:

the ideal wineglass

1. Be beautiful to look at, with simple, graceful lines

2. Be generous—9 ounces—so you can pour enough wine (4 ounces) for a satisfying drink and still have room in the glass to swirl the wine around and get the full benefit of its aroma

Wineglasses. LEFT: Oversize 23-ounce capacity. RIGHT: All-purpose 9-ounce capacity. Both contain 4 ounces of wine. (*Photo by Andrew B. Wile*)

3. Have a mouth that is slightly smaller than the widest part of the bowl so that the wine's bouquet is concentrated for maximum enjoyment, but wide enough so that the upper edge does not strike the nose when the glass is tilted for drinking

HOTEL SERVICE

In a hotel or restaurant the problem of glass service is entirely different. Tradition and showmanship enter the picture and the requirements are stricter and more numerous.

A fine hotel or restaurant must have conventional glassware for both its bar service and its wine service.

The bar must have available the following assortment with sizes and quantities determined by the needs of the operation:

Shot glass ($\frac{3}{4}$ to 2 ounces, lined)
Delmonico (5 ounces)
Old-fashioned or on-the-rocks (8 to 12 ounces)
Highball (8 to 10 ounces)
Tom Collins (12 ounces)
Cocktail (4 to $4\frac{1}{2}$ ounces, with a 3- or $3\frac{1}{2}$-ounce line)
Whisky sour (3 to 6 ounces)
Champagne cocktail (5 ounces)
Port (3 to 4 ounces)
Sherry (3 to 4 ounces)
Liqueur (3 ounces, with a 1-ounce line)
Pony brandy (2 ounces, with a 1-ounce line)
Brandy snifter (6 to 12 ounces, with a 2-ounce line)
Beer (8 to 12 ounces)
Punch bowl
Wine cooler

A hotel dining room or restaurant must have available the following assortment of glassware:

Water goblet
Rhine wine, tall, stemmed, squat-bowled (6 ounces)
Graves, Sauternes, white Burgundy (6 ounces)
Tulip Champagne goblet (8 ounces)
Claret, red Burgundy, and red Rhône (9 ounces)
Sherry (4 ounces)
Port (4 ounces)

While in a private home the all-purpose wineglass may serve nicely, a hotel or restaurant that serves formal dinners or banquets must serve each wine in its traditional glass. A wine will not taste better in it, but, just as dinner clothes invest a formal gathering with a dignity that is lacking when informal dress is the rule, so the proper glassware for each wine lends dignity and elegance to the affair. Some restaurants go the extreme in showmanship by using giant-size glasses containing up to twenty-four ounces. These glasses are often used as water goblets as well as for wine. Although oversized glasses are popular in many distinctive restaurants, some people consider them awkward and out of place in a formal setting.

Notwithstanding the foregoing, even in large luxury hotels the trend is to simplify, wherever possible, the service equipment, including glassware. Many new establishments have reduced wine glassware to three sizes: a six-ounce wine glass for serving rosé and white table wines; a round bowl glass with a capacity of nine to twelve ounces for serving red wines; and tulips or flutes for Champagne or sparkling wine.

Depending on the amount of space on the table, glasses may be placed in a line or grouped into triangles or diamonds. If they are placed in a line, the first glass to be used goes to the far right. The rest of the glasses will go on a diagonal toward the left and center of the table. *placement of glasses*

To save space when several glasses are required, create a triangle or diamond by placing the first glass to the right of the knife. The second glass should be to the left of the first and slightly toward the center of the table, above the knife. The third should be centered above the first two, forming a triangle. If a fourth glass is used, it goes above the second glass, but slightly to the left, forming a diamond. This pattern can be followed for as many glasses as are necessary. The water goblet should always be at the extreme left.

If several wines are served, each glass is removed when the course with which it is served is finished. After-dinner liqueurs, when offered with coffee, may be served from a cart or buffet that holds suitable glasses.

2. HOW TO SERVE WINE

What beverages are served chilled? All white wines, all sparkling wines, all rosé wines, some red wines, all beers, all cocktails, most mixed drinks, certain spirits that are consumed as apéritifs such as vodka and Aquavit, all apéritif wines, very dry sherry, very dry Madeira, and *eaux-de-vie* (clear, unaged fruit brandies). *temperature*

The following generally are served at room temperature: most red wines, medium and rich sherries, Madeira, port, Marsala, and all spirits when taken neat, such as whisky, gin, rum, brandy, and liqueurs. Exceptions are vodka and Aquavit. Exceptions make the rule, and even a liqueur, with all its sweetness, can be very pleasant in the summer if it is chilled. In fact, a liqueur such as crème de menthe is much more enjoyable if it is served over crushed ice.

LEFT TO RIGHT: 1. Saucer, 5 ounces, which is ideal for serving ice cream or fruit cups but not Champagne or sparkling wine. Its flat shallowness exposes too great a surface of wine, allowing the bubbles to escape too rapidly. 2. All-purpose 9-ounce wineglass for red table wines and all sparkling wines. 3. Tulip Champagne glass, 8 ounces, developed by the Champagne producers of France. 4. and 5. Two Champagne flute glasses. 6. Sherry glass, 2 ounces, which is popular but inadequate. The normal portion of sherry is 2 ounces, which means this glass must be filled to the brim. 7. The ideal 4½-ounce glass for sherry, port, or Madeira. The 2-ounce portion can be served cleanly in this glass. 8. Wine carafe, 20 ounces. (*Photo by Al Levine*)

LEFT TO RIGHT: 1. Wineglass, 4 ounces, is inadequate and should not be used. 2. and 3. All-purpose wineglasses, 6½ and 8½ ounces, which are recommended. 4. Excellent 9-ounce glass for red wine and Champagne. 5. The Grossman all-purpose 8-ounce lead crystal glass without the 4-ounce fill line. 6. Baccarat 10-ounce thin lead crystal wineglass suitable for home use but too fragile for restaurant service. 7. Traditional 7-ounce Roemer wineglass for serving German wines. 8. and 9. Dramatic lead crystal glasses for serving white wine and red wine, respectively. (*Photo by Al Levine*)

LEFT TO RIGHT: 1. Shot glass. The etched line marks the $\frac{5}{8}$-ounce fill. It is a dishonest glass, properly called a cheater in Canada. 2. Special shot glass approved by the Liquor License Board of Ontario that must be used by all Ontario licensees. The etched lines mark the 1-, $1\frac{1}{4}$-, and $1\frac{1}{2}$-ounce fill. 3. Pony brandy or liqueur glass, 1 ounce. The normal 1-ounce portion cannot be served in this glass without spilling. 4. and 5. The 2-ounce brandy glass with an etched line marking the 1-ounce fill and the 3-ounce snifter are much more practical for both brandy and liqueurs. 6. The large, dramatic, 20-ounce crystal snifter is sometimes used for Cognac and other fine brandies. 7. Traditional 10-ounce Pilsner beer glass. 8. Elegant 16-ounce footed beer shell. 9. Absinthe drip glass. 10. Porcelain singing saké bottle and whistling saké cup from Japan. (*Photo by Al Levine*)

LEFT TO RIGHT: 1. Cocktail glass, $2\frac{1}{2}$ ounces, is inadequate and should not be used. 2. Ideal $4\frac{1}{2}$-ounce cocktail glass has an etched line showing the proper 3-ounce fill. 3. Cocktail glass, 6 ounces, filled to within $\frac{1}{4}$ inch of the brim holds $4\frac{1}{2}$ ounces. 4. Waterford Irish crystal glass for serving Irish Coffee. 5. Sour glass, 6 ounces. 6. Highball glass, 8 ounces. 7. Collins glass, 12 ounces. 8. Delmonico glass, 5 ounces, better known today as a juice glass and rarely used in bars. 9. Old-fashioned or on-the-rocks glass, 6 ounces. 10. Footed old-fashioned glass, 7 ounces. (*Photo by Al Levine*)

How cold should wine be when it is served? It depends, in the last analysis, on the individual taste of the host in each case. The general rules are that sweeter wines should be served colder than dry and that no wine should be chilled below 42 degrees Fahrenheit (45 degrees is cold enough).

What does room temperature mean? In reality, not quite what it says. The room temperature criterion was established in Europe long before central heating was known. Even today rooms abroad are never heated as warmly as is customary in the United States, where 70 to 72 degrees Fahrenheit is usual. Room temperature for wine is 65 to 68 degrees Fahrenheit, which is the temperature at which red wines are most enjoyable. However, if you enjoy your red table wines either tepid (80 degrees) or very cold (45 degrees), by all means drink them that way, since it is your palate that must be pleased.

If the wine has been stored in a cellar where the temperature is lower, the wine may be brought to room temperature by standing the bottle for a few hours in the room where it is to be served. WARNING: Under no circumstances should the wine be warmed artificially, either by plunging the bottle in hot water or by placing it on or near a heater. This will harm the wine. It is better to drink a red wine too cool than to spoil it by heating it.

chilling the wine   There are two ways to chill wine for dining room service. One is to put still white and sparkling wines in the refrigerator. A wine will be properly chilled after two to three hours. In some restaurants, and for luncheon service in almost any restaurant, this is the only kind of chilling used. The other way is to serve the wine in the conventional table cooler or ice bucket, but this is not always used. Sparkling wines are nearly always served in coolers, however.

Dining rooms that use coolers usually have them available at the service bar together with stands or trays. Place a little shaved ice in the bottom of the cooler, then insert the bottle and add ice and water to fill the cooler. Water is added so the bottle can be reinserted in the cooler between servings. Also, water and ice together chill the bottle faster than ice alone. A wine will be properly chilled after twenty minutes in the cooler.

It is important to bring the wine to the table immediately after it is ordered. The cooler may be placed on the table if a stand is not available. When the bottle is removed from the cooler it should be wiped dry before the wine is poured.

An attentive waiter refills patrons' wineglasses promptly and spares the host the inconvenience of pouring the wine himself. But the cooler should be placed conveniently at the host's right so he may refill glasses in the waiter's absence. When the waiter empties the bottle, he should remove it and the cooler from the table. Turning the bottle upside down in the cooler is also practiced, although many guests (and wine stewards) feel that it is an impolite suggestion that it is time the host ordered another bottle of wine.

OPENING A BOTTLE OF WINE

After presenting the bottle, cut the capsule (the foil or plastic covering over the cork) to just below the bulge that is found on all wine bottles. Cut all the way around, pressing the knife firmly against the glass, and remove the capsule. Since the metal capsule is often corroded or moldy, the wine would taste tainted if it came in contact with the metal.

With a clean napkin wipe off any mold, debris, or seeped wine sometimes found between the cork and the capsule, since it is impossible to serve wine without pouring over the lip of the bottle, and possibly picking up an off-taste.

Insert the point of the corkscrew (we recommend the single-lever type°) slightly off center, so that the worm will go down into the center of the cork. Turn the corkscrew until all of the worm has entered the cork, hook the lever onto the rim of the bottle, and raise the body of the corkscrew until the cork emerges. For very long corks you may need to ease out the final length of cork with a rocking motion. Do not jerk it out nervously, as that will shake up the wine.

If you use the T corkscrew, turn it into the cork, then grasp the bottle firmly with the left hand; hold the bottle so that the shoulder rests in the palm of your hand. Grasp the corkscrew with your right hand, hold the bottle between your knees, and pull slowly and evenly. Pull straight out. Do not rock or twist the cork while withdrawing it.

When the cork is out, smell it to see whether it is sound. Then wipe the mouth of the bottle both inside and out with the napkin. You are ready to serve.

° There are many types of corkscrews or cork pullers available, several of which are illustrated on page 432, but only a few are really practical. The object is to extract the cork from the bottle in one piece and as easily as possible so as not to disturb the wine. Ideally, the screw, or worm, should be 2 to $2\frac{1}{4}$ inches long. The metal should be rounded, and the point should be a continuation of the spiral. Avoid a worm with a flattened, sharp cutting edge. Avoid any corkscrew that has the appearance of an auger. The single-lever type is the most practical cork puller for a waiter to use in a restaurant because it closes into a compact, flat instrument he can carry in his pocket. It is also practical for home use.

One of the best cork pullers we have found for older bottles is the wooden corkscrew with a counter screw. It functions easily and requires a minimum of effort to remove the cork, thus not disturbing any sediment. The screwpull is also excellent, as it has a 5-inch long, antifriction-coated worm, which is centered on the cork by an outer frame.

The two-pronged cork extractor works by inserting the prongs on either side of the cork, between the cork and the neck of the bottle, and rocking them all the way down the side of the cork. The handle is then twisted and the cork comes out, held between the two prongs. This method does not pierce the cork.

Serving a bottle of wine.
1. Present the bottle to the guest. The towel, if used, should not cover the label.

2. Cut the capsule below the bulge in the neck of the bottle and remove upper portion of capsule.

3. An older bottle of wine may have some mold on top of the cork.

4. If this is the case, *before* the cork is pulled, clean the top of the cork and the rim of the bottle with a towel.

5. Insert worm of corkscrew slightly off center and twist.

6. Hook lever onto rim of bottle.

(*Photos of Kevin Zraly, Wine Director for Inhilco, at Windows on the World, by Andrew B. Wile*)

7. Lift up until cork emerges.

8. Sniff the cork to see whether it is sound.

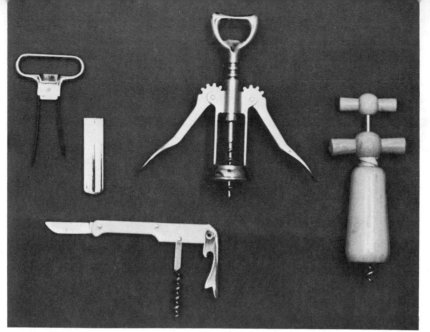

Cork pullers. CLOCKWISE FROM LEFT: 1. Two-tined extractor and case. 2. Metal wing type. 3. Wooden corkpuller with counterscrew. 4. Waiter's lever type with knife. (*Photo by Andrew B. Wile*)

Screwpull has long, smooth, coated worm. (*Courtesy Hallen Co.*)

OPENING A BOTTLE OF CHAMPAGNE OR SPARKLING WINE

If the bottle is presented in a cooler filled with fine ice or ice cubes and water, it should be stood upright. Holding a napkin in your hand, grasp the bottle by its neck and remove the bottle from the cooler. Wipe it dry and present it to the guest. It is incorrect to wrap the bottle in the napkin.

Locate and untwist the wire loop under the foil on the neck of the bottle. Loosen the wire cage, which will tear the foil or metal capsule covering the cork. Remove both together. (Some people prefer to remove the foil first.) Put your thumb over the cork immediately to prevent it from flying out. The pressure in a bottle of Champagne or sparkling wine is four to six atmospheres, or sixty to ninety pounds per square inch.

Holding the napkin in your hand, grasp the cork and tilt the bottle to a forty-five-degree angle away from your face. Twist the bottle and gently ease out the cork. After the cork is out, keep the bottle at an angle for about five seconds to let excess gas escape. If you return the bottle to its upright position too quickly, the gas will rush out and carry a good part of the wine with it.

Once the bottle is open, wipe the rim of the bottle with the napkin. Champagne and sparkling wines should be served in two motions. Pour wine until the froth almost reaches the brim of the glass. Stop. Wait a moment until this foaming froth subsides, then continue pouring to fill the glass one-third to one-half full. Be careful not to pour too rapidly or the wine will froth over.

SERVING WINE

In the Middle Ages a popular way of poisoning one's enemies was to ask them to dine and sometime during the festivities serve a goblet of poisoned wine. A guest had to be wary in those days.

Gradually the custom arose for the host to taste the wine before his guests to allay their fears. Today, too, the host samples the wine before his guests are served, but this practice now has a far more reasonable basis. It is the means of assuring the host that his wine is in perfect condition. At a dinner for twelve or more, the host and the sommelier or captain sample the wines beforehand. Wines are not presented for approval.

When serving at home, when there are no servants, the host should serve himself and then his guests. First he should fill his own glass about one-fourth full and satisfy himself on the quality of the wine. Then, around the table, counterclockwise, he should pour wine for everyone in turn. After everyone has been served, he should serve himself. The wineglass should not be more than one-third to one-half full.

When the wine is poured, the bottle should be held so that the label is always uppermost and can readily be seen. The bottle should be brought to the glass on the table—the glass should not be lifted to the bottle. When the glass is one-half full, the bottle should be twisted to distribute the last drop on the bottle's rim, preventing it from dripping. The wine should be served from the right side of the guest, as the glass is set at the right of the plate.

It is not necessary to drape either red or white wine in such a manner as to hide the label unless one is ashamed of the wine he is serving. However, a bottle that is in an ice bucket should be carefully wiped dry each time it is withdrawn to prevent drops of ice water from trickling down. It is a good idea to hold a napkin in your hand and place your hand under the bottle while pouring.

The open wine bottle may be kept at the right of the host. When there are servants, the bottle is usually placed on the sideboard until it is needed. Wines that are chilled should be kept at the right of the host in a cooler or, if there are servants, in a cooler on the sideboard. At every course the wine should be served before the food.

Red wine is a perfect companion to dark-meated fowl and all kinds of red meat however prepared and is excellent with cheese. As previously noted, it is generally served at room temperature. If brought directly from the wine cellar, it should be served at that temperature—*never warmed*. Some lighter-bodied red wines may be preferred when slightly chilled, particularly in summer.

Red wine often throws a sediment as it grows older. This is natural and shows that the wine is maturing in the bottle. For this reason, red wine should be handled carefully and gently. In fact, the Burgundy basket was created in

serving red wines

Serving a bottle of Champagne.
1. Bottle should be placed in cooler packed with ice and with a towel handy.

2. Present the bottle, wiping it off with the towel.

3. Locate and untwist the wire loop on cage.

4. Loosen and remove the wire cage.

5. Holding a towel, grasp the neck of the bottle and tilt it to a forty-five-degree angle.

6. Twist the bottle and ease the cork out.

7. Wipe the rim of the bottle.

8. Pour Champagne gently so as not to drive out too much gas.

Burgundy for the sole purpose of removing the bottle from the cellar bin in the horizontal position in which it lies, so that the sediment in the bottle is not disturbed. If the bottle in the basket is carried under the arm and stirred up, the object of the basket is wasted. Its sole purpose is to leave the wine undisturbed. Baskets should not be used for wines that do not have any sediment.

When red wine is presented to a restaurant guest for his approval before opening, care should be taken not to disturb any sediment present. When using a Burgundy basket the bottle should be left in the basket while presenting, opening, and serving the wine.

Very old red wines should be decanted to draw off the clear wine and leave any sediment there might be in the bottle. It is not necessary to decant white wines, as any light tartrates that might precipitate are odorless and tasteless. Avoid using a filter in decanting wine, since it takes out some of the taste and body.

In decanting, the decanter must be perfectly clean and dry. Remove the capsule on the wine bottle completely, draw the cork, then place a candle or a strong light behind the bottle neck for visibility while pouring gently and steadily. At the moment you see any sediment coming over, stop pouring.

Aeration is the second good reason for decanting. However, if a decanter is not available, a clean empty wine bottle will do. Decanting is particularly advisable if the wine is young or from an off year. Contact with the air expands the bouquet and enhances the enjoyment of the wine by permitting any undesirable volatile aromas to dissipate.

serving white and rosé wines in restaurants

As previously stated, white and rosé wines should be served chilled. Traditionally, they are served with white meats—fowl, fish, and seafood—but tradition does not rule out the possibility that white wine may be drunk with red meat or red wine with fowl. When a guest orders a particular type and brand of wine, he should be served the wine he orders with no comment by the waiter.

When a guest asks for white or rosé wine, the waiter—or sommelier (wine steward)—should obtain the bottle from storage, set it in an ice cooler filled with ice and water, cover it with a clean, folded napkin, and bring this service into the dining room. The ice bucket, placed on a stand, is set to the right of

Burgundy basket, for red wines with sediment only. (*Photo by Al Levine*)

the person who ordered the wine. The waiter or sommelier then takes the bottle out of the bucket and presents it to the guest with the label uppermost. The host thus has an opportunity to verify that his order has been filled correctly.

This bottle presentation is an important part of wine service and should not be overlooked. If the waiter has misunderstood the guest and brought the wrong wine—to which the guest will later object—the waiter can easily exchange this bottle for one the guest prefers. Had the waiter ignored this presentation ritual and opened the bottle without showing it to the guest for his approval, the bottle would have to be returned to storage and may become a loss. Furthermore, this bottle-presentation ceremony shows courtesy to the guest, regardless of his knowledge about wines, and adds to the atmosphere of the dining room.

Once the bottle is opened and the mouth cleaned, the waiter should pour about one ounce into the glass of the host (or whoever ordered the wine) so he or she can approve the wine. A towel should be held in the left hand when serving wine and used to wipe the bottle, particularly when it is taken out of the ice bucket. The bottle should not be wrapped in a towel since the guests may wish to see the label of the wine they are drinking.

When the host has approved the wine, it should be poured for the woman first, if a couple is being served. If a group is being served, then the person sitting to the host's right is served first. The waiter then proceeds around the table counterclockwise, filling the host's glass last. For white wine, the glasses should not be filled more than one-half full. This gives the guests an opportunity to savor the wine's aroma before sipping it.

When everyone has been served, the white wine bottle should be replaced in the ice bucket. Waiters should always see that every guest's glass is replenished. It often produces the sale of an extra bottle of wine.

A second bottle of a wine that has already been served should be checked as carefully as the first to make sure that it is sound, and tastes the same as the first bottle. Only then may the waiter pour it into glasses that have some of the first wine left in them, without fear of any possible contamination.

Appetizer and dessert wines are served in the manner of cocktails and other mixed drinks. It should be remembered that with wines—and cocktails and spirits too—no glass should ever be filled to the brim. It is impossible to carry it on a tray without spilling, and the result is sloppy service.

serving appetizer and dessert wines

An increasingly popular way of serving sherry, other appetizer wines, and cocktails is over ice cubes in an old-fashioned glass.

When serving sherry or any product ordered by brand name, it is our opinion that the bottle should be brought to the table. It is not always practical, but wherever it is possible it makes a better impression, and there is no question that the customer is getting what he ordered.

29
BAR OPERATION

Bar profits depend on the economical and practical operation of the bar. In most instances a bar represents a substantial investment in plant, furniture, and decoration. This investment must be protected by maintaining a standard of service and quality of beverages on a par with the decor and the investment.

wine bars   The recent American interest in tasting many different wines, combined with innovations in wine packaging, storage, and wine service, have led to the popularity of wine bars. Additionally, since many have a glass of wine as a substitute for a cocktail, eventually the desire to know just what wine was being poured and, if possible, to have a selection from which to choose, became important.

Wine bars with simple food menus have been responding to this interest. Instead of just being restaurants with extensive wine lists, a selection of wines are offered by the glass each day. In this way, the patron gets to taste or compare many different wines, without having to order a whole bottle.

The advantages to the customer are numerous: if he or she is considering buying the wine for a home cellar, it may be tasted with little risk to the budget. If a group of people are dining together, it is not necessary for all to agree on the wine. Each may have what he or she wants. It is also possible to have a glass of white wine with the first course, and then change to a glass of rosé or red for the main course. Dessert wines may also be available by the glass.

In addition, some wine bars even offer half portions, or tasting portions, so that a person doesn't even have to risk the price of a whole glass before deciding on what wine to have. It is possible to have tasting portions of several wines.

In the past, many restaurateurs have hesitated to open expensive or rare bottles, because of the possibility of the wine's oxidizing before being used up. New equipment, however, that uses nitrogen to blanket the wine in the bottle, thus keeping oxygen away from the wine, has enabled wine bar owners to

The 14-bottle Cruvinet (largest capacity at present) keeps open bottles of wine in perfect condition for service by the glass. At this resort, the selection of wines changes monthly. (*Courtesy The Colony Beach & Tennis Resort, Sarasota, Florida*)

serve a wider variety of costly wines. The Cruvinet, from France, is the most famous and expensive nitrogen system, but many wine bars have improvised their own. Blind taste-tests confirm that the nitrogen does not affect the taste of the wine, and does keep it stable.

Since the wines are poured at the bar and served in wine glasses, it is important for the owner to instruct the staff not to mix up the glasses when bringing them to the table.

Restaurants that do a large business in one single wine can also make use of nitrogen technology. At La Colline, in Washington, D.C., for example, the house wine is purchased in 3-liter containers, and put in 5-gallon stainless steel transfer tanks with sealed lines. Nitrogen replaces the wine as it is pumped to the bar. White wines remain fresh, and red wines, which sell less than whites, do not oxidize, and the tank does not have to be continually topped off.

types of spirits bars

There are two basic types of spirits bars: the front, or stand-up, bar, where drinks are made in front of the patrons; and the service bar never seen by the patrons, from which drinks are dispensed. A service bar is sometimes called a back bar. The space behind a front bar is also sometimes called a back bar, although we prefer to call it the back-of-the-bar space.

The working arrangement of a bar is of the utmost importance. This matter is too often overlooked when the installation plans are made, and nine times out of ten the people who work behind the bar are not consulted. The space between the front and the back of the bar should be wide enough so that two bartenders can pass each other without jostling. The front section should not be too low, but so arranged that the bartender can reach ice, mixing glass, and bottles with ease.

front bar

In laying out a bar, try to keep the working stations well off the floor. Plumbing repairs will have to be made, and if there is plenty of working space the repairs will be completed in less time and at much less expense. More importantly, people will have to work in the fairly cramped space between the front and the back of the bar. In practically every new large bar layout we have observed over the years the bartender's comfort has been forgotten. The fact that a man must be on his feet for eight hours or longer is not taken into account. Wooden or plastic racks or cushioned rubber on the floor makes the difference between a smiling, efficient bartender and one who is tired and grouchy after a couple of hours of standing on a cold cement floor.

Floor racks can be built using clear pine laths three inches wide by one inch thick by three feet long; allow a one-inch separation between laths and hold the rack together by crosspieces of the same laths. This produces racks with a two-inch clearance off the floor. If the racks are longer than three feet, they become too heavy to lift for cleaning the floor.

If the bar is oval or some other shape whereby the customers standing on one side can see the working stations on the other, a cover should be hung in front of the stations to conceal the pipes and other equipment. Under the same circumstances, special thought must be given to the floor covering.

The working space between the front and the back of the bar should be at least thirty inches, and thirty-six inches is ideal. Doors of refrigerators set into the back-of-the-bar space should not be so wide that they block traffic when opened.

The back-of-the-bar space should also have storage cabinets and shelves to hold bottles.

Do not have a lighting system that consists of electric bulbs under glass shelves on which bottles are placed. The heat generated by the lights will be detrimental to the liquid contents.

service bar

For service bars out of public sight, there need be no back work space. This space will be occupied by large refrigerators, while the bottles that ordinarily would be on the back of the bar are placed on overhead shelves above the counter.

The working space between the service bar and the back wall line must be at least ten feet, particularly if the bar services banquets. This provides the extra space needed for stacking cases of wines, liquors, and waters when they are to be served in quantities exceeding the capacity of the regular storage space.

A service bar should have one entrance and one exit. Some establishments prefer a turnstile at the entrance. If there is none, the rule must be enforced that once a waiter reaches the bar there can be no turning around and going out the way he came in. The waiter should exit past the service-bar manager.

THE BARTENDER'S JOB

the bartender

Beverage dispensing should be done quietly and with dignity, creating an atmosphere of refinement and good taste. The job of the bartender is no different from that of any other retail salesman except that, because of the character of the goods he is selling, extra care should be taken to please customers and look after their welfare.

The bartender's day really starts the night before, for without sufficient rest he cannot do his best work on the job.

The bartender is often in close contact with the guest, and it is therefore imperative that he practice scrupulous personal hygiene.

Uniform coats or vests, as appropriate for the operation, should be provided by the employer, but it is the responsibility of the bartender to provide a white shirt, black tie, and dark trousers, or a white blouse and dark skirt for women. The full uniform must always be kept clean and pressed. Colored shirts should never be worn unless they are part of a uniform. Jewelry should be limited. Aprons are not considered in good form today, unless they are part of a specific uniform.

Care of the feet is important for the bartender. He cannot show the customer a happy face if his feet are tired and aching. It is a good idea to have two pairs of comfortable shoes and change once or twice during the day. Shoes with built-in arches are available and help prevent fatigue. Rubber heels also relieve the strain.

When not busy, the bartender should not slouch or stand around with his hands in his pockets. The bartender should refrain from smoking while on duty. Customers as a rule do not like smoking behind the bar, and smoking while handling food or drink is extremely unsanitary. The same is true of drinking—do *not* drink while on duty. Many times the bartender is asked to take a drink with a customer, but he should pass it up.

the bar   The first duty of the day, of course, is to report for work on time, whether the bartender is to open the bar or to relieve someone else. The bar should be inspected to see that it is spotlessly clean, that the floor, walls, windows, and furniture for table service are in perfect condition, that the room temperature is right, and that there are no offensive odors.

At the bar the woodwork should be polished, the back of the bar dusted, and bottles and glasses neatly arranged. The mirrors should be clean and shining. Liquor bottles should be wiped off with a damp cloth each morning. The work area sinks and drain board and the storage cabinets under the bar should be clean and ready for use.

Supplies of wines and liquors should be carefully checked so that the stock is up to par for the day. Any orders should be sent to the storeroom and followed up to make sure all supplies are on hand before the first customer arrives. Ice boxes should be filled with ice. Bottles of liquor should be in the speed racks or in their proper places on the shelves. Then the working equipment and the draft beer system should be checked.

There should be a supply of clean towels, which are properly kept behind the bar, not stuck into the belt or over the shoulder of the bartender.

garnishes   Next, the fruit and other garnishes should be prepared. These include oranges, lemons, limes, pineapples, olives, cherries, cocktail onions, and any special items that are ordered frequently or that are unique to the operation.

This should be done just before opening time so that the garnishes will be as fresh as possible. If the bar opens an hour or two before lunch, it is well to prepare only the fruits for which there will be a call during the luncheon hour. During the afternoon lull there is time to prepare such additional fruits as might be necessary for the cocktail hour and the evening.

Oranges should be of uniform size—about 216 to the crate is a good size—and either California or Florida fruit may be used. Floridas have more juice, but Californias have a better color, which is better for slices and peel. Cut orange slices in half from top to bottom, about one-fourth inch thick, and discard the end pieces. Slices should be kept together as much as possible until used, to preserve their freshness. The main supply should be covered with a moist napkin and kept, if possible, in a refrigerator.

Lemon slices should also be about a quarter-inch thick. Begin by cutting the lemon in half in the middle as for juicing. Then slice each half, throwing the ends away.

Limes should be cut in wedges large enough to grasp and squeeze the juice into the drink. A forty-eight-to-fifty-four count lime (forty-eight to fifty-four

to the crate) should yield eight wedges. Begin by cutting each lime in half as for juicing. Place the flat side on the cutting board and cut into four equal wedges. Keep the finest fruits for slicing and peeling, reserving the less perfect fruit for squeezing.

Where twists of lemon or orange peel are called for, start at one end of the whole fruit and cut a strip about three-quarters of an inch wide, skin deep, the length of the fruit to the other end. If a long spiral piece of lemon or orange peel is called for, start at one end and cut a strip about three-quarters of an inch wide spirally, as when peeling an apple, until the other end is reached.

Fresh pineapple should be used for punches and special drinks. The best method of preparing this fruit is to cut it into strips about three inches long.

Olives and cherries should be placed in handy containers so they may be reached easily. Only small pitted green olives, especially prepared for cocktails, should be used, never stuffed olives. Maraschino cherries especially prepared for cocktail use, pitted but with the stems left on, are the best. No broken fruit should be used.

Never use anything but tongs or picks when serving ice or fruit. It is unsanitary and undignified to use the fingers.

the juices   Juices needed for most situations are lemon, orange, pineapple, tomato, and sometimes grapefruit. Freshly squeezed orange and lemon juices yield superior cocktails, but because of cost and/or convenience, frozen orange concentrate and frozen or bottled lemon juice are widely used.

Lemon juice mixes can be purchased presweetened with sugar or artificial sweetener. The artificially sweetened ones often leave a bitter aftertaste, so it is best to sample them in a cocktail before purchasing them in any significant quantity.

Tomato, pineapple, and grapefruit juices are usually purchased canned. It is best to transfer the liquid to a pitcher or bottle if it is to be kept opened for any length of time without being used. See Chapter 26 for guidelines to mixing cocktails.

the drink   The appearance of a drink should have great eye appeal, since eye appeal is a factor in your guests' enjoyment as well as in merchandising. The professional touch is given when a drink is well garnished with fruit. The glass should be filled to within one-eighth to one-fourth inch of the brim. Filling the glass to the brim or allowing it to overflow is sloppy.

Finally, the dishes on the bar should be filled with whatever appetizers the rules of the house call for—pretzels, cheese crackers, cheese, nuts, and so forth. One of the functions of these salty foods is to stimulate the guests to further beverage consumption and they should be placed within reach without guests' having to ask for them.

SOME RULES FOR THE BARTENDER

1. Your manners will be reflected in your sales. After you have served a drink, step back from your customer or move away. Never appear to listen to a conversation and never take part in it unless you are directly addressed.

2. Cultivate a good memory for the faces and tastes of your regular customers and greet them pleasantly when they come in.

3. Handle complaints courteously. At the bar the customer is always right. If he complains about his drink, fix it or mix another. A bar quickly gets a reputation for fine drinks and courteous service—and it can lose it just as quickly.

4. Never hurry a customer or show that you are impatient. Don't show by your manner that you think a customer is drinking too much—or too little. If he is intoxicated he should be refused service courteously. It may be against the law to serve him and you could lose your license to sell alcoholic beverages if you do so.

5. If you must answer a telephone at the bar, do so quietly. If the call is for a patron, *never* say that he is there. Instead, say that you will inquire and leave it up to the patron to decide whether or not he wishes to answer the telephone.

6. Be cooperative and friendly with the other employees.

7. Be sure you know how to mix standard cocktails without referring to a book. A helpful trick in starting is to take a glass cutter and make a few tiny marks on the outside of the bar glass, showing where the main ingredients for Martinis and Manhattans come to for one, two, three, and four drinks. It is simpler to gauge ingredients if you put them in before adding the ice. Practice until you can fill four glasses to just the right height and not have a drop left over in your bar glass.

8. When a drink is ordered, first place the required glass on top of the bar. If more than one drink is ordered, place the glasses in a straight row with the rims touching. Then place your mixing glass on the bar and pour the ingredients into it where the customer can see. Allow for ice melting during the shaking process.

9. In pouring more than one drink, run your mixing glass back and forth over the row of glasses, filling them all first quarter full, then half full, then full. Never fill one glass first and then another.

10. As soon as you have mixed a drink, put the bottles back in their proper places, no matter how rushed you are. Discard the ice, rinse your bar glass, shaker, and strainer, and you are ready for the next one. Good, efficient work habits will save time in the long run.

11. As a rule, follow standard recipes, but you should also study regular patrons' likes and dislikes and make their drinks the way they prefer.

12. Many houses now require the use of the shot glass or jigger, as modern bar controls make it necessary to account for every drink. An inexperienced bartender often has a little left over in the shaker, which goes down the sink. This waste is trifling on one drink, but if it is repeated often during a day, the loss is substantial. Therefore, measure to be sure.

13. When preparing standard cocktails such as the Martini and Manhattan, use cracked ice or ice cubes. Finely shaved ice melts too rapidly and dilutes the cocktail too much.

14. Cocktails that are shaken should be shaken briskly and not too long, since the ice melts and weakens the drink.

15. In the past it was proper to wipe all glasses twice, one to dry and again to give them a polish. In view of present-day sanitation codes, however, it is best that all glasses air dry on racks to avoid unsanitary handling by wiping.

closing procedures

1. Put all bottles in their proper places and lock the liquor cabinet if required.

2. Clean all bar tools and utensils.

3. Wash all dirty glasses and ashtrays.

4. Wipe down the bar and clean your station thoroughly, including the outside of ice bins, beer boxes, and so forth.

5. Drain and wipe off the sinks and drain boards.

6. Write up your liquor order for the next day's operation.

7. Count out and turn in your receipts for the night.

8. Turn out lights and lock up after making sure that all tables have been cleaned off and wiped down by the person responsible.

IMPLEMENTS FOR THE BAR

Aside from the necessary glassware, which is discussed in Chapter 28, the person behind the bar needs a number of tools of the trade, some of which are stationary, some movable. The stationary equipment is the province of the architects who design the bar.

The principal implements needed in a bar are:

Bar spoons—assorted sizes	Cutting board
Beer can openers	Electric blender
Beer scraper	Electric drink mixer
Bottle openers, cap lifters	Electric juice extractor
Cocktail picks	Fruit knives
Cocktail shakers	Fruit tongs
Corkscrews—automatic and	Ice crusher
waiter's type	Ice pick

Ice scoops	Saltshakers
Ice tongs	Speed pourers
Lemon and lime squeezers	Strainers
Mixing glasses—large and small	Sugar bowls
Muddlers—wooden	Swizzle sticks
Nutmeg shakers or graters	Towels
Pitchers	

SUGGESTIONS FOR MANAGERS

1. When you find a good bartender, make every effort to keep him.

2. It pays to listen to the bartender's suggestions.

3. If you have no confidence in your bartender, don't keep him on the job.

4. A good bartender is worth a good salary in the added business he brings you.

5. Show the bartender you are interested in him.

6. Set policy and guidelines, but avoid overly rigid rules, since exceptions are often necessary to please a customer.

7. Many organizations find they do better by training their own bartenders. After several weeks of group training, the best is gradually given more responsibility in accordance with his abilities.

DOS AND DON'TS IN MIXING

Do not make up more cocktails than are needed to fill the exact number of glasses. "Dividends," the remains in the shaker, are usually tasteless and watery from melting ice.

Cocktails taste better when freshly made. If allowed to stand, some of the ingredients will separate. This is particularly the case with mixed drinks that contain fruit juices and sugar.

Cocktails made of liquor and wine may be prepared in quantity in advance of a party, but those that include fruit juices are better if mixed just before drinking.

If the recipe calls for lime juice, use fresh green limes for best results. The only exception to this rule is the frozen Daiquiri mix. In many tests we have found it the equal of fresh lime juice and we recommend it highly. Do not substitute lemon juice for lime juice in a drink. This is particularly important with rum drinks, such as the Daiquiri, Planter's Punch, or Swizzle. Lemon juice will not give the sharp acid tang necessary for best results with rum.

30
PURCHASING

Confidence is the foundation on which the wine and spirits trade has been built. The wholesale distributor has confidence in the producer or shipper, the retailer has confidence in the wholesaler, and the consumer has confidence in the retailer. The basis for this confidence is a combination of quality, price, and service.

QUALITY VERSUS PRICE

Quality is foremost in importance, for if this is lacking the other factors will not interest the purchaser. A product may be of good, sound quality and yet be inexpensive, while a similar product of better quality may be more costly. In both cases the purchaser gets his money's worth. It is value the purchaser looks for when he buys a product. Value is quality in relation to price.

Determining the quality of a product presents some difficulties unless samples are available. It is important for the buyer to know the product he purchases by actually tasting it. Comparative qualities can be determined only by comparative tastings. It is important that the salesman, whether wholesale or retail, be sold on a product himself before he can sell it to someone else.

For instance, if two whiskies are under consideration and the price of one is 25 percent higher than the other, the buyer must be satisfied that it is at least 25 percent better in quality, or the values will not be equal. When quality and price are equal, intangibles enter the picture. For example, if similar products of similar value at a similar price are offered for sale by different houses, the firm that gives the best service will usually get the order.

While the foregoing applies to trade buyers, it is equally important that the consumer or nonlicensee purchaser should also sample before making a quantity purchase of a given type of beverage. In most states, however, sampling in a retail store is not permitted. It is wise, in this case, to follow the wine merchant's suggestions on several brands and purchase a bottle of each. After tasting them, perhaps with some friends, the purchaser can determine which he or she prefers and can rate its value in relation to its price.

DISTRIBUTOR'S SALES REPRESENTATIVE

The sales representative of the distributor or wholesaler is important to the retail trade buyer because he brings information about market changes. He can also provide merchandising ideas and render many little services that make the buyer's life easier than it might otherwise be.

The sales representative who approaches his work eager to render every reasonable service and assistance to his customer will find that the relationship will be a pleasant one of mutual confidence with profit to both. The greatest help a sales representative can give his customer is accurate, honest information about the products he is offering.

The B.A.T.F. and state A.B.C. board regulations are specific about what services a wholesaler is forbidden by law to render a retail establishment. There are many such prohibitions, but they are all designed with one broad principle in mind—to prevent offering inducements to the retailer to use a specific brand to the detriment of competing brands.

The salesman, in offering his brands, should use all the information he has about their quality and usefulness, but he should not disparage his competitor or his brands. This is bad salesmanship. It is always wise to remember that brands that have been selling successfully for generations have stayed on the market because the public has found them satisfactory. The salesman who bases his selling talk on the premise that the public does not know what it is buying is in for a sad awakening.

INVENTORY AND THE ECONOMICS OF TURNOVER

To operate successfully, a business establishment should have a variety and quantity of stock sufficient to meet all its normal needs. The amounts that must be kept in stock are governed by how near the source of supply is. If it is in the same city, and an order can be filled within the day, there is no point in carrying a very large stock. On the other hand, the farther away the source of supply, the greater must be the reserve stock to protect the business from losses because of lack of stock.

During periods when freight, insurance, and costs are likely to rise, it is good business to increase the stock of items affected by those conditions, as such purchasing is not a risky speculation.

A seven- to ten-time inventory turnover is considered normal business practice. That is, if the stock required to handle normal business is worth $20,000, the annual purchases should total $140,000; the stock turns over seven times during the year. A slower turnover means that either the establishment is overstocked or something should be done to stimulate more business.

A careful analysis of sales and keeping a perpetual inventory will soon indicate which types and brands of merchandise move most steadily and which are dead stock. With the exception of rare, fine-quality, high-priced brands on which a rapid turnover is not expected (but which may be compensated for by a larger profit), slow-moving brands or items should be removed from stock.

A profit is obtained on a given brand of merchandise only when it is sold. Bottles standing on the shelf or lying in a cellar bin cost money. They represent an investment, and unless the merchandise moves, it is costing at least 10 percent or more per annum on the purchase price, plus overhead.

Purchasing, therefore, is closely related to merchandising. Buying must always be done in proportion to the establishment's ability to sell. Where savings can be effected by quantity purchases and by cash discounts, it is elementary to avail oneself of the lower price; but if it takes six months to a year to sell a lot so purchased, the saving should be greater than the cost of carrying, as a portion of working capital has been tied up in dead stock that has been paid for but is not earning any income.

The proper stock for a store, restaurant, or distributor's cellar or warehouse depends entirely on the market it serves. In the East, for example, the public prefers vodka and Scotch whiskies, while throughout the Middle West, South, and Southwest the public prefers Bourbons.

It is good merchandising to have as complete and varied an assortment on hand as is commensurate with good business practice, as this will make customers feel that they can obtain anything they need. It is impossible, of course, for either a retail or a wholesale outlet to carry every brand. A fairly complete assortment of types is possible, however, without too great an investment.

CONSUMER PURCHASING

Quality should always be the first consideration—with the consumer as well as with the wholesaler and retailer—although its relation to price and value should not be overlooked.

The most satisfactory system for the consumer who has not had an opportunity to taste many products is to find a supplier in whom he has confidence and ask for advice. In time each individual discovers, by actual tasting, which products and brands are preferred.

While in the long run the contents of a bottle are more important than the label, it must not be forgotten that the brand is important. Any brand that has been marketed successfully for generations—and sometimes for centuries—has maintained its popularity because its quality is satisfactory. People do not continue to accept famous brands only because of their reputation and advertising; they continue to buy because of the consistent quality maintained by the manufacturers of these brands. The moment quality is lowered, the public turns away.

In purchasing spirits, there is little advantage in stocking more than the necessary requirements, as spirits do not gain in value or in quality after they have been bottled. Very rare old brandies, whiskies, or rums of which there are limited supplies may, however, gain in value.

It is a different story where wines are concerned. Some table wines and Champagnes do change and improve, and, in the case of very fine vintaged wines, increase in value with time (when properly stored and cared for) and therefore often are worth purchasing with a view to future use.

In general we recommend allowing red wines several days' rest after receipt before serving. In other words, do not buy a bottle of old red wine this afternoon to serve with tonight's dinner. If the wine has any deposit it will be stirred up, giving the wine an unattractive, dull appearance. Sturdier wines do not need all this care, but it is safer to err on the side of too much care than to risk handling wines carelessly.

When preparing to entertain, whether at a cocktail party, reception, or dinner, it is advisable to figure out in advance the quantities of beverages needed. Every host wishes to make sure his guests have as much as they wish. It is difficult to predict thirst accurately, but in general it is safe to approximate two drinks per person if the party lasts two hours, and three if it lasts three or four hours. Allow an extra half-drink per person, and there should be no shortage.

Guests' preferences should govern the beverages served. There must be enough soda water on hand for highballs, lemons and limes for cocktails, and so forth. Spirits and fortified wines do not spoil, so a few extra bottles may be purchased as a precaution against a shortage.

The following chart may help you calculate the number of bottles needed to entertain any number of guests.

PRODUCT	BOTTLE CONTENT	AVERAGE PORTION	NO. OF PORTIONS
Table wine	750 ml. (75 cl.)	4 oz. (125 ml.)	6
Champagne and sparkling wine	750 ml. (75 cl.)	4 oz. (125 ml.)	6
Sherry, Porto, and Madeira	750 ml. (75 cl.)	3 oz. (90 ml.)	8
Vermouth and apéritif wine	1000 ml. (1 liter)	3 oz. (100 ml.)	10
Cognac and brandy	750 ml. (75 cl.)	1 oz. (30 ml.)	25
Whisky, vodka, and gin	750 ml. (75 cl.)	1½ oz. (45 ml.)	17
Rum and Tequila	750 ml. (75 cl.)	1½ oz. (45 ml.)	17
Liqueurs	750 ml. (75 cl.)	1½ oz. (45 ml.)	17
Mixers: soda water or ginger ale	32.0 oz. (1 liter)	4 oz. (125 ml.)	8
Beer on draft (in kegs)	15.5 gal.	8 oz. (250 ml.)	250

In estimating the wine needed for a dinner party, one should bear in mind the enthusiasm and interest of the guests toward wine. A good rule of thumb is to figure on one-half bottle per person, and adjust either up or down. This amount should be considered as a total amount. If two or more wines are served at a dinner, less of each will be needed, rather than if one wine is served throughout.

Have a reserve of one-half glass per person in case the guests wish more. When sherry, Madeira, or Champagne is served as an apéritif before the meal, allow one and one-half glasses per person.

WHAT THE CELLAR SHOULD CONTAIN

When one is limited by space or inclination to an inexpensive cellar, it is better to have a small, compact assortment of wines and spirits that provides a sufficient quantity of a given product rather than a wide assortment of single bottles.

The cellars suggested on the following pages can only serve as guides; personal taste should govern the selection. The only reason for cellaring these products is to buy early when prices are lower, and the wines are still available.

THE STARTING CELLAR

3 bottles California red wine (Zinfandel, Cabernet Sauvignon, proprietary red)
3 bottles California or eastern white wine (Chardonnay, White Riesling, proprietary white)
3 bottles French red wine (Beaujolais, Borgogne, Rouge, claret)
3 bottles French white wine (Mâcon Blanc, Graves, Sauternes)
3 bottles Italian red wine (Bardolino, Chianti, Barolo)
2 bottles German white wine (Rhine, Moselle)
2 bottles rosé wine (Anjou, California rosé)
2 bottles Champagne or sparkling wine (French, California)

A basic collection of wines and spirits that do not have to be laid away and may be purchased as needed is:

1 bottle medium-dry sherry	2 bottles gin
1 bottle dry vermouth	2 bottles vodka
1 bottle sweet vermouth	2 bottles rum
2 bottles whisky—blended, Bourbon, or Canadian	2 half-bottles liqueurs (amaretto,
2 bottles Scotch whisky	peppermint schnapps)

If one has twice as much to invest, a wider assortment is possible. Quantities can also be increased. For example, one can include several different wines of the regions mentioned above. Additions to the list can include:

Madeira
Porto
Cognac
A wider assortment of liqueurs (Drambuie, Grand Marnier, B & B)

THE EXPANDED CELLAR

For one who enjoys a variety to please all tastes, this assortment should fill the bill:

6 bottles Champagne and sparkling wine (Brut French, California, *vin mousseux*)
6 bottles red California wine (Cabernet Sauvignon, Zinfandel, Petite Sirah)
6 bottles white California wine (Chardonnay, Johannisberg Riesling, Sauvignon Blanc)
3 bottles eastern white wine (Aurora, Seyval Blanc, Vidal Blanc)
12 bottles red and white regional Bordeaux wine (Médoc, Saint-Émilion, Graves, Sauternes)
6 bottles château-bottled Bordeaux wine, second and third growths (Cos d'Estournel, Gruaud-Larose, etc.)
3 bottles château-bottled Bordeaux wine, first growths (Latour, Margaux, Lafite-Rothschild, etc.)
6 bottles red Burgundy wine (Beaune, Gevrey-Chambertin, Chambolle-Musigny)
6 bottles white Burgundy wine (Mâcon Blanc;, Puligny-Montrachet, Meursault)
6 bottles Rhine and Moselle wines (Liebfraumilch and Bernkasteler Riesling)
3 bottles rosé wine (Tavel, Portuguese, California)
6 bottles red Italian wine (Barolo, Valpolicella, Merlot)
6 bottles white Italian wine (Soave, Orvieto, Est! Est!! Est!!!)
6 bottles red and white Spanish wine (Rioja, Rueda, Catalonia)

A complementary liquor cabinet would include the following:

3 bottles Canadian whisky	1 bottle Cointreau or Grand Marnier
3 bottles Scotch whisky	1 bottle aromatic bitters
3 bottles vodka	2 bottles Cognac
3 bottles gin	1 bottle Madeira
1 bottle Tequila	2 bottles Porto
2 bottles rum (light, dark)	3 bottles sherry—dry, medium, sweet
1 bottle Calvados or applejack	2 bottles dry vermouth
1 bottle Bénédictine or B & B	2 bottles sweet vermouth

THE COLLECTOR'S CELLAR

The wine and spirits collector can stock his cellar with the assortment of wines mentioned in the starting and expanded cellars, but in greater quantities and with emphasis on the ones indicated in parentheses below, or vary it as his experience dictates. It is a good idea to try wines from the same grape or region from different producers.

18 bottles red California wine (Cabernet Sauvignon, Zinfandel, Pinot Noir, etc., from different regions)

18 bottles white California wine (Chardonnay, white Riesling, Sauvignon Blanc, Gewürztraminer, etc., from different regions)

6 bottles eastern varietal white wine (white Riesling, Chardonnay, Seyval Blanc)

12 bottles red and white regional Bordeaux wine (Médoc, Saint-Émilion, Graves, Sauternes)

12 bottles Bordeaux wine, second and third growths (Lascombes, Léoville-Lascases, Kirwan, Palmer, etc.)

12 bottles Bordeaux wine, first growths (Lafite-Rothschild, Mouton-Rothschild, Margaux, Haut Brion, Latour)

6 bottles château-bottled white Graves wine (Olivier, Carbonnieux, etc.)

6 bottles Sauternes wine (d'Yquem, Suduiraut, Coutet, etc.)

12 bottles Mâcon and Beaujolais wine (Mâcon Viré, Brouilly, Moulin à Vent, etc.)

6 bottles red Côte de Nuits wine (Chambertin, Clos de Vougeot, Richebourg, etc.)

6 bottles red Côte de Beaune wine (Volnay, Beaune, Corton, etc.)

12 bottles white Burgundy wine (Meursault, Montrachet, Corton Charlemagne, Chablis, etc.)

6 bottles white Loire wine (Muscadet, Sancerre, Pouilly-Fumé)

6 bottles rosé wine (Côtes de Provence, Tavel, California varietal, etc.)

6 bottles Alsace wine (Riesling, Gewürztraminer, etc.)

6 bottles Moselle-Saar-Ruwer wine (Bernkasteler Doctor, Wehlener Sonnenuhr, Scharzhofberger, etc.)

6 bottles Rhine wine (Schloss Johannisberg, Oestricher Lenchen, Niersteiner Orbel, Forster Jesuitengarten, etc.)

6 bottles red Spanish wine (Rioja, Catalonia)

6 bottles Italian white wine (Verdicchio, Pinot Grigio, etc.)

12 bottles Italian red (Brunello, Valpolicella Amarone, Vino Nobile di Montepulciano, Barolo, Gattinara, Chianti Classico Riserva)

A complementary fortified wines and spirits cabinet would contain the following:

6 bottles sherry—dry, medium, sweet

3 bottles Vintage Porto

6 bottles Tawny and Ruby Porto

2 bottles Sercial and Malmsey Madeira

4 bottles apéritif wines (Dubonnet, St. Raphaël, Lillet, or Campari)

2 bottles dry vermouth

2 bottles sweet vermouth

2 bottles Cognac

2 bottles Puerto Rican rum

2 bottles Jamaican rum

2 bottles Calvados or applejack

4 bottles Scotch whisky (all malt, aged, etc.)

4 bottles American whisky (Bourbon, blended, Tennessee, etc.)

2 bottles Canadian whisky

1 bottle Irish whiskey

3 bottles gin (English, American, Dutch)

1 bottle Aquavit

3 bottles vodka (imported and domestic)

2 bottles Tequila

12 bottles assorted liqueurs (amaretto, apricot, Bénédictine, Chartreuse, Cointreau, Grand Marnier, crème de menthe, Kahlúa, Irish creams, etc.)

2 bottles Kirsch, Framboise, or Poire

1 bottle aromatic bitters (Angostura or Peychaud)

1 bottle orange bitters

beer
ale   } Quantities vary with personal requirements and coolness of
stout   storage conditions—these should not be held too long

THE HOME BAR

In addition to the wines and spirits suggested above, one should not forget the supplies needed to create a good working bar that hosts and guests will enjoy. The following list is offered in the nature of a guide.

USEFUL EQUIPMENT FOR A HOME BAR

Cocktail, highball, and all-purpose wine glasses	Ice bucket
Cocktail shaker	Lemon and lime squeezer
Corkscrew, bottle opener, and beer can opener	Jigger or measuring cup
Electric blender	Long mixing spoons
Flat bar strainer	Mixing glass
	Muddler
	Stainless steel fruit knife

USEFUL SUPPLIES FOR A HOME BAR

Lemons	Club soda
Limes	Mineral water
Oranges	Bitter lemon
Maraschino cherries	Cola
Small cocktail olives	Ginger ale
Small cocktail onions	Quinine water
Fresh mint	Aromatic bitters
Sugar, granulated (superfine)	Grenadine or Falernum

The foregoing are only suggestions we offer as a beginning, but the collector's cellar and bar can be varied and expanded as much as his taste, wishes, and pocketbook allow. It can include many finer wines, some in magnums, both table wines and Champagne, and increased quantities of less costly wines, as well as a supply of older spirits. The selection can be modified considerably, to include Armagnac, some of the rare Rhines and Moselles, and some of the other very interesting Italian wines, Hungarian Tokays, and so forth.

The sweeter-tasting white table wines such as Sauternes, Spätlese, Auslese, and even richer Beerenauslese and Trockenbeerenauslese German wines of the Moselle and Rhine districts can be quite long lived. We have enjoyed and found such wines magnificent after forty years in the bottle. This does not mean that all such rich white table wines will always last so long. They, like all white wines, tend to maderize with time, but when they are good, they can be extraordinarily good.

There is one recommendation we wish to make with regard to building up a private cellar. Do not purchase wines or spirits merely for the sake of collecting and storing them. Store them only for the purpose of aging. Wines, beers, and spirits are produced for only one purpose, and that is to be drunk, thereby giving pleasure, enjoyment, and satisfaction to appreciative consumers. Buy them, buy them generously, so that you may enjoy them generously with your guests. We make the admonition because on more than one occasion we have had the sad experience of having to appraise cellars filled with wines that bore magnificent names and vintages but had been hidden away and perhaps forgotten until, when we examined them, they were finished and worthless, no longer capable of being drunk and giving enjoyment.

As a final observation, we suggest purchasing only young vintages of white table wines, rosé wines, and Beaujolais. They are at their best, most attractive, and most enjoyable while they possess the fresh fruity charm of youth. This also means you should drink them young. You may find them disappointing if you keep them four or five years.

31
STORAGE AND CELLAR TREATMENT

T he care of wines, beers, and spirits is an important but fairly simple task. In a commercial establishment these beverages represent an investment on which a profit is expected, and they should be treated both with care and with regard for their perishable qualities. Just as a restaurant operator takes care to store dairy products, meats, and vegetables in a properly refrigerated room, so beverages must be carefully stored. While this applies more to beers and wines than it does to spirits, even the latter need to be safeguarded, preferably under lock and key, for otherwise the profits in them tend to "evaporate" mysteriously.

Assuming proper security, attention must be paid to the actual physical environment that surrounds the bottles. The most important factors are temperature, humidity, light, and vibrations. These should be considered when choosing a place for storing wines, beers, and spirits.

WINE STORAGE

The cardinal requirement of a cellar or storage space where wines are to be kept for some time is an even temperature. There is no single ideal temperature, but instead a range of acceptable storage temperatures that vary with the length of time the wines will be stored. For long-term storage (fifteen to thirty years) 55 to 60 degrees Fahrenheit would be the best range. For moderately long storage (five to fifteen years), anywhere from 55 to 65 degrees Fahrenheit would be satisfactory if the temperature is kept fairly constant and any changes are simply gradual seasonal changes. Violent swings in temperature should be avoided. For short-range laying away of wines (up to five years), the temperature can go as high as 70 degrees Fahrenheit, and any fluctuations must still be gradual. It is not advisable to store wine for any length of time in a room where the temperature goes above 70 degrees Fahrenheit. The storage area should be away from a heating plant or hot-water unit.

temperature

Whether the cellar is below ground or in the closet of an apartment, it should be ventilated to keep it free of odors and to maintain uniform conditions throughout the area.

Air conditioning makes ideal cellar conditions possible in any part of a building, provided the space is large enough. Air conditioning not only maintains the proper temperature, but it can provide needed ventilation to filter the air and maintain humidity control, both of which are important. One mistake that many people make is to install an air-conditioning unit in a small room or closet. This can lead to poor humidity control and excessive air currents and temperature fluctuations, which are bad for wine. Also, the coils of the unit may freeze, which will make the air conditioner unreliable. If you are thinking of installing an air conditioner, call in an expert who will select the proper-size unit or who may even suggest using a refrigeration system that can be adapted to smaller spaces.

White wines, either still or sparkling, may be stored in the refrigerator so that they will be properly chilled and immediately available. Nothing will happen to them if they are left in the refrigerator for a few months.

Large hotels and restaurants that sell a considerable amount of wine daily find it economical to have special refrigerators in which the white and sparkling wines for daily use are kept at serving temperature. This ensures prompt service to guests. Such refrigerators are also useful for chilling large numbers of bottles for banquet service.

humidity   Proper humidity is the most nebulous of all the physical conditions that affect wines. If the air is too damp, molds are encouraged to grow and labels, foils, and corks may deteriorate.

Air at different temperatures can hold different amounts of water vapor. The biggest problem occurs when the outside air is significantly warmer (20 to 30 degrees Fahrenheit) than the air inside the cellar. The cooler air holds less water vapor than the warmer air. If the cool cellar is ventilated (to avoid stale odors), the outside air mixes with the cooler cellar air. Condensation can occur when the outside air is cooled to the temperature existing in the cellar. To avoid the mustiness caused by the condensation, the cellar should not only be ventilated but it should also be dehumidified, keeping the air at a practical relative humidity of approximately 50 percent.

light   Sunlight is an indispensable friend of the vine but an implacable enemy of the wine it yields. Wines are injured by light, which is why most wine bottles are made of colored glass. Actually, all bright light is bad, and a wine cellar or storage location should be as dark as possible. No wine, of course, will be damaged by an hour or a day or even a week of any light except bright sunlight.

The proprietors of the Four Seasons restaurant in New York, Tom Margittai (left) and Paul Kovi (right), inside the wine cellar. (*Photo by S. Karin Epstein*)

Wine cellar and tasting room of Theodore Hutton's famous La Doña Luz Restaurant at Taos, New Mexico. (*Courtesy La Doña Luz Restaurant*)

vibrations   Constant vibrations can damage wine. For this reason do not put wine bottles directly on the floor, but rather keep them on shelves or in racks that are free of vibrations. If possible, locate the wine cellar away from machinery or the rumble of traffic.

manner of storing   Bottles of still and sparkling wines should always be stored on their sides so the wine is in contact with the inner surface of the cork. This keeps the cork expanded and prevents it from drying out. If the bottles are stored upright and the cork dries out, air could seep through and spoil the wine. In the case of Champagne and sparkling wines, a dried-out cork permits the gas to escape, resulting in flat wine.

Fortified wines and any spirits that are closed with corks should be stored in an upright position, since the alcohol, which is at a higher strength than that of table wine, has an adverse effect on the cork, resulting in seepage. The one exception is Vintage Porto, which is closed with an extralong cork for long-term horizontal storage.

Wines and spirits closed with plastic or metal stoppers or screw caps may be stored in any position. Upright is preferable, however, as there is a slight chance that a bottle with a loose cap may leak.

White and sparkling wines should be stored in the coolest part of the cellar in the lower bins or shelves, while red wines may be stored in the bins above them, with the topmost bins for fortified wines and spirits.

The arrangement should be determined by your own practical needs, with items most frequently in demand within easy reach.

Cased goods should be stored in an orderly fashion, stacked off the floor to permit ventilation and to prevent mold from forming. This can be accomplished by laying down two parallel two-by-four runners below the stacks.

corking   Eventually corks deteriorate. It is generally felt that a good cork will last about twenty-five years and should be changed after that. The best way to tell whether a cork needs to be changed is to examine the bottle for signs of *ullage* resulting from slight leaking.

Recorking is best left to a professional. Extracting a damaged cork is critical, and several tools are needed; the standard waiter's corkscrew can rarely be used. If there are several bottles of the same wine, all are usually recorked at the same time; one of the bottles is used to top off the others and reduce the amount of air space.

Sweet wines tend to "weep" more than clarets or red Burgundies, and the presence of some sticky liquid on the neck of a bottle of Sauternes or great German wine is usually not cause for alarm. Those corks need be replaced only if there is a substantial loss in the bottle.

Recently, the "21" Club in New York had its large, valuable cellar checked by a professional. Old bottles from the last century were recorked. They were also relabeled with the date and the name of the person who performed the recorking. These wines are part of "21's" carefully maintained wine museum.

All the adjuncts to beverage service, such as mineral water, ginger ale, and tonic water, may be stored in the wine cellar. Wine baskets and wine coolers may be stored there too, but the wine cellar should never become the repository for broken furniture and odds and ends.

adjuncts to beverage service

The wine cellar should be separated from the rest of the cellar so it can be locked. In large establishments a time lock may be used or it will be difficult to maintain correct inventory balances.

PACKAGE STORES

Generally speaking, the same principles of cellar storage apply to stores as to hotels and restaurants.

In each case the cellar should be arranged so that the patrons of the establishment may be shown through the cellar. This is good sales promotion, since it arouses greater interest in the beverages, and viewing bottles and cases in a well-maintained storage area is far more enticing than a mere printed list.

Entrances to fine wine shop are flanked with wine artifacts in a museum-like setting. (*Courtesy Corti Brothers, Sacramento, California*)

LEFT: Wines stored in prefabricated triangular modules in apartment closet designed by Greg Lentz. (*Courtesy Harold J. Baron*) ABOVE: A wine vault unit that can be installed in a home. (*Courtesy Wine Vault, Inc.*)

HOME CELLAR

The home cellar can vary from simple racks to elaborately controlled environments. But whether it is a cupboard, a closet, or an actual cellar, it should serve the purposes of the owner.

For an apartment, select a closet that is not near any heating apparatus. Shelves can be built in of strong, three-fourths-inch-thick boards. Leave plenty of space above the top shelves on which to stand fortified wines and spirits. These bottles average thirteen to fourteen inches in height when the cork is half out. Then build the other shelves from twelve to fourteen inches apart, making them fourteen inches deep, for the wines to be stored on their sides.

When a cellar is in a house, a room away from the heating plant or hot-water unit should be selected. Bins made of wood planking or of metal should be installed along the walls, fourteen inches deep. If the room is large and is to store large quantities of wine, it is advisable to build additional rows of bins in the center of the room. If these are made of wood, we recommend crisscross bins. If made of metal, the bins should be square. Honeycomb units made of metal, wood, or plastic are available in different shapes and capacities and are useful if you have a large number of individual bottles. The disadvantage of individual binning is that it is difficult to tell what is in each cubicle without pulling out the bottle. One way to avoid this is to use press-on labels, available at most stationery stores, which can be placed on the capsule of the bottle or on the bottom, depending on which way the bottle is placed in the rack. This label should tell the name of the wine, or its bin number, and will eliminate excessive handling of bottles.

The cellar should have an adequate light source and contain a table and a cellar book in which a record is kept of all purchases of wines and spirits. A cellar book might also contain menus of dinner parties and guest lists, with notes on the wines that were served and their condition. In time this will become a record of some of your most pleasant memories.

For more controlled cellar conditions, although at greater expense, some self-contained storage units are available. Two brands that have given satisfactory service for a long time are the Wine Vault and the Cramer Wine Steward. Both have refrigeration units to maintain constant temperature and humidity.

Whether an elaborate system or simple shelves, remember to keep a strong lock on the cellar door.

32
MERCHANDISING

The principles of successful promotion and selling are fundamental. When the public clamors for a particular brand it is usually not only a good product but one that has been intelligently and aggressively merchandised. In the wine and spirits trade the brands most in demand are those that are most widely advertised and intensively merchandised.

The first important consideration is the salesman. Everyone engaged in the wine and spirits trade, whether producer, distributor, retailer, or owner of a restaurant, is necessarily a salesman. The whole object of producing, distributing, or selling these products is to make a profit from them. No one can sell anything about which he knows nothing. The more the salesman knows about the product he is selling, the more successfully he will sell it.

Therefore, it is basic that the members of the sales staff, from the president through the newest salesman down to the telephone operator, who very often takes orders and answers questions, should know as much as possible about the wines, beers, or spirits (and their uses and service) that are being sold.

RESTAURANT MERCHANDISING

We are convinced that if the food is good and the prices of the beverages are reasonable, the public will buy wine or other beverages when dining out, because in the proper atmosphere wine is enjoyed with well-cooked, well-presented meals.

We have never been able to understand why American restaurants work so hard at selling ice water. This is a beverage service that produces no revenue or profit, and yet this "service" is costly to the management. On the other hand, the nearest the restaurant comes to "selling" profitable beverages is "Do you wish a drink before dinner?" or "Do you want your coffee now or later?"

Another sales deterrent is overpricing. In far too many cases, wine sales in a restaurant are discouraged by outrageous prices. Wine is the only item

464

restaurants list that is sold in its original package. It is an item whose price the patron can compare with a known retail price. While he is willing to pay for service and surroundings, he is not prepared—nor should he be expected—to pay an excessively high premium. Most people resent any pricing that appears to take advantage of them. The average patron will enjoy good wines with his dinner if the price is not prohibitive. Marking up premium-quality wine 100 percent over the wholesale price yields the restaurant a small profit and is acceptable to the patron. We also suggest the cost-plus system as a suitable alternative.

The following table compares the most-used markup systems, showing them with various percentage markups for each. For a given wholesale cost of a bottle of wine (column A), the table shows the retail store price (column B), figuring the usual 50 percent markup taken by the retail wine merchant. Columns C and D show restaurant selling prices based on straight markups of 100 and 200 percent respectively.

Columns E and F, with 100 and 150 percent markups applied, also add $2 per bottle for fixed overhead expenses, which include wine service and glassware. With the cost-plus system, higher-priced wine, such as Champagne, can be offered at a more reasonable price and therefore increase sales and total profits. In fact, columns E and F are approximately double retail prices, with the more expensive bottles actually less than twice retail, which is an extremely reasonable price for a wine in a restaurant. Many restaurateurs use the straight markup system for their lower-priced wines and shift to the cost-plus system for the higher-priced wines.

BOTTLE COSTS AND MARKUPS

		RESTAURANT PRICE			
WHOLESALE	RETAIL	STRAIGHT MARKUP		COST PLUS	
COST	STORE	100%	200%	100%	150%
	PRICE			PLUS $2.00	PLUS $2.00
A	B	C	D	E	F
2.00	3.00	4.00	6.00	6.00	7.00
2.50	3.75	5.00	7.50	7.00	8.25
3.00	4.50	6.00	9.00	8.00	9.50
4.00	6.00	8.00	12.00	10.00	12.00
5.00	7.50	10.00	15.00	12.00	14.50
6.00	9.00	12.00	18.00	14.00	17.00
7.00	10.50	14.00	21.00	16.00	19.50
8.00	12.00	16.00	24.00	18.00	22.00
10.00	15.00	20.00	30.00	22.00	27.00
12.00	18.00	24.00	36.00	26.00	32.00

One should remember, however, that a restaurant or hotel that uses more expensive glassware, linens, and other furnishings, may have to use higher markups on wines and spirits, to cover replacement costs.

How is the restaurant owner going to sell beverages? This is a serious problem, for obviously it is difficult to get the sales staff to learn about something in which they are not interested. How can the interest of the sales staff be aroused so that every member will want to know more about wines and spirits? The answer is money.

As an example, compare two dinner checks. The first check, for dinner without wine, amounts to $20.00, and the tip is $3.00. The second check includes a cocktail and a half-bottle of wine and amounts to $30.00. Now the tip is $4.50.

Of course, before waiters can sell wines they must be familiar with what they are selling. Here are a few points they should learn:

1. Waiters should know exactly what wines and spirits the restaurant has to offer.

2. They must know which of these are red and which are white, as well as which are dry or sweet.

3. They must know which of the wines are table wines, such as claret, Sauternes, Burgundy, Rhine, and Moselle; which are sparkling wines; and which are fortified wines, such as sherry, port, and Madeira.

4. They must know which wines should be chilled and which should be served at room temperature.

5. They should know what wines to suggest for the various dishes on the menu.

6. When they do sell a bottle of wine, they should know the correct manner of presenting, opening, and serving the wine—described in Chapter 28. Too frequently wine is casually, sloppily, or incorrectly served. A great deal of absurd ritual has grown up about serving wines and spirits and it is necessary that a hotel, restaurant, or club know the correct procedure in presenting, opening, and serving wine.

These are the bare essentials that a good staff should know in order to sell wines; any additional information given them will help. No one can expect a staff to learn everything overnight. The best way to equip them is to have a weekly class where these things are explained repeatedly until the staff is thoroughly versed. When waiters are trained, they in turn will be better able to serve guests.

OPPOSITE: One of two pages from an extensive wine list that is devoted exclusively to Cognacs available by the snifter. Other spirits are also impressively detailed. (*Courtesy Narsai's Restaurant, N. Berkeley, California*)

NARSAI'S

COGNACS

	Snifter (1-3/4 oz. portion)
Remy Martin VSOP Fine Champagne	3.75
Remy Martin Centuar Royal	6.00
Remy Martin Napoleon Grande Fine Champagne	7.50
Remy Martin Louis XIII	35.00
Martell VSP	3.25
Martell VSOP	3.75
Martell Cordon Bleu	5.75
Martell Extra	15.00
Hennessey Bras Arme VS	3.50
Hennessey VSOP Fine Champagne	4.00
Hennessey Bras D'Or Napoleon	6.25
Hennessey XO	7.75
Hennessey Paradis	19.00
Courvoisier VS	3.25
Courvoisier VSOP	4.00
Courvoisier Napoleon	5.75
Courvoisier Grande Fine	10.50
Hine VS	3.25
Hine VSOP	3.75
Hine Triomphe Fine Grande Champagne	9.00
(See also listing for Avery's Early-Landed Vintage Cognacs below.)	
Monnet Four Star	3.25
Monnet Napoleon	6.00
Monnet Anniversaire	7.50
Prunier's Reserve Fine	4.25
Delmain Grande Champagne	4.50
Logis de la Mothe Grande Champagne	7.50
Eclipse VSOP Fine Champagne	3.25
Bisquit VS	3.25
Bisquit Napoleon VSOP Fine Champagne	3.75

Now for a few practical selling ideas:

1. A good, well-rounded wine list that is suited to the needs of the establishment's clientele is a must. A list is often placed on each table. Avoid repetition in listings. For example, one Sauternes may be quite adequate.

2. Describe each wine as to taste in two or three words—especially the white wines, which vary greatly between sweet and dry.

3. Mention wines on the food menu. An appropriate wine suggestion printed next to the plat du jour will sell wine.

4. Certain dishes have an affinity for specific beverages. For example, one way to boost Porto sales is to offer a combination of cheese and Porto for one price. Beer goes well with sauerkraut dishes; offer them together.

5. Arrange a table at the entrance to the dining room with a few wines attractively displayed. This in itself suggests gracious dining, and it starts the guest thinking about wine before he is seated.

6. Table tents and menu riders will sell cocktails, wines, beer, and cordials.

7. We are in favor of measuring all ingredients when making cocktails so they will always be uniform. This encourages repeat business.

8. Specialize in two or three cocktails made better than other restaurants make them.

9. Feature seasonal drinks. Tie in holidays with beverage merchandising.

10. Finally, and most important, while the foregoing ideas will help, the actual sale must still be made by the person taking the food order. The wine must be suggested. The wine list or wine card should be presented when the guest finishes ordering the food, if not before, and while he is psychologically in the ordering mood. It should be presented naturally, without fanfare, but as a matter of course, with a suggestion such as "Would you like to enjoy a pleasant bottle of Riesling with the fish you have ordered?" In other words, *suggest* a wine. You will be surprised by the number of sales.

From experience we know that the best advertisement for wine is the wine itself. We have long maintained that if the wine trade could distribute samples, as the food and cigarette industries do, our country would be much more of a wine-drinking nation.

The best approach to sampling wine in a restaurant is the one of offering a selection of wines by the glass. This makes it possible for a person who has never tasted a certain wine to do so without risking too great a sum.

Serving house wine in small carafes or decanters also helps to promote wine sales, as this does not require studying the wine list, and is easy to order.

The price is usually reasonable. Unfortunately, with wine served by the glass or in a carafe, the customer does not get to see the actual bottle or label, and it is a less successful selling tool.

Wine available in half-bottles is declining, with the increase in popularity of wine by the glass—particularly when the restaurant has a good selection of these wines from which to choose. Half-bottles are still in demand for dessert wines, when a small amount of a rich, sweet wine is all that is required.

Another way to promote wine sales that has been used successfully is to offer small six- to eight-ounce decanters. These perform the same function as the half-bottle but are not as successful as selling tools, however, because the customer cannot see the actual bottle or label.

Splits and half-bottles have also been merchandised with equal success in retail stores and have produced repeat sales of regular-size bottles.

Wine sales are best when *all* waiters or waitresses suggest and serve wine to customers. For added showmanship some leading hotels and restaurants like to designate one person to specialize in the sale and service of wine, paying him a commission on the wine he sells. Usually, for practical purposes, this

A suitable display for either a liquor store or a restaurant. (*Courtesy* Liquor Store *Magazine*)

person is simply called the wine waiter, and his uniform need differ only in color from that of the other waiters. Any experienced waiter can acquire a knowledge of wine types and uses with a little extra training and inducement from the management. In turn, he can then aid the management in training other waiters in wine use. Since he is a wine salesman, it is important that the wine waiter have a pleasant personality and the ability to sell without high-pressure tactics.

There is another, more traditional, type of wine waiter, known as the sommelier, preferred by hotels or restaurants that want the maximum attention given to wine. The sommelier is more of a true wine expert, by custom, and he often wears a leather cellar apron and a silver chain, with a tasting cup and a medallion or giant key attached. These accessories are available from some restaurant supply firms.

It should be emphasized that neither the wine waiter nor the sommelier is necessary to a successful wine-selling program if the regular waiters or waitresses are properly trained. When a wine specialist is used, however, he can still work hand in hand with the regular waiter, and both benefit from the wine sale: one from his wine commission, one from his increased tip. In such an operation the regular waiter finds out quickly in taking the food order whether the customer likes the idea of wine with dinner. He then summons the wine waiter or sommelier to the table. The latter presents the wine list, suggests a specific type and brand, brings the wine promptly, and serves it. The wine price is added to the regular food check.

An important factor in any merchandising policy is maintaining a uniform and constant source of supply. The standard quality merchandise should be available to customers at all times. Bargains and close-outs do not build permanent trade. The customer who is pleased by a wine or spirit wants the same quality when he comes back a second time. If he is shifted from one brand or one quality to another, he will lose confidence in the establishment. This is a basic point that applies equally to restaurants and to retail establishments, and it should be stressed by the distributor's salesman.

STORE MERCHANDISING AND ADVERTISING

To sell you must tell. This may be accomplished by various methods:

1. In personal conversation with a customer
2. By a newspaper or magazine advertisement
3. By broadcasting the message over radio and television
4. By a letter
5. By catalogs and price lists
6. By displaying the merchandise both in the store and in the windows

ABOVE: Morrell & Company in New York City has a counter constructed of wooden liquor cases and displays oversize bottles atop its liqueur and brandy shelves. BELOW: A "supermarket" liquor store with a good selection of wines divided by regions. Note the displays at the end of each aisle of full and open cartons. (*Courtesy* Liquor Store *Magazine*)

The ideal method, of course, is personal discussion, during which the salesman may use arguments and counterarguments, answer questions, and render service in the most complete fashion. This method is necessarily limited to the number of people who enter the establishment because of a specific need for merchandise.

When a customer does come into an establishment, however, half of the selling problem has been solved because the customer has come to buy. The other half of the problem is to have the salesman serve the customer's needs if they are specific or to offer helpful suggestions if he is not certain what he wishes to purchase. In direct personal selling, even if the customer knows exactly what he wants, the alert merchant can find out by adroit questioning how the beverage will be used and base his selling on this information.

For example, if the merchandise is intended for a party, the merchant can advise the customer as to the quantities required for the number of guests expected. If it is for daily use, the merchant will be able to tell whether the customer should buy in half-bottle, bottle, or gallon sizes, depending on the customer's needs.

Merchants can inform customers, for example, that white wine, if promptly recorked after opening, may be kept in the refrigerator and will not spoil for a week or ten days, while red wine, if tightly recorked after opening, especially if decanted into a smaller bottle, will keep almost as long stored in a dark cabinet. Champagne and sparkling wines should be consumed when they are opened, as they cannot be recorked and will lose most of their effervescence in a few hours. Loss of gas can be retarded if the sparkling wine is kept very cold at all times. Offering this kind of useful information inspires customer confidence.

As desirable as personal contact with prospective customers is, it is limited, and therefore other media are useful and, when properly employed, profitable. Advertising reaches a far greater audience. Every advertisement should convey the personality of the store and reflect its reputation.

What sort of trade does the establishment wish to attract? Are low prices, or special offerings, or a complete range from low-priced to finest-quality products to be featured? Even if all three types of merchandise are stocked, start with one and feature it above the others.

Once store advertising policy is decided, select the medium best suited to reach the widest audience: local magazines, club magazines, fraternal publications, newspapers, local radio stations, or direct mail. First, of course, determine what audience these vehicles reach and what audience contains the largest proportion of potential customers. Check this against the cost of the medium you have chosen to determine the most profitable method.

It is advisable to find some merchandising device—a slogan, an illustration, a crest, or the store name—that will always associate the advertisement with the store at first glance.

In the advertisement feature your merchandise or simply the enjoyment the purchaser will derive from it. Perhaps the selling point is a very convenient location, or a fine telephone and delivery service; or perhaps the store specializes in certain types of beverages or sizes of packages. If so, feature these points.

This is known as institutional advertising—that is, selling primarily the store name, its policies, and its services to the public rather than employing the special offering form of advertisement where the primary attraction is price or availability of extraordinary items.

All advertising has a cumulative effect, and therefore repetition will, in time, produce the wanted sales.

An important consideration in newspaper advertising is deciding on the right spot for the advertisement. There are society and women's pages, sports pages, food pages, and general news sections. Specify in what part of the paper your ad is to appear. The wine column page and pages 2, 3, and 4 are premium spots and cost more than the general run of the paper. Some dealers prefer to specify these positions and pay the extra rate, as a small advertisement so placed will often be more productive than a larger one in another spot. Try this by test. The advertisement should be timed with the buying habits of the public.   *newspapers*

To get double value for your advertising dollar, post a blow-up of an ad in the store after it has appeared in the newspaper. (*Courtesy* Liquor Store *Magazine*)

radio and television   The National Association of Broadcasters accepts wine and beer advertisements for radio and television, but not spirits advertising. There are a number of different methods of using air time. Most popular are thirty- and sixty-second radio spots and ten- and thirty-second television spots.

direct mail   Direct solicitation by means of a convincingly worded letter has many advantages, although it is one of the costlier methods of advertising. Its principal advantage is that the list of names to which a letter is addressed is made up of either customers who have actually purchased wines or spirits in the store or those believed to be consumers of alcoholic beverages. The productiveness of this form of advertising will only be as good as the list itself. In view of this fact, and considering the cost of mailing, the list must be updated constantly.

catalogs and price lists   The primary object of a catalog or price list is to inform the customer of the products stocked and the prices at which they are sold. Price lists fall into two classes—a general catalog listing every item in inventory and condensed offerings of specific products or groups of products.

The general price list or catalog should be revised periodically. In addition to the prices and the list of products, it should contain information that is useful to the customer, such as cocktail recipes, punch recipes, and uses of wines and spirits. The more useful this information is to the customer, the longer he will keep the catalog and the more often he will refer to it and be reminded of the name of the store and its products.

special offerings   The special offering should state clearly that it is for a limited time only. Its object is to stimulate quick sales, and therefore it should be concise, direct, and dramatic.

These points may be accomplished in several ways. If a lower price than normal is offered, show the regular price and indicate the savings involved.

If it is a new product, describe it briefly.

If it is a seasonal or holiday offering, an illustration or a short paragraph about the seasonal use of the product may be effective.

The main point is that to be effective, the special-offering price list must encourage people to buy at once, to take advantage of a special opportunity.

window displays   Every window display should be designed to be an "interrupting factor" to the eye of the passerby. What accomplishes this? Certainly not a display of standard merchandise with standard prices arranged in rows. Arrange a window so that attention is focused on some one thing. That may be an item of merchandise or it may be some related subject, a well-set table, for instance, that indicates how a beverage can be used, such as:

1. A brilliant scarlet riding coat, a pair of boots, a riding crop, and bottles of Bourbon whisky; or a punch bowl, Jamaican rum, and the other ingredients for several different punches.

2. A casserole, an artificial chicken, and a bottle of claret; or a chafing dish, pancakes, and bottles of brandy and Triple Sec.

3. A top hat, a pair of white gloves, a cane, and a bottle of Champagne and a couple of tulip glasses.

4. A bottle of Rock and Rye, a pair of rubbers, and an umbrella.

5. Bottles of wines that would be interesting to compare, along with wineglasses and a tasting list, can suggest ideas for wine tastings.

All of the objects used can be obtained from local merchants, who will usually be glad to lend them, providing a credit is placed in the window.

In states where standard merchandise prices are fixed, there is no advantage in displaying bottles with prices that are identical to competitors'; therefore, it is better merchandising to display fewer bottles but arrange the display attractively, either with a quantity of a given item, a picture background, or a seasonal motif with the merchandise of the season featured.

A promotional wine-of-the-month display encourages people to try a variety of wines throughout the year. (*Courtesy* Liquor Store *Magazine*)

Were a person to be placed in a window under the direct rays of the sun, he would get sunburned and possibly sunstruck. Wine is also affected by too much light. Wherever possible, use dummy bottles for window displays; if they are unobtainable, keep the awnings down so that the direct rays of the sun do not strike the wines. They become blind, or dull looking, and lose their brilliance. The flavor of the wine is affected in the same manner—the wine becomes flat in taste. Sparkling wine may become overheated and the bottle may burst.

Liqueurs that are artificially colored may change or lose their color if exposed too long to the sun. The afternoon sun is worse than that of the morning, because the actinic rays are stronger after midday. This is partly the reason for using colored glass in wine bottles. The dark green, brown, or black glass protects the wine against the light. (The original reason for dark-colored glass in wine bottles, however, was to hide the cloudy condition of the wines themselves.)

interior displays

Several effective merchandising principles should be considered. One well-recognized and highly productive principle is the related sale, that is, grouping items in relation to each other. For example, cocktail ingredients, the wine for a meal, and the cordial or brandy to finish it can make an attractive island display set in a central spot in the store to attract attention.

Grouping a dozen half-bottles of wine of different types encourages a customer to buy a few bottles in order to find out which wine he or she likes best.

The intimate sale display, where merchandise is arranged helter skelter in a basket so customers will not hesitate to pick up and examine a bottle, helps them to overcome the hesitancy they feel about disturbing a neatly arranged stack.

chilled wines

A selection of more popular white and rosé table wines and Champagne and sparkling wines should be kept in refrigerated storage. This is an accommodation for the customer who wants a bottle for lunch or dinner and does not have the facilities for chilling one on short notice. If the shop is located near a pier for cruise ships, having chilled Champagne on hand for bon voyage parties is a must.

OPPOSITE: "The Ultimate Wine List," a 21″ x 29″ poster, is used as a merchandising tool by a Rhode Island retailer. Rhode Island state law prohibits price advertising for alcoholic beverages, and the poster serves as a catalog of this retailer's extensive wine selection. (*Courtesy Town Wine & Spirits, Rumford, Rhode Island*)

Rock-Solid Value from Stony Ridge

By now it must seem obvious that we are very impressed with the efforts of Stony Ridge Winery. Their attempt to provide the consumer with top-quality California varietals at everyday prices has been singularly successful. Your response to their last two Chardonnays was overwhelming so we know you feel the same way. (We still have a little of the 1981 Chardonnay in stock.)

This Zinfandel is to red what those Chardonnays were to white. It has that spicy, raspberry intensity that is the hallmark of a really good Zin. It is juicy and supple, just the wine for quaffing by the flagon. Zinfandel with this much flavor interest is hard to find anyway, and at this price you just have to have some.

1980 Stony Ridge   Zinfandel   case: 35.10   bottle: 3.25

Pure and Charming Chardonnay

There you are in the hills of Veneto trying to persuade a 65-year old wine-maker to get out of the top of a persimmon tree. Your train station Italian told him you liked them ripe, but you can't remember how to say forget it. The Empsons said the Zeni's were friendly and accommodating, but things are slightly out of hand. Back on earth, finally, the Zeni family continues to charm. Romano and his two sons Roberto and Andrea make extraordinary wines with real character.

This Chardonnay of theirs is the product of almost fanatical dedication. The tiny winery contains nothing but the latest, best equipment, all shiny and spotless. Very soon you realize that here everything takes second place to what goes into the bottle. No other producer in the entire region designates single vineyards for white wines. Here there is no blending, period. The wine reflects their central credo, devotion to true varietal character. The wine really tastes like Chardonnay--not an oak tree from central France. The accent is on rich, round fruit with a gentle lemon tang. Pure and long, this is what Italian Chardonnay is all about. P.S. Their persimmons are good too.

1981 Chardonnay   Zeni   case: 61.02   bottle: 5.65

Pages from two attractive retail wine catalogs. (RIGHT: *Courtesy Draper & Esquin, San Francisco.* LEFT: *Courtesy Sherry-Lehmann, Inc., New York*)

Well-designed stores put the customer at ease. ABOVE: Fluorescent lighting and natural wood panels create a bright, modern decor in this store. Wines from each country are located under shipping-case signs. Designer: Display Fixtures, Inc., Minneapolis, Minnesota, photograph by H. M. Schawang. BELOW: This Northfield, Illinois, store is classical and traditional. Each alcove holds wines from a different country, and expensive wines are locked in a "rare-wine" cellar. Designer: Florio, Inc., Franklin Park, Illinois. (*Photos courtesy* Liquor Store *Magazine*)

shelf display   Merchandise with which the customer is not familiar and which has a slow sale should be placed in the most prominent part of the store—in the front—while the standard merchandise can be placed in the center or rear so as to draw the customer back into the store to see the island displays as well as the shelf merchandise.

Put signs on floor stackings, on middle-of-the-floor and island displays, and in the windows. Signs should tell more than just the price and should have a professional look. Keep them clean and neat.

seasonal promotions   There is a holiday or a seasonal merchandising motif in nearly every month of the year, and these should be tied up with advertising and window displays.

The gift-giving holidays should be featured with the logical type of merchandise for the season or holiday. Other holidays indicate weekend parties and entertaining. Stress these facts.

New Year's is a Champagne holiday.

In the spring rums and gins should be featured with the lighter wines.

In May begin promoting Champagne for June weddings and summer garden parties.

In June prestigious brands should be displayed for Father's Day.

In the summer feature beverages that may be used in preparing cooling drinks; also promote light white table wines.

In the fall, with approaching cold weather, whiskies, brandies, and fuller-bodied wines should be promoted.

For the football season feature whiskies and brandies.

Throughout the winter the richer products will be more popular.

At Christmastime, the peak selling season in the trade for the entire year, be sure to bring out the finest-quality merchandise and the fancy packaged liqueurs. This is the best season for these products; anyone giving wines and spirits as a gift wants to feel he is making a gift of something that is not only fine but that will give pleasure and enjoyment to the recipient.

sales   Special offerings of slow-moving merchandise help inventory turn over.

Keep duplicates of sales slips and, at the end of each month or at the end of six months, find out how many customers bought two bottles of an item and how many were pint buyers. From these sales slips you can determine the buying habits of customers. If you find that a good portion of them are multiple buyers, try the device, which has proved very successful in certain large stores, of offering a small discount over the one-bottle price in lots of three bottles. Customers who are constant group-bottle buyers may be interested in buying a case of the same item if they can save something by doing so.

how to sell oneself to one's customers   There is only one road to the goal of a flourishing neighborhood business, and that is confidence. The soundest ways to establish confidence are knowledge of the products, courtesy to customers, quality and value in the merchandise stocked, and the service given. Added to this is personality, a great intan-

IF YOU CAN TASTE FOOD, YOU CAN TASTE WINE.

Contrary to popular belief, you don't have to come from Oxford or talk funny in order to taste wine.

Anyone, man or woman, with a nose, a mouth and a tongue can become proficient in the art of wine tasting. All it takes is a desire to learn, some practice and the discipline to stick to the guidelines which we are now going to set forth for you free of charge.

There is something in it for us, however, in that if more people developed their palates, more Inglenook Wine would probably be sold, because the taste of our wine is complex enough to challenge the best of wine tasters.

8 PALATES ARE BETTER THAN 1.

If you're just getting into wine tasting, do it among friends.

For one thing, it's cheaper because the cost of the wines can be defrayed. And this is one case where too many cooks don't spoil the broth, for it helps to have several opinions on a wine that is particularly difficult to judge. So select 6 or 8 friends who are as interested in learning how to taste wine as you are and get them together. But tell them to check their cigarettes at the door. Wine tasting is a difficult enough business under ideal conditions, and the last thing you need is a smoke screen between you and the wine.

TO SPIT OR TO SWALLOW.

A good wine list should include a selection of related wines. They should have something in common, such as vintage, region, varietal, or brand. This gives the palate a better chance to compare one wine with another and it gives the tasting a theme. Eight to ten wines is about right for a good tasting. Any more than this and your taste buds start to get confused. Always cover the labels when tasting and spit, don't swallow. Remember, this is a wine tasting, not a drinking bout, and if you swallow the wine your impressions of the last few wines will be anything but clear. A wine case half-full of sawdust can serve as an excellent make-shift spitoon.

NEVER TRUST YOUR MEMORY.

Even the best of wine tasters will forget a wine's name if he forgets to take notes. So always have paper and pen handy. Note the date of the tasting, name of the wine, vintage year, bottler, price, and a description of the wine's appearance, bouquet, and taste.

Try to keep your descriptions brief and to the point. Describe the wine as clearly as possible so that later, when you refer to your notes, you will be able to recall the wine.

> **ACIDITY:** Natural sourness which bites the tongue.
> **AROMA:** The perfume of the grape.
> **BOUQUET:** The smell of the wine itself.
> **BODY:** The feeling of weight in the mouth.
> **CHARACTER:** Complexity in a wine.
> **CLEAN:** Absence of foreign matter.
> **DEEP:** A bouquet of full, rich and lasting quality.
> **DRY:** Complete absence of sweetness.
> **EARTHY:** A mineral or organic taste of the soil.
> **FRUITY:** A ripe but not necessarily grapy smell.
> **FULL-BODIED:** Thick in the tactile sense.
> **MELLOW:** Soft, ripe and well-matured.
> **WOODY:** A smell derived from aging in oak casks.

Armed with this information and willing to put in several hours a week, you should be able to tuck away 25 to 30 wines a year in your memory. Considering the fact that there are over 5,000 wines in the world, this should keep you busy until around the year 2169.

WINE IS LIKE MUSIC.

There are only two kinds of wine: wine you gulp and wine you taste. Trying to learn wine tasting with a "gulp" wine is like trying to learn music theory on a kazoo.

In our opinion, the better tasting wines should be the following:

A. Estate bottled. This means that every grape used in the wine's production was grown, picked and crushed under the direct supervision of the vintner. It takes this kind of care to produce a truly great wine.

B. Napa Valley. The Napa Valley of California is, in our opinion, the finest wine producing area outside of France, and it consistently produces wines worthy of tasting.

C. Vintage dated. Sunshine and rainfall have a tremendous effect on a wine's taste, and only when a wine is marked with its year of production will you begin to make an association between its taste and the weather.

One wine which fulfills all of these requirements is Inglenook Estate Bottled Wine.

We mention this because any ad that explains wine tasting would have been incomplete without it.

INGLENOOK

In Europe, there are many great wines.
In America, there is Inglenook.

In a four-part advertising series, Inglenook concentrated on education. This ad gives the basics of wine tasting. (*Courtesy Inglenook Vineyards*)

gible. Some people have this faculty of approach, the ready smile, the confident air—and it is helpful for the store owners to develop a pleasant manner.

Before customers can be convinced that the merchant's advice is sound, that he is honest in his suggestions, he must know something about the products and how they should be used. Some customers want advice, others feel they know more about it than the merchant does. Let them have their own way about it or they will go elsewhere.

community relations   Watch the daily announcements in the newspaper and keep alert to the happenings in your neighborhood. In the society page announcements there are valuable leads for large sales: not only for events such as coming-out parties, engagements, weddings, and births, but for organization outings, conventions, and so forth.

sales representatives   The foregoing discussion of merchandising is as applicable to the producer's or distributor's representatives as it is to the retail trade. The services that these experts, calling on an account, can render will have a great deal to do with the volume of business the account will produce. The services include helping prepare wine and price lists, giving the customer new display or advertising ideas, suggestions for and placement of point-of-sale material, and new or varied factual information about the products the representative has sold to the customer. The salesman who brings a customer ideas he can use profitably is the one who will get the bulk of the business.

TRADE TASTINGS

One of the best methods of introducing or promoting wines is through wine tastings. Importers and producers of domestic products often hold tastings for their wholesalers and retailers. Retailers, in some states, may also hold tastings for their customers.

A range of wines from one shipper or producer might be shown—either to potential buyers at the various levels, the company's own sales force in order to familiarize them with the line, or, perhaps, to local journalists. These tastings can be of particular advantage to retailers, who can then advise their customers with greater confidence.

Each tasting must be tailored to the specific purpose of the occasion. Points to be considered are which wines or spirits are to be shown, to whom they are to be shown, and how they will be presented. Tastings may be held with everyone standing or seated and may or may not have a commentator.

33
BEVERAGE
CONTROL

1. ACCOUNTING FOR HOTELS, RESTAURANTS, AND BARS

A watchful eye makes any business prosper. If you could buy, receive, and sell without depending on anyone else, you would need few beverage controls; but this is never possible. You must have help from others, and you can maintain a watchful eye over your business by establishing an orderly control over each phase.

Beverage control encompasses all the records and checks on the movement of beverages from their purchase, receipt, and storage to their use or sale. It is important, since the information obtained reflects the health—the profit or loss—of your business.

We believe strongly in a practical beverage control system keyed to your specific needs. You should employ the necessary inventory and sales records to keep you informed at all times of the state of your business but avoid excessive, costly control systems that go beyond your needs.

WINE STEWARDS AND BEVERAGE MANAGERS

A wine steward need not have spent a lifetime in the business and sport a set of symbolic cellar keys hung about his neck. Today the wine steward, in addition to being thoroughly experienced in his own specialty, is an accredited executive with responsibility for accounting records and statistical information in his department and for supervising personnel.

Today even the title itself has been changed and the position is better known as beverage manager, and the person who has charge of the wine cellar is known as the wine steward. The function of the beverage manager is to maintain constant supervision over all divisions of the department. He usually has a wine steward, an assistant, and a supervisor for the bartenders to help him. The beverage manager's responsibility should extend over the wine cellar, service bars, and public bars up to the point of service. He should have charge of employing and discharging employees in this department.

483

WINE CELLARS

Wine cellars need not be cellars at all but may be located many floors above street level as long as they are air conditioned to maintain the proper temperature for storing cases of wines. The layout of a cellar must, of course, be based on the physical condition of the building, but there are a number of points regarding its construction that can be applied generally.

security Square foot for square foot, the bottled-goods storeroom is the most valuable space in the house, except perhaps for the office safe. In one operation, for example, the average value of merchandise in the food storage rooms and refrigerators was $25 per square foot, while in the cellar it was $150. Therefore, all possible safeguards are mandatory.

There should be only one entrance to the beverage storage room, and the refrigerators and bins should be inside this area. The door should be strongly locked. Some clubs even have old safe doors, complete with combination and/or time locks, to protect this important space. Time locks are useful, as they print the time and the code of the key used to unlock the door on a tape inside a locked box. This tape can be inspected for the length of time the door was open, the number of times it was opened, who opened it, and any unusual occurrences.

Traffic in this space should be kept to a minimum, and nothing from any other department should be stored therein.

A layout that permits physical contact with all or a majority of the bars, through either small pass-through windows or a dumbwaiter if the cellar is on a lower level, is ideal. Such interior contact prevents bottles from "disappearing" from the halls, keeps cases and empties out of the guest areas, and speeds up filling requisitions. All supplemental entrances should also be well locked.

If the cellarman orders the wine, a telephone should be available, and if there are more than two bars, some system of communication between them is necessary.

tools The cellar should be equipped with these tools:

> Wire and metal tape cutter
> Carton cutter (for cardboard)
> Case hammer (not a regular hammer)
> Dustpan and broom
> Mop and bucket
> Marking pens
> Thumbtacks
> Bottle breaker and trash cans
> Desk or work table and chair
> Flat truck for delivery

BEVERAGE DEPARTMENT PROCEDURES

In a large hotel or restaurant the beverage department is in charge of every aspect of acquiring and controlling stock. The beverage manager must oversee purchasing, receiving, and sometimes returning goods, security, case and bottle storage, bottle tags, and issuing stock.

When the wine cellar needs an item, whether it be a new one or a reorder, a small establishment may order it directly, while a large hotel or restaurant generally calls central purchasing to place the order. Working with a central purchasing system has many advantages for a large establishment. For one thing, central purchasing can check prices from several companies that may be selling the same thing and can obtain the lowest prices. Some companies may be more competitive than others and offer certain price reductions and post-offs. In addition, the grouping of orders allows for quantity discounts. Delivery dates can also be coordinated for the restaurant's or hotel's needs. Lastly, the wine steward does not have to spend time with salesmen, and there is also less opportunity for the offering of bribes to place merchandise.

purchasing

Central purchasing completes a purchase order form, which is made out in triplicate. This form should provide plenty of room for writing in the names of the items. Some wines have long names, and when the vintage and shipper's name are added, as should always be done, ample space is needed. The form may also state conditions of the purchase. The original copy of the order is sent to the purveyor; the duplicate goes to the accounting office; and the third copy is sent back to the wine cellar receiving clerk as a receiving copy.

When the goods arrive, the wine cellar receiving clerk receives them and completes a receiving clerk's daily report (RCDR), listing the items fully and accurately. He also checks the copy of the original order against the invoice to verify correct prices, extensions, totals, and the merchandise being delivered. The invoices and the RCDR are now sent to the beverage manager's office and are compared again with the original purchase order for price and quantity. After scrutinizing the invoices, the beverage manager should approve each bill, if correct, and return it to the accounting department for payment.

receiving

A copy of the RCDR, with all pertinent details on it, is kept by the beverage manager. These details include the date, quantity, vendor, price, discount, tax, additional charges, order number, net cost per case and per bottle, and selling price per bottle. This record gives a complete history of the beverage department's purchases. While the accounting department may duplicate some of the records maintained by the beverage manager's office, the RCDR has the advantage of containing all the information on one form. By referring to it while ordering new stock, the beverage manager can easily find out how many cases of a certain product were purchased previously and at what price.

returned goods   The receiving clerk is also responsible for returning goods to a purveyor. On a pick-up order form (which should be prepared in duplicate, with the sets numbered consecutively) he enters the name of the dealer, the date, and the items being returned. Both copies must be signed by the trucker making the pickup. The original is sent to the dealer with the merchandise. The duplicate RCDR is then handed to the beverage manager, who holds it pending receipt of credit advice from the dealer, and then lists it. Inventory records can be adjusted from the duplicate copy.

Liquor bills must be paid as is, and may not be changed or adjusted, even if some of the bottles or cases are refused. You must request a credit. The unchanged bill is posted on the RCDR as is, with a notation, in red ink, requesting a credit item for the number of bottles or cases, with the reason.

Occasionally, "dry breakage" (bottles broken in shipment from which the wine has evaporated without leaving stains on the outside of the case), "leakers" (bottles from which part of the wine has drained because of a poor cork), "dummies" (unfilled bottles), and bad or spoiled bottles may be encountered. The wine steward must call the company immediately if these are found at the

The Waldorf-Astoria
REQUEST FOR CREDIT   0926

To _____

_____   _____ 19 ___

PLEASE ISSUE YOUR CREDIT MEMO FOR ITEMS LISTED BELOW					

REASON FOR REJECTION IN DETAIL _____

Signature of party to whom delivered

AC-372 | Per _____

time of delivery. The purveyor will replace the bottles or issue a credit memo, providing the still-sealed necks are presented. If breakage or dummies are found later, the hotel or restaurant must absorb the loss. Obviously, spoilage may not be detected until the wines are opened.

As soon as any wines or spirits are received, they are marked with a uniform coding number, which is used whenever referring to them. For example, if an item is marked "1516," that number is used on the case, on the RCDR, any requisitions, and for inventory. The first two numbers refer to the category, and the second two numbers refer to the actual item. Different sizes have the same number, such as 1516 Bot (750 ml), 1516 Mag (1.5 L), or 1516 L.

case storage

The cases should be stacked so that the bottles within are on their sides, so the corks will be kept moist. All cases should be stacked on 2-by-4-inch slats. If stored next to a wall, they should be placed at least 2 inches from the wall to permit air circulation.

Shelves are also needed for the standing storage of liquors and the horizontal storage of wines. Liquors may also be stored horizontally, if that is more convenient, but some may leak.

bottle storage

When the wines are binned, we suggest one round tag be placed on the end of the capsule, with the code number and the selling price. These tags should be self-sticking labels. The price is a helpful reminder to the server.

bottle tags

Bottles should also be tagged with hotel identification. This is important, particularly for full-bottle sales at banquets, since all bottles carrying this identification are proved property of the house. In instances where corkage is charged, this procedure is of the utmost importance, since it eliminates the possibility of an argument and a disgruntled guest.

Perpetual inventory is not practical for storerooms that carry a large number and variety of items. This is true both for food storerooms and beverage storerooms. All bars and the wine cellar should be inventoried once a month.

inventory

The price book is maintained by inventory control. The information contained in it is garnered from invoices posted on the RCDR for merchandise received, and is used to cost out requisitions. It shows all receipts, issues, and the amount of stock on hand for all items at any time. These amounts are checked periodically against the actual stock on the shelves in order to uncover any discrepancies. The maximum and minimum guidelines act as signals that stock is running low and indicate what amounts to reorder.

Writing issues and receipts on bin cards is time consuming and serves little practical value. Information about usage can be obtained from delivery dates

HILTON

BEVERAGE REQUISITION   117026

Bar _____   Date _____

QUANTITY	SIZE	STOCK NUMBER	DESCRIPTION	✓	UNIT COST	TOTAL COST	UNIT SALE VALUE	TOTAL SALE VALUE
				TOTAL				

ORDERED BY _____   ISSUED BY _____

RECEIVED BY _____

F/B-112 (2-80)

Requisition form filled out by bartender to replace the bar parstock. (*Courtesy Hilton Corp.*)

and a physical count or by referring to an inventory sheet. The monthly inventory should be taken on pretyped sheets or in a book from which the previous month's figures have been transferred. This forces the cellarman to count each bottle each month and prevents him from skipping a bin or a bank of bins.

One of the best methods of issuing stock from the storeroom to the bar is using a requisition and a bottle-for-bottle exchange system.   *issuing stock*

The bartender fills out a requisition slip any time a bottle is sold and taken from the bar. This slip is used to replace the empty bottles for requisitioning and maintaining the bar parstock, which will be described shortly. The night barman, or whoever checks the bar inventory, makes out the requisition in triplicate based on the number of empty bottles from that day's sales.

One copy of the requisition is kept at the bar for record purposes. The original and the other copy are sent, along with the empty bottles, to the storeroom. The storeroom clerk issues a new bottle only upon receipt of the requisition and an empty bottle for each item listed. This is known as a bottle-for-bottle exchange. When the empty bottles have been received and checked, they are destroyed, usually by breaking them. This ensures that the bottles will not be reused for illicit purposes.

The bottles that go to the different bars in a large operation are often coded with different colored stickers that are pasted on the labels. Each bar receives bottles with just one color. This system of color-coding the bottles prevents bartenders from the different bars from switching stock among themselves. The storeroom clerk can quickly check the colored stickers on the empty bottles to make sure that they have been sent from the proper bar, when the bottles come in for replacement. This also verifies that the bottles are house property.

Requisition form filled out by the bartender to replace any broken bottles. This slip must be accompanied by the neck of the bottle. (*Courtesy Waldorf-Astoria*)

3-7   **The WALDORF-ASTORIA**
BAR REQUISITION

BAR_____DATE_____

LIST NO.	SIZE	DESCRIPTION	QUAN. ORDERED	TOTAL COST

ISSUED BY:_____DELIVERED BY:_____RECEIVED O. K._____

Wm. Allen & Co., N. Y. Stock Form 7042

BAR REQUISITION   No. 25055

Bar_____   **Date**_____

List No.	Size	Description	Quantity	COST		SALE VALUE	
				Unit	Total	Unit	Total

Requisitioned by: Issued by: Received by:

_____   _____   _____

The storeroom clerk signs the original and the copy of the requisition, verifying that the order is filled. The copy is then sent to inventory control for daily cost records.

The original requisition is taken back to the bar with the filled order and signed by the bartender on duty to acknowledge receipt, after he has checked it against the order and his copy of the requisition. It is then turned in to the inventory control office, with that day's receipts, for their records.

This requisitioning procedure ensures good control by assigning responsibility to specific individuals throughout the ordering and receiving process.

Another essential element in control that supports the bottle-for-bottle exchange is maintaining what is known as bar parstock.

The bar parstock is a list used to maintain a safe level of bar stock. Parstock levels are one and a half times the greatest amount used of any bottle on the busiest day. The par levels may, from time to time, have to be modified, and a current list should always be kept on hand; but they virtually guarantee that there is adequate stock at the bar at all times.

A bar parstock can also be used to make periodic comparisons between the parstock list and the number of bottles—full, empty, or partial—at the bar. There should be no discrepancies. The bottle-for-bottle exchange system, as explained previously, makes this possible. If there is a difference, something has gone awry, and it is the beverage manager's responsibility to correct the problem.

DRINK PRODUCTION CONTROLS

One of the most important aspects of good bar management is uniformity of drinks. This uniformity ensures that drinks taste the same each time they are ordered and that the proper beverage cost is maintained. Drink production controls have three components: standard recipes, standard serving-glass sizes, and standard measures.

Standard recipes that provide for the same ingredients and amounts to be used are essential if cocktails are to taste and cost the same each time they are made.

When the same drink is served in different-size glasses, it leads to the appearance of a slipshod operation and may cause guests to be dissatisfied with their drinks. Use standard sizes and shapes of glasses for specific drinks.

Standard measures are necessary so that recipe quantities and costs are adhered to. Many different methods, such as shot glasses, measured pourers, and automatic bars, can be used to measure spirits accurately. Shot glasses or jiggers are the most common. One of the best types to use is the lined glass, which has a thin line printed at some height around the glass to indicate a specific amount. Measured pourers that can be attached to the bottle can be purchased. When the bottle is turned for pouring, a specific amount flows into the pourer and then into the glass. Automatic bars have become popular recently and are gaining more and more acceptance in the trade. Some automatic bars are based on gravity: the bottles are placed upside down in a rack and a premeasured shot is poured when a lever is pushed or pulled. Others use a pump to get the spirits to a dispensing head. At the push of a button, spirits that are kept in a separate storeroom are pumped, through lines, to a spigot head at the bar. *measuring*

All of these measuring methods have their individual advantages and disadvantages, which must be weighed according to the specific operation before you decide which to use. All are preferable to free pouring, however, which is practical only if the bartender can pour accurately. Free pouring is even frowned upon by some guests who wish to see that they are getting the proper amount. Others, who don't like to see measuring and like free pouring, can be reassured by using lined shot glasses and pouring slightly above the line. The main problem with free pouring, from the standpoint of good bar management, is that it leaves a large gap in the control system and can be exploited by an unscrupulous bartender.

SALES CONTROLS

Sales controls enable the beverage manager to know whether revenue and costs are in line with what has been planned and budgeted.

There are many areas of sales controls, all of which depend, either largely or in part, on the use of cash registers and checks.

cash register   The most practical business control agent ever devised was invented by a tavern owner in Dayton, Ohio, and was patented on November 4, 1879. It was called Ritty's Incorruptible Cashier, later improved and sold as James Ritty's New Cash Register and Indicator. Today James Ritty's invention, somewhat improved to be sure, is known throughout the world as the National Cash Register. While there are quite a number of cash register manufacturers in the world, National is the leading producer, supplying the majority of all cash registers used anywhere.

Today's cash registers are computerized electronic marvels. In our opinion, no matter how large or small the business operation, the cash register and check are your most important beverage control tools. The register issues an itemized, mechanically added receipt, prints separate and total charges on a waiter's check, and accumulates and stores totals of the several kinds of information you desire for daily verification. Many of the newer registers help reduce losses from human error. Those that are programmed with the prices of every food and drink item can avoid waiters' mistakes in prices, as well as addition mistakes, undercharges, illegible figures, and overlooked items.

Registers can be equipped with eight or more separate category keys and can total separately the transactions of each category. They can even separate the sales made by each cash drawer, when there are several.

Just how you use the cash register is up to you and your individual needs, whether your business is a small tavern, a restaurant, a retail store, or a large hotel whose entire data-processing system from bar checks, room bills, large banquets, and payrolls is handled by a whole assortment of registers, including an electronic computer that collates and analyzes the data from all of the small registers.

Only one control form is used behind the bar. This is to account for losses through accidents. When drinks are spilled, either by employees or by customers, a regular check must be made for it and the word *accident* written across its face and signed by the bar captain. If for any reason a drink is not acceptable and is returned, the same procedure is followed. In both instances the cause for the loss or the return of the drink should be stated. Most of these losses can be prevented, and the beverage manager's office should scrutinize such records daily and initiate remedial action within the department if necessary.

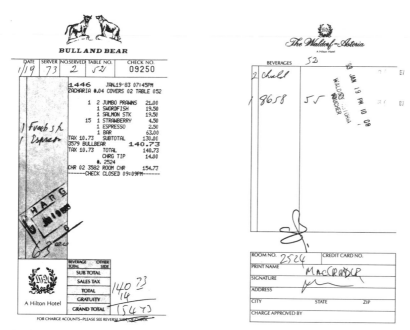

A check from the Bull & Bear Restaurant at the Waldorf-Astoria Hotel in New York. Notice that the wine and liquor charges are entered and totaled on the back of the check. These charges are then entered on the front of the check when the total bill is rung up on the cash register. (*Courtesy Waldorf-Astoria Hotel, New York*)

Another control is to compare actual consumption with revenue taken in for the amount supposedly consumed. This control can be done three ways.

The inventory, or ounce, method compares ounces used (determined by physical inventory) with ounces sold (determined by counting drinks written on sales checks). There should be only slight differences.

A mechanical counting system incorporated into an automatic pouring head is another method. As the mechanical device pours the premeasured shot, it also records how many shots or ounces have been poured. Revenues taken in must tally with these recorded amounts. Some systems are so advanced that either the machine will not dispense the drink until a check is placed in the cash register and rung up as the drink is poured, or the register will deliver a chit with the name of the drink and the price that must be presented to the bartender before he may dispense the drink.

In the third control method potential revenues and cost percentages are projected for each bottle sold at the bar. These potentials are compared with the actual revenue received, and there should be very little difference, if any.

banquet sales   A separate division of the beverage department that is of great importance to a hotel is the banquet bar. Ordering and stocking this bar follow the procedure previously outlined for bars in general, except that a banquet bar requires a larger stock, both of wine and of liquor items, because the bulk of the business is done in full-bottle sales. This fact also necessitates keeping a complete record of all full bottles of liquor sold so that the proper internal financial adjustment can be made. Since the bar has been debited for all beverages at selling prices per drink, the bottle sales show a decrease from this debit total. For example:

The bar is charged with 16 drinks at $3.00 each	$48.00
And sells a bottle at	37.00
Full-bottle sales adjustment due the bar is	$11.00

From the record of bottles sold at each party, data are obtained for the beverage manager's future use. Here is a splendid chance to procure a detailed record of these parties and form a comparison for the following year. A list of the wines sold should also be added to the records. One of the most convenient ways to keep such data is on five-by-eight cards. The name of the person or organization giving the party is essential. The day and date are important for future comparison, as is the type of function, for if the next party should be a dance instead of a dinner, the beverage requirements would be entirely different. The number of persons attending and the original number guaranteed would be useful, too. Use the term *bar cash* to indicate à la carte sale of beverages and *bar signed* to denote the inclusive items that the party may have ordered in advance. On the face of the card in the left-hand column enter the number of bottles sold, followed by the type of beverage:

54 B Scotch
10 B Rye
9 B Champagne

To know the brands used, refer to the bar captain's figures. With a large volume operation, you must know the brands, and not just the numbers of bottles. In addition, attention must be paid as to whether the host is using premium brands or the less expensive popular brands, or even house brands at the function.

While a choice of cocktails is invariably offered at receptions for banquets, receptions are moving towards serving either more wine, or just wine receptions. In large establishments where there can be anywhere from five to a dozen parties going on at the same time, this basic choice should be limited. If we consider the possibility not only of this choice of drinks, but of sherry with the soup, dry white wine with the fish, red wine with the roast, and sweet wine with dessert, then we can understand how complicated the service can be-

MONDAY, MARCH 21, 1983   METROPOLITAN LIFE
THE STARLIGHT ROOF/GOLD ROOM   BOARD OF DIRECTORS (DNL)
TIME: 11:00AM - 11:00PM   RECEPTION/DINNER
                                       MR. D. JANELLI, IN CHARGE

EXTRA ITEMS AND ARRANGEMENTS

TIME: RECEPTION - Gold Room............. 6:00PM
                         DINNER - Starlight Roof........... 7:00PM
                          (Dancing Between Courses)
                         SHOW............................. 9:15PM
                         ADJOURNMENT......................11:00PM

CHECKROOM: Charge $1.00 per person, based upon the Final
                         Guarantee or actual attendance, whichever
                         exceeds with the "NO TIPPING" Sign displayed.

RESTROOMS: Charge 25¢ per person, with the "NO TIPPING"
                         Sign displayed. Provide Toiletries.

CONTROL: By invitation only. Provide one (1)
                         committee table, head if entrance to
                         Starlight Roof.

SEATING: Formal. Own place cards.

BEVERAGES: RECEPTION - Provide two (2) bars and
                         bartenders, charge $50.00 each to serve
                         assorted Highballs at current bottle prices
                         and Cocktails at current drink prices of
                         $4.10 per drink. Use NAME BRANDS. Have
                         Light and Heineken Beers available. White
                         Wine at bar to be Special Joseph Phelps
                         Chardonnay, charge $40.00 per bottle.
                         Waiters to take drink orders from guests. Be
                         sure to use Gold Glasses.
                         DINNER - WITH THE FISH COURSE, we are to
                         serve Special Joseph Phelps Chardonnay,
                         charge $40.00 per bottle.   WITH THE ENTREE,
                         We are to serve Jordon Cabernet Sauvignon,
                         Bin #8223, 1978, charge $40.00 per bottle.
                         WITH THE COFFEE, we are to offer the guests a
                         full line of Cordials and Liqueurs, charge
                         $5.00 each. Be sure to have Bailey's Irish
                         Cream. Bar to remain open throughout the
                         entire evening for drinks upon request.

ROOM ARRANGEMENTS: GOLD ROOM - RECEPTION - Crescent shaped
                         buffet opposite entrance, bar on east side,
                         bar on west side, provide upright Piano.
                         Remainder of room set vanderbilt style with
                         cocktail tables and chairs.
                         STARLIGHT ROOF - DINNER - Music on North
                         Terrace, provide Baby Grand Piano. Dance
                         Floor in front of North Terrace.
                         Entertainment on South Terrace. Provide Baby
                         Grand Piano. Curtains closed. Remainder of
                         rooms with rounds of ten (10) as per special
                         diagram. Standing lectern on South Terrace.

DECORATIONS: LINEN - Floralia Florists to provide floor
                         lenght White Tablecloths, Waldorf-Astoria to
                         provide Blue Napkins in Fan Fold.
                         SEATBACKS - Floralia Florists to provide.

Some of the banquet list requirements furnished to beverage manager and wine cellar
in advance of a function. (*Courtesy Waldorf-Astoria Hotel, New York*)

come and how necessary it is to give this phase careful advance attention. The detailed information concerning the beverage service of each banquet is, of course, collected at the banquet department, where it originates. It should be typed on a list ten days before the date of the function, with copies to everyone in the beverage department and to others connected with any of the functions. This includes the wine cellar, each bar, and the beverage manager's office. This ensures sufficient time to order and receive the proper beverages. In the event that an item is out of stock, the host will have time to select another.

2. ACCOUNTING FOR RETAIL STORES

Accounting for stock and sales in a retail liquor store depends to a great extent on the size of the store and the statutory requirements of the state in which it is located. There usually are prescribed forms, too numerous to cite here, in state-controlled stores. It is our intent to outline the internal control any liquor store needs to ensure intelligent operation, without stressing any type of record keeping.

Individual practices may vary, but in general the previously described routine used by hotels and restaurants for requisitioning, purchasing, receiving, stocking, and recording broken merchandise is applicable to a retail store.

unit control ticket

In a large number of retail stores it is the custom to have a unit control ticket pasted on the bottle before it is placed in stock. The price is entered from the duplicate purchase order, and the ticket also states the type of merchandise, the size of the bottle, the bin, and the purchase order number for identification. When the bottle is sold, half the ticket is torn off and either attached to the sales slip or collected for further classification.

inventory

A retail store should maintain a perpetual inventory record for each individual brand and size of product. For example, if you have 750 ml, 375 ml, and 187 ml bottles of a Scotch whisky, you should have an inventory sheet for each size.

Since many stores today are self-service, the computerized cash register has assumed new importance. As in supermarkets, after customers make their selections, they take them to the cash register. It can keep a running account of sales in all categories. This information will then be used to purchase new goods.

In addition, those stores that have optical scanning equipment can make use of the 10-digit UPC price codes that are appearing on labels of many bottled goods. The price is automatically tallied, and the information on the price code helps the retailer to keep track of sales and depletions.

It must be mentioned that while this system simplifies record keeping for the retailer, not every store can make use of it. More traditional stores, with the reputation for personal service, do not send their customers to a line to pay for merchandise. They may use computers behind the scenes for their inventory and bookkeeping, but not at the point where the customers settle their accounts.

A manual record sheet should provide columns for entering dates, purchase order numbers, and sales ticket numbers; columns for the units purchased and units sold; and a column for units in stock at the close of each day. At the bottom of the sheet there should be space for the unit cost price, if the proprietor wishes to enter it; the selling price per unit and per case, and the maximum and minimum stock to be carried. This last, of course, is not constant but varies according to the time of the year.

The perpetual inventory record works as follows:

1. Enter in an "in" column merchandise received as shown by the vendor's invoice and the receiving department ticket. Also enter sales returns from the duplicate tickets.

2. Enter in an "out" column total unit daily sales, arrived at by classifying the duplicate sales ticket and/or the unit control tickets; also enter merchandise returned to vendors as shown on the duplicate return ticket. Sales prices should be carefully compared with schedules on inventory sheets, as these provide an opportunity to audit daily sales. Breakages should be entered individually and so labeled.

3. Stock on hand, as reflected in the perpetual inventory at the end of a day, is arrived at by adding to the previous day's inventory the merchandise put into stock and by deducting the sales, returns to vendors, and breakages.

Physical inventory of the merchandise should be taken at regular intervals and the results checked against the perpetual inventory.

vendor's invoices

Invoices should be compared with the bills of lading from the receiving department, and the condition of the wines and spirits should be checked. After the person who made the purchase checks the price, discount if any, quantity, and type of merchandise, the invoices are approved for payment, attached to the bills of lading, and entered in the regular purchase register.

returned goods   Merchandise to be returned to vendors should be taken out of stock and the unit tickets removed and attached to the returned goods memorandum, which is made out in triplicate. One copy of this memorandum is to be sent to the accounting department. The merchandise, with the original and the remaining copy of the return ticket, should be sent to the shipping department, from where it is either delivered by the store itself or picked up by the vendor, at which time a receipt is obtained and sent to the accounting department. On the return slip should be indicated the originating department, the date, the vendor, the quantity and description of merchandise, and the reason for the return. Returns should always be made promptly.

The manager or owner of the store is held responsible for all merchandise returned by customers. The regular returned goods slip may be used for this purpose and on it should be entered the goods returned, the reason for the return, and the amount of the refund involved. The merchandise should then be entered back into stock, unless it is faulty.

sales   In states permitting sales on credit, stores should use a standard accounts-receivable system, with a separate account being maintained for each customer. In some states credit cards may now be used as well.

At the end of each day an analysis of sales shows the types of merchandise sold. These quantities must agree with the unit control tickets and the perpetual inventory.

customer
orders   When a customer orders wine to be sent C.O.D., the wines are packed immediately and the order is written up on a C.O.D. order form, which has instructions that the amount due should be collected before the wines are left at their destination. This transaction is completed quickly.

If a customer telephones for some wines for which he will send payment before they are delivered, a memo is kept of the order, but nothing is written up and the wines are not necessarily held aside. After the customer's check arrives, the wines are packed and the order is written up on a paid-send order form. The wines are then delivered to the customer.

SHERRY-LEHMANN, INC.
WINE & SPIRITS MERCHANTS
679 Madison Ave. At 61 St., New York, N.Y. 10021 · TEmpleton 8-7500

ORDERS TO BE SENT TO OTHERS

Name..................

Address..................

FOR DELIVERY TO YOUR OWN ADDRESS

Quantity	NO.	DESCRIPTION	UNIT	AMOUNT
			TAX	
			TOTAL	

☐ Check Enclosed (Add 8% Sales Tax Within City Limits)
☐ Send C.O.D. (Add applicable % in remainder of N.Y. State)

DELIVERY INFORMATION

WITHIN U.P.S. ZONE: No charge for delivery within west U.P.S. zone on orders of $25 or more. This includes the five boroughs — Long Island, Westchester, and most of Rockland County. Below $25, kindly add $3.00 for each delivery.

BEYOND U.P.S. ZONE: (but within New York State). No charge for delivery on orders of $200 or more. Below $200, kindly add $19 for each delivery. — The minimum charge that trucking companies impose for upstate deliveries. During mid-winter some upstate areas may not be serviced by truck. If there are any questions as to trucking facilities, kindly inquire.

Quantity	DESCRIPTION	SEND TO	AMOUNT
		Name	
		Address	
		City	
		Name	
		Address	
		City	
		Name	
		Address	
		City	
		Name	
		Address	
		City	
		TAX →	
		TOTAL →	

☐ Send Card to each with my name
☐ Cards Enclosed

Convenient Order Form — Tear Out and Mail

Prompt Delivery Service Throughout United Parcel Zone

INTERSTATE BUSINESS FORMS

S12191

PLEASE PRINT-USE PRESSURE

LICENSE No. L-1131

TO..................
ADDRESS..................
CITY..................

APARTMENT

NO. OF BOTTLES
NO. OF PACKAGES
DATE

52158

COD

Telephone
TEMPLETON 8-7500

FROM **SHERRY LEHMANN, INC.**
WINE & SPIRITS MERCHANTS
679 MADISON AVE. at 61st ST., NEW YORK 10021 ·

THE WINE AND SPIRIT CENTER OF NEW YORK

QUANTITY	SIZE	BIN	DESCRIPTION	PRICE	AMOUNT
		A			
		B			
		C			
		D			
		E			
		F			
		G			
		H			
		J			
		K			
		L			
		M			

COLLECT →

NOTE: Payment in advance, or C.O.D. . . . Section 100, New York State Alcoholic Beverage Control Law Provides . . . "No retail licensee shall sell any alcoholic beverages on credit."

34
REGULATORY
BODIES AND LAWS

Agreat many volumes could be written on the regulation of the alcoholic beverage trade in the United States and the rest of the world. For the purposes of this book, a brief history of the laws and regulations concerning alcoholic beverages will illustrate American attitudes toward these products and how our present-day laws have developed.

history   Liquor restrictions in our country go back to colonial days. At that time the legislative regulations regarding liquor were mainly for revenue and, later, to encourage sobriety among the Indians, the slaves, and finally the working classes.

In 1630, only ten years after the Pilgrims landed, some agitation against the use of strong liquor began. The first organized attempt to curtail the consumption of hard liquor, however, came in 1733 when Governor Oglethorpe of Georgia prohibited the importation of hard liquors into that colony.

Probably the strongest impetus given to the organized temperance movement was caused by the publication, in 1785, of "The Effects of Ardent Spirits upon the Human Mind and Body" by Dr. Benjamin Rush of Philadelphia. The publication of this essay converted many medical as well as nonmedical persons to the temperance ideal.

Both for revenue and as a deterrent, a tax was levied on the selling of distilled liquors in 1790. This led to the Whiskey Rebellion in 1794 in Pennsylvania, an uprising that was put down by federal troops.

In 1816 the first prohibitory law, forbidding the selling of liquor on Sundays, was passed in Indiana. By the end of 1833 there were more than five thousand organized temperance groups, with a membership totaling more than one million people. In 1838 Massachusetts limited the amount of liquor that one person could buy at a time. Many people in this country felt that drinking was a problem and that it should be controlled or stopped.

500

In 1846 Maine passed the first statewide prohibition law. As the opposition to hard liquor increased, people began to drink more malt and vinous beverages, and brewing operations developed into a major industry.

The groundswell against alcohol consumption reached such proportions that on January 16, 1920, the National Prohibition Amendment (the Eighteenth Amendment to the Constitution) became law. Although the amendment was adopted nationwide, the public was not ready for such drastic controls and violations flourished. It has been estimated that the cost to the government alone approached $1 billion per year, including loss in federal, state, county, and municipal revenues. It is also estimated that the American people spent a total of $36 billion for bootleg and smuggled liquor during Prohibition. Clearly some other form of control was necessary.

On December 5, 1933, the Twenty-first Amendment repealed the Eighteenth Amendment, and the way was cleared for new controls. A system of federal regulations concerning trade practices and requiring permits was set up. This concern for regulations to avoid any possible return to prohibition marked the start of a new period for liquor control.

FEDERAL CONTROLS

Under authority of the 1933 National Industrial Recovery Act (N.I.R.A.), the president approved codes of fair competition for the industry, which continued in force until 1935, when the Federal Alcohol Control Administration, which had been previously established to administer the codes, was abolished and the N.I.R.A. was invalidated by the Supreme Court. The Federal Alcohol Administration (F.A.A.) was created and 1935, 1936, and 1937 saw a new legislative trend. Much fair trade legislation was passed, both by the federal government and by individual states, but this is no longer the trend.

In 1940 the F.A.A. was abolished, and its functions were transferred to the Alcohol Tax Unit (A.T.U.) of the Treasury Department. In 1952, when the functions of the A.T.U. were increased by adding responsibilities for tobacco administration, the name was enlarged to the Alcohol and Tobacco Tax Division of the U.S. Treasury Department (A.T.T.D.). In 1968, with increased responsibilities for firearms control, the name was further enlarged to the Alcohol, Tobacco, and Firearms Division of the U.S. Treasury Department (A.T.F.D.). In 1972 the name was changed to the Bureau of Alcohol, Tobacco, and Firearms (B.A.T.F.), still a division of the Treasury Department.

In 1983 the B.A.T.F. was restructured into two branches: the FAA, Wine and Beer Branch, relating to the Federal Alcohol Administration Act, which handles all regulations for wine and beer; and the Distilled Spirits and Tobacco Branch.

There are three broad areas where the B.A.T.F. exercises control over the alcoholic beverage industry: public protection, trade practices, and revenue collection.

The public is protected by the prevention of adulteration and/or mis-branding of products and from the misuse of advertising.

labeling   Control of labeling° is a prime function of the B.A.T.F. All alcoholic beverage labels must conform to certain regulations and must have B.A.T.F. approval before they may be used. Labels *must* include such information as the identity of the product; the manufacturer, bottler, or importer; the liquid contents; and the alcohol content—except for wine containing 14 percent or less alcohol by volume. In this special case the percentage of alcohol may be stated, or the label may simply mention the type designation (table wine or light wine). Distilled spirits must indicate the percentage of neutral spirits used and the source of those neutral spirits (except for cordials, liqueurs, and specialties).

Certain statements are also specifically prohibited, such as those that disparage a competitor's product; those that are false, misleading, indecent, or obscene; or those that use the name of a person or organization to imply that the product has been endorsed by such a person or organization. There may also not be any consumer deception regarding the age, manufacturing processes, analyses, guarantees, or other irrelevant matters.

These labeling regulations require a certificate of label approval or a specific exemption from this requirement if the product is sold only within the state where it is produced. Once a product is sold interstate, it must comply with federal codes.

Imported products are also controlled by the B.A.T.F. in close cooperation with the customs branch of the Treasury Department. All stipulations listed previously apply, and the country of origin must be clearly marked.

The certificate of label approval must conform, to the last period and comma, with the actual labels on the bottles. If an imported or domestic product does not conform, except for certain allowed variables, the product may be withheld from the market by Internal Revenue and customs officials.

advertising   Advertisements of any alcoholic beverages must contain much of the mandatory label information, such as the class and type of the product, the percentage of alcohol as it appears on the label, and the source of any neutral spirits in distilled products when it appears on the label. The lettering of this information must be clear and legible, and the name and address of the advertiser must be present.

As with the labeling regulations, there may be no false or misleading assertions, disparagement of a competitor's product, or any other statements that would be prohibited on a label. There may be no medicinal or therapeutic claims that might be misleading. Also, a label is not allowed to imply that a

°For a basic federal document on labeling information and requirements, write to the U.S. Government Printing Office for Document 27CFR-4.

product is from a country other than that where it was produced. Confusion of brands is forbidden, and two or more products may not be advertised together if the advertisement implies that what is said about one product also applies to the other. The American flag or other government symbol may not be used to mislead the consumer into thinking that the product has been produced for or supervised by the government.

trade practices

The B.A.T.F. exercises a further protective control over the many branches of the industry by regulating just what services a distiller, brewer, rectifier, blender, producer, importer, or wholesaler may or may not render a retailer. A retailer may not be induced to purchase certain alcoholic beverages to the exclusion of competing beverages by bribery, bonuses, premiums, or direct or indirect compensation.

Also prohibited are consignment sales, conditional sales with the privilege of return, or sales involving the acquisition of other alcoholic beverages. The bona fide return of merchandise to a vendor for usual commercial reasons arising after the merchandise is sold is permitted.

controls

While distilled spirits in the possession of a retail dealer have had to be in bottles or similar containers with Internal Revenue tax stamps, new legislation is eliminating this system. This applies to whisky, gin, rum, brandy, vodka, alcohol, cordials containing distilled spirits, and other similiar liquors.

With the elimination of the strip stamp, there are now a variety of tamperproof closures developed for spirits. These include shrink-wrapping of the entire cap, and perforated metal caps that shear apart when twisted for the first time. These closures must be approved by the B.A.T.F. on a case by case basis. As an interim measure, strip stamps were imprinted on these closures, but that is being eliminated also.

A retail liquor dealer must for a period of two years keep all records that relate to purchases of, and payment for, distilled spirits, wines, and fermented malt beverages. Invoices and bills must be kept in book form showing the quantity, from whom received, and the date received.

For specific tax information, see Appendix R.

STATE CONTROL

In addition to the federal government's control of the industry, the individual states exercise a secondary control. Laws vary from state to state but cannot conflict with federal laws, and each state must meet all federal regulations. State regulations may be stricter than federal regulations, however. For example, federal law allows a wine from any state to be labeled with the name of that state if 75 percent of the wine in the bottle is from there. California law, however, requires that 100 percent of the wine be from California.

State control of the sale of alcoholic beverages falls into three types:

OPEN-LICENSE STATES, where private business makes both on-premise (restaurants, bars, and some retail outlets where consumption is permitted) and off-premise (retail or package stores) sales of alcoholic beverages to all types of consumers.

The operations vary in these states because of different taxes imposed on wines, spirits, and beers and because of different license fees imposed on wholesalers and retailers. Furthermore, each state and, as a rule, each municipality, may have different hours for opening and closing, and different provisions with respect to the number of licenses permitted.

CONTROL (MONOPOLY) STATES that control the sale of all alcoholic beverages distributed in their territories.

CONTROL (MONOPOLY) STATES that control the sale of distilled spirits and certain kinds of wines.

In the open-license states trade is conducted as in other competitive businesses. Open states collect revenues from excise taxes and sales tax. In the control states, however, whether those that control the sale of all alcoholic beverages or those that control only a part of the trade and permit the open sale of other beverages, it must be borne in mind that the states themselves are in the liquor business and their function, public statements to the contrary, is to make money. As a result, these states stock only those brands they believe will have the most sales, thereby limiting consumer choice.

CONTROLS OF OTHER COUNTRIES

The European Economic Community (EEC) or Common Market, has done a great deal to standardize the wine regulations of its member countries. For one thing, regions have been divided into six zones—A, B, C Ia, C Ib, C II, and C III—based on climate. These regions have specific minimum alcohols for the level of wine produced, and limits on the amount of chaptalization that may be done.

A massive undertaking has been the production of a four-volume *Cadastre Viticole*, with member countries reporting the grapes they are growing, along with acreage. In addition to this register of grapes from all producing countries, place-names have also been registered.

The lowest level of wine is called Typical Wine or Table Wine. This is followed by VQPRD wines. VQPRD is now a Common Market term that covers AOC wines of France, DOC wines of Italy, and Qualitätsweins of Germany. The letters VSQPRD do the same for sparkling wines.

Some wines are made from grapes or wine from more than one country. These are known as "Euroblends," and must be clearly labeled as to the origin of the grapes or wines. The bottler or shipper must be identified by a code number.

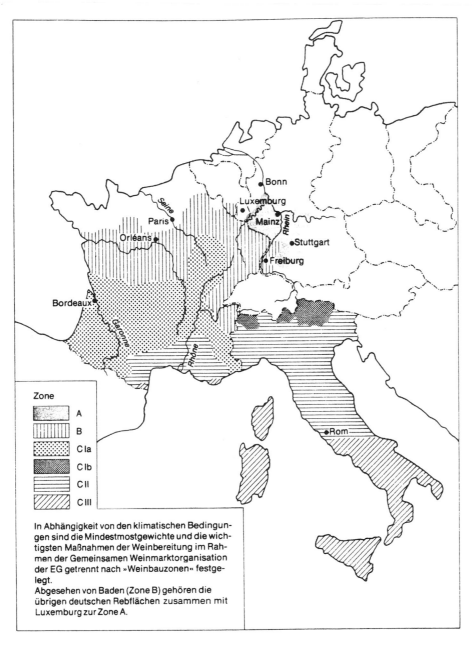

Zone

A
B
C Ia
C Ib
C II
C III

In Abhängigkeit von den klimatischen Bedingungen sind die Mindestmostgewichte und die wichtigsten Maßnahmen der Weinbereitung im Rahmen der Gemeinsamen Weinmarktorganisation der EG getrennt nach »Weinbauzonen« festgelegt.
Abgesehen von Baden (Zone B) gehören die übrigen deutschen Rebflächen zusammen mit Luxemburg zur Zone A.

Viticultural regions of the EEC. (*From Ambrosi and Becker's* Der Deutsche Wein, *courtesy Gräfe and Unzer Verlag, München*)

35
SUMMARY

Since Repeal the wine and spirits trade has established the fact that the American public drinks its alcoholic beverages in moderation. Consumption of spirits has gradually increased to a moderate 2 gallons per capita, while that of wine and beer has increased progressively to $2\frac{1}{4}$ gallons and 25 gallons respectively. This does not mean that individuals are drinking a great deal more, but rather than a greater number of people are enjoying the pleasant relaxation that wines, beers, and spirits offer. It reflects as well the states, counties, and cities that have shifted from "dry" to "wet" areas.

We are convinced that our consumption of spirits will remain fairly steady and that beer drinking will increase, and we see every indication that wine consumption will increase steadily. The popularity of white wine as an apéritif is a step in this direction.

A dinner complemented with wine gives the diner greater enjoyment and makes the food more appetizing. Both the diner and the restaurant (or host if it is a home dinner) will be pleased, and everyone benefits.

The trade itself, as a matter of protection, must advocate temperance. Temperance education is becoming a function of our public school systems, and we are seeing some cooperative action between the beverage trade and the educational boards to teach children the real meaning of moderation and the value as well as the dangers of alcoholic beverages of all types.

The trade has made little attempt to place before the medical community the value of wines and spirits in the treatment of patients. In other countries alcoholic beverages have a place in this field and in time many doctors in the United States may prescribe them in similar ways.

The increased knowledge and technology of viniculture are spreading throughout the world, and with them the interest of the general public has grown. Wine publications and articles on alcoholic beverages in leading popular magazines contain specific information demanded by the consumer. Another happy occurrence is the space devoted to both the use and the service of these beverages in the food sections of our important daily newspapers. Editors are satisfying their readers' demands for information and are also tacitly showing that wine is, indeed, considered a food.

The more accurate information people have about alcoholic beverages, the better off they are. Much educational work has been done but there is much more still to be done. The future should usher in an era of freedom, but *not* one of unlimited license and abuse.

Of one thing we are convinced: the American public demands the best. It is the best-informed buying public in the world. The person who attempts to fool the public with poor quality or shoddy imitations is fooling only himself. Any brand can be sold, provided it has the quality claimed for it. No company can stay in the wine and spirits trade unless people are convinced that the firm's products are good.

The more the wine and spirits merchant learns about the product he is presenting, the prouder he will be to find himself engaged in a profession whose honorable and ancient traditions have evolved through the centuries.

Our aim has been to compress into this book available information on alcoholic beverages required for the producer, seller, and consumer. The crowning knowledge about the beverages we have described can come only firsthand by actual tasting.

We lift our glass to wish you profit in the reading, pleasure in the tasting, and your very good health!

APPENDICES

APPENDIX A
QUICK GUIDE TO WINES AND SPIRITS

Any wine can accompany any food, and you should choose a wine according to personal preference. Certain combinations of wine and food have developed, however, because they are generally pleasing. These are listed here for general guidance but should not be taken as hard and fast rules. Remember also that many chilled wines, either still or sparkling, may be enjoyed by themselves, as hospitality wines, or as apéritifs.

NAME	PHONETIC SPELLING	SOURCE	TYPE	COLOR	TASTE	SERV. TEMP.	SERVE WITH
Adabag	ah-DAH-bah	Turkey	Table wine	Red	Dry	°	Ch, G, & RM
Adom Atic	ah-DOHM ah-TEEK	Israel	Table wine	Red	Dry	°	Ch, G, & RM
Advocaat	AHD-voh-kaht	Holland	Prepared eggnog	Yellow	Sweet	° or °°°	AD
Afames	ah-FAHM-ees	Cyprus	Table wine	Red	Dry	°	Ch, G, & RM
Affentaler	AH-fen-tah-lehr	Baden, Ger.	Table wine	Red	Dry	°	RM
Aigle	AY-gul	Switzerland	Table wine	White	Med. dry	°°°	F, P, & LM
Albana di Romagna	ahl-bahn-eh dee ro-MAHN-yeh	Emilia, It.	Table wine	White	Dry to med.	°°°	F, P
Ale		Various	Malt beverage	Straw to dark amber	Bittersweet	°°°	Hosp
Aleatico	ah-leh-AH-tee-koh	California & Italy	Dessert wine	Red	Sweet	°	AD
Alella	ah-LAY-yah	Spain	Table wine	Red or white	Dry	° or °°°	Varies with color
Aloxe-Corton	ah-lohs-kor-toh(n)	Côte de Beaune, Fr.	Table wine	Red	Dry	°	Ch, G, & RM
Amarone della Valpolicella	ah-mah-roh-neh deh-lah vahl-poh-lee-CHAY-lah	Veneto, It.	Table wine	Red	Dry	°	Ch, G, & RM
Amer Picon	ah-mehr pee-koh(n)	France	Aperitif	Dark	Bitter	°°°	BD
Amontillado	ah-mohn-tee-YAH-doh	Jerez, Sp.	Sherry	Amber	Dry	°°	Hosp
Angelica	ahn-JEL-ee-kah	California	Fortified wine	Gold	Sweet	°	Hosp
Angostura Bitters	ahn-gus-TOO-rah	Trinidad	Aromatic bitters	Reddish brown	Bitter	°	C & Pun
Anisette	ah-nee-zet	Various	Liqueur	White	Aniseed	°	AD
Anjou	ah(n)-zhoo	Loire, Fr.	Table wine	White or pink	Med. sweet	°°°	F, P, & LM
Anninger Perle	on-ing-ehr PEHR-luh	Austria	Table wine	White	Dry	°°°	F, P, & LM
Applejack		U.S.	Apple brandy	Amber	Dry, fruity	°	AD
Apricot liqueur		Various	Liqueur	Amber	Sweet, fruity	°	AD
Aquavit	AHK-wa-veet	Denmark	Spirit	White	Caraway	°°°	BD
Armagnac	ar-mah-nyahk	Gers, Fr.	Brandy	Amber	Dry	°	AD
Assmannshausen	AHS-mahnz-howz-en	Rheingau, Ger.	Table wine	Red	Dry	°	RM
Asti Spumante	ahs-tee spoo-MAHN-teh	Piedmont, It.	Sparkling wine	White	Sweet	°°°	Desserts
Aurora	oh-RORE-uh	New York State	Table wine	White	Dry	°°°	F, P, & LM
Avdat	AHV-daht	Israel	Table wine	Red or white	Dry	° or °°°	Varies with color
Baco Noir	bah-koh nwahr	New York State	Table wine	Red	Dry	°	P & RM
Badacsonyi Rizling	BAHD-ah-choh-nee reez-ling	Hungary	Table wine	White	Dry	°°°	F, P, & LM
Badacsonyi Szürkebarát	BAHD-ah-choh-nee tsoor-keh-BAH-raht	Hungary	Table wine	White	Med. dry	°°°	F, P, & LM
Banyuls	bah-nyuls	Banyuls, Fr.	Fortified wine	White	Sweet	°	AD
Barack Palinka	BAR-ahks PAH-leen-kah	Hungary	Apricot brandy	Orange	Dry	°	AD

Service temperature: °—Room temperature / °°—Slightly Chilled / °°°—Cold
Serve with: AD—After dinner / BD—Before dinner / C—Cocktails / Ch—Cheese / F—Fish / Fr—Fruits / G—Game / H—Highballs / Hosp—Hospitality / LM—Light meats / P—Poultry / Pun—Punches / RM—Red meats / S—Straight

NAME	PHONETIC SPELLING	SOURCE	TYPE	COLOR	TASTE	SERV. TEMP.	SERVE WITH
Barbaresco	bar-bah-REHZ-koh	Piedmont, It.	Table wine	Red	Dry	°	Ch, G, & RM
Barbera	bar-BEH-rah	Piedmont, It., California	Table wine	Red	Dry	°	Ch, G, & RM
Bardolino	bar-doh-LEEN-oh	Veneto, It.	Table wine	Red	Dry	°	Ch, G, & RM
Barolo	bah-ROH-loh	Piedmont, It.	Table wine	Red	Dry	°	Ch, G, & RM
Barsac	bar-sahk	Barsac, Fr.	Table wine	White	Sweet	° ° °	Fr & desserts
Batard-Montrachet (GC)	bah-tar-moh(n)-rah-shay	Côte de Beaune, Fr.	Table wine	White	Dry	° ° °	F, P, & LM
Batavia arak	bah-TAY-vee ah AHR-ahk	Java, Indonesia	Spirit	Straw	Dry, aromatic	° ° °	C, Pun, & H
Beaujolais	boh-zhoe-lay	Beaujolais, Fr.	Table wine	Red	Dry	° or ° °	All foods
Beaune	bone	Côte de Beaune, Fr.	Table wine	Red	Dry	°	Ch, G, & RM
Beaune-Grèves (PC)	bone-grehv	Côte de Beaune, Fr.	Table wine	Red	Dry	°	Ch, G, & RM
Beaune-Les Fèves (PC)	bone-lay-fehv	Côte de Beaune, Fr.	Table wine	Red	Dry	°	Ch, G, & RM
Beer, lager	LAH-gur	Various	Malt beverage	Pale gold	Dry	° ° °	Hosp
Bénédictine	bay-nay-deek-teen	Fécamp, Fr.	Liqueur	Gold	Spicy, sweet	°	AD
Bernkasteler Doctor	behrn-kahs-tel-ehr DAWK-tohr	Moselle, Ger.	Table wine	White	Med. dry	° ° °	F, P, & LM
Bianco di Custoza	bee-AHN-koh dee kus-TOES-eh	Veneto, It.	Table wine	White	Dry	° ° °	F, P
Bienvenue-Bâtard-Montrachet (GC)	bya(n)-veh-noo-bah-tahr-moh(n)-rah-shay	Côte de Beaune, Fr.	Table wine	White	Dry	° ° °	F, P, & LM
Binger Scharlachberg	bing-ehr SHAHR-lahk-behrk	Rheinhessen, Ger.	Table wine	White	Dry	° ° °	F, P, & LM
Bitters		Various	Spirit	Reddish brown	Bitter	° ° °	C, H, & Pun
Blackberry liqueur		Various	Liqueur	Dark red	Sweet, fruity	°	AD
Blanc de Blancs	blah(n) duh blah(n)	Champagne, Fr.	Sparkling wine	White	Dry	° ° °	All foods & Hosp
Bonnes Mares, Les (GC)	lay bun mahr	Côte de Nuits, Fr.	Table wine	Red	Dry	°	Ch, G, & RM
Bordeaux Blanc	bor-doh blah(n)	Bordeaux, Fr.	Table wine	White	Dry, semisweet	° ° °	F, P, & LM
Bordeaux Rouge	bor-doh roozh	Bordeaux, Fr.	Table wine	Red	Dry	°	Ch, G, & RM
Bourbon whisky		U.S.	Spirit	Brown	Dry		S, C, H, & Pun
Bourgogne Blanc	boor-gun-yeh blah(n)	Burgundy, Fr.	Table wine	White	Dry	° ° °	F, P, & LM
Bourgogne Rouge	boor-gun-yeh roozh	Burgundy, Fr.	Table wine	Red	Dry	°	Ch, G, & RM
Brachetto	brah-KET-oh	Piedmont, It.	Table wine	Red	Dry	°	Ch, G, & RM
Brandy	BRAN-dee	Various	Fruit spirit	Amber	Dry, fruit	°	BD, C, & H
Brauneberger Juffer	brown-uh-behrk-ehr YOO-fehr	Moselle, Ger.	Table wine	White	Dry	° ° °	F, P, & LM
Brouilly	brwee-yee	Beaujolais, Fr.	Table wine	Red	Dry	°	Ch, G, & RM
Brunello di Montalcino	broo-NEHL-oh dee mohn-tahl-CHEE-noh	Tuscany, It.	Table wine	Red	Dry	°	Ch, G, & RM
Bual (Boal)	boo whal	Madeira	Fortified wine	Gold	Sweet	°	Hosp
Bucelas	boo-SEL-ush	Portugal	Table wine	White	Med. sweet	° ° °	LM & Fr
Buzbag	BOOZ-bah	Turkey	Table wine	Red	Dry	°	Ch, G, & RM
Cabernet Sauvignon	kah-behr-nay soh-vee-nyoh(n)	Various	Table wine	Red	Dry	°	Ch, G, & RM
Calvados	kahl-vah-dohs	Normandy, Fr.	Apple brandy	Brown	Dry, fruit	°	AD
Campari	kahm-PAR-ee	Italy	Aperitif	Red	Bitter	° ° °	BD
Canadian whisky		Canada	Spirit	Brown	Dry, rich	° or ° ° °	C, H, Pun, & S

Service temperature: °—Room temperature / ° °—Slightly chilled / ° ° °—Cold
Serve with: AD—After dinner / BD—Before dinner / C—Cocktails / Ch—Cheese / F—Fish / Fr—Fruits / G—Game / H—Highballs / Hosp—Hospitality / LM—Light meats / P—Poultry / Pun—Punches / RM—Red meats / S—Straight
1855 classification: 1st—First growth / 2nd—Second growth, etc.; *wines of Burgundy:* GC—*Grand Cru* / PC—*Premier Cru*

NAME	PHONETIC SPELLING	SOURCE	TYPE	COLOR	TASTE	SERV. TEMP.	SERVE WITH
Capri	KAH-pree	Capri, It.	Table wine	White	Dry	° ° °	F, P, & LM
Carcavelos	kar-sah-VEL-ush	Portugal	Fortified wine	White	Sweet	° ° °	AD
Carema	kah-RAY-mah	Piedmont, It.	Table wine	Red	Dry	°	Ch, G, & RM
Carruades de Château Lafite-Rothschild	kah-rwahd duh shah-toh lah-feet-roh-sheeld	Médoc, Fr.	Table wine	Red	Dry	°	Ch, G, & RM
Catawba	kuh-TAW-bah	New York State & Ohio	Table or sparkling wine	White	Sweet	° ° °	Fr & Hosp
Cava	cah-vah	Spain	Sparkling	White	Dry	° ° °	Hosp
Chablis	shah-blee	Chablis, Fr.	Table wine	White	Dry	° ° °	Oysters, P, & LM
Chablis Blanchots (GC)	shah-blee blah(n)-shoh	Chablis, Fr.	Table wine	White	Dry	° ° °	Oysters, P, & LM
Chablis Bougros (GC)	shah-blee boo-groh	Chablis, Fr.	Table wine	White	Dry	° ° °	Oysters, P, & LM
Chablis Grenouilles (GC)	shah-blee grah-nwee	Chablis, Fr.	Table wine	White	Dry	° ° °	Oysters, P, & LM
Chablis Les Clos (GC)	shah-blee lay kloh	Chablis, Fr.	Table wine	White	Dry	° ° °	Oysters, P, & LM
Chablis Les Preuses (GC)	shah-blee lay pruhz	Chablis, Fr.	Table wine	White	Dry	° ° °	Oysters, P, & LM
Chablis Valmur (GC)	shah-blee vahl-moor	Chablis, Fr.	Table wine	White	Dry	° ° °	Oysters, P, & LM
Chablis Vaudésir (GC)	shah-blee voh-day-zeer	Chablis, Fr.	Table wine	White	Dry	° ° °	Oysters, P, & LM
Chambertin, Le (GC)	luh shah(m)-behr-ta(n)	Côte de Nuits, Fr.	Table wine	Red	Dry	°	Ch, G, & RM
Chambertin-Clos de Bèze (GC)	shah(m)-behr-ta(n)-klohd-behz	Côte de Nuits, Fr.	Table wine	Red	Dry	°	Ch, G, & RM
Chambolle-Musigny	shah(m)-bohl-moo-see nyee	Côte de Nuits, Fr.	Table wine	Red	Dry	°	Ch, G, & RM
Chambolle-Musigny-Les Amoureuses (PC)	shan(m)-bohl-moo-see-nyee layz ah-muh-ruhz	Côte de Nuits, Fr.	Table wine	Red	Dry	°	Ch, G, & RM
Champagne	shah(m)-pah-nye	Champagne, Fr.	Sparkling wine	White or light red	Dry to sweet	° ° °	All foods & Hosp
Chapelle-Chambertin (GC)	shah-pehl-shah(m)-behr-ta(n)	Côte de Nuits, Fr.	Table wine	Red	Dry	°	Ch, G, & RM
Charbono	shar-BOH-noh	California	Table wine	Red	Dry	° ° °	Ch, G, & RM
Chardonnay	shahr-doh-NAY	Various	Table or sparkling	White	Dry	° ° °	F, P, & LM
Charmes-Chambertin (GC)	shahrm-shah(m)-behr-ta(n)	Côte de Nuits, Fr.	Table wine	Red	Dry	°	Ch, G, & RM
Chartreuse	shahr-truhz	Voiron, Fr.	Liqueur	Yellow or green	Spicy, sweet	°	AD
Chassagne-Montrachet	shah-sah-nyuh-moh(n)-rah-shay	Côte de Beaune, Fr.	Table wine	White or red	Dry	° or ° ° °	Varies with color
Château Ausone	shah-toh oh-sohn	Saint-Emilion, Fr.	Table wine	Red	Dry	°	Ch, G, & RM
Château Bataillce (5th)	shah toh bah-tie-yay	Médoc, Fr.	Table wine	Red	Dry	°	Ch, G, & RM
Château Beauséjour	shah-toh boh-say-zhewr	Saint-Emilion, Fr.	Table wine	Red	Dry	°	Ch, G, & RM
Château Belair	shah-toh bel-ehr	Saint-Emilion, Fr.	Table wine	Red	Dry	°	Ch, G, & RM
Château Belgrave (5th)	shah-toh bel-grahv	Médoc, Fr.	Table wine	Red	Dry	°	Ch, G, & RM
Château Bellevue	shah-toh bel-vuh	Saint-Emilion, Fr.	Table wine	Red	Dry	°	Ch, G, & RM
Château Beychevelle (4th)	shah-toh baysh-vehl	Médoc, Fr.	Table wine	Red	Dry	°	Ch, G, & RM
Château Bouscaut	shah-toh boo-skoh	Graves, Fr.	Table wine	Red or white	Dry	° or ° ° °	Varies with color

NAME	PHONETIC SPELLING	SOURCE	TYPE	COLOR	TASTE	SERV. TEMP.	SERVE WITH
Château Boyd-Cantenac (3rd)	shah-toh-bwahd-kah(n)-teh-nahk	Médoc, Fr.	Table wine	Red	Dry	°	Ch, G, & RM
Château Branaire-Ducru (4th)	shah-toh brah-nehr-doo-croo	Médoc, Fr.	Table wine	Red	Dry	°	Ch, G, & RM
Château Brane-Cantenac (2nd)	shah-toh brahn kah(n)-teh-nahk	Médoc, Fr.	Table wine	Red	Dry	°	Ch, G, & RM
Château Broustet (2nd)	shah-toh broo-stay	Barsac, Fr.	Table wine	White	Sweet	°°°	Desserts
Château Caillou (2nd)	shah-toh kah-yoo	Barsac, Fr.	Table wine	White	Sweet	°°°	Desserts
Château Calon-Ségur (3rd)	shah-toh kah-loh(n) say-goor	Médoc, Fr.	Table wine	Red	Dry	°	Ch, G, & RM
Château Camensac (5th)	shah-toh kah-men-sahk	Médoc, Fr.	Table wine	Red	Dry	°	Ch, G, & RM
Château Canon	shah-toh kah-noh(n)	Saint-Emilion, Fr.	Table wine	Red	Dry	°	Ch, G, & RM
Château Cantemerle (5th)	shah-toh kha(n)-teh-mehrl	Médoc, Fr.	Table wine	Red	Dry	°	Ch, G, & RM
Château Cantenac-Brown (3rd)	shah-toh kha(n)-teh-nahk-brown	Médoc, Fr.	Table wine	Red	Dry	°	Ch, G, & RM
Château Carbonnieux	shah-toh car-boh-nyuh	Graves, Fr.	Table wine	Red or white	Dry	° or °°°	Varies with color
Château Certan-Giraud	shah-toh sehr-ta(n)-zhee-roh	Pomerol, Fr.	Table wine	Red	Dry	°	Ch, G, & RM
Château Châlon	shah-toh-shah-loh(n)	Jura, Fr.	Table wine	White	Dry	°°°	BD
Château Cheval-Blanc	shah-toh sheh-vahl-blah(n)	Saint-Emilion, Fr.	Table wine	Red	Dry	°	Ch, G, & RM
Château Clerc-Mil-on-Mondon (5th)	shah-toh klehr-mee-loh(n)-moh(n)-doh(n)	Médoc, Fr.	Table wine	Red	Dry	°	Ch, G, & RM
Château Climens (1st)	shah-toh klee-mah(n)	Barsac, Fr.	Table wine	White	Sweet	°°°	Desserts
(Château) Clos Fourtet	shah-toh kloh foor-tay	Saint-Emilion, Fr.	Table wine	Red	Dry	°	Ch, G, & RM
(Château) Clos Haut-Peyraguey (1st)	shah-toh kloh oh-pay-rah-gay	Sauternes, Fr.	Table wine	White	Sweet	°°°	Desserts
Château Cos d'Estournel (2nd)	shah-toh koh deh-toor-nel	Médoc, Fr.	Table wine	Red	Dry	°	Ch, G, & RM
Château Cos-Labory (5th)	shah-toh koh-lah-boh-ree	Médoc, Fr.	Table wine	Red	Dry	°	Ch, G, & RM
Château Couhins	shah-toh k wah(n)	Graves, Fr.	Table wine	White	Dry	°°°	F, P, & LM
Château Coutet (1st)	shah-toh koo-tay	Barsac, Fr.	Table wine	White	Sweet	°°°	Desserts
Château Croizet-Bages (5th)	shah-toh krwah-zeh-bahzh	Médoc, Fr.	Table wine	Red	Dry	°	Ch, G, & RM
Château d'Arche (2nd)	shah-toh dahrsh	Sauternes, Fr.	Table wine	White	Sweet	°°°	Desserts
Château Dauzac (5th)	shah-toh doh-zahk	Médoc, Fr.	Table wine	Red	Dry	°	Ch, G, & RM
Château de Malle (2nd)	shah-toh duh mahl	Sauternes, Fr.	Table wine	White	Sweet	°°°	Desserts
Château d'Issan (3rd)	shah-toh dee-sah(n)	Médoc, Fr.	Table wine	Red	Dry	°	Ch, G, & RM
Château de Rayne-Vigneau (1st)	shah-toh duh rayn-vee-nyoh	Sauternes, Fr.	Table wine	White	Sweet	°°°	Desserts
Château Doisy-Daene (2nd)	shah-toh dwah-zee-dane	Barsac, Fr.	Table wine	White	Sweet	°°°	Desserts
Château Doisy-Védrines (2nd)	shah-toh dwah-zee-vay-dreen	Barsac, Fr.	Table wine	White	Sweet	°°°	Desserts
Château Ducru-Beaucaillou (2nd)	shah-toh doo-croo-boh-kah-yoo	Médoc, Fr.	Table wine	Red	Dry	°	Ch, G, & RM

Service temperature: °—Room temperature / °°—Slightly chilled / °°°—Cold
Serve with: AD—After dinner / BD—Before dinner / C—Cocktails / Ch—Cheese / F—Fish / Fr—Fruits / G—Game / H—Highballs / Hosp—Hospitality / LM—Light meats / P—Poultry / Pun—Punches / RM—Red meats / S—Straight
1855 classification: 1st—First growth / 2nd—Second growth, etc.; *wines of Burgundy:* GC—*Grand Cru* / PC—*Premier Cru*

NAME	PHONETIC SPELLING	SOURCE	TYPE	COLOR	TASTE	SERV. TEMP.	SERVE WITH
Château Duhart-Milon-Rothschild (4th)	shah-toh doo-ar-mee-loh(n)-roh-sheeld	Médoc, Fr.	Table wine	Red	Dry	*	Ch, G, & RM
Château Durfort-Vivens (2nd)	shah-toh duhr-for-vee-vah(n)	Médoc, Fr.	Table wine	Red	Dry	*	Ch, G, & RM
Château du Tertre (5th)	shah-toh doo tehrtr	Médoc, Fr.	Table wine	Red	Dry	*	Ch, G, & RM
Château d'Yquem (1st)	shah-toh dee-kem	Sauternes, Fr.	Table wine	White	Sweet	***	Desserts
Château Ferrière (3rd)	shah-toh fehr-yehr	Médoc, Fr.	Table wine	Red	Dry	*	Ch, G, & RM
Château Fieuzal	shah-toh fyuh-zahl	Graves, Fr.	Table wine	Red	Dry	*	Ch, G, & RM
Château Figeac	shah-toh fee-zhahk	Saint-Émilion, Fr.	Table wine	Red	Dry	*	Ch, G, & RM
Château Filhot (2nd)	shah-toh fee-loh	Sauternes, Fr.	Table wine	White	Sweet	***	Desserts
Château Gazin	shah-toh gah-za(n)	Pomerol, Fr.	Table wine	Red	Dry	*	Ch, G, & RM
Château Giscours (3rd)	shah-toh zhis-koor	Médoc, Fr.	Table wine	Red	Dry	*	Ch, G, & RM
Château Grand-Puy-Ducasse (5th)	shah-toh grah(n)-pwee-doo-kahs	Médoc, Fr.	Table wine	Red	Dry	*	Ch, G, & RM
Château Grand-Puy-Lacoste (5th)	shah-toh grah(n)-pwee-lah-kohst	Médoc, Fr.	Table wine	Red	Dry	*	Ch, G, & RM
Château Grillet	shah-toh gree-yay	Côtes du Rhône, Fr.	Table wine	White	Dry	***	F, P, & LM
Château Gruaud-Larose (2nd)	shah-toh groo-oh-lah-rohz	Médoc, Fr.	Table wine	Red	Dry	*	Ch, G, & RM
Château Guiraud (1st)	shah-toh zhwee-roh	Sauternes, Fr.	Table wine	White	Sweet	***	Desserts
Château Haut-Bages-Libéral (5th)	shah-toh oh-bahzh-lee-beh-rahl	Médoc, Fr.	Table wine	Red	Dry	*	Ch, G, & RM
Château Haut-Bailly	shah-toh oh-bay-yee	Graves, Fr.	Table wine	Red	Dry	*	Ch, G, & RM
Château Haut-Batailley (5th)	shah-toh oh-bah-tie-yay	Médoc, Fr.	Table wine	Red	Dry	*	Ch, G, & RM
Château Haut-Brion (1st)	shah-toh oh-bree-oh(n)	Graves, Fr.	Table wine	Red	Dry	*	Ch, G, & RM
Château Haut-Brion Blanc	shah-toh oh-bree-oh(n) blah(n)	Graves, Fr.	Table wine	White	Dry	***	F, P, & LM
Château Kirwan (3rd)	shah-toh kir-wah(n)	Médoc, Fr.	Table wine	Red	Dry	*	Ch, G, & RM
Château La Conseillante	shah-toh lah koh(n)-say-ah(n)t	Pomerol, Fr.	Table wine	Red	Dry	*	Ch, G, & RM
Château Lafaurie-Peyraguey (1st)	shah-toh lah-foh-ree-pay-rah-gay	Sauternes, Fr.	Table wine	White	Sweet	***	Desserts
Château Lafite-Rothschild (1st)	shah-toh lah-feet-roh-sheeld	Médoc, Fr.	Table wine	Red	Dry	*	Ch, G, & RM
Château La Fleur-Pétrus	shah-toh lah fluhr-pay-troos	Pomerol, Fr.	Table wine	Red	Dry	*	Ch, G, & RM
Château Lafon-Rochet (4th)	shah-toh lah-foh(n)-roh-shay	Médoc, Fr.	Table wine	Red	Dry	*	Ch, G, & RM
Château La Gaffelière	shah-toh lah gah-fel-yehr	Saint-Émilion, Fr.	Table wine	Red	Dry	*	Ch, G, & RM
Château La Garde	shah-toh lah gahrd	Graves, Fr.	Table wine	Red	Dry	*	Ch, G, & RM
Château Lagrange (3rd)	shah-toh lah-grah(n)zh	Médoc, Fr.	Table wine	Red	Dry	*	Ch, G, & RM
Château La Lagune (3rd)	shah-toh lah lah-goon	Médoc, Fr.	Table wine	Red	Dry	*	Ch, G, & RM
Château La Mission Haut Brion	shah-toh lah mee-syoh(n) oh bree-oh(n)	Graves, Fr.	Table wine	Red	Dry	*	Ch, G, & RM
Château Lamothe (2nd)	shah-toh lah-moht	Sauternes, Fr.	Table wine	White	Sweet	***	Desserts

NAME	PHONETIC SPELLING	SOURCE	TYPE	COLOR	TASTE	SERV. TEMP.	SERVE WITH
Château Langoa-Barton (3rd)	shah-toh lah(n)-goh ah-bahr-toh(n)	Médoc, Fr.	Table wine	Red	Dry	*	Ch, G, & RM
Château Laroze	shah-toh lah-rohz	Saint-Emilion, Fr.	Table wine	Red	Dry	*	Ch, G, & RM
Château Larrivet Haut Brion	shah-toh lah-ree-veh oh-bree-oh(n)	Graves, Fr.	Table wine	White	Dry	***	F, P, & LM
Château Lascombes (2nd)	shah-toh lahs-coh(m)b	Médoc, Fr.	Table wine	Red	Dry	*	Ch, G, & RM
Château Latour (1st)	shah-toh lah-toor	Médoc, Fr.	Table wine	Red	Dry	*	Ch, G, & RM
Château La Tour-Blanche (1st)	shah-toh lah toor-blah(n)sh	Sauternes, Fr.	Table wine	White	Sweet	***	Desserts
Château La Tour-Carnet (4th)	shah-toh lah toor-car-nay	Médoc, Fr.	Table wine	Red	Dry	*	Ch, G, & RM
Château La Tour Haut Brion	shah-toh lah toor oh bree-oh(n)	Graves, Fr.	Table wine	Red	Dry	*	Ch, G, & RM
Château La Tour-Martillac	shah-toh lah toor-mahr-tee-yahk	Graves, Fr.	Table wine	Red or white	Dry	* or ***	Varies with color
Château Latour-Pomerol	shah-toh lah-toor-pohm-rohl	Pomerol, Fr.	Table wine	Red	Dry	*	Ch, G, & RM
Château Laville Haut Brion	shah-toh lah-vee yoh bree-oh(n)	Graves, Fr.	Table wine	White	Dry	***	F, P, & LM
Château Léoville-Barton (2nd)	shah-toh lay-oh-veel-bar-toh(n)	Médoc, Fr.	Table wine	Red	Dry	*	Ch, G, & RM
Château Léoville-Lascases (2nd)	shah-toh lay-oh-veel-lahs-kahz	Médoc, Fr.	Table wine	Red	Dry	*	Ch, G, & RM
Château Léoville-Poyferré (2nd)	shah-toh lay-oh-veel-pwah-feh-ray	Médoc, Fr.	Table wine	Red	Dry	*	Ch, G, & RM
Château L'Évangile	shah-toh lay-vah(n)-zheel	Pomerol, Fr.	Table wine	Red	Dry	*	Ch, G, & RM
Château Lynch-Bages (5th)	shah-toh leensh-bahzh	Médoc, Fr.	Table wine	Red	Dry	*	Ch, G, & RM
Château Lynch-Moussas (5th)	shah-toh leensh-moo-sah	Médoc, Fr.	Table wine	Red	Dry	*	Ch, G, & RM
Château Magdelaine	shah-toh mahg-duh-lehn	Saint-Émilion, Fr.	Table wine	Red	Dry	*	Ch, G, & RM
Château Malartic-Lagravière	shah-toh mah-lahr-teek-lah-grahv-yehr	Graves, Fr.	Table wine	Red or white	Dry	***	Varies with color
Château Malescot-Saint-Exupéry (3rd)	shah-toh mah-lehs-koh-sa(n)-tex-oo-peh-ree	Médoc, Fr.	Table wine	Red	Dry	*	Ch, G, & RM
Château Margaux (1st)	shah-toh mahr-goh	Médoc, Fr.	Table wine	Red	Dry	*	Ch, G, & RM
Château Marquis d'Alesme-Becker (3rd)	shah-toh mahr-kee dah-lehm-beh-ker	Médoc, Fr.	Table wine	Red	Dry	*	Ch, G, & RM
Château Marquis de Terme (4th)	shah-toh mahr-kee duh tehrm	Médoc, Fr.	Table wine	Red	Dry	*	Ch, G, & RM
Château Montrose (2nd)	shah-toh moh(n)-rohz	Médoc, Fr.	Table wine	Red	Dry	*	Ch, G, & RM
Château Mouton-Baron-Philippe (5th)	shah-toh moo-taw(n)-bah-roh(n)-fee-leep	Médoc, Fr.	Table wine	Red	Dry	*	Ch, G, & RM
Château Mouton-Rothschild (1st)	shah-toh moo-taw(n)-roh-sheeld	Médoc, Fr.	Table wine	Red	Dry	*	Ch, G, & RM

Service temperature: *—Room temperature / **—Slightly chilled / ***—Cold
Serve with: AD—After dinner / BD—Before dinner / C—Cocktails / Ch—Cheese / F—Fish / Fr—Fruits / G—Game /
      H—Highballs / Hosp—Hospitality / LM—Light meats / P—Poultry / Pun—Punches / RM—Red meats / S—Straight
1855 classification: 1st—First growth / 2nd—Second growth, etc.; *wines of Burgundy:* GC—*Grand Cru* / PC—*Premier Cru*

NAME	PHONETIC SPELLING	SOURCE	TYPE	COLOR	TASTE	SERV. TEMP.	SERVE WITH
Château Myrat (2nd)	shah-toh mee-rah	Barsac, Fr.	Table wine	White	Sweet	***	Desserts
Château Nairac (2nd)	shah-toh nay-rahk	Barsac, Fr.	Table wine	White	Sweet	***	Desserts
Château Nenin	shah-toh nuh-neen	Pomerol, Fr.	Table wine	Red	Dry	*	Ch, G, & RM
Châteauneuf-du-Pape	shah-toh-nuf-doo-pop	Rhône, Fr.	Table wine	Red	Dry	*	Ch, G, & RM
Château Olivier	shah-toh oh-lee-vyay	Graves, Fr.	Table wine	Red or white	Dry	* or ***	Varies with color
Château Palmer (3rd)	shah-toh pahl-mehr	Médoc, Fr.	Table wine	Red	Dry	*	Ch, G, & RM
Château Pape-Clément	shah-toh pop-klay-mah(n)	Graves, Fr.	Table wine	Red	Dry	*	Ch, G, & RM
Château Pavie	shah-toh pah-vee	Saint-Émilion, Fr.	Table wine	Red	Dry	*	Ch, G, & RM
Château Pédesclaux (5th)	shah-toh pay-dehs-kloh	Médoc, Fr.	Table wine	Red	Dry	*	Ch, G, & RM
Château Petit-Village	shah-toh puh-tee-vee-lahzh	Pomerol, Fr.	Table wine	Red	Dry	*	Ch, G, & RM
Château Pétrus	shah-toh peh-troos	Pomerol, Fr.	Table wine	Red	Dry	*	Ch, G, & RM
Château Pichon-Longueville (Baron) (2nd)	shah-toh pee-shoh(n)-loh(n)g-veel (bah-roh(n))	Médoc, Fr.	Table wine	Red	Dry	*	Ch, G, & RM
Château Pichon-Longueville-Comtesse (2nd)	shah-toh pee-shoh(n)-loh(n)g-veel-coh(m)-tehs	Médoc, Fr.	Table wine	Red	Dry	*	Ch, G, & RM
Château Pontet-Canet (5th)	shah-toh poh(n)-teh-kah-neh	Médoc, Fr.	Table wine	Red	Dry	*	Ch, G, & RM
Château Pouget (4th)	shah-toh poo-zhay	Médoc, Fr.	Table wine	Red	Dry	*	Ch, G, & RM
Château Prieuré-Lichine (4th)	shah-toh pree-uh-ray-lee-sheen	Médoc, Fr.	Table wine	Red	Dry	*	Ch, G, & RM
Château Rabaud-Promis (1st)	shah-toh rah-boh-proh-mee	Sauternes, Fr.	Table wine	White	Sweet	***	Desserts
Château Rausan-Ségla (2nd)	shah-toh roh-zah(n)-say-glah	Médoc, Fr.	Table wine	Red	Dry	*	Ch, G, & RM
Château Rauzan-Gassies (2nd)	shah-toh roh-zah(n)-gah-see	Médoc, Fr.	Table wine	Red	Dry	*	Ch, G, & RM
Château Rieussec (1st)	shah-toh ree-uh-sehk	Sauternes, Fr.	Table wine	White	Sweet	***	Desserts
Château Ripeau	shah-toh ree-poh	Saint-Émilion, Fr.	Table wine	Red	Dry	*	Ch, G, & RM
Château Romer (2nd)	shah-toh roh-mehr	Sauternes, Fr.	Table wine	White	Sweet	***	Desserts
Château Saint-Pierre (4th)	shah-toh sa(n)-pyehr	Médoc, Fr.	Table wine	Red	Dry	*	Ch, G, & RM
Château Sigalas-Rabaud (1st)	shah-toh see-gah-lah-rah-boh	Sauternes, Fr.	Table wine	White	Sweet	***	Desserts
Château Smith-Haut-Lafitte	shah-toh smith-oh-lah-feet	Graves, Fr.	Table wine	Red	Dry	*	Ch, G, & RM
Château Suau	shah-toh soo-oh	Barsac, Fr.	Table wine	White	Sweet	***	Desserts
Château Suduiraut (1st)	shah-toh soo-dwee-roh	Sauternes, Fr.	Table wine	White	Sweet	***	Desserts
Château Talbot (4th)	shah-toh tahl-boh	Médoc, Fr.	Table wine	Red	Dry	*	Ch, G, & RM
Château Trimoulet	shah-toh tree-moo-lay	Saint-Émilion, Fr.	Table wine	Red	Dry	*	Ch, G, & RM
Château Troplong-Mondot	shah-toh troh-loh(ng)-moh(n)-doh	Saint-Émilion, Fr.	Table wine	Red	Dry	*	Ch, G, & RM
Château Trotanoy	shah-toh trwah-tah-nwah	Pomerol, Fr.	Table wine	Red	Dry	*	Ch, G, & RM
Château Trottevieille	shah-toh troht-vyay	Saint-Émilion, Fr.	Table wine	Red	Dry	*	Ch, G, & RM
(Château) Vieux Château Certan	(shah-toh) vyuh shah-toh sehr-ta(n)	Pomerol, Fr.	Table wine	Red	Dry	*	Ch, G, & RM

NAME	PHONETIC SPELLING	SOURCE	TYPE	COLOR	TASTE	SERV. TEMP.	SERVE WITH
Chefoo	chay-foo	China	Dessert wine	Red or white	Sweet	°°°	Desserts
Chelois	shel-wah	New York State	Table wine	Red	Med. dry	°°	P & RM
Chenin Blanc	sheh-neen blah(n)	California & France	Table wine	White	Med. dry	°°	F, P, & LM
Cherry liqueur		Various	Liqueur	Red	Sweet, cherry	°	AD
Chevalier-Montrachet (GC)	sheh-vahl-yay moh(n)-rah-shay	Côte de Beaune, Fr.	Table wine	White	Dry	°°°	F, P, & LM
Chianti	kee-AHN-tee	Tuscany, It.	Table wine	Red	Dry	°	All foods
Chiaretto del Garda	kee-ah-RET-oh del gar-dah	Veneto, It.	Table wine	Pink	Med. dry	°°°	All foods
Cider		Spain & England	Sparkling or still wine	Straw	Sweet, fruity	°°°	Hosp
Clos de la Roche (GC)	kloh duh lah rohsh	Côte de Nuits, Fr.	Table wine	Red	Dry	°	Ch, G, & RM
Clos des Lambrays (PC)	kloh day lah(m)-bray	Côte de Nuits, Fr.	Table wine	Red	Dry	°	Ch, G, & RM
Clos des Mouches (PC)	kloh day moosh	Côte de Beaune, Fr.	Table wine	Red	Dry	°	Ch, G, & RM
Clos de Tart (GC)	kloh-duh tahr	Côte de Nuits, Fr.	Table wine	Red	Dry	°	Ch, G, & RM
Clos de Vougeot (GC)	kloh duh voo-zhoh	Côte de Nuits, Fr.	Table wine	Red	Dry	°	Ch, G, & RM
Clos Saint-Denis (GC)	kloh sa(n)-duh-nee	Côte de Nuits, Fr.	Table wine	Red	Dry	°	Ch, G, & RM
Clos Sainte-Odile	kloh sa(n)-toh-deel	Alsace, Fr.	Table wine	White	Med. dry	°°°	All foods
Clos Saint-Jacques (PC)	kloh sa(n)-zhahk	Côte de Nuits, Fr.	Table wine	Red	Dry	°	Ch, G, & RM
Cognac	koh-nyahk	Cognac, Fr.	Brandy	Brown	Dry	°	AD
Cointreau	kwa(n)-troh	Angers, Fr.	Liqueur	White	Sweet, orange	°	AD
Colares	koh-LAHR-esh	Portugal	Table wine	Red	Dry	°	Ch, G, & RM
Combettes, Les (PC)	lay co(m)-bet	Côte de Beaune, Fr.	Table wine	White	Dry	°°°	F, P, & LM
Commandaria	koh-mahn-dah-REE-ah	Cyprus	Dessert wine	White	Sweet	°	AD
Cortaillod	kohr-tie-oh	Switzerland	Table wine	Red	Dry	°	Ch, & RM
Cortese di Gavi	kohr-TAY-zee	Piedmont, It.	Table wine	White	Dry	°°°	F, P, & LM
Corton, Le (GC)	luh kohr-toh(n)	Côte de Beaune, Fr.	Table wine	Red	Dry	°	Ch, G, & RM
Corton-Charlemagne (GC)	kor-toh(n)-shahr-leh-mah-nyuh	Côte de Beaune, Fr.	Table wine	White	Dry	°°°	F, P, & LM
Corton-Clos du Roi (GC)	kor-toh(n)-kloh doo rwah	Côte de Beaune, Fr.	Table wine	Red	Dry	°	Ch, G, & RM
Corton-Pougets (GC)	kor-toh(n)-poo-zheh	Côte de Beaune, Fr.	Table wine	Red	Dry	°	Ch, G, & RM
Corvo	kohr-voh	Sicily, It.	Table wine	Red or white	Dry	° or °°°	Varies with color
Côteaux de la Loire	koh-toh duh lah lwahr	Loire, Fr.	Table wine	White	Med. sweet	°°°	All foods
Côte Rôtie	koht roh-tee	Rhône, Fr.	Table wine	Red	Dry	°	Ch, G, & RM
Cotnari Grasa	koht-NAR-ee GRAH-sah	Romania	Dessert wine	Gold	Sweet	°°°	Desserts, AD
Crème de bananes	krehm deh bah-nahn	Various	Liqueur	Gold	Sweet, banana	°	AD
Crème de cacao	krehn duh kah-kah_oh	Various	Liqueur	Brown or white	Sweet, chocolate	°	AD

Service temperature: ° —Room temperature / ° ° —Slightly chilled / ° ° ° —Cold
Serve with: AD—After dinner / BD—Before dinner / C—Cocktails / Ch—Cheese / F—Fish / Fr—Fruits / G—Game / H—High-balls / Hosp—Hospitality / LM—Light meats / P—Poultry / Pun—Punches / RM—Red meats / S—Straight
1855 classification: 1st—First growth / 2nd—Second growth, etc.; *wines of Burgundy:* GC—*Grand Cru* / PC—*Premier Cru*

NAME	PHONETIC SPELLING	SOURCE	TYPE	COLOR	TASTE	SERV. TEMP.	SERVE WITH
Crème de cassis	krehm duh kah-sees	Various	Liqueur	Red	Sweet, currant	° ° °	H & C, aperitifs
Crème de menthe	krehm duh mah(n)t	Various	Liqueur	White or green	Sweet, mint	° ° °	AD
Crème de noyaux	krehm duh noy-oh	Various	Liqueur	Cream	Sweet, nut	°	AD
Crème de violettes	krehm duh vee-oh-let	Various	Liqueur	Violet	Sweet, violet	°	AD
Crème Yvette	krehm ee-vet	Connecticut	Liqueur	Blue or violet	Sweet, violet	°	AD
Criots-Bâtard-Montrachet (GC)	kree-ut-bah-tahr-moh(n)-rah-shay	Côte de Beaune, Fr.	Table wine	White	Dry	° ° °	F, P, & LM
Csopaki Furmint	CHO-pah-kee foor-mint	Hungary	Table wine	White	Dry	° ° °	F, P, & LM
Curaçao	kuh-rah-soh	Various	Liqueur	Orange	Sweet, orange	°	AD
Cynar	CHEE-nar	Italy	Aperitif	Brown	Bitter	° ° °	BD
Danziger Goldwasser	dahnt-zeeg-ehr GOHLD-vahs-ehr	Danzig, Ger.	Liqueur	White	Sweet	°	AD
Dão	dow	Portugal	Table wine	Red or white	Dry	° or ° ° °	Varies with color
Debröi Hárslevelü	DEH-broy harsh-leh-vel-yoo	Hungary	Table wine	White	Med. sweet	° ° °	All foods
Deidesheimer Leinhöhle	die-dehs-hie-mehr LINE-hoyl-eh	Rheinpfalz, Ger.	Table wine	White	Med. dry	° ° °	F, P, & LM
Demeraran rum	dem-eh-RAH-rahn	Guyana	Spirit	Dark brown	Med. sweet	° ° °	C, H, Pun & S
Demestica	deh-MES-tee-kah	Greece	Table wine	Red or white	Dry	° or ° ° °	Varies with color
Dézaley	day-zah-lay	Switzerland	Table wine	White	Dry	° ° °	F, P, & LM
Dolcetto	dohl-CHET-oh	Piedmont, It.	Table or sparkling wine	Red	Dry or sweet	° or ° ° °	All foods
Dôle de Sion	dohl duh see oh(n)	Switzerland	Table wine	Red	Dry	°	Ch, G, & RM
Domaine de Chevalier	duh-men duh sheh-vahl-yay	Graves, Fr.	Table wine	Red or white	Dry	° or ° ° °	Varies with color
Drambuie	dram-BOO EE	Scotland	Liqueur	Gold	Sweet, spicy	°	AD
Dubonnet	doo-boh-nay	France & U.S.	Aperitif	Red or white	Sweet	° ° °	BD
Dürkheimer Michelsberg	doork-hie-mehr MEEK-els-behrk	Rheinpfalz, Ger.	Table wine	White	Med. dry	° ° °	F, P, & LM
Dürkheimer Spielberg	doork-hie-mehr SHPEEL-behrk	Rheinpfalz, Ger.	Table wine	White	Med. dry	° ° °	F, P, & LM
Eau de Vie de Marc	ode-vee duh mahr	France	Brandy	Brown	Dry	°	AD
Eau de Vie de Poire	ode-vee duh pwahr	Various	Pear brandy	White	Dry, pear	° ° °	AD
Echézeaux, Les (GC)	lays ay-sheh-zoh	Côte de Nuits, Fr.	Table wine	Red	Dry	°	Ch, G, & RM
Egri Bikavér	eg-ree BEE-kah-vehr	Hungary	Table wine	Red	Dry	°	Ch, G, & RM
Eiswein	ICE-vine	Rhine & Moselle, Ger.	Table wine	White	Sweet	° ° °	Desserts
Erbacher Marcobrunn	EHR-bahk-ehr MAHR-koh-bruhn	Rheingau, Ger.	Table wine	White	Med. dry	° ° °	F, P, & LM
Erdener Treppchen	ehrd-eh-nehr TREPF-shen	Moselle, Ger.	Table wine	White	Med. dry	° ° °	F, P, & LM
Escherndorfer Lump	eh-shehrn-dorf-ehr LOOMP	Franconia, Ger.	Table wine	White	Med. dry	° ° °	F, P, & LM
Est! Est!! Est!!!	ehst-ehst-EHST	Latium, It.	Table wine	White	Dry	° ° °	F, P, & LM
Falerno	fah-LEHR-noh	Campania, It.	Table wine	Red or white	Dry	° or ° ° °	Varies with color
Fendent de Sion	fah(n)-dah(n) duh see oh(n)	Switzerland	Table wine	White	Dry	° ° °	F, P, & LM

NAME	PHONETIC SPELLING	SOURCE	TYPE	COLOR	TASTE	SERV. TEMP,.	SERVE WITH
Fernet Branca	fehr-net BRAHN-kah	Italy & U.S.	Bitters	Reddish brown	Bitter	°	C & H
Fiano di Avellino	FYAN-oh dee ah-veh-LEEN-oh	Campania, It.	Table wine	White	Dry	°°°	F, P, LM, & Ch
Fino	FEE-noh	Jerez, Sp.	Sherry	Straw	Dry	°°	BD
Fior d'Alpe	fyor DAHL-pay	Italy	Liqueur	Gold	Sweet	°	AD
Fleurie	fluh-ree	Beaujolais, Fr.	Table wine	Red	Dry	°	All foods
Folle Blanche	fohl blah(n)sh	California	Table wine	White	Dry	°°°	F, P, & LM
Forster Kirchenstück	forsh-ter KEER(KH)-en-shtuk	Rheinpfalz, Ger.	Table wine	White	Med. dry	°°°	F, P, & LM
Forster Ungeheuer	forsh-ter OONG eh-hoy-er	Rheinpfalz, Ger.	Table wine	White	Med. dry	°°°	F, P, & LM
Fraise	frehz	Various	Strawberry brandy	White	Dry	°°°	AD
Framboise	frah(m)-bwahz	Various	Raspberry brandy	White	Dry, raspberry	°°°	AD
Frascati	frahs-KAH-tee	Latium, It.	Table wine	White	Med. sweet	°°°	F, P, & LM
Frecciarossa	freh-chah-ROH-sah	Lombardy, It.	Table wine	Red or white	Dry	° or °°°	Varies with color
Freisa	FRAY-sah	Piedmont, It.	Table wine	Red	Dry	°	Ch, G, & RM
French vermouth		Midi, Fr.	Aromatized wine	White	Dry	°°°	BD & C
Galestro	gah-LEHS-troh	Tuscany, It.	Table wine	White	Dry	°°°	F, P, LM
Galliano	gahl-YAH-noh	Milan, It.	Liqueur	Gold	Sweet	°	AD
Gamay	gah-may	France & California	Table wine	Red	Dry	°°	Ch, G, & RM
Gamay Beaujolais	Gam-aye boh-zhoe-lay	California, U.S.	Table wine	Red	Dry	°	P, LM, & Ch
Gattinara	gah-tee-NAH-rah	Piedmont, It.	Table wine	Red	Dry	°	Ch, G, & RM
Gavi	GAH-vee	Piedmont, It.	Table wine	White	Dry	°°	F, P, LM, & Ch
Geisenheimer Mäuerchen	gie-zen-hie-mehr MOY-er-shen	Rheingau, Ger.	Table wine	White	Med. dry	°°°	F, P, & LM
Geisenheimer Rothenberg	gie-zen-hie-mehr RAHTH-en-behrk	Rheingau, Ger.	Table wine	White	Med. dry	°°°	F, P, & LM
Genever (gin)		Holland	Spirit	White	Dry	°°	BD, S, & H
Gevrey-Chambertin	zhev-ray-shah(m)-behr-ta(n)	Côte de Nuits, Fr.	Table wine	Red	Dry	°	Ch, G, & RM
Gewürztraminer	geh-VURTZ-trah-meen-er	Alsace, Fr., & California	Table wine	White	Med. dry	°°°	All foods
Gin, dry	jin	Various	Spirit	White	Dry	°°°	C, H, & S
Girò	zhee-roh	Sardinia, It.	Dessert wine	Red	Sweet	°	AD
Graacher Himmelreich	grah-kehr HIM-el-rie(kh)	Moselle, Ger.	Table wine	White	Med. dry	°°°	F, P, & LM
Gragnano	grah-NYAH-noh	Campania, It.	Table wine	Red	Dry	°	Ch, G, & RM
Grand Marnier	grah(n) mahr-nyay	Cognac, Fr.	Liqueur	Orange	Sweet, orange	°	AD
Grands Echézeaux, Les (GC)	lay grah(n) zay-sheh-zoh	Côte de Nuits, Fr.	Table wine	Red	Dry	°	Ch, G, & RM
Graves	grahv	Bordeaux, Fr.	Table wine	Red or white	Dry	° or °°°	Varies with color
Greco di Tufo	greh-koh dee TOO-foh	Campania, It.	Table wine	White	Med. dry	°°°	F, P, & LM
Grenadine	GREHN-ah-deen	Various	Syrup	Red	Sweet	°°°	C & Pun
Grignolino	gree-nyoh-LEE-noh	Piedmont, It.	Table wine	Red	Dry	°	Ch, G, & RM
Grinzinger	GRINT-zing-ehr	Austria	Table wine	White	Dry	°°°	F, P, & LM
Griotte-Chambertin (GC)	gree-ut-shah(m)-behr-ta(n)	Côte de Nuits, Fr.	Table wine	Red	Dry	°	Ch, G, & RM
Grumello	groo-MEL-oh	Lombardy, It.	Table wine	Red	Dry	°	Ch, G, & RM

Service temperature: °—Room temperature / °°—Slightly chilled / °°°—Cold
Serve with: AD—After dinner / BD—Before dinner / C—Cocktails / Ch—Cheese / F—Fish / Fr—Fruits / G—Game / H—Highballs / Hosp—Hospitality / LM—Light meats / P—Poultry / Pun—Punches / RM—Red meats / S—Straight
1855 classification: 1st—First growth / 2nd—Second growth, etc.; *wines of Burgundy:* GC—*Grand Cru* / PC—*Premier Cru*

NAME	PHONETIC SPELLING	SOURCE	TYPE	COLOR	TASTE	SERV. TEMP.	SERVE WITH
Gumpoldskirchner	GOOM-pohls-keer(kh)-nehr	Austria	Table wine	White	Dry	° ° °	F, P, & LM
Haitian rum	hay-shun	Haiti	Spirit	Straw	Dry	° ° °	C, Pun, H, & S
Hallgartener Schönhell	hahl-gar-ten-ehr SHOYN-hel	Rheingau, Ger.	Table wine	White	Med. dry	° ° °	F, P, & LM
Hattenheimer Nussbrunnen	haht-ten-hie-mehr NOOS-broon-en	Rheingau, Ger.	Table wine	White	Med. dry	° ° °	F, P, & LM
Hermitage	ehr-mee-tahzh	Rhône, Fr.	Table wine	Red or white	Dry	° or ° ° °	Varies with color
Hochheimer Domdechaney	hok-hie-mehr DOHM-deh-shah-nay	Rheingau, Ger.	Table wine	White	Med. dry	° ° °	F, P, & LM
Hochheimer Kirchenstück	hok-hie-mehr KEER(KH)-en-shtuk	Rheingau, Ger.	Table wine	White	Med. dry	° ° °	F, P, & LM
Hohenwarther	HOH-hen-vahr-tehr	Austria	Table wine	White	Dry	° ° °	F, P, & LM
Hollands (gin)		Holland	Spirit	White	Dry	°	BD, S, & H
Hospices de Beaune	ohs-pees duh bone	Côte de Beaune, Fr.	Table wine	Red or white	Dry	° or ° ° °	Varies with color
Inferno	een-FEHR-noh	Lombardy, It.	Table wine	Red	Dry	°	Ch, G, & RM
Iphofener Julius-Echter-Berg	ip-hah-fehn-er YOOL-yuhs-eh(kh)t-ehr-behrk	Franconia, Ger.	Table wine	White	Dry	° ° °	F, P, & LM
Irish whiskey		Ireland	Spirit	Brown	Dry, rich	° or ° ° °	C, H, AD, & S
Ischia	EESK-yah	Campania, It.	Table wine	White	Dry	° ° °	F, P, & LM
Italian vermouth		Italy	Aromatized wine	Red	Bittersweet	° ° °	C & BD
Jamaican rum	jah-MAY-kuh	Jamaica, W.I.	Spirit	Dark brown	Med. sweet	° ° °	C, H, Pun, & S
Johannisberger Erntebringer	yoh-hahn-is-behrk-ehr EHRN-teh-bring-ehr	Rheingau, Ger.	Table wine	White	Med. dry	° ° °	F, P, & LM
Johannisberg Riesling	yoh-hahn-is-behrk REES-ling	California	Table wine	White	Med. dry	° ° °	F, P, & LM
Juliénas	yoo-lee-eh-nahs	Beaujolais, Fr.	Table wine	Red	Dry	°	All foods
Kadmon	KAHD-mahn	Israel	Dessert wine	Amber	Sweet	°	AD
Kahlúa	kah-LOO-ah	Mexico	Liqueur	Brown	Sweet, coffee	°	AD
Kalebag	kah-LAY-bah	Turkey	Table wine	Red	Dry	°	Ch, G, & RM
Kéknyelü	KAYK-nee-el-yoo	Hungary	Table wine	White	Dry	° ° °	F, P, & LM
Kirsch	keersh	Various	Cherry brandy	White	Dry, cherry	° ° °	AD
Kirschwasser	KEERSH-vahs-ehr	Various	Cherry brandy	White	Dry, cherry	° ° °	AD
Klosterneuburger	klos-tir-NOY-boorg-ehr	Austria	Table wine	White	Dry	° ° °	F, P, & LM
Knipperlé	k_nip-ehr-lay	Alsace, Fr.	Table wine	White	Dry	° ° °	All foods
Kokineli	koh-kee-NAY-lee	Cyprus	Table wine	Red	Dry, non-resinated	°	Ch, G, & RM
Kokineli	koh-kee-NAY-lee	Greece	Table wine	Red	Dry, resinated	° °	F, P, & LM
Kremser	KREHM-zer	Austria	Table wine	White	Dry	° ° °	F, P, & LM
Kröver Nacktarsch	kroy-vehr-NAHK-tarsh	Moselle, Ger.	Table wine	White	Med. dry	° ° °	F, P, & LM
Kümmel	KUHM-mel	Various	Liqueur	White	Sweet, caraway	°	AD
Lacryma Christi	lah-creem-ah KREES-tee	Campania, It.	Table wine	White	Med. dry	° ° °	All foods
Lambrusco	lahm-BROOS-coh	Emilia, It.	Sparkling wine	Red	Med. sweet	° ° °	All foods
Latricières-Chambertin (GC)	lah-tree-syehr-shah(m)-behr-ta(n)	Côte de Nuits, Fr.	Table wine	Red	Dry	°	Ch, G, & RM
Leányka Edes	LAY-ahn-kyah a-dehsh	Hungary	Table wine	White	Med. sweet	° ° °	F, P, & LM
Leányka Szaras	LAY-ahn-kyah ZHAH-rahzh	Hungary	Table wine	White	Dry	° ° °	F, P, & LM
Liebfraumilch	LEEB-frow-mil(kh)	Rhine, Ger.	Table wine	White	Med. dry	° ° °	F, P, & LM
Lillet	lee-lay	France	Aperitif	White	Bitter	° ° °	BD
Lugana	loo-GAHN-ah	Veneto, It.	Table wine	White	Dry	° ° °	F, P, & LM

NAME	PHONETIC SPELLING	SOURCE	TYPE	COLOR	TASTE	SERV. TEMP.	SERVE WITH
Mâcon	mah-coh(n)	Burgundy, Fr.	Table wine	White	Dry	°°°	F, P, & LM
Madeira	mah-DEHR-ah	Madeira	Fortified wine	Dark brown	Dry or sweet	°	Hosp
Málaga	MAH-lah-gah	Málaga, Sp.	Fortified wine	Dark brown	Sweet	°	Hosp
Malmsey	MALM-zee	Madeira	Fortified wine	Dark brown	Sweet	°	Hosp
Malvasia	mahl-vay-see ah	Sicily, It.	Fortified wine	Gold	Sweet	°	Hosp
Manzanilla	mahnt-sah-NEE-yah	Sanlúcar, Sp.	Sherry	Straw	Dry	°°	Hosp
Maraschino	mah-rahs-KEE-no	Various	Liqueur	White	Sweet, cherry	°	AD
Marsala	mahr-SAH-lah	Sicily, It.	Dessert wine	Brown	Sweet	°	Hosp
Mastikha	MAHS-tee-kah	Greece	Liqueur	Cloudy white	Sweet	°°°	BD & H
Mavrodaphne	mahv-roh-DAHF-nee	Greece	Dessert wine	Red	Sweet	°	AD
Maximim Grünhauser Herrenberg	mahx-ee-meen GRUHN-hoyz-ehr HEHR-ehn-behrk	Moselle, Ger.	Table wine	White	Med. dry	°°°	F, P, & LM
May wine		Germany & U.S.	Table wine	White	Med. sweet	°°°	All foods
Mazis-Chambertin (GC)	mah-zee-shah(m)-behr-ta(n)	Côte de Nuits, Fr.	Table wine	Red	Dry	°	Ch, G, & RM
Médoc	may-dohk	Médoc, Fr.	Table wine	Red	Dry	°	Ch, G, & RM
Mercurey	mehr-kyu-ray	Chalonnais, Fr.	Table wine	Red	Dry	°	Ch, G, & RM
Merlot	mehr-LOH	Various	Table wine	Red	Dry	°	Ch, P, LM, & RM
Meursault	muhr-soh	Côte de Beaune, Fr.	Table wine	White	Dry	°°°	F, P, & LM
Meursault-Charmes (PC)	muhr-soh-shahrm	Côte de Beaune, Fr.	Table wine	White	Dry	°°°	F, P, & LM
Meursault-Genevrières (PC)	muhr-soh-zhah(n)-eh-vryehr	Côte de Beaune, Fr.	Table wine	White	Dry	°°°	F, P, & LM
Meursault-Perrières (PC)	muhr-soh-pehr-yehr	Côte de Beaune, Fr.	Table wine	White	Dry	°°°	F, P, & LM
Mirabelle	mee-rah-bel	Alsace, Fr.	Plum brandy	White	Dry, plum	°°°	AD
Montilla	mohn-TEE-yah	Cordoba, Sp.	Aperitif wine	Straw	Dry	°°°	Hosp & BD
Montrachet, Le (GC)	luh moh(n)-rah-shay	Côte de Beaune, Fr.	Table wine	White	Dry	°°°	F, P, & LM
Moore's Diamond		New York State	Table wine	White	Dry	°°°	F, P, & LM
Moscatel de Setúbal	mohs-kah-tel duh seh-TOO-bahl	Portugal	Fortified wine	Gold	Sweet	°°°	AD
Moscatel de Sitges	mohs-kah-tel duh SEET-yes	Catalonia, Sp.	Fortified wine	Gold	Sweet	°	Hosp
Moscato di Salento	mohs-KAH-toh dee sah-LEN-toh	Apulia, It.	Fortified wine	Gold	Sweet	°	Hosp
Moscato Fior d'Arancio	mohs-KAH-toh fyor dah-RAHN-choh	Sicily, It.	Fortified wine	Gold	Sweet	°	Hosp
Moselblümchen	MOH-zel-bloom-shehn	Moselle, Ger.	Table wine	White	Med. dry	°°°	F, P, & LM
Moulin-à-Vent	moo-la(n)-ah-vah(n)	Beaujolais, Fr.	Table wine	Red	Dry	°	Ch, G, & RM
Muscadet	moos-kah-day	Loire, Fr.	Table wine	White	Dry	°°°	F, P, & LM
Muscatel	mus-kah-tel	California	Fortified wine	Gold	Sweet	°	AD
Musigny, Les (GC)	lay moo-see-nyee	Côte de Nuits, Fr.	Table wine	Red	Dry	°	Ch, G, & RM
Muskotaly	MOOSH-koh-tah-lee	Hungary	Table wine	White	Dry	°°°	F, P, & LM
Nackenheimer Rothenberg	nok-en-hie-mehr ROTH-ehn-behrk	Rheinhessen, Ger.	Table wine	White	Med. dry	°°°	F, P, & LM

Service temperature: °—Room temperature / °°—Slightly chilled / °°°—Cold
Serve with: AD—After dinner / BD—Before dinner / C—Cocktails / Ch—Cheese / F—Fish / Fr—Fruits / G—Game / H—Highballs / Hosp—Hospitality / LM—Light meats / P—Poultry / Pun—Punches / RM—Red meats / S—Straight
1855 classification: 1st—First growth / 2nd—Second growth, etc.; *wines of Burgundy:* GC—*Grand Cru* / PC—*Premier Cru*

NAME	PHONETIC SPELLING	SOURCE	TYPE	COLOR	TASTE	SERV. TEMP.	SERVE WITH
Nebbiolo	nehb-yoh-loh	Piedmont, It.	Table wine	Red	Dry	°	Ch, G, & RM
Neuchâtel	nuh-shah-tel	Switzerland	Table wine	White	Dry	°°°	F, P, & LM
Niersteiner Auflangen	neer-shtine-ehr OWF-lahngen	Rheinhessen, Ger.	Table wine	White	Med. dry	°°°	F, P, & LM
Niersteiner Heiligenbaum	neer-shtine-ehr HIE-lee-gen-bowm	Rheinhessen, Ger.	Table wine	White	Med. dry	°°°	F, P, & LM
Niersteiner Hipping	neer-shtine-ehr HIP-ing	Rheinhessen, Ger.	Table wine	White	Med. dry	°°°	F, P, & LM
Niersteiner Oelberg	neer-shtine-ehr OHL-behrk	Rheinhessen, Ger.	Table wine	White	Med. dry	°°°	F, P, & LM
Niersteiner Rehbach	neer-shtine-ehr RAY-bahkh	Rheinhessen, Ger.	Table wine	White	Med. dry	°°°	F, P, & LM
Nuits-Saint-Georges	nwee-sa(n)-zhorzh	Côte de Nuits, Fr.	Table wine	Red	Dry	°	Ch, G, & RM
Nussberger	NOOS-behrk-ehr	Austria	Table wine	White	Dry	°°°	F, P, & LM
Oeil de Perdrix	oy duh pehr-dree	Burgundy, Fr., Switzerland, & U.S.	Sparkling or still wine	Pale pink	Med. dry	°°°	All foods
Oloroso	oh-loh-ROH-soh	Jerez, Sp.	Sherry	Gold	Sweet	°	Hosp
Opol	oh-POHL	Yugoslavia	Table wine	Light red	Dry	°°°	All Foods
Oppenheimer Daubhaus	ah-pen-hie-mehr DOWB-howss	Rheinhessen, Ger.	Table wine	White	Med. dry	°°°	F, P, & LM
Oppenheimer Herrenberg	ah-pen-hie-mehr HEHR-en-behrk	Rheinhessen, Ger.	Table wine	White	Med. dry	°°°	F, P, & LM
Oppenheimer Kreuz	ah-pen-hie-mehr KROYTS	Rheinhessen, Ger.	Table wine	White	Med. dry	°°°	F, P, & LM
Oppenheimer Sackträger	ah-pen-hie-mehr ZAHK-tray-gehr	Rheinhessen, Ger.	Table wine	White	Med. dry	°°°	F, P, & LM
Orgeat	or-zhah	France	Syrup	Gray	Sweet, almond		C & Pun
Orvieto (abboccato)	orv-YEHT-oh (ah-boe-KAHT-oh)	Umbria, It.	Table wine	White	Dry (or semisweet)	°°°	F, P, & LM
Othello	oh-THEL-loh	Cyprus	Table wine	Red	Dry	°	Ch, G, & RM
Ouzo	OO-zoh	Greece	Liqueur	Cloudy white	Sweet, licorice	°°°	H & C
Partom	PAR-tohm	Israel	Dessert wine	Red	Sweet	°	Desserts, AD
Passito	pahs-EET-oh	Italy	Fortified wine	Amber	Sweet	°°	Fr, AD
Pastis de Marseilles	pahs-tees duh mahr-say	Marseilles, Fr.	Liqueur	Cloudy white	Sweet, licorice	°°°	H & BD
Pavillon Blanc du Château Margaux	pah-vee-yoh(n) blah(n) doo shah-toh mahr-goh	Médoc, Fr.	Table wine	White	Dry	°°°	F, P, & LM
Peach liqueur		Various	Liqueur	Brown	Sweet, fruity	°	AD
Perlan	pehr-lah(n)	Switzerland	Table wine	White	Dry	°°°	F, P, & LM
Pernand-Vergelesses	pehr-nah(n)-vehrzh-uh-les	Côte de Beaune, Fr.	Table wine	Red	Dry	°	Ch, G, & RM
Pernod	pehr-noh	France	Liqueur	Green gold	Sweet, licorice	°°°	BD & H
Perry		England	Sparkling or still pear wine	Straw	Sweet	°°°	Desserts
Peter Heering		Denmark	Liqueur	Red	Sweet, cherry	°	AD
Petit Sirah	puh-tee sih-rah	California	Table wine	Red	Dry	°	Ch, G, & RM
Pfaffstätter	FAHF-shtay-tehr	Austria	Table wine	White	Dry	°°°	F, P, & LM
Picolit	PEE-coh-leet	Friuli, It.	Table wine	White	Sweet	°°°	Ch, Fr
Piesporter Goldtröpfchen	pees-port-ehr GOHLD-trehpf-shen	Moselle, Ger.	Table wine	White	Med. dry	°°°	F, P, & LM

NAME	PHONETIC SPELLING	SOURCE	TYPE	COLOR	TASTE	SERV. TEMP.	SERVE WITH
Pineau des Charentes	pee-noh day shah-rah(n)t	Cognac, Fr.	Fortified wine	White	Sweet	° ° °	BD
Pinot Blanc (Bianco)	pee-noh blah(n) (bee-yahn-koh)	France, Italy, California	Table wine	White	Dry	° ° °	F, P, & LM
Pinot Grigio	pee-noh gree-zho	Italy	Table wine	White	Dry	° ° °	F, P, & LM
Pinot Noir	pee-noh nwahr	Various	Table wine	Red	Dry	°	Ch, G, & RM
Pisco	PEES-koh	Pisco, Peru	Brandy	Gold	Dry	°	AD & Pun
Pommard	poh-mahr	Côte de Beaune, Fr.	Table wine	Red	Dry	°	Ch, G, & RM
Pommard-Clos-de-la-Commareine (PC)	poh-mahr-kloh-duh-lah-kuhm-ah-rehn	Côte de Beaune, Fr.	Table wine	Red	Dry	°	Ch, G, & RM
Pommard-Garollières (PC)	poh-mahr-gah-rohl-yehr	Côte de Beaune, Fr.	Table wine	Red	Dry	°	Ch, G, & RM
Pommard-Les-Epenots (PC)	poh-mahr-lay-zay-puh-noh	Côte de Beaune, Fr.	Table wine	Red	Dry	°	Ch, G, & RM
Pommard-Platière (PC)	poh-mahr-plah-tyehr	Côte de Beaune, Fr.	Table wine	Red	Dry	°	Ch, G, & RM
Pommard-Rugiens (PC)	poh-mahr-roo-zhyens	Côte de Beaune, Fr.	Table wine	Red	Dry	°	Ch, G, & RM
Port		U.S.	Fortified wine	Red	Sweet	°	Hosp
Porter		England & Ireland	Malt beverage	Dark brown	Bitter	° °	Hosp
Porto		Portugal	Fortified wine	Red	Sweet	°	Hosp
Pouilly-Fuissé	pwee-yee-fwee-say	Mâconnais, Fr.	Table wine	White	Dry	° ° °	F, P, & LM
Pouilly-Fumé	pwee-yee-foo-may	Loire, Fr.	Table wine	White	Med. sweet	° ° °	F, P, & LM
Pousse-Café	poos-kah-fay	France	Liqueur	Various	Sweet	°	AD
Prunelle	proo-nel	France	Liqueur	Brown	Sweet, plum	°	AD
Puerto Rican rum		Puerto Rico	Spirit	White	Dry	° ° °	C, H, Pun, & S
Puligny-Montrachet	poo-lee-nyee-moh(n)-rah-shay	Côte de Beaune, Fr.	Table wine	White	Dry	° ° °	F, P, & LM
Quetsch	kwehtch	Alsace, Fr.	Plum brandy	White	Dry	° ° °	AD
Quinquina	ka(n)-ka(n)-nah	France	Aperitif	Red or white	Bittersweet	° ° °	BD
Raki	RAHK-ee	Turkey	Liqueur	White	Sweet, licorice	° ° °	AD
Randersackerer Teufelskeller	rahn-dehr-zahk-ehr-ehr TOY-fels-kel-ehr	Franconia, Ger.	Table wine	White	Dry	° ° °	F, P, & LM
Rauenthaler Baiken	row-en-tahl-ehr BY-ken	Rheingau, Ger.	Table wine	White	Med. dry	° ° °	F, P, & LM
Rauenthaler Gehrn	row-en-tahl-ehr GAYRN	Rheingau, Ger.	Table wine	White	Med. dry	° ° °	F, P, & LM
Rauenthaler Langenstück	row-en-tahl-ehr LAHNG-en-shtuk	Rheingau, Ger.	Table wine	White	Med. dry	° ° °	F, P, & LM
Rauenthaler Wülfen	row-en-tahl-ehr VIL-fen	Rheingau, Ger.	Table wine	White	Med. dry	° ° °	F, P, & LM
Recioto	reh-chee-OH-toh	Veneto, It.	Table wine	Red	Sweet	° °	All foods
Retsina	reht-SEE-nah	Greece	Table wine	White	Dry resinated	° ° °	All foods
Rhodity	roh-DEE-tis	Greece	Table wine	White red	Dry	° ° °	All foods
Ricard	ree-kahr	France	Liqueur	Brown	Semisweet	° ° °	BD
Richebourg, Le (GC)	luh reesh-boor	Côte de Nuits, Fr.	Table wine	Red	Dry	°	Ch, G, & RM
Riesling	REES-ling	Various	Table wine	White	Dry or sweet	° ° °	Varies with sweetness

Service temperature: °—Room temperature / ° °—Slightly chilled / ° ° °—Cold
Serve with: AD—After dinner / BD—Before dinner / C—Cocktails / Ch—Cheese / F—Fish / Fr—Fruits / G—Game / H—Highballs / Hosp—Hospitality / LM—Light meats / P—Poultry / Pun—Punches / RM—Red meats / S—Straight
1855 classification: 1st—First growth / 2nd—Second growth, etc.; *wines of Burgundy:* GC—*Grand Cru* / PC—*Premier Cru*

NAME	PHONETIC SPELLING	SOURCE	TYPE	COLOR	TASTE	SERV. TEMP.	SERVE WITH
Rioja	ree-OH-hah	Spain	Table wine	Red or white	Dry	° or °°°	Varies with color
Rizling Szemelt	REEZ-ling tseh-mehlt	Hungary	Table wine	White	Dry	°°°	F, P, & LM
Romanée, La (GC)	lah roh-mah-nay	Côte de Nuits, Fr.	Table wine	Red	Dry	°	Ch, G, & RM
Romanée-Conti (GC)	roh-mah-nay-kah(n)-tee	Côte de Nuits, Fr.	Table wine	Red	Dry	°	Ch, G, & RM
Romanée-Saint-Vivant (GC)	roh-mah-nay-sa(n)-vee-vah(n)	Côte de Nuits, Fr.	Table wine	Red	Dry	°	Ch, G, & RM
Rubesco	roo-BEHS-coh	Umbria, It.	Table wine	Red	Dry	°	Ch, G, & RM
Ruby Porto		Portugal	Fortified wine	Red	Sweet	°	Hosp
Ruchottes-Chambertin (GC)	roo-shot-shah(m)-behr-ta(n)	Côte de Nuits, Fr.	Table wine	Red	Dry	°	Ch, G, & RM
Rüdesheimer Berg Rottland	roo-des-hie-mehr behrk ROHT-lahnt	Rheingau, Ger.	Table wine	White	Med. dry	°°°	F, P, & LM
Rüdeshemer Berg Schlossberg	roo-des-hie-mehr behrk SHLAWS-behrk	Rheingau, Ger.	Table wine	White	Med. dry	°°°	F, P, & LM
Rüdesheimer Klosterberg	roo-des-hie-mehr KLOHS-tehr-behrk	Rheingau, Ger.	Table wine	White	Med. dry	°°°	F, P, & LM
Rum		Various	Spirit	Various	Slightly sweet	°°°	C, H, Pun, & S
Ruppertsberger Hoheburg	roo-pehrts-behrk-ehr HOH-heh-boorg	Rheinpfalz, Ger.	Table wine	White	Med. dry	°°°	F, P, & LM
Ruppertsberger Nussbien	roo-pehrts-behrk-ehr NOOS-been	Rheinpfalz, Ger.	Table wine	White	Med. dry	°°°	F, P, & LM
Saint-Amour	sa(n)-tah-moor	Beaujolais, Fr.	Table wine	Red	Dry	°	Ch, G, & RM
Saint-Emilion	sa(n)-tay-meel-yohn	Saint-Emilion, Fr.	Table wine	Red	Dry	°	Ch, G, & RM
Saint-Estèphe	sa(n)-tehs-tef	Médoc, Fr.	Table wine	Red	Dry	°	Ch, G, & RM
Saint-Julien	sa(n)-zhul-yen	Médoc, Fr.	Table wine	Red	Dry	°	Ch, G, & RM
Saint-Raphaël	sa(n)-rah-fah-el	France	Aperitif	Red	Bitter	°°°	BD
Saké	SAH-kee	Japan	Rice beer	White	Dry	100°F	All foods
Sancerre	sa(n)-sehr	Loire, Fr.	Table wine	White	Dry	°°°	F, P, & LM
Santenay	sa(n)-teh-nay	Côte de Beaune, Fr.	Table wine	Red	Dry	°	Ch, G, & RM
Sassella	sah-SAY-lah	Lombardy, It.	Table wine	Red	Dry	°	Ch, G, & RM
Saumur	soh-moor	Anjou, Fr.	Still or sparkling wine	White	Med. sweet	°°°	F, P, & LM
Sauterne	soh-tehrn	U.S.	Table wine	White	Dry	°°°	All foods
Sauternes	soh-tehrn	Sauternes, Fr.	Table wine	White	Sweet	°°°	Desserts
Sauvignon Blanc	soh-vee-nyoh(n) blah(n)	California & France	Table wine	White	Dry or sweet	°°°	F, P, & LM
Scharzhofberg	shartz-huf-behrg	Moselle, Ger.	Table wine	White	Med. dry	°°°	F, P, Hosp
Schaumwein	SHOHM-vine	Germany	Sparkling wine	White	Dry or sweet	°°°	All foods
Scheidam (gin)	SKEE-dahm	Holland	Spirit	White	Dry	°°°	S & H
Schloss-Bockelheimer-Mühlberg	shlawss-BUHK-el-hie-mehr-mewl-behrk	Nahe, Ger.	Table wine	White	Dry	°°°	F, P, & LM
Schloss Johannisberg	shlawss yoh-hahn-is-behrk	Rheingau, Ger.	Table wine	White	Med. dry	°°°	F, P, & LM
Schloss Vollrads	schlawss FAWL-rahds	Rheingau, Ger.	Table wine	White	Med. dry	°°°	F, P, & LM
Scotch whisky		Scotland	Spirit	Brown,	Dry, smoky	° or °°°	C, H, & S
Scuppernong		Southeastern U.S.	Table wine	White	Sweet	°°°	All foods
Sekt	sehkt	Germany	Sparkling wine	White	Dry or sweet	°°°	All foods
Sémillon	seh-mee-yoh(n)	California	Table wine	White	Dry or sweet	°°°	All foods
Sercial	SIR-shahl	Madeira	Fortified wine	Gold	Med. dry	°°	Hosp

NAME	PHONETIC SPELLING	SOURCE	TYPE	COLOR	TASTE	SERV. TEMP.	SERVE WITH
Sherry		Jerez, Sp., & various	Fortified wine	Amber	Dry to sweet	° or °°	Hosp
Sidra	SEE-drah	Northern Spain	Sparkling cider	Gold	Sweet, apple	°°°	Hosp
Slivovitz	SHLIV-oh-wits	Various	Plum brandy	Brown	Dry, plum	°	AD
Sloe gin		England & U.S.	Liqueur	Red	Sweet, astringent	° or °°°	AD & C
Soave	suah-veh	Veneto, It.	Table wine	White	Dry	°°°	F, P, & LM
Somlói Furmint	SHOHM-loy ye foor-mint	Somlói, Hungary	Table wine	White	Dry	°°°	F, P, & LM
Spanish brandy		Spain	Brandy	Brown	Med. dry	°	AD
Spanna	SPAHN-neh	Piedmont, It.	Table wine	Red	Dry	°	Ch, G, & RM
Sparkling Burgundy		Burgundy, Fr., & U.S.	Sparkling wine	Red or white	Med. sweet	°°°	All foods
Steinberger	SHTINE-behrk-ehr	Rheingau, Ger.	Table wine	White	Med. dry	°°°	F, P, & LM
Stout		England & Ireland	Malt beverage	Dark brown	Bitter	°°	Hosp
Strega	STRAY-gah	Benevento, It.	Liqueur	Gold	Sweet	°	AD
Suze	sooz	France	Aperitif	Brown	Bittersweet	°°°	BD
Swedish Punsch		Sweden	Liqueur	Yellow	Sweet, rummy	°°°	AD
Sylvaner (Silvaner)	zil-vah-nehr	Alsace, Fr., & Germany	Table wine	White	Med. dry	°°°	All foods
Szilvanyi Zold	ZIL-vahn-yuh zuhld	Hungary	Table wine	White	Med. sweet	°°°	F, P, & LM
Tâche, La (GC)	lah tahsh	Côte de Nuits, Fr.	Table wine	Red	Dry	°	Ch, G, & RM
Taurasi	touw-RAH-zi	Campania, It.	Table wine	Red	Dry	°	Ch, G, & RM
Tavel	tah-vel	Rhône, Fr.	Table wine	Pink	Dry	°°°	All foods
Tawny Porto		Portugal	Fortified wine	Red	Sweet	°	Hosp
Tequila	teh-KEE-lah	Jalisco, Mex.	Spirit	White	Dry	°	C & S
Tia Maria	tee-ah mah-REE-ah	Jamaica	Liqueur	Brown	Sweet, coffee	°	AD
Tignanello	tee-nyan-EHL-oh	Tuscany, It.	Table wine	Red	Dry	°	Ch, G, & RM
Tocai	tohk-ahye	Friuli, It.	Table wine	White	Dry	°°°	F, P, & LM
Tokaji Aszú	TOHK-ah ye ah-zoo	Hungary	Dessert wine	Amber	Sweet	°°	Hosp & AD
Tokaji Szamorodni	TOHK-ah ye SAH-mah-rohd-nee	Hungary	Dessert wine	White	Med. dry	°°°	Hosp
Trakya	TRAHK-yah	Turkey	Table wine	White	Dry	°°°	F, P, & LM
Triple Sec		Various	Liqueur	White	Sweet, orange	°	AD
Trittenheimer Altärchen	trit-en-hie-mehr AHLT-ehr-shen	Moselle, Ger.	Table wine	White	Med. dry	°°°	F, P, & LM
Trittenheimer Apotheke	trit-en-hie-mehr ah-poh-TAY-kuh	Moselle, Ger.	Table wine	White	Med. dry	°°°	F, P, & LM
Tsingtao	TSEENG-tow	China	Malt beverage	Amber	Dry	°°°	Hosp.
Ürziger Würzgarten	oor-tsee-gehr VURTZ-gahr-ten	Moselle, Ger.	Table wine	White	Med. dry	°°°	F, P, & LM
Valdepeñas	vahl-day-PAYN-yahs	La Mancha, Sp.	Table wine	Red	Dry	°	Ch, G, & RM
Valgella	vahl-ZHEHL-eh	Lombardy, It.	Table wine	Red	Dry	°	Ch, G, & RM
Valpolicella	vahl-poh-lee-CHAY-lah	Veneto, It.	Table wine	Red	Dry	°	Ch, G, & RM
Valtellina	vahl-tel-LEE-nah	Lombardy, It.	Table wine	Red	Dry	°	Ch, G, & RM
Van Der Hum	VAN der huhm	South Africa	Liqueur	Gold	Sweet	°	AD
Verdelho	vehr-DEL-yo	Madeira	Fortified wine	White	Sweet	°	AD & Hosp
Verdicchio	vehr-DEEK-yoh	Marches, It.	Table wine	White	Dry	°°°	Shellfish
Vernaccia	vehr-NAH-chah	Italy	Table wine	White	Dry	°	F & LM

Service temperature: °—Room temperature / °°—Slightly chilled / °°°—Cold
Serve with: AD—After dinner / BD—Before dinner / C—Cocktails / Ch—Cheese / F—Fish / Fr—Fruits / G—Game / H—Highballs / Hosp—Hospitality / LM—Light meats / P—Poultry / Pun—Punches / RM—Red meats / S—Straight
1855 classification: 1st—First growth / 2nd—Second growth, etc.; *wines of Burgundy:* GC—*Grand Cru* / PC—*Premier Cru*

NAME	PHONETIC SPELLING	SOURCE	TYPE	COLOR	TASTE	SERV. TEMP.	SERVE WITH
Villányi-Pècs	VIL-ahn-yee-pehch	Hungary	Table wine	Red	Dry	°	G & RM
Vinho Verde	VEE-nyoh vehr-deh	Portugal	Table wine	Red or white	Dry	° or °°°	Varies with color
Vin (Vino) Santo	veen (VEE-noh) SAHN-toh	Italy	Table wine	White	Sweet	°°°	All foods
Vino Nobile di Montepulciano	vee-noh NOH-beel-eh dee mohn-teh-puhl-chi-AHN-oh	Tuscany, It.	Table wine	Red	Dry	°	Ch, G, & RM
Vodka	VAHD-kah	Various	Spirit	White	Dry	°°°	C, H, & S
Volnay	vuhl-nay	Côte de Beaune, Fr.	Table wine	Red	Dry	°	Ch, G, & RM
Vöslau	FOYS-low	Austria	Table wine	Red	Dry	°	Ch, G, & RM
Vosne-Romanée	vohn-roh-mah-nay	Côte de Nuits, Fr.	Table wine	Red	Dry	°	Ch, G, & RM
Vouvray	voo-vreh	Loire, Fr.	Table wine	White	Med. sweet or sweet	°°°	Fr
Wachenheimer Schlossberg	vah(kh)-en-hie-mehr shlawss-behrk	Rheinpfalz, Ger.	Table wine	White	Med. dry	°°°	F, P, & LM
Wehlener Sonnenuhr	VAY-len-ehr ZAWN-en-oor	Moselle, Ger.	Table wine	White	Med. dry	°°°	F, P, & LM
Whisky	WISS-kee	Various	Spirit	Brown	Dry, rich	° or °°°	C, H, Pun, & S
White Porto		Portugal	Aperitif	Gold	Sweet	°	Hosp & BD
Wiltinger Schlangengraben	vilt-ing-ehr SHLAHNG-en-grah-ben	Moselle, Ger.	Table wine	White	Med. dry	°°°	F, P, & LM
Wisniowka	vish-nyoof-kah	Poland	Liqueur	Red	Sweet, cherry	°°	AD
Würzburger Stein	vurtz-behrk-ehr SHTINE	Franconia, Ger.	Table wine	White	Dry	°°°	F, P, & LM
Zeller Schwarze Katz	tsel-ehr SHVAHRT-seh kahts	Moselle, Ger.	Table wine	White	Med. dry	°°°	F, P, & LM
Zeltinger Himmelreich	tselt-ing-ehr HIM-mel-rie(kh)	Moselle, Ger.	Table wine	White	Med. dry	°°°	F, P, & LM
Zeltinger Schlossberg	tselt-ing-ehr SHLAWSS-behrk	Moselle, Ger.	Table wine	White	Med. dry	°°°	F, P, & LM
Zeltinger Sonnenuhr	tselt-ing-ehr ZAWN-en-oor	Moselle, Ger.	Table wine	White	Med. dry	°°°	F, P, & LM
Zinfandel	TZIN-fan-del	California	Table wine	Red	Dry	°	Ch, G, & RM
Zubrowka	zoo-BROHV-kah	Russia & Poland	Flavored spirit	Straw	Dry	°°°	C, H, & S

APPENDIX B

VINTAGE INFORMATION—
FRANCE, ITALY, GERMANY, PORTUGAL,
AND THE UNITED STATES

Every vintage chart is a compilation of many opinions that tends to even out the extremes. There are often exceptional bottles in average years and average bottles in excellent years. The vintage chart must always be considered the indicator of the general quality.

FRENCH AND GERMAN VINTAGE CHART

	'59	'60	'61	'62	'63	'64	'65	'66	'67	'68	'69	'70	'71	'72	'73	'74	'75	'76	'77	'78	'79	'80	'81	'82
Red Bordeaux	9C	6D	10C	8C	2D	8C	X	9B	7C	X	6C	9B	8B	5B	6B	6A	10A	8A	5B	8A	8A	8A	8A	10A
Dry White Bordeaux	X	X	X	X	X	9	X	8	X	X	5	9	9	7	7	7	8	7	7	9	8	8	8	9
Sweet White Bordeaux	9D	X	10D	9D	X	X	X	7C	9C	X	7C	9C	9C	6C	6D	6C	9B	7B	6B	8A	8A	8A	9A	8A
Red Côte d'Or Burgundy	9D	X	10C	8C	X	9C	X	8C	6D	X	9B	8C	8C	8C	7C	7C	5C	10B	7B	9B	7B	7A	7A	9A
Red Beaujolais Burgundy	X	X	X	X	X	X	X	X	X	X	X	8D	9D	7C	7C	6C	5B	10B	X	8A	9D	6D	8C	8B
White Burgundy	X	X	X	X	X	X	X	9D	7D	X	9D	8D	9C	7D	7D	7D	8C	8C	6C	9B	9B	7B	9B	9A
Loire	X	X	X	X	X	X	X	X	X	X	X	X	X	X	X	X	X	X	9C	9C	8C	7B	8B	8A
Red Rhône	8D	10D	9C	8D	8D	8D	X	9C	9C	X	9C	10C	8C	8C	7C	7C	7C	9B	6B	10A	8A	8A	8A	9A
Rhine	X	X	X	X	X	X	X	9D	7D	X	9D	8D	10C	6D	7D	6D	9C	10C	6D	6D	7B	5D	7C	8A
Mosel-Saar-Ruwer	X	X	X	X	X	X	X	X	X	X	8D	8D	10C	6D	7D	6D	9C	10C	6D	6D	7C	5D	7C	8A

Number ratings:

1 to 10 relate to potential quality when fully mature. A mature wine of modest rating should be preferred to an immature wine whatever its potential quality (10 is finest grade).

Letter code for red Bordeaux and Burgundy:

A = Not at present ready for drinking
B = Can be drunk now but development still to come
C = Fully ready for drinking
D = Approach with caution; could be good, but could be past best

Many of this charts ratings were collected by the late Gordon Bass.

NOTES ON RED BORDEAUX VINTAGES

1945   Very small yield, but quality superb. Excellent to drink now, but will continue to develop.

1946   Generally very light wines.

1947   A great vintage. Big, fine wines that are long lived. Some are starting to decline.

1948   A good vintage that was overshadowed by those of '47 and '49.

1949   An important vintage although the quantity was somewhat below average. Very fine wines.

1950   Abundant vintage. Quality good. Now old.

1951   Small yield, but wines were better than average. Now old.

1952   Wines somewhat hard and slow in developing, long lived. In general a great year.

1953   Big vintage produced under optimum conditions. Wines much softer and earlier developing than the '52s. They are still excellent.

1954   Small crop. Some useful wines but on the whole thin and short lived.

1955   Smaller vintage than '54, but the wines have body. Many good wines and some great wines were produced.

1956   A very small vintage because of severe frosts. Very light, thin wines.

1957   Quantity small. Quality fairly good. Quite hard wines that are now starting to soften.

1958   Quantity small. Light, pleasant, drinkable wines. Now old.

1959   Good harvest. Quality excellent. On the whole big, balanced wines that have developed quickly and are now fully mature.

1960   Better than average quantity. Wines somewhat light and not long lived.

1961   Very small vintage because of rains at time of flowering. Excellent quality. Wines show concentration and are well balanced. These will be very long lived.

1962   Better than average quantity. Well-made wines, pleasant, soft. At their peak now.

1963   Quality generally poor. A few pleasant light wines were produced.

1964   Rains at harvest time produced wines of variable quality. In Saint-Emilion and Pomerol and in those parts of the Médoc that harvested early some very good wines were made.

1965   A rainy summer produced thin wines.

1966   An excellent year. Big, full-bodied, well-balanced wines. Will be long lived.

1967   A larger harvest than in '66. The wines are lighter than those of '66, maturing earlier, but have charm and elegance.

1968   Generally a very poor year.

1969   Light wines that are generally pleasant.

1970   Very good quantity. Quality excellent. Big wines with character. Will be long lived.

1971   Quantity small but quality excellent. Big, concentrated wines, in many cases comparable to '70s.

1972   Light wines. Many lack fruit and charm. Some pleasant wines. Not long lived.

1973   Very abundant quantity. Variable quality. Some good light wines but will not be long lived.

1974   Good quantity. Quality average. Sound wines that will mature quickly.

1975   Small quantity, less than half that of '74. Quality is excellent. Wines have high alcohol and tannin and should be long lived.

1976   Large quantity. Wines are rich and dark with a great deal of fruit. Lack tannin and consequently may mature early.

1977   Small crop. Quality less than average. Wines predominantly Cabernet Sauvignon were more successful.

1978   Average crop. Variable vintage with lesser wines disappointing. Wines harvested later were more successful.

1979   Enormous quantity. Early maturation. Quality has some elegance—typically claret.

1980   Less than average quantity. Quality affected by bad weather. Some rot, little fruit, Merlot suffered the most.

1981   Small crop. Better than average quality. Wines are soft and have good color and body.

1982   Very large harvest. Quality good to excellent.

NOTES ON WHITE BORDEAUX VINTAGES

1959 Sauternes excellent—sweet, rich, and luscious. Dry wines were very good.

1960 Dry wines were very good. Sweet wines poor.

1961 Some excellent sweet wines produced. These should be long lived. Dry whites were very good to excellent. High in alcohol.

1962 Very good for sweet wines, many excellent. Good to very good for dry wines, which are now too old.

1963 Fair for dry wines, poor for sweet.

1964 Some good dry wines were produced. Very poor sweet wines.

1965 Very poor year for Sauternes. Dry wines were fair to good.

1966 Some very good sweet wines were produced. The dry wines were good to very good.

1967 Very good Sauternes—sweet, rich, and luscious. Some very good dry wines were produced.

1968 Generally poor year for sweet and dry wines.

1969 Good dry wines. Sweet wines are variable, but generally good.

1970 An excellent year. Sauternes are rich and elegant, will live long. Graves are well balanced and elegant.

1971 Excellent vintage for Sauternes—elegant, outstanding, long-lived wines. Dry wines also excellent—good depth and character.

1972 Quality is variable. Dry wines generally better than the sweet.

1973 Very large quantity. Dry wines better than the sweet.

1974 Abundant quantity. Quality only fair.

1975 Excellent, luscious sweet wines. Dry wines also excellent and high in alcohol.

1976 September rain washed away the noble rot, and few quality sweet wines were produced. Some good dry wines, high in acidity, were made from grapes harvested before the rain.

1977 Dry wines better than average. Tiny yield of sweet wines of fair quality.

1978 Very dry year produced less than average yield and quality of sweet wines. Dry whites were very good.

1979 Dry wines were abundant and fruity. Sweet wines were good and in some cases excellent.

1980 Dry wines of good quality but quantity very small. Sweet wines were very fine.

1981 Both dry and sweet wines in short supply. Good noble rot produced great concentration in the sweet wines. Dry wine delicate in style.

1982 Abundant harvest for both whites. Dry whites exemplary. Sweet wines very promising.

NOTES ON RED AND WHITE BURGUNDY VINTAGES

1945 Small quantity. A great year. Slow maturing.

1946 Quick-maturing wines.

1947 Wines made with sufficient care were of excellent quality.

1948 A very good vintage.

1949 Excellent vintage.

1950 Above average quantity. Light red wines. White wines good.

1951 Poor quality.

1952 Good, sturdy wines of fine color and bouquet.

1953 Very fine, balanced wines of finesse, body, and flavor.

1954 Very large quantity. Quality variable. Some good wines produced.

1955 Good, well-rounded wines.

1956 Very poor quality. Light wines.

1957 Fair quantity. Good wines of fine color and good body.

1958 Reds fair—some wines have good, fruity flavor. Whites were good.

1959 A great vintage in all respects. One of the best of the century. White wines tend to be overrich.

1960 Fair.

1961 Excellent quality for both red and white wines. Grand Cru reds still excellent for present consumption.

1962 Quality almost up to 1961 wines.

1963 Large quantity. Quality variable.

1964 Large quantity. Well-made wines. Early maturing.

1965 Poor quality.

1966 Abundant quantity. Quality was good. Big, full wines. Some fast-maturing wines produced; others will live a long time.

1967 Generally light and fast-maturing wines.

1968 Generally light wines. Whites better than reds.

1969 Low quantity. A great year. Deeply colored, big, full wines. Reds matured faster than expected.

1970 Good quantity. Good quality. Fast-maturing wines.

1971 Small quantity. Full-bodied, concentrated wines. Good color, long lived. Perhaps comparable to the '69s.

1972 Good quantity. Wines somewhat hard, but generally good quality. Will be long lived.

1973 Very large quantity. Variable quality. Many light wines produced. Fast maturing.

1974 A long period of heavy rains lowered the quality.

1975 Quantity small. With good grape selection some good reds were made. Whites tend to be better than the reds, with Chablis producing excellent, full wines.

1976 Average quantity. Very hot summer required early harvest. Red wines are dark in color, have good alcohol, and are well balanced. They have exceptional potential and should be long lived. Some whites may lack acidity but are very full and round.

1977 Average year. Spotty quality. Taste before you purchase.

1978 Bad weather led to short crop in some areas. Whites very aromatic—reds robust and round. Very good to excellent vintage.

1979 Record crop with whites showing surprisingly high quality for this size yield. Reds show good color but lack body.

1980 Adverse weather reduced crop and produced wines for early maturation. Some reds impressive, while Chablis best of the whites.

1981 White wine year. Short crop but aromatic wines.

1982 Very good weather, abundant harvest and outlook excellent for both reds and whites.

NOTES ON CHAMPAGNE VINTAGES°

1961 Good quantity. Top quality, light and delicate wines.

1962 Good quantity. Excellent quality. Wines are full bodied.

1963 Not a vintage year.

1964 Good quantity. Excellent quality, very full-bodied wines.

1965 Not a vintage year.

1966 Very good quality, well-balanced wines.

1967 Good quality when grapes carefully selected by the producer. Not a vintage year.

1968 Not a vintage year.

1969 Small quantity. Good quality, full-bodied wines.

1970 Large quantity. Good quality, light, fragrant wines.

1971 Very small quantity. Very good quality, full-bodied wines.

1972 Not a vintage year.

1973 Large quantity. Well balanced wines with good bouquet.

1974 Not a vintage year.

1975 Large quantity. Good quality, very full wines.

1976 Large quantity. Good quality, very full wines. Unusual to have two such years in a row.

°Some houses may produce a vintage Champagne in years when the majority of houses do not. The decision is up to each producer. When vintage wines are not produced, the wines of that year are used to replenish blending stocks, so that each house may maintain its unique style and continuity.

1977 Small quantity. Not a vintage year.

1978 Very small crop. High acid wines.

1979 Abundant crop. Quality high.

1980 Not a vintage year. Inadequate crop from devastating weather.

1981 Not a vintage year. Poor weather led to very small yield.

1982 Large quantity. First vintage in several years.

NOTES ON RHÔNE VINTAGES

1945
1949
1952 } All long-lived, full-bodied wines.
1955
1957

1959 Selectivity needed in choosing wines.

1960 A very good year.

1961 Good wines produced.

1962 Quantity small. Quality fair.

1963 Quantity very small. Quality poor.

1964 Quality average.

1965 One of the few regions to produce good wines during this year.

1966 An excellent year. Long-lived wines.

1967 Well-balanced, long-lived wines.

1968 Some pleasant, drinkable wines were produced.

1969 Quantity small. Variable quality. Excellent in the north, good in the south.

1970 Large quantity. Excellent quality. Long-lived wines with great potential.

1971 Small quantity. Very good quality. Full body and high alcohol. Need some time.

1972 Big, full-bodied wines. Need time to soften.

1973 Enormous quantity. Most areas suffered from overproduction. Most wines pleasant and light. Some good wines produced.

1974 In general, good-quality wines.

1975 Limited quantity and variable quality in the northern Rhône. Good quantity as well as good quality in the south.

1976 Quantity good. Very good quality because of very warm growing conditions. Wines should be long lived with high alcohol and very full body.

1977 Abundant crop. Very good color but lacking fruit.

1978 Superb crop. Superb quality. Superb future.

1979 Generous crop. Wines have fine color, body but less concentration than '78.

1980 Most successful region of this year. Consistently high quality with record-breaking quantity.

1981 Shorter crop than 1980. Good quality overall.

1982 Very abundant crop. Full-bodied, high-alcohol, deeply colored wines.

NOTES ON ALSATIAN VINTAGES

1970 Very large quantity. Quality good.

1971 Excellent quality. Wines high in alcohol.

1972 Quality fair.

1973 Quantity very large. Quality good.

1974 Quality good.

1975 Quantity about average. Quality good. Well-balanced wines.

1976 Average quantity, with above average amount of Beerenauslesen produced. Excellent quality with delicate bouquet and superior elegance.

1977 Light vintage. Ordinary quality.

1978 Mixed harvest. Riesling did well. Gewürztraminer good but small crop.

1979 Fine vintage. All varieties successful.

1980 Poor weather diminished all varieties except for Sylvaner.

1981 Dry season producing all-around fine wines.

1982 Extremely large harvest. Potentially great year, repeating the success of 1981.

RED ITALIAN VINTAGE CHART

	64	65	66	67	68	69	70	71	72	73	74	75	76	77	78	79	80	81	82
Aglianico del Vulture (Basilicata)							6c	6c	2e	8c	6c	8b	2d	8b	8a	6a	8c	8a	6b
Amarone (Veneto)	10c	5d	7c	8c	6c	8c	6c	6c	6b	6b	8b	7b	6a	8a	6a	8a	7a	6a	10a
Barbaresco (Piedmont)	10c	6e	2e	7d	6d	6c	8c	10b	2e	5c	9b	5b	5b	5b	10a	8a	7a	6a	10a
Barbera (Piedmont)	8d	4e	2e	6d	6d	7d	7c	8c	4e	5d	8c	5c	4b	2c	9a	7a	7b	7b	10a
Bardolino (Veneto)	8e	4e	6e	8e	7e	9e	7e	8e	5e	7e	7e	6e	8e	8e	6d	8c	7c	7c	8c
Barolo (Piedmont)	9c	8c	2e	8d	6d	7b	8b	10a	2e	5c	9a	5b	5b	5b	10a	8a	7a	6a	10a
Brunello di Montalcino (Tuscany)	10c	—	8c	8c	6c	5c	10a	7b	2c	6c	5c	10a	2c	8a	8a	8a	8a	10a	7a
Cannonau (Sardinia)	8e	2e	6d	6d	8d	4d	6d	4d	8c	6c	6c	4c	4c	8c	8c	6c	7c	8c	4c
Carema (Piedmont)							8c	8c	4d	6d	8c	6c	8c	2c	8a	8a	7a	8a	10a
Chianti (Tuscany)	6e	4e	4e	6e	7d	7d	8d	8d	4e	4e	5d	6c	2c	6b	8b	8a	8a	4c	8a
Chianti Classico Riserva (Tuscany)	8d	6d	6d	8c	8c	8c	8c	10c	4e	4d	7c	8b	4c	8b	10a	8b	8a	6b	10a
Ciro Rosso (Calabria)	4e	6e	—	6d	10c	2e	6d	6d	6c	8c	8b	6c	2d	8b	8b	6b	8b	8b	6b
Friuli-Venezia Giulia Varietals (I)	8e	4e	6e	6e	4e	7e	7e	8d	8d	8d	7d	6c	5c	7c	7c	8c	6c	8c	5c
Gattinara (Piedmont)	10c	6d	4e	6d	8c	8c	8c	4d	2e	4c	10a	6b	8a	4c	6b	8a	7a	6a	10a
Ghemme (Piedmont)	9c	4e	2e	6d	4c	6c	8c	8c	6c	8b	10b	6c	7b	2c	10a	8a	7a	4b	10a
Gutturnio (Emilia-Romagna)	10e	4e	6e	6d	6d	6d	8d	8d	2e	4e	6c	4c	4c	4c	6b	8a	7b	8a	8a
Montepulciano d'Abruzzo (Abruzzo)	2e	8e	6e	6e	10e	2e	4e	4e	4e	8c	8c	8c	4c	8c	6c	8c	8c	6c	5c
Nebbiolo d'Alba (Piedmont)	8e	4e	2e	8e	6e	6e	6e	10c	2e	4d	6c	4c	4c	4c	6b	4b	7a	6a	10a
Sangiovese di Romagna (Emilia-Romagna)	6e	8e	8d	8d	8d	4e	8d	8d	6e	6e	6e	8c	6c	10c	8b	8b	6c	8b	10b
Taurasi (Campania)	8e	6e	8e	8e	10c	6d	8c	8c	6c	8b	6c	8a	6b	10a	6a	8a	8a	8a	10a
Torgiano Rubesco (Umbria)	6d	6d	10c	8c	10c	8c	10c	10c	7c	8c	8b	10a	2d	8a	8a	8a	8a	8a	8a
Trentino-Alto Adige Varietals (II)	9e	2e	6e	6e	5e	10c		8d	4d	5d	6d	8c	7c	6c	5c	5c	8c	6c	6c
Valpolicella (Veneto)	10e	4e	6e	8e	6e	8e	6e	6e	4e	7e	6e	4e	6d	8c	6c	8c	7c	6c	8c
Valtellina (Lombardy) (III)	10d	2e	4d	6d	4e	8c	7c	8c	4d	6c	4c	6c	4b	2b	8b	6a	6a	6a	10a
Vino Nobile di Montepulciano (Tuscany)	8d	2e	6d	10c	8c	7c	10c	4d	4d	8c	6c	10a	2b	8a	6a	8a	7a	8a	7a

KEY TO READING TABLE
I. Cabernet, Merlot, Pinot Nero, and Refosco are grown in 6 D.O.C. areas: Aquileia, Collio Goriziano or Collio, Colli Orientali de Friuli, Isonzo, and Latisana.

II. Cabernet, Lagrein, Marzemino, Merlot, Pinot Nero, Schiava, and Teroldego are grown in 2 D.O.C. areas: Alto Adige and Trentino.

III. Valtellina embraces 5 sub-denominations: Inferno, Grumello, Sassella, Valgella, and Sfursat.

Number ratings:
2: Less than average vintage
4: Average vintage
6: Good vintage
8: Very good vintage
10: Exceptional vintage

Letter ratings:
a. Best with further aging
b. Can improve with further aging
c. Ready for drinking
d. Caution advised if aged further
e. Wine may be too old to drink

NOTES ON GERMAN VINTAGES

(1921 was considered one of the greatest vintages ever.)

1971 A great vintage. *Edelfäule* produced wines of great concentration and depth. Spätlesen and higher will be very long lived.

1972 Generally light, attractive wines. Rhine wines better than Moselles.

1973 Extremely large quantity. Fruity and well-balanced wines best consumed young.

1974 Small quantity. Agreeable but undistinguished.

1975 Average quantity. Great vintage. Extremely high proportion of top-category wines. Almost no Tafelwein was produced.

1976 Small quantity. Long, hot summer produced predominantly Spätlesen and higher-quality wines, but some lack acid.

1977 Generally light wines for quick drinking.

1978 Moderate vintage. Good year for Qualitätswein, and a few late harvest specialties.

1979 Small quantity. Successful Prädikat wines up to Auslese level.

1980 Small quantity of Riesling and Prädikat wines. Rhine wines fared better.

1981 Above average quantity. Good QbA and Kabinett wines.

1982 Superlative vintage in both quantity and quality.

NOTES ON PORTO VINTAGES

Vintage Porto is made only in fine years, and even then not every producer makes a Vintage Porto. The number of producers who declare a vintage has ranged from two (in 1931) to thirty (in 1927). The average number of producers who declare a vintage is fourteen.

1945 Classic vintage; wines are rich with good color and body.

1947 Good year; wines are fruity and delicate.

1948 Wines are full and powerful with depth.

1950 Lighter wines, faster to mature.

1955 Good year; wines are long lasting and full.

1958 Lighter wines, more delicate.

1960 Good quality, not too dark, can be drunk now.

1963 Big, fat wines, good fruity bouquet, dark color. Drink in 1980s.

1966 Fresh and fruity, not as big as '63s. Drink from 1980 on.

1967 Borderline vintage, few declared; on the light side.

1970 Superb year, good color and body. Drink in the 1990s.

1975 Exceptional year; wines are very dark and intense.

1977 Outstanding year; expected to rank with 1963.

1978 Borderline vintage; most shippers undecided.

1980 Another very good year; many declared due to full, rich wines.

California North Coast Vintage Chart SECOND EDITION

Napa

Red Wines

	'68	'69	'70	'71	'72	'73	'74	'75	'76	'77		'78	'79
CABERNET SAUVIGNON	18	17	19	13	12	16	18	16	15	16		17	16
PETITE SIRAH	16	16	17	14	12	15	16	17	16	15		17	17
PINOT NOIR	16	15	17	13	13	14	15	16	17	16		16	17
ZINFANDEL	18	15	18	14	14	16	17	15	18	17		16	17

White Wines

	'74	'75	'76	'77	'78		'79	'80
CHARDONNAY	15	18	15	17	17		18	17
SAUVIGNON BLANC	15	16	15	16	18		17	18
CHENIN BLANC	16	16	15	17	17		16	17
JOHANNISBERG RIESLING	14	17	15	16	17		16	18

Sonoma

Red Wines

	'68	'69	'70	'71	'72	'73	'74	'75	'76	'77		'78	'79
CABERNET SAUVIGNON	17	16	18	14	10	15	17	15	16	16		17	15
PETITE SIRAH	17	17	17	14	13	15	16	17	16	15		17	16
PINOT NOIR	16	15	17	14	13	15	15	16	17	17		16	17
ZINFANDEL	18	16	18	14	13	16	18	16	19	17		18	17

White Wines

	'74	'75	'76	'77	'78		'79	'80
CHARDONNAY	16	17	17	16	18		17	19
SAUVIGNON BLANC	15	16	17	16	18		16	18
CHENIN BLANC	16	16	15	16	16		16	17
JOHANNISBERG RIESLING	15	17	17	16	18		17	18

Mendocino

Red Wines

	'68	'69	'70	'71	'72	'73	'74	'75	'76	'77		'78	'79
CABERNET SAUVIGNON	15	16	16	14	12	15	17	16	15	17		17	16
PETITE SIRAH	16	17	16	15	13	16	18	18	16	17		18	15
PINOT NOIR	16	15	15	14	13	14	15	16	15	16		16	17
ZINFANDEL	17	15	16	15	14	15	17	15	17	16		17	18

White Wines

	'74	'75	'76	'77	'78		'79	'80
CHARDONNAY	17	18	16	17	16		16	17
SAUVIGNON BLANC	15	16	15	17	17		16	17
CHENIN BLANC	17	17	16	17	18		16	18
JOHANNISBERG RIESLING	15	16	15	17	17		16	17

INTERPRETATION

20-18 EXCEPTIONAL
17-16 VERY GOOD
15-14 AVERAGE
13-12 FAIR
11-10 POOR

©Vintage Wine Merchants 1981

APPENDIX C

THE CLASSIFIED GROWTHS OF BORDEAUX

OFFICIAL CLASSIFICATION OF 1855

The Official Classification of 1855 listed the red wines of the Médoc and the sweet white wines of the Sauternes in order of quality. The one exception was the inclusion of Château Haut-Brion, from Graves, among the first growths of Médoc. The following list, which uses the current spelling of the names of some of the châteaux, also lists some châteaux that were not originally part of the 1855 classification but which came into existence when a château that had been originally listed was divided up. These wines are shown bracketed, signifying that they were once a single château.

Château Mouton-Rothschild, which is now listed as a first growth, was listed as a second growth from 1855 to 1973, although it always brought prices commensurate with those of the first growths.

MEDOC WINES

FIRST GROWTHS
Château Lafite-Rothschild
Château Margaux
Château Latour
Château Haut-Brion
Château Mouton-Rothschild

SECOND GROWTHS
Château Rausan-Ségla
Château Rauzan-Gassies
{ Château Léoville-Lascases
Château Léoville-Poyferré
Château Léoville-Barton
Château Durfort-Vivens
Château Gruaud-Larose
Château Lascombes
Château Brane-Cantenac
{ Château Pichon-Longueville, Baron de Pichon
Château Pichon-Longueville, Comtesse de
  Lalande
Château Ducru-Beaucaillou
Château Cos d'Estournel
Château Montrose

THIRD GROWTHS
Château Kirwan
Château d'Issan
Château Lagrange
Château Langoa-Barton
Château Giscours
Château Malescot-Saint-Exupéry
{ Château Boyd-Cantenac
Château Cantenac-Brown
Château Palmer
Château La Lagune

Château Desmirail
Château Calon-Ségur
Château Ferrière
Château Marquis d'Alesme-Becker

FOURTH GROWTHS
Château Saint-Pierre
Château Talbot
Château Branaire-Ducru
Château Duhart-Milon-Rothschild
Château Pouget
Château La Tour-Carnet
Château Lafon-Rochet
Château Beychevelle
Château Prieuré-Lichine
Château Marquis de Terme

FIFTH GROWTHS
Château Pontet-Canet
{ Château Batailley
Château Haut-Batailley
{ Château Grand-Puy-Lacoste
Château Grand-Puy-Ducasse
Château Lynch-Bages
Château Lynch-Moussas
Château Dauzac
Château Mouton-Baron-Philippe
Château du Tertre
Château Haut-Bages-Libéral
Château Pédesclaux
Château Belgrave
Château Camensac
Château Cos-Labory
Château Clerc-Milon-Mondon
Château Croizet-Bages
Château Cantemerle

SAUTERNES (INCLUDING BARSAC)

FIRST SUPERIOR GROWTH
Château d'Yquem

FIRST GROWTHS
Château La Tour-Blanche
{ Château Lafaurie-Peyraguey
{ Clos Haut-Peyraguey
Château de Rayne-Vigneau
Château Suduiraut
Château Coutet
Château Climens
Château Guiraud
Château Rieussec
{ Château Rabaud-Promis
{ Château Sigalas-Rabaud

SECOND GROWTHS
Château Myrat
{ Château Doisy-Daene
{ Château Doisy-Dubroca
{ Château Doisy-Védrines
Château d'Arche
Château Filhot
{ Château Broustet
{ Château Nairac
Château Caillou
Château Suau
Château de Malle
{ Château Romer (R. Farges, prop.)
{ Château Romer (A. du Hayot, prop.)
{ Château Lamothe
{ Château Lamothe-Bergey

OFFICIAL CLASSIFICATIONS OF OTHER BORDEAUX

The wines of Graves and Saint-Émilion were not classified until 1953 and 1955, respectively. The 1955 list still holds for Saint-Émilion, but the Graves list was redone and finalized in 1959. All of these wines are listed in alphabetical order, with the exception of Châteaux Ausone and Cheval-Blanc, which are listed ahead of the other Premiers Grands Crus Classés of Saint-Émilion. In the list of the classified wines of the Graves, Château Haut-Brion appears in Crus Classés—Red, even though it remains listed as a first growth of the 1855 classification.

The wines of Pomerol have never been officially classified. Château Pétrus, however, is considered to be an outstanding growth, equal to the first growths of the Médoc. The rest of the listed Pomerol wines are those generally considered to be the best wines after Château Pétrus.

GRAVES
1959 Official Classification

CRUS CLASSÉS—RED
Château Bouscaut
Château Carbonnieux
Domaine de Chevalier
Château Fieuzal
Château Haut-Bailly
Château Haut-Brion
Château La Mission Haut Brion
Château La Tour Haut Brion
Château La Tour-Martillac
Château Malartic-Lagravière
Château Olivier

Château Pape-Clément
Château Smith-Haut-Lafitte

CRUS CLASSÉS—WHITE
Château Bouscaut
Château Carbonnieux
Domaine de Chevalier
Château Couhins
Château La Tour-Martillac
Château Laville Haut Brion
Château Malartic-Lagravière
Château Olivier

SAINT-ÉMILION
1955 Official Classification

PREMIERS GRANDS CRUS CLASSÉS
Château Ausone
Château Cheval-Blanc

Château Beauséjour (Lagrosse, prop.)
Château Beauséjour (Fagouet, prop.)
Château Belair

Château Canon
Château Figeac
Château La Gaffelière
Château Magdelaine
Château Pavie
Château Trottevieille
Clos Fourtet

GRANDS CRUS CLASSÉS
Château L'Angélus
Château L'Arrosée
Château Balestard-La Tonnelle
Château Bellevue
Château Bergat
Château Cadet-Bon
Château Cadet-Piola
Château Canon-La Gaffelière
Château Cap-de-Mourlin
Château Chapelle-Madeleine
Château Chauvin
Château Corbin (Giraud, prop.)
Château Corbin (Michotte, prop.)
Château Coutet
Château Croque-Michotte
Château Curé-Bon
Château Fonplégade
Château Fonroque
Château Franc-Mayne
Château Grand-Barrail-Lamarzelle-Figeac
Château Grand-Corbin-Despagne
Château Grand-Corbin-Pécresse
Château Grand-Mayne
Château Grand-Pontet
Château Grandes-Murailles
Château Guadet-Saint-Julien
Château Jean-Faure
Château La Carte
Château La Clotte
Château La Cluzière
Château La Couspaude

Château La Dominique
Château Larcis-Ducasse
Château Lamarzelle
Château Larmande
Château Laroze
Château Lassere
Château La Tour-du-Pin-Figeac (Bélivier, prop.)
Château La Tour-du-Pin-Figeac (Moueix, prop.)
Château La Tour-Figeac
Château Le Châtelet
Château Le Couvent
Château Le Prieuré
Château Mauvezin
Château Moulin-du-Cadet
Château Pavie-Décesse
Château Pavie-Macquin
Château Pavillon-Cadet
Château Petit-Faurie-de-Souchard
Château Petit-Faurie-de-Soutard
Château Ripeau
Château Sansonnet
Château Saint-Georges-Côte-Pavie
Château Soutard
Château Tertre-Daugay
Château Trimoulet
Château Trois-Moulins
Château Troplong-Mondot
Château Villemaurine
Château Yon-Figeac
Clos des Jacobins
Clos La Madeleine
Clos Saint-Martin

POMEROL

CRU EXCEPTIONNEL
Château Pétrus

PREMIERS CRUS
Château Beauregard
Château Certan-Giraud
Château Certan-de-May
Château Gazin
Château La Conseillante
Château La Croix-de-Gay
Château Lafleur
Château La Fleur-Pétrus
Château Lagrange

Château La Pointe
Château Latour-Pomerol
Château L'Église-Clinet
Château L'Évangile
Château Nenin
Château Petit-Village
Château Rouget
Château Trotanoy
(Château) Vieux Château Certan

Source: *Bordeaux et Ses Vins* by Ch. Cocks et Éd. Féret, 12th edition, 1968, 1974.

APPENDIX D

PRINCIPAL VINEYARDS OF THE CÔTE D'OR, BURGUNDY

The ranking of wines of Burgundy has developed by tradition. Over the years, the best wines were judged to be Grands Crus, followed by Premiers Crus. These opinions have generally held to this day.

In this compilation of Grands and Premiers Crus, which is arranged by communes from north to south, Grand Cru vineyards appear in **boldface** type. Where the spelling of a vineyard has changed slightly from the original, the current spelling is used.

Unlike the great châteaux of Bordeaux, the names of Grands Crus vineyards are controlled appellations.

CÔTE DE NUITS

COMMUNE	VINEYARD (CLIMAT)	
FIXIN (mostly red)	Les Arvelets Aux Cheusots Le Clos-du-Chapitre	Les Hervelets Les Meix-Bas La Perrière
GEVREY- CHAMBERTIN (only red)	**Chambertin** **Chambertin-Close de Bèze** **Chapelle-Chambertin** **Charmes-Chambertin** **(Mazoyères-Chambertin)**	**Griotte-Chambertin** **Latricières-Chambertin** **Mazis-Chambertin** **Ruchottes-Chambertin**
	Au Closeau Aux Combottes Bel-Air Cazetiers Champeaux Champitonnois Champonnets Cherbaudes Clos-du-Chapitre Clos-Prieur Le Clos Saint-Jacques Combe-aux-Moines	Les Corbeaux Craipillot Ergots Estournelles Le Fonteny Les Gemreaux Les Goulots Issarts Lavaut La Perrière Poissenot Les Véroilles
MOREY-SAINT- DENIS (mostly red)	**Bonnes Mares** (partly in Chambolle-Musigny) **Clos de la Roche**	**Clos de Tart** **Clos Saint-Denis**
	Aux Charmes Les Bouchots Calouères Chabiots Les Chaffots Les Charrières Les Chénevery Le Clos-Baulet Clos-Bussière Clos-des-Lambrays Le Clos-des-Ormes Le Clos-Sorbès Côte Rôtie	Les Façonnières Les Fremières Les Froichots Les Genevrières Les Gruenchers Maison-Brûlée Les Mauchamps Meix-Rentiers Les Millandes La Riotte Les Ruchots Les Sorbès

537

COMMUNE	VINEYARD (CLIMAT)	
CHAMBOLLE-MUSIGNY (mostly red)	**Bonnes Mares** **Musigny**	
	Les Amoureuses	Les Fousselottes
	Aux Beaux-Bruns	Les Fuées
	Aux Combottes	Les Gras
	Les Baudes	Les Groseilles
	Les Bonnes Mares	Les Gruenchers
	Les Borniques	Les Hauts-Doix
	Les Charmes	Les Lavrottes
	Les Chatelots	Les Noirots
	Les Combottes	Les Plantes
	Derrière-la-Grange	Les Sentiers
VOUGEOT (mostly red)	**Clos de Vougeot** Le Clos-Blanc (white) Clos-de-la-Perrière	Les Cras Les Petits-Vougeots
VOSNE-ROMANÉE (only red)	**Richebourg** **Romanée** **Romanée-Conti**	**Romanée-Saint-Vivant** **La Tâche**
	Aux Brûlées	La Grande Rue
	Aux Malconsorts	Les Petits-Monts
	Les Beaumonts	Les Reignots
	Les Chaumes	Les Suchots
	Le Clos des Réas	
FLAGEY-ECHÉZEAUX (only red)	**Echézeaux** **Grands Echézeaux**	
NUITS-SAINT-GEORGES (mostly red)	Les Argillats	Clos-des-Forêts
	Aux Argillats	Clos-des-Grandes-Vignes
	Aux Boudots	Le Clos Saint-Marc
	Aux Bousselots	Les Corvées-Paget
	Aux Chaignots	Les Didiers
	Aux Champs-Perdrix	En la Chaine-Carteau
	Aux Cras	Les Hauts-Pruliers
	Aux Crots	La Perrière
	Aux Damodes	Perrière-Noblet
	Aux Murgers	Les Porets
	Aux Perdrix	Les Poulettes
	Aux Thorey	Le Procès
	Aux Vignes-Rondes	Les Pruliers
	Les Cailles	La Richemone
	Les Chaboeufs	La Roncière
	Clos-Arlots	Rue-de-Chaux
	Clos-de-la-Maréchale	Les Saint-Georges
	Clos-des-Argillières	Les Vallerots
	Clos-des-Corvées	Les Vaucrains

CÔTE DE BEAUNE

COMMUNE	VINEYARD (CLIMAT)	
ALOXE-CORTON (mostly red)	**Corton** or **Corton** plus vineyard name: Bressandes, Clos du Roi, Languettes, Perrières, Pougets, Renardes, La Vigne-au-Saint, etc. **Corton-Charlemagne** (white)	
	Les Chaillots En Pauland Les Fournières Les Guérets	Les Maréchaudes Les Meix Les Valozières Les Vercots
LADOIX-SERRIGNY (mostly red)	Basses-Mourettes La Coutière Les Grandes-Lolières	La Maréchaude Les Petites Lolières La Toppe-au-Vert
PERNAND- *VERGELESSES* (mostly red)	Les Basses-Vergelesses Creux-de-la-Net	En Caradeux Les Fichots
SAVIGNY-LES- *BEAUNE* (mostly red)	Aux Clous Aux Fourneaux Aux Grands-Liards Aux Gravains Aux Guettes Aux Guettes Aux Petits-Liards Aux Serpentières Aux Vergelesses Basses-Vergelesses Bataillière Les Charnières	La Dominode Les Hauts-Jarrons Les Hauts-Marconnets Les Jarrons Les Lavières Les Marconnets Les Narbantons Petits-Godeaux Les Peuillets Redrescuts Les Rouvrettes Les Talmettes
BEAUNE (mostly red)	Les Aigrots A l' Ecu Aux Coucherias Aux Cras Les Avaux Le Bas-des-Teurons Les Blanches-Fleurs Les Boucherottes Les Bressandes Les Cent-Vignes Champs-Pimont Les Chouacheux Le Clos-de-la-Mousse Le Clos-des-Mouches Clos-du-Roi En Genêt En l'Orme	Les Épenottes Les Fèves Les Grèves Les Marconnets La Mignotte Montée-Rouge Les Montrevenots Les Perrières Pertuisots Les Reversées Les Seurey Les Sisies Sur-les-Grèves Les Teurons Tiélandry or Clos-Landry Les Toussaints Les Vignes-Franches

COMMUNE	VINEYARD (CLIMAT)	
POMMARD (only red)	Les Argillières	Les Épenots
	Les Arvelets	Ès-Charmots
	Les Bertins	Les Fremiers
	Les Boucherottes	Les Garollières
	La Chanière	Les Petits-Épenots
	Les Chanlins-Bas	Les Pézerolles
	Les Chapponières	La Platière
	Clos-Blanc	Les Poutures
	Clos-de-la-Commareine	La Refène
	Clos-du-Verger	Les Rugiens
	Le Clos-Micot	Les Rugiens-Bas
	Les Combes-Dessus	Les Rugiens-Hauts
	Les Croix-Noires	Les Sausilles
	Derrière-Saint-Jean	
VOLNAY (only red)	Les Angles	En l'Ormeau
	Les Aussy	En Verseuil
	La Barre or Clos-de-la-Barre	Fremiers
	Bousse-d'Or	Les Lurets
	Les Brouillards	Les Mitans
	Caillerets-Dessus	Les Petures (red)
	Carelle-Dessous	Les Pitures-Dessus
	Carelle-sous-la-Chapelle	Pointe-d'Angles
	Chanlin	Robardelle
	Le Clos-des-Chênes	Ronceret
	Les Clos-des-Ducs	Les Santenots (red)
	En Caillerets	Taille-Pieds
	En Champains	Village-de-Volnay
	En Chevret	
MONTHÉLIE (mostly red)	Le Cas-Rougeot	Le Meix-Bataille
	Les Champs-Fulliot	Les Riottes
	Le Château-Gaillard	Sur Lavelle
	Le Clos-Gauthey	La Taupine
	Duresse	Les Vignes-Rondes
AUXEY-DURESSES (predominantly red)	Les Bas-des-Duresses	Les Duresses
	Les Bretterins	Les Écusseaux
	La Chapelle	Les Grands-Champs
	La Chapelle	Reugne
	Clos-du-Val	
MEURSAULT (mostly white)	Aux Perrières	Les Perrières-Dessous
	Les Bouchères	Les Perrières-Dessus
	Les Caillerets	Les Petures
	Les Charmes-Dessous	La Pièce-sous-le-Bois
	Les Charmes-Dessus	Le Poruzot
	Les Cras	Le Poruzot-Dessus
	Les Genevrières-Dessous	Les Santenots-Blancs
	Les Genevrières-Dessus	Les Santenots-du-Milieu
	La Goutte d'Or	Sous-le-dos-d'Ane
	La Jennelotte	

COMMUNE	VINEYARD (CLIMAT)	
PULIGNY-MONTRACHET (mostly white)	**Bâtard-Montrachet** (partly in Chassagne-Montrachet) **Bienvenues-Bâtard-Montrachet**	**Chevalier-Montrachet** **Montrachet** (partly in Chassagne-Montrachet)
	Le Cailleret Les Chalumeaux Le Champ-Canet Clavoillons Les Combettes Les Folatières	La Garenne Hameau-de-Blagny Les Pucelles Les Referts Sous-le-Puits
CHASSAGNE-MONTRACHET (majority red)	**Bâtard-Montrachet** (partly in Puligny-Montrachet) **Criots-Bâtard-Montrachet**	**Montrachet** (partly in Puligny-Montrachet)
	Abbaye-de-Morgeot La Boudriotte Les Brussoles Les Champs-Gain Les Chenevottes Clos-Saint-Jean En Cailleret	Grandes-Ruchottes Les Macherelles La Maltroie Morgeot La Romanée Les Vergers
SAINT-AUBIN (predominantly red)	Champlot La Chatenière Les Combes En Remilly	Les Frionnes Les Murgers-des-Dents-de-Chien Sur Gamay Sur-le-Sentier-du-Clou
SANTENAY (mostly red)	Beauregard Beaurepaire Clos-de-Tavannes La Comme	Les Gravières La Maladière Le Passe-Temps

Source: Pierre Poupon and Pierre Forgeot, *The Wines of Burgundy*, 5th ed. (Paris: Presses Universitaires de France, 1974).

PRINCIPAL VINEYARDS OF CHABLIS

GRAND CRU VINEYARDS:

Blanchots
Bougros
Grenouilles
Les Clos
Les Preuses
Valmur
Vaudésir

PREMIER CRU VINEYARDS (boldface),

Beauroy
Troesmes
Côte de Léchet
Fourchaume
Côte de Fontenay
L'Homme Mort
Vaulorent
Vaupulent
Les Fourneaux
Côtes des Prés-Girots
Morein
Mélinots
Les Epinottes
Roncières

SUBDIVISIONS (lightface):

Montée de Tonnerre
Chapelot
Pieds-d'Aloup
Montmains
Butteaux
Forêts
Monts de Milieu
Vaillons
Beugnons
Châtains
Les Lys
Séché
Vaucoupin
Vosgros
Vaugiraut

PRINCIPAL VINEYARDS OF BEAUJOLAIS

GRAND CRU VINEYARDS:

Brouilly
Chénas
Chiroubles
Côte de Brouilly
Fleurie
Juliénas
Morgon
Moulin-à-Vent
Saint-Amour

Source: Pierre Poupon et Pierre Forgeot, *Les Vins de Bourgogne,* 8eme ed. (Paris: Presses Universitaires de France, 1977)

APPENDIX E

D.O.C. WINES, D.O.C.G. WINES, AND PRINCIPAL GRAPE VARIETIES OF ITALY

D.O.C. WINES OF ITALY

(by region from north to south)

VALLE D'AOSTA

Donnaz
Enfer d'Arvier

PIEDMONT

Barbaresco
Barbera d'Alba
Barbera d'Asti
Barbera del Monferrato
Barolo
Boca
Brachetto d'Acqui
Bramaterra
Carema
Colli Tortonesi (Barbera, Cortese)
Cortesi dell'Alto Monferrato
Dolcetto d'Acqui
Dolcetto d'Alba
Dolcetto d'Asti
Dolcetto delle Langhe Monregalesi
Dolcetto di Diano d'Alba
Dolcetto di Dogliani

Dolcetto di Ovada
Erbaluce di Caluso or Caluso Passito
Fara
Freisa d'Asti
Freisa di Chieri
Gabiano
Gattinara
Gavi or Cortese di Gavi
Ghemme
Grignolino d'Asti
Grignolino del Monferrato Casalese
Lessona
Malvasia di Casorzo d'Asti
Malvasia di Castelnuovo Don Bosco
Moscato d'Asti Spumante
Moscato Naturale d'Asti
Nebbiolo d'Alba
Rubino di Cantavenna
Sizzano

LOMBARDY

Botticino
Capriano del Colle (Bianco, Rosso)
Cellatica
Franciacorta Pinot
Franciacorta Rosso
Lugana
Oltrepò Pavese (Barbacarlo, Barbera, Bonarda, Buttafuoco, Cortese, Moscato, Pinot, Riesling, Rosso, Sangue di Giuda)

Riviera del Garda Bresciano (Rosso and Chiaretto)
Tocai di San Martino della Battaglia
Valcalepio
Valtellina (Rosso, Sfursat)
Valtellina Superiore (Inferno, Grumello, Sassella, Valgella)

TRENTINO-ALTO ADIGE

Alto Adige (Cabernet, Lagrein, Malvasia, Merlot, Moscato Giallo, Moscato Rosa, Müller-Thurgau, Pinot Bianco, Pinot Grigio, Pinot Nero, Riesling Italico, Riesling Renano, Sauvignon, Schiava, Sylvaner, Traminer Aromatico)
Caldaro or Lago di Caldaro
Casteller
Colli di Bolzano
Meranese or Meranese di Collina
Santa Maddalena
Sorni
Terlano
Teroldego Rotaliano
Valdadige
Valle Isarco (Müller Thurgau, Pinot Grigio, Sylvaner, Traminer Aromatico, Veltliner)
Vini del Trentino (Cabernet, Lagrein, Marzemino, Merlot, Moscato, Pinot Bianco, Pinot Nero, Riesling, Traminer Aromatico, Vin Santo)

VENETO

Bardolino
Bianco di Custoza
Breganze (Bianco, Cabernet, Pinot Bianco, Pinot Grigio, Pinot Nero, Rosso, Vespaiolo)
Colli Berici (Cabernet, Garganega, Merlot, Pinot Bianco, Sauvignon, Tocai Bianco, Tocai Rosso)
Colli Euganei (Bianco, Moscato, Rosso)
Gambellara (Bianco, Recioto, Vin Santo)
Lugana
Montelloe Colli Asolani (Cabernet, Merlot, Prosecco)
Pramaggiore (Cabernet, Merlot)
Prosecco di Conegliano-Valdobbiadene
Soave (Recioto, Soave, Soave Classico)
Tocai di Lison
Valpolicella (Valpolicella, Valpolicella Classico, Recioto, Recioto Amarone)
Vini del Piave (Cabernet, Merlot, Tocai, Verduzzo)

FRIULI-VENEZIA-GIULIA

Aquileia (Cabernet, Merlot, Pinot Bianco, Pinot Grigio, Refosco, Riesling Renano, Tocai)
Colli Goriziano or Collio (Bianco Cabernet France, Malvasia, Merlot, Pinot Bianco, Pinot Grigio, Pinot Nero, Riesling Italico, Sauvignon, Tocai Traminer)
Colli Orientali del Friuli (Cabernet Franc, Cabernet Sauvignon, Merlot, Picolit, Pinot Bianco, Pinot Grigio, Pinot Nero, Ribolla, Riesling Renano, Refosco, Sauvignon, Tocai, Verduzzo)
Grave del Friuli (Cabernet Franc, Cabernet Sauvignon, Merlot, Pinot Bianco, Pinot Grigio, Refosco Tocai, Verduzzo)
Isonzo (Cabernet, Malvasia Istriana, Merlot, Pinot Bianco, Pinot Grigio, Riesling Renano, Sauvignon, Tocai, Traminer Aromatico, Verduzzo)
Latisana (Cabernet, Merlot, Pinot Bianco, Pinot Grigio, Refosco, Tocai, Verduzzo)

LIGURIA

Cinqueterre
Cinqueterre Sciacchetrà
Rossese di Dolceacqua or Dolceacqua

EMILIA-ROMAGNA

Albana di Romagna
Biano di Scandiano
Colli Bolognesi (Monte San Pietro or Castelli Medioevali)
Gutturnio dei Colli Piacentini
Lambrusco di Sorbara
Lambrusco Grasparossa di Castelvetro
Lambrusco Reggiano
Lambrusco Salamino di Santa Croce
Monterosso Val d'Arda
Sangiovese di Romagna
Trebbianino Val Trebbia
Trebbiano di Romagna

TUSCANY

Bianco della Valdinievole
Bianco di Pitigliano
Bianco Vergine Val di Chiana
Brunello di Montalcino
Carmignano
Chianti (Classico, Colli Aretini, Colli Fiorentini, Colline Pisane, Colline Senesi, Montalbano, Rufina)
Elba (Bianco and Rosso)
Montecarlo
Montescudaio
Morellino di Scansano
Parrina
Rosso delle Colline Lucchesi
Vernaccia di San Gimignano
Vino Nobile di Montepulciano

MARCHES

Bianchello del Metauro
Bianco dei Colli Maceratesi
Falerio dei Colli Ascolani
Rosso Conero
Rosso Piceno
Sangiovese dei Colli Pesaresi
Verdicchio dei Castelli di Jesi
Verdicchio di Matelica
Vernaccia di Serrapetrona

UMBRIA

Colli Altotiberini
Colli del Trasimeno
Colli Perugini

Montefalco (Rosso, Sagrantino)
Orvieto
Torgiano (Bianco, Rosso)

LATIUM

Aleatico di Gradoli
Aprilia (Merlot, Sangiovese, Trebbiano)
Bianco Capena
Cerveteri (Bianco, Rosso)
Cesanese del Piglio or Piglio
Cesanese di Affile or Affile
Cesanese di Olevano Romano or Olevano Romano
Colli Albani
Colli Lanuvini

Cori (Bianco, Rosso)
Est! Est!! Est!!! di Montefiascone
Frascati
Marino
Montecompatri Colonna
Orvieto
Velletri (Bianco Rosso)
Zagarolo

ABRUZZI AND MOLISE

Montepulciano d'Abruzzo
Trebbiano d'Abruzzo

CAMPANIA

Capri (Bianco, Rosso)
Fiano di Avellino
Greco di Tufo

Ischia (Bianco, Bianco Superiore, Rosso)
Solopaca (Bianco, Rosso)
Taurasi

APULIA

Aleatico di Puglia
Brindisi (Rosso, Rosato)
Caccé Mmitte di Lucera
Castel del Monte (Bianco, Rosso, Rosato)
Coperatino (Rosso, Rosato)
Leverano (Bianco, Rosso, Rosato)
Locorotondo
Martina or Martina Franca
Matino (Rosso, Rosato)

Moscato di Trani
Ostuni (Bianco, Ottavianello)
Primitivo di Manduria
Rosso Barletta
Rosso Canosa
Rosso di Cerignola
Salice Salentino (Rosso, Rosato)
San Severo (Bianco, Rosso, Rosato)
Squinzano (Rosso, Rosato)

BASILICATA

Aglianico del Vulture

CALABRIA

Cirò (Classico, Bianco, Rosso, Rosato
Donnici
Greco di Bianco
Lamezia

Melissa (Bianco, Rosso)
Pollino
Sant'Anna di Isola Capo Rizzuto
Savuto

SICILY

Bianco Alcamo or Alcamo
Cerasuolo di Vittoria
Etna (Bianco, Rosso, Rosato)
Faro
Malvasia delle Lipari

Marsala
Moscato di Noto
Moscato di Pantelleria
Moscato di Siracusa
Moscato Passito di Pantelleria

SARDINIA

Campidano di Terralba
Cannonau di Sardegna
Carignano del Sulcis
Girò di Cagliari
Malvasia di Bosa
Malvasia di Cagliari
Mandrolisai (Rosso, Rosato)
Monica di Cagliari

Monica di Sardegna
Moscato di Cagliari
Moscato di Sardegna
Moscato di Sorso-Sennori
Nasco di Cagliari
Nuragus di Cagliari
Vermentino di Gallura
Vernaccia di Oristano

Source: Anderson, Burton, "The Simon and Schuster Pocket Guide to Italian Wines" (1982); Hazan, Victor, "Italian Wine" (Knopf, 1982).

D.O.C.G. WINES OF ITALY

Barbaresco	Piedmont
Barolo	Piedmont
Brunello di Montalcino	Tuscany
Chianti	Tuscany
Vino Nobile di Montepulciano	Tuscany

PRINCIPAL GRAPE VARIETIES OF ITALY

dark grapes

GRAPE	REGIONS WHERE GROWN°	WINES
Aglianico	Basilicata	Aglianico del Vulture
	Campania	Taurasi
Aleatico	Latium	Aleatico di Gradoli
(Muscato Nero)	Apulia	Aleatico di Puglia
Barbera	Piedmont	Barbera d'Alba
		Barbera d'Asti
		Barbera del Montferrato
	Lombardy	Botticino
		Cellatica
		Franciacorta
		Oltrepò Pavese
		Riviera del Garda
	Emilia-Romagna	Gutturnio dei Colli Piacentini
Bombino Nero	Apulia	Castel del Monte
Bonarda	Piedmont	Boca
		Fara
		Ghemme
		Sizzano
Brachetto	Piedmont	Brachetto d'Acqui
		Brachetto d' Asti
Brunello di Montalcino	Tuscany	Brunello di Montalcino
Cabernet Sauvignon or	Veneto	Breganze Cabernet
Cabernet Franc	Trentino–Alto Adige	Trentino Cabernet
	Friuli-Venezia-Giulia	Grave del Friuli Cabernet
		Colli Orientale del Friuli Cabernet
Calabrese	Sicily	Cerasuolo di Vittoria
Canaiolo Nero	Tuscany	Chianti
		Vino Nobile di Montepulciano
Cannonau	Sardinia	Cannonau di Sardegna
Cesanese	Latium	Cesanese del Piglio
		Cesanese di Affile
Corvina	Veneto	Bardolino
Veronese		Valpolicella
Dolcetto	Piedmont	Dolcetto d'Acqui
		Dolcetto di Ovada
Freisa	Piedmont	Freisa d'Asti
Girò	Sardinia	Girò di Cagliari
Grignolino	Piedmont	Grignolino d'Asti
Gropello	Lombardy	Gropello Amarone
		Riviera del Garda
Lagrein	Trentino–Alto Adige	Trentino Lagrein
Lambrusco	Emilia-Romagna	Labrusco Reggiano
(several varieties)		Lambrusco di Sorbara, etc.

°These are the regions where the grapes are most important. Many of these grapes are grown elsewhere in Italy in smaller amounts.

GRAPE	REGIONS WHERE GROWN	WINES
Merlot	Friuli-Venezia-Giulia	Colli Orientale del Friuli Merlot
		Grave del Friuli Merlot
	Trentino—Alto Adige	Trentino Merlot
	Veneto	Breganze Rosso
Montepulciano	Abruzzo	Monepulciano d'Abruzzo
	Marches	Rosso Conero
		Rosso Piceno
	Apulia	San Severo
Nebbiolo	Piedmont	Barbaresco
(called Spanna around		Barolo
Gattinara)		Boca
		Carema
		Fara
		Gattinara
		Ghemme
		Sizzano
(here called Chiavennasca)	Lombardy	Grumello
		Inferno
		Sassella
		Vagella
Negroamaro	Apulia	Brindisi
		Copertino
		Leverano
		Matino
		Salice Salentino
		Squinzano
Perricone	Sicily	Corvo Rosso
Pinot Nero	Friuli-Venezia-Giulia	Colli Orientale del Friuli Pinot Nero
		Collio Pinot Nero
	Lombardy	Oltrepò Pavese Pinot
	Trentino–Alto Adige	Trentino Pinot Nero
	Veneto	Breganze Pinot Nero
Primitive	Apulia	Primitivo di Manduria
Refosco	Friuli-Venezia-Giulia	Colli Orientali del Friuli Refosco
		Aquilea Refosco
		Grave del Friuli Refosco
		Latisana Refosco
Rondinella	Veneto	Bardolino
		Valpolicella
Sangiovese	Emilia-Romagna	Sangiovese di Romagna
(several varities)	Latium	Sangiovese di Aprilia
	Marches	Sangiovese dei Colli Pesaresi
	Tuscany	Chianti
		Elba Rosso
		Vino Nobile di Montepulciano
	Umbria	Torgiano Rosso
	Veneto	Riviera del Garda
Schiava	Lombardy	Botticino
(several varieties)		Cellatica
	Trentino–Alto Adige	Caldaro
		Santa Maddalena
Uva di Troia	Apulia	Castel del Monte Rosso
		Rosso Barletta
		Rosso Canosa
Vespolina	Piedmont	Boca
		Fara
		Ghemme
		Sizzano

light grapes

GRAPE	REGIONS WHERE GROWN	WINES
Albana	Emilia-Romagna	Albana di Romagna
Ansonica (Inzolia)	Sicily	Corvo
		Marsala
	Tuscany	Parrina Bianco
Biancolella	Campania	Ischia Bianco
Bombino Bianco	Abruzzo	Trebbiano d'Abruzzo
	Apulia	San Severo Bianco
Catarratto	Sicily	Alcamo
		Corvo
		Etna Bianco
		Marsala
Cortese	Lombardy	Oltrepò Pavese Cortese
	Piedmont	Cortese di Gaul
Erbaluce	Piedmont	Caluso Passito
		Caluso Passito Liquoroso
Fiano	Campania	Fiano di Avellino
Garganega	Veneto	Gambellara
		Soave
Greco	Calabria	Cirò Bianco
	Campania	Greco di Tufo
	Latium	Frascati
Grillo	Sicily	Marsala
Malvasia (several varieties)	Latium	Colli Albani
		Est! Est!! Est!!!
		Frascati
		Marino
	Tuscany	Chianti
		Vin Santo
	Umbria	Orvieto
	Marches	Verdicchio
	Sardinia	Malvasia di Bosa
Moscato Bianco	Piedmont	Asti Spumante
	Sardinia	Moscato di Cagliari
Müller-Thurgau	Trentino–Alto Adige	Trentino Riesling
Nuragus	Sardinia	Nuragus di Cagliari
Picolit	Friuli-Venezia Giulia	Colli Oriental del Friuli-Picolit
Pinot Bianco	Friuli Venezia Giulia	Collio Pinot Bianco
		Colli Orientale del Friuli Pinot Bianco
		Grave del Friuli Pinot Bianco
	Trentino–Alto Adige	Trentino Pinot Bianco
	Veneto	Berganze Pinot Bianco
Pinot Grigio	Friuli-Venezia Giulia	Collio Pinot Grigio
		Colli Orientale del Friuli Pinot Grigio
		Grave del Friuli Pinot Grigio
	Trentino–Alto Adige	Trentino Pinot Grigio
	Veneto	Breganze Pinot Grigio
Prosecco	Veneto	Prosecco di Conegliano-Valdobbiadene

GRAPE	REGIONS WHERE GROWN°	WINES
Riesling Italico Riesling Renano	Friuli-Venezia-Giulia Lombardy Trentino–Alto Adige	Colli Orientale del Friuli Riesling Oltrepò Pavese Riesling Trentino Riesling
Tocai Friulano	Friuli-Venezia-Giulia Lombardy Veneto	Colli Orientale del Friuli Tocai Collio Tocai Tocai di San Martino della Battaglia Tocai di Lison Breganze Bianco Piave Tocai
Traminer Aromatico (Gewürztraminer)	Friuli-Venezia-Giulia Trentino–Alto Adige	Collio Traminer Aromatico Trentino Traminer Aromatico
Trebbiano (several varities)	Emilia-Romagna Latium Lombardy Tuscany Umbria Veneto	Trebbiano di Romagna Est! Est!! Est!!! Frascati Lugana Chianti Elba Bianco Montecarlo Vin Santo Orvieto Torgiano Bianco Lugana Soave
Verdicchio (several varieties)	Marches	Verdicchio dei Castelli di Jesi Verdicchio di Matelica
Verduzzo Friulano	Friuli-Venezia-Giulia Veneto	Colli Orientale del Friuli Verduzzo Grave Del Friuli Verduzzo Piave Verduzzo
Vernaccia (several varieties)	Sardinia Tuscany	Vernaccia di Oristano Vernaccia di San Gimignano
Vespaiolo	Veneto	Breganze Vespaiolo
Zibibbo (Moscato di Alessandria)	Sicily	Marsala Moscato di Pantelleria Moscato Passito di Pantelleria

Source: Pier Giovanni Garoglio, *Enciclopedia Vitivinicola Mondiale* (Milan: Unione Italiana Vini, 1973).

APPENDIX F
PRINCIPAL GERMAN WINE REGIONS
AND GRAPE VARIETIES

AHR
0.5 percent of Germany's harvest

1 subregion (*Bereich*): Walporzheim/Ahrtal
1 collective vineyard (*Grosslage*): Klosterberg
43 single vineyards (*Einzellagen*) around 11 villages (*Gemeinden*)
409 hectares under cultivation
Main grapes: Spätburgunder (red), 29 percent; Portugieser (red), 29 percent; Riesling, 18 percent; Müller-Thurgau, 16 percent
No principal wines distributed in the United States

MOSEL-SAAR-RUWER
13 percent of Germany's harvest

5 subregions (*Bereiche*): Zell, Bernkastel, Saar-Ruwer, Obermosel, Moseltor
20 collective vineyards (*Grosslagen*): Weinhex, Goldbäumchen, Rosenhang, Grafschaft, Schwarze Katz, vom Heissen Stein, Schwarzlay, Nacktarsch, Münzlay, Badstube, Beerenlay, Kurfürstlay, Michelsberg, St. Michael, Probstberg, Römerlay, Schwarzberg, Königsberg, Gipfel, Schloss Bübinger
524 single vineyards (*Einzellagen*) around 161 villages (*Gemeinden*)
12,297 hectares under cultivation
Main grapes: Riesling, 58 percent; Müller-Thurgau, 22 percent; Elbling, 9 percent
Principal wines distributed in the United States: Zeller Schwarze Katz (*Grosslage*), Erdener Treppchen, Zeltinger Himmelreich, Zeltinger Sonnenuhr, Wehlener Sonnenuhr, Graacher Domprobst, Graacher Himmelreich, Bernkasteler Badstube (*Grosslage*), Bernkasteler Doctor und Graben, Bernkasteler Kurfürstlay (*Grosslage*), Piesporter Michelsberg (*Grosslage*), Piesporter Goldtröpfchen, Maximin Grünhauser Herrenberg, Scharzhofberger, Trittenheimer Apotheke, Ockfener Bockstein, Ürziger Würzgarten, Ayler Kupp, Eitelsbacher Kronenberg, Kröver Nacktarsch (*Grosslage*), Brauneberger Juffer

MITTELRHEIN
1 percent of Germany's harvest

3 subregions (*Bereiche*): Rheinburgengau, Siebengebirge, Bacharach
11 collective vineyards (*Grosslagen*): Burg Hammerstein, Lahntal, Marksburg, Gedeonseck, Burg Rheinfels, Loreleyfelsen, Schloss Schönburg, Herrenberg, Petersberg, Schloss Stahleck, Schloss Reichenstein
120 single vineyards (*Einzellagen*) around 55 villages (*Gemeinden*)
762 hectares under cultivation
Main grapes: Riesling, 75 percent; Müller-Thurgau, 12 percent
No principal wines distributed in the United States

RHEINGAU
3 percent of Germany's harvest

1 subregion (*Bereich*): Johannisberg
10 collective vineyards (*Grosslagen*): Burgweg, Steil, Erntebringer, Honigsberg, Gottesthal, Deutelsberg, Mehrhölzchen, Heiligenstock, Steinmächer, Daubhaus
117 single vineyards (*Einzellagen*) around 28 villages (*Gemeinden*)
2,900 hectares under cultivation
Main grapes: Riesling, 80 percent; Müller-Thurgau, 8 percent
Principal wines distributed in the United States: Rüdesheimer Bischofsberg, Rüdesheimer Berg Rottland,

Rüdesheimer Rosengarten, Geisenheimer Rothenberg, Johannisberger Erntebringer (*Grosslage*), Johannisberger Klaus, Schloss Johannisberg, Schloss Vollrads, Oestricher Lenchen, Hattenheimer Nussbrunnen, Steinberger, Erbacher Marcobrunn, Eltviller Rheinberg, Eltviller Sonnenberg, Rauenthaler Baiken, Hochheimer Domdechaney, Hochheimer Kirchenstück

NAHE
5 percent of Germany's harvest

2 subregions (*Bereiche*): Kreuznach, Schloss Böckelheim
7 collective vineyards (*Grosslagen*): Schlosskapelle, Sonnenborn, Pfarrgarten, Kronenberg, Rosengarten, Burgweg, Paradiesgarten
340 single vineyards (*Einzellagen*) around 79 villages (*Gemeinden*)
4,486 hectares under cultivation
Main grapes: Müller-Thurgau, 29 percent; Riesling, 22 percent; Silvaner, 19 percent
Principal wines distributed in the United States: Schloss Böckelheimer Kupfergrube, Schloss Böckelheimer Mühlberg

RHEINHESSEN
25 percent of Germany's harvest

3 subregions (*Bereiche*): Bingen, Nierstein, Wonnegau
24 collective vineyards (*Grosslagen*): Sankt Rochuskapelle, Abtey, Rheingrafenstein, Adelberg, Kurfürstenstück, Kaiserpfalz, Sankt Alban, Domherr, Gutes Domtal, Spiegelberg, Rehbach, Auflangen, Güldenmorgen, Krötenbrunnen, Vogelsgärten, Petersberg, Rheinblick, Sybillenstein, Bergkloster, Pilgerpfad, Gotteshilfe, Burg Rodenstein, Domblick, Liebfrauenmorgen
430 single vineyards (*Einzellagen*) around 140 villages (*Gemeinden*)
23,500 hectares under cultivation
Main grapes: Müller-Thurgau, 28 percent; Silvaner, 18 percent; Scheurebe, 8 percent; Bacchus, 6 percent; Faberrebe, 6 percent; Riesling, 5 percent
Principal wines distributed in the United States: Niersteiner Gutes Domtal (*Grosslage*), Niersteiner Spiegelberg (*Grosslage*), Niersteiner Rehbach (*Grosslage*), Niersteiner Pettenthal, Niersteiner Hipping, Niersteiner Auflangen (*Grosslage*), Niersteiner Orbel, Oppenheimer Krötenbrunnen (*Grosslage*)

RHEINPFALZ
23 percent of Germany's harvest

2 subregions (*Bereiche*): Mittelhaardt Deutsche Weinstrasse, südliche Weinstrasse
26 collective vineyards (*Grosslagen*): Schnepfenflug vom Zellertal, Grafenstück, Höllenpfad, Schwarzerde, Rosenbühl, Kobnert, Feuerberg, Saumagen, Honigsäckel, Hochmess, Schenkenböhl, Schnepfenflug an der Weinstrasse, Mariengarten, Hofstück, Meerspinne, Rebstöckel, Pfaffengrund, Mandelhöhe, Schloss Ludwigshöhe, Ordensgut, Trappenberg, Bischofskreuz, Königsgarten, Herrlich, Kloster Liebfrauenberg, Guttenberg
Approximately 330 single vineyards (*Einzellagen*) around 160 villages (*Gemeinden*)
21,850 hectares under cultivation
Main grapes: Müller-Thurgau, 24 percent; Silvaner, 13 percent; Riesling, 14 percent; Portugieser (red), 8 percent; Kerner, 9 percent; Morio-Muskat, 8 percent
Principal wines distributed in the United States: Forster Mariengarten (*Grosslage*), Forster Jesuitengarten, Deidesheimer Herrgottsacker, Deidesheimer Hohenmorgen, Deidesheimer Paradiesgarten, Ruppertsberger Hoheburg, Ungsteiner Herrenberg, Bad Dürkheimer Feuerberg (*Grosslage*), Wachenheimer Gerümpel

HESSISCHE BERGSTRASSE
0.5 percent of Germany's harvest

2 subregions (*Bereiche*): Umstadt, Starkenburg
3 collective vineyards (*Grosslagen*): Rott, Wolfsmagen, Schlossberg
19 single vineyards (*Einzellagen*) around 9 villages (*Gemeinden*)
350 hectares under cultivation
Main grapes: Riesling, 53 percent; Müller-Thurgau, 20 percent; Silvaner, 10 percent
No principal wines distributed in the United States

FRANKEN
5 percent of Germany's harvest

3 subregions (*Bereiche*): Mainviereck, Maindreieck, Steigerwald

17 collective vineyards (*Grosslagen*): Rauschberg, Heiligenthal, Burg, Rosstal, Ravensburg, Ewig Leben, Olspiel, Teufelstor, Hofrat, Honigberg, Kirchberg, Schild, Herrenberg, Schlossberg, Burgweg, Schlosstück, Kapellenberg

Approximately 130 single vineyards (*Einzellagen*) around 115 villages (*Gemeinden*)

4,300 hectares under cultivation

Main grapes: Müller-Thurgau, 49 percent; Silvaner, 26 percent; Bacchus, 6 percent

Principal wines distributed in the United States: Escherndorfer Lump, Sommerhausen Ölspiel (*Grosslage*)

WÜRTTEMBERG
9 percent of Germany's harvest

4 subregions (*Bereiche*): Kocher-Jagst-Tauber, Württembergisch Unterland, Remstal-Stuttgart, Bayerischer-Bodensee

17 collective vineyards (*Grosslagen*): Tauberberg, Kocherberg, Staufenberg, Lindelberg, Salzberg, Schozachtal, Wunnenstein, Kirchenweinberg, Heuchelberg, Stromberg, Schalkstein, Weinsteige, Kopf, Wartbühl, Sonnenbühl, Hohenneuffen, Lindauer Seegarten

Approximately 200 single vineyards (*Einzellagen*) around 230 villages (*Gemeinden*)

8,670 hectares under cultivation

Main grapes: Riesling, 24 percent; Trollinger (red), 22 percent; Müller-Thurgau, 11 percent; Müllerrebe, 11 percent

Principal wines distributed in the United States: Stettener Heuchelberg, Cannstatter Zuckerle (red wine)

BADEN
15 percent of Germany's harvest

7 subregions (*Bereiche*): Badisches Frankenland, Badische Bergstrasse Kraichgau, Bodensee, Ortenau, Breisgau, Kaiserstuhl-Tuniberg, Markgräflerland

16 collective vineyards (*Grosslagen*): Tauberklinge, Hohenberg, Mannaberg, Stiftsberg, Rittersberg, Sonnenufer, Fürsteneck, Schloss Rodeck, Burg Zähringen, Burg Lichteneck, Schutterlindenberg, Attilafelsen, Vulkanfelsen, Vogtei Rötteln, Burg Neuenfels, Lorettoberg

Approximately 340 single vineyards (*Einzellagen*) around 300 villages (*Gemeinden*)

14,300 hectares under cultivation

Main grapes: Müller-Thurgau, 39 percent; Blauer Spätburgunder (red), 19 percent; Ruländer, 13 percent; Gutedel, 8 percent; Riesling, 7 percent; Silvaner, 4 percent

Principal wines distributed in the United States: Affentaler Spätburgunder, Kenzinger Hummelberg, Attilafelsen Niederrimsinger (*Grosslage*), Freiburger Lorettoberg Gutedel (*Grosslage*)

Source: Statistisches Bundesamt, Wiesbaden, 1980

MOST WIDELY GROWN GRAPE VARIETIES
(in hectares)

GRAPE	Ahr	Mittelrhein	Mosel-Saar-Ruwer	Nahe	Rhein-hessen	Rhein-pfalz	Rhein-gau	Hessische Berg-strasse	Baden	Württem-berg	Franken	Total
Müller-Thurgau	64	88	2,741	1,311	6,632	5,302	229	72	5,542	938	2,109	25,028
Riesling	74	576	7,166	981	1,243	3,066	2,334	201	1,051	2,080	90	18,862
Silvaner	—	9	•	841	4,285	2,771	34	37	546	543	1,136	10,209
Kerner	•	39	456	231	1,218	1,938	33	5	73	727	149	4,871
Scheurebe	•	8	14	266	1,960	1,219	14	6	•	•	121	3,669
Ruländer	•	•	•	119	•	688	23	30	1,833	115	•	3,390
Morio-Muskat	—	•	•	57	1,104	1,820	—	—	•	—	•	3,012
Bacchus	•	•	256	198	1,521	410	•	•	•	—	•	2,681
Faberrebe	—	•	—	122	1,366	•	•	•	•	—	•	1,874
Huxelrebe	—	—	—	•	794	617	—	—	—	—	—	1,487
Gutedel	•	—	—	—	—	—	—	—	1,222	—	—	1,222
Elbling	•	—	1,105	—	—	—	—	—	—	—	54	1,115
Ortega	•	•	158	•	•	•	18	•	303	•	42	1,047
Traminer	•	•	•	58	•	•	•	5	•	•	—	942
Weiss-Burgunder	—	•	194	•	•	•	•	•	375	•	—	838
Optima	—	—	•	—	•	•	•	—	—	•	—	496
Ehrenfelser	—	—	—	—	—	•	73	5	•	—	—	420
Perle	—	—	—	—	—	—	•	—	—	—	90	271
Siegerrebe	—	—	•	—	—	•	•	—	—	—	•	266
Reichensteiner	•	•	60	—	—	•	18	—	—	—	—	245
Other whites	—	—	—	—	—	—	—	—	—	—	—	1,323
Spätburgunder	120	•	—	—	•	•	98	—	2,740	274	•	3,572
Portugieser	118	•	—	—	713	1,648	—	—	•	380	•	2,965
Trollinger	—	—	—	—	—	—	—	—	—	1,902	—	1,902
Müllerrebe	—	—	—	—	—	—	—	—	—	912	•	1,015
Limberger	—	—	—	—	—	—	—	—	—	408	—	408
Other reds	—	—	—	—	—	—	—	—	—	—	—	723
Wine Grapes Total	409	762	12,297	4,486	23,499	21,830	2,932	375	14,295	8,665	4,303	93,853

• = less than 1% of vineyards

Source: Statistisches Bundesamt, Wiesbaden, 1980

APPENDIX G
COMMERCIALLY IMPORTANT
BONDED WINERIES
AND BONDED WINE CELLARS
OF THE UNITED STATES*

Perdido Vineyards, Inc.
Perdido, AL 36562

ARKANSAS

De Salvo's Winery
Center Ridge, AR 72027

Heckmann's Winery
Harrisburg, AR 72432

Mount Bethel Winery
Altus, AR 72821

Post Winery, Inc.
Altus, AR 72821

Wiederkehr Wine Cellars, Inc.
Altus, AR 72821

CALIFORNIA

Acacia Winery
Napa, CA 94558

Adler Fels
Santa Rosa, CA 95405

Ahern Winery, Ltd.
San Fernando, CA 91340

Almaden Vineyards
San Jose, CA 95118

American Industries Co, Inc.
Guasti, CA 91743

B & R Vineyards, Inc./Rapazzini Winery
Gilroy, CA 95020

Baldinelli Shenandoah Valley Vineyards
Plymouth, CA 95669

Balverne Winery & Vineyards
Windsoe, CA 95492

Bargetto's Santa Cruz Winery
Soquel, CA 95073

Beaulieu Vineyard
Rutherford, CA 94573

Bella Napoli Winery
Manteca, CA 95336

Bellerose Vineyard
Healdsburg, CA 95448

Belevedere Wine Co.
Healdsburg, CA 95448

Beringer Vineyards/Los Hermanos Vineyards
(Division of Wine World, Inc.)
St. Helena, CA 94574

Bernardo Winery
Escondido, CA 92128

Bianchi Vineyards
Kerman, CA 93630

Bisceglia Bros. Wine Co.
(Canandaigua Wine Company, Inc.)
Madera, CA 93639

Boeger Winery, Inc.
Placerville, CA 95667

Bogle Vineyards, Inc.
Clarksburg, CA 95612

Borelli, Ciriaco Winery
Stockton, CA 95205

Bouchane Vineyards
Napa, CA 94558

J.F.J. Bronco Winery
Ceres, CA 95307

Brookside Enterprises, Inc.
Guasti, CA 91743

David Bruce Winery, Inc.
Los Gatos, CA 95031

Buena Vista Winery and Vineyards
(The Harazthy Cellars)
Sonoma, CA 95476

Burgess Cellars
St. Helena, CA 94574

Davis Bynum Winery
Healdsburg, CA 95448

* Wineries that have a minimum of 20,000 gallons capacity of storage, as declared in *Wines & Vines Directory*, 1983.

Cadenasso Winery
Fairfield, CA 94533

Cadlolo Winery
Escalon, CA 95320

Cakebread Cellars
Oakland, CA 94606

Calera Wine Company
Hollister, CA 95023

California Cellar Masters
Lodi, CA 95240

California Growers Winery, Inc.
San Francisco, CA 94111

California Wine Company
Cloverdale, CA 95425

California Wine Service Cooperative
San Jose, CA 95112

J. Carey Cellars
Solvang, CA 93463

Carneros Creek Winery
Napa, CA 94558

Caymus Vineyards
Rutherford, CA 94573

Chalone Vineyard
Soledad, CA 93960

Chappellet Winery
St. Helena, CA 94574

Chateau Chevalier Winery
St. Helena, CA 94574

Chateau De Leu Winery
Suisun, CA 94585

Chateau Montelena Winery
Calistoga, CA 94515

Chateau St. Jean, Inc.
Kenwood, CA 95452

Cilurzo Vineyard & Winery
Temecula, CA 92390

Clos du Bois
Healdsburg, CA 95448

Clos du Val Wine Co., Ltd.
Napa, CA 94558

Concannon Vineyard
Livermore, CA 94550

Congress Springs Vineyards
Saratoga, CA 95070

Conn Creek Winery
St. Helena, CA 94574

Anselmo Conrotto Winery
Gilroy, CA 95020

R & J Cook
Clarksburg, CA 95612

Cordtz Brothers Cellars, Inc.
Cloversdale, CA 95425

Cresta Blanca Winery
Ukiah, CA

Cribari & Sons Winery
Fresno, CA 93711

Cribari Vineyards, Inc.
Fresno, CA 93711

John Culberston Winery
Fallbrook, CA 92038

Cuvaison, Inc.
Calistoga, CA 94515

Cygnet Cellars
Hollister, CA 95023

D'Agostini Winery
Plymouth, CA 95669

Dehlinger Winery
Sebastopol, CA 95472

Delano Growers Cooperative Winery
Delano, CA 93215

Delicato Vineyards
Manteca, CA 95336

DeLoach Vineyards
Santa Rosa, CA 95401

Devlin Wine Cellars
Soquel, CA 95073

Diamond Creek Vineyards
Calistoga, CA 94515

Diamond Oaks Vineyard
Cloverdale, CA 95425

J.E. Digardi Winery
Martinez, CA 94553

Domaine Chandon
(d.b.a. of M & H Vineyards)
Yountville, CA 94599

Domaine Laurier
Forestville, CA 95436

Donna Maria Vineyards
Healdsburg, CA 95448

Dry Creek Vineyard, Inc.
Healdsburg, CA 95448

Durney Vineyard
Carmel, CA 93922

East-Side Winery
Lodi, CA 95240

Edmeades Vineyards
Philo, CA 95466

Edna Valley Vineyards
San Luis Obispo, CA 93401

Enz Vineyards
Hollister, CA 95023

Estrella River Winery
Paso Robles, CA 93446

Far Niente Winery
Sausalito, CA 94955

Ferrara Winery
Escondido, CA 92025

Fetzer Vineyards
Redwood Valley, CA 95470

Ficklin Vineyards
Madera, CA 93637

Field Stone Winery
(d.b.a. of Redwood Ranch & Vyd., Inc.)
Healdsburg, CA 95448

J. Filippi Vintage Co.
Mira Loma, CA 91752

Filsinger Vineyards & Winery
Temecula, CA 92390

The Firestone Vineyard
Los Olivos, CA 93441

Fisher Vineyards
Santa Rosa, CA 95404

Flora Springs Wine Co.
St. Helena, CA 94574

L. Foppiano Wine Co.
Healdsburg, CA 95448

Forman Winery
St. Helena, CA 94574

Fortino Winery
Gilroy, CA 95020

Franciscan Vineyards
Rutherford, CA 94573

Franzia Brothers Winery
(Franzia Brothers Champagne Cellars)
Ripon, CA

James Frasinetti and Sons
Sacramento, CA 95828

Chris A. Fredson Winery
Geyersville, CA 95441

Freemark Abby Winery
St. Helena, CA 94574

Fritz Cellars
Cloverdale, CA 94574

Galleano Winery, Inc.
Mira Loma, CA 91752

E. & J. Gallo Winery
Modesto, CA 95353

Gemello Winery Corp.
Mountain View, CA 94040

Geyser Peak Winery
San Rafael, CA 95441

Gibson Wine Co.
Sanger, CA 93657

Girard Winery
Oakville, CA 94562

Giumarra Vineyards Corp.
Bakersfield, CA 93303

Glen Ellen
Glen Ellen, CA 95412

Grand Cru Vineyards
Glen Ellen, CA 95412

Grand Pacific Vineyard Co.
San Rafael, CA 94901

Granite Springs Winery
Somerset, CA 95684

Grgich Hills Cellar
Rutherford, CA 94573

Emilio Guglielmo Winery
Morgan Hill, CA 95037

Guenoc Winery
Middletown, CA 95461

Guild Wineries and Distilleries
Lodi, CA 95240

Gundlach-Bundschu Winery
Vineberg, CA 95487

Hacienda Wine Cellars
Sonoma, CA 95476

Allan S. Haley
Nevada City, CA 95959

Hanns Kornell Champagne Cellars
St. Helena, CA 94574

Hanzell Vineyards
Sonoma, CA 95476

Haywood Winery, Sonoma
Corte Madera, CA 94925

Hecker Pass Winery
Gilroy, CA 95020

Heitz Wine Cellars
St. Helena, CA 94574

Herrera Cellars
Sacramento, CA 95825

Heublein Wines
San Francisco, CA 94107

William Hill Winery
Napa, CA 94558

HMR-Hoffman Vineyards
Paso Robles, CA 93446

Hop Kiln Winery, Griffin Vyd.
Healdsburg, CA 95448

Hopper Creek Winery
Napa, CA 94558

Hultgren & Samperton
Healdsburg, CA 95448

Husch Vineyards
Philo, CA 95466

Iron Horse Vineyards
Sebastopol, CA 95472

Jekel Vineyard
Studio City, CA 91604

Johnson's Alexander Valley Wines
Healdsburg, CA 95448

Robert Keenan Winery
St. Helena, CA 94574

Kenwood Vineyards
Kenwood, CA 95452

Kirgin Cellars
Gilroy, CA 95020

Kistler Vineyards
Glen Ellen, CA 95442

Knights Valley Vineyards
Ukiah, CA 95482

Konocti Cellars
(d.b.a. Lake County Vintners)
Kelseyville, CA 95451

F. Korbel & Bros.
Guerneville, CA 95446

Charles Krug Winery
(C. Mondavi & Sons)
St. Helena, CA 94574

La Crema Vinera
Petaluma, CA 94953

Lakespring Winery
Napa, CA 94558

Lambert Bridge
Healdsburg, CA 95448

La Mont Winery, Inc.
Di Giorgio, CA 93217

Landmark Vineyards
Windsor, CA 95448

La Purisma Winery
Menlo Park, CA 94025

Las Tablas Winery
Templeton, CA 93465

Lawrence Winery
San Luis Obispo, CA 93406

Le Bay Cellars
Cloverdale, CA 95425

Liberty Winery, Inc.
Acampo, CA 95220

Llords & Elwood Winery, Inc.
Beverly Hills, CA 91364

Los Vineros Winery, Inc.
Pasadena, CA 91101

Lyeth Vyd. & Winery Ltd.
Geyserville, CA 95441

Madrona Vineyards
Camino, CA 95709

Marietta Cellars
Healdsburg, CA 95448

Markham Winery
St. Helena, CA 94574

Mark West Vineyards
Forestville, CA 95436

Martin Brothers
Paso Robles, CA 93446

Louis M. Martini
St. Helena, CA 94574

Martini & Prati Wines, Inc.
Santa Rosa, CA 95401

Paul Masson Vineyards
Saratoga, CA 95070

Mastantuono
Paso Robles, CA 93446

J. Mathews Napa Valley Winery
Newport Beach, CA 95070

Mayacamas Vineyards
Napa, CA 94558

Giuseppe Mazzoni
Cloverdale, CA 95425

McDowell Valley Vineyards and Cellars
Hopland, CA 95449

Louis K. Mihaly Vyd.
Napa, CA 94558

Milano Winery
Hopland, CA 95449

Mill Creek Vineyards
Healdsburg, CA 95448

Robert Mondavi Winery
Oakville, CA 94562

Robert Mondavi Winery Woodbridge
Woodbridge, CA 95258

R. Montali Winery
Oakland, CA 94610

Monterey Peninsula Winery
Monterey, CA 93940

The Monterey Vineyard
Gonzales, CA 93926

Montevina Wines
Plymouth, CA 95669

Monticello Cellars
Yountville, CA 94599

Mont La Salle Vineyards
Napa, CA 94558

Mont St. John Cellars
Napa, CA 94558

J.W. Morris Port Works
Emeryville, CA 94608

Mount Eden Vineyards
Saratoga, CA 95070

Mount Palomar Winery
Temecula, CA 92390

Mt. Veeder Winery and Vineyards
Napa, CA 94558

Napa Creek Winery
St. Helena, CA 94574

Napa Cellars
Oakville, CA 94562

Napa Valley Cooperative Winery
St. Helena, CA 94574

Navarro Vineyards
Philo, CA 95466

Newton Vineyard
St. Helena, CA 94574

Nichelini Vineyards
St. Helena, CA 94574

Niebaum-Coppola Estate
Rutherford, CA 94573

Noble Vineyards, Inc.
Kerman, CA 93630

A. Nonini Winery
Fresno, CA 93630

Nordman of California
Fresno, CA 93727

Novitiate Wines
Los Gatos, CA 95031

Numano Sake Co.
Berkeley, CA 94710

Oak Barrel Winery
Berkeley, CA 94702

Old Casteel Vineyards
Paso Robles, CA 93446

Opici Winery, Inc.
Alta Loma, CA 91701

Ozeki San Beito, Inc.
Hollister, CA 95023

Pannonia Winery, Inc.
Napa, CA 94558

Papagni Vineyards
Madera, CA 93637

Parducci Winery, Ltd.
(d.b.a. Paraducci Wine Cellars)
Ukiah, CA 95482

Parsons Creek Winery
Ukiah, CA 95425

Pastori Winery
Cloverdale, CA 95425

Pat Paulsen Vineyards
Cloverdale, CA 95425

Robert Pecota Winery
Calistoga, CA 94515

Pedrizzetti Winery
Morgan Hill, CA 95037

J. Pedroncelli Winery
Geyserville, CA 95441

Pendleton Winery
San Jose, CA 95131

Robert Pepi Winery
Oakville, CA 94562

Pesenti Winery
Templeton, CA 93465

Joseph Phelps Vineyards
St. Helena, CA 94574

Piconi Winery Ltd.
Temecula, CA 92390

Pine Ridge
Napa, CA 94558

Piper-Renfield
(d.b.a. Piper Sonoma Cellars)
Windsor, CA 95492

L. Pocai & Sons
Calistoga, CA 94515

Pope Valley Winery
Pope Valley, CA 94567

Preston Vineyards
Healdsburg, CA 95448

Quady Winery
Madera, CA 93637

Quail Ridge
Napa, CA 94558

Rancluit Oaks Winery, Inc.
Lodi, CA 95240

Ravenswood
Sonoma, CA 95476

Martin Ray Vineyards, Inc.
Palo Alto, CA 94303

Raymond Vineyard & Cellar
St. Helena, CA 94574

Renaissance Vineyard and Winery, Inc.
Renaissance, CA 95962

Ridge Vineyards, Inc.
Cupertino, CA 95015

River Oaks Vineyards
Healdsburg, CA 95448

Rombauer Vineyards
St. Helena, CA 94574

Ross Winery
Napa, CA 94558

Round Hill Cellars
St. Helena, CA 94574

Roudon-Smith Vineyards, Inc.
Santa Cruz, CA 95066

Rubidoux Winery
Riverside, CA 92506

Rutherford Hill Winery
St. Helena, CA 94574

Rutherford Vintners, Inc.
Rutherford, CA 94573

Saint Andrew's Winery
Napa, CA 94558

St. Clement Vineyards
St. Helena, CA 94574

St. Helena Wine Co.
(d.b.a. Duckhern Vineyards)
St. Helena, CA 94574

Saintsbury
St. Helena, CA 94574

San Antonio Winery, Inc.
Los Angeles, CA 90031

San Benito Vineyards, Inc.
Hollister, CA 95023

Sanford & Benedict Vineyards
Lompoc, CA 93436

San Joaquin Warehousing Co.
Lodi, CA 95240

San Martin Winery
San Martin, CA 95046

San Pasqual Winery
San Diego, CA 92025

Santa Barbara Winery
Santa Barbara, CA 93101

Santa Cruz Mountain Winery
Santa Cruz, CA 95065

Santa Ynez Valley Winery
Santa Ynez, CA 93460

V. Sattui Winery
St. Helena, CA 94574

Sausal Winery
Healdsburg, CA 95448

Peter Scagliott
(d.b.a. Live Oaks Winery)
Gilroy, CA 95026

Scharffenberger Cellars
Ukiah, CA 94582

Schenley Distillers, Inc.
Fresno, CA 93725

Schramsberg Vineyards Co.
Calistoga, CA 94515

Sebastini Vineyards
Sonoma, CA 95476

Seghesio Winery, Inc.
Cloverdale, CA 95425

Sequoia Grove Vineyards
Napa, CA 94558

Charles F. Shaw Vineyard and Winery
St. Helena, CA 95669

Shenandoah Vineyards
Plymouth, CA 95669

Sherrill Cellars
Woodside, CA 94062

Shown & Sons Vineyards
Rutherford, CA 94573

Sierra Wine Corporation
Delano, CA 93215

Silverado Vineyards
Napa, CA 94558

Siver Oak Wine Cellars
Oakville, CA 94562

Simi Winery
Healdsburg, CA 95448

Smith & Hook Winery
Gonzales, CA 93926

Snow Mountain Winery
Nevada City, CA 95959

Soda Rock Winery
Healdsburg, CA 95448

Sommelier Winery
Mountain View, CA 94043

Sonoma County Cellars
Healdsburg, CA 95448

Sonoma County Cooperative Winery
Windsor, CA 95492

Sonoma County Vintners Cooperative
Windsor, CA 95492

Sonoma Vineyards
Windsor, CA 95492

Sotoyome Winery
Healdsburg, CA 95448

Souverain Cellars
Geyserville, CA 95441

Spring Mountain Vineyards
St. Helena, CA 94574

Stag's Leap Wine Cellars
Napa, CA 94558

Stag's Leap Winery, Inc.
Napa, CA 94558

Sterling Vineyards
Calistoga, CA 94515

Stevenot Winery
Murphys, CA 95247

Stonegate, Inc.
Calistoga, CA 94515

Stony Ridge Winery
Pleasanton, CA 94566

Storybook Mountain Vineyards
Calistoga, CA 94515

Summerhill Vineyards
Gilroy, CA 95020

Sunrise Winery
Santa Cruz, CA 95060

Sutter Home Winery, Inc.
St. Helena, CA 94574

Taylor California Cellars
Gonzales, CA 93926

Thomas Vineyards
Cucamonga, CA 91730

Topolos at Russian River
Forestville, CA 95436

Trefethen Vineyards
Napa, CA 94558

Trentadue Winery
Geyerville, CA 94541

Turgeon-Lohr Winery
San Jose, CA 95126

Turner Winery
Acampo, CA 95220

Tyland Vineyards
Ukiah, CA 95482

Valley of the Moon Winery
Glen Ellen, CA 95442

Veedercrest
Emeryville, CA 94608

Ventana Vineyards Winery, Inc.
Soledad, CA 93960

Verdugo Vineyards, Inc.
Acampo, CA 95220

Nicholas G. Verry, Inc.
Parlier, CA 93648

Vichon Winery
Oakville, CA 94562

Vie-Del Company
Plant No. 1: Fresno, CA
Plant No. 2: Kingsburg, CA

Villa Armando Winery
Pleasanton, CA 94566

Villa Baccala Winery
Ukiah, CA 95482

Villa Mt. Eden Winery
Oakville, CA 94562

Vintage Wine Warehouse
San Jose, CA 95054

Vose Vineyards
Napa, CA 94558

Weibel Champagne Vineyards
Mission San Jose, CA 94538

Wente Brothers
Livermore, CA 94550

Westcom Industries
Pleasant Hill, CA 94523

Whitehall Lane Winery
St. Helena, CA 94574

William Wheeler Winery
Healdsburg, CA 95448

The Wine Group
San Francisco, CA 94108

The Wine Service Cooperative, Inc.
St. Helena, CA 94574

Woodbury Winery
San Rafael, CA 94901

Wooden Valley Winery
Suisun, CA 94585

York Mountain Winery
Templeton, CA 93465

Yverdon Vineyards
St. Helena, CA 94574

Zaca Mesa Winery
Santa Maria, CA 92456

ZD Wines
Napa, CA 94558

CONNECTICUT

Heublein Spirits and Wine Co.
Farmington, CT 06032

FLORIDA

Florida Heritage Winery
Anthony, FL 32617

Fruit Wines of Florida, Inc.
Tampa, FL 33602

National Distr. Co. Incs
(d.b.a. Consolidated Dist. Co., Inc.)
Jacksonville, FL 32218

Todhunter International, Inc.
West Palm Beach, FL 33401

GEORGIA

Monarch Wine Co. of Georgia
Atlanta, GA 30315

The Wine Spectrum
(d.b.a. General Beverage Co.)
Atlanta, GA 30339

IDAHO

Ste. Chapelle Winery, Inc.
Caldwell, ID 83605

Consolidated Distilled Products, Inc.
Chicago, IL 60623

Mogen David Wine Corp.
Chicago, IL

Gem City Vineland Co., Inc.
Nauvoo, IL 62354

Thompson Winery
Monee, IL 60449

INDIANA

Banholzer Winecellars Ltd.
New Carlisle, IN 46350

Oliver Wine Co., Inc.
Bloomington, IN 47401

Golden Rain Tree Winery, Inc.
Wadesville, IN 47638

Schenley Distillers, Inc.
Lawrenceburg, IN 47025

Huber Orchard Wines
Borden, IN 47106

Villa Medeo Vineyards Winery
Madison, IN 47250

IOWA

Ackerman Winery, Inc.
South Amana, IA 52234

Village Winery
Amana, IA 52203

Colony Village Winery
Williamsburg, IA 52361

The Wankon Corporation
Wankon, IA 52172

Colony Wines, Inc.
Amana, IA 52203

KENTUCKY

Kontinental Spirits Kompanie
Bardstown, KY 40004

Laine Vineyards & Winery
Fulton, KY 42041

MARYLAND

Berrywine Plantations Winery
Mt. Airy, MD 21771

Boordy Vineyard
Riderwood, MD 21082

MASSACHUSETTS

Chicama Vineyards
West Tisbury, MA 02575

Commonwealth Wines
Plymouth, MA 02360

MICHIGAN

Bronte Champagne & Wines Co., Inc.
Detroit, MI 48220

Leelanan Wine Cellars, Ltd.
Traverse City, MI 49684

Chateau Grand Travers, Inc.
Travers City, MI 49684

Milan Wineries
Detroit, MI 48210

Fenn Valley Vineyards
Fennville, MI 49408

St. Julian & La Salle Wine Co., Inc.
Paw Paw, MI 49079

Frontenac Vineyards, Inc.
Paw Paw, MI 49079

Tabor Hill Vineyard and Winecellar, Inc.
Buchanan, MI 49107

Heublein Inc.
Allen Park, MI 48101

Warner Vineyards, Inc.
Paw Paw, MI 49079

Lakeside Vineyard, Inc.
Harbert, MI 49115

MISSISSIPPI

Almarla Vineyards
(d.b.a. Alex P. & Margaret E. Mathers)
Matherville, MS 39360

The Winery Rushing
Merigold, MS 38759

Thousand Oaks Vineyard & Winery
Starkville, MS 39759

MISSOURI

Bowman Wine Cellars
Weston, MO 64098-0097

Green Valley Vineyards
Portland, MO 65067

Hermannhof
Hermann, MO 65041

McCormick Distilling Co.
Kansas City, MO 64161

Mount Pleasant Vineyards
Augusta, MO 63332

Ozark Vineyards
Chestnut Ridge, MO 65630

Rosati Winery
St. James, MO 65559

St. James Winery
St. James, MO 65559

Stone Hill Wine Co., Inc.
Hermann, MO 65041

NEW HAMPSHIRE

White Mountain Vineyards
Laconia, NH 03246

NEW JERSEY

Antuzzi's Winery
Delran, NJ 08075

Balic Winery
Mays Landing, NJ 08330

Gross' Highland Winery
Abescon, NJ

Jacob Lee Winery
Bordentown, NJ 08505

Regina Wine Co.
Newark, NJ 07105

Renault Winery, Inc.
Egg Harbor City, NJ 08215

Tomasello Winery
Hammonton, NJ 08037

NEW MEXICO

Vina Madre
Roswell, NM 88201

NEW YORK

Benmarl Wine Co.
Marlboro, NY 12542

Brotherhood Corp., Inc.
Washingtonville, NY 10992

Bully Hill
Hammondsport, NY 14840

Cagnasso Winery
Milton, NY 12547

Canandaigua Wine Co., Inc.
Canandaigua, NY 14424

Cascade Mountain Vineyards
Amenia, NY 12501

Chadwick Bay Wine Company
Fredonia, NY 14063

Chateau Esperanza Winery, Ltd.
Bluff Point, NY 14417

Delmonico's
Brooklyn, NY 11215

DeMay Wine Cellars
Hammondsport, NY 14840

Dr. Konstantin D. Frank & Sons
(Vinifera Wine Cellars)
Hammondsport, NY 14840

Fredonia Products Co., Inc.
Dunkirk, NY 14048

Glenora Wine Cellars, Inc.
Dundee, NY 14837

Gold Seal Vineyards, Inc.
Hammondsport, NY 14840

Hammondsport Wine Co., Inc.
(Canandaigua Wine Co., Inc.)
Hammondsport, NY 14840

Heron Hill Vineyards, Inc.
Hammondsport, NY 14840

Hudson Valley Wine Co., Inc.
Highland, NY 12528

Italian & French Wine Co. of Buffalo, Inc.
Buffalo, NY 14215

Frederick S. Johnson Vineyards
Westfield, NY 14787

Long Island Vineyards, Inc.
Cutchogue, NY 11935

Merritt Estate Winery, Inc.
Forestville, NY 14062

Monarch Wine Co., Inc.
Brooklyn, NY 11232

Niagara Wine Cellars
Cambria, NY 14094

Penn Yan Wine Cellars
Penn Yan, NY 14527

Poplar Ridge Vineyards
Valois, NY 14888

Robin Fils & Cie, Ltd.
Batavia, NY 14020

Royal Wine Corporation
Bronx, NY 11211

Schapiro's Wine Co., Ltd.
New York, NY 10002

Distillerie Stock U.S.A., Ltd.
Woodside, NY 11377

The Taylor Wine Co., Inc.
Hammondsport, NY 14840

Transamerica Wine Corp.
New York, NY 10012

Villa D'Ingianni Winery, Inc.
Dundee, NY 14837

Wagner Vineyards
Lodi, NY 14860

Wickham Vineyards Ltd.
Hector, NY 14841

Widmer's Wine Cellars, Inc.
Naples, NY 14512

Windsor Vineyards & Great River Winery
Marlboro, NY 12542

Woodbury Vineyards
Dunkirk, NY 14048

NORTH CAROLINA

Duplin Wine Cellars, Inc.
Rose Hill, NC 28458

La Rocca Wine Company
Fayetteville, NC 28204

Wine Cellars, Inc.
Edenton, NC 27932

OHIO

American Vineyards Co., Inc.
Cleveland, OH 44113

Breitenbach Wine Cellars
Dover, OH 44622

Leslie J. Bretz
Middle Bass, OH 43446

Chalet Debonne Vineyards
Madison, OH 44057

Dover Vineyards, Inc.
Westlake, OH

E & K Wine Company
Sandusky, OH 44870

Grand River Wine Co.
Madison, OH 44057

Hafle Vineyards
Springfield, OH 45502

The Hammer Company
Cleveland, OH 44114

Heineman Winery
Put-in-Bay, OH 43456

Heritage Vineyards
W. Milton, OH 45383

Klingshirn Winery
Avon Lake, OH 44012

Mantey Vineyards, Inc.
Sandusky, OH 44870

Markko Vineyard
Conneaut, OH 44030

Meier's Wine Cellars, Inc.
Cincinnati, OH 45236

Mon Ami Champagne
(d.b.a. Catawba Island Wine Co.)
Port Clinton, OH 43452

Pompei Winery, Inc.
Cleveland, OH 44105

Rini Wine Company
Cleveland, OH 44113

Tarula Farms
Clarksville, OH 45113

Valley Vineyards Farm, Inc.
Morrow, OH

Willoughby Winery
Willoughby, OH 44094

Wyandotte Wine Cellars, Inc.
Gahanna, OH 43230

OKLAHOMA

Pete Schwarz Winery
Okarche, OK 73762

OREGON

Amity Vineyards
Amity, OR 97101

Bjelland Vineyards
Roseburg, OR 97470

Chateau Benoit Winery
Carlton, OR 97111

De Martini Wine Co.
Roseburg, OR 97470

Elk Cove Vineyards
Gaston, OR 97119

Henry Endres Winery
Oregon City, OR 97045

Forgeron Vineyard
Elmira, OR 97437

Hillcrest Vineyard
Roseburg, OR 97470

Honeywood Winery
Salem, OR 97309

Knudsen-Erath Winery
Dundee, OR 97115

Nehalem Bay Wine Co.
Nehalem, OR 97131

Oak Knoll Winery, Inc.
Hillsboro, OR 97123

Ponzi Vineyards
Beaverton, OR 97007

Scott Henry's Winery
Umpqua, OR 97486

Siskiyou Vineyards
Cave Junction, OR 97253

Sokol Blosser Winery
Dundee, OR 97115

Valley View Vineyard
Jacksonville, OR 97530

PENNSYLVANIA

Bucks County Vineyards, Inc.
New Hope, PA 18938

Conestoga Vineyards, Inc.
Birchrunville, PA 17603

Heritage Wine Cellars
North East, PA 16428

Kasser Distillers Prod. Corp.
Philadelphia, PA 17603

La Fayette Vintners, Ltd.
Philadelphia, PA 19140

Lancaster County Winery, Ltd.
Willow Street, PA 17584

James Moroney, Inc.
Philadelphia, PA 19139

Mount Hope Estate & Winery
Cornwall, PA 17016

Naylor Wine Cellars
York, PA 17403

Nissley Vineyards
Bainbridge, PA 17502

Nittany Valley Winery
State College, PA 16801

Penn-Shore Vineyards, Inc.
North East, PA 16428

York Springs Winery
York Springs, PA 17372

RHODE ISLAND

Sakonnet Vineyards
Little Compton, RI 02877

SOUTH CAROLINA

Foxwood Wine Cellars
Woodruff, SC 29388

Tenner Brothers, Inc.
(Canandaigua Wine Co., Inc.)
Patrick, SC 29584

Truluck Vineyards & Winery
Lake City, SC 29560

TEXAS

Fall Creek Vineyards
Tow, TX 78672

Moyer Texas Champagne Co.
New Braubfels, TX 78130

Oberhellmann, Inc.
Fredericksburg, TX 78624

VIRGINIA

K.C. Arey & Co., Inc.
Danville, VA 24541

Barboursville Winery, Inc.
Barboursville, VA 22923

Dixie Wine Company
Richmond, VA

Ingleside Plantation Vineyards
Oak Grove, VA

Laird & Company
North Garden, VA 22959

Meredyth Vineyard
Middleburg, VA 22117

Oasis Vineyard
Hume, VA 22639

Piedmont Vineyards & Winery
Middleburg, VA 22117

Rapidan River Vineyards
Culpepper, VA 22701

Richard's Wine Cellars, Inc.
(Canandaigua Wine Co., Inc.)
Petersburg, VA 23803

Shenandoah Vineyards
Edinburg, VA 22824

WASHINGTON

Associated Vintners, Inc.
Bellevue, WA 98005

Chateau Ste. Michelle Vintners
(d.b.a. National Wine Co. & Pommerelle Co.)
Woodinville, WA 98072

Hinzerling Vineyards, Inc.
Prosser, WA 99350

Preston Wine Cellars
Paco, WA 99301

Mt. Rainier Vintners, Inc.
Puyallup, WA 98371

Paul Thomas Wines
Bellevue, WA 98005

Manfred J. Vierthaler Winery
Sumner, WA 98390

Worden's Washington Winery
Spokane, WA 99204

WISCONSIN

Bonduel Pickling Co., Inc.
Bonduel, WI 54107

Christina Wine Cellars
LaCrosse, WI 54601

Wisconsin Winery
Lake Geneva, WI 53147

The Wollersheim Winery, Inc.
Prairie Du Sac, WI 53578

APPENDIX H
EXPLANATION OF
ALCOHOLIC FERMENTATION

The juice from the freshly crushed grape berry contains sugars, acids, and other cell-sap-soluble components of the easily disrupted cells. Juice-insoluble substances and the contents of cells not easily broken, which may be important to the composition and quality of the wine, are dissolved in the wine by the alcohol and by other effects produced by fermentation. The metabolic activities of the fermenting wine yeast produce a theoretical conversion of 51 percent of the weight of sugar fermented to ethanol and the rest to carbon dioxide. Actual yields are slightly lower because the yeast produces a series of compounds other than alcohol. Some of the sugar is used to synthesize new yeast cells. The energy necessary for this synthesis and waste heat energy are produced by the yeast during the sequence of fermentation reactions terminating in ethanol, a by-product of the activity of anaerobic yeast. The ethanol, acetaldehyde, higher alcohols (fusel oils), and other products of alcoholic fermentation are important attributes of wine. The variable proportions of them contribute to type, flavor, and quality differences among wines. Some yeast cells die and "leak" or break up (autolyze) to contribute their soluble constituents to the solution. Therefore, the composition of the wine may be affected by the grape, by the direct and indirect reactions of alcoholic fermentation on grape must, by yeast-cell breakdown products, by activity of other microorganisms, and by reactions during processing.

The biochemistry of fermentation not only beautifully illuminates and clarifies the ancient art of making wine, but also explains and makes possible a calculated control of many of the "mysteries" which baffled the artisan winemaker. Aesthetics, however, is still a part of (and should not be displaced from) wine production and wine appreciation, but mystique should not remain if knowledge can be substituted.

* * *

The word *yeast* is believed to have reached English from the Anglo-Saxon *gist* via Greek *zestos* ("boiled") and Sanskrit *yasyati* ("it seethes"). To ferment is to seethe, or "boil" without a great deal of heat. The term *fermentation* today is used loosely to include all processes in which chemical changes are brought about in organic substances by the action of microorganisms (or less commonly by other cells or free enzymes). Important commercial examples include the production of antibiotics by submerged aerobic mold and actinomycete fermentations. With some exceptions, such as vinegar production, the "natural" food fermentations observed by housewives and farmers of long ago were usually capable of changing foods in sealed or deep containers—that is, were anaerobic. This includes sauerkraut, pickle, and olive fermentations by lactic-acid bacteria, as well as the alcoholic fermentation by yeasts. This "boiling" without heat was a great mystery to the ancients and was one of the first subjects studied in the emerging life sciences. The knowledge resulting from the study of wine fermentations and the so-called diseases of wine was a major contributor to the development and early progress of the modern sciences of microbiology and biochemistry.

Only a little over a hundred years ago it was discovered that alcoholic fermentation could occur naturally only in the presence of small living "ferments," the yeasts. Pasteur, from his studies in the 1860s, defined fermentation as life without air (anaerobic life), in contrast to the respiration of animals and higher plants which require air (are aerobic). In 1897 Edward Buchner reported that yeasts could be broken up and the cell-free juice would still produce alcohol from sugar. Thus the idea arose that there were "organized" ferments (cells of microorganisms) which could be broken down to "unorganized" ferments. These we know now as the enzymes, proteinaceous molecules which catalyze each of the metabolic reactions of the cell. Originally it was assumed that one enzyme of the yeast produced alcohol from sugar, but further study revealed that separate enzymes carry on steps in the process. The process of sugar catabolism to ethyl alcohol by yeasts and to lactic acid by the muscles of animals was eventually found to be essentially the same process except for the very last steps. This pathway of carbohydrate utilization by living organisms is usually called the Embden-Meyerhof pathway, after two of the many scientists who have contributed to our present understanding of this biochemical process.

The process of fermentation of one molecule of a simple sugar to alcohol was shown to result in two molecules of ethyl alcohol (more simply called ethanol) and two molecules of carbon dioxide. This was formulated by Gay-Lussac in 1810 into the equation which bears his name. This equation on the overall process can be written in a slightly modernized version as:

$$1 \text{ glucose } (C_6H_{12}O_6) \rightarrow 2 \text{ ethanol } (CH_3CH_2OH) +$$
$$2CO_2 + \text{ about 56 kilocalories of energy}$$

Thus 180 grams of glucose (the molecular weight in grams computed from the atomic weights of carbon 12, hydrogen 1, and oxygen 16) should produce a total of 92 grams of ethanol and 88 grams of carbon dioxide when completely fermented. This represents the maximum theoretical ethanol yield, which is 51.1 percent of the weight of the sugar (hexose) fermented. Although actual yields in winemaking approach this level, they are slightly lower owing to the diversion of some of the sugar's atoms to other products, incorporation of sugar derivatives into the yeast cells, losses by volatilization, and so on.

The Embden-Meyerhof pathway of conversion of sugars to ethanol does not require oxygen, and in fact the mixture of air into the fermenting solution decreases the yield of ethanol. Under truly aerobic conditions no alcohol is produced even though yeast growth is excellent, and if ethanol is already present the yeast cells, in the presence of air, can eventually metabolize it completely to carbon dioxide and water. The normal condition for alcoholic fermentation, then, is the absence of air or oxygen. This is relatively simple to accomplish, since any oxygen dissolved in the solution to be fermented is rapidly consumed by the yeast cells during initial (aerobic) multiplication. Access of further oxygen during fermentation in the typical deep liquid layer is not usually a serious problem, particularly since carbon dioxide is produced in large volume, and as it escapes it sweeps away the air.

The 56 kilocalories of energy indicated in the Gay-Lussac equation as a product of fermentation of one gram molecular weight of glucose represents the total energy change during the reaction. If glucose is "burned" either actually or by complete metabolic combustion to carbon dioxide and water, the total heat energy released is 673 kilocalories. The yeast cell ferments sugar *not* to get alcohol and carbon dioxide; it has no use for them and thus they accumulate or escape. It does need energy, and this is the "profit" the yeast gains from fermenting the sugar. The energy is needed to do the chemical work of synthesizing the substances of more yeast cells; without it no reproduction of the yeast can occur. It is obvious that if 673 kilocalories are produced when yeast converts 180 grams of glucose to carbon dioxide and water by complete oxidation, and only 56 kilocalories are produced by alcoholic fermentation, more than twelve times the amount of energy is potentially available for producing new yeast cells aerobically than anaerobically. To put it another way, yeasts must metabolize more than twelve times as much sugar to produce the same amount of cellular growth when growing anaerobically as they would if oxygen were available to them. This is fortunate for us, because it means that during alcoholic fermentation the yeasts must "process" a great deal of sugar to alcohol with relatively little cell multiplication and therefore relatively little consumption of the sugar and other nutrients to build cells. If our object is to produce a large number of yeast cells, whether for use in inoculation of musts for wine fermentation or as pressed yeast cakes for the baker, the pumping of oxygen (air) through the solution containing the yeast will produce up to twelvefold more cells per unit of sugar consumed and lower or eliminate the production of ethanol. The fact that the addition of oxygen to fermenting yeasts inhibits the conversion of glucose to ethanol, and gives more cells per unit of glucose consumed, was observed by Pasteur and is termed the Pasteur effect.

The total amount of energy released during conversion of glucose to ethanol by yeasts (about 56 kilocalories/mole) is not available to the yeast for metabolic work. About 40 percent of this amount, or 22 kilocalories, is captured in a usable form by the yeast. The rest is lost to the yeast and appears as heat. Thus the temperature of the fermenting solution is increased significantly. The usable energy is captured and transferred to other uses by the yeast cell in the form of a complex chemical, adenosine triphosphate, usually abbreviated ATP. A phosphate ion from the fermenting solution is combined by enzymes of the yeast with adenosine diphosphate, ADP, to give ATP. This illustrates one important reason why yeasts require the presence of phosphate for growth. The formation of ATP requires energy, and the energy is obtained by the yeast from specific steps in the conversion of sugar to ethanol. Once "built into" ATP, this energy can be temporarily stored, transferred, and used by the yeast for a multitude of metabolic reactions requiring energy. In fact, ATP is the primary energy-exchanging substance for all activities of living organisms including the muscular work you are doing right now as you breathe.

Converting sugar to alcohol requires at least a dozen enzymes, each of which catalyzes one step in the process sequence of the Embden-Meyerhof pathway. The enzymes acting first are those necessary to get the particular sugar being fermented phosphorylated and isomerized into the form of fructose-1,6-diphosphate. This hexose phosphate is necessary for starting the remainder of the breakdown reactions, and two molecules of ATP are consumed in its formation from the fermentable simple sugars. The next reaction splits the 6-carbon unit, fructose-1,6-diphosphate, into two 3-carbon triose phosphates. These are dihydroxyacetone phosphate and glyceraldehyde-3-phosphate, which can be converted one into the other by the action of an isomerase (enzyme). A series of reaction steps, each with its own enzyme, then occurs, and eventually two molecules of pyruvic acid result. During these reactions hydrogen is transferred to a coenzyme carrier and two new molecules of ATP are formed for each 3-carbon unit, or a total of four, giving a net gain of two ATP per sugar molecule fermented. Each new gram molecule of ATP represents about 11 kilocalories of useful energy gained by the yeast and therefore accounts for the 22 kilocalories of energy yeasts gain in converting one mole of glucose to two moles of ethanol.

The pyruvic acid (CH_3—CO—COOH) is converted to acetaldehyde (CH_3CHO) by loss of one molecule of carbon dioxide (or two per original hexose sugar.) This escaping carbon dioxide is one of the major products of fermentation. The acetaldehyde is ordinarily reduced by the addition to it of the hydrogen transferred to the coenzyme carrier at the earlier step mentioned. This final reaction—

$$CH_3CHO + H_2 \rightarrow CH_3CH_2OH$$

—is catalyzed by the enzyme alcohol dehydrogenase. It is a reversible reaction, and acetaldehyde can be produced from ethanol. All the reactions in this sequence are reversible if the proper conditions, enzymes, and energy are supplied, except that of the decarboxylation (carbon dioxide loss) of pyruvic acid. The reversal of the sequence would produce sugars from smaller molecules and has several features in common with the way in which the grapevine makes its sugar.

This reaction system may seem a bit complicated, but it has been substantiated by chemists and is one of the fundamentals of modern biochemistry. It clearly explains the origin of the major products of alcoholic fermentation. It also explains the presence of at least small amounts of many of the intermediate compounds in the sequence, such as acetaldehyde and pyruvic acid. Acetaldehyde reacts with sulfur dioxide, or rather the bisulfite ion in solution, to form an addition product which cannot be reduced to ethanol by the coenzyme hydrogen carrier system. The hydrogen is diverted under this condition to reduce the triose dihydroxyacetone to glycerol. Some glycerol (also called glycerine, $CH_2OH—CHOH—CH_2OH$) is produced to the extent of about 0.2 to 1.5 percent in every wine fermentation, but considerably more may be produced under certain conditions, including the presence of high amounts of bisulfite. Glycerol production for explosives (nitroglycerine) by fermentation was an important development in the First World War. Glycerol is a slightly sweet substance and *may* contribute to the viscosity and apparent "body" of some wines.

Glycerol is a constituent of fats, and as such some of it is incorporated into the yeast cell. Pyruvic acid is partly converted to alanine, one of the amino acids of yeast proteins. Reactions such as these divert some of the atoms from the original sugar molecule into yeast-cell constituents and decrease the yield of ethanol. Other reactions, such as the enzymatic reduction of a small amount of pyruvic acid to lactic acid or the conversion of some acetaldehyde to acetic acid, not only divert some of the carbon source to products other than alcohol, but also explain the presence of small amounts of these compounds which may contribute to a wine's flavor.

Yeasts are able to grow aerobically and can convert ethanol to acetaldehyde and then, via a series of reactions known as the Krebs cycle, after its discoverer, to carbon dioxide and water. Various degrees of temporary, partial, or incomplete aerobic metabolism can occur or be produced in wine fermentation. In the production of *flor* sherry, for example, the level of acetaldehyde and certain other flavor-producing substances is much increased by aerobic growth of yeast in or on the surface of previously fermented wine. In any typical wine fermentation, some oxygen gains access to the wine even though relatively anaerobic conditions must exist to produce wine. Again, as a result, more or less of the carbon source is diverted from ethanol production to other products. Among these products are citric acid, succinic acid, fumaric acid, malic acid, and α-ketoglutaric acid. Not all compounds that are found in wine got there from the action of yeasts, however, for the Krebs cycle occurs in grapes, too, and produces the greater part of the total acids found in wine.

These many possible and actual diversions of the carbon of sugar during wine fermentation explain the fact that whereas 51.1 percent of the weight of glucose theoretically should appear as ethanol, only about 48 percent actually does so. Since the yeast does produce 90 to 95 percent of the theoretical amount of ethanol, it might be assumed that the small amounts of other products are unimportant. This is far from the truth, because many of the constituents minor in amount in wine are major in importance to flavor and aroma. Many of the important esters and other odorous constituents are present in very small amounts and in complex mixtures which are difficult to analyze; yet they determine the quality and distinctiveness of wines and most other food products. In wines many of these important trace compounds arise from the grapes themselves, but many are produced or are modified as the yeasts play their role in the process of winemaking.

Higher alcohols, sometimes called fusel oils, occur in fermented beverages. By higher alcohols is meant those like ethanol, but with more than two carbon atoms. Particularly the 5-carbon or amyl alcohols, 4-carbon butanols, and 3-carbon propyl alcohols or propanols may occur in wine in various isomers and proportions. These compounds arise in large part during alcoholic fermentation, and their relative concentration in wines and spirits is a factor in the flavor and quality of the product, although they ordinarily total rather less than 0.1 percent of the wine. It was believed, based upon the work of Ehrlich, that these compounds arose by the action of the yeast enzymes upon the amino acids in wine musts. An example is the conversion of leucine into isoamyl alcohol:

$$(CH_3)_2—CH—CH_2—CH(NH_2)—COOH + H_2O$$
$$\rightarrow (CH_3)_2—CH—CH_2—CH_2OH + NH_3 + CO_2$$

This is an oversimplification because, among other things, more higher alcohols are produced under some conditions than can be accounted for by complete conversion of all the respective amino acids present in the medium. Rather, it is now known, the carbon skeletons which the yeast produces to make its amino acids can also be diverted to produce these alcohols. This is another example of the complex and intimate interplay among the numerous chemical reactions which characterize the metabolism of living cells, and alcoholic fermentation in particular.

As we have seen, the grape berry contains sugars, acids, pigments, tannins, and odorous compounds; and some of these ingredients, particularly sugars and amino-acid derivatives, are used and transformed by yeasts during fermentation. Fermentation, particularly the alcohol produced, affects the solvent powers of the fluid and influences the composition of the wine. The pigments, many of the odorous compounds, and part of the tannin compounds are localized within the cells of the skin of the grape berry. Another large portion of the total tannin of the berry is found in the seeds. Some of these compounds are not released at all and some do not go completely into the solution merely as a result of the crushing of the grapes. Time for diffusion from the cells and the extractive effect of alcohol are both provided during fermentation, if the solid parts of the berry remain in the must during this period. The turbulence in the fermentation vessel and perhaps the enzymic actions of the yeast also affect the transfer of less soluble grape-cell components to the solution. Thus, although the grape produces the tannin, anthocyanin pigment, and aroma compounds, and the yeast may not produce any synthesis or chemical change of these compounds, their content in the wine can be strongly influenced by events during the fermentation process.

Source: Maynard Amerine and V.L. Singleton, *Wine: An Introduction*. Copyright © 1965, 1977 by The Regents of the University of California; reprinted by permission of the University of California Press.

APPENDIX I
MUST WEIGHT AND
SUGAR CONTENT MEASUREMENTS

The specific gravity of a liquid is the relative density of the liquid compared with water, the specific gravity of which is designated as 1.000.

The German *Öchsle* reading is a hydrometer determination of the specific gravity of the grape must. The hydrometer is calibrated to indicate the specific gravity directly, with the number 1 to the left of the decimal point understood. In the table below the average minimum *Öchsle* values for must that can produce Kabinett, Spätlese, Auslese, Beerenauslese, and Trockenbeerenauslese wines are indicated by the letters within parentheses. Slightly lower values are allowed in the Moselle region.

The Brix or Balling hydrometer readings are calibrated to indicate directly the sugar content of the unfermented must. Thus a Balling reading of 22 indicates 22 percent sugar by weight in the unfermented grape must.

The Dujardin hydrometer, when inserted in the unfermented must, indicates the potential alcoholic percentage by volume of the finished wine, assuming that all of the sugar is converted to alcohol. Since high must weight wines usually have residual sugar, their alcohol content would be lower than indicated in the table, as not all of the sugar is converted to alcohol by the yeast.

Specific gravity	German Öchsle reading	Percent sugar by weight	Brix or Balling hydrometer reading	Approximate Dujardin hydrometer reading
1.035	35	9	9.0	4.0
1.039	39	10	10.0	4.5
1.043	43	11	11.0	5.0
1.047	47	12	12.0	5.5
1.052	52	13	13.0	6.3
1.056	56	14	14.0	7.1
1.059	59	15	15.0	7.5
1.064	64	16	16.0	8.2
1.068	68	17	17.0	9.0
1.072	72(K)	18	18.0	9.5
1.077	77	19	19.0	10.3
1.081	81	20	20.0	11.0
1.086	86(S)	21	21.0	11.6
1.090	90	22	22.0	12.2
1.095	95(A)	23	23.0	13.0
1.099	99	24	24.0	13.9
1.104	104	25	25.0	14.4
1.109	109	26	26.0	15.2
1.113	113	27	27.0	16.0
1.118	118	28	28.0	16.7
1.123	123(BA)	29	29.0	17.5
1.127	127	30	30.0	18.2
1.150	150(TBA)	35	35.0	21.0

APPENDIX J
CALORIC VALUES OF
ALCOHOLIC BEVERAGES

Wines	Calories per ounce (approx.)
Light wine	less than 18
Red table wine	25
Dry white table wine	25
Champagne (brut)	25
Champagne (extra dry)	29
Catawba (sweet)	30
Madeira (dry)	35
Porto	50
Sherry (dry)	35
Sherry (sweet)	50
Vermouth (dry)	35
Vermouth (sweet)	46

Malt beverages	Calories per 8 ounces
Light Beer	75
Beer	100
Ale	150

Spirits	Calories per ounce (approx.)
Vodka, gin, whiskies, etc.	65–85

Liqueurs	Calories per ounce (approx.)
Bénédictine, Chartreuse, Drambuie, and other proprietary and generic liqueurs	100–120

Bitters	Calories per teaspoon
Aromatic bitters	10

TEMPERATURE CONVERSIONS

Degrees Fahrenheit (°F) to Degrees Celsius (°C)*

°F	°C	°F	°C	°F	°C
+ 0	− 17.78	+ 60	+ 15.56	+ 120	+ 48.87
1	17.22	61	16.11	121	49.44
2	16.67	62	16.67	122	50.00
3	16.11	63	17.22	123	50.56
4	15.56	64	17.78	124	51.11
+ 5	− 15.00	+ 65	+ 18.33	+ 125	+ 51.67
6	14.44	66	18.89	126	52.22
7	13.89	67	19.44	127	52.78
8	13.33	68	20.00	128	53.33
9	12.78	69	20.56	129	53.89
+ 10	− 12.22	+ 70	+ 21.11	+ 130	+ 54.44
11	11.67	71	21.67	131	55.00
12	11.11	72	22.22	132	55.56
13	10.56	73	22.78	133	56.11
14	10.00	74	23.33	134	56.67
+ 15	− 9.44	+ 75	+ 23.89	+ 135	+ 57.22
16	8.89	76	24.44	136	57.78
17	8.33	77	25.00	137	58.33
18	7.78	78	25.56	138	58.89
19	7.22	79	26.11	139	63.44
+ 20	− 6.67	+ 80	+ 26.67	+ 140	+ 60.00
21	6.11	81	27.22	141	60.56
22	5.56	82	27.78	142	61.11
23	5.00	83	28.33	143	61.67
24	4.44	84	28.89	144	62.22
+ 25	− 3.89	+ 85	+ 29.44	+ 145	+ 62.78
26	3.33	86	30.00	146	63.33
27	2.78	87	30.56	147	63.89
28	2.22	88	31.11	148	64.44
29	1.67	89	31.67	149	65.00
+ 30	− 1.11	+ 90	+ 32.22	+ 150	+ 65.56
31	0.56	91	32.78	155	68.33
32	0.00	92	33.33	160	71.11
33	+ 0.56	93	33.89	165	73.89
34	1.11	94	34.44	170	76.67
+ 35	+ 1.67	+ 95	+ 35.00	+ 175	+ 79.44
36	2.22	96	35.56	180	82.22
37	2.78	97	36.11	185	85.00
38	3.33	98	36.67	190	87.78
39	3.89	99	37.22	195	90.56
+ 40	+ 4.44	+ 100	+ 37.78	+ 200	+ 93.33
41	5.00	101	38.33	205	96.11
42	5.56	102	38.89	210	98.89
43	6.11	103	39.44	215	101.67
44	6.67	104	40.00	220	104.44
+ 45	+ 7.22	+ 105	+ 40.56	+ 225	+ 107.22
46	7.78	106	41.11	230	110.00
47	8.33	107	41.67	235	112.78
48	8.89	108	42.22	240	115.56
49	9.44	109	42.78	245	118.33
+ 50	+ 10.00	+ 110	+ 43.33	+ 250	+ 121.11
51	10.56	111	43.89	255	123.89
52	11.11	112	44.44	260	126.67
53	11.67	113	45.00	265	129.44
54	12.22	114	45.56	270	132.22
+ 55	+ 12.78	+ 115	+ 46.11	+ 275	+ 135.00
56	13.33	116	46.67	280	137.78
57	13.89	117	47.22	285	140.56
58	14.44	118	47.78	290	143.33
59	15.00	119	48.33	295	146.11

Water freezes

$$\begin{bmatrix} 32°F \\ 0°C \end{bmatrix}$$

Ethyl alcohol boils

$$\begin{bmatrix} 173°F \\ 78.5°C \end{bmatrix}$$

Water boils

$$\begin{bmatrix} 212°F \\ 100°C \end{bmatrix}$$

The formula used to derive the table is:

$$°C = 5/9\,[°F − 32]$$

*Degrees Celsius was formerly called degrees Centigrade. The change was made to honor Anders Celsius (1701-1744) in accordance with the scientific custom of naming units of measurement after famous scientists who have contributed to that field.

APPENDIX L

CONVERSIONS
FOR WEIGHTS AND MEASURES IN
THE UNITED STATES, ENGLAND,
AND ALL OTHER COUNTRIES
USING THE METRIC SYSTEM

CONVERSION TABLES BETWEEN U.S. AND METRIC SYSTEMS

	To Change	To	Multiply by
LENGTH	centimeters	inches	0.394
	inches	centimeters	2.540
	meters	feet	3.281
	feet	meters	0.305
	kilometers	miles	0.621
	miles	kilometers	1.609
AREA	square centimeters	square inches	0.155
	square inches	square centimeters	6.451
	square meters	square feet	10.764
	square feet	square meters	0.093
	hectares	acres	2.471
	acres	hectares	0.405
	square kilometers	square miles	0.386
	square miles	square kilometers	2.590
VOLUME	cubic centimeters	cubic inches	0.061
	cubic inches	cubic centimeters	16.387
	cubic meters	cubic feet	35.315
	cubic feet	cubic meters	0.0283
LIQUID	centiliters	fluid ounces	0.338
CAPACITY	fluid ounces	centiliters	2.957
	liters	gallons	0.264
	gallons	liters	3.785
	hectoliters	gallons	26.418
	gallons	hectoliters	0.0378
WEIGHT	grams	ounces	0.035
	ounces	grams	28.35
	kilograms	pounds	2.205
	pounds	kilograms	0.454
	metric ton	long ton	0.984
	long ton	metric ton	1.016
	metric ton	short ton	0.907
	short ton	metric ton	1.102

CONVERSION TABLES WITHIN EACH SYSTEM

For most purposes the modern units used for measures and weights in the United are the same as those used in Great Britain. The major exception is in the measurement of capacity. In the following tables, therefore, there are three systems for liquid capacity—U.S., British, and metric—instead of the two major systems—U.S.-British combined and metric.

The S.I. system (*Système Internationale*), a refinement of the long-used metric system, will in time become the universal system of measurement. Britain is already committed to a complete transfer to this system, and the United States has approved transfer on a voluntary, industry-by-industry, basis.

United States
Great Britain   *Metric or S.I.*

LENGTH

12 inches	= 1 foot	10 millimeters	= 1 centimeter
3 feet	= 1 yard	10 centimeters	= 1 decimeter
1,760 yards	= 1 mile	10 decimeters	= 1 meter
5,280 feet	= 1 mile	10 meters	= 1 dekameter
6,080 feet	= 1 nautical mile	10 dekameters	= 1 hectometer
		10 hectometers	= 1 kilometer

AREA

144 square inches	= 1 square foot	100 square centimeters	= 1 square decimeter
9 square feet	= 1 square yard	100 square decimeters	= 1 square meter (centare)
4,840 square yards	= 1 acre	100 square meters	= 1 square dekameter (are)
43,560 square feet	= 1 acre	10,000 square meters	= 1 hectare
640 acres	= 1 square mile	100 hectares	= 1 square kilometer

VOLUME AND DRY CAPACITY

1,782 cubic inches	= 1 cubic foot	1,000 cubic centimeters	= 1 cubic decimeter
27 cubic feet	= 1 cubic yard	1,000 cubic decimeters	= 1 cubic meter
1 dry pint	= 33.6 cubic inches	1,000 cubic meters	= 1 cubic dekamter
1 dry quart (2 pints)	= 67.201 cubic inches	1,000 cubic dekameters	= 1 cubic hectometer
1 peck (8 quarts)	= 537.6 cubic inches	1,000 cubic hectometers	= 1 cubic kilometer
1 bushel (4 pecks)	= 2,150.42 cubic inches		

United States
Great Britain
(avoirdupois weight)

Metric or S.I.

WEIGHT

437.5 grams	= 1 ounce		1,000 milligrams	= 1 gram
16 ounces	= 1 pound		1,000 grams	= 1 kilogram
100 pounds	= 1 cental		100 kilograms	= 1 quintal
2,000 pounds	= 1 short ton		1,000 kilograms	= metric ton
2,240 pounds	= 1 long ton			

(Also in Great Britain)

14 pounds	= 1 stone
2 stones	= 1 quarter
4 quarters	= 1 hundredweight
20 hundredweights	= 1 long ton

LIQUID CAPACITY

United States   *Great Britain*

16 fluid ounces	= 1 pint		20 fluid ounces	= 1 imperial pint
2 pints	= 1 quart		2 imperial pints	= 1 imperial quart
4 quarts	= 1 gallon		4 imperial quarts	= 1 imperial gallon°
5 fifths	= 1 gallon			
1 fluid ounce	= 1.8 cubic inches		1 fluid ounce	= 1.735 cubic inches
1 pint	= 28.88 cubic inches		1 imperial pint	= 34.68 cubic inches
1 quart	= 57.75 cubic inches		1 imperial quart	= 69.35 cubic inches
1 gallon	= 231 cubin inches		1 imperial gallon	= 277.4 cubic inches
			°1.2 American gallons	= 1 imperial gallon

Metric or S.I.

10 milliliters	= 1 centiliter
100 centiliters	= 1 liter
100 liters	= 1 hectoliter
10 hectoliters	= 1 kiloliter
1 milliliter	= 1 cubic centimeter
1 liter	= 1,000 cubic centimeters
1 hectoliter	= 100,000 cubic centimeters

APPENDIX M
BEVERAGE CONTAINER CAPACITIES
BOTTLES SIZES

Pre-metric terminology		Metric terminology	Metric capacity	Number of bottles	Fluid-ounce capacity
WINES					
Split		Small	187 ml°	¼	6.3
Tenth		Medium	375 ml	½	12.7
Fifth		Regular	750 ml	1	25.4
Bottle	(Champagne)			1	26.0
Quart		Large	1.0 L†	1⅓	33.8
Magnum		Magnum	1.5 L	2	50.7
Marie-Jeanne	(Bordeaux)			3	72.0
Tappit Hen	(Oporto)			3	72.0
Double Magnum		Extra Large	3.0 L	4	101.4
Jeroboam	(Burgundy, Champagne)		3.0 L	4	101.4
—		—	4.0 L	5⅓	135.2
Jeroboam	(Bordeaux)		4.5 L	6	152.1
Rehoboam	(Champagne)		4.5 L	6	156.0
Imperial	(Bordeaux)		6.0 L	8	202.8
Methuselah	(Burgundy, Champagne)		6.0 L	8	202.8
Salmanazar	(Champagne)		9.0 L	12	307.2
—		—	18.0 L	24	614.4
SPIRITS					
Miniature		Miniature	50 ml°		1.7
Half-Pint		Small	200 ml		6.8
Pint		Medium	500 ml		16.9
Fifth		Regular	750 ml		25.4
Quart		Large	1.0 liter†		33.8
Half-Gallon		Extra Large	1.75 liters		59.2

Note: Liqueurs and cordials previously were exempt from standards of fill requirements and the number of available bottle sizes eventually reached an extreme of thirty-nine. Liqueur and cordial bottles must now conform to metric sizes, and as with other spirits the permitted number is six.

° *ml* means milliliters, or 1/1000 liter.

† 1 liter equals 1,000 milliliters.

TRADITIONAL WINE AND SPIRIT CASK STANDARDS
WITH LITER EQUIVALENTS

	Approx. gallons	Approx. liters
Barrique of Bordeaux (24 cases)	59	225
Tonneau of Bordeaux (4 *barriques*)	238	900
Pièce* of Burgundy (24-25 cases)	60	228
Queue of Burgundy (2 *pièces*)	120	456
Pièce* of Champagne	54	200
Fuder of the Moselle	264	1,000
Stück of the Rhine	317	1,200
Halbstück (Fass) of the Rhine	158	600
Pipe of Porto or Tarragona	138	522
Pipe of Madeira	110	418
Butt of sherry	132	500
Hogshead of sherry (one-half butt)	66	250
Hogshead of Cognac	72	272
Puncheon of rum (varies in value)	112	422

*The term *pièce* is also used in the Loire and Rhône and denotes varying capacities, all approximately 60 gallons.

HISTORICAL BEVERAGE CAPACITIES
IN GREAT BRITAIN

2 mouthfuls	= 1 jigger (handful)
2 jiggers	= 1 jack (jackpot)
2 jacks	= 1 jill (gill)
2 jills	= 1 cup (half-pint)
2 cups	= 1 pint (jug)
2 pints	= 1 quart
2 quarts	= 1 pottle
2 pottles	= 1 wine gallon
2 gallons	= 1 peck (flagon)
4 pecks	= 1 bushel
2 bushels	= 1 cask
2 casks	= 1 barrel
2 barrels	= 1 hogshead
2 hogsheads	= 1 pipe (butt)
2 pipes	= 1 tun

The units listed in this table, whose order is essentially derived from a doubling process, varied greatly throughout English history. One of the measurements that varied most was the barrel. Originally there were two types of barrels, the ale barrel and the beer barrel. The ale barrel contained 32 corn gallons (1 corn gallon = 268 cubic inches). It then was changed to hold 32 ale gallons (1 ale gallon = 282 cubic inches). The original beer barrel contained 36 wine gallons (1 wine gallon = 231 cubic inches). Thus the later ale barrel contained 32 x 282 = 9,024 cubic inches, as against the beer barrel's 36 x 231 = 8,316 cubic inches. One had to know what type of barrel one was dealing with to avoid being confused or cheated.

The conversion of all capacities to metric measurements eventually should eliminate the inconsistencies of the past.

Source: H. Arthur Klein, *The World of Measurements* (New York: Simon & Schuster, 1974).

APPENDIX N
VINEYARD AND WINERY YIELDS AND CONVERSIONS

The weight of grapes grown in a unit area of a vineyard is known as *grape yield*. The units used to measure this yield in some of the major wine regions of the world are:

GRAPE YIELD CONVERSION FACTORS	UNITED STATES	FRANCE	ITALY	GERMANY
	$1 \dfrac{\text{short ton}}{\text{acre}}$	$= 2.25 \dfrac{tonne}{\text{hectare}}$	$= 22.5 \dfrac{quintale}{\text{hectare}}$	$= 22.5 \dfrac{Doppelzentner}{Hektar}$

Weight conversion factors:

$$1 \text{ short ton} = 0.9 \text{ metric } tonne = 9 \; quintale = 9 \; Doppelzentner$$

The *grape yield* (or *harvest yield*) can range from 1 ton per acre to 16 tons per acre, depending upon grape variety, climate, soil, rainfall, pruning methods, and many other vineyard practices.

The volume of table wine that is produced from a specific quantity of grapes varies from winery to winery and from region to region. The range is from 150 to 200 gallons of table wine produced from a short ton of grapes crushed. An average yield is 170 gallons per ton. With this average figure as a base, some conversions into other units are:

WINE YIELD	UNITED STATES	FRANCE	ITALY	GERMANY
	$170 \dfrac{\text{gallons}}{\text{ton}}$	$= 7 \dfrac{\text{hectoliters}}{tonne}$	$= 70 \dfrac{\text{liters}}{quintale}$	$= 70 \dfrac{\text{liters}}{Doppelzentner}$

Perhaps the most important winery production term is the *winery yield*, since the wine laws of France and Italy place a limit on this value. The *winery yield* is determined by multiplying the *grape yield* by the *wine yield*. For example, assume a *grape yield* of 1 ton per acre, then:

WINERY YIELD (grape yield × wine yield)	UNITED STATES	FRANCE	ITALY	GERMANY
	(1×170) $170 \dfrac{\text{gallons}}{\text{acre}}$	$= \dfrac{(2.25 \times 7)}{15.75 \dfrac{\text{hectoliters}}{\text{hectare}}}$	$= \dfrac{(22.5 \times 70)}{1575 \dfrac{\text{liters}}{\text{hectare}}}$	$= \dfrac{(22.5 \times 70)}{1575 \dfrac{\text{Liters}}{Hektar}}$

OTHER USEFUL CONVERSIONS ARE:

Gallons per acre × 0.0925 = hectoliters per hectare
Hectoliters per hectare × 10.7 = gallons per acre
Cases° × 2.4 = gallons
Gallons per ton × 0.42 = cases per ton
Gallons per acre × 0.42 = cases per acre
Hectoliters per hectare × 11.1 = cases per hectare
Total tonnage at grape harvest × 70 = potential cases
Acres planted × *Harvest Yield* (tons per acre) × 70 = potential cases
  Example: 10 acres planted × 3 tons per acre × 70 = 2100 potential cases

° A case is 12 bottles at 75 centiliters (750 milliliters).

Source: William Lembeck.

APPENDIX O

COMPARISON OF U.S. PROOF, BRITISH "SIKES," AND METRIC "GAY-LUSSAC" TABLES OF ALCOHOLIC STRENGTHS—at 60° F

U.S. PROOF	BRITISH SIKES U.P.*	GAY-LUSSAC Alcohol by volume	U.S. PROOF	BRITISH SIKES U.P.*	GAY-LUSSAC Alcohol by volume	U.S. PROOF	BRITISH SIKES U.P.*	GAY-LUSSAC Alcohol by volume	U.S. PROOF	BRITISH SIKES O.P.*	GAY-LUSSAC Alcohol by volume
0	100	0	52	54.5	26.0	104	8.9	52.0	149	30.5	74.5
1	99.1	0.5	53	53.6	26.5	105	8.1	52.5	150	31.3	75.0
2	98.2	1.0	54	52.7	27.0	106	7.2	53.0	151	32.2	75.5
3	97.4	1.5	55	51.8	27.5	107	6.3	53.5	152	33.1	76.0
4	96.5	2.0	56	51.0	28.0	108	5.4	54.0	153	34.0	76.5
5	95.6	2.5	57	50.1	28.5	109	4.6	54.5	154	34.9	77.0
6	94.7	3.0	58	49.2	29.0	110	3.7	55.0	155	35.7	77.5
7	93.9	3.5	59	48.3	29.5	111	2.8	55.5	156	36.6	78.0
8	93.0	4.0	60	47.5	30.0	112	1.9	56.0	157	37.5	78.5
9	92.1	4.5	61	46.6	30.5	113	1.1	56.5	158	38.4	79.0
10	91.2	5.0	62	45.7	31.0	114	0.2	57.0	159	39.2	79.5
11	90.4	5.5	63	44.8	31.5				160	40.1	80.0
12	89.5	6.0	64	44.0	32.0	114.3	0.0	57.1	161	41.0	80.5
13	88.6	6.5	65	43.1	32.5		Proof		162	41.9	81.0
14	87.7	7.0	66	42.2	33.0	U.S. PROOF	BRITISH SIKES O.P.*	GAY-LUSSAC Alcohol by volume	163	42.7	81.5
15	86.9	7.5	67	41.3	33.5				164	43.6	82.0
16	86.0	8.0	68	40.5	34.0				165	44.5	82.5
17	85.1	8.5	69	39.6	34.5				166	45.4	83.0
18	84.2	9.0	70	38.7	35.0	115	0.7	57.5	167	46.2	83.5
19	83.4	9.5	71	37.8	35.5	116	1.6	58.0	168	47.1	84.0
20	82.5	10.0	72	37.0	36.0	117	2.3	58.5	169	48.0	84.5
21	81.6	10.5	73	36.1	36.5	118	3.3	59.0	170	48.9	85.0
22	80.7	11.0	74	35.2	37.0	119	4.2	59.5	171	49.7	85.5
23	79.9	11.5	75	34.3	37.5	120	5.1	60.0	172	50.6	86.0
24	79.0	12.0	76	33.5	38.0	121	6.0	60.5	173	51.5	86.5
25	78.1	12.5	77	32.6	38.5	122	6.8	61.0	174	52.4	87.0
26	77.2	13.0	78	31.7	39.0	123	7.7	61.5	175	53.2	87.5
27	76.4	13.5	79	30.8	39.5	124	8.6	62.0	176	54.1	88.0
28	75.5	14.0	80	29.9	40.0	125	9.5	62.5	177	55.0	88.5
29	74.6	14.5	81	29.1	40.5	126	10.3	63.0	178	55.9	89.0
30	73.7	15.0	82	28.2	41.0	127	11.2	63.5	179	56.7	89.5
31	72.9	15.5	83	27.3	41.5	128	12.1	64.0	180	57.6	90.0
32	72.0	16.0	84	26.4	42.0	129	13.0	64.5	181	58.5	90.5
33	71.1	16.5	85	25.6	42.5	130	13.8	65.0	182	59.4	91.0
34	70.2	17.0	86	24.7	43.0	131	14.7	65.5	183	60.2	91.5
35	69.4	17.5	87	23.8	43.5	132	15.6	66.0	184	61.1	92.0
36	68.5	18.0	88	22.9	44.0	133	16.5	66.5	185	62.0	92.5
37	67.6	18.5	89	22.1	44.5	134	17.3	67.0	186	62.9	93.0
38	66.7	19.0	90	21.2	45.0	135	18.2	67.5	187	63.7	93.5
39	65.8	19.5	91	20.3	45.5	136	19.1	68.0	188	64.6	94.0
40	65.0	20.0	92	19.4	46.0	137	20.0	68.5	189	65.5	94.5
41	64.1	20.5	93	18.6	46.5	138	20.8	69.0	190	66.4	95.0
42	63.2	21.0	94	17.7	47.0	139	21.7	69.5	191	67.3	95.5
43	62.3	21.5	95	16.8	47.5	140	22.6	70.0	192	68.1	96.0
44	61.5	22.0	96	15.9	48.0	141	23.5	70.5	193	69.0	96.5
45	60.6	22.5	97	15.1	48.5	142	24.3	71.0	194	69.9	97.0
46	59.7	23.0	98	14.2	49.0	143	25.2	71.5	195	70.8	97.5
47	58.8	23.5	99	13.3	49.5	144	26.1	72.0	196	71.6	98.0
48	58.0	24.0	100	12.4	50.0	145	27.0	72.5	197	72.5	98.5
49	57.1	24.5	101	11.6	50.5	146	27.8	73.0	198	73.4	99.0
50	56.2	25.0	102	10.7	51.0	147	28.7	73.5	199	74.3	99.5
51	55.3	25.5	103	9.8	51.5	148	29.6	74.0	**200**	**75.1**	**100.0**

*U.P. = Underproof; O.P. = Overproof.

APPENDIX P
U.S. STANDARDS OF IDENTITY
FOR DISTILLED SPIRITS

Subpart C—Standards of Identity for Distilled Spirits

§ 5.21   Application of standards.

The standards of identity for the several classes and types of distilled spirits set forth in this part shall be applicable only to distilled spirits for beverage or other nonindustrial purposes.

§ 5.22   The standards of identity.

Standards of identity for the several classes and types of distilled spirits set forth in this section shall be as follows . . . :

(a) *Class 1; neutral spirits or alcohol.* "Neutral spirits" or "alcohol" are distilled spirits produced from any material at or above 190° proof, and, if bottled, bottled at not less than 80° proof.

(1) "Vodka" is neutral spirits so distilled, or so treated after distillation with charcoal or other materials, as to be without distinctive character, aroma, taste, or color.

(2) "Grain spirits" are neutral spirits distilled from a fermented mash of grain and stored in oak containers.

CAUTION: Section 5.22(a) (2) becomes effective July 1, 1972.

(b) *Class 2; whisky.* "Whisky" is an alcoholic distillate from a fermented mash of grain produced at less than 190° proof in such manner that the distillate possesses the taste, aroma, and characteristics generally attributed to whisky, stored in oak containers (except that corn whisky need not be so stored), and bottled at not less than 80° proof, and also includes mixtures of such distillates for which no specific standards of identity are prescribed.

(1)(i) "Bourbon whisky," "rye whisky," "wheat whisky," "malt whisky," or "rye malt whisky" is whisky produced at not exceeding 160° proof from a fermented mash of not less than 51 percent corn, rye, wheat, malted barley, or malted rye grain, respectively, and stored at not more than 125° proof in charred new oak containers; and also includes mixtures of such whiskies of the same type.

(ii) "Corn whisky" is whisky produced at not exceeding 160° proof from a fermented mash of not less than 80 percent corn grain, and if stored in oak containers stored at not more than 125° proof in used or uncharred new oak containers and not subjected in any manner to treatment with charred wood; and also includes mixtures of such whisky.

(iii) Whiskies conforming to the standards prescribed in subdivisions (i) and (ii) of this subparagraph, which have been stored in the type of oak containers prescribed, for a period of 2 years or more shall be further designated as "straight"; for example, "straight bourbon whisky," "straight corn whisky," and whisky conforming to the standards prescribed in subdivision (i) of this subparagraph, except that it was produced from a fermented mash of less than 51 percent of any one type of grain, and stored for a period of 2 years or more in charred new oak containers shall be designated merely as "straight whisky." No other whiskies may be designated "straight." "Straight whisky" includes mixtures of straight whiskies which are homogeneous under section 5025(e) (5), Internal Revenue Code (26 U.S.C. 5025 (e) (5)), and implementing regulations in 26 CFR Part 201, and also mixtures of straight whiskies of the same type produced by the same proprietor at the same distillery all of which are not less than 4 years old.

(2) "Whisky distilled from bourbon (rye, wheat, malt, or rye malt) mash" is whisky produced in the United States at not exceeding 160° proof from a fermented mash of not less than 51 percent corn, rye, wheat, malted barley, or malted rye grain, respectively, and stored in used oak containers; and also includes mixtures of such whiskies of the same type. Whisky conforming to the standard of identity for corn whisky must be designated corn whisky.

(3) "Light whisky" is whisky produced in the United States at more than 160° proof, on or after January 26, 1968, and stored in used or uncharred new oak containers; and also includes mixtures of such whiskies. If "light whisky" is mixed with less than 20 percent of straight whisky on a proof gallon basis, the mixture shall be designated "blended light whisky" (light whisky—a blend).

Section 5.22(b) (3) effective July 1, 1972.

(4) "Blended whisky" (whisky—a blend) is a mixture which contains at least 20 percent of straight whisky on a proof gallon basis and, separately or in combination, whisky or neutral spirits. A blended whisky containing not less than 51 percent on a proof gallon basis of one of the types of straight whisky shall be further designated by that specific type of straight whisky; for example, "blended rye whisky" (rye whisky—a blend).

(5) "A blend of straight whiskies" (blended straight whiskies) is a mixture of straight whiskies. A blend of straight whiskies consisting entirely of one of the types of straight whisky, and not conforming to the standard for "straight whisky," shall be further designated by that specific type of straight whisky; for example, "a blend of straight rye whiskies" (blended straight rye whiskies).

(6) "Spirit whisky" is a mixture of neutral spirits and not less than 5 percent on a proof gallon basis of whisky, or straight whisky, or straight whisky and whisky, if the straight whisky component is less than 20 percent on a proof gallon basis.

(7) "Scotch whisky" is whisky which is a distinctive product of Scotland, manufactured in Scotland in compliance with the laws of the United Kingdom regulating the manufacture of Scotch whisky for consumption in the United Kingdom: *Provided*, That if such product is a mixture of whiskies, such mixture is "blended Scotch whisky" (Scotch whisky—a blend).

(8) "Irish whisky" is whisky which is a distinctive product of Ireland, manufactured either in the Republic of Ireland or in Northern Ireland, in compliance with their laws regulating the manufacture of Irish whisky for home consumption: *Provided*, That if such product is a mixture of whiskies, such mixture is "blended Irish whisky" (Irish whisky—a blend).

(9) "Canadian whisky" is whisky which is a distinctive product of Canada, manufactured in Canada in compliance with the laws of Canada regulating the manufacture of Canadian whisky for consumption in Canada: *Provided*, That if such product is a mixture of whiskies, such mixture is "blended Canadian whisky" (Canadian whisky—a blend).

(c) *Class 3; gin.* "Gin" is a product obtained by original distillation from mash, or by redistillation of distilled spirits, or by mixing neutral spirits, with or over juniper berries and other aromatics, or with or over extracts derived from infusions, percolations, or maceration of such materials, and includes mixtures of gin and neutral psirits. It shall derive its main characteristic flavor from juniper berries and be bottled at not less than 80° proof. Gin produced exclusively by original distillation or by redistillation may be further designated as "distilled." "Dry gin" (London dry gin), "Geneva gin" (Hollands gin), and "Old Tom gin" (Tom gin) are types of gin known under such designations.

(d) *Class 4; brandy.* "Brandy" is an alcoholic distillate from the fermented juice, mash, or wine of fruit, or from the residue thereof, produced at less than 190° proof in such manner that the distillate possesses the taste, aroma, and characteristics generally attributed to the product, and bottled at not less than 80° proof. Brandy, or mixtures thereof, not conforming to any of the standards in subparagraphs (1) through (8) of this paragraph shall be designated as "brandy," and such designation shall be immediately followed by a truthful and adequate statement of composition.

(1) "Fruit brandy" is brandy distilled solely from the fermented juice or mash of whole, sound, ripe fruit, or from the standard grape, citrus, or other fruit wine, with or without the addition of not more than 20 percent by weight of the pomace of such juice or wine, or 30 percent by volume of the lees of such wine, or both (calculated prior to the addition of water to facilitate fermentation or distillation). Fruit brandy shall include mixtures of such brandy with not more than 30 percent (calculated on a proof gallon basis) of lees brandy. Fruit brandy, derived from grapes, shall be designated as "grape brandy" or "brandy," except that in the case of brandy other than neutral brandy, pomace brandy, marc brandy, or grappa brandy) distilled from the fermented juice, mash, or wine of grapes, or the residue thereof, which has been stored in oak containers for less than 2 years, the statement of class and type shall be immediately preceded, in the same size and kind of type, by the word "immature." Fruit brandy, other than grape brandy, derived from one variety of fruit, shall be designated by the word "brandy" qualified by the name of such fruit (for example, "peach brandy"), except that "apple brandy" may be designated "applejack." Fruit brandy derived from more than one variety of fruit shall be designated as "fruit brandy" qualified by a truthful and adequate statement of composition.

(2) "Cognac," or "cognac (grape) brandy," is grape brandy distilled in the Cognac region of France, which is entitled to be so designated by the laws and regulations of the French Government.

* * *

(e) *Class 5; blended applejack.* "Blended applejack" (applejack—a blend) is a mixture which contains at least 20 percent of apple brandy (applejack) on a proof gallon basis, stored in oak containers for not less than 2 years, and not more than 80 percent of neutral spirits on a proof gallon basis if such mixture at the time of bottling is not less than 80° proof.

(f) *Class 6; rum.* "Rum" is an alcoholic distillate from the fermented juice of sugarcane, sugarcane syrup, sugarcane molasses, or other sugarcane by-products, produced at less than 190° proof in such manner that the distillate possesses the taste, aroma, and characteristics generally attributed to rum, and bottled at not less than 80° proof; and also includes mixtures solely of such distillates.

(g) *Class 7; Tequila.* "Tequila" is an alcoholic distillate from a fermented mash derived principally from the Agave Tequilana Weber ("blue" variety), with or without additional fermentable substances, distilled in such manner that the distillate possesses the taste, aroma, and characteristics generally attributed to Tequila and bottled at not less than 80° proof, and also includes mixtures solely of such distillates. Distinctive product of Mexico.

(h) *Class 8; cordials and liqueurs.* Cordials and liqueurs are products obtained by mixing or redistilling distilled spirits with or over fruits, flowers, plants, or pure juices therefrom, or other natural flavoring materials, or with extracts derived from infusions, percolation, or maceration of such materials, and containing sugar, dextrose, or levulose, or a combination thereof, in an amount not less than 2½ percent by weight of the finished product.

(1) "Sloe gin" is a cordial or liqueur with the main characteristic flavor derived from sloe berries.

(2) "Rye liqueur," "bourbon liqueur" (rye, bourbon cordial) are liqueurs, bottled at not less than 60° proof, in which not less than 51 percent, on a proof gallon basis, of the distilled spirits used are, respectively, rye or bourbon whisky, straight rye or straight bourbon whisky, or whisky distilled from a rye or bourbon mash, and which possess a predominant characteristic rye or bourbon flavor derived from such whisky. Wine, if used, must be within the 2½ percent limitation provided in § 5.23 for coloring, flavoring, and blending materials.

(3) "Rock and rye," "rock and bourbon," "rock and brandy," "rock and rum" are liqueurs, bottled at not less than 48° proof, in which, in the case of rock and rye and rock and bourbon, not less than 51 percent, on a proof gallon basis, of the distilled spirits used are, respectively, rye or bourbon whisky, straight rye or straight bourbon whisky, or whisky distilled from a rye or bourbon mash, and, in the case of rock and brandy and rock and rum, the distilled spirits used are all grape brandy or rum, respectively; containing rock candy or sugar syrup, with or without the addition of fruit, fruit juices, or other natural flavoring materials, and possessing, respectively, a predominant characteristic rye, bourbon, brandy, or rum flavor derived from the distilled spirits used. Wine, if used, must be within the 2½ percent limitation provided in § 5.23 for harmless coloring, flavoring, and blending materials.

(4) The designation of a cordial or liqueur may include the word "dry" if the sugar, dextrose, or levulose, or a combination thereof, are less than 10 percent by weight of the finished product.

(5) Cordials and liqueurs shall not be designated as "distilled" or "compound."

(i) *Class 9; flavored brandy, flavored gin, flavored rum, flavored vodka, and flavored whisky.* "Flavored brandy," "flavored gin," "flavored rum," "flavored vodka," and "flavored whisky" are brandy, gin, rum, vodka, and whisky, respectively, to which have been added natural flavoring materials, with or without the addition of sugar, and bottled at not less than 70° proof. The name of the predominant flavor shall appear as a part of the designation. If the finished product contains more than 2½ percent by volume of wine, the kinds and percentages by volume of wine must be stated as a part of the designation, except that a flavored brandy may contain an additional 12½ percent by volume of wine, without label disclosure, if the additional wine is derived from the particular fruit corresponding to the labeled flavor of the product.

(j) *Class 10; imitations.* Imitations shall bear, as a part of the designation thereof, the word "imitation" and shall include the following:

(1) Any class or type of distilled spirits to which has been added coloring or flavoring material of such nature as to cause the resultant product to simulate any other class or type of distilled spirits;

(2) Any class or type of distilled spirits (other than distilled spirits required under § 5.35 to bear a distinctive or fanciful name and a truthful and adequate statement of composition) to which have been added flavors considered to be artificial or imitation. In determining whether a flavor is artificial or imitation, recognition will be given to what is considered to be "good commercial practice" in the flavor manufacturing industry;

(3) Any class or type of distilled spirits (except cordials, liqueurs, and specialties marketed under labels which do not indicate or imply that a particular class or type of distilled spirits was used in the manufacture thereof) to which has been added any whisky essence, brandy essence, rum essence, or similar essence or extract which simulates or enhances, or is used by the trade or in the particular product to simulate or enhance, the characteristics of any class or type of distilled spirits;

(4) Any type of whisky to which beading oil has been added;

(5) Any rum or Tequila, to which neutral spirits or distilled spirits other than rum or Tequila, respectively, have been added;

(6) Any brandy made from distilling material to which has been added any amount of sugar other than the kind and amount of sugar expressly authorized in the production of standard wine; and

(7) Any brandy to which neutral spirits or distilled spirits other than brandy have been added, except that this provision shall not apply to any product conforming to the standard of identity for blended applejack.

(k) *Class 11; geographical designations.* (1) Geographical names for distinctive types of distilled spirits (other than names found by the Director under subparagraph (2) of this paragraph to have become generic) shall not be applied to distilled spirits produced in any other place than the particular region indicated by the name, unless (i) in direct conjunction with the name there appears to the word "type" or the word "American" or some other adjective indicating the true place of production, in lettering substantially as conspicuous as such name, and (ii) the distilled spirits to which the name is applied conform to the distilled spirits of that particular region. The following are examples of distinctive types of distilled spirits with geographical names that have not become generic: Eau de Vie de Dantzig (Danziger Goldwasser), Ojen, Swedish punch. Geographical names for distinctive types of distilled spirits shall be used to designate only distilled spirits conforming to the standard of identity, if any, for such type specified in this section, or if no such standard is so specified, then in accordance with the trade understanding of that distinctive type.

(2) Only such geographical names for distilled spirits as the Director finds have by usage and common knowledge lost their geographical significance to such extent that they have become generic shall be deemed to have become generic. Examples are London dry gin, Geneva (Hollands) gin.

(3) Geographical names that are not names for distinctive types of distilled spirits, and that have not become generic, shall not be applied to distilled spirits produced in any other place than the particular place or region indicated in the name. Examples are Cognac, Armagnac, Greek brandy, Pisco brandy, Jamaica rum, Puerto Rico rum, Demerara rum.

(4) The words "Scotch," "Scots," "Highland," or "Highlands," and similar words connoting, indicating, or commonly associated with Scotland, shall not be used to designate any product not wholly produced in Scotland.

(1) *Class 12; products without geographical designations but distinctive of a particular place.* (1) The whiskies of the types specified in paragraph (b), (1), (4), (5), and (6) of this section are distinctive products of the United States and, if produced in a foreign country, shall be designated by the applicable designation prescribed in such paragraphs, together with the words "American type" or the words "produced (distilled, blended) in ___," the blank to be filled in with the name of the foreign country: *Provided*, That the word "bourbon" shall not be used to describe any whisky or whisky-based distilled spirits not produced in the United States. If whisky of any of these types is composed in part of whisky or whiskies produced in a foreign country there shall be stated, on the brand label, the percentage of such whisky and the country of origin thereof.

(2) The name for other distilled spirits which are distinctive products of a particular place or country, an example is Habanero, shall not be given to the product of any other place or country unless the designation for such product includes the word "type" or an adjective such as "American," or the like, clearly indicating the true place of production. The provision for place of production shall not apply to designations which by usage and common knowledge have lost their geographical significance to such an extent that the Director finds they have become generic. Examples are Slivovitz, Zubrovka, Aquavit, Arrack, and Kirschwasser.

§ 5.23   **Alteration of class and type.**

(a) *Additions.* (1) The addition of any coloring, flavoring, or blending materials to any class and type of distilled spirits, except as otherwise provided in this section, alters the class and type thereof and the product shall be appropriately redesignated.

(2) There may be added to any class or type of distilled spirits, without changing the class or type thereof, (i) such harmless coloring, flavoring, or blending materials as are an essential component part of the particular class or type of distilled spirits to which added, and (ii) harmless coloring, flavoring, or blending materials such as caramel, straight malt or straight rye malt whiskies, fruit juices, sugar, or wine, which are not an essential component part of the particular distilled spirits to which added, but which are customarily employed therein in accordance with established trade usage, if such coloring, flavoring, or blending materials do not total more than 2½ percent by volume of the finished product.

(3) "Harmless coloring, flavoring, and blending materials" shall not include (i) any materials which would render the product to which it is added an imitation, or (ii) any material whatsoever in the case of neutral spirits or straight whisky, or (iii) any material, other than caramel and sugar, in the case of Cognac brandy.

(b) *Extractions.* The removal from any distilled spirits of any constituents to such an extent that the product does not possess the taste, aroma, and characteristics generally attributed to that class or type of distilled spirits alters that class and type thereof, and the product shall be appropriately redesignated. In addition, in the case of straight whisky the removal of more than 15 percent of the fixed acids, or volatile acids, or esters, or soluble solids, or higher alcohols, or more than 25 percent of the soluble color, shall be deemed to alter the class or type thereof.

(c) *Exceptions.* This section shall not be construed as in any manner modifying the standards of identity for cordials and liqueurs, flavored brandy, flavored gin, flavored rum, flavored vodka, and flavored whisky or as authorizing any product which is defined in § 5.22(j), Class 10, as an imitation to be otherwise designated.

Source: "Regulations under the Federal Alcohol Administration Act, Title 27, Code of Federal Regulations, Part 5, Subpart C."

APPENDIX Q

PRODUCTION AND CONSUMPTION OF WINES, BEERS, AND SPIRITS

PRODUCTION OF WINE IN VARIOUS COUNTRIES°

Position in 1981	Country	1974 (millions of U.S. gallons)	1979 (millions of U.S. gallons)	1980 (millions of U.S. gallons)	1981 (millions of U.S. gallons)
1	Italy	2031	2228	2218	1863
2	France	1994	2222	1839	1506
3	USSR	730	810	851	909
4	Spain	961	1322	1150	909
5	Argentina	718	712	636	572
6	USA	310	352	376	392
7	Portugal	365	378	269	234
8	South Africa	132	177†	185†	204
9	Romania	211	234	201	201
10	West Germany	182	216	127	188
11	Yugoslavia	155	178	178	169
12	Greece	151	140†	145†	145
13	Chile	123	145	132†	143
14	Hungary	117	137	132†	129
15	Bulgaria	85.8	66†	66†	128
16	Australia	77.9	91.2	93†	125
17	Brazil	53†	75†	75†	76.6
18	Algeria	195†	71	66†	70.6
19	Austria	44.0	81.5	79.3†	55.1
20	Poland	40†	40†	40†	39.6
21	Czechoslovakia	22.6	38.1	37†	37.6
22	Cyprus	13†	24†	24†	25.1
23	Switzerland	18.3	29.3	29†	22.5
24	Tunisia	32.7	16.2	18†	14.7
25	Uruquay	24†	12†	12†	14.5

° In some cases much of the total wine production is distilled into brandy.
† Estimated.

Position in 1981	Country	1974 (millions of U.S. gallons)	1979 (millions of U.S. gallons)	1980 (millions of U.S. gallons)	1981 (millions of U.S. gallons)
26	Canada	15†	10†	10†	13.7
27	Morocco	34.3	28.2	29†	13.6
28	Japan	6.2	5†	5†	12.0
29	New Zealand	9†	11.2	11†	9†
30	Turkey	14†	9†	11†	9.0
31	Albania	4.5†	6†	5†	5.6
32	Israel	10.6	10†	10†	5.4
33	Mexico	41.4	4†	4†	5.0
34	Cuba	2.5†	3†	3†	2.6
35	Madeira	2.5†	3†	3†	2.6
36	Peru	2†	2†	2†	2.6
37	Luxembourg	3.6	1.7	1.3	2.6
38	Venezuela	0.7†	2†	2†	2.6
39	Paraguay	0.2†	2†	2†	2†
40	Syria	0.2†	2†	2†	2†
41	Libya	0.8†	1†	1†	2.1
42	Bolivia	0.15†	.5†	.5†	.5†
43	Malta	0.5†	.4†	.4†	.4†
44	Madagascar	0.5†	.3†	.3†	.3†
45	Jordan	0.4†	.3†	.3†	.26
46	Belgium	0.18	.1†	.1†	.11
	World Production	9,035	10,017	9,275	8,323

Source: *Produktschap Voor Gedistilleede Dranken,* 1982.

CONSUMPTION OF WINE PER CAPITA
IN VARIOUS COUNTRIES

POSITION	COUNTRY	YEAR	LITERS	U.S. GALLONS
1	France	1981	90	23.8
2	Portugal	1981	77	20.3
3	Italy	1981	74	19.5
4	Argentina	1981	73	19.3
5	Spain	1981	60	15.8
6	Switzerland	1981	48.4	12.8
7	Greece	1981	44.9	11.9
8	Chile	1981	43.7	11.5
9	Luxembourg	1981	40.2	10.6
10	Austria	1981	35.1	9.3
11	Hungary	1981	35	9.2
12	Romania	1981	28.9	7.6
13	Yugoslavia	1980	28.2	7.4
14	Uruguay	1980	25.0	6.6
15	West Germany	1981	24.7	6.5
16	Bulgaria	1980	22.0	5.8
17	Belgium	1981	20.97	5.5
18	Australia	1981	18.3	4.8
19	Denmark	1981	16.1	4.3
20	Czechoslovakia	1981	16.0	4.2
21	New Zealand	1981	14.5	3.8
22	USSR	1981	±14.5	3.8
23	Netherlands	1981	12.9	3.4
24	Cyprus	1981	10.8	2.9
25	Sweden	1981	9.7	2.6
26	East Germany	1981	±9.5	2.5
27	South Africa	1981	9.4	2.48
28	Finland	1981	8.8	2.32
29	Canada	1981	8.5	2.25
30	U.S.A.	1981	8.2	2.17
31	England	1981	7.6	2.01
32	Poland	1981	7.5	1.98
33	Iceland	1981	6.2	1.64
34	Israel	1981	4.5	1.19
35	Norway	1981	4.2	1.11
36	Ireland	1981	3.6	0.95
37	Tunisia	1981	3.1	0.82
38	Brazil	1981	±2.6	0.7
39	Paraguay	1980	1.9	0.50
40	Peru	1981	1.1	0.29
41	Algeria	1980	1.1	0.28
42	Turkey	1981	0.8	0.21
43	Venezuela	1980	±0.7	0.2
44	Japan	1981	±0.55	0.15
45	Cuba	1977	±0.5	0.1
46	Mexico	1981	±0.25	0.07
47	Morocco	1981	0.2	0.05

Source: *Produktschap voor Gedistilleede Dranken*, 1982.

CONSUMPTION OF BEER PER CAPITA
IN VARIOUS COUNTRIES

POSITION	COUNTRY	YEAR	LITERS	U.S. GALLONS
1	West Germany	1981	147.0	38.8
2	Czechoslovakia	1981	140.1	37.0
3	East Germany	1981	±138	±36
4	Australia	1981	134.1	35.4
5	Belgium	1981	124.2	32.8
6	Luxembourg	1981	123.0	32.5
7	Denmark	1981	122.2	32.3
8	New Zealand	1981	121.8	32.2
9	Ireland	1981	116.4	30.8
10	England	1981	111.5	29.5
11	Austria	1981	104.8	27.7
12	U.S.A.	1981	93.3	24.6
13	Netherlands	1981	89.5	23.6
14	Hungary	1981	±87	±23
15	Canada	1981	85.0	22.5
16	Switzerland	1981	70.5	18.6
17	Venezuela	1980	62.5	16.5
18	Bulgaria	1980	60.9	16.1
19	Finland	1981	57.2	15.1
20	Spain	1981	56.0	14.8
21	Sweden	1981	45.0	12.0
22	Colombia	1981	±45	±12
23	Romania	1981	±45	±12
24	Norway	1981	44.8	11.8
25	Yugoslavia	1980	44.2	11.7
26	France	1981	44.0	11.6
27	Mexico	1981	40.0	10.6
28	Japan	1981	±40	±10
29	Portugal	1981	37.0	9.8
30	Cyprus	1981	34.7	9.2
31	South Africa	1981	33.3	8.8
32	Greece	1981	30.1	8.0
33	Peru	1981	±29	±8
34	Poland	1981	28.6	7.6
35	Cuba	1977	±25	±7
36	USSR	1981	23.5	6.2
37	Uruguay	1980	22.6	6.0
38	Brazil	1981	±19	±5
39	Paraguay	1980	18.9	5.0
40	Italy	1981	17.9	4.7
41	Chile	1981	17.0	4.5
42	Israel	1981	±14	±4
43	Iceland	1981	±14	±4
44	Argentina	1981	7.9	2.1
45	Turkey	1981	6.7	1.8
46	Tunisia	1981	5.1	1.3
47	Algeria	1980	±3	±0.8
48	Morocco	1981	±2	±0.5

Source: *Produktschap voor Gedistilleede Dranken*, 1982.

CONSUMPTION OF DISTILLED SPIRITS
PER CAPITA IN
VARIOUS COUNTRIES

POSITION	COUNTRY	YEAR	LITERS PURE ALCOHOL (200 PROOF)	U.S. GALLONS (80 PROOF)
1	Luxembourg	1981	°9.5	°6.28
2	East Germany	1981	±4.7	3.1
3	Hungary	1981	±4.5	3
4	Poland	1981	4.3	2.84
5	Czechoslovakia	1981	3.6	2.38
6	Canada	1981	3.5	2.31
7	USSR	1981	±3.3	2.18
8	U.S.A.	1981	3.04	2.01
9	Peru	1981	±3	2
10	Spain	1981	±3	2
11	West Germany	1981	2.90	1.95
12	Finland	1981	2.76	1.82
13	Netherlands	1981	2.52	1.67
14	Sweden	1981	2.48	1.64
15	Iceland	1981	2.23	1.47
16	Belgium	1981	2.13	1.41
17	Switzerland	1981	2.11	1.39
18	Cyprus	1981	2.1	1.39
19	New Zealand	1981	2.0	1.32
20	France	1981	±2	1.3
21	Yugoslavia	1980	±2	1.3
22	Romania	1981	±2	1.3
23	Italy	1981	1.9	1.26
24	Japan	1981	±1.9	1.2+
25	Ireland	1981	1.89	1.25
26	England	1981	1.69	1.12
27	Norway	1981	1.61	1.06
28	Denmark	1981	1.59	1.05
29	Austria	1981	1.51	1.00
30	South Africa	1981	1.40	0.93
31	Argentina	1981	1.3	0.86
32	Australia	1981	1.1	0.73
33	Portugal	1981	±0.9	0.6
34	Cuba	1977	±0.7	0.5
35	Turkey	1981	0.46	0.30

° This statistic is misleading since the figure does not distinguish between actual consumption and depletions. Luxembourg has become a convenient source of alcoholic beverages for many of its neighboring countries.

Source: *Produktschap voor Gedistilleede Dranken*, 1982.

TOTAL ALCOHOL CONSUMPTION
(WINES, BEERS, AND SPIRITS)
IN VARIOUS COUNTRIES
(in order of per capita consumption)

POSITION	COUNTRY	YEAR	LITERS OF PURE ALCOHOL (200 PROOF)	U.S. GALLONS (AT 80 PROOF)
1	Luxembourg	1981	°18.0	11.9
2	France	1981	13.7	9.1
3	Spain	1981	13.0	8.6
4	West Germany	1981	12.5	8.3
5	Portugal	1981	11.9	7.9
6	Hungary	1981	11.6	7.9
7	Switzerland	1981	11.0	7.3
8	Austria	1981	11.0	7.3
9	Italy	1981	10.9	7.2
10	Belgium	1981	10.5	6.9
11	Argentina	1981	10.5	6.9
12	Australia	1981	10.0	6.6
13	East Germany	1981	±10	±6.5
14	Czechoslovakia	1981	9.9	6.5
15	New Zealand	1981	9.8	6.5
16	Denmark	1981	9.6	6.3
17	Canada	1981	9.1	6.0
18	Netherlands	1981	8.8	5.8
19	U.S.A.	1981	8.3	5.5
20	Romania	1981	±7.7	±5
21	Yugoslavia	1980	7.6	5.0
22	Ireland	1981	7.0	4.6
23	Greece	1981	6.9+	4.5+
24	England	1981	6.8	4.5
25	Poland	1981	6.6	4.4
26	Finland	1981	6.5	4.3
27	USSR	1981	6.2	4.1
28	Chile	1981	6.1+	4.0+
29	Bulgaria	1980	5.7+	3.8+
30	Japan	1981	±5.6	±3.7
31	Sweden	1981	5.4	3.6
32	Cyprus	1981	5.1	3.4
33	Peru	1981	4.6	3.0
34	South Africa	1981	4.2	2.8
35	Norway	1981	4.2	2.8
36	Uruguay	1980	4.1+	2.7+
37	Iceland	1981	3.9	2.6
38	Venezuela	1980	3.2	2.1
39	Colombia	1981	2.3+	1.5+
40	Mexico	1981	2.0	1.3
41	Cuba	1977	±2	±1.3
42	Brazil	1981	1.3+	0.9+
43	Paraguay	1980	1.2+	0.8+
44	Israel	1981	1.2+	0.8+
45	Turkey	1981	0.9	0.6
46	Tunisia	1981	0.7+	0.5+
47	Algeria	1980	0.3+	0.2+
48	Morocco	1981	0.1+	0.07+

° This statistic is misleading since the figure does not distinguish between actual consumption and depletions. Luxembourg has become a convenient source of alcoholic beverages for many of its neighboring countries.

Source: *Produktschap Voor Gedistilleede Dranken*, 1982.

APPENDIX R
CUSTOMS DUTIES
AND INTERNAL REVENUE TAXES

HISTORY OF FEDERAL EXCISE (INTERNAL REVENUE) TAXES ON ALL ALCOHOLIC BEVERAGES

WINES
(rates are per wine gallon)

Date effective	0-14% alcohol	14-21% alcohol	21-24%* alcohol	Sparkling wine	Carbonated wine
Sept. 9, 1916	$0.04	$0.10	$0.25	$1.92	$0.96
Feb. 25, 1919	0.16	0.40	1.00	7.68	3.84
Jan. 12, 1934	0.10	0.20	0.40	0.80	0.40
June 26, 1936	0.05	0.10	0.20	0.40	0.20
July 1, 1938	0.10	0.15	0.20	0.40	0.10
July 1, 1940	0.06	0.18	0.30	0.48	0.24
October 1, 1941	0.08	0.30	0.65	1.12	0.56
November 1, 1942	0.10	0.40	1.00	1.60	0.80
April 1, 1944	0.15	0.60	2.00	2.40	1.60
November 1, 1951	0.17	0.67	2.25	2.72	1.92
January 1, 1955, to present	0.17	0.67	2.25	3.40	2.40

The Internal Revenue Code imposes a tax upon all wines, including imitation, standard, or artificial wine, and compounds sold as wine, produced in or imported into the United States. These taxes are determined at the time of removal for consumption or sale.

The tax imposed on wines does not apply to wine produced by the duly registered head of a family for family use and not for sale, or to wine removed from a bonded wine cellar for family use where the head of a family operates the bonded wine cellar as an individual owner. The quantity produced or removed during a year may not exceed 200 gallons per family.

*All wines containing more than 24 percent alcohol by volume are classified as distilled spirits and are taxed accordingly.

BEERS
(per barrel of 31 gallons)

Date effective	Tax	Date effective	Tax
Sept. 1862	$1.00	Oct. 4, 1917	$3.00
Mar. 3, 1863	0.60	Feb. 25, 1919	6.00
Apr. 1, 1864	1.00	Jan. 12, 1934	5.00
Jun. 14, 1898	2.00	Jul. 1, 1940	6.00
Jul. 1, 1901	1.60	Nov. 1, 1942	7.00
Jul. 1, 1902	1.00	Apr. 1, 1944	8.00
Oct. 23, 1914	1.50	Nov. 1, 1951, to present	9.00

DISTILLED SPIRITS

Date effective	Amount per tax gallon (proof gallon)
July 1, 1791	$0.09-0.25 according to proof
July 1, 1792	$0.07-0.18 according to proof
July 1, 1802	No tax
Jan. 1, 1814	No tax
Feb. 1, 1815	$0.20
Jan. 1, 1818	No tax
Sept. 1, 1862	$0.20
March 7, 1864	0.60
July 1, 1864	1.50
Jan. 1, 1865	2.00
July 20, 1868	0.50
Aug. 1, 1872	0.70
March 3, 1875	0.90
Aug. 27, 1894	1.10
Oct. 3, 1917—World War I	
Basic rate	2.20
Withdrawn for beverage use	3.20
Feb. 25, 1919—Prohibition	
Basic rate	2.20
Withdrawn for (from Nov. 23, 1921, if "diverted to") beverage use	6.40*
Jan. 1, 1927	1.65
Diverted to beverage use	6.40*
Jan. 1, 1928	
Basic rate	1.10
Diverted to beverage use (prior to repeal of Prohibition, Dec. 6, 1933)	6.40*
Jan. 12, 1934	2.00
July 1, 1938	
Distilled spirits generally	2.25
Brandy	2.00
July 1, 1940	
Distilled spirits generally	3.00
Brandy	2.75
Oct. 1, 1941	4.00
Nov. 1, 1942—World War II	6.00
April 1, 1944	9.00
Nov. 1, 1951, to present time	10.50

*During Prohibition.

CUSTOMS DUTIES AND INTERNAL REVENUE TAXES ON IMPORTED ALCOHOLIC BEVERAGES

WINES	Customs duties (per wine gallon)		Internal Revenue taxes (per wine gallon)
Champagne and other sparkling wines	$1.17	($6.00)	$3.40
Artificially carbonated wines	1.17	($6.00)	2.40
Cider:			
Still	0.03	($1.25)	0.17
Sparkling	0.05	($6.00)	2.40
Rice wine or saké	0.25	($1.25)	°
Still wines produced from grapes:			
Containing not over 14 percent alcohol by volume:			
In containers holding each			
Not over one gallon	0.37½	($1.25)	0.17
Over one gallon	0.62½	($1.25)	0.17
Containing over 14 alcohol percent by volume:			
Marsala or Marsala types in containers each holding not over one gallon	0.31½	($1.25)	0.67†
Sherry	1.00	($1.25)	0.67†
Other	1.00	($1.25)	0.67†
Vermouth, in containers holding each			
Not over one gallon	0.21	($1.25)	0.67†
Over one gallon	0.32	($1.25)	0.67†
Other fermented alcoholic beverages	0.25	($1.25)	§

Imitation wines are subject to the highest rate of duty for the product to be represented, but not less than $3.75 per proof gallon; the Internal Revenue tax is payable at the same rate as genuine wine according to the latter's classification, that is, Champagne, still wine, and so on. Still wines containing over 24 percent alcohol by volume are dutiable and taxable as distilled spirits.

BEER	Customs duties		Internal Revenue tax
Beer, ale, porter, and stout	$0.06	($0.50)	At the rate of $9.00 per 31 gallons computed upon the actual quantity in a container

° Internal Revenue tax same as for beer when product is made like beer; when alcohol has been added, it is taxed as distilled spirits.

† Internal Revenue tax on still wines containing more than 21 percent and not exceeding 24 percent alcohol by volume, $2.25 per wine gallon.

§ Internal Revenue tax same as for still wines according to alcohol content thereof.

DISTILLED SPIRITS	Customs duties (proof gallon)	Internal Revenue taxes°° (proof gallon)
Aquavit	$0.42	$10.50
Arak		
In containers each holding not over 1 gallon	2.28	10.50
In containers each holding over 1 gallon	1.00	10.50
Bitters of all kinds containing spirits:		
Not fit for use as beverages	0.38	
Fit for use as beverages	0.50	10.50
Brandy:		
Pisco and Singani:		
In containers each holding not over		
1 gallons:		
Valued not over $9 per gallon	0.43	10.50
Valued over $9 per gallon	0.87	10.50
In containers each holding over 1 gallon:		
Valued not over $9 per gallon	0.35	10.50
Valued over $9 per gallon	0.70	10.50
Slivovitz and other:		
In containers each holding not over 1 gallon:		
Valued not over $9 per gallon	3.40	10.50
Valued over $9 but not over $13 per		
gallon	1.25	10.50
Valued over $13	0.87	10.50
In containers each holding over 1 gallon:		
Valued not over $9 per gallon	0.50	10.50
Valued over $9 but not over $13	0.70	10.50
Cordials, liqueurs, Kirschwasser, and Ratafia	0.50	10.50
Ethyl alcohol for beverages purposes	1.12	10.50
Gin	0.50	10.50
Rum	1.57	10.50
Whisky:		
Irish and Scotch	0.35	10.50
Canadian and other	0.43	10.50
Tequila:		
In containers each holding not over 1 gallon	2.27	10.50
In containers each holding over 1 gallon	1.25	10.50

°° Customs duties and Internal Revenue Tax rates are based upon proof gallon, or wine gallon when below proof.

Other spirits and preparations in chief value of distilled spirits, fit for use in beverages or for beverage purposes:		
Vodka:		
In containers each holding not over 1 gallon:		
Valued not over $7.75 per gallon	2.56	10.50
Valued at over $7.75 per gallon	0.87	10.50
In containers each holding over 1 gallon:	1.25	10.50
Spirits:		
In containers each holding not over 1 gallon:	2.56	10.50
In containers each holding over 1 gallon:	1.25	10.50
Other:	1.25	10.50
Imitations of brandy and other spirituous beverages:		
In containers each holding not over 1 gallon:	5.75	10.50
In containers each holding over 1 gallon:	2.50	10.50

Source: National Association of Alcoholic Beverage Importers, Inc., Statistical Report, Table 23, 1982.

The duties on imported alcoholic beverages are in *addition* to federal and state excise taxes that are also charged for alcoholic beverages. To determine the total tax on an imported beverage, add the federal tax for its category, then add the state tax, which varies from state to state, and finally add the import duty. There may also be local sales taxes.

Rates of duties shown in parentheses on page 592 are the full rates that were in effect on January 1, 1934, or as revised by Public Law 96-39, which applies to products of all countries not benefiting from most-favored-nation status.

Proclamation 4991, October 27, 1982, concerns all products of Communist countries.

Source: *General Headnotes and Rules of Interpretation of the Tariff Schedules of the United States,* January, 1983.

APPENDIX S
GLOSSARY

The abbreviations Aus., Eng., Fr., Hun., It., Port., Sp., and Yug. represent the countries of origin Austria, England, France, Hungary, Italy, Portugal, Spain, and Yugoslavia respectively.

abboccato (It.). Semidry.

Abfüllung, Abf. (Ger.). Bottling.

Abstich (Ger.). Racking.

acerbe (Fr.). Green, acid.

acid, acidity. Compounds in wine that provide a tart freshness and contribute to the wine's ability to age.

acqua vita, aqua vitae (It., Latin). Water of life—spirits.

adega (Port.). Equivalent of *bodega*, wine warehouse.

aftertaste. The taste in the back of the throat after a wine has been swallowed. A lingering aftertaste is an indication of a complex wine.

agrafes (Fr.). Metal clips used in Champagne cellars to hold the temporary corks in place.

aguardiente (Sp.). Spirits, primarily brandy or whisky.

aigre (Fr.). An acid undertone.

albariza (Sp.). Chalky-white soil of best Jerez sherry vineyards in Spain.

alcohol (ethyl). Chemically C_2H_5OH, one of the results of fermenting liquids containing sugar.

aldehydes. By-products of alcoholic liquids resulting from the combination of alcohol, acid, and air.

alembic, *alambic, alambique* (Eng., Fr., Sp.). Still.

alt (Ger.). Old.

amabile (It.). Semisweet.

amaro (It.). Bitter or very dry.

amélioré (Fr.). Improved, usually by the addition of sugar to the must before fermentation.

amertume. (Fr.). Bitter.

amontillado (Sp.). Dry type of sherry.

amoroso (Sp.). Medium-dry type of sherry.

ampelography. Science of grapevine culture.

añada (Sp.). Wine of one vintage.

ansprechend (Ger.). Attractive, engaging.

aperitif. Appetizer wine or spirit.

Appellation d'Origine Contrôlée (Fr.). Term that appears on labels of fine French wines signifying origin and right to the name it bears, guaranteed by French law.

âpre (Fr.). Harsh, rough.

arenas (Sp.). Sandy soils of the Jerez sherry vineyards in Spain.

arome, aroma (Fr., Sp.). Odor or bouquet of a wine or spirit.

arroba (Sp.). Wine measure holding 16⅔ liters.

arrope (Sp.). Concentrated wine used to sweeten and give color to sherries. See also *vino de color.*

artig (Ger.). Smooth, rounded.

asciato (It.). Dry.

astringence. Puckering or drying sensation in the mouth after drinking certain tannic wines.

aszú (Hun.). Sweeter type of Tokay wine.

Auslese (Ger.). A wine made from selected grapes.

balance. The harmony of a wine in which none of the components is overly apparent.

Balthazar. Oversize Champagne bottle, holding 16 regular bottles, or 416 ounces.

Banvin, Ban de Vendange (Fr.). Ancient French custom of fixing the date when the gathering of the grapes might begin.

barrique, barrica (Fr., Sp.). Hogshead, cask.

barros (Sp.). Clayish soils of the Jerez sherry vineyards in Spain.

basto (Sp.). Coarse.

B.A.T.F. Bureau of Alcohol, Tobacco, and Firearms, U.S. Treasury Department.

Baumé. Measurement of the degree of sweetness in wines and spirits. Hydrometer and scales invented by the French chemist Antoine Baumé.

Beerenauslese (Ger.). A wine made from individually selected, perfectly ripe grapes.

beste (Ger.). Best.

bianco (It.). White.

binning. Storing wines in bins in a cellar for development.

blanc de blancs (Fr.). Wine made from the juice of white grapes only.

blanco (Sp.). White.

blending. Marrying two or more similar products to obtain a better and more uniform quality.

Blume (Ger.). Bouquet, aroma.

blumig (Ger.). Good bouquet.

Bocksbeutel (Ger.). Squat, flasklike bottle used for Frankenwein.

bocoy (Sp.). Large cask holding approximately 162 gallons.

bodega (Sp.). Ground-level wine warehouse.

body. The term employed to describe the consistency of beverages. For example, a thin wine has less body than a full one.

bond, in. A wine or spirit on which duty and Internal Revenue tax has not been paid must remain under government supervision as "bond" that same will be paid.

bonded warehouse. Warehouse under government supervision.

bon goût (Fr.). Good or pleasant taste.

bor (Hun.). Wine. *Fehérbor* is white wine; *Vörösbor* is red wine. Both are pluralized with the suffix *-ok*, as in *borok*.

bota (Sp.). Butt, sherry cask, holding 132 gallons.

bottle, *bouteille, botella* (Eng., Fr., Sp.). A wine bottle containing from 23 to 26 ounces.

Bottled in Bond. U.S.: Term signifying a straight whisky, at least four years old, bottled at 100 proof, under government supervision, before taxes have been paid on same. Canada: Term signifying a blended whisky, at least three years old, bottled at 100 proof, under government supervision, before taxes have been paid on same.

bouchonné (Fr.). Corky, as a wine that has taken on an unpleasant taste of cork.

bouquet. Aroma or fragrance of a wine or spirit.

Bowle (Ger.). Wine cup prepared with fresh fruit, wine, herbs, and liqueurs or brandy.

brandewijn, Branntwein (Dutch, Ger.). Brandy; literally, "burned wine."

breed. The character or degree of excellence a wine attains.

brouilli (Fr.). The middle distillate (about 24 to 32 percent alcohol), collected for the second distillation in Cognac.

brut (Fr.). Dry. Also, the driest type of Champagne.

bukettreich (Ger.). Rich, pronounced bouquet.

butt. Standard shipping cask for sherry, 132 gallons.

Cabinet-wein (Ger.). Term used before 1971 to denote the finest quality of certain Rhine wines, specially reserved and so marked.

cantina (It.). Cellar, winery, or bar.

cantina sociale (It.). Wine growers' cooperative.

capataz (Sp.). Foreman or *bodega* master in Jerez.

capiteux (Fr.). Spirity, heady.

capsule. Protector made of metal or plastic for wine and spirit bottle cork.

caque (Fr.). Basket in which grapes are carried from the vineyard to the press.

casco (Sp.). Cask or large barrel, usually made of oak, used for developing (aging) and/or shipping wines and spirits.

cask. Large container, usually made of oak, for wines or spirits.

casse (Fr.). Chemical disease of wines resulting from excess iron.

catalyst. Chemical agent that induces chemical changes in other substances by its presence but itself remains unchanged.

cave, celler, cellier (Fr.). Warehouse (usually underground) or cellar for storing wines and/or spirits.

cellar. Warehouse for storing wines.

centiliter. 1/100 part of a liter.

cep (cépage), cepa (Fr., Sp.). The vinestock.

chai (Fr.). Ground-level or aboveground warehouse, usually kept totally dark, for wines and/or spirits.

chambrer (Fr.). To bring red wine to room temperature (65-68 degrees Fahrenheit) gradually.

chaptalization. The practice of increasing the natural sugar content of the grape juice, before fermentation begins, by the addition of sugar or concentrated grape must when there is such a deficiency, especially in poor vintage years.

charnu (Fr.). Full bodied.

château-bottled. Wine bottled at the château, estate, or vineyard where grapes from which it was made are grown. Applies to Bordeaux wines primarily.

chiaretto (It.). Very light red.

clarete (Sp.). Light red or dark rose.

classified growths. Bordeaux wines listed according to merit in 1855, 1955, and 1959.

climat (Fr.). Vineyard.

cochylis. A disease of the vine.

collage (Fr.). Fining or clearing a wine.

commune (Fr.). Parish, a subdivision of a district.

Confréries (Fr.). Wine and gastronomic fraternities, mostly of ancient "guild" origin, such as Burgundy's *Confrérie des Chevaliers du Tastevin* (Brotherhood of Gentlemen of the Tasting Cup) and the *Confrérie de la Chaîne des Rôtisseurs* (Fraternity of the Turners of the Roasting Spit).

consejo regulator (Sp.). Organization for the control and promotion of the *Denominacion de Origen*.

consorzio (It.). Local growers' association with legal standing.

consumo (Port., Sp.). Ordinary wine for local consumption.

cordial. See liqueur.

corks. Stoppers for bottles made from the spongy bark of the cork oak. Portuguese cork is the finest for this purpose.

corky wine. A wine with an unpleasant odor imparted by a diseased cork. This can happen to even the finest wines.

corps (Fr.). Body, richness in alcohol and other substances.

corsé (Fr.). Full bodied.

cosecha (Sp.). Crop or vintage.

coulant (Fr.). Easy, pleasant.

couleur, color (Fr., Sp.). The color of a wine.

coupage (Fr.). Blending or mixing of wines.

coupé (Fr.). A blended wine.

courtier, corredor (Fr., Sp.). Wine broker.

crémant (Fr.). Crackling or slightly sparkling. Given appellation status by I.N.A.O.

criadera (Sp.). Nursery stage in the sherry maturing system.

criado y embotellado por (Sp.). Grown and bottled by.

cru (Fr.). Vineyard, growth.

cru classé (Fr.). See classified growths.

crust. The heavy deposit thrown off by red wines that have been long in bottles. Applies principally to Vintage Portos.

cuit, cotto (Fr., It.). A wine that has been heated or "cooked."

cup. Iced wine flavored with fresh fruits, brandy, liqueurs, and/or herbs.

cuvaison (Fr.). The period of first or violent fermentation during which the must remains in contact with the grape skins to obtain its color. Applies only to red wines.

cuvée (Fr.). The blend.

decanter. A glass bottle or container into which wines or spirits are poured from their original containers, for serving.

decanting. Transferring a wine or spirit from one bottle to another.

dégorgement (Fr.). Disgorging process used in production of Champagne to remove the sediment.

délicat (Fr.). Delicate, not harsh or coarse.

delimited area. A certain area whose regional name by law is given to the wine or spirit produced within the geographical limits of the region.

demi (Fr.). Half.

demijohn. A fat-bellied, wicker-encased bottle holding 4 to 10 gallons.

demi-muid (Fr.). Cask holding 157 gallons used in Cognac.

demi-queue (Fr.). A Burgundy cask measuring 228 liters, a half-*queue*.

demi-sec (Fr.). Semidry. Also, a fairly sweet type of Champagne.

Denominacion de Origen (Sp.). Guarantee of origin and authenticity of a wine.

density. See specific gravity.

deposit. Normal sediment precipitated by a wine as it matures in the bottle.

dépôt (Fr.). Natural sediment that all wines deposit; more visible in red wines.

dextrin. One of the sugars resulting from starch being exposed to the action of malt.

diastase. The enzyme, formed by malting barley, that causes the starch in grains to be converted into sugars.

dolce (It.). Sweet.

domaine (Fr.). Followed by a name, it denotes ownership. For example, Domaine de la Romanée-Conti.

Domäne (Ger.). Usually a state-owned and/or state-managed vineyard property.

dosage (Fr.). The amount of sugar used in preparing Champagne.

douil (Fr.). An open cask holding 7 to 8 hectoliters in which the grapes are carted from the vineyard to the pressing house in the Bordeaux wine region.

doux (Fr.). Sweet. Also, the sweetest type of Champagne.

dry. The opposite of sweet, literally, lacking in sugar.

duftig (Ger.). Fragrant, fine bouquet.

dulce (Sp.). Sweet.

dulce apagado (Sp.). See mistelle.

dunder. Sugarcane juice remains, used in making full-bodied rums.

dur (Fr.). Hard, harsh.

earthy. A flavor in wines reminiscent of earth or soil, highly prized in Burgundy where it is called *goût de terroir*.

eau de vie (Fr.). Spirits, generally brandy. Literally, "water of life."

eau de vie de marc (Fr.). A brandy distilled from the fermented pomace or husks of grapes after they have been pressed for wine.

echt (Ger.). Genuine.

edel (Ger.). Noble, extra fine.

Edelbeerenauslese (Ger.). Term used before 1971 to denote an especially fine Beerenauslese.

Edelfäule (Ger.). Noble mold that settles on overripe grapes. See also *pourriture noble*.

Edelsüsse (Ger.). Great natural, noble sweetness.

edes (Hun.). Sweet.

égrappage (Fr.). Process of destemming grapes before they are pressed.

égrappoir (Fr.). Apparatus used to perform the *égrappage*.

Ehrwein (Ger.). Very fine wine.

Eigene abfüllung (Ger.). Bottled by the producer.

Eiswein (Ger.). A wine produced from perfectly ripened grapes that have been partially frozen while still hanging on the vine. Eiswein used to be very rare, appearing perhaps once every twenty or twenty-five years. It is now made more often but only in very limited quantities. Eiswein is quite elegant and very rich and may be considered between an Auslese and an Edelbeerenauslese.

élégance (Fr.). A term used to denote a wine of a poor vintage with delicacy and lightness but that does not promise longevity.

éleveur (Fr.). See *négociant-éleveur*.

élixir (Fr.). Old term used in France for liqueur.

enology, oenology. The science or study of wines.

enzymes. The organic catalysts of yeasts and other substances, which cause various reactions, including alcoholic or vinous fermentation.

Erben (Ger.). Heirs of, or estate of.

erdig (Ger.). Earthy.

espumoso (Sp.). Sparkling.

Essenz, Eszencia (Hun.). Essence. The rarest and richest Tokay wine.

estate-bottled. Produced and bottled by the vineyard owner-producer, traditionally in Burgundy.

esters. The volatile compounds formed by the combination of organic acids with the alcohols. Esters give the bouquet of a wine or spirit.

estufa (Port.). Hothouses or heated cellars where Madeiras are baked when young.

ether. A sweet-smelling compound that contributes to the bouquet of a wine, formed by the dehydration of alcohol molecules.

ethyl alcohol. The principal alcohol found in alcoholic beverages.

extra sec. Extra dry. Also, a type of dry Champagne, somewhat sweeter than *brut*.

fad (Ger.). Insipid.
faible (Fr.). Thin, weak.
Fass (Ger.). A cask of 600-liter capacity employed in all German wine regions except the Moselle, where the cask is called *Fuder*.
fein, feine, feinste (Ger.). Fine, very fine, finest.
feints. The first and last parts of a distillation, also called the heads and tails.
ferme (Fr.). Firm, full.
fermentation. The chemical process whereby sugars are broken down into ethyl alcohol, carbon dioxide, and other by-products.
fett (Ger.). Full, big; literally, fat.
fiasco (It.). Raffia-wrapped flask employed for bottling Chianti, Orvieto, and some other Italian wines. Plural *fiaschi*.
filter. To clarify liquids by passing them through a fine screen or permeable membrane.
finage (Fr.). All of the vineyards of a given subdistrict.
fine. To clarify wine by adding materials that combine with the particles floating in it and, after a short period, settle to the bottom, leaving the wine clear.
fine maison (Fr.). The house brandy served in a restaurant.
finesse (Fr.). Fineness, delicacy.
fino (Sp.). The driest type of sherry.
flagon. An ancient wine flask.
flask. A flat-sided bottle usually holding 12½ ounces but with a capacity of anywhere from 8 to 32 ounces.
flinty. See *pierre-à-fusil*.
flor (Sp.). See flower.
flower, flowering. Unique property of the yeast in the Jerez sherry region of Spain. Multiplying profusely, the yeast forms a film on the surface of the wine in the cask, especially in the case of the drier, more delicate fino types, giving sherry its nutty character. A similar flowering of the yeast also occurs in the casks of the *vin jaune* and *vin de paille* of Château-Châlon and Château-d'Arlay, in the Côtes de Jura region of France, and in South Africa.
flowery. A pleasing, fragrant perfume in some white wines.
fort (Fr.). Strong, with high alcohol.
fortified wines. Wines whose natural alcoholic strength is increased by the addition of brandy. Term not recognized by the B.A.T.F.
foudre (Fr.). A large storage cask for wines.
foxiness. The very pronounced grapey flavor found in wines produced from American grapes in the eastern United States.
franc (Fr.). Natural-tasting, clean.
frappé (Fr.). Iced. A liqueur served with finely cracked ice.
Freiherr (Ger.). Baron.
frisch (Ger.). Fresh, sprightly.

frizzante (It.). Semisparkling, crackling.
fruity, *fruité, fruchtig* (Eng., Fr., Ger.). Describes the frank taste of the grape found in good wines.
Fuder (Ger.). A Moselle wine cask holding 1,000 liters.
Fülle (Ger.). Richness, fullness.
fumet (Fr.). A pronounced bouquet.
fumeux (Fr.). Spirited, heady.
fungus. Mold that appears when wine is kept carelessly and when the most careful hygiene is not observed.
Fürst (Ger.). Prince.
fusel oil. The higher alcohols found in all spirits.

gallon. A liquid measure containing 128 fluid ounces.
Gay Lussac. French inventor of the alcoholometer and the standard metric measures of alcoholic strengths, in use today, that bear his name.
gefällig (Ger.). Pleasing, harmonious.
gefüllt (Ger.). Full, rich.
Gemarkung (Ger.). The boundary of a district in which wine is grown.
généreux (Fr.). Generous, warming.
Gewächs (Ger.). Growth or vineyard. Always followed by the name of the proprietor, to denote ownership.
gezuckert (Ger.). Sugared or improved.
glatt (Ger.). Smooth.
goût (Fr.). Taste.
goût américain (Fr.). Sweet Champagne to please the South American market.
goût anglais (Fr.). A very dry Champagne for the English market.
goût de bois (Fr.). Woody taste.
goût de bouchon (Fr.). Corky taste.
goût de paille (Fr.). Straw, musty taste.
goût de pique (Fr.). Vinegary taste.
goût de terroir (Fr.). Earthy taste.
goût d'évent (Fr.). Flat, lifeless taste.
gradi, gradi alcool, grado alcoolico (It.). Followed by a number, percentage of alcohol by volume.
Graf (Ger.). Count.
grain spirits. Patent still spirits obtained from malted and unmalted grain.
grappa (It.). Brandy distilled from grape pressings in Italy and California. See also *marc*.
green. Very young, light, such as *vinho verde* ("green wine") of Portugal.
gros producteur (Fr.). A vine variety that produces large quantities of grapes but not fine-quality wines.
grossier (Fr.). Harsh, coarse.
growth. A vineyard (*cru* in French).
grün (Ger.). Young, green, immature.
gut (Ger.). Good.

habzó (Hun.). Sparkling.
Halb-fuder (Ger.). The standard Moselle wine cask containing 500 liters, a half-*Fuder*.
Halb-stück (Ger.). The standard Rhine wine cask containing 600 liters, a half-*Stück*.

harmonisch (Ger.). Harmonious, well-balanced.

hart (Ger.). Hard, acid, even vinegary.

heads. The spirits obtained at the beginning of distillation.

hecho (Sp.). Made. A completed wine ready for bottling and shipping.

hectare. 100 ares, equaling 2.47 acres.

hectoliter. 100 liters, equaling 26.418 gallons.

herb (Ger.). Bitter.

high wines. The useful spirits obtained in distillation after eliminating heads and tails.

Hochgewächs (Ger.). Superior vineyard or growth.

Hock. The English abbreviation for Hochheimer that today denotes any Rhine wine.

hogshead. Cask of varying measure. A hogshead of sherry contains 66 gallons.

honigartig (Ger.). Honeylike.

Hospices de Beaune (Fr.). A charitable hospital in Beaune, Burgundy, supported by an annual public sale of wine.

hübsch (Ger.). Nice, delicate.

hydrometer. An apparatus used to measure the density of alcoholic beverages and other liquids.

imbottigliato (It.). Bottled.

impériale (Fr.). An oversize Bordeaux bottle with a capacity of 8 bottles, or 6 liters; known as a Methuselah when used for Champagne.

I.N.A.O. (Fr.). *Institut National des Appellations d'Origine des Vins et Eaux-de-Vie.*

informing grape. The principal grape that gives a wine its varietal character.

isinglass. Substance made from fish gelatine; used as a fining material.

jarra (Sp.). Wooden or metal jar holding 11½ to 12½ liters, used in all sherry blending operations as the basic unit of measure.

Jeroboam or double magnum. Oversize Bordeaux or Champagne bottle, holding 4 regular bottles or 104 ounces.

jigger. The standard 1½-ounce measure used in cocktail and mixed drink recipes.

jung (Ger.). Young, immature.

Kabinett (Ger.). The driest wine of Qualitätswein mit Prädikat.

keg. A small, stout cask.

Keller (Ger.). Cellar.

Kellerabfüllung, kellerabzug (Ger.). Bottled at the cellar or estate.

kilogram, kg. 1,000 grams, or 2.2 pounds.

klein (Ger.). Small.

Körper (Ger.). Body.

kräftig (Ger.). Robust, rich in alcohol.

kräusen (Ger.). A method of carbonating beers.

lagar (Sp., Port.). The pressing and treading trough.

Lage (Ger.). Vineyard site.

lager. To store beer for aging and sedimentation. All American beers today are lagered.

lebendig (Ger.). Fresh, racy.

lees. The sediment that settles on the bottom of a cask of wine.

léger (Fr.). Light, lacking in body.

levante (Sp.). Hot, searing wind that blows over the sherry region, said to originate in the Sahara Desert.

lías (Sp.). Wine lees.

licoroso (Sp.). Rich, sweet, fortified.

Limousin (Fr.). The oak used for the casks in which Cognac is aged.

liqueur (Fr.). A sweetened, flavored distilled spirit.

liqueur de tirage (dosage) (Fr.). In Champagne, the sugar solution added at the time of bottling to ensure a proper secondary fermentation.

liqueur d'expédition (Fr.). In Champagne, the sugar solution added at the time of disgorging to give the varying degrees of sweetness.

liquoreux (Fr.). Rich, sweet.

lodges. The warehouses where Porto wines are stored in Vila Nova de Gaia, Portugal. Also, the warehouses where Madeira wines are stored in Funchal, Madeira.

low wines. In pot still distillation, the spirits obtained from the first operation.

maderisé (Fr.). A white wine that has become very dark and taken on a woody character because of oxidation and exposure to heat.

mager (Ger.). Thin, lacking in body, undistinguished.

magnum. A double-size bottle.

maigre (Fr.). Thin, weak.

malt. Grain, generally barley, that has been allowed to germinate for a short period so that the enzyme diastase may be formed.

malts. Scotch whisky made entirely from malted barley.

marc (Fr.). The grapes required to load a Champagne press for a pressing; also a distillate of skins, pips, or husks remaining after the grapes have been pressed.

mashing. The operation of mixing ground meal and malt with water to liquefy the starches so they may be converted into sugars by the diastase in the malt.

Master of Wine, M.W. Professional title in England acquired by members of the trade after many years of study and rigorous examinations.

metallic. See *pierre-à-fusil.*

Methuselah. Oversize Champagne bottle, holding 7 to 8 regular bottles or 179 to 208 ounces.

mildew. A disease that attacks the vines in rainy or damp seasons.

millésime (Fr.). Vintage year.

mise d'origine (Fr.). Bottled by the shipper.

mis en bouteille à la propriété (Fr.). Bottled by the shipper.

mis en bouteille au château (Fr.). Bottled at the château where the grapes are grown in Bordeaux.

mis en bouteille au domaine (Fr.). Bottled at the property where it is made in Burgundy; estate-bottled.

mistelle (Fr.). Grape must whose fermentation is halted by adding sufficient brandy to give it an alcohol content of 15 percent. The natural unfermented grape sugar remains as sweetening. *Mistelles* are used as sweetening wines, particularly in making vermouths and aperitif wines.

moelleux (Fr.). Soft, velvety.

Monimpex (Hun.). The Hungarian state export monopoly.

monopole (Fr.). A trademark name.

mou (Fr.). Flabby, lacking in character.

mousseux (Fr.). Sparkling.

mûr (Fr.). Balanced, fruity.

must, *moût, Moot, mosto* (Eng., Fr., Ger., Sp.). Grape juice before and during fermentation.

mustimeter. See saccharometer.

musty. Moldy, unpleasant.

muté (Fr.). *Mistelle* or a sweet wine whose fermentation has been inhibited by the addition of brandy.

Mycodermae aceti. The vinegar yeast.

Mycodermae vini. The yeast responsible for vinous fermentation.

Natur, Naturrein, Naturwein (Ger.). Completely natural wine to which no sugar has been added.

nature (Fr.). Term used in Champagne labeling interchangeably with *brut.* Also denotes still Champagne.

Nebuchadnezzar. Extraordinary Champagne bottle size holding 20 regular bottles or 520 ounces.

négociant-éleveur (Fr.). A merchant who buys wine from the grower, blends, bottles, and then markets it.

nero (It.). Very dark red.

nerveux (Fr.). Vigorous, with long-keeping qualities.

nervig (Ger.). Good, full-bodied.

neutral spirits. Spirits distilled out from any material at a proof of 190 or more, regardless of whether they are later reduced in proof.

Nicolauswein (Ger.). Denotes a wine produced from grapes gathered on December 6, St. Nicholas Day.

nip. Miniature bottle of spirits.

nose. The bouquet or aroma of a wine or spirit.

nu (Fr.). "Bare." Term denoting that the price quoted for a barrel of wine does not include the cost of the cask.

nube (Sp.). Cloudiness.

Öchsle (Ger.). The German scale for measuring the sugar content of the grape must before fermentation. The determination is made by the higher weight in grams of the must in relation to an equal volume of water, or its specific gravity. Twenty-five percent of this greater weight is known to be sugar. Thus, 100 liters of must with a reading of 100 *Öchsle* contains 25 kilograms of natural grape sugar.

octave, *octavilla* (Eng., Sp.). An eighth of a cask. In the sherry trade, 16½ gallons.

oeil de perdrix (Fr.). Partridge eye. Describes pale or still pink sparkling wine, usually from Burgundy, Switzerland, or California.

oenology. See enology.

oïdium. A fungus disease that attacks the vines.

ölig (Ger.). Having high consistency that gives wine the impression of being oily as it is poured..

oloroso (Sp.). The full-bodied, deeper-colored sherries. Although very dry in their *soleras,* they are usually shipped as sweet-tasting sherries by blending sweet wines with them.

organoleptic examination. The method of judging the quality of wines, beers, and spirits by the human organs of sight, smell, and taste.

Originalabfüllung, Originalabzug (Ger.). Term used before 1971 to denote original bottling. Equivalent to estate bottling.

overproof. A spirit whose alcoholic strength is more than 100 proof.

palma (Sp.). The special chalk marking used to identify a very fine fino sherry (𝗒).

palo cortado (Sp.). The special marking used to denote *dos rayas,* sherries that have developed fino characteristics (⟋).

Passe Tout Grains (Fr.). A Burgundy wine made of a mixture of at least one-third Pinot Noir and the balance Gamay grapes.

passito (It.). A wine made from partially dried grapes.

Pasteur, Louis (1822-1895). Great French scientist whose studies on malt and vinous fermentations gave the first complete explanation of these phenomena.

pasteurization. A process discovered by Louis Pasteur of arresting, making inactive, or killing the ferments in wine, beer, milk, and other liquids through heating the liquid and holding it for a brief time at 131 to 158 degrees Fahrenheit.

patent still. The two-column or continuous still "patented" by Aeneas Coffey in 1832.

pelure d'oignon (Fr.). Onion skin. The brown tinge that certain red wines take on after aging.

perfume. The fragrance of a wine or spirit.

Perlwein (Ger.). Slightly sparkling wine.

pétillant (Fr.). Crackling or semisparkling.

petit (Fr.). Small, thin.

Pfarrgut (Ger.). Vineyard owned by a church whose product is given to the parson or preacher as part of his remuneration.

Phylloxera vastatrix. The American grape louse.

pièce (Fr.). A cask holding approximately 60 gallons, used in many French wine regions.

pierre-à-fusil (Fr.). Gun flint. A sharp, metallic tang sometimes noticed in bone-dry wines, especially those from Chablis.

pikant (Ger.). Attractive, intriguing.

pint. Liquid measure of 16 ounces.

pipe. The cask used in the Porto, Lisbon, and Tarragona wine trades containing 138 gallons and in the Madeira trade where a pipe holds 110 gallons.

piquant (Fr.). A pleasant point of acidity. Generally applied to dry white wines.

piqué (Fr.). A term used to describe a wine that has begun to turn and whose only use is for vinegar.

piquette (Fr.). A common, ordinary wine used in certain parts of France.

pisador (Sp.). One who treads the grapes at vintage time in the sherry region.

plastering. The system of adding *yeso* or gypsum to grapes when they are treaded and pressed in the *lagar* in Jerez, Spain.

plat (Fr.). Dull, flat, lifeless.

plein (Fr.). Full bodied.

pony. One-ounce brandy or liqueur glass.

portes-greffes (Fr.). The hardy *Phylloxera*-resistant American rootstocks on which the fine vines of Europe are grafted.

pot still. The old-fashioned, fat-bellied, taperedneck still that requires two distinct operations to produce the spirit that is eventually bottled.

pourriture noble (Fr.). "Noble rot," the state of overripeness of the grapes of the Sauternes region of Bordeaux. It is in reality a yeast or mold known scientifically as *Botrytis cinerea*.

précoce (Fr.). Precocious, maturing rapidly.

pressoir, prensa (Fr., Sp.). Wine press.

proof. An arbitrary system of measuring the alcoholic strength of a liquid. In America, a spirit of 100 proof is one that contains exactly 50 percent alcohol by volume at 60 degrees Fahrenheit. Each degree of proof represents ½ percent alcohol.

puncheon. A large cask of varying capacities.

pupitres (Fr.). The special racks used in the Champagne cellars during *remuage* (shaking sediment onto the cork).

puttony (Hun.). The measure in which grapes are gathered in Tokay-Hegyalja. Plural *puttonos*.

Qualitätswein (Ger.). Superior table wine subject to certain controls, from any of eleven designated regions.

Qualitätswein mit Prädikat (Ger.). As above, but with more stringent controls and special attributes.

quart. Liquid measure of 32 ounces.

quarter bottle. Wine bottle containing 6 to 6½ ounces, one-fourth the size of a regular bottle.

quarter cask. In cases where the standard cask, pipe, or butt is too large for a merchant, casks containing one-fourth the original are used. Quarter casks vary in contents, depending on the wine region where they are used.

queue (Fr.). Burgundy casks holding 2 *pièces*, a total of 120 gallons or 456 liters.

quinquina (Fr.). Quinine. Most French aperitif wines use the word as a description because they are quinined wines.

quinta (Port.). Vineyard or winery estate in Portugal, similar to château in the Bordeaux wine region.

quintal, quintale (Fr., It.). 100 kilograms.

race (Fr.). Breed.

racking. The drawing of wine off its lees into a fresh, clean cask. Also, the transference of any alcoholic beverage from one cask or vat to another.

rancio (Sp.). A term used to describe a sweet fortified wine that has lost some color through age in the bottle. Such a wine acquires a special aroma.

rassig (Ger.). With race and breed.

rauh (Ger.). Raw, harsh.

raya (Sp.). The chalk mark used in the sherry region to identify wines that will become finos or amontillados (/).

récemment dégorgé (Fr.). Recently disgorged.

récolte (Fr.). Vintage.

rectifying. Anything that changes the natural state of a spirit, such as redistilling after it has been barreled or adding coloring matter, sweetening, or any other flavoring material. Adding water to reduce proof does not constitute rectifying.

redondo (Sp.). Round, well-balanced.

reduce. To lower alcoholic strength of a spirit by the addition of water.

red wine. Any wine that has the slightest part of red coloring, obtained from the pigment found on the inside of the grape skin.

refresh. To add young wine to an older one (in cask) to give the old wine new life. This term is also used in the same manner with respect to spirits, particularly brandies.

Rehoboam. Oversize Champagne bottle holding 6 regular bottles or 156 ounces.

reif (Ger.). Ripe, fine, sweet.

rein (Ger.). Pure.

reintönig (Ger.). Well-balanced, very good.

remuage (Fr.). The "shaking-down" operation employed in the production of Champagne, whereby the bottles are placed head downward and periodically shaken and turned slightly to cause the sediment to settle on the cork. In the United States the term used is *riddling*.

Rentamt (Ger.). Collection office.

reserva (Sp.). Mature quality.

riche (Fr.). Having a generous bouquet, flavor, and fullness of body.

rick. Framework or rack in a warehouse in which barrels of distilled spirits are stored for aging. Also, to place or rack barrels.

riddling. See *remuage*.

riserva (It.). Mature quality.

robe. The sheen of color left on the inside of a glass from a highly pigmented red wine.

rociar (Sp.). To refresh an old solera with young new wine.

rondeur (Fr.). Roundness.

rosé, *rosato, rosado* (Eng., It., Sp.). A pale red wine obtained by removing the grape skins as soon as the required amount of color has been attained.

rosso (It.). Red.

Rotwein (Ger.). Red table wine.

ruby. A port of a very deep red color, usually quite young, in contrast to one that has been aged for some time in wood and has become "tawny," pale in color, through repeated finings.

rund (Ger.). Round, harmonious.

saccharometer. Instrument used to measure the sugar content of must or of wines or liqueurs.

saftig (Ger.). Juicy, succulent.

Salmanazar. Oversize Champagne bottle holding 10 to 12 regular bottles or 270 to 312 ounces.

sancocho (Sp.). Syrup produced by simmering or cooking must to one-third its original volume. Used in the sherry blend to sweeten and color the wine.

sauber (Ger.). Clean, pure.

scantling. The stout wooden beams or supports on which the casks rest in the cellar.

schal (Ger.). Musty, tired.

Schaumwein (Ger.). Sparkling wine.

Schloss (Ger.). Castle.

schlossabzug (Ger.). Bottled at the castle's cellars, equivalent to estate-bottled.

schnapps. Generic Dutch and German term denoting spirituous liquors.

Schwefel (Ger.). Sulfur smell in the bouquet of the wine.

sec (Fr.). Dry. Also, a medium-sweet Champagne.

secco, seco (It., Sp.). Dry.

sediment. The natural deposit found in wines as they mature, formed by the crystallization and settling or precipitation of bitartrates, tannins, and pigments.

Sekt (Ger.). Sparkling wine.

self whiskies. Used in the Scotch whisky trade to denote a "straight" or unblended Scotch malt whisky.

sève (Fr.). Sappy, aromatic, vigorous.

Sikes (Sykes). Hydrometer and tables for measuring alcoholic strengths that are in use in England; invented by Bartholomew Sikes.

skunky. Describing the off aroma in beer that has been exposed to excessive light and heat.

slatko (Yug.). Sweet.

solear (Sp.). Sunning. The exposure of the grapes to the sun (*sol*) for 24 to 48 hours in the sherry region.

solera (Sp.). The system of tiered casks used to blend sherry.

sophistiquer (Fr.). To falsify a wine or to ameliorate a defective wine with anything that will cover up its defects.

souche (Fr.). *Cep* or vine rootstock.

sour mash. Yeasting process in which at least one-quarter of the working yeast from a previous fermentation *and* fresh yeast may be added to the mash to induce fermentation.

soutirer (Fr.). To rack clear wine from one cask into a fresh one.

soyeux (Fr.). Silky, smooth, soft roundness. Lacking in roughness.

Spätlese (Ger.). Late gathered. A wine made from late-picked bunches of grapes. Generally sweeter than wine made from grapes gathered earlier.

specific gravity. A measure of the density of a liquid or solid; the ratio of the weight of any volume of a liquid or solid to the weight of an equal volume of water.

spirits. The generic term for distilled beverages.

split. See quarter bottle.

spritzig (Ger.). Prickling, slightly effervescent.

spumante (It.). Sparkling.

stahlig (Ger.). Steely, austere.

still. The apparatus in which, by application of heat, the alcohol in a liquid may be separated and recovered. Pot still is the original form of still or alembic; Coffey still, patent still, and double-column still are three names applied to the continuous-operation still.

still wine. Table wine without any additional alcohol, carbon dioxide, or flavorings.

stirrup-cup. A cup for the parting drink. The name comes from an old custom of having a last drink with a guest after he had mounted his horse.

stolno vino (Yug.). Table wine.

Stück, Stückfasser (Ger.). The standard of cask measure, used in the Rhine, containing 1,200 liters.

suho (Yug.). Dry.

süss (Ger.). Sweet.

sweet mash. Yeasting process in which fresh yeast is added to the mash to induce fermentation.

Tafelwein (Ger.). Ordinary table wine from any of the five Tafelwein regions.

tannin, tannic. Organic compounds found mostly in red grapes, their woody stems, and new wood casks used for aging wines. They give the wine astringency and some bitterness when young, and they give the wine the ability to develop and age. Tannin is a large part of the sediment that eventually forms in sturdy red wines.

tawny. The quality of paleness that Portos acquire when matured in wood. This loss of red color comes from repeated finings. Such wines are Tawny Portos.

teinturier (Fr.). Grapes used primarily for the abundance of color they contribute to the must.

tendre (Fr.). A rather light and delicate wine, usually a young wine.

tête de cuvée (Fr.). Outstanding growth; generally used in Burgundy.

tierce, terzo, tercero (Fr., It., Sp.). A cask holding one-third of a butt or pipe.

tilts. Bars used for adjusting casks or scantlings to the desired position.

tinto (Sp.). Red.

tirage (Fr.). Drawing off wines or spirits into other containers, usually from casks into bottles.

tonelero (Sp.). Cooper.

tonneau (Fr.). Tun. Term used in the Bordeaux wine trade representing 4 *barriques* of 225 liters, or 900 liters. This is the unit of measure in which wines are sold in the bulk trade, the equivalent of 96 cases of finished wine.

Traube (Ger.). Bunch of grapes.

Traubenkelter (Ger.). Hydraulic grape press.

trocken (Ger.). Dry.

Trockenbeerenauslese (Ger.). Wine made from individually selected, dry, raisinlike grapes. Weather conditions must be perfect throughout the summer and the late vintage season for a Trockenbeerenauslese wine to be made. It is very rare and very sweet.

uisgebeatha, uisgebaugh (Celtic). Water of life, whisky.

ullage. The air space in a cask or bottle due to evaporation or leakage. May result in deterioration of contents.

underproof. Describes a spirit whose alcoholic strength is below proof. In the United States this is a spirit of less than 100 proof, as opposed to an overproof spirit having a strength of over 100 proof.

ungezuckert (Ger.). Unsugared, pure.

usé (Fr.). A wine that has passed its peak and is on the decline.

uva (Sp.). Grape.

vats. The containers in which alcoholic beverages are fermented or blended.

vatting. Mixing or blending in a vat.

velouté (Fr.). Rich, mellow, velvety, soft.

vendange (Fr.). Grape harvest.

vendange tardif (Fr.). Late-picked wine, implying more strength and/or sweetness.

vendangeur (Fr.). Grape harvester.

vendemmia, vendimia (It., Sp.). Vintage or harvest.

venencia (Sp.). The special cup used for drawing samples from the sherry butts in the *bodega*. It is a cylindrical silver cup attached to a long, flexible strip of whalebone.

viejo (Sp.). Old.

vif (Fr.). Lively, brisk.

vigne (Fr.). Vine.

vigneron (Fr.). Vine grower.

vignoble (Fr.). Vineyard.

vin (Fr.). Wine.

viña (Sp.). Vine. Also, vineyard in Argentina and Chile.

vin blanc (Fr.). White wine.

vin cuit (Fr.). A concentrated wine used to improve thin wines.

vin de garde (Fr.). A wine worth keeping, for laying down.

vin de goutte (Fr.). Wine made from the last pressing. It is generally of poor quality.

vin de messe (Fr.). Altar wine.

vin de paille (Fr.). White wine made from grapes that have been spread on straw (*paille*) mats to dry in the sun, before pressing.

vin de pays (Fr.). Small wines of each region, consumed locally.

vin doux (Fr.). A sweet wine.

vine. Climbing plant, one variety of which produces grapes.

viñedo (Sp.). Vineyard.

vineux (Fr.). Vinosity.

vin gris (Fr.). A pale pink wine made in Lorraine.

vinho (Port.). Wine.

vinho claro (Port.). Natural wine.

vinho estufado (Port.). Madeira wine after it has been baked in the *estufa*.

vinho generoso (Port.). Fortified wine.

vinho surdo (Port.). Fortified wine. According to Portuguese law, Porto wine must be a *vinho surdo*.

vinho verde (Port.). Light, young white or red wine produced in northern Portugal.

viniculture. The science of making wine.

vini tipici (It.). Typical or standard wines.

vin mousseux (Fr.). Sparkling wine.

vin nature (Fr.). Natural, unsweetened wine.

vino (It., Sp.). Wine.

vino corriente (Sp.). Ordinary wine for local consumption.

vino crudo (Sp.). Young or immature wine.

vino de añada (Sp.). Young wine of one vintage, ready for the *criadera* reserves.

vino de color (Sp.). Concentrated wine used in the sherry *bodega* to give color and sweetness to the final blend.

vino de crianza (Sp.). A suitable wine destined to become sherry.

vino de mesa (Sp.). Table wine.

vino frizzante (It.). A lightly sparkling type of wine in Italy.

vino liquoroso (It.). Very sweet wine.

vino maestro (Sp.). Master wine. A sweet, full wine used to lend character and body to weaker, thinner wine.

vin ordinaire (Fr.). Ordinary cheap wine for immediate consumption.

vinosity. The character of a wine, the balance of its bouquet, flavor, and body.

vino spumante (It.). Sparkling wine.

vinous. Pertaining to wine.

vin rosé (Fr.). Pink wine.

vin rouge (Fr.). Red wine.

Vin (Vino) Santo (It.). Sweet white wine produced from dried grapes in the Chianti region of Tuscany.

vin sec (Fr.). Dry wine.

vintage. Gathering the grape crop and making the wine. Also, the year when the wine is made, which often appears on wine labels.

vintage wine. In certain wine regions, particularly Champagne and Porto, the product of exceptional years only is dated. In other regions wines are dated each year.

virgin brandy. Unblended Cognac brandy.

viticulture. The science of growing grapes.

vitis (Latin). Vine.

vornehm (Ger.). Noble, aristocratic.

vörös (Hun.). Red.

Wachstum (Ger.). See *Gewächs.*

wash. In a distillery (usually whisky), the fermented liquor when it is ready to go to the still. In a Scotch distillery, the still that receives the wash is known as the wash still.

weepers. Bottles that show leakage through the cork.

Wein (Ger.). Wine.

Weinbau (Ger.). Viticulture.

Weingut (Ger.). Vineyard or estate.

Weinkeller (Ger.). Wine cellar.

Weisswein (Ger.). White wine.

wernig (Ger.). Vinous, vinosity.

wine. The fermented juice of fruit, usually grapes unless otherwise specified. Ideally, wine is the naturally fermented juice of freshly gathered ripe grapes that have been pressed at or near the place where gathered.

wine broker. An intermediary who acts for buyers and for a vineyard owner.

Winzergenossenschaft (Ger.). Wine growers' cooperative.

woody. The taste of a wine or spirit that has spent too much time in wood, sometimes called *goût de bois.*

wormwood. A perennial herb, *Artemisia absinthium,* aromatic, tonic, and bitter. Formerly used in the preparation of absinthe, certain liqueurs, and vermouths.

würzig (Ger.). Spicy, desirable, flowery.

yayin. A biblical Hebrew term for wine.

yeast. The plant organism whose fermentative qualities cause sugars to break down into alcohol and carbon dioxide gas.

yema (Sp.). The must resulting from the treading before the grapes are subjected to pressure. *Yema* is Spanish means "yolk of an egg" or the core of any product.

yeso (Sp.). Powdered gypsum (calcium sulfate) sprinkled on the grapes in the *lagar* at the time of treading and pressing to fix the tartaric acid during fermentation of the must into sherry wine.

zapatos de pisar (Sp.). Special nail-studded shoes worn by the men who tread the grapes in the *lagar* in the Jerez sherry region.

zymase. The enzyme in yeast cells that causes vinous fermentation and whose catalytic action converts sugars into alcohol and carbon dioxide gas.

APPENDIX T
BIBLIOGRAPHY

This bibliography reflects, as much as possible, the great explosion in books about wines. We have tried to be as complete as possible, considering limitations of space, using the latest *Books in Print* as a reference.

Books listed have been separated into different sections as follows: audiovisual wine information; computer software on wines and spirits; general books on wine; general books on spirits and beers; wines of the United States (with a separate section on California); wines of France, Germany, Italy; wines of Spain, Portugal, and other European countries; wines of the Middle East, Africa, Far East, and Australia; wine service and marketing; wine and health; a how-to section that includes making wines, beers, and liqueurs at home; technical books; mixed drinks; and cooking with wines and spirits.

AUDIOVISUAL WINE INFORMATION

Balzer, Robert Lawrence. *Adventures in Wine.* Tustin, Calif.: The Wine Press, Ltd., 1982. Two hours on 3 video cassettes.

Brison, Fred R., and Jones, A. Eric. *The Video Wine Guide.* Mill Valley, Calif., and Houston, Tex.: Serendipity Productions, 1982. One ninety-minute video cassette.

Lembeck, Harriet. *A Wine Tasting Journey with Harriet Lembeck: An Adventure in Wine Educa-* tion. New York: Wine Wisdom, Inc., 1983. Six hours on 4 audio cassettes.

Lichine, Alexis. *The Joy of Wine.* New York: David Geller Associates, 1982. Eighty minutes on 2 audio cassettes or records.

The Wines of California. Indianapolis, Ind.: Kartes Video Communications, 1982. Four hours on 4 video cassettes.

COMPUTER SOFTWARE ON WINES AND SPIRITS

Cellar Master. Salem, Ore.: Vintage Information Systems, 1982.

International Standard Wine Identification System (*"ISWIS"*). Included with *Cellar Master* or available separately.

Micro Barmate. Rockport, Maine: Virtual Combiatics, 1982.

Wine Cellar. Chico, Calif.: WE Software, 1982.

Wine Record. Salem, Ore.: Vintage Information System, 1983.

Wine Steward. Salem, Ore.: Vintage Information System, 1983.

GENERAL BOOKS ON WINE

Adams, Leon D. *The Commonsense Book of Wine.* Boston: Houghton Mifflin, 1975. Paper.

Allen, H. Warner. *Romance of Wine.* New York: Dover, 1971. Paper.

Asher, Gerald. *On Wine.* New York: Random House, 1982.

Bespaloff, Alexis. *New Signet Book of Wine.* New York: New American Library, 1980. Paper.

———. *Guide to Inexpensive Wines.* New York: Simon & Schuster, 1975. Paper.

Blum, Howard L. *The Wines and Vines of Europe.* Elmsford, N.Y.: Benjamin Co., n.d.

Brillat-Savarin, Jean A. *Physiology of Taste.* Translated by M. F. K. Fisher. New York: Alfred A. Knopf, 1971.

Broadbent, Michael. *Wine Tasting: Enjoying and Understanding,* 6th ed. New York: International Publications Service (Christie Wine Publications), 1979.

———. *The Great Vintage Wine Book.* New York: Alfred A. Knopf, 1980.

Churchill, Creighton. *The New World of Wines,* 2nd rev. ed. New York: Macmillan, 1980. Paper.

de Blij, Harm J. *Wine: A Geographic Appreciation.* n. p.: Rowman & Allanheld, 1983.

DiGiacomo, Louis. *The Clear and Simple Wine Guide.* Harrisburg, Pa.: Stackpole Books, 1981.

Ensrud, Barbara. *The Pocket Guide to Wine,* rev. ed. New York: Perigee (Putnam), 1982. Paper.

Escritt, L. B. *The Wine Cellar,* 2nd ed. New York: International Publications Service, 1972. Paper.

Fingerhut, Bruce M., and Haskin, Steve. *Read That Label: How to Tell What's Inside a Wine Bottle from What's on the Outside.* South Bend, Ind.: Icarus, 1982. Paper.

Gillette, Paul. *Enjoying Wine.* New York: New American Library, 1976. Paper.

Hanssen, Maurice, and Dineen, Jacqueline. *Wines, Beers and Spirits.* New York: Baronet, 1978. Paper.

Henriques, E. Frank. *The Signet Encyclopedia of Wine.* New York. New American Library, 1975. Paper.

Hillman, Howard. *The Diner's Guide to Wines.* New York: Hawthorn Books, 1978. Paper.

Hogg, Anthony. *The Winetaster's Guide to Europe: How to Visit Over 300 Vineyards and Cellars on Your European Vacation.* New York: Dutton, 1980.

Hunderfund, Richard. *Wines, Spirits and Fermentations.* Palo Alto, Calif.: Star Publishing Co., 1982.

Jeffs, Julian. *Dictionary of World Wines, Liqueurs, and Other Drinks.* Toronto: Pagurian Press, 1973.

———. *Wines of Europe.* New York: Taplinger, 1971.

Johnson, Frank E. *The Professional Wine Reference.* New York: Beverage Media, 1978. Paper.

Johnson, Hugh. *Wine,* rev. ed. New York: Simon & Schuster, 1975.

———. *World Atlas of Wine,* rev. ed. New York: Simon & Schuster, 1981.

Kleinsinger, Irene J. *Wine Log.* White Plains, N. Y.: Kleinsinger, 1980. Paper.

Lamb, Richard, and Mittelberger, Ernest. *In Celebration of Wine and Life,* 2nd ed. San Francisco: Wine Appreciation, 1980. Paper.

Lee, Susan. *Signet Book of Inexpensive Wine,* rev. ed. New York: New American Library, 1979. Paper.

Lender, Mark Edward, and Martin, James Kirby. *Drinking in America.* New York: The Free Press (Macmillan), 1983.

Lester, Mary. *Hand Me That Corkscrew, Bacchus.* New York: Piper, 1973.

Lichine, Alexis. *New Encyclopedia of Wines and Spirits,* 3rd ed. New York: Alfred A. Knopf, 1981.

Massee, William E. *Massee's Wine Almanac.* Englewood Cliffs, N. J.: Prentice-Hall, 1980. Paper.

Misch, Robert J. *Quick Guide to Wine,* rev. ed. New York: Cornerstone Library, 1976.

Mittelberger, Ernest. *The Wine Cellar Record.* Edited by Sullivan, Morris and Roux. San Francisco: Wine Appreciation, 1979.

Modern Encyclopedia of Wine, rev. ed. New York: Simon & Schuster, 1982.

Morris, Roger. *The Genie in the Bottle: Unraveling the Myths about Wine.* New York: A & W Pubs., 1981.

The New Great Book of Wine. New York: A & W Pubs., 1982.

Paterson, John. *Choosing Your Wine.* New York: Larousse, 1981.

Peppercorn, David, *et al. Drinking Wine: A Complete Guide with Ratings.* New York: Harbor House Books, 1979.

Postgate, Raymond. *The Plain Man's Guide to Wine.* Revised by John Arlott. New York: Paul S. Eriksson, 1976.

Pratt, James N., and De Caso, Jacques. *The Wine Bibber's Bible,* rev. ed. San Francisco: 101 Productions, 1981. Paper.

Prial, Frank. *Wine Talk.* New York: Times Books, 1978.

Price, Pamela V. *Dictionary of Wines and Spirits.* Mystic, Conn.: Verry, 1981.

———. *Entertaining with Wine.* Philadelphia: International Ideas, 1976.

———. *The Taste of Wine.* New York: Random House, 1975.

Ramey, Bern C. *The Great Wine Grapes and the Wines They Make.* San Francisco: Great Wine Grapes, n.d.

Robards, Terry. *The New York Times Book of Wine.* New York: Avon, 1981. Paper.

———. *Wine Cellar Journal.* New York: Times Books, 1974.

Robinson, Jancis. *The Great Wine Book.* New York: Morrow, 1982.

Saintsbury, George. *Notes on a Cellar Book,* rev. ed. Reprint of 1920 ed. New York: W. H. Smith Pub., 1978.

Seldon, Philip. *How to Buy Wine.* New York: Doubleday, 1982. Paper.

Seward, Desmond. *Monks and Wine.* New York: Crown, 1979.

Sharp, William J., and Martin, Joseph. *Wines: How to Develop Your Taste and Get Your Money's Worth.* Englewood Cliffs, N. J.: Prentice-Hall, 1976. Paper.

Sichel, Peter M. F., and Ley, Judy. *Which Wine? The Wine Drinker's Buying Guide.* New York: A & W Pubs., 1977. Paper.

Simon, André L. *All About Wines,* 8 vols. Brooklyn, N. Y.: Shalom, n.d. Paper.

———. *History of the Wine Trade in England,* 3 vols. Williamstown, Mass.: Corner House, n.d.

———. *Wine Primer,* 18th ed. Levittown, N. Y.: n.p., n.d.

———. *Wines of the World.* New York: McGraw-Hill, 1981.

Stockley, Tom. *Great Wine Values.* n.p. 1982. Paper.

Storm, John. *An Invitation to Wines,* rev. ed. New York: Fireside (Simon & Schuster), 1971. Paper.

Sutcliffe, Serena. *The Wine Handbook.* New York: Fireside (Simon & Schuster), n.d.

Todd, William J. *Handbook of Wines: How to Buy, Serve, Store and Drink It.* Brooklyn, N. Y.: Revisionist Press, 1974.

Turner, William. *Book of Wines.* Reprint of 1568 ed. Delmare, N. Y.: Scholar's Facsimiles Reprints, 1980.

Wagenvoord, James. *The Wine Diary.* Indianapolis, Ind.: Bobbs-Merrill, 1979.

Wagenvoord, James. *The Wine Book.* New York: Quick Fox (Music Sales), 1980.

Wallace, Forest, and Cross, Gilbert. *The Game of Wine.* New York: Harper & Row, 1977. Paper.

Wasserman, Sheldon, and Wasserman, Pauline. *White Wines of the World.* Briarcliff Manor, N. Y.: Stein & Day, 1980. Paper.

———. *Guide to Fortified Wines.* San Diego: Marlborough Pub., 1983.

Waugh, Alec. *Wines and Spirits.* New York: Time-Life, 1968.

Waugh, Harry. *Diary of a Winetaster: Recent Tastings of the Wines of France and California.* New York: Quadrangle, 1972.

Wile, Julius. *Frank Schoonmaker's Encyclopedia of Wine.* New York: Hastings House, 1978.

Williamson, Darcy. *Wild Wines.* n.p. 1980. Paper.

Wine Album. Adapted from *Monseigneur Le Vin.* Paris, 1927. New York: Metropolitan Museum of Art—Coward, McCann & Geoghegan, 1982.

Yoxall, Harry W. *The Enjoyment of Wine.* New York: Drake, 1972.

GENERAL BOOKS ON SPIRITS AND BEERS

Baron, Stanley W. *Brewed in America: A History of Beer & Ale in the United States.* New York: Arno, 1972.

Eames, Alan. *The Beer Book.* New York: Music Sales, 1981.

Eckhardt, Fred, and Takita, Itsuo. *Beer Tasting and Evaluation for the Amateur.* Portland, Ore.: F. Eckhardt, 1977. Paper.

Gorman, Marion, and Figuerosa, C. L. *The Tequila Book.* Chicago: Henry Regnery, 1976. Paper.

Greenberg, Emanuel, and Greenberg, Madeline. *Pocket Guide to Spirits and Liqueurs.* New York: Perigee (Putnam), 1983. Paper.

Hallgarten, Peter. *Liqueurs.* New York: International Publications Service, 1973.

———. *Spirits and Liqueurs.* London: Faber and Faber, 1979.

Hanssen, Maurice, and Dineen, Jacqueline. *Wines, Beers, and Spirits.* New York: Baronet, 1978. Paper.

Jackson, Michael. *The World Guide to Beer.* Philadelphia: Running Press, 1977. Paper.

Price, Pamela V. *Penguin Book of Spirits and Liqueurs.* London: Penguin, 1978. Paper.

Ray, Cyril. *Cognac.* Briarcliff Manor, N. Y.: Stein & Day, 1973.

———. *Complete Book of Spirits and Liqueurs.* New York: Macmillan, 1978.

Robertson, James D. *The Connoisseur's Guide to Beer.* Aurora, Ill.: Caroline House, 1982. Paper.

———. *Great American Beer Book.* New York: Warner Books, 1981. Paper.

Weiner, Michael A. *The Taster's Guide to Beer: Brews and Breweries of the World.* New York: Macmillan, 1977.

WINES OF THE UNITED STATES

Abel, Dominick. *Guide to the Wines of the United States.* New York: Cornerstone (Simon & Schuster), 1981.

Adams, Leon O. *The Wines of America,* 2nd ed. New York: McGraw-Hill—San Francisco Book Co., 1978.

Better Homes & Gardens Books, ed. *Better Homes & Gardens Favorite American Wines and How to Enjoy Them.* Des Moines, Iowa: Meredith Corp., 1979.

Brown, Sanborn C. *Wines and Beers of Old New England: A How-to-Do-It History.* Hanover, N. H.: University Press of New England, 1978.

Cattell, Hudson, and Miller, Lee. *Wine East of the Rockies.* Lancaster, Pa: L & H Photojournalism, 1982.

Church, Ruth Ellen. *Wines of the Midwest.* Athens, Ohio: Swallow Press, 1981. Paper.

Mishkin, David J. *The American Colonial Wine Industry: An Economic Interpretation,* 2 vols. New York: Arno Press, 1975.

Stockley, Tom. *Winery Tours in Oregon, Washington, Idaho, and British Columbia.* Seattle: Writing Works, 1978. Paper.

WINES OF CALIFORNIA

Balzer, Robert L. *Wines of California.* New York: Harry N. Abrams, 1978.

Blumberg, Robert S., and Hannum, Hurst. *The Fine Wines of California.* New York: Doubleday, 1973. Paper.

Brennan, John M., ed. *Buying Guide to California Wines,* 3rd rev. ed. San Diego: Wine Consultants of California, 1982.

De Groot, Roy Andries. *The Wines of California.* New York: Summit, 1982.

Emmery, Lena, and Taylor, Sally. *Grape Expeditions: Bicycle Tours of the California Wine Country,* vol. 2. San Francisco: Taylor and Friends, 1980.

Gordon, Alvin. *Of Vines and Missions.* Flagstaff, Ariz.: Northland Press, 1971.

Gorman, Robert. *Gorman on California Premium Wines.* Berkeley, Calif.: Ten Speed Press, 1976. Paper.

Haynes, Irene W. *Ghost Wineries of Napa Valley.* n.p. 1980. Paper.

Hinkle, Richard P. *Central Coast Wine Tour.* St. Helena, Calif.: Vintage Image, 1977. Paper.

Kaufman, William I. *Pocket Encyclopedia of California Wine.* Maurice T. Sullivan, ed. San Francisco: Wine Appreciation, 1982. Paper.

Latimer, Patricia. *California Wineries: Sonoma and Mendocino Valley.* St. Helena, Calif.: Vintage Image, 1976.

———. *Sonoma–Mendocino Wine Tour.* St. Helena, Calif.: Vintage Image, 1977. Paper.

Olken, Charles, *et al. The Connoisseur's Handbook of California Wines,* 2nd rev. ed. New York: Alfred A. Knopf, 1980. Paper.

Pieroth, K. F. *The Great California Wine Book.* New York: Sterling, 1983.

Robards, Terry. *California Wine Label Album.* New York: Workman Publishing Co., 1982.

Schoenman, Theodore, ed. *Father of California Wine: Agoston Haraszthy.* Santa Barbara, Calif.: Capra Press, 1979.

Silverman, Harold I., ed. *Pride of the Wineries: The California Living Wine Report.* San Francisco: California Living Books, 1980. Paper.

Sunset Editors. *Guide to California's Wine Country,* rev. ed. Menlo Park, Calif.: Sunset–Lane, 1982. Paper.

Teiser, Ruth, and Harron, C. *Winemaking in California.* n.p., 1982.

Thompson, Bob, and Johnson, Hugh. *The California Wine Book.* New York: William Morrow, 1976.

Thompson, Robert. *The Pocket Encyclopedia of California Wines.* New York: Simon & Schuster, 1980.

WINES OF FRANCE

Benson, Jeffrey, and MacKenzie, Alastair. *Sauternes: A Study of the Great Wines of Bordeaux.* London: Sotheby–Park Bernet, 1979.

Brown, Michael. *Food and Wine of Southwest France.* n.p.: Batsford, 1981.

Brunel, Gaston. *A Guide to the Vineyards of the Côte du Rhône.* New York: St. Martin's, 1981.

Cocks, Ch., et Féret, ed. *Bordeaux et ses vins,* 12th ed. Bordeaux: Féret et Fils, 1969, 1974.

Hallgarten, Peter. *Guide to the Wines of the Rhône.* London: Pitman Publishing, 1979.

Lichine, Alexis. *Alexis Lichine's Guide to the Wines and Vineyards of France,* rev. ed. New York: Alfred A. Knopf, 1982.

Loubère, Leo. *The Red and the White: History of Wine in France and Italy in the 19th Century.* Albany, N. Y.: State University of New York, 1978.

Penning-Rowsell, Edmund. *Wines of Bordeaux,* rev. ed. New York: Scribners, 1981. Paper.

Poupon, Pierre, et Forgeot, Pierre. *The Wines of Burgundy,* 5th rev. ed. Paris: Presses Universitaires de France, 1974. Paper.

Price, Pamela. *Monarch Guide to the Wines of Bordeaux.* New York: Monarch Press, 1978. Paper.

Ray, Cyril. *Lafite.* Briarcliff Manor, N. Y.: Stein & Day, 1969.

———. *Bollinger.* London: Heinemann—Peter Davies, 1982.

Société d'Action et de Gestion Publicitaire. *Les Grands Vins de Bordeaux.* Bordeaux: Delmas, 1972.

Warner, Charles K. *The Wine Growers of France and the Government since 1875.* Reprint of 1960 ed. Westport, Conn.: Greenwood Press, 1975.

Wildman, Frederick S., Jr. *A Wine Tour of France: A Convivial Guide to French Vintages and Vineyards,* rev. ed. New York: Random House, 1976. Paper.

Woon, Basil. *The Big Little Wines of France,* 2 vols. New York: International Publications Service, 1976.

Yoxall, Harry W. *The Wines of Burgundy: The International Wine and Food Society's Guide,* rev. ed. Briarcliff Manor, N. Y.: Stein & Day, 1980.

WINES OF GERMANY

Ambrosi, Hans. *Where the Great German Wines Grow.* Transl. by Gavin Hamilton and Thom Pringle. New York: Hastings House, 1976.

German Wine Atlas and Vineyard Register. Introduction by Edmund Penning-Rowsell. New York: Hastings House, 1977. Paper.

Hallgarten, Fritz S. F. *German Wines.* n.p., 1981.

Meinhard, Heinrich. *German Wines.* Boston: Routledge and Kegan Paul, 1971.

———. *The Wines of Germany.* Briarcliff Manor, N. Y.: Stein & Day, 1980.

Raelson, Jeffrey E. *Getting to Know German Wines.* Miami, Fla.: Banyan Books, 1979. Paper.

Sichel, Peter M. F. *The Wines of Germany: Completely Revised Edition of Frank Schoonmaker's Classic.* New York: Hastings House, 1980.

Siegel, Hans. *Guide to the Wines of Germany.* New York: Cornerstone, 1979. Paper.

WINES OF ITALY

Anderson, Burton. *The Simon & Schuster Pocket Guide to Italian Wines.* New York: Simon & Schuster, 1982. Paper.

———. *Vino: The Wine and Winemakers of Italy.* Boston: Little, Brown. 1981.

Bode, Charles. *Wines of Italy.* New York: Dover, 1974.

Dallas, Philip. *The Great Wines of Italy.* New York: Doubleday, 1982.

Garoglio, Pier Giovanni. *Enciclopedia Vitivinicola Mondiale,* 10 vols. Milan: Unione Italiana Vini, 1973.

Hazan, Victor. *Italian Wine.* n.p., 1982.

Roncarati, Bruno. *Viva Vino: Doc Wines of Italy.* London: Wine & Spirit Publications, Ltd., 1976.

Sarles, John D. *ABC's of Italian Wines.* San Marcos, Calif.: Wine Books, 1981. Paper

WINES OF SPAIN, PORTUGAL AND OTHER EUROPEAN COUNTRIES

Casas, Penelope. *The Food and Wine of Spain.* n.p., 1982.

Gunyon, R. E. *The Wines of Central and Southeastern Europe.* New York: International Publications Service, 1971.

Halász, Zoltán. *Hungarian Wine Through the Ages.* New York: International Publications Service, 1962.

———. *The Best of Hungarian Wines.* n.p., 1981.

Hallgarten, Peter, and Hallgarten, F. L. *Wines and Wine Gardens of Austria.* New York: International Publications Service, 1979.

Ordish, George. *Vineyards in England and Wales.* Julian Jeffs, ed. London: Faber and Faber, 1978.

Read, Jan. *Monarch Guide to the Wines of Spain and Portugal.* New York: Monarch Press, 1978. Paper.

Stanislawski, Dan. *Landscapes of Bacchus: The Vine in Portugal.* Austin, Tex.: University of Texas Press, 1969.

Waterson, Mike. *The U.K. Market for Beers, Wines, and Spirits: Nineteen Seventy-Seven to Nineteen Eighty-Five.* London: Graham and Trotman, 1978.

WINES OF THE MIDDLE EAST, AFRICA, FAR EAST, AND AUSTRALIA

Antcliff, A. J. *Major Wine Grape Varieties of Australia.* n.p., State Mutual Books (CSJRO), 1980.

Bosdari, C. D. *Wines of the Cape,* 3rd rev. ed. New York: International Publications Service, 1966.

Hallicky, James. *Wines and Wineries of South Australia.* n.p., 1981.

Lesko, Leonard H. *King Tut's Wine Cellar.* Berkeley, Calif.: B. C. Scribe, 1977. Paper.

Simon André L. *All about South Africa.* (*All About Wines,* vol. 8) Brooklyn, N. Y.: Shalom, n.d.

WINE SERVICE AND MARKETING

Braunig, M. *Wine Service Procedures.* New York: Radio City Book Store, 1974.

Gavin-Jobson Associates. *Liquor Handbook.* New York: Jobson, annually.

Hasler, G. F. *Wine Service in the Restaurant: Professional Guide for the Sommelier,* 4th ed. New York: International Publications Service, 1977. Paper.

Haszonics, J. J., and Barratt, S. *Wine Merchandising.* New York: Radio City Book Store, n.d.

Horwath, Ernest B., *et al. Hotel Accounting,* 4th ed. New York: Wiley, 1978.

Shanken, Marvin R., ed. *The Impact American Wine Market Review and Forecast,* 2nd ed. New York: M. Shanken Pub., 1982.

Shepard, John. *Shepard's Wine and Liquor Pricing Guide.* Boston: Herman Publishing, 1982.

Stokes, John. W. *How to Manage a Restaurant or Institutional Food Service,* 3rd ed. Dubuque, Iowa: William C. Brown, 1978.

WINE AND HEALTH

Abrahamson, E. M., and Pezet, A. W. *Body, Mind and Sugar,* rev. ed. New York: Avon, 1977. Paper.

Kohniechner, Manfred. *Healing Wines: Celebrating Their Creative Powers.* Trans. Heidi Blocher. Brookline, Mass.: Autumn Press, 1981.

Lucia, Salvatore P. *Wine and Your Well Being.* Reprint of 1971 ed. San Francisco: Wine Appreciation Guild, 1980.

Michaels, Marjorie. *Stay Healthy with Wine: Natural Cures and Beauty Secrets from the Vineyards.* New York: Dial, 1981.

MAKING WINES, BEERS, AND LIQUEURS

Alexander, Frank. *How to Make Your Own Trail Wines.* Byron, Calif.: Kokono, 1978. Paper.

Anderson, Stanley F., and Hull, Raymond. *Art of Making Beer.* New York: Hawthorn Books, 1971. Paper.

———. *Art of Making Wine.* New York: Hawthorn Books, 1971. Paper.

Beadle, Leigh. *The New Brew It Yourself: A Complete Guide to the Making of Beer, Wine, Liqueurs and Soft Drinks,* rev. ed. New York: Farrar, Straus & Giroux, 1981.

Belt, T. Edwin. *Plants Unsafe for Winemaking.* Elmsford, N. Y.: British Book Center, 1973. Paper.

Bravery, H. E. *Home Booze.* Brooklyn Heights, N. Y.: Beekman, n.d.

———. *Successful Winemaking at Home.* New York: Arc Books, 1967. Paper.

Brown, Sanborn C. *Wines and Beers of Old New England: A How-to-Do-It History.* Hanover, N.H.: University Press of New England, 1978. Paper.

De Chambeau, André. *Creative Winemaking.* Robert A. Fowler, ed. Rochester, N. Y. WWWWW Info. Services, 1972.

Foster, Charles. *Home Winemaking.* Brooklyn Heights, N. Y.: Beekman, 1975. Paper.

Hill, Kenneth. *Wine and Beer Making at Home.* Buchanan, N. Y.: Emerson, 1976.

Jagendorf, Moritz. *Folk Wines, Cordials and Brandies: How to Make Them, Along with the Pleasures of Their Lore.* New York: Vanguard Press, 1963.

McIllnay, Annabelle. *Making Wine at Home.* Secaucus, N. J.: Citadel, 1976. Paper.

Morse, Roger A. *Making Mead (Honey Wine): History, Recipes, Methods.* New York: Scribners, 1981.

Nury, F. S., and Fugelsang, K. C. *Winemaker's Guide: Essential Information for Winemaking from Grapes or Other Fruits.* Santa Cruz, Calif.: Western Tanager, 1978. Paper.

Orton, Vrest. *The Homemade Beer Book.* Rutland, Vt.: C. E. Tuttle, 1973. Paper.

Palmer, Bruce. *Wine-Making at Home,* rev. ed. New York: Workman, 1975. Paper.

Papazian, Charlie. *Joy of Brewing,* rev. ed. Boulder, Col.: Log Boom, 1980. Paper.

Reese, M. R. *Better Beer and How to Brew It.* Charlotte, Vt.: Garden Way, 1981. Paper.

Roate, Mettja C. *How to Make Wine in Your Own Kitchen,* 12th ed. New York: Woodhill, 1975. Paper.

Simon, André L. *How to Make Wine and Cordials.* Magnolia, Minn.: Peter Smith, n.d.

Slater, Leslie G. *Secrets of Making Wine from Fruits and Berries.* Olympia, Wash.: Terry Publishing, n.d. Paper.

Tritton, S. M. *Tritton's Guide to Better Wine and Beer Making for Beginners*, 2nd rev. ed. New York: Book Service, 1969. Paper.

Turner, Ben. *Winemaking and Brewing*. St. Lawrence, Mass.: Merrimack Book Service, 1976.

Turner, Ben and Roycroft, Roy. *The Winemaker's Encyclopedia*. London: Faber and Faber, 1979. Paper.

Vine, Richard P. *Commercial Winemaking: Processing and Controls*. Westport Conn.: AVI, 1981.

Watkins, Derek. *Wine and Beer Making*. North Pomfret, Vt.: David & Charles, 1978.

Whitehouse, Albert. *Home Brewing: An Illustrated Guide*. North Pomfret, Vt.: David & Charles, 1981.

Zanelli, Leo. *Beer and Winemaking Illustrated Dictionary*. San Diego, Cal.: A. S. Barnes, 1979.

TECHNICAL BOOKS

Amerine, M. A., ed. *Wine Production Technology in the United States*. American Chemical Society Symposium Series, 1981.

————, and Joslyn, M. A. *Table Wines: The Technology of Their Production*, 2nd rev. ed. Berkeley, Calif.: University of California Press, 1970.

————, and Ough, C. S. *Methods for Analysis of Wines and Musts*. New York: John Wiley, 1980.

————, and Roessler, Edward B. *Wines: Their Sensory Evaluation*. San Francisco: W. H. Freeman, 1976.

————, and Singleton, V. L. *Wine: An Introduction*, rev. ed. Berkeley, Calif: University of California Press, 1977, 1978. Paper.

————, Berg, H. W., and Cruess, W. V. *Technology of Winemaking*, 4th rev. ed. Westport, Conn.: AVI, 1980.

Conant, James B., ed. *Pasteur's Study of Fermentation*. Cambridge, Mass: Harvard University Press, 1952. Paper.

Galet, Pierre. *Practical Ampelography: Grapevine Identification*. Translated by Lucie Morton. Ithaca, N. Y.: Cornell University Press, 1979.

Joslyn, M. A., and Amerine, M. A. *Dessert, Appetizer, and Related Flavored Wines*. Richmond, Calif.: Agricultural Sciences, 1964.

Marcus, Irving H. *How to Test and Improve Your Wine Judging Ability*, 2nd ed. Berkeley, Calif.: Wine Publications, 1974. Paper.

Wagner, Philip M. *American Wines and Winemaking*, rev. ed. New York: Alfred A. Knopf, 1974.

————. *Grapes into Wine: The Art of Winemaking in America*. New York: Alfred A. Knopf, 1976. Paper.

————. *Wine-Grower's Guide*, rev. ed. New York: Alfred A. Knopf, 1965.

Weaver, Robert J. *Grape Growing*. New York: John Wiley, 1976.

Webb, A. Dinsmore, ed. *Chemistry of Winemaking*. Washington, D.C.: American Chemical Society, 1974.

Winkler, A. J., *et al*. *General Viticulture*. Berkeley, Calif: University of California Press, 1975.

MIXED DRINKS

Bergerae, Victor J. *Trader Vic's Bartender's Guide*, rev. ed. New York: Doubleday, 1972.

Esquire Magazine Editors. *Esquire Drink Book*. New York: Bantam Books, 1967. Paper.

Haimo, Oscar. *Cocktail and Wine Digest: The Barman's Bible*, 39th rev. ed. New York: Oscar Haimo, 1979.

Herbert, Malcolm R. *California Brandy Drinks: The One Bottle Bar*. San Francisco: Wine Appreciation Guild, 1981.

Kaufman, William I. *California Wine Drinks*. M. T. Sullivan, ed. San Francisco: Wine Appreciation Guild, n.d. Paper.

McNulty, Henry. *The Vogue Cocktail Book*. New York: Harmony Books, 1982.

Ramos, Adam, and Ramos, Joseph. *California Brandy: The Winedrinker's Spirit*. Berkeley, Calif.: Apple Pie, 1981.

————. *Mixed Wine Drinks: 700 Recipes for Punches, Hot Drinks, Coolers, and Cocktails*, 2nd ed. Berkeley, Calif.: Apple Pie, 1982.

Smith, C. Carter, Jr. *The Art of Mixing Drinks*. New York: Warner, 1981.

COOKING WITH WINES AND SPIRITS

Beard, James A. *Fireside Cookbook*. New York: Simon & Schuster, 1969.

————. *How to Eat and Drink Your Way Through a French or Italian Menu*. New York: Atheneum, 1971. Paper.

Caruba, Rebecca. *Cooking with Wine and Higher Spirits*. New York: Crown, n.d.

Chamberlain, Samuel. *Clementine in the Kitchen*, rev. ed. New York: Hastings House, 1963.

Chase, Emily. *Pleasures of Cooking with Wine*. Englewood Cliffs, N. J.: Prentice-Hall, 1960. Paper.

Child, Julia. *From Julia Child's Kitchen*. New York: Alfred A. Knopf, 1975.

————, *et al*. *Mastering the Art of French Cooking*, vol. 1. New York: Alfred A. Knopf, 1961.

————, and Beck, Simone. *Mastering the Art of French Cooking*, vol. 2. New York: Alfred A. Knopf, 1970.

Church, Ruth Ellen. *Entertaining with Wine*. New York: Rand McNally, 1979. Paper.

Claiborne, Craig. *Craig Claiborne's Kitchen Primer*. New York: Random House, 1972. Paper.

————. *The New York Times Cookbook.* New York: Harper & Row, 1975.

Curnonsky. *Cuisine et Vins de France.* New York: Larousse, n.d.

Délu, Christian Roland. *French Provincial Cuisine,* rev. ed. New York: Barrons, 1981.

Franey, Pierre, and Claiborne, Craig. *Craig Claiborne's New York Times Cookbook.* New York: Times Books, 1979.

Greenberg, Emanuel, and Greenberg, Madeline. *Whisky in the Kitchen.* Indianapolis, Ind.: Bobbs-Merrill, 1968.

Hatch, Ted. *American Wine Cook Book.* New York: Dover, 1971. Paper.

Kafka, Barbara. *American Food and California Wine.* Irene Chalmers Cookbooks, n.p., 1981.

Kerr, Graham. *The Complete Galloping Gourmet Cookbook.* New York: Grosset & Dunlap, 1972.

Montagne, Prosper. *The New Larousse Gastronomique: The Encyclopedia of Food, Wine, and Cooking.* Edited by Charlotte Turgeon. New York: Crown, 1977.

Root, Waverly. *Food of France.* New York: Random House, 1977. Paper.

Stockli, Albert. *Splendid Fare: The Albert Stockli Cookbook.* New York: Alfred A. Knopf, 1970.

Sunset Editors. *Country French Cooking,* 2nd ed. Menlo Park, Calif.: Sunset–Lane, 1981. Paper.

Van Zuylen, Guirne. *Eating with Wine.* Levittown, N. Y.: Transatlantic Arts, 1972.

Wine Advisory Board. *Easy Recipes of California Winemakers.* Marjorie K. Jacobs, ed. Blue Earth, Minn.: Piper Publishing, 1970.

————. *Epicurean Recipes of California Winemakers.* Donna Bottrell, ed. Blue Earth, Minn.: Piper Publishing, 1978.

————. *Wine Cookbook of Dinner Menus.* Compiled by Emily Chase. Blue Earth, Minn: Piper Publishing, 1978.

Wood, Morrison. *More Recipes with a Jug of Wine.* New York: Farrar, Straus & Giroux, 1956.

APPENDIX U
APHORISMS OF BRILLAT-SAVARIN*

The world would have been nothing if it were not for life; and all who live, eat.

Animals feed, man eats; only a man of culture knows how to dine.

Tell me what you eat and I will tell you what you are.

The pleasure of the table belongs to all ages, conditions, countries, and times; it accompanies all other joys and remains the last to console us for the loss of them.

Good living is an act of our judgment by which we show preference for those things that are agreeable to the taste over those that do not have this quality.

The discovery of a new dish is more beneficial to humanity than the discovery of a new star.

The dyspeptic and the drunkard do not know how to eat or drink.

The order of drinking is from the mildest to the fuller-bodied, and to the richest in bouquet.

Punctuality is the most important quality of the cook, and it should also be that of the guests.

To wait too long for a tardy guest denotes a lack of consideration for those who are present.

He who invites his friends and then neglects to give his personal attention to the food served to them does not deserve to have friends.

The hostess should always see to it that the coffee is excellent, and the host that the liqueurs are of first quality.

When we invite someone, we make ourselves responsible for his happiness while he is under our roof.

*Jean Anthelme Brillat-Savarin (1755-1826), a renowned French epicure, was a lawyer, political economist, mayor of the town of Belley, magistrate, musician, and literary man. His book *Physiologie du Goût* is a classic. The *Académie de Gastronomie Brillat-Savarin*, in Paris, is a culinary academy named in his honor.

INDEX

NOTE: The extensive material in the Appendices has not been incorporated into this index. For further information, the reader might wish to review the Appendices as well as studying the main body of the text.